AN INCONSTANT LANDSCAPE

AN INCONSTANT LANDSCAPE

The Maya Kingdom of El Zotz, Guatemala

Edited by
THOMAS G. GARRISON AND STEPHEN HOUSTON

UNIVERSITY PRESS OF COLORADO
Louisville

© 2018 by University Press of Colorado

Published by University Press of Colorado
245 Century Circle, Suite 202
Louisville, Colorado 80027

 ASSOCIATION of UNIVERSITY PRESSES   The University Press of Colorado is a proud member of
the Association of University Presses.

The University Press of Colorado is a cooperative publishing enterprise supported, in part,
by Adams State University, Colorado State University, Fort Lewis College, Metropolitan
State University of Denver, Regis University, University of Colorado, University of Northern
Colorado, University of Wyoming, Utah State University, and Western Colorado University.

∞ This paper meets the requirements of the ANSI/NISO Z39.48-1992 (Permanence of Paper).

ISBN: 978-1-60732-763-9 (cloth)
ISBN: 978-1-64642-077-3 (paperback)
ISBN: 978-1-60732-764-6 (ebook)
DOI: https://doi.org/10.5876/9781607327646

Library of Congress Cataloging-in-Publication Data

Names: Garrison, Thomas G. (Thomas Gardner), editor. | Houston, Stephen D., editor.
Title: An inconstant landscape : the Maya kingdom of El Zotz, Guatemala / edited by Thomas
    G. Garrison and Stephen Houston.
Description: Boulder : University Press of Colorado, [2018] | Includes bibliographical
    references and index.
Identifiers: LCCN 2018006247| ISBN 9781607327639 (hardcase) | ISBN 9781646420773
    (paperback) | ISBN 9781607327646 (ebook)
Subjects: LCSH: Zotz Site (Guatemala) | Mayas—Antiquities. | Guatemala—Antiquities.
Classification: LCC F1435.1.Z68 I53 2018 | DDC 972.81/01—dc23
LC record available at https://lccn.loc.gov/2018006247

The University Press of Colorado gratefully acknowledges the generous support of Brown
University toward the publication of this book.

Cover photograph by J. Pérez de Lara.

For Don Anatolio López and, over many years,
our peerless workers in the Peten.

Without them . . . nothing.

Contents

PART I: THE CULTURE HISTORY
OF THE PA'KA'N DYNASTY

Figures

Tables

Preface

STEPHEN HOUSTON AND
THOMAS G. GARRISON

Many archaeologists, in private comment, regret the passing of the monograph series, the specialist publications of high quality and expense (if negligible sales) issued on individual aspects of a dig. For complex projects, as at Tikal, Guatemala, that effort has been incomparable and breathtaking, reaching well over a dozen volumes of highest quality. Other manuscripts wait in the wings. But consider the problems. Such publications are, at times, so ambitious as to outlive the authors waiting in queue. Plans for dissemination lose their urgency when few remain of the original project—quite simply, authors are no longer around to guide their manuscripts to print. Moreover, research questions may shift to new topics, and less pricey, electronic modes of sharing evidence come into existence. For their part, dissertations can easily be downloaded from websites hosting such distribution. As directors of a dig, we are all too mindful of these matters.

There are alternatives, however. Of late, in Guatemala, such details may be explored online, through voluminous reports created and posted on an annual basis (http://www.mesoweb.com/zotz/resources.html). The current volume aims to craft another substitute: an edited volume that presents in timely manner and manageable cost the summations of work by talented archaeologists on the project. In this, it follows models from Motul de San José (Foias and Emery 2012) and El Perú-Waka' (Navarro-Farr and Rich 2014). The outcome cannot be encyclopedic—that option curls back to the now-obsolete monograph series. But it does represent the very kernel of what we found, in honest overview, and with results still fresh in mind. The archival life of the dig has been further assured by sturdy packaging and labeling of artifacts for future consultation in the main storage facility (Salón 3) in Guatemala City. At a later date, field records will, after consultation with colleagues, be archived in an appropriate university or library setting.

Support for the dig came from the National Endowment for the Humanities (Grant RZ–50680–07, to Houston), the National Science Foundation (BCS 0840930, to Houston and Garrison), and the Paul Dupee Family Professorship held by Houston at Brown University. Other funds were available from the Waitt Foundation (to Garrison), and, residually, from support given to Houston by Dr. Kenneth Woolley and Spencer Kirk while he was still the Jesse Knight University Professor at Brigham Young University. Colleagues not directly involved in this publication helped greatly in the field or in providing timely advice or technical consultation: Tessa de Alarcon, Omar Alcover, Kazuo Aoyama, Ana Lucía Arroyave, Rae Beaubien, Ronald Bishop, Kate Blankenship, Rafael Cambranes, Mary Clarke, Anabela Coronado, David Del Cid, Arturo Godoy, Alejandro Guillot Vassaux, Ioanna Kakoulli (and her team at the Cotsen Institute), Alex Knodell, Catherine Magee, Elizabeth Marroquín, Juan Carlos Meléndez, Margaret Ordoñez, Griselda Pérez, Fabiola Quiroa, Morgan Ritter-Armour, Elizabeth Sibley, Katie Simon (and her group at CAST, University of Arkansas), Alexander Smith, as well as Caitlin Walker. We could simply not have done this without them, or without a perceptive, tenacious, and hard-working set of excavators, cooks, and drivers from Cruce Dos Aguadas, Dolores, and Uaxactun. Permission came from the Instituto de Antropología e Historia de Guatemala, with the kind help over the years from, above all, Héctor Escobedo Ayala, for a time Minister of Culture and Sports in Guatemala, and also Juan Carlos Pérez Calderón, Eric Ponciano, Mónica Urquizú, Daniel Aquino, and Pedro Pablo Burgos. The Casa Herrera in Antigua, Guatemala, run by the University of Texas Mesoamerican Center, with David Stuart as director, has been of enormous help over the years. Houston and Garrison have benefited from stays there, as have Alyce de Carteret, James Doyle, Melanie Kingsley, Sarah Newman, and Edwin Román.

Although this volume reports primarily on data collected during the first phase of the Proyecto Arqueológico El Zotz (PAEZ), limited information from a second phase of research directed by Garrison and Román since 2012 is also incorporated. The Fundación Patrimonio Cultural y Natural Maya (PACUNAM) has been instrumental in supporting recent investigations. In particular, warm thanks go to Marianne Hernández, José Pivaral, Claudia Rosales, and Claudia Cruz for their support over the years. Hernández was instrumental in realizing the 2016 PACUNAM LiDAR Initiative, whose data are discussed in the epilogue to chapter 13 and have far-reaching implications for future research at not only El Zotz but the Maya Lowlands as a whole. Further conservation and excavation support was awarded to Garrison through a National Geographic Society Conservation Trust Grant (#C233-13); a further suite of AMS dates was provided by a grant to Houston from the National Geographic Society's Committee for Research and Exploration (#9643-15, Christopher Thornton, Program Officer). Darden Hood and Ron Hatfield at Beta Analytic, Inc., were very helpful in clarifying radiocarbon discrepancies and recalibrating all of our dates to the 2013 calibration curve. The University of Southern California has assisted in Garrison's participation at El Zotz since 2013, and he received support from Ithaca College and Alicia Ranney during the final stages of editing.

Individual authors also have specific thanks to offer: Ewa Czapiewska-Halliday (UCL Institute of Archaeology and the Graduate School); James Doyle (National Science Foundation. BCS #1023274, Doctoral Dissertation Improvement Grant; Wenner-Gren Foundation for Anthropological Research; Brown University Graduate School and Department of Anthropology; Tinker Foundation with the Brown University Center for Latin American and Caribbean Studies); Melanie Kingsley (Waitt Foundation and National Geographic Society, Grant #W90–10); Sarah Newman (Tinker Grant from the Center for Latin American and Caribbean Studies at Brown University; Jane C. Waldbaum scholarship from the Archaeological Institute of America; National Science Foundation, BCS #1240737, Doctoral Dissertation Improvement Grant; Zooarchaeology Lab at Harvard University, directed by Richard Meadow and Ajita Patel; Wenner-Gren Foundation for Anthropological Research, Dissertation Fieldwork Grant and Osmundsen Initiative Award #8603; US State Department Fulbright IIE Research/Study Grant to Guatemala, with thanks to Juan Carlos Meléndez, then at the National Museum, and Monica Urquizú, then at IDAEH, for sponsoring the Fulbright; IDAEH for use of Salón 3, loan of materials; summer research funds from the Department of Anthropology and the Graduate School at Brown University); and Edwin Román (CECON and the Universidad de San Carlos, for their help in the Biotopo San Miguel la Palotada). Andrew Scherer, for his part, was assisted greatly in his analysis by Chelsea Garrett as well as Sarah Newman and Alyce de Carteret. He received travel grants from Baylor University and Brown University, and acknowledges the skilled work of the archaeologists who excavated the El Zotz skeletal collection in the field.

We mentioned our workers before. Let us return to them again, in final recognition. To them and to Garrison's mentor, that fine gentleman and "gentle man," Don Anatolio López, indefatigable explorer and guardian of Guatemala's *patrimonio*, we dedicate this book with respect, affection, and awe.

PART I

The Culture History of the Pa'ka'n Dynasty

Every Maya city in the Classic period has modest settlement in the vicinity, blended with the center into a
single surface. The relations between the two, the large
poised against the small, remain a central concern of
Maya archaeology: were the interactions constant, col-
laborative, and amiable, or did they follow a path of
inconstancy, exploitation, and antagonism? To a notable extent, too, the nature of a larger city and its region
requires attention to boundaries. Frontiers and edges
are where interactions took place. On them, near them,
hostilities flared; flow occurred in people and resources.
To examine a boundary is to evaluate its porosity, to
ask about control of land and the varied intensity of
efforts to ease or impede movement. As a product of
boundaries, the Maya kingdom of El Zotz, Guatemala,
compels such inquiries. Six seasons of fieldwork, as
reported in this book, help to answer them.

As a city and a polity, El Zotz exists because of, even
despite, its position near the large dynastic capital of
Tikal (figure 1.1). In the central Peten of Guatemala,
Tikal is the ineluctable giant. It is mentioned, cop-
ied, fought, exalted, and deliberately ignored by other
kingdoms near by or farther afield (Martin and Grube
2008:24–53). After decades of research, perhaps the
most extensive at any Maya site, Tikal also offers a
vast body of comparative evidence for El Zotz, along
with growing understanding of a key conflict during
the Classic period (e.g., Haviland 2014, on modest
remains at Tikal). This was the sustained, often violent

A Fortress in Heaven

*Researching the Long Term
at El Zotz, Guatemala*

STEPHEN HOUSTON,
THOMAS G. GARRISON,
AND EDWIN ROMÁN

DOI: 10.5876/9781607327646.c001

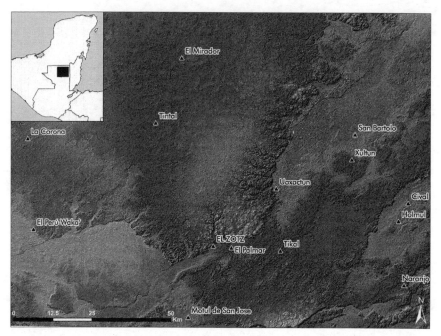

FIGURE 1.1. *El Zotz's regional setting in the Maya Lowlands (map by T. Garrison).*

competition between Tikal and Calakmul, a power of yet larger size to the north, in Campeche, Mexico (Carrasco Vargas and Cordeiro Baqueiro 2012). In this light, research at El Zotz poses oblique questions about Tikal's western frontier, building on similar research of high intensity and duration at the sites of Uaxactun, to the north of Tikal, and Yaxha, a prominent, lakeside city to the southeast (e.g., A. L. Smith 1950; R. Smith 1955; also Gámez 2013; Kováč and Arredondo 2011). To study El Zotz is to ponder Tikal and its other neighbors (Beach et al. 2015:278–279). No isolate, Tikal needs equal framing against El Zotz. Few areas in the neotropical New World offer comparable detail on the tumult of kingdoms and their frontiers; few projects draw regionally on such density of excavation, survey, ecological reconstruction, and history, or on such well-attested lengths of time and solid study of artifacts.

The comparatively small size of El Zotz offers a decided advantage to research. Among its other relevant traits are its limited history of research, its proximity to Tikal athwart a crucial valley, and the savage looting and broad, international dispersal of its thieved material. This destruction is irremediable, yet some evidence of value comes from addressing it. The mapping by Pennsylvania State University of a wall or set of ditches between Tikal and

El Zotz confirmed that the Maya sought definition between the two polities (Webster et al. 2004:figure 25). From these assembled data came, after a planning trip in 2004, a mapping project, sponsored by Brown University and the Instituto de Antropología e Historia de Guatemala (IDAEH), that took to the field for short-term reconnaissance and recording of looter pits in 2006 and 2007. This was followed by more intensive seasons, from 2008 to 2011, of deeper excavation and regional survey. Just as Tikal and Uaxactun had great antiquity, the area of El Zotz now attests to over two millennia of Maya occupation. At times the city was populous, at others leaving only a faint footprint of dedicated visits or low ebb of settlement among the ruins. Earlier hints of agricultural clearance from pollen profiles pushes occupation back at least another millennium (Beach et al., chapter 7, this volume). Only at regional scale, with work by several sub-projects, can long-term developments reveal their sequence.

THE VALLEY OF GOOD VIEWS

El Zotz perches on an elevation to the northern side of the Buenavista Valley (N17.23265 W-89.82425), a feature some 3 km across (figure 1.2). The valley runs for 30 km or so from the area of Tikal to the western flatlands around the San Pedro Martír River. That direction leads eventually to the Tabasco plains and the Gulf of Mexico. During colonial times, the *camino real* to Mérida hugged the edge of this opening on its way from Flores to points north (Jones 1998:map 3). Today, the northerly route coincides in part with the all-weather road passing toward Carmelita in the northern Peten. It serves also as the turnoff to the San Miguel la Palotada Biotope reserve that holds El Zotz. The Buenavista Valley is anomalous for the Peten. Only one other east–west passage of comparable size exists, and that is the south shore of Lake Peten Itza, an area well-populated with substantial ancient settlement, from Ixlu to Tayasal and the fortified peninsula of Nixtun-Ch'ich' (Pugh et al. 2016). The valley, with El Zotz situated halfway through it, represents one of the few routes by which the eastern side of the Maya Lowlands communicated readily with the west and vice versa. Other routes are possible but beset by broken karst and uplands. El Zotz has another attribute. To the north runs a valley (see figure 3.1) funneling contact with the so-called Mirador Basin (in fact an upland plateau) and its cluster of large Preclassic cities and scattered Classic settlement (Hansen et al. 2008).

Explored in 2015, another such valley exists approximately 8 km west of El Zotz. Similar in some respects to El Zotz is a site at the mouth of that

Figure 1.2. *Settlements of the Buenavista Valley (map by T. Garrison).*

valley. Our team labeled it "La Brisanta" after the local vegetation, a resilient grass. This ancient community proved to be substantial, with plain stelae and altars, copious quantities of Terminal Classic ceramics spilling out of looter trenches, at least two elevated palace areas, and a scattering of mound groups exposed by removal of the local forest. To the north, 5 km from La Brisanta, lies another site, called "Tikalito" because of its relatively large size and fancied similarity to the temples of Tikal. Tikalito consists of two elevated buildings, one a multiroomed palace with lateral rooms, some still standing. Across an elevated court is a massive platform raised on an outcropping of bedrock. The settlement sits outside the biotope park and, as a result, has been swept by occasional fires from agriculture. Dense regrowth stymies any easy mapping of its core or perimeter. Tikalito is also within an area of disputed ownership. Just prior to our visit, one owner, a purported drug *capo*, had been gunned down and his property markers removed with a chainsaw. But, in the long term, work at La Brisanta and Tikalito would pay a strong dividend. In 2015, survey near El Zotz by Omar Alcover Firpi of Brown University confirmed a general pattern shared by large sites on the northern portion of the Buenavista Valley.

El Zotz and La Brisanta both have settlement on either side of their valley opening, yet the dynastic or elite cores sprawl to one side only. That placement was probably conditioned by access to water in reservoirs or cisterns, cavities known as *chultunes* that in some cases likely held water for the humbler residences (Beach et al. 2015). Alcover Firpi (2016) also mapped a defensive feature east of El Zotz. Most likely, this circular redoubt, El Fortín, monitored movement in the north–south valleys and the low-lying areas beyond. Momentous finds from lidar, a technology to be described in the final chapter, through measurements determined as this book went to press, show that such redoubts encircled the El Diablo sector of El Zotz, and an especially extensive area due north from El Palmar. This last, since named La Cuernavilla, had walls to the north, on a route leading to Bejucal, and what appears to be a double-moated, garrison facility with orderly buildings at the base of the escarpment. At present, this may be one of the largest citadels in the Maya region. Our hunch, too, is that it dates largely to the Early Classic period, by direct analogy with the chronology of El Diablo.

The valley itself presents severe obstacles to vehicular traffic. Depending on the rains, even off-road pickups quickly bog down in the *bajo* mud characteristic of these seasonal swamps. The low-lying *bajos* were probably not a focus of settlement by Classic times, which favored hillsides or prominences. If the flatlands did have settlement, it was mostly of perishable construction. The overriding impression, while atop palace complexes like Las Palmitas or El Diablo, or while viewing from the Str. L7-11 pyramid, is the optical reach of El Zotz and its environs (Doyle et al. 2012). By Late Classic times, those on pyramids or the Buenavista escarpment could see clearly to Tikal, even in stormy conditions. Today, the naked eye can perceive Tikal's Temple IV and, from El Diablo, all major pyramids. Nonetheless, it is well to add that the major features during most of El Zotz's occupation were not those buildings at Tikal but the Mundo Perdido complex or the South Acropolis. They appeared on a far horizon as large, mounded heaps of masonry, not up-thrust architecture with high roofcombs. Bejucal (figure 1.3) to the northeast was also visible from the El Diablo hill, at least hypothetically. For much of its existence, the city of El Zotz and its outliers was a place to see and be seen. When cleared of vegetation, even a casual pedestrian would be glimpsed far below while moving along the valley floor. The intent was more to control a central, dry route through the valley and to position the major settlement, El Palmar (figure 1.4), with respect to the Laguna El Palmar as a water source. There must also have been striking effects of sunrise and sunset on the Laguna. The "E-Group," solar temple built close to its edge took full advantage of that

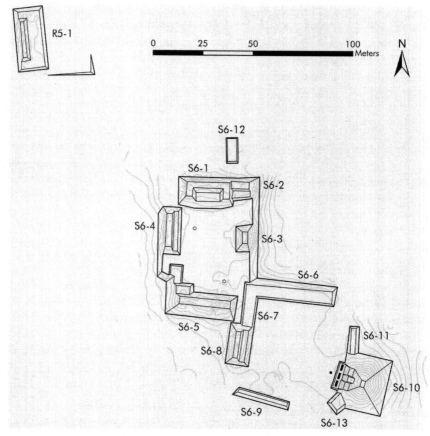

FIGURE 1.3. *Map of Dejucal (map by T. Garrison).*

shimmering view (Doyle 2012, 2013a, 2013b; Doyle and Piedrasanta, chapter 2, this volume).

The site layout of El Zotz is distinctive from other settlements in the central lowlands. At its main pyramid, El Zotz lies 23 km from the main plaza at Tikal, by far the largest settlement in this part of Guatemala (figure 1.5). The known epicenter embraces an area ca. 700 × 700 m, with a major causeway or ceremonial path connecting pyramids to the east and south. A ballcourt lies at the point where the causeway turns to the south. Possibly it aligned with an as-yet-undetected tomb under Str. L7-11 to the north (Houston 2014): energetic excavation by Arredondo cleared out a looter tunnel within but found only a single cache (see Carter et al., chapter 4, this volume). The orientation

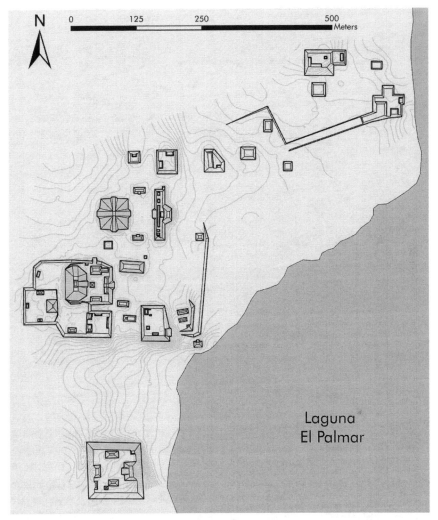

FIGURE 1.4. *Map of El Palmar (map by J. Doyle, O. Alcover Firpi, and T. Garrison).*

of the east–west causeway corresponded to the direction of the sinkhole where El Zotz's bat population resides as well as the site's main *aguada* (man-made water source); sight-lines from the Diablo complex to other monumental features of Early Classic El Zotz may also have informed the layout of the city (Houston, Newman, Román and Garrison 2015:figure 1.5). Such causeways went far back indeed. In 2016, Alcover Firpi found a Preclassic road leading northeast from El Palmar, perhaps indicating that the early urban

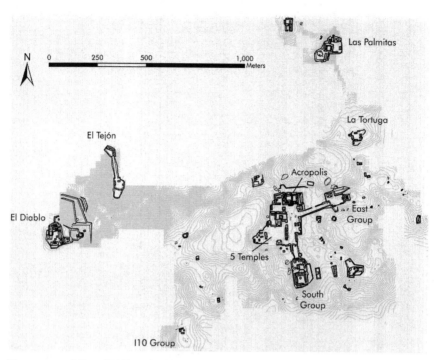

FIGURE 1.5. *Map of El Zotz (map by T. Garrison).*

planners of El Zotz determined to mimic the earlier center. Data from the 2016 PACUNAM LiDAR Initiative showed yet other causeways, revealing that El Palmar was far larger than earlier thought. Preclassic buildings have a distinctive, formal "signature," with gentle, modulated shapes that come from centuries of added erosion; by contrast, Classic buildings exhibit crisp edges and corners. At El Zotz, several plazas, most likely the setting of civic rituals such as royal dances or processions, occur near its main causeway (Grube 1992; Inomata 2006). Pyramids of considerable size cluster in the northern area of the site, just by the palace complex, or "Acropolis" (Carter et al., chapter 4, this volume). Structure L7-11, for example, reaches at least 27 m in height, with well-preserved room foundations. Its construction greatly changed the visual properties of El Zotz, and its bulk loomed over the Acropolis to dominate the city epicenter. The palace is an area of many courtyards near the juncture where the causeway turns south. It is easily the most massive construction at the site and the probable residence of the local dynasty (see Martin 2001, for comparative examples in the Maya region). A string of palaces atop the

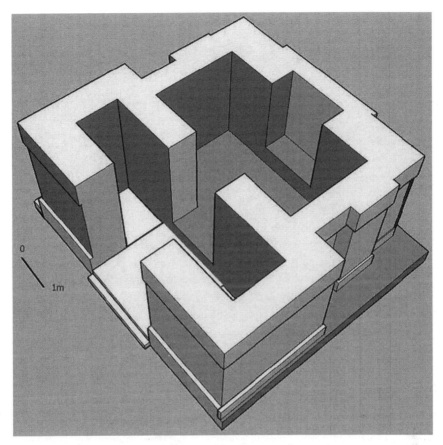

FIGURE 1.6. *Structure L7-11 summit (model by S. Houston).*

escarpment was later documented by Edwin Román, Rony Piedrasanta, and Nicholas Carter (see Carter 2014). Possibly these were alternative residences for royalty or the seats of minor members of the dynasty. The lidar campaign in 2016 highlighted even more grandiose buildings to the north of Carter's dissertation work in the Las Palmitas Group.

An important feature of El Zotz is that its pyramids bear close similarities to pyramids built later at Tikal (figure 1.6). That is, El Zotz demonstrates a pattern of local innovation in architecture. The summits display large axial passages and small lateral rooms (Coe 1967:29). Evidently, the vaults over the rooms helped to stabilize the central passage, but they were not themselves very spacious or useful for storage or ritual use. What has become even more apparent, however, is the role of water supply in founding the community. A team led by Timothy Beach and Sheryl Luzzadder-Beach discovered evidence for the sudden construction of large reservoirs near the South Group at El Zotz, possibly with sequenced pools to filter water by removing sediment (see Beach et al., chapter 7, this volume). Minor settlement too, of the sort to house non-elites and supporting staff for the royal court, were probed in Alyce de Carteret's (2017) doctoral research at Brown. Test pits and focused excavations of the I10 Group to the west of the main reservoirs at El Zotz shows robust occupation in the Late to Terminal Classic periods. The paradox is that monumental construction at El Zotz diminished when such modest settlement went into active phases of building, at limited scale to be sure. The suspicion is strong that El Zotz was, in this sense, inversely related to Tikal. With the decline of the latter city's power, settlement rebounded at El Zotz, albeit in selective ways. De Carteret's dissertation made this pattern eminently clear, with abundant, late settlement across the city. This was also when El Zotz began to re-erect stela, if soon to be broken up and incorporated into masonry (see below; Carter et al., chapter 4, this volume; Newman et al., chapter 5, this volume). Prior research by Houston and his team at Piedras Negras, Guatemala, hinted at a similar trajectory, royalty in active decay but with a surprising degree of trade and humbler construction (e.g., Golden 2002).

THE PLUNDERING OF EL ZOTZ

The first notice of El Zotz and its area comes from the Tikal Project of the University Museum at the University of Pennsylvania. Robert Carr (personal communication, 2012), a mapper of that effort, sent a reliable worker to do a sketch map of rumored ruins to the west of Tikal. This proved to be El Palmar (Doyle and Piedrasanta, chapter 2, this volume). Thereafter, reports became more distressing, from the late 1960s on. Large-scale looting, supposedly sponsored by a brother to the then-president, Kjell Laugerud García, punctured almost every mound or building in the region. Not even El Palmar escaped such damage, which included the violation of an Early Classic royal tomb in its main triadic group (Doyle and Piedrasanta, chapter 2, this volume). This destruction affected all sites from the smallest, such as La Avispa (figure 1.7), to the largest, El Zotz. Direct reports exist from those who stumbled across soldiers massed into platoons for looting. The current tally of such trenches, tunnels, and pits far exceeds 200, leaving, as at Bejucal, an entire pyramid gutted from the inside (Str. S6-3), held together by tree roots and some rubble or fill in between. A conservative tally soon rises to over 100

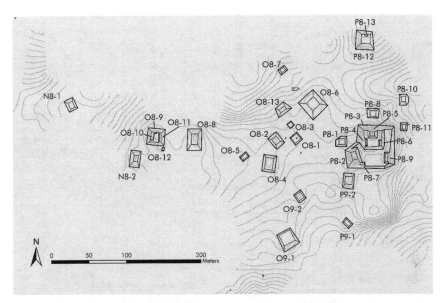

FIGURE 1.7. *Map of La Avispa (map by T. Garrison).*

looter trenches across El Zotz, many more in the region, with well over 1,000 m³ of fill removed.

The looters pillaged at least 10 royal tombs and several elite ones (Román et al., chapter 3, this volume; see also Garrison et al. 2016; Houston, Newman, Román, and Garrison 2015). These yielded pots that were eventually incorporated into private and public collections after their theft from Guatemala. One ceramic of Early Classic date, fully equipped with the titles of a ruler of El Zotz, found its way into the National Gallery of Art in Canberra, Australia (figure 1.8, K8458, NGA 78.1293.A–B). Other bowls possibly from El Zotz also ornament collections around the world (e.g., Berjonneau and Sonnery 1985:plates 339–340; Looper and Polyukhovych 2016:figures 1–3; Villela 2011:145, plate 65; also Denver Art Museum 1998.33A–B, 1998.34A–B; 1998.35A–B). A set of red- or buff-background pots likely came from the region during this wave of destruction. Most date to the beginnings of the Late Classic period, ca. AD 575–625, in "hands" of varying expertise but often sharing a distinctive variant of the **u** sign, "his, hers, its," as a "split-sky" sign (K679, 2669, 3924, 5350, 5460, 5465, 5509, 6618, 7147, 7220, 7525, 8393, 8418; see Carter et al., chapter 4, this volume). Those in red build on a longstanding, local emphasis on that color (de Carteret 2013). The red-background vessels in particular are noteworthy for presenting

FIGURE 1.8. *Canberra Bowl, from the area of El Zotz (photo by J. Kerr).*

the first depiction of a supernatural being known as the *way*, a co-essence or co-spirit of Maya royalty whose nature is still under discussion (K1743, 3060, 3387). In a few cases, they also show use of the local royal title (see below), along with a set of royal names. A queen, one of three known at El Zotz, appears in both text and image on a pot formerly in the Museu Barbier-Mueller in Barcelona (figure 1.9, Barbier et al. 1997:288–289). Most likely, she also occurs on a vessel now in the San Diego Museum of Man (Looper and Polyukhovych 2016:5–6, figure 8). One stela in the El Zotz plaza is sawn (Stela 3). This would presumably only have been done if there were a carved surface to steal.

A logging road driven through in the 1970s helped remove such objects from El Zotz and furthered invasive settlement to the north of the city and

FIGURE 1.9. *Late Classic vessel, El Zotz region, ca.* AD *625, ex–Museu Barbier-Mueller, Barcelona (photo by J. Kerr).*

near El Palmar. These communities were only removed by biotope authorities in the early 2000s. At least one village lay as far north as Pucte, a source of water on the road to Bejucal. But there was one small benefit to such a track. It still affords rugged access to El Zotz, and the logging camp itself, on a terrace bulldozed into the hillside, provides a dry location for archaeological labs and tenting. The camp is maintained today by CECON (Centro de Estudios Conservacionistas, Universidad de San Carlos de Guatemala). For the moment, the San Miguel la Palotada Biotope, at 35,468 ha, set aside by decree of the Guatemalan Congress in 1989, has year-round protection by IDAEH guards, as well as some seasonal rangers with CECON. Yet the biotope is also imperiled by routine, aggressive burning on its margins and into its core. These intrusions are unlikely to be casual, being rather, by common report, the stratagems of drug kingpins wishing to acquire land as part of money-laundering operations. Destroying a biotope, promoting settlements, and suborning a judge for "legal" title are, it seems, quick paths to that aim. Evidently, the process seeks to shift possession from public holdings to private. Patrols by the Guatemalan army, such as those mounted in 2010 and 2011 during the first phase of the El Zotz Project, may prevent further invasion. Tourists trekking from the biotope entrance to Tikal could provide a concrete incentive for preserving the local jungle.

CRAFTING AND COMPLETING A PROJECT

Most Maya sites of any size undergo cycles of research. First there is "discovery," although, of course, ruined cities are often known long before to farmers and foresters. This stage is followed by occasional forays and, in a few cases, a substantial project of some five years in length. In academic settings, that span is about the time necessary to train graduate students,

Guatemalan and international, and to bring theses and dissertations to fruition. In this, Gordon Willey of Harvard set a useful precedent, starting at Barton Ramie, Belize, then passing on to Altar de Sacrificios and Ceibal (Seibal) in Guatemala, to conclude his career of distinguished fieldwork at Copan, Honduras. On most projects, a generation passes before another, equivalent team returns to work again. The alternative, of continuous work by governments or intellectual "heirs" of the first project, takes place only at the largest sites or those with touristic potential. At El Zotz, the first effort, phase 1, has drawn to a close, succeeded by a phase 2 under two of us (Garrison and Román), with general sponsorship by the University of Southern California. Brown University, the National Endowment for the Humanities, the National Science Foundation, and private sources funded the majority of phase 1. PACUNAM, a research foundation created by generous benefactors in Guatemala, supported most of phase 2. Houston has continued to serve as a special advisor. Some phase 2 results are included here, but this book largely reports on phase 1.

The name of the site, El Zotz, "bat" (the flying mammal) in several Mayan languages, is a modern invention. After its rediscovery in recent times, El Zotz seems to have been called "Dos Aguadas" after the two natural reservoirs (*aguadas*) within a kilometer of the ruins. To avoid confusion with many places of the same name, this was changed in 1977 to "El Zotz," an epithet alluding to a large population of bats living in a partly collapsed sinkhole nearby (Laporte 2006:878). The first forays into the site involved Ian Graham and, at about the same time, the architect George Andrews (1986:123–124; see also Houston, Newman, Román, and Garrison 2015:figure 2.53) and Marco Antonio Bailey of IDAEH. Graham also recorded texts on the stelae still at El Zotz and urged Houston to investigate the spectacular, exposed stuccos in the El Diablo complex of the city (see also Mayer 1993). Graham showed that a carved lintel of chicozapote wood, at that point in the Denver Art Museum, came originally from Str. M7-1, a fact proved by matching the size, pigment, and carving style of fragments left at El Zotz with the sculpture at Denver. With this compelling evidence, and the enlightened cooperation of the Denver Art Museum, Guatemala secured the return of the lintel in 1998. The monument is now on display in the National Museum (MUNAE), Guatemala City. A crucial addition to Graham's work was the documentation in 1978 of three stelae and a carved altar at Bejucal, some 7 km to the northeast of El Zotz. In 1977, at Bailey's initiative, the site entered the rolls of officially registered sites in Guatemala. Later salvage work, by Juan Pedro Laporte (2006) in the early 1980s and, separately, by Oscar Quintana, retrieved caches and backfilled the acutely threatened summit of Str. M7-1 (Quintana and Wurster 2001:38–40). The final episode of major looting seems to have taken place between 1978, when Andrews took photos of the Diablo complex, and 1980, when the coffee importer Martin Diedrich visited the site, showing considerable damage in between. Diedrich was most generous in sharing his photos from that visit (Houston, Newman, Román, and Garrison 2015:figure 2.54). Small-scale looting continues to be problematic to this day, with fresh pits discovered as recently as 2017.

The Brown Project was designed and executed in cooperation with Héctor Escobedo, with later codirection by Ernesto Arredondo, and from 2009 onward, Román, Garrison, and Beach. Initial mapping and recording of looter tunnels, assisted by Zachary Nelson, was followed by a test-pitting program in all plazas of El Zotz and El Palmar. This was augmented with detailed work in the South Group, a focus of the Postclassic period, the El Diablo and Bejucal loci of the Early Classic, and the Classic constructions of the Str. L7-11 pyramid and the adjacent Acropolis, the evident royal palace at El Zotz. In the meantime, Garrison coordinated and directed a program of regional survey. Graduate students from Brown, Brandeis, University College London, the University of Texas at Austin, as well as professionals from the Universidad de San Carlos de Guatemala completed our research in 2011. The endpoint was logical. Funding had come to a close, and all doctoral students had sufficient data for their dissertations, with full coverage of all periods and most categories of artifact. To date, eight doctoral dissertations have resulted from the dig (Carter 2014; Czapiewska-Halliday 2018; de Carteret 2017; Doyle 2013a; Kingsley 2014; Mesick 2012; Newman 2015b; Román 2017). Ten master's theses are also in hand (Alcover Firpi 2016; Blankenship 2012; Cheung 2014; Czapiewska 2011b; de Carteret 2013; Lopez-Finn 2014; Newman 2011b; G. Pérez Robles 2014; Román-Ramírez 2011; Walker 2010), along with a licenciatura thesis on malacology (Gutiérrez Castillo 2015) and a technical thesis on object resoration (E. Pérez Robles 2013).

The overall concerns of the project were themes of longstanding interest in historical and anthropological research: the control of people and land, and how, under certain conditions, that dominion might shift over time. In political theory the more common orientation is to see such control as the result of central decision-making, with two variant forms of hierarchical organization or domination in polities of the past (Weber 1978:53–56, 948–953, 1013–1015, 1055–1059). The first form of organization is *sovereignty*, an arrangement of direct rule that depends on the allegiance of sectional interests, particularly elites (Hansen and Stepputat 2006:298–299). The second might be called *suzerainty*, which acknowledges the role of authority as a fluid byproduct of uneven relations between people or groups (Lincoln 1994:4; Smith 2003:106). Sovereignty hints at coercion and command over substantive resources, the so-called objective bases of power (Blanton 1998:table 152) that revolve around production, exchange, and consumption, usually vested in one person and the institution he or she represents (Wolf 1982:97). In contrast, suzerainty tends, in its classic formulation by Max Weber, to involve a variety of supports, including symbolic underpinnings, claims to legitimacy, and perceptions of social contract.

Ideally, the two systems of rule converge in one person or group of people. Despite the apparent contrast between the systems of rule, sovereignty and suzerainty can, in almost every circumstance, exist at the same time, thus creating more effective governance of people and land. But there is a difficulty with such formulations. They rely on abstract concepts that, when applied to actual examples, bear multiple exceptions (Smith 2003:93). This is a common problem in all disciplines that seek to provide terminology for systematic comparisons between societies. An example of this would be a term like *state*, which would seem self-evident in meaning. In point of fact, the term conveys a sense of pervasive, thoroughgoing bureaucratic control that often pertains, not to earlier episodes of rule, but to the modern period; even there, according to Clifford Geertz (2004:580), states can be confused and dysfunctional associations of people and groups that are not easy to reduce to a single logic of organization. Some scholars would go so far as to say that the very terms of political theory do not have much utility away from particular settings viewed at particular moments of time (e.g., Aretxaga 2003:398; see also Migdal 1988 and Yoffee 2005 for further critiques). In response to such criticisms, and to the idea that many societies were organized in a streamlined, top-down fashion, there is another, opposed perspective that seeks to capture the subtlety, even "messiness," of complex interactions between humans in settled and functionally diverse societies. The aim is to reflect what are, in most instances, unstable balances of sovereignty and suzerainty or, in more extreme cases, settings where such concepts apply weakly, if at all. This opposed perspective involves *heterarchy*, a label that describes simultaneous rule or decision-making by distinct, often cross-cutting groups of people (Crumley 1995, 2003:137; Crumley and Marquardt 1987; Yoffee 2005:179; for Mayanist discussion, see Martin 2016). An important feature of heterarchy is its suggestion that people choose either to cooperate or to clash, in patterns of decision-making that resemble the real complexity of human behavior and its often unexpected consequences. As a concept, heterarchy does another thing: it raises doubts about the self-descriptions of polities, which tend to perceive or describe themselves as smoothly functioning organizations.

Heterarchy thus emphasizes: (1) the relative autonomy of constituent groups; (2) *self-organization*, a technical term that expresses how non-centralized, non-hierarchical decision-making takes place; (3) multiple frictions between groups; and (4) ruptures between the declared operation of states and their actual performance, which can be both inefficient and ill-informed in dominating land, people, or things (Blanton 1998:167; Scott 1998:352–345; Yoffee 2005:92–94). Heterarchy is a logical offshoot of two intellectual tendencies in scholarship, a Marxist or materialist one that stresses conflict and compromise between groups or classes of people, and a "postmodern" perspective that lays emphasis on multiple interests and points of view. It also has a decided appeal for Maya scholarship. The dispersed nature of resources in the Maya region has been said to be ideal for heterarchical organization, in that multiple interactions of a non-hierarchical sort are necessary to exploit this mosaic of ecological microzones (Scarborough 1998:137). The opposition of hierarchy to heterarchy helps refine thinking about the ancient world. But even proponents of "heterarchy" would acknowledge a central challenge—the difficulty of drawing a strong line between the two kinds of organization. All complex polities display elements of both arrangements—heterarchical components of society (i.e., opposed groups or institutions) seldom exist without their own forms of hierarchical organization; and, with few exceptions, hierarchies consist of multiple, often conflicting elements that can subvert the aims of people at other levels of decision-making (Crumley and Marquardt 1987:618–619; Crumley 2003:144; Yoffee 2005:179). Rather, the pressing question becomes, which tendency—conflictive and consensual (often deliberate and slow in its operation) or top-down (often fast-paced and decisive in application)—comes to dominate ancient polities? And under what kinds of conditions does one system operate more strongly than the other?

The Classic Maya, who lived in the millions across the Yucatan Peninsula and adjacent regions from about AD 250 to 850, have attracted their own set of modern labels, depending on local patterns in the archaeology and scholarly frames of mind. The most cautious terms are *polity* or *kingdom* (Webster 2002:164). Many others make an appearance (Lucero 1999:212–216)—*regional state* (Adams 1990:figure 1), *superstate* (Martin and Grube 1995:45; since modified persuasively to *overkingship* or *hegemony*, Martin and Grube 2008:19–20), *segmentary state* (Houston 1987), *city-state* (Webster 1997), or *territory* (Garrison and Dunning 2009)—all of which savor of diverse opinion, ranging from centralized to non-centralized models of governance (Fox et al. 1996).

Some of the models are doubtful, such as the versions positing a large-scale polity governed from Tikal, Guatemala, during the late first millennium AD (e.g., Adams 1999:17). Fine-grained historical evidence does not support such a view, although hieroglyphic texts confirm the existence of broad and orderly patterns of overlordship and subordinates, some with the highest social rank, that of k'uhul ajaw, or "holy lord." One city in particular, Calakmul, clearly deserves the label of a hegemonic polity, rather like parts of the Aztec empire in that it employed a "grand strategy" of expansive influence over a century or so (Martin and Grube 2008:101; Parker 1998:1). Nonetheless, all models have some validity in capturing the diverse realities of political organization during the Classic period. No polity escapes the interplay of centripetal and centrifugal forces—those that bring together and those that pull apart (for more recent reviews, see Foias 2013; Jackson 2013, offers a court-oriented perspective, as do Houston and Inomata 2009:131–192; also Houston and Martin 2016).

An abstract model is a dry exercise in typology without cultural and historical detail. This is where process, a series of operational principles (e.g., "rulers seek allies," "elites wish for greater autonomy from rulers," "non-elites tend to farm," "giving and taking creates bonds within communities"), becomes refined by sequence, the actual flow of processes over time in certain political and ecological settings. This refinement must be done, however, with good control over evidence and thorough consideration of the social thrust and pull within polities. One exposition has attempted to deal with such forces by crafting a *dynamic model*, a label that seeks to describe the aggregation and decomposition of Maya polities as an almost physical process of ebb and flow (Marcus 1998:59–60). The drawback is that this model does not provide a clear presentation of process and sequence. For example, one chart offered in support of the dynamic model presents a horizontal pattern of specified time and an unspecified vertical dimension of undulating lines that are meant to show "consolidation and breakdown" (Marcus 1998:figure 3.2). Yet, a chart with determined x-axis and undetermined y-axis is neither a useful illustration nor an adequate explanation—it is merely an impression, a graphic imprecision dressed up in spurious exactitude. The purpose of the chart is to show small-scale polities being absorbed into large ones that eventually fracture back into constituent polities. This is not by itself a productive formulation, as it skirts attention to the internal structure of polities or the processes that shape them (e.g., Marcus 1998:figures 3.4, 3.5, 3.8, 3.13, 3.14). Nor does it reveal the actors, values, beliefs, institutions, social distinctions, or physical setting that factor into a sequenced account of how land and people are governed or control of them is relinquished. Each case requires its own discussion of process and sequence before scholars can address larger questions of comparison.

A second, principal orientation of the project has been a "landscape" approach, one that looks at broad patterns involving many sites against a backdrop of environmental change, human actors, and a range of meanings imputed to that landscape. Since the early 1990s there has been an increased focus on such studies in world archaeology (Tilley 1994), coinciding with the use of Geographic Information Systems (GIS) in regional archaeological investigations (Aldenderfer and Maschner 1996). These tools allow archaeologists to recognize variability in landscapes arising from cultural historical diversity (Wilkinson et al. 2005), natural changes (Schuldenrein et al. 2004), and conditions imposed by local social perspectives (Bauer et al. 2007; Mack 2004). The research at El Zotz places the Maya among the growing number of complex societies being studied for their landscape dynamics. Excellent models include the Mesopotamian research of Wilkinson and colleagues (2005), who have identified landscape "signatures" for different cultural historical phases of the Neo-Assyrian Empire during the eighth and seventh centuries BC or, in south India, the differing class perspectives studied by Mack (2004). Similarly, the El Zotz project sought to identify changes in landscape in the Maya Lowlands over two millennia. Here, a giant loomed, casting its shadow over the Buenavista Valley. The interruptions, bursts of energetic construction, and general oscillations in settlement were surely in part the result of being so close to Tikal. These and other patterns will be brought to a synthetic conclusion in the final chapter.

A SCRIM OF HISTORY

The El Zotz dig not only has its own history. It also extracted accounts of the Classic Maya from a difficult glyphic record (see Carter et al., chapter 4, this volume). The major, now "classic" synthesis of Classic history organizes its chapters by major city, namely, the capitals with full sequences of kings and textured reports of events (Martin and Grube 2008). El Zotz would never deserve a chapter in that volume. It fits instead into a category of sites—most belong to this class—with piecemeal evidence and a need for speculative inference to make sense of its history (e.g., Altar de Sacrificios, Guatemala, Houston 2016). At present, El Zotz and Bejucal have only six texts with moderate-to-good legibility, historical content, and firm provenience. These are (1) El Zotz Stela 1, a fragmentary, mutilated stela dating, probably, to December 6, AD 573; (2) El Zotz Wooden Lintel 1 (figure 3.4), a carving with a style-date in the early

FIGURE I.IO. *Text from vessel from El Zotz Burial 30, Str. L8-13 (drawing by S. Houston).*

500s; (3) El Zotz Stela 4 (figure 5.2), from March 12, AD 830; (4) a sherd with the local "Emblem Glyph" of El Zotz (figure 4.3), from a tunnel under Str. L7-1 in the Acropolis; (5) a pot excavated from a crypt in front of Str. L8-13 by the Garrison project in 2015 (figure 1.10); and (6) Bejucal Stela 2 (figure 3.2), with dates of July 24, AD 393, and an accession some 12 years before, on, probably, September 3, AD 381. A pot belonging to a ruler of El Zotz has also been found on the outskirts of El Perú-Waka' by Fabiola Quiroa (Héctor Escobedo, personal communication, 2006); another likely to have come from the region of El Zotz was excavated at Uaxactun, Guatemala (Smith 1955:figure 80k).

Each text contributes a key piece of information. Although damaged, Stela 1 provides the first datable sculptor's signature in the Classic Maya corpus. With the *way* cult, if it can termed as such, this spotlights El Zotz as a region of innovation, an attribute that might be expected in border zones. Perhaps they felt the need to reward agility and innovation more than inertia and supine tradition. Found in 2011, Stela 4 confirms that the Emblem of the site continued well into the final years of the Late Classic period, and two pots, excavated in 2010 and 2015 respectively, fix that Emblem on a provenienced piece of pottery (see also the same name on a vessel in the Museo Popol Vuh, Guatemala City, #1140). It is probably no coincidence that use of the "holy" epithet (*k'uhul*) seems only to occur with *pa'k'a'n*, a place name meaning "split" or "fortified sky" (see below), in the later sixth century AD, perhaps signaling a new, more exalted status. Had the newfound ties to the so-called Snake dynasty resulted in an acknowledged elevation in royal status? (To be sure, Emblems with *k'uhul* become more common generally at this time.) Bejucal Stela 2 is crucial for showing the broad reach of the dynasty into the uplands northeast of El Zotz, recording a figure who has precisely the same names as other rulers at El Zotz (Garrison et al. 2016:536–537). At the same time, it reveals the apparent subordination of the dynasty to the enigmatic Sihyaj K'ahk', an individual associated with Teotihuacan and deeply linked to the regional power of Tikal (Stuart 2000). Neighbors to the west, especially the important city of El Perú-Waka', refer to the same lord at about the same time (see, e.g., El Perú-Waka' Stela 9). In fact, the date of this reference may predate the figure's appearance at Tikal—unfortunately, the glyphs for this event are poorly preserved, and the stela itself carries a dedicatory date some 40 years

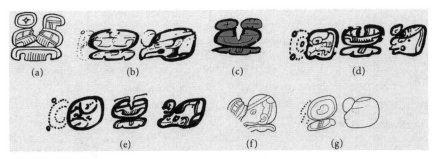

FIGURE I.II. *El Zotz Emblem Glyphs (drawings by S. Houston): (a) Canberra Bowl; (b) Hellmuth files; (c) K6618; (d) K8383; (e) "Vase of the Eleven Gods," lid of Tepeu I vase (based on Coe 1973:Plate 38); (f) El Zotz Wooden Lintel I:A7, Str. M7–I; and (g) "earspool" Emblem, El Zotz Wooden Lintel I:C7–C8, Str. M7–I.*

later (Stuart 2000:479–480). A later monument at El Perú-Waka', Stela 44, from 9.6.10.0.0 (AD 564), subordinates the local ruler to a recently detected ruler of the Snake dynasty, a power that governed Dzibanche, Quintana Roo, and, later still, Calakmul, Campeche (Castañeda Tobar 2013:197–202). According to a vase excavated at Uaxactun, Guatemala, this Snake lord was also an overlord in that region, perhaps of some splinter branch of the Tikal dynasty (Martin and Beliaev 2016).

From these data come clear proof, first marshaled by David Stuart on the basis of clues on the wooden lintel, that El Zotz uses two Emblems, a locally supreme title. One is the so-called split-sky glyph, probably read *pa'ka'n* ("Split Sky" or "Fortress-Sky"); the other shows an earspool subfixed by a **ji** syllable (figure 1.11; see also Ek' Balam Vault 15 capstone). These titles serve also as the Emblems of the royal family of Yaxchilan, a dynastic connection that has yet to be understood. A link is likely but cannot be demonstrated, we fear, on any available evidence. Another distant connection may embellish a jade belt ornament from Calakmul. Seemingly, the text refers to an "arrival" at an "earspool" location, with the event shown in an unusual form more often tied to the observation of the first crescent of the moon (Fields and Tokovinine 2012:figure 99a). Akte, a site closer to El Zotz, just south of Cruce Dos Aguadas (and just west of the road between San Andrés and Carmelita), may also have some bond with El Zotz (Krempel and Davletshin 2014:figure 2). Fragment 2 of its Stela 5 appears to show the "earspool" Emblem at position pF3. To judge from its style, the dating of that monument veers toward the end of the Classic period. A lidded vessel that belonged to an older youth (**ke-le-ma ch'o[ko]**) presents a possible third Emblem, perhaps read *Chak Nutz*, a spelling that occurs in varying form on at least two other vessels (Coe 1973:86, positions O to D; see also K8393, Coe 1973:87). As at Yaxchilan, these Emblems may have been agglomerative, referring to different, sovereign zones within a kingdom. At times they appear singly with particular lords, at others joined in the person of a single ruler. A comparison might be the crowns of England and Scotland: King James (1566–1625) was the "First" of England but the "Sixth" of Scotland.

The reading for the "split-sky" sign was proposed by Simon Martin (2004): *pa'-chan* or *pa'-ka'n*. For plausible reasons, Martin interpreted *pa'* as an expression in several Mayan languages for "split," literally present in the form of a sky glyph ripped asunder. He also mentions *pa'*, "an enclosing wall or fortress" (Martin 2004:4). The high location of El Zotz and its obvious defensive properties at the citadel of El Diablo trend to the latter meaning—indeed, data from the 2016 PACUNAM LiDAR Initiative now hint that such high-elevation fortifications characterized much of the northern escarpment and middle reaches of the Buenavista Valley. As a place name, *pa'* occurs on Naranjo Stela 10:B4, not in reference to El Zotz, but to a **TI'-pa'-'a**, *ti' pa'*, "edge of the fortress," or, in a more complex rendering, *ti' pa'a*, "edge of the fortified water/lake." The use of *pa'* in a place name lends weight to its meaning as "fortress" or "citadel."

Although only loosely tied to dates, eight or more dynasts are known from the patchwork epigraphy of El Zotz environs. Much depends on the puzzling welter of names on looted pots from the initial years of the Late Classic period. Some occur in one case only (K6618), others mark at least two vessels (*Baahkab K'inich*; see the Popol Vuh pot above, and that excavated from El Zotz Str. L8-13 (figure 1.10)). They prompt speculation: are they sequent rulers, the same ruler with different names, or concurrent lords holding the same august title? Of foreign mention there is only a little. One example, an unprovenanced slate mirror back from Los Bagaces, Costa Rica, doubtless brought there by ancient trade, reveals that a ruler of El Zotz had received a gift (**sih*) from a ruler of El Perú-Waka', one K'inich Bahlam, the **wa-ka AJAW** (figure 1.12; Schmidt et al. 1998:plate 434, Museo del Jade Lic. Fidel Tristán, INS#6528; the El Perú-Waka' Emblem was identified by Houston in 1983, cf. Guenter 2007:20). Although the pot from El Zotz that was found at El Perú-Waka' is at least 100 or more years later, it bespeaks a longstanding amity with an enemy of Tikal's and a friend of the Snake dynasty's (Martin and Grube 2008:46; see also Guenter 2014:165–166). Tikal Stela 31 may, in a passage alluding to events after the arrival of Sihyaj K'ahk' (at, possibly, November 27, AD 411), mention the funerary temple of El Diablo (Houston, Newman, Román, and Garrison 2015:232, figure 6.2). It identifies a place linked to the Jaguar God of the Underworld,

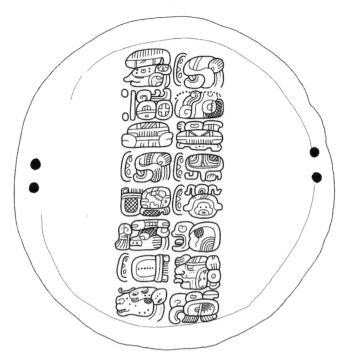

FIGURE 1.12. *Slate mirror back, close-up rubbing, Los Bagaces, Costa Rica (drawing by S. Houston based on Stone 1977:figure 44).*

seemingly at a location other than Tikal. The temple at El Diablo abounds in such imagery.

The ex–Museu Barbier-Mueller pot is equally intriguing because the ruler has a name that often appears at the site (see below), but it is the *mother* who bears the Pa'ka'n Emblem. The only other queen, possibly Yik'al Ahk, on the wooden lintel, employs the *Sak Wayis* title linked to the Calakmul region. The bowl in the San Diego Museum of Man (see above) is almost certainly of the same set of people, but with an important twist. In a surprising development, the son is now linked overtly to the Emblem Glyph of El Perú-Waka' (Looper and Polyukhovich 2016:4–5). This is a period in which many Maya dynasties appear to have been sending out cadet lines, splintering into multiple branches or experiencing breaks in father-to-son succession (e.g., Martin and Beliaev 2016). The significance here is unclear. The San Diego bowl could refer to a prince at El Perú-Waka'—he uses the title of youths, *Chak Ch'ok Keleem*, if in glyphs overly retouched by a restorer—taking a name from his maternal line. Or, as an alternative, the dynasty of El Zotz had been revived *through* a local woman. In the first scenario, the prince uses his title because he simply forms part of local royalty at El Perú-Waka'; in the second, the prince continued to lay claim to royal status at his home city but had shifted to another seat in the Buenavista Valley. At the least, the bowl both confirms close ties between the two kingdoms at the beginnings of the Late Classic period and shows them, with the evidence from Los Bagaces, to be exceptionally long lasting.

One name commonly repeated at El Zotz is composed of three to four glyphs. The first element is *chak*, meaning "red" or "great." The second glyph is a fish in a vertical position usually connected to the head of a dog or other mammal. This compound has not yet been deciphered, although it makes an appearance on a block in the Maegli Collection, Guatemala City, and on Copan Stela H, east side. A glyphic substitution on an unlabeled pot photographed by Justin Kerr appears to complete the spelling with an 'a syllable, a probable clue to the final of this sign. Finally, the name sometimes ends in *ahk*, or "turtle," often spelled out as 'a-ku (Houston 2008a).

The epigraphy can be summarized and extended as follows:

- Bejucal and Tikal displayed subordination to an enigmatic, foreign personage, "Born-from-Fire." Bejucal was an early seat of the dynasty that flourished also at El Zotz.

- In general, El Zotz had poor-to-uncertain relations with Tikal, its close, vastly larger neighbor. An earthwork of uncertain date and function separated the two, perhaps as a marker of territory. Notably, the lidar from 2016 also reveals a dearth of settlement between the two, though much of the lowland area is *bajo* swamps.

- El Zotz had amicable relations with a third city, El Perú-Waka', with close bonds of marriage and, we presume, cousinage. In the Late Classic, this city battled Tikal and, for much of its history, served as an ally of Tikal's archenemy, the Snake dynasty (Martin and Grube 2008:108–111). The mother of a ruler of El Zotz—the lord on the wooden lintel—was most likely from an area under the Snake dynasty's control, at least to judge from her title, an epithet common to its dependencies.

- Large quantities of looted vessels reveal that new religious themes emanated from the area of El Zotz. New forms of pyramid construction also appear first at El Zotz.

- Vessels referring to figures in the El Zotz royal family have an astonishing number in the final years of the sixth century AD. The meaning of this variety remains unclear, but there may have been either a rapid turnover of rulers or multiple, concurrent use of the local Emblem by competing lords—or an arrangement, unlike other cities, by which amicable dispersion of titles was the norm. It is noteworthy that use of "holy," *k'uhul*, comes in relatively late, at a time of close ties to the Snake dynasty, suggesting some heightened prestige as a result of that connection.

• The prodigiously rich Burial 9 at El Zotz (Houston, Newman, Román, and Garrison 2015) probably belonged to a founder, but had no legible text with which to prove that claim.

CONCLUSION

The El Zotz project addresses such history and its setting within a landscape that shifted dramatically over the course of millennia (see the Radiocarbon Appendix below and table 1.1 for a compilation of ^{14}C dates from the project). Yet there is a bald reality: El Zotz is a site in which the archaeology is far more eloquent than the epigraphy. A regional perspective, rooted in varied digs and suboperations, along with cross-cutting study of ceramics, lithics, human remains, and faunal material, composes a rich portrait of a kingdom at the uncomfortable margins of larger capitals. Tikal is the force here, but there are also clues to subordination and alliance with the enemies of Tikal, at El Perú-Waka' and even into the Mirador uplands, toward Calakmul. In more general terms, El Zotz possesses the features of what French and Italian scholars call a *fondation* or *fondazione* (Elisséeff 1983:151; Margueron 1994:4; Mazzoni 1991:319–321): a sudden establishment, not only of a large settlement, but, in the Maya case, of expensive facilities to house a royal court and to service royal cults. Burial 9 and its various dynastic conceits, including royal mergers with the sun, accord well with this scenario. Anthropological researchers have used another term for such urban creations, *disembedded capitals* or, in what may be a more accurate label, *reembedded capitals* (Joffe 1998). According to one recent review, these represent: (1) sudden foundations that (2) depart from previous settlement by (3) rearranging the layout and distribution of human populations and by (4) adding centralized facilities (such as palaces) with strong evidence of (5) planning and (6) "new symbolic vocabular[ies]" (Joffe 1998:551). Some of these points resonate with the data that follow, others diverge from evidence. The relative weight of top-down or bottom-up change forms the crux of later chapters by those who know those data best.

RADIOCARBON APPENDIX

The Proyecto Arqueológico El Zotz submitted 60 carbon samples for radiometric dating between 2008 to 2016. The dates help to anchor the complex cultural and environmental contexts discussed throughout this volume. All dates were run by Beta Analytic, Inc., in Miami, Florida, under the direction of Darden Hood. The dates are presented chronologically, in tabular format in table 1.1. It offers the lab sample number, appendix reference section, the excavation context, 2-sigma calibrated date ranges, and a brief description of the significance of the date and range probabilities where appropriate. In 2016, Darden Hood and Ron Hatfield recalibrated all of the project dates using the IntCal13 calibration curve (Reimer et al. 2013) and provided date-range probabilities based on Bayesian statistics (Bronk Ramsey 2009). El Zotz is by far the best-represented site from the suite of dates with 44 samples; 12 coming from El Diablo. El Palmar has 13 dates, although six of those are from paleoenvironmental investigations relating to the Laguna El Palmar (see Beach et al., chapter 7, this volume). Two more dates derive from Bejucal, and there is a single sample from the minor center of La Avispa.

The suite of dates covers the totality of human occupation in the region from possible Archaic-period disturbances as early as the eighteenth century BC to the deposition of Lacandon god pots in the Str. L7-11 temple at El Zotz, perhaps as late as the sixteenthn century AD. With a span of over 3,000 years, the Buenavista Valley has one of the longest records of ancient occupation in the Maya Lowlands. There are three dates from the Archaic, although two of them are bulk sediments and cannot be conclusively tied to human activity. In the Preclassic period, there are two dates in the Middle Preclassic and a further nine from the Late Preclassic. Five of these dates come from El Palmar, which had the largest Preclassic occupation in the valley. With 22 dates, the Early Classic is the best-represented time period, reflecting the importance of the rise of the Pa'ka'n dynasty at El Zotz and the growth of the city; this was also a focal period for many of our excavations. Nine dates come from the Late Classic period, which saw the continued expansion of the El Zotz polity. There are four dates from the critical Terminal Classic period, when dynastic kingship collapsed in the region. An additional 10 dates come from a small Early Postclassic settlement that remained at El Zotz, extending perhaps into the fourteenth century AD. Finally, there is a single date associated with the Lacandon pots mentioned above. Beginning in the fifth century BC, there are overlapping date ranges in every century until the fourteenth century AD, making this a relatively thorough series of radiometric assays for the Buenavista Valley. This appendix highlights the significance of these dates and is organized by location.

TABLE 1.1. Radiocarbon dates from the Proyecto Arqueológico El Zotz processed by Beta Analytic, Inc. All ranges are based on a 2σ standard deviation.

Beta Sample	Appendix Reference	Context	Date Range		Description and Range Probabilities
			Early	Late	
Earliest Dates					
285474	El Palmar E-Group	EP 8A-15-12	1876 BC	1617 BC	Sediment on top of bedrock below El Palmar Str. E4-1-6th. This bulk sediment is not likely cultural. 1782–1617 BC (85.9%); 1876–1841 BC (6.5%); 1821–1797 BC (3%)
284408	El Palmar Paleonvironment	Z10-1	1731 BC	1511 BC	Base of 2010 El Palmar sediment core. 1693–1511 BC (93.6%); 1731–1721 BC (1.8%)
285473	El Palmar E-Group	EP 8A-12-3	1617 BC	1440 BC	Sediment from fill of El Palmar Str. E4-1-4th. This bulk sediment is not likely cultural
Middle Preclassic (800–300 BC)					
262057	El Zotz Aguada	Zotz Guatemala 3 200	747 BC	389 BC	Sediment sample from the base of the El Zotz Aguada in 2009. 556–389 BC (81.1%); 747–685 BC (11%); 666–642 BC (3.3%)
262061	El Palmar Paleonvironment	Zotz Guatemala 7 110	723 BC	236 BC	El Palmar ravine. 541–357 BC (91.7%); 283–255 BC (2.5%); 245–236 BC (0.6%); 703–696 BC (0.4%); 723–721 BC (0.1%)
Late Preclassic (300 BC–AD 300)					
284409	El Palmar Paleonvironment	Z10-2	405 BC	208 BC	El Palmar sediment core. 405–348 BC (48.3%); 317–208 BC (47.1%)
265817	El Palmar E-Group	EP 1B-3-5	388 BC	202 BC	Fill beneath floor on top of El Palmar Str. E4-4

continued on next page

Table 1.1.—*continued*

Beta Sample	Appendix Reference	Context	Date Range		Description and Range Probabilities
			Early	Late	
285472	El Palmar E-Group	EP 8A-3-4	352 BC	43 BC	Fill of El Palmar Str. E4-1-1st. 212–43 BC (84.1%); 352–297 BC (10.6%); 229–221 BC (0.8%)
265816	Bejucal	BL 2B-4-3	164 BC	AD 56	Leveling of the bedrock in front of Bejucal Str. S6-1. 121 BC–AD 56 (87.9%); 164–128 BC (7.5%)
284410	El Palmar Paleonvironment	Z10-3	88 BC	AD 124	Date from 2010 El Palmar sediment core. 56 BC–AD 92 (91%); AD 98–124 (3.3%); 88–77 BC (1%)
288297	Bejucal	BL 1B-6-7	AD 58	AD 238	Fill of Bejucal Str. S6-10-Sub.2
262058	El Palmar Paleonvironment	Zotz Guatemala 4 49	AD 127	AD 344	Deepest paleosol recovered in 2009 core at El Palmar near the Water Temple
289493	El Zotz Aguada	Z10-6 Aguada 80 cm Pit 4	AD 128	AD 322	On top of the lower floor in the El Zotz Aguada. AD 128–258 (86.6%); AD 284–322 (8.8%)
262060	El Diablo Aguada	Zotz Guatemala 6 130	AD 128	AD 381	Sample from 130 cm in the El Diablo Aguada

Early Classic (AD 300–550)

Beta Sample	Appendix Reference	Context	Date Range		Description and Range Probabilities
431441	El Diablo Palace	EZ 19D-9-1	AD 137	AD 334	Fill of Str. F8-7
265821	El Palmar Water Temple	EP 3E-1-4	AD 220	AD 405	Deposit in front of El Palmar Str. F5-1 ("Water Temple")
288303	El Diablo Pyramid	EZ 5B-29-V13B	AD 240	AD 410	Vessel inside royal tomb (El Zotz Burial 9)

continued on next page

TABLE 1.1.—*continued*

Beta Sample	Appendix Reference	Context	Date Range Early	Date Range Late	Description and Range Probabilities
431445	El Zotz I10 Group	EZ 25C-17-11	AD 256	AD 396	Burial 28 in Str. I10-4. This is a problematic date that is inconsistent with the Terminal Classic context of the burial. AD 320–396 (74.7%); AD 256–297 (20.7%)
433097	El Diablo Pyramid	EZ 5B-36-1	AD 256	AD 400	Inside the columnar altar associated with El Zotz Burial 9. AD 316–400 (74.8%); AD 256–300 (20.6%)
262059	El Diablo Aguada	Zotz Guatemala 5 95	AD 252	AD 530	Sample from 95 cm in the El Diablo Aguada. AD 252–430 (90.7%); AD 492–530 (4.7%)
288304	El Diablo Plaza	EZ 5J-4-2	AD 252	AD 530	Ash on top of the plaza floor in front of Str. F8-18. This is not a sealed context. AD 252–430 (90.7%); AD 492–530 (4.7%)
431443	El Zotz East Group	EZ 21C-8-1	AD 258	AD 422	Final remodeling of Str. M7-1-Sub. 1-1st. AD 321–422 (85.2%); AD 258–296 (10.2%)
288298	El Zotz Acropolis	EZ 2G-7-8	AD 260	AD 536	El Zotz Burial 5, an intrusive burial placed into cut floors prior to the construction of the final phase of Str. L7-1. The date is likely from the fill of the cut floors rather than the burial itself. AD 325–475 (77.6%); AD 484–536 (14.2%); AD 260–280 (3.5%)

continued on next page

TABLE 1.1.—*continued*

Beta Sample	Appendix Reference	Context	Date Range Early	Date Range Late	Description and Range Probabilities
437467	El Zotz East Group	EZ 21E-2-3	AD 335	AD 502	Amplification of central *adosado* associated with Burial 25. This is a problematic date that is inconsistent with other dates within Str. M7-1's stratigraphic profile. AD 335–428 (95%); AD 498–502 (0.4%)
265823	El Diablo Pyramid	EZ 5B-8-1	AD 266	AD 538	Fill in front of the posterior central mask of the Temple of the Night Sun; AD 332–538 (94.6%); AD 266–271 (0.8%)
437466	El Zotz East Group	EZ 21A-9-1	AD 336	AD 534	Carbon residue found in the beak of the northern *Ux Yop Huun* mask of Str. M7-1-Sub. 2. AD 336–436 (75.8%); AD 486–534 (15.9%); AD 446–472 (3.8%)
433095	El Diablo Pyramid	EZ 5B-30-2	AD 338	AD 502	Construction of the floor connecting the Temple of the Night Sun and the Shrine. AD 338–428 (94.9%); AD 498–502 (0.5%)
265822	El Diablo Pyramid	EZ 5B-7-2	AD 402	AD 572	Fill from an early destroyed platform found underneath two plaza floors in front of Str. F8-1
431444	El Zotz East Group	EZ 21E-1-5	AD 410	AD 546	El Zotz Burial 25, located in a remodeling of the central *adosado* of Str. M7-1
265818	El Zotz Acropolis	EZ 2A-13-3	AD 410	AD 583	Fill beneath penultimate floor in the interior of Str. L7-6-Sub. 1

continued on next page

TABLE 1.1.—*continued*

Beta Sample	Appendix Reference	Context	Date Range Early	Date Range Late	Description and Range Probabilities
431439	El Diablo Palace	EZ 19B-4-4	AD 422	AD 574	Fill covering the last palace phase of Str. F8-6. Combined with other dates the fill was likely placed between AD 428–574
284412	El Zotz Aguada	Z10-5	AD 424	AD 606	Above the lower floor in the El Zotz Aguada
437465	El Diablo Palace	EZ 19C-2-6	AD 428	AD 598	Fill covering the last palace phase of Str. F8-9. Combined with other dates the fill was likely placed between AD 428–574
431440	El Diablo Palace	EZ 19C-4-1	AD 428	AD 598	Fill covering the last palace phase of Str. F8-9. Combined with other dates the fill was likely placed between AD 428–574
431442	El Zotz East Group	EZ 21C-1-2	AD 430	AD 622	Fill of Str. M7-1-Sub. 2 (the Accession Platform). AD 528–622 (74.8%); AD 430–494 (19.7%); AD 510–517 (0.9%)
288299	El Zotz Acropolis	EZ 2G-23-3	AD 433	AD 650	Fill of a possible substructure in the acropolis (Str. L7-1-Sub. 1?). AD 532–650 (88.4%); AD 433–457 (3.6%); AD 468–488 (3.4%)

Late Classic (AD 550–850)

Beta Sample	Appendix Reference	Context	Date Range Early	Date Range Late	Description and Range Probabilities
292997	El Palmar Paleonvironment	Z Palmar 09 42 cm core 4: sapric peat	AD 614	AD 763	Date from 2010 El Palmar sediment core, 42 cm. AD 614–694 (92.2%); AD 747–763 (3.2%)
265825	La Avispa	IR 9A-1-4	AD 648	AD 770	Beneath the final floor of the La Avispa platform

continued on next page

TABLE 1.1.—*continued*

Beta Sample	Appendix Reference	Context	Date Range		Description and Range Probabilities
			Early	Late	
262056	El Zotz Aguada	Zotz Guatemala 2 105	AD 651	AD 869	Sample from 105 cm in the El Zotz Aguada in 2009; below the upper floor. AD 651–779 (83.1%); AD 790–869 (12.3%)
262055	El Zotz Aguada	Zotz Guatemala 1 87	AD 656	AD 864	Sample from 87 cm in the El Zotz Aguada in 2009; above the upper floor. AD 656–778 (87.4%); AD 790–828 (4.7%); AD 838–864 (3.3%)
285471	El Palmar E-Group	EP 8A-2-6	AD 656	AD 864	Soil on top of El Palmar Str. E4-1-1st. This is not a sealed context. AD 656–778 (87.4%); AD 790–828 (4.7%); AD 838–864 (3.3%)
250881	El Zotz L7-11	EZ 3A-3-2	AD 666	AD 874	Fill surrounding the shark teeth cache found in the base of Str. L7-11. AD 666–780 (74.1%); AD 788–874 (21.3%)
250883	El Zotz L7-11	EZ 3B-1-8	AD 672	AD 879	Burnt wood, possibly from the collapsed roof of the temple on top of Str. L7-11
288300	El Zotz Acropolis	EZ 2H-5-8	AD 680	AD 881	Fill of remodeling that covered the Early Classic base (talud) of Str. L7-1
288301	El Zotz Acropolis	EZ 2H-9-3	AD 687	AD 940	Fill between final phases of Strs. L7-1 and L7-6. AD 687–895 (93.7%); AD 928–940 (1.7%)

continued on next page

TABLE 1.1.—*continued*

Beta Sample	Appendix Reference	Context	Date Range Early	Date Range Late	Description and Range Probabilities
Terminal Classic (AD 850–1000)					
433098	El Zotz I10 Group	EZ 25C-17-9	AD 771	AD 965	Capstones of El Zotz Burial 28 in Str. I10-4. AD 771–903 (80.8%); AD 918–965 (14.6%)
311992	El Zotz South Group	EZ 6K-4-7	AD 773	AD 968	Midden to the north-west of the South Group platform. AD 773–906 (71.8%); AD 916–968 (23.6%)
265819	El Zotz Acropolis	EZ 2G-2-2	AD 774	AD 978	Ritual deposit on top of Str. L7-1
265820	El Zotz Acropolis	EZ 2G-4-5	AD 776	AD 990	Ritual deposit on top of Str. L7-1
Early Postclassic (AD 1000–1300)					
288302	El Zotz Las Palmitas	EZ 4F-11-3	AD 900	AD 1152	Interior of room in Str. M3-6. This is not a sealed context. AD 947–1051 (76.5%); AD 1082–1128 (11.4%); AD 900–922 (4.2%); AD 1134–1152 (3.4%)
250880	El Zotz South Group	EZ 1D-1-1	AD 996	AD 1164	Near-surface deposit of utilitarian materials at the base of the South Group platform. This is not a sealed context
307271	El Zotz South Group	EZ 6L-5-4	AD 1033	AD 1204	Lot with postholes in Str. L9-11. AD 1033–1190 (94%); AD 1198–1204 (1.4%)
288306	El Zotz South Group	EZ 6K-2-3	AD 1034	AD 1220	South Group midden
288305	El Zotz South Group	EZ 6A-3-5	AD 1052	AD 1274	Leveling of the bedrock at the western edge of the plaza entrance to the South Causeway. AD 1151–1274 (91.1%); AD 1052–1081 (4.3%)

continued on next page

TABLE 1.1.—*continued*

Beta Sample	Appendix Reference	Context	Date Range Early	Date Range Late	Description and Range Probabilities
311991	El Zotz South Group	EZ 6A-18-4	AD 1190	AD 1278	From fill in the horizontal excavation of Str. L8-28
265824	El Zotz South Group	EZ 6E-1-3	AD 1190	AD 1294	Final floor of platform in front of Str. L9-3 in the South Group
307270	El Zotz South Group	EZ 6K-2-6	AD 1222	AD 1286	Base of South Group midden
285470	El Palmar E-Group	EP 1B-10-6	AD 1220	AD 1387	Mixed in a deposit of ceramic, obsidian, and faunal remains near the surface north of El Palmar Str. E4-4. This is not a sealed context. AD 1220–1310 (84.2%); AD 1360–1387 (11.2%)
307269	El Zotz South Group	EZ 6A-28-2	AD 1265	AD 1388	Context with toad pot in South Group on top of possible floor. AD 1265–1312 (68.9%); AD 1358–1388 (26.5%)

Late Postclassic (AD 1300–1519)

Beta Sample	Appendix Reference	Context	Date Range Early	Date Range Late	Description and Range Probabilities
250882	El Zotz L7-11	EZ 3B-1-6	AD 1426	AD 1632	Lot just above the Lacandon pots found on top of Str. L7-11. AD 1426–1524 (71.9%); 1558–1632 (23.5%)

EL PALMAR

Paleoenvironmental Dates

Six radiocarbon dates were obtained for paleoenvironmental studies around El Palmar. Four of these (284408, 284409, 284410, 292997) date a sediment core taken at El Palmar in 2010. A fifth date (262061) came from a unit excavated in a ravine to the south-southeast of the Triadic Group. The sample was associated with an alignment of boulders that may have served a terracing function; it returned possible date ranges of 723–236 BC (with a 91.7% probability of falling between 541 and 357 BC), consistent with human activity at other areas of the site during the Middle Preclassic. A final date (262058) comes from a core near the El Palmar Water Temple (Str. F5-1). It dates a paleosol layer (AD 127–344) that would have been in use during the Late Preclassic period before being buried by sedimentation. Further results from these dates are reported in Beach et al. (2015; Beach et al., chapter 7, this volume) and Luzzadder-Beach et al. (2017).

E-Group Dates

Six radiocarbon dates came from excavations directed by James Doyle in the El Palmar E-Group. The earliest from the group (285474) comes from bulk sediment on top of bedrock and beneath the earliest version of the E-Group pyramid (Str. E4-1-6th); it issues from the Archaic period (1876–1617 BC with an 85.9% probability of falling between 1782 and 1617 BC). This is not a demonstrably cultural date. A second bulk sediment date (285473) from Str. E4-1-4th is also very early (1617–1440 BC) and does not date the architecture; indeed, it may simply correspond to the soil used as construction fill. Two other dates relate to unsealed surface contexts associated with the El Palmar E-Group. A date (285471) from the summit of the final-phase pyramid (Str. E4-1-1st) returned a Late Classic date (AD 656–864 with an 87.4% probability of falling between AD 656 and 778), while a sample (285470) from debris found on top of the eastern platform (Str. E4-4) dates to the Early Postclassic (AD 1220–1387 with an 84.2% probability of falling between AD 1220 and 1310). These are either unreliable dates or evidence of later, quite light occupation at El Palmar.

Two more secure dates were obtained from stratigraphic excavations within the El Palmar E-Group. The earlier sample (265817) is from the penultimate construction phase of the eastern platform (Str. E4-4) and returned a date of 388–202 BC, indicating that the bulk of the structure must have been built in the Middle Preclassic. The fill (285472) of the final E-Group pyramid (E4-1-1st) dates to 352–43 BC (with an 84.1% probability of falling between 212 and 43 BC), with ceramics supporting the tighter range. These dates buttress Doyle's (2013a; Doyle and Piedrasanta, chapter 2, this volume) chronology for the Preclassic construction of the El Palmar E-Group.

Water Temple Dates

Right on the edge of the Laguna El Palmar sits a small pyramid, nicknamed the Water Temple (Str. F5-1) because of its location. In 2009, Varinia Matute excavated a substantial offering at the base of the structure that consisted of ceramics, obsidian, faunal remains, and ash (Doyle and Matute Rodríguez 2009; Román et al., chapter 3, this volume). A carbon sample (265821) from the deposit confirmed the Early Classic date cued by ceramic analysis, returning a range of AD 220–405. The offering appears to be a termination ritual that coincides with the abandonment of El Palmar at the beginning of the Early Classic period.

BEJUCAL DATES

Two radiocarbon samples were dated for the hilltop site of Bejucal, which served as a royal country house for the Classic-period rulers of Pa'ka'n (Garrison et al. 2016). The dates come from the earliest occupation of the site, when it seems to have been a sacred hilltop where temples were constructed and important individuals buried. A date from the site's northwestern courtyard (265816) indicates that the bedrock was leveled for construction between 164 BC and AD 56 (with an 87.9% probability of falling between 121 BC and AD 56). A second sample (288297), from the fill of a round temple (Str. S6-10-Sub.-2), dates the construction of that structure to AD 58–238, which is consistent with the architectural form and the associated ceramics. The two dates confirm the Late Preclassic establishment of Bejucal within the sacred geography of the Buenavista Valley. The site grew in importance with the rise of the Early Classic dynasty at El Zotz.

EL DIABLO GROUP

El Diablo Aguada Dates

The El Diablo Group is a part of El Zotz itself, but the large quantity of dates associated with this important complex merits its own section. Further dates from El Zotz are discussed below. The El Diablo Group was built in multiple levels on a hilltop overlooking the Buenavista Valley. One of these levels has a large depression and a leveled area that supports Str. G8-1 (figure 3.3). The depression served as a limestone quarry to build much of the architecture located at the group's center. We hypothesized that the quarry was then converted into an *aguada* (a pond for drinking water) that would have served a newly established royal court. Paleoenvironmental studies could not confirm whether the depression was ever actually capable of holding water, but two dates, one from 0.95 m (262059) and another from 1.3 m (262060), date the onset of activity in the group. The deeper date has a range of AD 128–381, while the shallower date could be AD 252–530 (with a 90.7% probability of falling between AD 252 and 430). These dates are consistent with the Early Classic date of the El Diablo Group, and the earlier date may indicate a Late Preclassic presence, which has been confirmed by ceramics if not by architecture.

EL DIABLO PALACE DATES

The El Diablo palace is composed of a number of structures on the north and west side of the group. Investigations by Edwin Román and, later, Yeny Gutiérrez confirm the Early Classic use of the complex based on ceramics. A date (431441) from the fill of Str. F8-7 came back as AD 137–334. Early Classic ceramic evidence suggests that the date falls later in this range (Garrison and Houston, chapter 13, this volume; Román et al., chapter 3, this volume).

Three more dates come from the abandonment of the El Diablo palace. A large fill deposit was encountered on top of all of the palace structures, probably indicating the cessation of the remodeling, though Román-Ramírez (2011) believes that the deposit has ritual overtones. A sample (431439) from the deposit on Str. F8-6 dates to AD 422–574, while dates (437465, 431440) from two different contexts on Str. F8-9 each had a range of AD 428–598. Assuming the deposit occurred at the same time across the structures, the abandonment of the El Diablo palace must have occurred between AD 428 and 574. This range accords with site growth in the El Zotz epicenter at around the same time.

EL DIABLO PYRAMID DATES

A series of five dates come from the El Diablo pyramid (Str. F8-1) and its substructures, which includes the Temple of the Night Sun and the associated royal tomb (El Zotz Burial 9; Houston, Newman, Román, and Garrison 2015). Two dates are associated directly with the tomb. The first (288303) corresponds to a vessel within the tomb itself and dates to AD 240–410, while the second (433097) comes from a columnar altar that was used as the tomb offerings were being made: its range is AD 256–400 (with a 74.8% chance of falling within AD 316–400). This second date gives a tighter bracket for the interment of the El Zotz royal founder. Combined with other data sets, including a text from Bejucal Stela 2, Teotihuacan iconography on a vessel lid in Burial 9, and the aging of the king's skeleton, it is possible that the tomb's occupant died sometime between AD 378 and 381 (see Garrison and Houston, chapter 13, this volume, for further discussion).

The founder's tomb was covered by a large platform (Str. F8-1-Sub. 1) that supported the Temple of the Night Sun (built in two stages: Strs. F8-1-Sub. 1B and F8-1-Sub. 1C) and a smaller, slightly later structure that we called the "Shrine" (F8-1-Sub. 1A; see Houston, Newman, Román, and Carter 2015:figure 2.3 for detailed stratigraphy). A date (433095) from a floor linking the Temple of the Night Sun and the Shrine returned as AD 338–502 (with a 94.9% probability of falling between AD 338 and 428). Presuming the king died in the early AD 380s, the temple, its expansion, and the Shrine would have been built within four decades at most.

Two more dates are relevant to establishing the construction sequence of the pyramid. The first (265822) dates the raising of the El Diablo plaza level in front of Str. F8-1-Sub. 1 to the elevation of the Shrine in AD 402–572. The second (265823) comes from architectural fill from Str. F8-1-2nd, which represents the most massive remodeling of the pyramid. This sample, recovered from in front of the central rear mask of the Temple of the Night Sun, dates to AD 266–538 (with a 94.6% probability of falling within AD 332–538). Since this construction occurred stratigraphically later than the raising of the plaza, the range in which both Str. F8-1-2nd was built and the plaza was raised must have extended from AD 402 to 538.

El Diablo Plaza Date

A final radiocarbon assay (288304) from El Diablo comes from an unsealed context in an ash layer on top of the plaza floor in front of Str. F8-18. This small platform in the plaza was likely built by squatters living in the abandoned group. The ash layer dates to AD 252–530 (with a 90.7% probability of falling within AD 252–430), but the meaning of this date is unclear because of the poorly understood context. One possibility is that Str. F8-18 was added late, but was filled with earlier material from middens on the edges of the El Diablo Group. This seems more likely than having a residential platform situated in the center of the plaza during the group's primary royal occupation. Overall, the pattern of dates from all settings at El Diablo indicate that it was the seat of royal power at El Zotz beginning in the early fourth century AD, and continued in that role until its sudden abandonment around 200 years later.

EL ZOTZ

El Zotz Aguada

Five carbon samples were dated from the El Zotz Aguada, located west of the Five Temples Group, as part of paleoenvironmental investigations directed by Timothy Beach and Sheryl Luzzadder-Beach; these are extensively reported in

Beach et al. (2015; Beach et al., chapter 7, this volume). The earliest date (262057) appears to have washed into the *aguada* at some point: it is stratigraphically and contextually inconsistent with the rest of the dates. This assignment is 747–389 BC (with an 81.1% probability of falling between 556 and 389 BC). The lack of context is frustrating, in that it is one of only two dates firmly in the Middle Preclassic.

The other four samples from the El Zotz Aguada date the two floors uncovered during excavations in 2009 and 2010. Those floors doubtless aided in water retention. For the lower floor, a sample (289493) taken directly on top of the surface came back as AD 128–322 (with an 86.6% probability of falling within AD 128–258). A clear Early Classic jar found within the floor's matrix suggests that the first surface was laid down around the turn of the fourth century AD. A sample (284412) higher up in the sediment profile dates to AD 424–606, consistent with the sedimentation of the Early Classic *aguada*, likely accelerated by the relocation of the royal court from El Diablo around the turn of the sixth century AD.

The upper *aguada* floor is bracketed by two dates. The upper date (262055) was AD 656–864 (with an 87.4% probability of falling within AD 656–778), while the lower sample (262056) returned a date of AD 651–869 (with an 83.1% probability of falling within AD 651–779). Most likely, the upper floor was constructed between AD 650–780, perhaps as part of an acceleration of building activity in the El Zotz epicenter during the eighth century AD (Carter et al., chapter 4, this volume; Garrison and Houston, chapter 13, this volume).

EAST GROUP DATES

A series of five dates derive from the East Group at El Zotz, all from within the Pyramid of the Wooden Lintel (Str. M7-1) and its substructures. One of the samples (437467) is stratigraphically incongruent with the rest, despite falling in the Early Classic at AD 335–502 (with a 95% probability of falling within AD 335–428). Coming from a fill context, the carbon may represent older burnt wood that was incorporated in the later building. The other four dates provide a tidy sequence for the successive remodelings of the pyramid. A date (431443) from the final phase of the earliest platform in this location, Str. M7-1-Sub. 1-1st, places it between AD 258 and 422 (with an 85.2% probability of falling within AD 321–422). Fragments of painted modeled stucco from the destroyed portions of this platform indicate that it was built in a style similar to fourth-century AD architecture in the El Diablo Group.

Two dates are associated with the Accession Platform (Str. M7-1-Sub. 2). The first (431442) links to the building's construction fill and dates to AD

430–622 (with a 74.8% probability of falling within AD 528–622). The second (437466) comes from carbon found within the beak of the northern *Ux Yop Huun* mask on the platform and is related to the structure's use or abandonment. Its date was AD 336–534 (with a 75.8% probability of falling within AD 336–436). Using the shorter high-probability ranges for these two dates puts them into stratigraphic conflict, so we are required to use the full 2-sigma ranges for interpretation. Based on this, the range for the construction of the Accession Platform and the royal tomb (El Zotz Burial 16) that it houses is AD 436–534. The platform is architecturally distinct from earlier constructions at El Diablo, but is oriented toward the Temple of the Night Sun. It is possible that the structure was built around the turn of the sixth century AD as part of the shift of the seat of power from the El Diablo Group to the valley floor.

A final date (431444) from the East Group comes from El Zotz Burial 25, an elite interment associated with a remodeling of the central *adosado* (outset building) that was added to the first pyramidal form of the structure (Str. M7-1-2nd). The burial dates to AD 410–546, which accords with the Early Classic pots found in the tomb. The central *adosado* was remodeled numerous times and with fair regularity. The East Group was clearly a zone of the site that experienced rapid growth in the second half of the Early Classic period.

ACROPOLIS

A suite of seven dates from the El Zotz Acropolis spans its earliest constructions in the Early Classic to its eventual abandonment in the Terminal Classic as dynastic kingship ceased. The Classic-period palace consisted of 13 different structures (figure 4.1), but all of the dates correspond to the two largest buildings, Strs. L7-1 and L7-6, which were the focus of intensive investigation by the project. The earliest date (288298) fixes to El Zotz Burial 5, which was an intrusive, on-axis deposit at the base of Str. L7-1. The date of AD 260–536 (with a 77.6% probability of falling within AD 325–475) suggests that the sample is dating, not the later burial, but the fill of the earliest floor cut to prepare for this deposit.

There are two dates for early constructions in the Acropolis. The clearest early masonry building is Str. L7-6-Sub. 1, which was investigated in 2009 (Pérez Robles et al. 2009). A date (265818) from the penultimate floor inside of this structure returned as AD 410–583. This finely made Early Classic building may have been the first palace construction in epicentral El Zotz, following the abandonment of the El Diablo Group. A tunnel excavated in Str. L7-1 (figure 4.2) revealed a possible substructural platform (Str. L7-1-Sub. 1?; Marroquín et al. 2011), and a sample (288299) from the fill dates to AD 433–650 (with an 88.4% probability of falling within AD 532–650). Slightly later than Str. L7-6-Sub. 1, this could represent the beginning of the palace's expansion at the onset of the Late Classic period (see Carter et al., chapter 4, this volume; Garrison and Houston, chapter 13, this volume). It is also one of the few massive constructions from the so-called Tepeu 1 period, when many vases appear to have come from the kingdom (Carter et al., chapter 4, this volume).

An additional two dates are tethered to Late Classic amplifications of the Acropolis. A sample (288300) from the fill covering the Early Classic talud of Str. L7-1's platform dates to AD 680–881. A second date (288301) from architectural fill connecting Strs. L7-1 and L7-6 places the final construction of the palace between AD 678–940 (with a 93.7% probability of falling within AD 687–895). These dates confirm the Acropolis as the seat of the Late Classic royal court of Pa'ka'n.

Two final dates illuminate the ritual deposit that covered portions of the Acropolis in preparation for a remodeling that was never completed (Newman 2015b; Newman et al., chapter 5, this volume). These dates from two separate excavation contexts of the same deposit are virtually identical. The first (265819) has a range of AD 774–978, while the second (265820) is just slightly different at AD 776–990. With the evidence from El Zotz Stela 4 (Newman et al., chapter 5, this volume), it appears probable that the ritual deposit dates to around AD 850 and signals the end of dynastic kingship and the onset of the Terminal Classic period.

Structure L7-11

Three dates assist in understanding El Zotz's largest pyramid, Str. L7-11. Two dates are associated with the pyramid's construction. The first (250881) is associated with a dedicatory cache found at the center base of the pyramid: this deposit runs from AD 666 to 874 (with a 74.1% probability of falling within AD 666–780). The second (250883) comes from the probable remains of a perishable roof from the pyramid's upper temple, with a range of AD 672–879. To judge from stratigraphic evidence, the pyramid was almost certainly built in a single construction phase, probably during the expansion of the site during the eighth century AD. Most likely, too, it was coeval with the expansion of the Acropolis. The final date (250882) comes from just above the two Lacandon god pots offered in the ruined temple. The date is from the Late Postclassic at AD 1426–1632 (with a 71.9% probability of falling within AD 1426–1524) and provides a coda for activity at El Zotz before it was rediscovered by archaeologists in the twentieth century.

I10 Group

Two dates were obtained from Burial 28 located within Str. I10-4 in a small residential group on the El Zotz periphery (de Carteret 2016). The first date (431445) from inside the burial is inconsistent with the Terminal Classic context of the structure, returning an Early Classic date of AD 256–396 (with a 74.7% probability of falling within AD 320–396). This date must be considered spurious, given the other evidence associated with the burial. A second date (433098) from the level of Burial 28's capstones is more reliable, having a range of AD 771–965 (with an 80.8% chance of falling within AD 771–903). This date is consistent with a trend of increasing residences around El Zotz in the Terminal Classic, perhaps as land became more accessible after the collapse of dynastic kingship.

Las Palmitas Group

A single date (288302) from the Las Palmitas Group comes from an unsealed context within Str. M3-6 (figure 4.11). Dating to AD 900–1152 (with a 76.5% probability of falling within AD 947–1051), it accords with a small Early Postclassic occupation of the group. However, the archaeology indicates that most of Las Palmitas was constructed during the Late Classic period (Carter et al., chapter 4, this volume).

South Group

A series of nine dates derives from the El Zotz South Group, which saw the latest population at the site, well into the Early Postclassic. Ceramic data indicate that this was also, in all likelihood, the earliest location occupied at El Zotz, with occupation as early as the Middle Preclassic. The presence of the nearby El Zotz Aguada, perhaps beginning as a natural feature, is a likely explanation for the persistence of the South Group as a settlement over millennia. One date (250880) comes from near the surface at the northern base of the group's platform. Although consistent with other dates from the area, with a range of AD 996–1164, it should not, because of its surface context, be considered reliable. In general, it seems, the late settlement began on top of the South Group's abandoned Classic-period platform and then spread to the western edge of the Southern Causeway.

A suite of three dates originate in a midden located northwest of the South Group platform. The midden probably began in the Terminal Classic, indicated by a date (311992) between AD 773 and 968 (with a 71.8% probability of falling within AD 773–906). Real expansion did not occur until the Early Postclassic, however. A date (288306) from the middle of the midden returned as AD 1034–1220, while another sample (307270) from the base of the deposit came back as AD 1222–1286. The organic growth of midden deposits through time makes it difficult to clarify the chronology of the deposit. A sample (307271) from the platform of a perishable structure above the midden (Str. L9-11) is consistent with the trash deposit, returning a date of AD 1033–1204 (with a 94% probability of falling within AD 1033–1190). Another sample (265824) from a small platform at the base of Str. L9-3 dates to AD 1190–1294, indicating that the Early Postclassic presence diffused across the top of the South Group platform.

A second area of Postclassic activity was west of El Zotz's Southern Causeway. Three dates reflect the occupation of that area through time. The first (288305) comes from the leveling of the bedrock at the western edge of intersection of the Southern Causeway and the plaza. This dates between AD 1052 and 1274 (with a 91.1% probability of falling within AD 1151–1274). A second sample (311991) from the fill of Str. L8-28 along the causeway's western edge dates to AD 1190–1278. Finally, the latest date (307269) at the site before it was completely abandoned is associated with a toad-effigy pot found along the western edge of the causeway, possibly on top of a floor. This final date has a range of AD 1265–1388 (with a 68.9% probability of falling within AD 1265–1312), making El Zotz one of the latest occupied Peten sites outside of the lakes region.

LA AVISPA DATE

A single radiocarbon sample (265825) dates the final of eight floors that resurfaced a small triadic group at La Avispa. While most of the settlement dates to the Preclassic period, this sample returned a range of AD 648–770, situating the final construction firmly in the Late Classic.

2

Monumental Beginnings

The Preclassic Maya of El Palmar and the Buenavista Valley, Peten, Guatemala

JAMES A. DOYLE
AND RONY E. PIEDRASANTA

The first florescence of Maya civilization in the Preclassic period (ca. 2000 BC–AD 250) has received much attention since the twentieth century, when it became clear that early materials lay under the great Classic cities (Estrada-Belli 2011:33–38). Today, a general consensus exists that during the first millennium BC peoples across the Maya Lowlands shared a cultural inventory that included language, monumental architecture, aesthetic canons, and material technologies (Houston and Inomata 2009:65). However, despite over 75 years of research after the recognition of "early Maya" (Ricketson, Jr. and Ricketson 1937) or "pre-Classic" Maya settlement (Smith 1950:4), many unanswered questions remain about the origins of civilization in the central Lowlands. Evidence from the Buenavista Valley Preclassic period is beginning to address some of these major questions. This chapter reports on material and architectural findings from the Preclassic period at the sites of El Palmar, El Zotz, La Avispa, and Bejucal (see figures 1.3–1.5, 1.7).

The Proyecto Arqueológico El Zotz (PAEZ) recovered strong evidence that a significant population occupied the Buenavista Valley as far back as the Middle Preclassic period (ca. 1000–300 BC). During this time, the site of El Palmar grew into a major civic center lying in the path of east–west trade corridors, and residents constructed E-Group architecture comparable to Tikal and other Middle Preclassic sites. A building boom of the Late Preclassic period (dated

DOI: 10.5876/9781607327646.c002

locally to ca. 300 BC–AD 300) occurred as populations expanded the E-Group at El Palmar and invested in significant site planning, likely the result of the establishment of an early political authority in the valley. Aside from El Palmar, the populations of El Zotz, La Avispa, and Bejucal also constructed platforms and produced ceramics during the Preclassic period. At the end of the Late Preclassic (ca. AD 100–300), populations left behind the low-lying centers of the valley and moved to upland, defensible locations such as the El Diablo and El Tejón Groups at El Zotz and the site of Bejucal. However, evidence of revisiting or reoccupying abandoned Preclassic centers signifies that the Classic populations of the Buenavista Valley shared a connection with their monumental Preclassic past.

PRECLASSIC CERAMICS

To understand the settlement chronology for the Preclassic period and create a preliminary ceramic sequence for comparison, the authors undertook analysis of the ceramic materials from El Palmar by using the type-variety method. Analysis demonstrates that the majority of the occupation of El Palmar dates from the Middle and Late Preclassic periods (ca. 800 BC–AD 300) with ceramic production traits common to the wider Maya Lowland traditions (figure 2.1, table 2.1, 8.1). Currently, the artifacts remain with the Instituto de Antropología e Historia in Guatemala City, pending further analyses. For example, a modal analysis (see Rands 1961) of the El Palmar ceramics, along with household excavations, could yield productive results for the understanding of Preclassic Lowland ceramic traditions over time.

Ceramicists performed limited mineralogical analysis on sherds from El Palmar and El Zotz in 2009 (Walker 2009). Thin-section petrography, which uses high-powered optical microscopes to identify mineral inclusions within pottery, revealed temper compositions that resembled those reported for Tikal, including sherd grog, limestone, and volcanic ash in the Preclassic. Preliminary results from Instrumental Neutron Activation Analysis (INAA) performed by Ronald Bishop of the Smithsonian Institution confirm that the Preclassic sherds include both carbonate and non-carbonate temper. Carbonate-tempered sherds contained calcium levels consistent with having been produced from calcareous clays (figure 2.2a).

Bishop has also identified distinct signatures of elemental ratios (Fe/Cr) for the Classic-period PAEZ samples, the samples from the Mundo Perdido Group at Tikal, and other samples from Tikal (figure 2.2b). When compared with these groups, the Middle and Late Preclassic sherds from the Buenavista

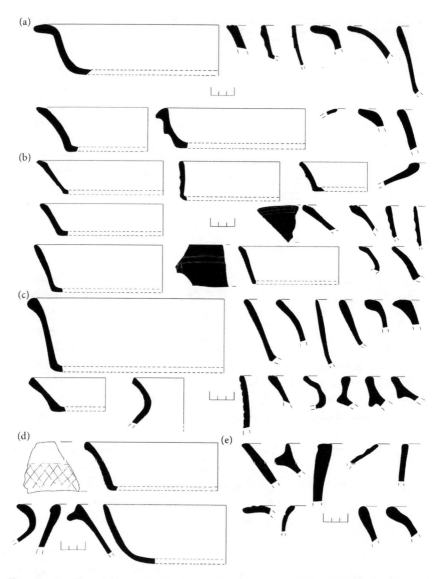

FIGURE 2.1. *Representative Preclassic ceramic vessels recovered from El Palmar and the Buenavista Valley, scales in centimeters: (a) Joventud Group; (b) Chunhinta Group; (c) Sierra Group; (d) Flor Group; (e) Polvero Group (drawings by J. Doyle).*

TABLE 2.1. Ceramics from El Palmar by time period

Time Period	Number	Category (%)	Total (%)
Eroded	14,423		55.53
Unslipped Total	5,468		21.05
Preclassic	1,211	22.15	4.66
Early Classic	4,257	77.85	16.39
Slipped Total	6,083		23.42
Early Middle Preclassic (possible)	6	0.00	0.00
Middle Preclassic	2,211	36.35	8.51
Late Preclassic	1,792	29.46	6.90
Early Classic	1,582	26.01	6.09
Undetermined	492	8.09	1.89
Total	**25,974**		

Valley demonstrate that Preclassic residents of the valley used a wide variety of clay sources. The diversity of sources has implications for the overall organization of clay gathering in the Preclassic period versus that of the Classic period. During the Middle and Late Preclassic periods, residents at El Palmar and smaller settlements throughout the valley may have been experimenting with their own clay sources. In contrast, when population coalesced around the nascent royal court at El Zotz in the Early Classic, the reduction in source diversity signaled yet tighter control over clay procurement.

Coupled with radiocarbon dates (see table 1.1), the ceramic sequence of sherds recovered from sealed construction fills at El Palmar confirms a heavy investment in monumental architecture beginning in the middle of the Middle Preclassic period (ca. 700–600 BC), followed by another heavy investment in enlarging the monumental center in the Late Preclassic (ca. 300 BC). For example, in the radial pyramid of the E-Group (Str. E4-1), three phases contained Middle Preclassic types, two phases contained mixed Middle Preclassic and Late Preclassic ceramics, and the final phase contained mostly Late Preclassic types (see figure 2.1). Excavations from across the site recovered very few Terminal Preclassic (or "Protoclassic") types. Very few sealed contexts yielded Early Classic or mixed Preclassic-Classic ceramic types, but some ceramics found in unsealed collapse and mixed-surface contexts date to the Early Classic, as discussed below. Although investigations did not determine the size of the Early Classic population at El Palmar, the deposit of a large quantity of ceramic material occurred at the site around AD 300. A very

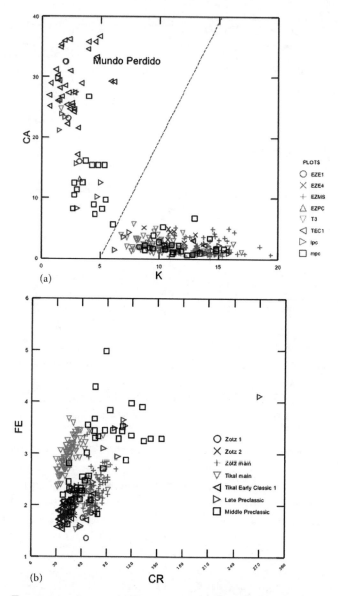

FIGURE 2.2. *Instrumental Neutron Activation Analysis (INAA) on Preclassic sherds: (a) comparison of calcium/potassium ratios. (b) comparison of iron/chromium ratios (figures by R. Bishop).*

small sample of Late Classic, Terminal Classic, and Postclassic ceramic materials indicates that although people may have periodically visited El Palmar, no substantial population occupied the site during these periods. What follows is a summary of the Preclassic occupation of the Buenavista Valley drawn from survey data, excavation results, and laboratory analysis.

EARLIEST SETTLEMENT IN THE BUENAVISTA VALLEY

The environmental evidence from the Laguna El Palmar (see Beach et al., chapter 7, this volume) confirms that populations were in the valley growing maize at least as early as 1300 BC. These preceramic settlers in the Buenavista Valley bear similarities to other Archaic populations found across the Lowlands. Although little evidence remains about the culture of the early residents of the valley, it is likely that the descendants of these agriculturalists established the earliest detectable settlements in the Buenavista Valley. In fact, a recent synthesis of Archaic and early Middle Preclassic radiometric dates and materials concluded that "some component of the earliest sedentary villagers in Belize and adjacent Petén were descended from preceramic populations" (Lohse 2010:315). Populations in the valley probably remained small and dispersed in the early Middle Preclassic (ca. 800–600 BC). Radiocarbon evidence combined with pollen data indicate that the water source was a perennial wetland with low erosion rates from 1400 to 300 BC, signaling low levels of deforestation-induced runoff into the lagoon. Settlers thus lived near the lagoon but did not heavily alter the environment for large-scale constructions or agriculture.

Wider patterns across the Maya Lowlands show that Middle Preclassic populations built more permanent residences with stone-lined walls and plaster floors (Doyle 2012:356–58). Although the evidence from this time in the Buenavista Valley is scant and confined to El Palmar, it seems that the early settlers also had a material desire for more durable domiciles and durable containers. The earliest ceramics are possible early Middle Preclassic (ca. 800–600 BC) sherds from the site of El Palmar, found in the deepest strata of architectural fills. Some of these pre-Mamom sphere ceramics might exhibit incised designs derivative of similar designs on pottery from other parts of Mesoamerica. However, research shows that local potters produced and decorated pottery in different styles that remain to be adequately identified and analyzed (Cheetham 2005; Clark and Cheetham 2002). The similarity in incised decorations underscores "the unlikelihood of these styles having been introduced to the Lowlands by a more developed group of migrants" (Estrada-Belli 2011:41). Associated with the sherds at El Palmar were some possible early Middle Preclassic (or earlier) lithic materials, including a heat-treated biface fragment. Thus the Buenavista Valley Middle Preclassic peoples likely shared ritual practice and craft specialization with other Lowland communities.

MIDDLE PRECLASSIC EL PALMAR CIVIC CENTER AND THE EL ZOTZ SOUTH GROUP

After many generations, the agriculturalists who lived near the Laguna El Palmar began cooperating to build civic spaces on the edge of the water source. During the middle years of the Middle Preclassic (ca. 700–500 BC), the residents of the Buenavista Valley constructed a large plaza by leveling an elevated area above the lakeshore. The civic center of El Palmar during the Middle Preclassic period conforms to the widely known E-Group typology (Aimers and Rice 2006; Chase and Chase 1995; Doyle 2012; Ruppert 1940). E-Groups occur throughout the Maya Lowlands and are significant for both their large plazas that served as gathering spaces and their architecture that is oriented toward the movement of the sun. From a western structure, the residents could view the sunrise on the equinoxes and solstices marked by a long building on the eastern edge of the plaza. These architectonic configurations are a hallmark of early Maya centers, perhaps originating after 1000 BC from Lowland settlers' interaction with peoples from the Isthmian region (Inomata et al. 2013).

The chronology of the El Palmar E-Group comes from stratigraphic excavations and subsequent ceramic analysis (figure 2.3). An excavation program aimed to understand the construction sequence of the largest pyramid at El Palmar, including a tunnel that penetrated to the earliest phases of Str. E4-1. The tunnel began approximately 3 m to the south of the probable east–west axis of the structure with the purpose of locating different façade construction techniques rather than the sequence of staircases. One excavation on the summit of the structure addressed the final stage of use. Finally, a third excavation on the east–west axis targeted the sequence of floors and staircases to confirm the tunnel findings.

The site of El Palmar (figure 1.4) was a Middle Preclassic civic center, comparable to its contemporaries like Tikal, Yaxha, Cival, and Nakbe, where community life focused around this plaza and the gatherings and activities that happened therein (Doyle 2012). At least three out of six known phases of the large E-Group pyramid (Str. E4-1) correspond to the Middle Preclassic time period from approximately 700 to 300 BC. The earliest-encountered structure (Str. E4-1-6th) contained a corner of the façade or staircase made

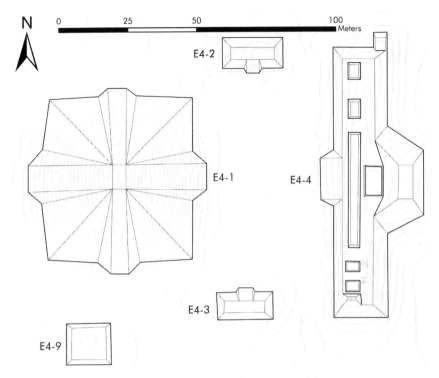

FIGURE 2.3. *Detail of the El Palmar E-Group (map by J. Doyle).*

out of hard limestone blocks constructed above bedrock. This structure was built very close to bedrock, perhaps as one of the earliest, if not the earliest, version of the western pyramidal platform. A polished biface-reduction flake of blue-green jadeite (figure 2.4a) associated with this earliest structure is consistent with types of jade used in offerings during this time periods, such as at Cival or Ceibal (Estrada-Belli 2006; Willey 1978). However, future investigations are necessary to confirm a possible pre-Mamom architectural sequence, such as that found at the site of Ceibal (Inomata et al. 2013). Fill of the subsequent phase (Str. E4-1-5th) was tightly packed and yielded the earliest waxy-slipped Mamom ceramics from El Palmar. One semi-complete bowl (figure 2.4b) was perhaps a dedicatory offering on the axis, cached when builders constructed the earthen floor. It seems that builders at El Palmar in the Middle Preclassic did not yet incorporate plaster into the façades of the earliest two phases, a practice similar to that reported at Nakbe (Hansen 1998:figures 6 and 9).

The subsequent generations of El Palmar residents modified the existing plaza and associated structures between 500 and 300 BC and constructed large platforms, which possibly served as early elite residences. As they built new phases of the pyramidal platforms, the builders took measures to preserve the footprint of the E-Group plaza over time (figure 2.5; Doyle 2012:363). The final Middle Preclassic construction phase, Str. E4-1-4th, contained an intricate façade with inset corners composed almost entirely of long, flat, cut stones, similar to techniques noted at Nakbe (Doyle 2017:figure 4.11; Hansen 1998:figure 6). The very dark fill of this building also contained large amounts of Mamom-sphere ceramics and Middle Preclassic figurines (figure 2.4c). The stratigraphy of this layer and the exceptional preservation of the ceramics indicate that the artifacts were included in the fill as the builders covered Str. E4-1-5th, rather than in refuse that ended up in the mud before extraction. The excavation unit placed on axis to reach bedrock demonstrated at least six floors or surfaces of occupation. The earliest floor was composed of compacted sandy soil, similar to those found in the tunnel excavations. The ceramic material confirms a Middle Preclassic date for the earliest floors.

One building practice to note during the Middle Preclassic is that, after encasing Str. E4-1-5th in the dark mud, builders deposited a layer composed almost entirely of worked chert, raw chert nodules, and hammerstones (see Doyle 2012:370–372; Hruby, chapter 9, this volume). Similar layers were also noted by excavators in the Las Ventanas pyramid at San Bartolo (Urquizú and Saturno 2004:611) and at other sites. This evidence could suggest an important role of chert in the development of El Palmar as a civic center, wherein early-stage stone-tool craft production occurred in or near these early gathering places, and the production refuse then became construction fill (Doyle 2012:372). Overall, Middle Preclassic materials from El Palmar are consistent with the kinds of objects and modes of production found at other settlements in the central Lowlands, including figurines, stucco, jade, and Mamom-type ceramics, such as examples from the Joventud, Chunhinta, and Pital groups (see figures 2.1 and 2.4).

Platform construction during the Middle Preclassic period also occurred at the site of El Zotz itself, in the South Group (Gámez 2009). There, settlers excavated down to bedrock to create level spaces, presumably for residences. Environmental studies of the *aguada* water source, a modified depression near the South Group, show that Preclassic settlers at El Zotz practiced small-scale maize agriculture until Early Classic population growth forced farmers out of the city center (Beach et al., chapter 7, this volume). The scant evidence confirms that the El Zotz South Group population engaged in ceramic

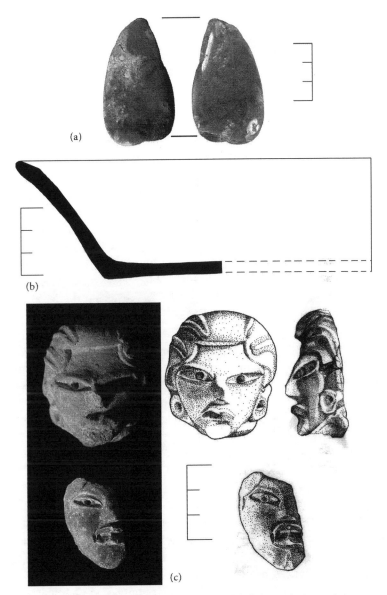

(a)

(b)

(c)

FIGURE 2.4. *Middle Preclassic artifacts from El Palmar, scales in centimeters: (a) polished biface-reduction flake of blue-green jade, Middle Preclassic period (photos by A. Godoy); (b) semi-complete bowl, Chunhinta Group, Middle Preclassic period (drawing by J. Doyle); (c) Middle Preclassic figurine fragments (photos by A. Godoy; drawings by M. Ritter-Armour).*

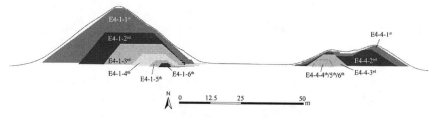

FIGURE 2.5. *North profile of reconstructed building sequence, Structures E4-1 and E4-4, El Palmar E-Group (drawing by J. Doyle).*

production consistent with the Mamom complex across the central Lowlands (see Czapiewska-Halliday et al., chapter 8, this volume). The El Zotz South Group evidence could be representative of a wider pattern of small, dispersed hillock settlements around the Buenavista Valley, as noted at other Middle Preclassic sites such as Cival (Estrada-Belli and Wahl 2010:25). The contrast in the volume of investment during the Middle Preclassic between El Palmar, with its level site core of approximately 200 × 200 m, and the El Zotz South Group, measuring less than 50 × 50 m, underscores the primacy of El Palmar as the Buenavista Valley civic center during the valley's early history. Furthermore, the significant lack of Late Preclassic ceramics from South Group excavations could mean that the Late Preclassic period was marked by intracommunity movement toward the end of the Middle Preclassic (ca. 300 BC) between the South Group and other areas of El Zotz (particularly the El Diablo and Las Palmitas Groups), or perhaps even Bejucal and El Palmar.

LATE PRECLASSIC MONUMENTALITY
IN THE BUENAVISTA VALLEY

Deposition of sediment in the Laguna El Palmar accelerated greatly between 300 BC and AD 200, according with the probability that high populations existed at the site of El Palmar in the Late Preclassic, with lower populations in the Classic period (Beach et al., chapter 7, this volume). Pollen and phytolith evidence also demonstrates that residents cultivated economic species during the Late Preclassic period in the vicinity of the Laguna El Palmar. In addition to maize, El Palmar farmers grew cultigens such as arrowroot (*Maranta arundinacea*) and squash (*Cucurbita* sp.).

Several Late Preclassic developments are evident in the construction sequence at El Palmar. First, the residents enlarged the E-Group pyramid and eastern platform to the extent visible today, probably doing so between 300 and 100 BC. Second, during this same time, residents constructed a massive 19-m-tall Triadic Group, a pyramidal hallmark of Late Preclassic architecture in the central Lowlands. Many have noted that the appearance of Triadic Groups, which possibly had mortuary functions, coincides with the emerging dynastic kingship known from the Classic period, although more investigation is necessary to trace back such institutions of authority (Hansen 1998:77–81). Finally, these monumentalization efforts culminated in a widespread planning event that extended common axes and orientations of structures across the entire El Palmar center.

Excavations at the E-Group at El Palmar revealed that the buildings are contemporaries of Str. E-VII-Sub at Uaxactun and Str. 5D-86 at Mundo Perdido, Tikal (see figure 2.5). Topographic evidence of symmetric protrusions from extensive survey indicates the likely presence of large masks on either side of the primary eastern staircase (Nelson and Doyle 2008:figure 7–6). Architecture in the three final phases of the E-Group at El Palmar is consistent with the large-block construction and heavily stuccoed façades noted at many other sites (Hansen 1998:94–102). The earliest Late Preclassic construction (Str. E4-1-3rd) was later cut and destroyed to construct the penultimate phase of the pyramid (Str. E4-1-2nd), a practice also reported at El Mirador and Tikal (Laporte and Fialko 1995:50).

The exterior walls of Str. E4-1-2nd contained very large stones and a cap of stucco of the highest quality (figure 2.6a), similar to Str. 5C-54-3B in Mundo Perdido, Tikal. The final enlargement of the radial pyramid (Str. E4-1-1st), which possibly occurred between 200 and 100 BC, involved a heavy investment in architectural fill, primarily cut blocks and *bajo* mud (figure 2.6b). Despite limited exposure of the façade of E4-1-1st, excavations recovered remnants of stucco architectural features such as apron molding and modeled sculpture, as found elsewhere in the central Lowlands. In the final phase of the summit of the Str. E4-1 pyramid was a building with two narrow rooms. At least three floors in the eastern room may represent a very long use for the building, with resurfacing occurring at least twice. The ceramic chronology confirms that the final phase of use occurred in the Late Preclassic. The final modification of Str. E4-1-1st was the addition of a plaza floor in the Terminal Preclassic period.

Investigations in looter trenches in Str. E4-4, the eastern long platform of the E-Group, demonstrated at least three major phases of later architectural investment and renovation, presumably encasing earlier unexcavated phases. Residents augmented the penultimate phase of the long platform, radiocarbon dated to 388–202 BC, to include a central building that extended eastward from the original long platform, very similar to the Chuen-phase

(a)

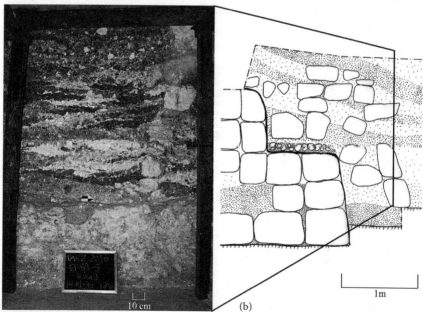

(b)

FIGURE 2.6. *Excavations in Str. E4-1: (a) east exterior wall of Str. E4-1-2nd, Late Preclassic period (photo by A. Godoy); (b) western profile and north profile, fill of Str. E4-1-1st (photo and drawing by J. Doyle).*

(350–1 BC) modifications of the equivalent building at Mundo Perdido. The best-preserved mask in the Mundo Perdido architecture is one with feline features, found in the corresponding building (Str. 5D-86) in the Cauac phase (ca. 1 BC–AD 150; Laporte and Fialko 1995:figure 14). Although the final floors of the El Palmar platform correspond to the Late Preclassic, evidence exists of an intrusive event, the deposit of Burial 1, an individual, whose remains had been scattered in fill (see Scherer 2009).

Investigations within the Triadic Group at El Palmar confirmed that the group fit the pattern of Late Preclassic monumentality described at El Mirador and elsewhere. Excavations uncovered evidence of heavy investment in platform architecture; an excavation unit placed in the northern boundary of the Triadic Group platform produced evidence of large lattice-block construction as the builders created a level surface out of the uneven bedrock. A superficial cleaning of a looter trench in Str. E4-7 produced several pieces of modeled stucco sculpture, at least one with red paint that included flecks of specular hematite (figure 2.7a). The looter trench also exposed an earlier phase of the Triadic Group, including red-painted apron molding (figure 2.7b). More evidence of stucco sculpture and mural painting in the El Palmar Triadic Group came from a horizontal exposure of the southern face of Str. E4-7. The excavation revealed a complex stairway and landing façade, with a destroyed stucco frieze on the central axis. The dimensions of the frieze recall those of the El Mirador Chahk friezes, which also date to the same time period (Doyle and Houston 2012; cf. Hansen et al. 2011:190). Explorations also uncovered a looted tomb, probably from the Early Classic period, described further below, in the context of the reoccupation of El Palmar in the third-to-fourth centuries AD.

Concurrent with the monumentalization of the E-Group and the construction of the Triadic Group in the Late Preclassic were wider efforts to integrate the site of El Palmar with an extensive site plan (Doyle et al. 2011). Although alignments based on astronomical observation may have played a role in Late Preclassic site planning (e.g., Šprajc et al. 2009), the El Palmar site plan also demonstrates that the dimensions of the final E-Group plaza, approximately 48.5 × 78.5 m, might have been the planar proportions used to expand all platforms and avenues in the Late Preclassic (Doyle 2013a:figure 4b). This effort was the final monumental construction episode at El Palmar, where residents seemed to have ceased building before the first century AD.

Excavations and intersite survey in the Buenavista Valley show that the Late Preclassic population was widespread and not confined to the vicinity of the El Palmar monumental center. The nearby site of La Avispa is perhaps emblematic of the Late Preclassic population increase, as residents seemed to

FIGURE 2.7. *Details from Str. E4-7: (a) modeled and painted stucco fragments, structure E4-7; (b) red-painted apron molding, Str. E4-7 (photos by J. Doyle).*

have constructed Late Preclassic platforms and pyramids about 2 km to the west of El Palmar. The growth of El Palmar and neighboring La Avispa could have been related to the growth of probable trade routes to Tikal that might have passed through the center of the valley (Doyle et al. 2012). In fact, the builders of La Avispa possibly used similar plaza proportions as El Palmar, suggesting an administrative link between the two sites (Thomas Garrison, personal communication 2012).

La Avispa consists of at least 32 structures and eight *chultunes* (storage chambers cut into bedrock), built upon large basal platforms. These modifications of the hilltops at the site produced level surfaces with straight edges that were originally detected using airborne radar elevation data (Garrison, Chapman, et al. 2011). The ceramic evidence, although scant, confirms a possible Middle Preclassic presence, with firmly Late Preclassic construction for the wide plazas and monumental platforms (Garrison and Garrido 2009a:266–274). Atop the largest platform at La Avispa is a clear example of a Late Preclassic Triadic Group, consisting of Strs. P8-4, P8-5, and P8-6. The existence of the only other Triadic Group outside of El Palmar marks the site of La Avispa as an important Late Preclassic center (see Hansen 1998:77–80). One factor in the growth of La Avispa as a Late Preclassic settlement may have been the visible surveillance of exchange routes to the west of El Palmar, as it was perhaps desirable to have visual contact with the footpaths (Doyle et al. 2012:figure 3).

Late Preclassic populations also occupied the site of El Zotz, although they did not construct monumental architecture on the scale of El Palmar and La Avispa. Data from two excavation units that accessed the earliest levels of construction in the El Zotz Acropolis revealed Late Preclassic ceramic material in construction fills, although the excavator dated the early floors to the Early Classic with the Preclassic sherds mixed in from prior occupations (Meléndez and Houston 2008:69). Excavations and environmental studies of soils at the El Zotz Aguada showed agricultural activity in the Late Preclassic before Early Classic peoples had begun to modify the water source with paving stones and containment barriers (Beach and Luzzadder-Beach 2009:figure 12.2). The Late Preclassic investment at El Zotz was the result of a variety of factors, such as population growth and the need for water reserves for the dry season. Perhaps the paving of the El Zotz Aguada signals a wider problem in the valley in the Terminal Preclassic with natural water sources, such as the Laguna El Palmar and other local *civales* (perennial wetland swamps).

Another *aguada* might have been constructed to the west of the El Zotz site center, where Preclassic residents had also begun leveling the hilltop of the El Diablo Group. There, excavations recovered possible—albeit difficult to identify positively—Late Preclassic sherds, (Román and Carter 2009:94; de Carteret 2015:table 1). At the Las Palmitas Group, an excavation in the plaza between Strs. M3-1, M3-4, M3-5, and M3-7 produced a few Late Preclassic sherds as well, indicating that settlement also extended to the elevated out-crops to the north of El Zotz proper (Gillot Vassaux 2008b:113).

The site of Bejucal was also a monumental center constructed in the Late Preclassic, perhaps by a modest population drawn to the natural min-iature cave entrances on the hilltop of the site. Excavations returned radio-carbon dates of 164 BC–AD 56 (with an 87.9% probability of falling within 121 BC–AD 56) and AD 58–238, consistent with the later Late Preclassic period (table 1.1). Furthermore, a small temple, visible in illicit excavations, exhibit rounded façades typical of Late Preclassic architecture (Garrison and Del Cid 2012:220–230). Bejucal Burial 1, a cist burial excavated in the bedrock, con-tained Late Preclassic ceramics from the Savana and Polvero groups (Garrison and Garrido López 2009b; Garrison et al. 2016:537). Semi-complete vessels of the Polvero and Sierra Groups recovered from outside Burial 3 show surface treatment more consistent with Late Preclassic types, but are forms associated with later time periods, such as the Protoclassic (or possibly Early Classic) "potstands" (Brady et al. 1998:figure 1d). Under the rounded temple mentioned above, Bejucal residents interred a female in Burial 3 toward the end of the second century AD (Garrison et al. 2016:538–540). Early Classic epigraphic evidence indicates connections with the Preclassic residents of El Zotz during this earlier time period as well. The Late Preclassic materials from El Palmar, La Avispa, Bejucal, and the groups at El Zotz provide a glimpse into the ori-gins of the Classic-period Pa'ka'n dynasty.

THE PRECLASSIC–CLASSIC TRANSITION IN THE BUENAVISTA VALLEY

Some evidence of continuity between El Palmar and the sites in the north-ern part of the valley comes from neutron activation analyses (Ronald Bishop, personal communication 2012). First, the same paste recipe was used for a Sierra rim recovered in the eastern platform of the E-Group at El Palmar and a Sierra sherd from the lowest levels of the El Zotz acropolis, mentioned above (Meléndez and Houston 2008:50–51; Walker 2008:164). Furthermore, a Polvero black sherd from El Palmar was a 100 percent composition match—that is, from the exact same clay source—with one of the vessels recovered from the El Diablo tomb (see Roman et al., chapter 3, this volume). As Newman (2011b:57–58) noted, it seems to be possibly earlier than the other cache vessels placed in the tomb, and was heavily worn on its rim and interior, suggesting prior use. One interpretation of this evidence is that Classic populations used some of the very same clay sources as residents of El Palmar, or, possibly, that the vessel itself was an heirloom from El Palmar that was important to the early royal court at El Zotz.

More evidence of movement from El Palmar to the area around El Zotz comes from the intersite survey (Garrison and Garrido López 2012). As mentioned above, Preclassic settlements in the valley seemed to concentrate near the sites along the likely footpath corridor; however, the residents of the valley constructed settlements in the Early Classic (ca. AD 300–550), especially those with extant architecture, along the ridge and away from the likely footpaths. At this same time, post–AD 100, there is evidence that Tikal was growing because of in-migration—possibly related to the coalescence of the dynastic court there (Scherer and Wright 2013; Wright 2005, 2012). One plausible hypothesis is that the Late Preclassic residents of the Buenavista Valley moved away from El Palmar and La Avispa because of Tikal's growing population and likely political power, resulting in increased foot traffic in the Buenavista Valley corridor (Doyle et al. 2012:804).

Despite the dominance of Preclassic material at El Palmar, it is apparent from superficial and intrusive contexts that the abandonment of all areas of the site was not simultaneous. In fact, certain parts of structures continued to be used and remodeled within the E-Group, while other parts remained unaltered until the jungle took over sometime during the Late Classic period. Farming actually increased, with pollen evidence from a soil core at El Palmar showing that maize levels peaked around the Late Preclassic to Early Classic transition (see Beach et al., chapter 7, this volume). Large concentrations of Early Classic polychrome pottery came from excavations in the south-central portion of the site, especially on the platform Str. E5-7 and Str. F5-1. Excavations in the E-Group and at the water's edge revealed two different periods of post-Preclassic occupation, two occupations that are not necessarily continuous or interrelated.

Residents constructed the main building at the summit of Str. E4-1 during the Preclassic period, but resurfaced the floor at least twice in later time periods. The lack of cultural material from the summit excavations makes these remodeling events difficult to date, but eroded sherds on the surface possibly give an Early Classic date for the final use of the structure. Other evidence supports the interpretation of Early Classic use of the main pyramid. Excavations on the east–west axis on the eastern pyramid-plaza interface recovered a complete Cubierta Impressed pot (figure 2.8a) associated with a typically Early Classic chert biface (Zachary Hruby, personal communication, 2011; figure 2.8b).

Further evidence for a continuous occupation comes from the long platform of the E-Group, Str. E4-4. On the central east–west axis of the structure,

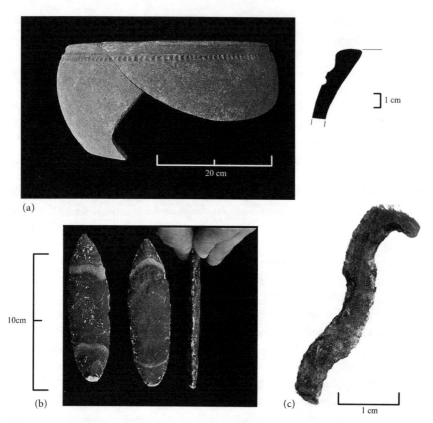

FIGURE 2.8. *Artifacts from Str. E4-1: (a) Cubierta Impressed pot, Str. E4-1 (photo and drawing by J. Doyle); (b) Early Classic chert biface, Str. E4-1 (photo by J. Doyle); (c) green obsidian eccentric, Str. E4-4 (photo by A. Guluy).*

residents completed several modifications after the Late Preclassic boom. Primarily, they constructed a final staircase after placing a dedicatory offering of two plates, classified as belonging to the Late Preclassic Flor group, based on surface treatment, but perhaps with a form more typical of the Late Preclassic–Early Classic transitional period. This deposit most likely occurred between AD 150 and 250, corresponding to the Cimi phase at Tikal, characterized in turn by tetrapod plates similar to the ones recovered at El Palmar (Culbert 1993:figure 139; Culbert 1999:70–71; Culbert 2003:57–59).

Further alterations on the upper platforms of Str. E4-4 demonstrated a possible reoccupation at a later date than the final staircase. Unlike post–AD 150 modifications at nearby E-Groups at Uaxactun and Tikal, the El Palmar

E-Group exhibits small, low platforms, with no apparent comparisons in the region. Two lines of evidence indicate that these platforms were later than the staircase-building event: (1) an intrusive burial (El Palmar Burial 1) on the east–west axis of an individual with Early Classic ceramics of the Balanza and possibly Dos Arroyos polychrome groups (Doyle and Matute Rodríguez 2009; Scherer 2009), and (2) surface collections near the platforms that included Early Classic materials, the most diagnostic of which was a miniature eccentric made out of green obsidian, likely imported from the Pachuca source near Teotihuacan, common in Early Classic Maya contexts (figure 2.8c).

The possibility that the small platforms on Str. E4-4 and associated burial were Early Classic in date, and not connected with any early occupation, was borne out in the excavations on platform Str. E5-7 and Str. F5-1. Evidence shows a possible lens of abandonment—in the form of darkened soil with little cultural content—directly overlying the final Late Preclassic stucco floor of platform Str. E5-7. The layer of soil is distinct from the extensive floor construction in the Preclassic period, in which stucco was either laid directly on top of a prior layer, or on top of a thin layer of compact fill (including sherds). This dark lens was later covered with a crude stone layer that contained Early Classic sherds, perhaps signaling that people returned to a platform that had been partially covered in vegetation for some time. Furthermore, excavations on the small mounds in the northwest and south-central edges of the platform showed solid Late Preclassic house foundations reutilized by Early Classic people. Although they were living on the same platforms, they did not use similar techniques of floor construction or ceramic production. A burial of two individuals (El Palmar Burial 2) was apparently excavated down to the Late Preclassic floor, where the bodies had been laid, only to be filled in and paved over by the final Early Classic occupational surface (Doyle and Piedrasanta 2012:211–212).

The people living on platform Str. E5-7 were clearly participating in wider networks of ceramic production, long-distance trade, and ritual practice. The nearby small temple, Str. F5-1, became the scene of repeated offerings that show strong characteristics of commensality, or ritual gathering and feasting, and possibly even a conscious termination of daily life at the site. Excavations at Str. F5-1 revealed a massive deposit around AD 300 of ceramic vessels, faunal material, and other artifacts in the floor of the northwest corner of the building. A large quantity of striated jars probably held water or liquids, and a number of polychrome serving vessels would have held other consumables. The fact that vessel refits were found across all lots of the deposit, with stratigraphically higher sherds showing more weathering than others, leads to the conclusion that the deposit occurred as one event, or at least over a short period of time during one generation. The volume of material does not support possible alternatives such as intermittent visitors, or "pilgrims," as argued by researchers at El Mirador (Hansen et al. 2008). Rather, the people probably lived on platform Str. E5-7, produced ceramics, and conducted a termination ritual at El Palmar—perhaps as the ultimate result of the migrations that happened for generations after authorities enacted the final monumental building plan.

One final aspect of Early Classic life at El Palmar deserves mention. During the fourth-century expansion of El Zotz and Bejucal, a group of residents, not necessarily the same who had reoccupied platform Str. E5-7, most likely constructed a small structure containing what was likely a royal tomb (El Palmar Burial 3). Looters pierced the small structure in the middle of the Triadic Group plaza, Str. E5-1, and encountered a sizable tomb (approximately 1 × 3 m) with an intact vaulted ceiling (figure 2.9a). The tomb was oriented north–south and had been looted in the late twentieth century. Found inside were only a few fragments of what was likely a jade-and-shell mosaic mask, probably part of a pectoral or belt (figure 2.9b). The placement of the small burial temple, slightly askew from the final central axis of the largest pyramid in the Triadic Group, the construction of the tomb and subsequent superstructure, and the meager artifacts left by the looters all date to the Early Classic. During the fourth century in the region, many similar tombs contained important royal individuals, including an intact tomb at El Zotz (see Román et al., chapter 3, this volume), and looted tombs found at Bejucal (Garrison and Del Cid 2012). This suggests that the residents of El Palmar, likely those who reoccupied platform Str. E5-7, were participating in the wider elite culture of the Buenavista Valley and beyond. Regardless of the exact timing of this entombment, the placement of the burial shows a distinct intent to reconnect with the major alignments of the Preclassic buildings, possibly as a nod to an ancestral connection with El Palmar.

CONCLUSION

The Preclassic populations in the Buenavista Valley were dynamic and widespread, participated in broader systems of production and exchange within a shared Maya Lowland culture, and, over time, engaged in cooperative efforts to gather people in monumental civic centers. Early agriculturalists grew maize and gathered other resources such as waterfowl and other game, fish, and perhaps other cultigens around the Laguna El Palmar

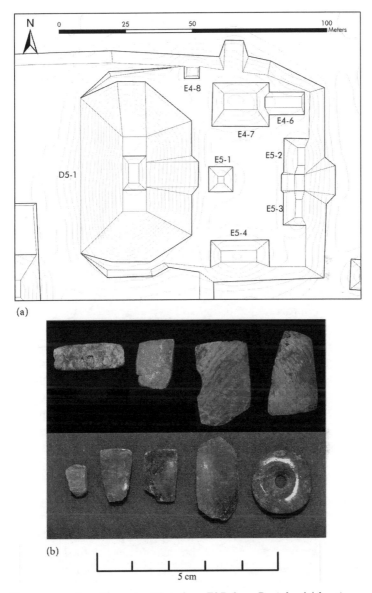

(a)

(b)

FIGURE 2.9. *Location and artifacts from El Palmar Burial 3: (a) location of Str. E5-1, El Palmar Triadic Group (map by J. Doyle); (b) finds from cleaning of looted tomb, Str. E5-1 (photos by J. Doyle).*

for several centuries before investing in permanent residential platforms and ceramic manufacturing. The water source probably became a vital place for gathering within the valley long before the monumentalization of the gathering place in the El Palmar E-Group, and the large plaza at the site represented the crystallization of a more permanent community center on the landscape in the Middle Preclassic. Over time, residents continued to improve the E-Group at El Palmar, owing to wider regional trends or internal developments that spurred on monumental construction. The parallel development of El Palmar and other sites such as Tikal, Nakbe, Uaxactun, and Cival, is at odds with a scenario in which one large community held sway over any others during the Middle Preclassic. In fact, the existence of a Middle Preclassic settlement in the South Group of El Zotz shows that people in the valley were not necessarily persuaded to move near the growing center of El Palmar, but rather to consciously position themselves in another point on the dynamic landscape.

The Late Preclassic period saw an increase in population throughout the valley, with the monumentalization of the civic center of El Palmar, construction of monumental platforms and pyramids at La Avispa, and investment in communities at El Zotz and its subsidiary groups El Diablo and Las Palmitas, and Bejucal. Across the Lowlands, populations began to coalesce around burgeoning royal courts, and the Pa'ka'n dynasty of Classic-period El Zotz owes its beginnings to the Late Preclassic societies in the valley. A possible scenario is that the individuals or groups who held authority over activities at the El Palmar center laid the foundations for the royal court at El Zotz. Some evidence of the reoccupation of El Palmar suggests a desire for Early Classic peoples to reconnect with the ruined center in the fourth century AD.

After AD 100, possible tensions in the valley between the residents of its centers and neighboring communities caused a rupture in settlement. Tikal likely began exerting influence in the area as its emerging dynastic leaders sought control over political territory and probable exchange routes. The same could have been true for the massive centers to the north of the Buenavista Valley, such as El Mirador, Nakbe, Tintal, and others, as all vied for control over landscape and labor in the Late Preclassic. Soon after the cessation of monumental building at the valley floor centers, populations migrated away from El Palmar and La Avispa, abandoning settlements that had been central to community life for centuries. The upland Late Preclassic centers of Bejucal and El Zotz possibly absorbed migrating families from El Palmar and La Avispa, who started anew in places on the landscape that were more defensible from encroaching ambition from the east and north. Ambitious funerary activities in the El Diablo group and the establishment of the acropolis at El Zotz in the Early Classic thus represent the resilience of local populations that shared a deep past with the valley they continued to watch over for centuries more.

3

Ruling through Defense

The Rise of an Early Classic Dynasty at El Zotz

Edwin Román,
Thomas G. Garrison
and Stephen Houston

DOI: 10.5876/9781607327646.c003

Scholars have studied the Early Classic period (ca. AD 250–600) in the Maya area for many years. It is well known for the technological and cultural changes following the chaos of the Late Preclassic. It is also during the Early Classic period that the great Maya dynasties were fully established (Houston and Inomata 2009); however, the evidence found in texts and iconography from sites in the southern Lowlands indicates that some of these royal courts were founded long before this time. The rulers of the Early Classic emphasized the deep roots of their dynastic histories, especially in the central Peten (Martin and Grube 2008; Saturno et al. 2006). Fortunately, in the last 30 years of investigation, the Maya area has provided new archaeological data about the beginning of dynasties in Classic centers, which can be verified with historical records enabled by advances in epigraphy, and the discovery of the tombs of the first rulers in some archaeological centers (Agurcia Fasquelle and Fash 2005; Freidel 1992; Freidel and Schele 1988; Houston and Inomata 2009; Houston, Newman, Román, and Garrison 2015; Román-Ramírez 2011; Román et al. 2011; Sharer et al. 2005; Stuart 2004).

This chapter presents information about the foundation of the royal lineage at El Zotz in the Early Classic. The epigraphic evidence of El Zotz reveals vital information regarding the local dynastic history (Carter et al., chapter 4, this volume; Garrison et al. 2016; Houston 2008a; Houston et al., chapter 1, this volume), which began to be attested in the Early Classic and is confirmed by archaeological material found in the area. Archaeological data from the Buenavista Valley suggest that the most extensive occupation in rural and urban areas occurred during the Early Classic (Garrison and Garrido López 2012; cf. epilogue in Garrison and Houston, chapter 13, this volume). However, the first evidence of human occupation in the region started in the Archaic, but with larger populations not appearing until the Middle Preclassic period (Doyle 2012, 2013a; Doyle and Piedrasanta 2011, 2012, and chapter 2, this volume). At the site of El Palmar, the monumental architecture is similar to the Preclassic architecture found in cities such as Tikal and Uaxactun (Laporte and Valdés 1993), indicating the possibility that a centralized authority commissioned these works. El Palmar suffered an abrupt abandonment toward the end of the Late Preclassic period (Doyle et al. 2011), a social phenomenon identified in other Preclassic centers, such as the great metropolises of El Mirador and Nakbe. Both were abandoned due to the overuse of natural resources (Hansen 1998; Hansen et al. 2002) and the effects of anthropogenic changes on the natural landscape (Dunning et al. 2002). After the abandonment of El Palmar, its inhabitants migrated west, establishing a new royal court at El Zotz.

Here, data collected by the Proyecto Arqueológico El Zotz (PAEZ) are used to model the emergence of a new dynasty in Early Classic El Zotz. This chapter uses two pieces of evidence to argue that the El Zotz (Pa'ka'n) dynasty started in the beginning of the Early Classic. The first is the presence of palaces and monumental structures at the sites of El Zotz and Bejucal, evidence that proves the existence of a centralized power and nascent kingship. The second set of data is the discovery of royal burials inside of temples, including the discovery of the tomb of the possible dynastic founder of Pa'ka'n (Houston, Newman, Román, and Garrison 2015). This chapter also examines the internal shifts of royal palaces within the El Zotz political landscape. The palace of the El Diablo Group was abandoned towards the end of the Early Classic, possibly because of restrictions to settlement growth dictated by its hilltop location. As a consequence, an Early Classic Pa'ka'n ruler decided to move the palace to the valley where the landscape was better suited and ampler for opulent architecture, like palaces and pyramids. These buildings helped the dynasty consolidate its identity and devise an arena for politics over the next 400 years.

THE BEGINNING OF A DYNASTY: EVIDENCE OF THE EARLY CLASSIC OCCUPATION OF THE BUENAVISTA VALLEY

Some of the best-known developmental changes between the Preclassic and Early Classic periods in the Maya area are in ceramics (which registered substantial alterations in forms and included the introduction of polychromes (Smith 1955)), site planning, the broad standardization of the writing system, and the overt establishment of hereditary dynastic kingship. In the Buenavista Valley all of these changes can be observed during the Late Preclassic to Early Classic transition, but investigations show that a shift in settlement locations in the landscape during the Early Classic in the central Maya Lowlands is another important feature worth considering.

During over 3,000 years of occupation of the Buenavista Valley, ceremonial centers rose and fell in a changing landscape. During the Preclassic period, the ancient inhabitants built their first settlements on flat areas, close to natural wetlands with potable water and abundant plant and animal resources. The best example is the site of El Palmar, constructed next to one of the biggest sources of water in the heart of the southern Lowlands (Doyle 2013b; Doyle and Piedrasanta, chapter 2, this volume). During the Late Preclassic period, however, the Maya abandoned the site and its habitants moved to other locations. This phenomenon has also been observed in other Preclassic centers, and in many cases a combination of climate change and anthropogenic influences on the environment have been implicated (Dunning 1995; Dunning et al. 2002, 2006; Hansen et al. 2002). Francisco Estrada-Belli (2011) proposed a second theory to explain the abandonment of Preclassic sites, arguing that the Preclassic Maya center of Cival was vacated during the end of the Late Preclassic because of warfare: a defensive wall around the site core supports that claim.

In the Buenavista Valley, the abandonment of El Palmar occurred before the first century AD (Doyle et al. 2011). The site's decline appears to have been caused by a combination of environmental and political stress in the region (Garrison, Garrido López, and de Carteret 2012; Houston, Román, et al. 2011; Román-Ramírez 2011). This precipitated a settlement shift in which the nobles created a defensive landscape by building their palaces on escarpment hilltops about 150 m higher than the main ruins of El Zotz (figure 3.1). A similar phenomenon is observed at Uaxactun. The site is located 26 km northeast of El Zotz, situated along the same escarpment, which takes a sharp turn to the north near Tikal. Valdés and Fahsen (1995:199–201) suggest that the seat of royal authority shifted repeatedly in the early periods of Uaxactun's history. Originally, the royal court was located in Group E, the first architectural group recognized as being used for solar observations in the Maya Lowlands. The Maya built a new palace in Group H between 150 BC and AD 250, decorated with monumental architectural masks. After a brief return to Group E from AD 250 to 300, the elites of Uaxactun moved

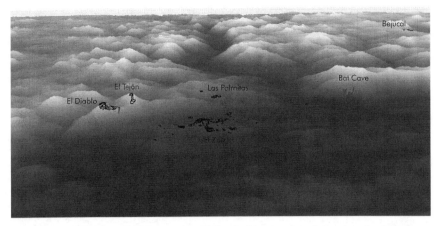

FIGURE 3.1. *3D view of the Buenavista Valley, looking north and showing the elevation differences between settlements (image by T. Garrison).*

the royal court to the highest hill at the site, establishing Group A as the seat of Classic-period authority (Valdés 2005). This group, classically rendered by Tatiana Proskouriakoff (in Smith 1950), also became the royal necropolis for the Uaxactun dynasty. These political changes in Uaxactun were highly localized in the landscape, but they still provide an analogy to concurrent processes in the Buenavista Valley. The movements indicate regional political instability that forced elites into a defensive posture, perhaps in response to the energetic polity at Tikal.

BEGINNING OF THE EARLY CLASSIC
IN THE BUENAVISTA VALLEY

In the Buenavista Valley evidence of the Early Classic period was found at the sites of El Palmar, Bejucal, and El Zotz. Data from excavations and mapping between El Zotz and El Palmar show that the Early Classic period saw the highest level of occupation in the valley's history (Garrison and Garrido López 2012; Houston, Román, et al. 2011), though this may need to be reconsidered in light of the 2016 lidar survey over the region (Garrison and Houston, chapter 13, this volume). The rural areas during this period were located in the valleys where the inhabitants had more access to water and more land for farming. There is not much evidence of rural architecture, perhaps because many of the structures were made of perishable materials. However, Garrison and Garrido López (2012) were able to confirm a strong Early Classic presence around El Zotz and El Palmar based on the amount of ceramic and lithic materials recovered from excavations, as well as the discovery of *chultunes* in the intersite area.

In the urban centers, some of the earliest constructions in the area were water sources (Houston, Román, et al. 2011). These *aguadas* were made by digging out big areas in the landscape (Beach and Luzzadder-Beach 2009; Houston, Román, et al. 2011). In the case of the El Zotz Aguada, the inhabitants constructed a massive dam that blocked a natural drainage, causing water to pool (Beach et al., chapter 7, this volume). The ancient inhabitants of El Zotz covered the walls and floor of the *aguada* with limestone blocks, waterproofing the surface with a layer of stucco (Beach and Luzzadder-Beach 2009; Garrison, Garrido López, et al. 2011).

El Palmar

The site of El Palmar is one of the three major centers in the Buenavista Valley that has an Early Classic occupation. This Preclassic site was largely abandoned by the first century AD but was briefly reoccupied at the beginning of the Early Classic. However, the new inhabitants did not build new monumental constructions, instead choosing to modify Preclassic architecture. They reused, for example, the east platform of the E-Group (Str. E5-7) as a residential area. Constructions on top of Str. E5-7 were small platforms supporting perishable superstructures (Doyle and Piedrasanta 2011, 2012). Another sector reused in the Early Classic period was the Triadic Group. In this case, the inhabitants of El Palmar built a small structure (Str. E5-1) in the middle of the group atop a Preclassic floor. Within the structure was a funerary chamber that had the remains of an elite individual. The tomb had been looted, but a fragment of a funerary jade mask and marine shells were recovered, indicating the prestige of the burial's occupant (Doyle et al. 2011; Doyle and Piedrasanta, chapter 2, this volume). Further evidence of a strong Early Classic presence comes from the shore of the *cival* (perennial wetland) where the so-called Water Temple (Str. F5-1) is located. A termination deposit containing ceramics mixed with obsidian, faunal remains, and ashes covered this structure.

Bejucal

Bejucal also has evidence of Early Classic occupation, and the site most likely served as a royal country house for the Pa'ka'n lords (Garrison and Beltrán 2011; Garrison and Garrido López 2009b; Garrison et al. 2016). The site was built 8 km northeast from El Zotz among the rolling hills fronted by the Buenavista Escarpment. Most of the site's architecture is arranged around two main courtyards, with 14 structures.

The first constructions at Bejucal date to the end of the Late Preclassic and were found under Str. S6-10. These small, round temples (Strs. S6-10-Sub. 1 and S6-10-Sub. 2), are the earliest of eight substructures identified at Bejucal (Garrison et al. 2016:figure 11). Structure S6-10-Sub. 1 contained a cist burial (Bejucal Burial 3) that might have belonged to one of the first elites living at the site. Although the burial had been looted, a nearby Sierra slipped pot and Polvero slipped ring base as well as a fragment of a pyrite mirror probably came from it (Garrison and Beltrán 2011). Structure S6-10-Sub. 2 contained a dedicatory infant burial (Bejucal Burial 6), interred in a stone cist with no funerary offerings.

An Early Classic pyramid (Str. S6-10-2nd), whose form was again replicated in the Late Classic (Str. S6-10-1st), covered these two early temples. The Early Classic phase contained a looted royal tomb (Bejucal Burial 2). The tomb was vaulted and had a possible psychoduct (a presumed passage for spirits) on the north end. Iconography from Bejucal Altar 1, which was set in front of Str. S6-10, suggests that the individual interred in the tomb may very well have been the ruler mentioned on Bejucal Stela 2 as having been installed by the Teotihuacan warrior, Sihyaj K'ahk' in AD 381 (Garrison et al. 2016:544, figure 5) (figure 3.2). A lip-to-lip Aguila Orange cache was found outside the chamber on the east side and contained an offering of marine shells, a stingray spine, jade and mica "Charlie Chaplin" fetishes, so-named for their bow-legged appearance, along with a sacrificed quail (Garrison and Beltrán 2011; Garrison et al. 2016:figure 8).

EL ZOTZ

El Zotz is a site of 224 known structures distributed in a site epicenter with at least three hilltop satellite groups (explorations by Omar Alcover in 2015 discovered further groups to the east of the transverse valley running north–south from the eastern edge of the city). The first construction at the site dates to the Preclassic period and consisted of a small settlement located in the South Group, about 300 m from the El Zotz Aguada (Gámez 2009). However, the apogee of the city occurred in the Classic period, during which the biggest structures were built. The Early Classic at El Zotz is found in five sectors. The first two, the Acropolis and the Five Temples Group, are located off the main plaza. The third area is in the East Group, dominated by the Pyramid of

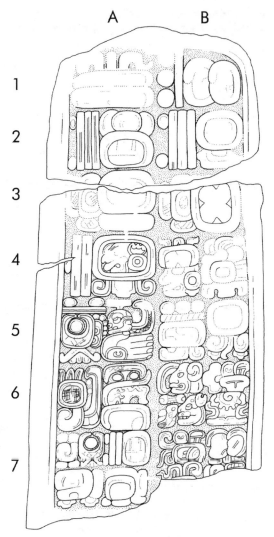

FIGURE 3.2. *Bejucal Stela 2 (drawing by N. Carter).*

the Wooden Lintel (Str. M7-1). The final two are the El Diablo and El Tejón Groups, located on adjacent hilltops about 500 m apart.

The Acropolis of El Zotz is located on the north end of the main plaza. Although the final phase dates to the Late Classic, earlier constructions beneath the palace date to the Early Classic (Czapiewska 2012; Marroquín et al. 2011; Meléndez and Houston 2008; Newman et al. 2012; Newman and Menéndez 2012; Pérez Robles et al. 2009). The excavation of two tunnels in Strs. L7-1 and L7-6 found evidence that the first structures of the palace were only small platforms with perishable buildings on top (Marroquín et al. 2011; Newman et al. 2012; Pérez Robles et al. 2009). The function of these Early Classic edifices is unclear. The architecture is modest compared to other locations in and around the Buenavista Valley, such as the palace at Bejucal (Str. S6-1) and the palace at the El Diablo Group (Strs. F8-6 to F8-10).

Despite its minimal architecture, the Acropolis location still appears to have been important from an early time. A dedicatory infant burial (El Zotz Burial 2) was found on the axis of Str. L7-6-Sub. 1 (Pérez Robles et al. 2009) (figure 12.2). The burial was located inside a cist dug into the fill of the first construction stage, and its remains consisted of a 2–3-year-old child in ventral extended position (see Scherer, chapter 12, this volume). A shell pendant was associated with the burial. It is possible that the interment was part of a ritual associated with the foundation of the Acropolis.

EL DIABLO GROUP

The El Diablo Group is located 1.2 km west from the Acropolis of El Zotz (figure 3.3). This was the first civic-ceremonial center of the Pa'ka'n dynasty and was most likely established after the collapse of El Palmar. El Diablo is composed of multiple terraces and patios, and a 2016 lidar survey indicates that substantial defensive fortifications protected the ascent to the group. A palace complex to the north and west, range structures to the east and south, and a funerary pyramid (Str. F8-1) at the southeast corner define the group's main plaza. East of Str. F8-1 is a small platform with three low mounds (Strs. F8-12 to F8-14), each of which housed an impressive vaulted tomb. Unfortunately, all of these mounds were looted, a persistent problem at El Zotz in general (Beltrán and Román 2012; Gillot Vassaux 2008a). The platform supporting these structures was repeatedly plastered over and may have served as an observation platform for viewing the sunrise on different points in the landscape (Garrison 2012). Descending east from this platform is another terrace with a large quarry, which may have also served as a water source for the El Diablo Group. A single structure (Str. G8-1) is located just to the southeast of the quarry. Another elevated group of three structures (Strs. G8-2 to G8-4) juts out east of the quarry platform. A lone building (Str. G8-5) is located on a terrace just northeast. Another group of low residential platforms (Strs. F8-15 to F8-17) is found north of the El Diablo palace complex. A series of

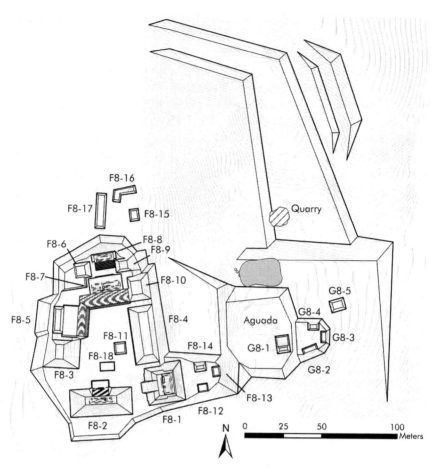

Figure 3.3. *Map of the El Diablo Group (map by T. Garrison).*

terraces descend to the northeast and includes a small quarry and three *chultunes* (Román-Ramírez 2011).

The El Diablo palace consists mainly of five, partially linked structures (Strs. F8-6 to F8-10), and was built in two construction phases (Román-Ramírez 2011; Román and Carter 2009). Structure F8-7, at the top of the stairs, faces to the south but also has doors to the north, which were probably used as entrances. A modeled stucco frieze decorated the palace, but it was removed and some of the stuccoes were cached in antiquity when El Diablo was abandoned. The north structure was a small building with access via a central door;

the temple had two small chambers, and also seems have been decorated with a stucco frieze (Román and Carter 2009).

The team also excavated Strs. F8-1, F8-2, F8-4, and F8-5. Only the final construction phase was investigated in the latter three structures, each one dating to ca. AD 400. These building may have been for administrative purposes, but this is uncertain and such general functions are nearly impossible to ascertain on present information (Román-Ramírez 2011). Structure F8-1 contains evidence of early building at El Diablo dating to the second century AD. However, this earliest construction (Str. F8-1-Sub. 2) was deliberately razed, making it impossible to know its shape and function (Houston, Newman, Román, and Carter 2015:38–39).

El Tejón Group

The El Tejón Group is located about 500 m northeast from El Diablo (Knodell and Garrison 2011), and the 2016 lidar survey shows that these two groups were linked by a curved causeway. Organized into three platforms, El Tejón is distributed vertically on a hilltop, with a rustic causeway connecting the highest buildings to lower ones. The lowest portion of El Tejón is a platform and does not show any evidence of architecture. However, there are associated *chultunes* that indicate that there may have been perishable structures in the vicinity (Garrison and Kwoka 2012:243–244). The middle terrace is where the causeway begins, connecting this sector with the hill summit. This middle level supports three low platforms with perishable structures. The summit of the El Tejón Group holds more elaborate edifices (Piedrasanta et al. 2014). These buildings extend across the north and east sides of the platform in the shape of an inverted L. The structures are masonry and served as elite residences, possibly for nobles associated with the El Diablo court (Román-Ramírez 2011). The elite nature of El Tejón is exemplified by two jade mosaic earflare plaques recovered from a looted tomb in Str. H6–2 (Carter et al. 2012; Piedrasanta 2012:191).

RISE OF A DYNASTY

The epigraphic evidence at El Zotz indicates that the Buenavista Valley was home to the royal family of Pa'ka'n (Houston 2008a). The names of the dynasty came from a variety of sources, including looted polychrome vessels in private collections and museums; an incised mirror back from Los Bagaces, Costa Rica; a wooden lintel from Str. M7-1 that is on display in the Museo Nacional de Arqueología y Etnología (MUNAE) in Guatemala City (figure

3.4); and stelae from El Zotz and Bejucal. With this information Houston (2008a; see also Carter et al., chapter 4, this volume; Houston et al., chapter 1, this volume) established a basic dynastic sequence for El Zotz. The Pa'ka'n dynasty begins around the mid-fourth century AD, and continues into the ninth century, with the latest securely dated monument coming in AD 830.

EXCAVATION OF AN EARLY CLASSIC TOMB

Archaeological data from looted and intact tombs helps to fill in some of the record that is unanswered by epigraphy. Structure F8-1 is located in the southeast corner of the main plaza of the El Diablo Group. The pyramid is 13-m-tall from the level of the plaza and served as a funerary monument (Houston, Newman, Román, and Garrison 2015; Román-Ramírez 2011; Román et al. 2011). George Andrews (1986) published the first images of this building soon after a large looter trench was dug into it, revealing a buried temple structure. Ian Graham mapped the pyramid and the rest of El Diablo in 1978 (Houston, Nelson, et al. 2006:1–2). In 1980, Martin Diedrich took pictures of some of the stucco found in the looter trench and Jacques VanKirk took another set of photos, also in the beginning of 1980.

The architectural stratigraphy of Str. F8-1 is well known, with three principal substructures (Temple of the Night Sun, Shrine, Red Temple) buried under two versions of a pyramid (Strs. F8-1-1st and F8-1-2nd; Houston, Newman, Román, and Carter 2015). All phases of Str. F8-1 date to the Early Classic period. The Red Temple (Str. F8-1-Sub. 2) may have been the earliest construction at El Diablo, but it is known only from a floor, possibly burned and red-painted, stones (Beltrán and Román 2012; Houston, Román, et al. 2011; Houston, Newman, Román, and Carter 2015; Román-Ramírez 2011). The Red Temple forms part of a small patio and faced another temple to the west. These two structures may date as early as the second century AD, at least to judge from the presence of unassociated Chicanel sherds at El Diablo (Román-Ramírez 2011). The Maya razed the Red Temple to construct the platform that supports the Temple of the Night Sun and the Shrine, revealing little of its history or function.

The Temple of the Night Sun was built in two phases. The main structure supports a large roofcomb (Str. F8-1-Sub. 1C), which saw a later addition to the front of the temple, adding a second vaulted room (Str. F8-1-Sub. 1B). The Shrine (Str. F8-1-Sub. 1A) was erected in front of the Temple of the Night Sun on the same Sub. 1 platform (Houston, Newman, Román, and Carter 2015). This platform and associated structures were built as a funerary monument for

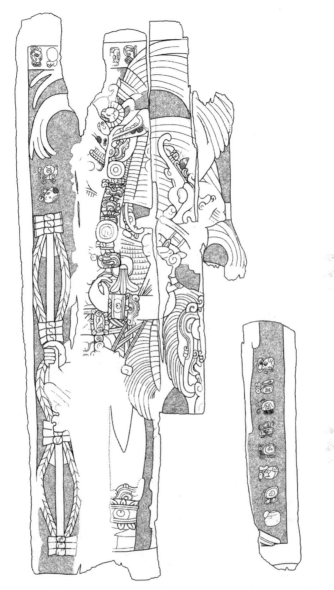

FIGURE 3.4. *El Zotz Wooden Lintel 1 (drawing by N. Carter).*

a Pa'ka'n ruler. In many ancient Maya cities, it was common practice to construct tomb chambers just above bedrock (Fitzsimmons 2009). For this reason, the inhabitants of El Diablo decided to dismantle the Red Temple, break the floor, and level the bedrock for the new burial. They put offerings around the chamber and enclosed the still-open tomb with two plaza floors. On top of the last floor, west of the funerary chamber, they built a columnar altar that had evidence of residue on top (Beltrán and Román 2012; Houston, Román, et al. 2011; Houston, Newman, Román, and Garrison 2015; Román-Ramírez 2011). After the interment, the platform and superstructures were built on top, sealing the king's tomb.

Initial investigations of the Temple of the Night Sun were carried out in 2009 (Román and Carter 2009) and 2010 (Román and Newman 2011). The temple has two rooms and faces to the west. The interior of the building presents a bench in the rear, the walls and ceiling painted red. This structure has one of the most elaborately decorated exteriors of the Early Classic period in the Maya area. The temple walls and upper frieze are covered with iconography presented in modeled stucco and painted in polychrome (Taube and Houston 2015) (figure 3.5). In 2011, the project discovered that the structure had two successive programs of art. The first, the original, was built in the late fourth century AD when the king was buried. A second iconographic program, which is the one most clearly revealed by the archaeological tunnels, then covered the earlier frieze as part of a new construction phase (Román-Ramírez 2011).

The decision to bury the Temple of the Night Sun appears to result from structural problems with the building. The weight of the roofcomb put excessive pressure on the relatively wide interior rooms. Not wanting to abandon the temple, the Maya attempted to engineer structural solutions. First, they thickened the interior dividing wall at the expense of the width of the front room. This provided additional support to the burdensome roofcomb. Second, they elevated the floors around the exterior of the temple, stabilizing the walls and making them stronger. These modifications affected the overall utility of the building, both structurally and in terms of its iconographic message. The raising of the floors partially obscured the complex stucco iconography of the temple walls. In addition, the damage from the roofcomb required a new program of masks to refresh the temple's imagery (Beltrán and Román 2012; Román-Ramírez 2011; Taube and Houston 2015). Eventually, the entrance to the building was reduced to just 1.40 m, further restricting access to this sacred temple.

The iconography of the temple is laden with solar and celestial themes (Taube and Houston 2015). Excavations have uncovered eight of 14 masks on the temple's frieze, a massive mask on the front wall of the temple, and other iconographic elements on other sections of the building's walls. In addition,

FIGURE 3.5. *Near-range photogrammetric image of the north façade of the Temple of the Night Sun (image by K. Simon).*

there is evidence of a royal couple on the sides of the roofcomb and a central ruler on its front. The building is called the Temple of the Night Sun because of the prominence of the Jaguar God of the Underworld (JGU) in the temple's imagery (Beltrán and Román 2012; Houston, Román, et al. 2011; Román-Ramírez 2011; Taube and Houston 2015). This being represents the sun on its nocturnal trip through the Maya underworld, a perilous journey that had to be performed each night. The temple itself faces toward the setting sun.

The best-preserved section of the Temple of the Night Sun is its upper frieze. Three out of five potential masks have been exposed on the eastern (rear) side of the temple. Assuming that there was symmetry in the iconography, this rear frieze is a giant skyband. Central to the band is an old god, with aged jaguar features (Stuart 1998:189–193; Taube and Houston 2015:216). This central deity is framed by two JGU shield masks positioned over descending serpent snouts that represent the ends of skybands in Late Preclassic and Early Classic contexts at Izapa, Takalik Abaj, San Bartolo, and Kohunlich (Taube and Houston 2015:212). The masks themselves are interconnected by a bejeweled skyband with a mask of the Sun God at the building's northeast corner, and likely another at the still-buried southeast corner. The crenelated feature around the Sun God's mouth shows that he fed on blood.

The northern frieze has two masks, one representing the storm god, Chahk, and the other a nighttime variant of a solar being known as GI. GI is a fish-like deity, representing the morning sun, but his nocturnal jaguar features on the Temple of the Night Sun suggest some alternative connection. A similar pair of masks was on the southern frieze, although only the Chahk survives the extensive damage by looters (Gutiérrez and Román 2014). The western frieze is on the front of the temple and the central mask, above the doorway, is a large JGU. The other two excavated masks, north of the JGU are in poor condition, but likely had identical pairs to the south. The ones near the corners may have been smaller, less elaborate versions of the JGU (Taube and Houston 2015:216–217). The temple walls, to the north and south of the doorway, were themselves decorated with two enormous JGU masks, further highlighting the central role this deity played in the building's iconographic program. The Shrine was built 1 m west of the Temple of the Night Sun. It is a small building with two doorways providing east–west passage. The structure was painted with red pigments and had a series of niches but no evidence of modeled stucco. The Shrine appears to have been built to mark the exact location of the royal tomb underneath and to afford seasonal cover or secrecy to rituals over the tomb (Román-Ramírez 2011; Román and Newman 2011).

El Zotz Burial 9

The discovery of Burial 9 during the 2010 field season represents the most intact royal tomb found at El Zotz to date. Located beneath the Shrine and within the same platform that supports the Temple of the Night Sun, this interment was the whole motivation for the iconographic program described above. The king, probably the founder of the Pa'ka'n dynasty, was buried with an array of objects, while additional offerings were made outside of the tomb chamber to consecrate the burial (Houston, Newman, Román, and Carter 2015:39–46).

The external offerings can be divided into two sectors. The first were found beneath the floor of the Shrine. Cache 1 consisted of two sets of lip-to-lip vessels, one of which contained a single human fingertip. Just to the south, Cache 2, was another lip-to-lip pair, this time with a complete finger (Román-Ramírez 2011; Román and Newman 2011; Román et al. 2011; Scherer 2015b; Scherer and Garrett 2011b). The Maya placed a second group of offerings outside the west wall of the tomb chamber. This deposit was more complex. A carved, columnar altar was positioned on top of five ceramic caches, perhaps configured in quadripartite fashion. Four of the caches were paired vessels, while one (Cache 8) was a single bowl. Inside the caches were various parts of human fingers, as well as two human incisors. Cache 5 also contained an obsidian blade, possibly the implement used to remove the fingers for the other offerings (Houston,

Newman, Román, and Garrison 2015; Román-Ramírez 2011; Román and Newman 2011; Scherer 2015b; Scherer and Garrett 2011b). The nature of the tunneling operation to reach Burial 9 prevented exploration of other sides of the tomb chamber. It is possible that other offerings were made to consecrate the space of the king's interment.

The Funerary Chamber

The funerary chamber was 3 m long, 1 m wide, and 1.58 m in height. Carbon from inside one of the tomb's vessels dated to the fourth century AD (table 1.1; Houston et al., chapter 1, this volume). The king was laid on a wooden bier above the funerary offerings (for a full description of the tomb contents see Newman et al. 2015). He was dressed in a dance costume, with an elaborate belt composed of 96 *Conus* shells (each with 1–4 canine teeth inside), and various *Spondylus* "clappers" (Gutiérrez Castillo 2015). Dancing was a key part of royal performance and a means of impersonating or interacting with deities. An elaborate belt assemblage, complete with jade celts and two mosaic jade masks, displayed the king's wealth (Román-Ramírez 2011; Román and Newman 2011). In his right hand, he held an obsidian sacrificial knife, highlighting the human offerings made both outside and inside the tomb (Aoyama 2011, 2015; Houston, Román, et al. 2011).

The ruler's body was coated in a layer of specular hematite, followed by cinnabar. It is also possible that he was then covered with a clay-like substance that was subsequently stuccoed, perhaps as a preventive measure against decomposition. The body was set upon the funerary bier with the head oriented to the north. The other offerings in the tomb consisted of 23 ceramic vessels, three organic vessels, 15 hematite cubes, six child sacrifices (four whole, two crania) within lip-to-lip vessel pairings, two stucco sculptural objects, a bone needle, and a series of degraded textile bundles (Newman et al. 2015). The preparation of the body, combined with the richness of the interior and exterior offerings, as well as the elaborate mortuary temple, all indicate the presence of a royal tomb (Fitzsimmons 2009).

First Ruler of El Zotz

The epigraphic record of El Zotz does not leave much in the way of personal names of rulers (Houston 2008a). The fourth century AD date of Burial 9 suggests that it contains one of the earliest rulers of El Zotz. Stratigraphic evidence proves that the king was buried when one of the site's earliest structures, the Red Temple, was destroyed. This sequence is similar to the burial of K'inich Yax K'uk' Mo', the dynastic founder of Copan, who was interred in the early Hunal structure of that city (Agurcia Fasquelle and Fash 2005). The large funerary chamber and the richness of its offerings underscore the importance of the personage. The iconography of the Temple of the Night Sun, with themes of royal ancestry, cycles of life and death, and royal authority, is fully appropriate to the monument of a dynastic founder (Houston, Newman, Román, and Garrison 2015). Excavations of later versions of the Str. F8-1 pyramid recovered broken pieces of modeled stucco that appeared to have similar iconographic content to the themes of the Temple of the Night Sun. At Copan, Temple 16, which covered the Hunal structure and the founder's tomb, was laden with iconography connected to the time of the dynastic founder himself and to his identification with the Sun God (Taube 2004b). These lines of evidence strongly suggest that Burial 9 contained the founder of the Pa'ka'n dynasty.

CONSOLIDATION OF A DYNASTY: THE END OF THE EARLY CLASSIC (AD 400–550)

Visit from a Foreigner

In AD 378, the enigmatic Sihyaj K'ahk' ("Born-from-Fire") entered the Maya lowlands (Stuart 2000). This event was first identified by Tatiana Proskouriakoff (1993), and later elaborated upon by Stuart (2000) who argued that he was a warrior from Teotihuacan who came to Tikal after a brief stop at El Perú-Waka', and most likely dethroned and executed the Tikal king, Chak Tok Ich'aak I. In his place, Sihyaj K'ahk' installed Yax Nuun Ahiin, the grandson of Spearthrower Owl, a possible ruler of Teotihuacan (Stuart 2000). In the years immediately following this Lowland *entrada* there are a number of Peten sites that make mention of Sihyaj K'ahk', including at nearby Uaxactun and on the murals of La Sufricaya (Estrada-Belli et al. 2009). El Zotz appears also to have come under the influence of Sihyaj K'ahk'. Stela 2 at Bejucal, a royal country house for the Pa'ka'n lords (Garrison et al. 2016), names an El Zotz ruler who came to the throne in AD 381 as a subordinate to Sihyaj K'ahk' (Houston 2008a). The times immediately following the Teotihuacan *entrada* may have been temporarily chaotic, but ultimately led to a century and a half of relative political stability in the central Lowlands under the guidance of a powerful Tikal dynasty. In this process, smaller dynasties like that of El Zotz, lost some of their independence and innovation, but still ruled as powerful local lords.

Process of Abandonment at El Diablo and El Tejón

Excavations at the hilltop groups of El Diablo and El Tejón reveal that they were abandoned towards the end of the Early Classic (ca. AD 450–500). At El Diablo this appears to have been a deliberate process as the inhabitants removed all of their possessions when they left the hill. At the time that this was occurring, other portions of El Zotz experienced growth, including the site's main Acropolis. This suggests that the polity remained strong, while the physical center of power shifted.

In the El Diablo Group there is evidence that the abandonment of the hilltop may have had a ritual component, as indicated by the deposition of a gray mixture of limestone blocks, pulverized limestone, dirt, and ceramics in various locations. Román-Ramírez (2011) believes that this was a structured process, taking place in three steps. First, the roofs and decorations were removed from the temple and palace structures. Next, the upper walls of buildings were dismantled. Finally, there was a ritual deposition resulting in the gray mixture described above. For his part, Houston wonders whether these practices existed to prepare for an aborted or incomplete episode of further construction, similar to that seen in the El Zotz Acropolis during the Terminal Classic (Newman et al., chapter 5, this volume).

In the El Diablo Acropolis, excavations revealed that the palace was abandoned during a new phase of construction activity (Román-Ramírez 2011; Román and Carter 2009) (figure 3.6). The front chamber of the south structure (Str. F8-7) was 40 percent dismantled, while the back chamber remained intact except for the roof. The rooms were packed with construction fill for the next phase, including pieces of stucco decoration, but then the whole operation was abandoned and covered with the gray mixture. A similar process was detected in excavations of Str. F8-5 (Román-Ramírez 2011; Román and Newman 2011).

In the cases of Strs. F8-4 and F8-2, the Maya completely destroyed the upper temples during the process of abandonment, leaving only very low remnants of the walls (Román-Ramírez 2011). These remaining partitions were then packed with the gray deposit (Román and Newman 2011). For Str. F8-1, the most important building at El Diablo (and perhaps all of El Zotz), the process of termination was slightly different (Román and Carter 2009). Here the upper temple was partially destroyed, but some of the stucco decoration was left intact before being covered in the gray mixture.

Excavations in 2011 at the El Tejón Group (Piedrasanta 2012) and in some of the humbler residences of El Diablo (Strs. F8-15 to F8-17) indicate that it was not just the royal court that moved during the Early Classic. Again, the abandoned structures were covered with the gray deposit. Ceramic evidence

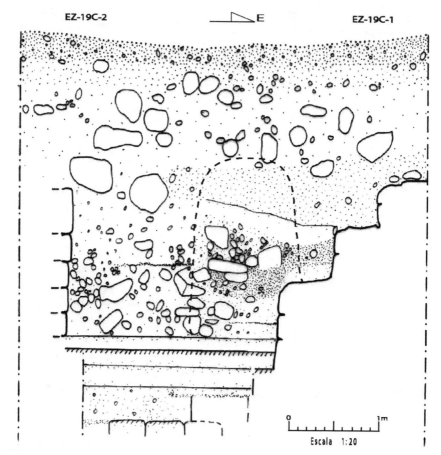

Escala 1:20

FIGURE 3.6. *North excavation profile of Str. F8-9 showing the abandonment debris associated with the El Diablo Group (drawing by Y. Gutiérrez).*

suggests that the residential abandonments may have been somewhat later, given the presence of possible Tzakol 3 sherds. However, the ceramic chronology of the Early Classic at El Zotz is insufficiently refined to assert a precise date. Strs. F8-11 and F8-18 were built in the El Diablo plaza on top of the gray deposit. These buildings also date to the Early Classic period, and their presence in the middle of the elite group's plaza indicates that it had lost importance for the royal family as a residence.

The cause of the abandonment of El Diablo and El Tejón by the end of the Early Classic was a decision made by the ruling lineage of El Zotz. The decision was certainly influenced by the difficulty of hilltop living. Access to resources was a constant strain, and the limited space for architectural expansion meant that the ruling family was living above and away from its subjects. Yet there is no evidence for violence in the Pa'ka'n polity at this time: other parts of the site continued to thrive and grow.

Ruling from the defensive hilltop landscape of the Buenavista Escarpment probably started to tax the growing population in terms of gaining access to sufficient water and other critical resources (Román-Ramírez 2011). This must have also meant that moving to the lower valley was not as fearful a military risk as it had been at the end of the Late Preclassic when the hills were originally settled. The key to this shift to lower elevations probably lies in the alliances forged by the Teotihuacan-influenced kingdom of Tikal after the AD 378 *entrada*. Without the immediate threat of military aggression—a *pax tikalensis?*—the El Zotz rulers were able to move to the valley and expand their kingdom. However, Tikal and its new regime were also probably responsible for limiting just how large El Zotz was allowed to grow, as evidenced by the subordination of the Pa'ka'n ruler mentioned at Bejucal.

CONSOLIDATION OF A DYNASTY IN A NEW LAND

For Lisa Lucero (2003), the consolidation of dynasties in the Early Classic period allowed for the creation and maintenance of power through the appropriation and utilization of domestic rituals, which later were performed in massive public displays. In the case of El Zotz this dynastic consolidation is, in Román's opinion, seen in the monumental religious architecture built and rebuilt during the Early Classic. The first monumental structures of the Acropolis were constructed at the end of the Early Classic as the seat of royal power shifted from the El Diablo Group down to the valley floor (Czapiewska 2012; Newman et al. 2012). These structures included monumental platforms around at least two patios. Newman and colleagues (2012) proposed that the east patio was a royal residence, while the west patio represented the administrative space of the early palace.

Another important building is Str. M7-1 (the Pyramid of the Wooden Lintel). The final version of this pyramid was the largest Early Classic structure at El Zotz and has direct connections to the Pa'ka'n dynasty. The structure is 23 m tall and had at least six major construction phases that saw it evolve from a small, elaborately decorated platform to a major funerary pyramid. Later additions were made to the front of Str. M7-1 in the Late and Terminal Classic, but these features are just auxiliary platforms attached to the front, presumably as the

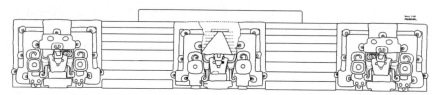

FIGURE 3.7. *West (front) profile of the Accession Platform (Str. M7-1-Sub.2)(drawing by M. Clarke and T. Linden).*

pyramid became a place of ancestral offerings (see Carter et al., chapter 4, this volume). Laporte (2006) proposed that the final phase of the pyramid dated to Tzakol 3, based on salvage work in looter excavations in the 1980s by members of the Tikal Project. Investigations by Garrison (2012; Garrison et al. 2012) found evidence of earlier phases. Structure M7-1-Sub. 1 is an eastward-facing platform that may be contemporary with the El Diablo Group. Though deliberately mutilated by the Maya, excavations recovered large pieces of modeled, painted stucco, similar in scale to the decorations on the Temple of the Night Sun. At a certain point, perhaps in the early fifth century AD, this platform was destroyed and a major royal tomb constructed (Burial 16). This tomb was then covered by Str. M7-1-Sub. 2, a large platform decorated with three masks depicting *Ux Yop Huun*, the embodiment of royal headbands and highest office (Garrison 2012; Stuart 2012b) (figure 3.7). This platform was aligned along the exact same centerline and orientation as the Temple of the Night Sun, forming the termini of a roughly east–west axis that defined Early Classic El Zotz.

The Maya deliberately destroyed the central mask of Str. M7-1-Sub. 2, presumably to reenter the royal tomb before burying the structure. The new construction at the site was a major amplification of the platform (Str. M7-1-4th), and eventually formed the base of the first pyramidal building at this location (Str. M7-1-3rd). The pyramid had an inset staircase, flanked by large apron-molding architectural tiers. The Maya began building central ancillary additions and expanding this pyramid, creating a low platform with an outset staircase that eventually ran in to the preexisting inset steps. One of these additions was partially dismantled to insert the tomb of an elite individual (Burial 25), buried with four Early Classic vessels (Garrison and Houston, chapter 13, this volume; Scherer, chapter 12, this volume).

The final construction at this site was the so-called Pyramid of the Wooden Lintel (Str. M7-1-1st). Its name comes from a carved wooden lintel that was looted in the 1970s and identified by Ian Graham in the collections of the Denver Art Museum. Graham was able to match the cut on the lintel to fragments found still *in situ*, and the piece was later repatriated to Guatemala, where it resides in the national museum. This is the earliest-known, carved wooden lintel in the Maya Lowlands, predating the famous examples from Tikal. The temple itself has three chambers, appearing very similar in plan to Tikal Temple I. The lintel depicts a Maya ruler and the associated text names him and his parents (Houston 2008a). Stylistically dated to the sixth century AD, this may depict the last great Early Classic king of El Zotz, before the Pa'ka'n dynasty fell on hard times, perhaps in the wake of the defeat of Tikal by the Snake dynasty (Martin and Grube 2008:28–31).

CONCLUSIONS

The sites of the Early Classic period in the Buenavista Valley participated in a number of pan-Lowland developments, such as the creation of polychrome pottery and the adoption of divine, dynastic kingship. However, three distinct local adaptations are worth highlighting. First, the transition to the Early Classic period saw a major change in building locations in the valley landscape as the elites moved to higher ground following the abandonment of El Palmar. Strained environmental conditions and competition from an emerging Tikal kingdom may have factored into the decision to leave El Palmar and move up onto the escarpment. Relocating into the hills provided greater natural defenses for the elites in the region. Complementing the relocation to the escarpment above El Zotz was, as a second major adjustment, the emergence of the Pa'ka'n dynasty. Evidence from El Palmar suggests that the kingdom existed as a centralized power with a clear urban plan during the Late Preclassic period (Doyle 2013b). However, while El Palmar remained important symbolically after its abandonment, El Zotz became the center of dynastic activity beginning in the fourth century AD. This is seen in the undisturbed royal tomb found in 2010 and the iconography of a founding couple associated with the funerary Temple of the Night Sun constructed over the interment (Houston, Newman, Román, and Garrison 2015). The dynasty expanded its power across the local landscape with the appropriation of the sacred hilltop of Bejucal as a royal residence (Garrison et al. 2016) and renewed activity at El Palmar, including an elite burial in front of the Triadic Pyramid (Doyle 2013b; Doyle and Piedrasanta, chapter 2, this volume). Architectural constructions from this period, such as Str. F8-1 at El Diablo and Str. S6-10 at Bejucal, were modest in terms of their size, while a greater emphasis was placed on the ornate stucco decoration of these early buildings, reflecting the artistry controlled by the ruling family.

The final adjustment made during the Early Classic period was the abandonment of the El Diablo and El Tejón Groups towards the end of the Early Classic period. Renovations to the buildings at these sites were incomplete, but the abandonment does not seem to have been sudden. Neither conflict nor climate change appears to have motivated the relocation to the valley floor. The reorganization of the royal court at El Zotz may have been related to the arrival of Sihyaj K'ahk' in the Maya Lowlands. A vessel lid from Burial 9 at El Diablo has probable connections to the Teotihuacan *ojo de reptil* motif (Newman et al. 2015:103–105), and the tomb probably dates to around the time of the Teotihuacan *entrada* in AD 378 (Stuart 2000). Once Sihyaj K'ahk' installed a new ruler at Tikal and began expanding that city's influence, the central and southern Maya Lowlands entered a period of general peace, almost like a *pax tikalensis*. Without the threat of immediate hostilities, the Pa'ka'n elites were comfortable in relocating the seat of royal authority to an area where expansion was possible and resources could be more easily obtained. After the relocation, much of the major architecture at El Zotz was constructed and the dynasty reached its Classic-period peak.

4

Contemporary understandings of Late Classic Maya polities are guided by two major models. One emphasizes the performative aspects of Maya kingship, the religious nature of political authority, and the centrality of royal courts rather than administrative bureaucracies in the operation of Classic kingdoms (Inomata and Houston 2001). The other model, potentially compatible with the first, posits that a few kings headed alliance networks that incorporated other polities great and small. During the Late Classic period, geopolitical struggles between two such hegemonic powers—the Mut dynasty of Tikal and the Snake dynasty of Calakmul—shaped the fortunes of less powerful polities (Martin and Grube 1994, 2008). Among these was the Pa'ka'n kingdom, which encompassed the larger site of El Zotz and the minor centers of Bejucal and La Avispa. Recent research at El Zotz offers insights into how the political strategies of the Mut and Snake rulers worked in practice on a local level.

A dearth of inscriptions at El Zotz and explicit references to it at other centers make it difficult to offer detailed proposals about Pa'ka'n rulers' activities during the Late Classic period, from ca. AD 550 to 850. It is not even certain that a Pa'ka'n dynasty ruled continuously at the site, especially during the eighth century (see below). Nevertheless, archaeological evidence from the site—architectural, lithic, environmental, and ceramic—makes it clear that elite activity was ongoing, and allows the kingdom's Late Classic history to be

Border Lords and Client Kings

El Zotz and Bejucal in the Late Classic Period

NICHOLAS P. CARTER,
YENY M. GUTIÉRREZ
CASTILLO, AND
SARAH NEWMAN

DOI: 10.5876/9781607327646.c004

93

sketched out in general terms. El Zotz's geographical position (figure 1.1)—situated between the territories of Tikal and the Snake kingdom ally El Perú-Waka', on the north edge of the Buenavista Valley, a natural travel route across the uplands of northern Peten—is key both to interpreting these data and to considering their implications for the political strategies of Classic Maya hegemonic powers.

ELITE CONSTRUCTIONS IN THE EARLY LATE CLASSIC PERIOD

The first major episodes of monumental construction during the Late Classic period, as early as AD 550, modified existing precincts in El Zotz's regal-ritual center (figure 1.5). Early Late Classic monumental works documented by the Proyecto Arqueológico El Zotz (PAEZ) included new constructions at the Acropolis and the Five Temples Group. A multi-courtyard compound at the northern edge of the El Zotz site core, the Acropolis is presumed to have been the residence of the Pa'ka'n royal family and the spatial center of courtly life (Newman et al. 2012). The Five Temples Group, southwest of the Acropolis, was a major public space covering about 7,700 m². It is bounded on the north and south by pyramids (Strs. L8-8 and L8-13); on the east by a line of lower buildings, perhaps shrines in the Late Classic (Strs. L8-9 to L8-11, and L8-19 to L8-20); and on the west by a residential patio group composed of Strs. K8-1 to K8-6 (Garrido López 2014).

In the Acropolis (figure 4.1), an early phase of Str. L7-1 was built that consisted of a platform about 3 m high and 50 m long from north to south. The associated radiocarbon date of AD 532–650 (88.4 percent probability) is consistent with associated Mo'-phase ceramics (table 1.1; Czapiewska-Halliday et al., chapter 8, this volume; Walker 2009). This stage of the building covered an earlier phase, perhaps Early Classic in date, represented by a low wall of worked stones with traces of stucco (figure 4.2). Prior to the construction of the Mo'-phase platform, a new stucco floor was laid down in front of the older building. A Saxche-Palmar orange polychrome sherd (figure 4.3) recovered from the fill of this floor bears the partial royal title k'uhul-Pa'ka'n [ajaw] ("holy Pa'ka'n [lord]"), confirming the existence of a royal court at El Zotz in the late sixth or early seventh century AD (Marroquín et al. 2011:27).

The same period saw new activity in the Five Temples Group. The major structures of the complex are currently under investigation, but their north–south orientation is consistent with that of the Late Classic pyramids Strs. M3-1 and L7-11, and differs from that of El Zotz's Early Classic temples. Excavations revealed an intrusive cist burial (El Zotz Burial 3) in the plaza

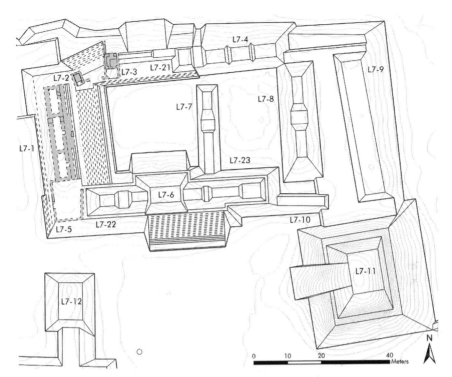

FIGURE 4.1. *Map of the El Zotz Acropolis (map by T. Garrison).*

floor in front of Str. K8-2 (Cambranes 2009:175–176). The grave contained the skeleton of an adult, probably male and over 50 years of age (Scherer, chapter 12, this volume), together with four monochrome slipped vessels—a vase, two bowls, and a plate—assigned to the Mo' phase (figure 4.4). Ceramics recovered from stratigraphically subsequent lots were also Mo', while earlier layers contained only Early Classic sherds. Sounding pits excavated in and around the residential group west of the Five Temples Group recovered substantial amounts of Mo'- and Caal-phase ceramics, indicating that the complex was occupied throughout the Late Classic period. In all likelihood, the buildings of this group were expanded during the seventh century AD, following Burial 3. This possibility, however, remains to be tested through future excavations.

EARLY SEVENTH-CENTURY KINGS AND THE CULT OF THE *WAY*

More than 30 polychrome vessels—most with red backgrounds, looted from the area of El Zotz and sold on the black market during the 1970s—depict

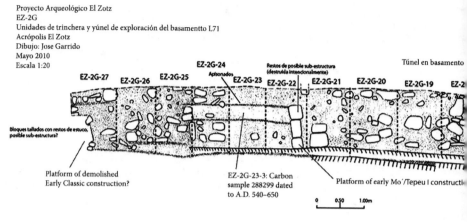

Proyecto Arqueológico El Zotz
EZ-2G
Unidades de trinchera y yúnel de exploración del basamentto L71
Acrópolis El Zotz
Dibujo: Jose Garrido
Mayo 2010
Escala 1:20

EZ-2G-27 EZ-2G-26 EZ-2G-25 EZ-2G-24 Apisonados Restos de posible sub-estructura (destruída intencionalmente) EZ-2G-23 EZ-2G-22 EZ-2G-21 EZ-2G-20 EZ-2G-19 EZ-2 Túnel en basamento

Bloques tallados con restos de estuco, posible sub-estructura?

Platform of demolished
Early Classic construction?

EZ-2G-23-3: Carbon
sample 288299 dated
to A.D. 540–650

Platform of early Mo´/Tepeu I constructi

0   0.50   1.00m

FIGURE 4.2. *Profile of excavations tunnel in Str. L7-1 (drawing by J. L. Garrido).*

frightening, frequently zoomorphic, supernatural beings called *way* (see Houston and Stuart 1989). Epigraphic, stylistic, and compositional data combine to suggest that these vessels were produced at El Zotz near the beginning of the seventh century and that this city was the first to depict and label such beings (Houston 2008a). Their dedicatory texts typically substitute what would otherwise be read **PA'KA'N-na** (*pa'ka'n*) for the third person ergative pronoun **U** (*u*, "his, her, its"), and several of the vessels are labeled as belonging to Pa'ka'n lords. Instrumental Neutron Activation Analysis (INAA) confirms that they were produced using the same clay sources as domestic vessels recovered from the El Zotz site area (Ronald Bishop, personal communication 2012).

Bearing names like "Eyeball Deer" and "Fire-Nosed Peccary," *way* may have been perceived as evil omens, personifications of illness, dangerous beings who could be controlled by magic, or some combination of the three (Houston and Inomata 2009:208). *Way* could "belong" to gods, individual kings or, most often, royal dynasties (the relevant expression is *u way*, "[it is] the *way* of . . ."). Vessels cataloguing and portraying *way* achieved importance in elite social settings during the seventh and eighth centuries, especially at Altar de Sacrificios and in the Mirador Basin. Even today, traditions of similar creatures, like the "Spine Man" (*ch'ix winik*) and the "Sucking Monkey" (*tz'u'max*), persist among some Mayan speakers (Aulie and de Aulie 1978:3; Hull 2005:111). As noted by Houston, the red-background vessels from El Zotz, however, mark the first appearance of *way* beings in Maya ceramic art. They point out the Pa'ka'n kings as ideological pioneers who asserted their power through fell beings in addition to more mundane political and military claims.

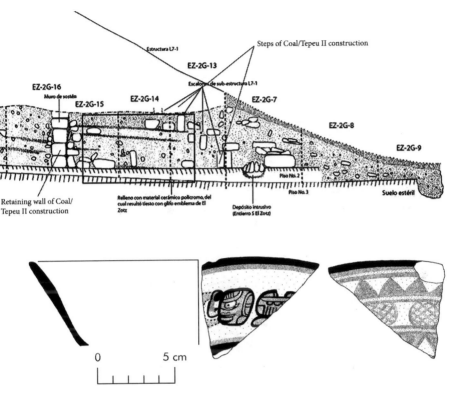

Figure 4.3 labels (within image):
Estructura L7-1 — Steps of Coal/Tepeu II construction — EZ-2G-13 — EZ-2G-16 — Muro de sostén — EZ-2G-15 — EZ-2G-14 — Escalones de sub-estructura L7-1 — EZ-2G-7 — EZ-2G-8 — EZ-2G-9 — Piso No.2 — Piso No.3 — Retaining wall of Coal/Tepeu II construction — Relleno con material cerámico policromo, del cual resultó tiesto con glifo emblema de El Zotz — Depósito intrusivo (Entierro 5 El Zotz) — Suelo estéril

0   5 cm

FIGURE 4.3. *Sherd with the El Zotz royal title* k'uhul Pa'ka'n *[ajaw] (drawing by N. Carter).*

This corpus of vessels names at least nine distinct owners plus two of their parents, the mother and father of two different individuals (figure 4.5). One name, *Ch'ich' Ti'is Chan [. . .] Kab Yopaat Chak Nutz Bahlam*, appears on several vessels. Another, *Chak [. . .] Ahk*, is the namesake of other Pa'ka'n or **EARSPOOL** kings named on the Canberra Vessel and El Zotz Lintel 1 (see Houston et al., chapter 1, this volume). His mother was a "holy lady, the lady of Pa'ka'n" (*k'uhul ixik, ix pa'ka'n*). Still a third individual bears a title, *Bolon Chan K'in*, also attested on an El Zotz–style vase found at Uaxactun (see below). Four vessel owners are called "Pa'ka'n lords" (*pa'ka'n ajaw*) or "holy Pa'ka'n lords" (*k'uhul pa'ka'n ajaw*); one is a "holy 'Earspool' [lord]" (**K'UHUL-[EARSPOOL]**). Several of the vessels emphasize their owners' youth with titles like *keleem* ("young man") or *ju'n winikha'b ajaw* ("twenty-year lord"; a lord in his first 20 years of life), consistent with a role as gifts marking entrance into young manhood (Houston 2009:165).

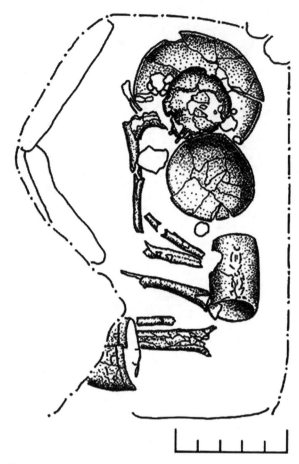

FIGURE 4.4. *El Zotz Burial 3 , scale in 10 cm increments (drawing by Z. Hruby).*

Most unprovenanced, El Zotz–style vessels correspond to the Mo' ceramic phase, ca. AD 550–700 (table 8.1; see Czapiewska-Halliday et al., chapter 8, this volume). Despite strong stylistic and paleographic similarities, there are definite stylistic differences between nine of the 10 vessels that bear the names of their owners and the rest, whose dedicatory texts break off after a description of the vessel (usually *u jay, yuk'ib*, "his clay vessel, his drinking-instrument"). Vessels without personal names tend to have red backgrounds, and their inscriptions frequently exhibit resist techniques or multiple coats of paint, yielding contrasting colors in the hieroglyphs. Often, though not always,

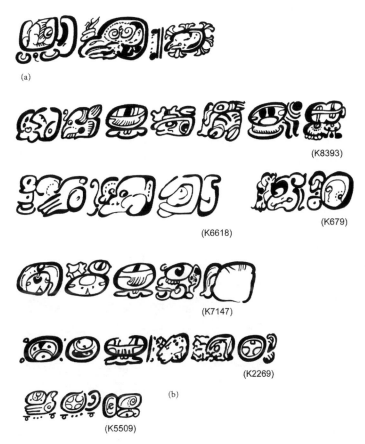

(a)

(K8393)

(K6618)

(K679)

(K7147)

(K2269)

(b)

(K5509)

FIGURE 4.5. *Names and titles from 10 unprovenanced El Zotz–style polychrome vessels (drawings by N. Carter).*

the proportions and lines of text and image are somewhat crude. Those with names rarely feature multicolored glyphs (the red-background, resist-painted K3924, numbered in a system of rollouts devised by Justin Kerr, is an exception), the texts instead being painted directly onto the background or filled with a single shade of red. These vessels' background colors and the subject matter of their scenes are more varied than is the case for the majority of those without personal names.

At least two schools or generations of artists can thus be posited for the El Zotz–style polychrome tradition, and most of the vessels with personal names appear to be later in date than many of those without them. The implication is that most of the nine individuals named on those vases were alive during a single, relatively narrow window of time—conservatively, ca. AD 600 to 650 (de Carteret 2013). If each of the five bearing the title *ajaw* or *k'uhul ajaw* ruled at El Zotz during that period, they would have enjoyed an average reign of 10 years, a little more than half of the average for kings of Tikal (19.3 tuns or 19.03 365-day years) between AD 426 and 768 (Culbert 1991:109). A better possibility is that members of the royal family other than current rulers and crown princes were entitled to call themselves *pa'ka'n ajaw* and to receive or commission polychrome vessels. Counting only *k'uhul ajaw* as rulers during the proposed second generation of polychrome artists yields an average reign of 16.6 years, closer to the figure for Tikal. The order in which those kings ruled, however, cannot yet be determined.

MONUMENTAL FLORESCENCE AT EL ZOTZ IN THE MID-EIGHTH CENTURY AD

Monumental constructions during the Caal ceramic phase—broadly supposed to correspond to the period from ca. AD 700 to 850 (table 8.1)—transformed built landscapes in the core of El Zotz and on its periphery. With the aid of radiocarbon dating, modal ceramic analysis, stratigraphic data, and epigraphic evidence from other Maya sites, it is possible to narrow the dates of the most ambitious projects down to between ca. AD 725 and 800. These projects followed an apparent hiatus in monumental works during the late seventh and early eighth centuries. They included multiple construction episodes at and near the Acropolis that increased the volume of many of its structures and added a third patio group (the Northwest Courtyard) to its western end. The Early Classic versions of Strs. L7-8 and L7-9, which form the eastern border of Courtyard 2, were partially demolished and covered over with new, stuccoed platforms that likely supported perishable buildings. Later, builders renovated the platform floor and added a staircase to its west side (Newman and Menéndez 2012:143).

Likewise, the platform of Str. L7-1 was partially dismantled and then doubled in size during this period (Marroquín et al. 2011:51–53). As the new phase of the building was being finished, a cist grave was cut in the plaza floor on its east–west axis, and the body of an adult (El Zotz Burial 5) interred (figure 4.6). The deceased was probably male, between 21 and 50 years of age, and exhibited both dental modification (notching in the front teeth) and perhaps tabular oblique cranial deformation (Scherer, chapter 12, this volume). The body was placed with the head oriented to the north, a common pattern in burials at El Zotz (Stephen

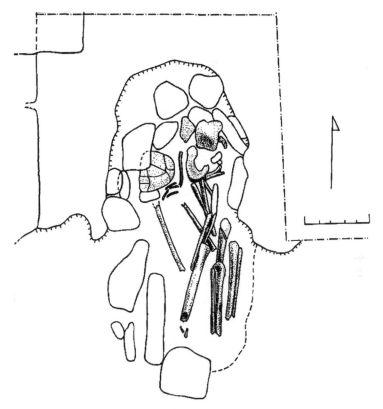

FIGURE 4.6. *El Zotz Burial 5, scale in 5 cm increments (drawing by S. Houston).*

Houston, personal communication, 2010). A single, small vessel was deposited just northeast of the head. The skeleton was found poorly preserved, but the positions of the surviving bones suggest the body was deposited in a seated position with the arms flexed toward the thoracic area, perhaps indicating that it was bundled at the time of burial. If so, it could have been kept in such a condition for some time while Str. L7-1 was being completed. A fragment of carbon recovered from the burial must have originally come from one of the cut floors, since its date—AD 325–475 (77.6 percent probability)—is potentially centuries earlier than that of the dismantled phase of L7-1 (see above).

Structure L7-2, an Early Classic platform adjacent to Str. L7-24 to the east, was also covered by a new construction phase during the Caal ceramic period. Another burial (Burial 8) of an elite male, more than 50 years old at death, was found under the Late Classic platform of Str. L7-2 (figure 4.7). Like the

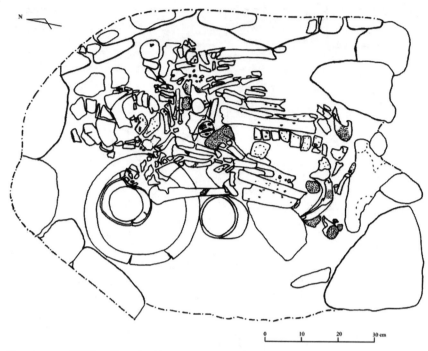

Figure 4.7. *El Zotz Burial 8 (drawing by E. Marroquín).*

occupant of Burial 5, this individual displayed tabular oblique cranial deformation, but had probably lost all his teeth by the time he died. The arms and legs were flexed as if the body had been wrapped when interred, and again the head was oriented to the north. Three vessels—a cylindrical vase, a tripod plate, and a small bowl set inside the plate—were placed just west of the body. The frontal and both parietal bones of the skull exhibited discoloration caused by exposure to intense heat, which occurred—presumably in a ritual context—prior to burial, while the skull was still articulated with the neck vertebrae (Scherer, chapter 12, this volume).

Other eighth-century architectural modifications reveal a concern with restricting and monitoring access to the Acropolis. The floor of a small patio at the southwest corner of Courtyard 1 was renovated twice, and the accessway between Strs. L7-1 and L7-6 was narrowed. A carbon sample from the fill beneath the first of Courtyard 1's two renovation floors dates to between AD 680 and 881, but the presence of Caal ceramics restricts this range to between AD 680 and 830 (table 1.1). To the east, a long, vaulted passage ran beneath Str.

L7-9 and an expanded version of L7-8, presenting a highly restricted entrance to Courtyard 2. While the Early Classic phase of L7-2 had offered relatively open access to Courtyard 1 from the north, its remodeled form included wide door-jambs that limited access and visibility. Recent investigations of Str. L7-7 suggest that passage between the two courtyards of the Acropolis may also have been restricted by mid-eighth-century constructions, with traffic channeled through the rooms of L7-7. The eastern Courtyard 2 could thus have served as a more private, domestic space for the Pa'ka'n royal family, with the larger and more accessible Courtyard 1 the scene of courtly gatherings (Newman et al. 2012).

Towards the end of the Caal phase, a new courtyard group, the Northwest Courtyard, was added to the west of the existing Acropolis (figure 5.1; Newman and Menéndez 2012:168–169). Basal platforms in this new group were built in a single construction phase—later modified during the Terminal Classic period (see Newman et al., chapter 5, this volume)—and probably supported perishable superstructures. The artifact assemblage recovered from excavations in the Northwest Courtyard suggest that it, like the Acropolis, was a domestic group inhabited by sociopolitical elites. The Late Classic architecture of the group supports this hypothesis: while it lacked masonry superstructures, its platforms were solidly built, using dressed limestone blocks of regular size, and its eighth-century floors are thick and well preserved.

In the East Group, a new phase of Str. M7-2 was built during the eighth century. A new stucco plaza floor followed this construction, and a low (~0.35 m), stone platform of undetermined function was built in front of the pyramid. Excavations during the 2012 field season revealed that a set of three ancillary platforms was built in stages on the front of Str. M7-1 (Garrison et al. 2012:59–65). First, the central platform, at the foot of the pyramid's stairway, was built to a height of about 0.25 m, with a niche housing the upper part of a blank stela. This first phase was stratigraphically subsequent to an old stucco floor laid down over leveled bedrock, but prior to a second stucco floor in front of Str. M7-1, which may well correspond to the new plaza floor encountered near Str. M7-1. Later, the central platform was raised to 1.1 m high, covering the stela; the platforms flanking it, which also stand about a meter tall but appear to have been built in a single phase, may date to this same construction event (figure 4.8).

Based on ceramic evidence—admittedly equivocal, since strongly diagnostic types like Pabellon Molded-carved or Ik'-style cream polychromes were not found in the fill—the first phase could correspond to the middle of the eighth century, while the second phase might date to the turn of the ninth. Fragments of ceramic censers recovered from the basal platforms may indicate

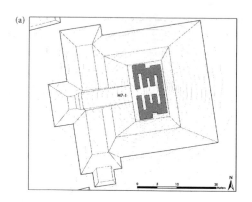

FIGURE 4.8. *(a) Plan and (b) profile of Str. M7-1 (map by T. Garrison, drawing by T. Garrison and A. de Carteret).*

that the whole pyramid served as an object of public adoration at the end of the Late Classic period, rather than as a venue for less-accessible rituals carried out inside its superstructure.

At the other end of the East Causeway, immediately south of the Acropolis, the inhabitants of El Zotz erected Str. L7-11, a terraced pyramid with a central staircase and temple superstructure (figure 4.9). With a footprint of almost 1,300 m² and a platform approximately 20 m high, L7-11 is the tallest building at El Zotz, and its superstructure and roofcomb would have raised it to an even more impressive height. Yet investigations of the multiple looter tunnels penetrating its base indicate that the pyramid was constructed in a relatively short period of time—conceivably even in a single, if complicated, building episode punctuated by the deposition of preparatory floors and ritual caches. There are no buried superstructures, and the pyramid underwent only minor modifications after its initial construction (Arredondo Leiva et al. 2008).

Str. L7-11 was built over a crevice in the bedrock in which a deposit of sand and Caal-phase ceramics had accumulated, perhaps washed in by rains. The builders packed this crevice with fill and laid down a series of leveling floors and a stuccoed basal platform before constructing the first terrace. Excavations in the fill between the final and penultimate floors of the basal platform

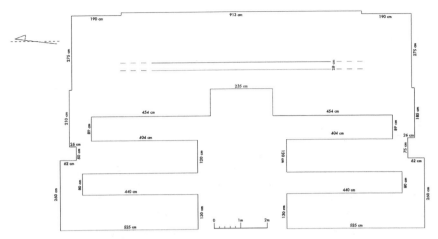

FIGURE 4.9. *Plan of Str. L7-11 temple (drawing by N. Carter).*

revealed a ritual cache contained in two small, outflaring bowls placed lip to lip. One of the bowls was a red-and-orange bichrome, the other a Zacatal Cream Polychrome painted with a basketweave pattern. They contained two plaques of muscovite, a drill-carved greenstone figurine pendant, and some fragments of unidentified animal bone (figure 4.10). Offerings of marine origin were also included in the cache: a polished *Spondylus*-shell pendant and 46 shark teeth probably belonging to a single individual of the genus *Carcharinus* (Arredondo Leiva et al. 2008:77–84; Blankenship 2012:9).

Since no fallen vault stones were found, the superstructure's lintel and roof were likely made of wood. All the walls are standing and well preserved. Its floor plan included a single front entrance and two tandem rooms connected by a central doorway. The two rooms were between 11 and 12 m long, but only 80 and 89 cm deep; a central niche stretching the whole height of the rear wall was 2.35 m wide and 0.98 m deep. The same back wall supported a stone roofcomb, now collapsed. The roofcomb's mass may have caused the builders some anxiety, since they buttressed the back wall at some point after its initial construction. The addition increased the wall's thickness by half, from ~2 to ~3 m, nearly three times that of the building's other walls. The temple's floors were renovated twice during its use-life, and a layer of charcoal found on top of the uppermost floor suggests that the building's perishable elements burned sometime after the second renovation (Arredondo Leiva et al. 2008:85).

A carbon sample recovered from the fill of the basal platform, associated with a dedicatory cache, yielded a date of AD 666–780 (74.1 percent probability;

FIGURE 4.10. *Contents of Str. L7-11 foundational cache (photo by S. Houston).*

table 1.1). A second sample, from the residue of the proposed burning event, returned a date range between AD 672 and 879. However, since the nature of the carbon was indeterminate, these dates may simply correspond to the age of the construction material that made up the temple's perishable elements. Sherds recovered from the crevice below the basal platform include a few so-called Ik'-style fragments. Characterized by cream backgrounds, expertly executed scenes of dancers or courtiers wearing elaborate masks or headdresses, and rich pink and purple paints and washes applied to figures and glyphs, Ik'-style ceramics are believed to have been produced in the area of Motul de San José beginning around AD 725 (Kerr 1989:32; Halperin and Foias 2010:396; Just et al. 2012:54–66; Tokovinine and Zender 2012:43).

A contemporary monumental construction consisting of two adjoining plazas—the North Group, or Las Palmitas—was built on a hilltop 1 km north of the East Group (figure 4.11; Carter and Gutiérrez Castillo 2011, 2012a,

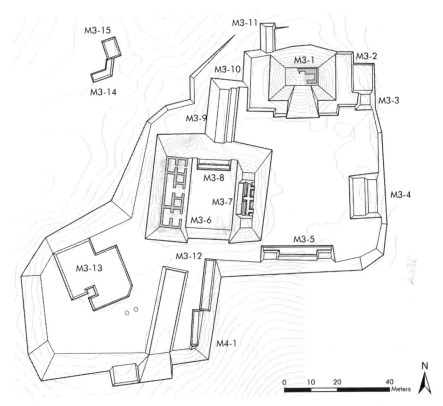

FIGURE 4.11. *Map of the Las Palmitas Group (map by T. Garrison).*

2012b). Las Palmitas's eastern plaza is bounded on the north by a pyramid (Str. M3-1) and smaller, associated buildings, including a raised tomb at the pyramid's southeast corner (Str. M3-3). Long, low buildings (Strs. M3-5 and M3-9) face the plaza on the southern and western sides. Abutting the plaza to the west is an elevated patio group delimited on the eastern and western sides by multi-roomed buildings (Strs. M3-6 and M3-7) believed to comprise an elite residence. A platform projecting south from this patio group likely served both as the access route for Las Palmitas's ritual and residential facilities and as the setting for humbler, perishable constructions.

Almost all the masonry buildings at Las Palmitas were erected in the same, single construction phase, with only minor later changes. Excavations to bedrock and the cleaning and documentation of looter tunnels produced no clear evidence of earlier structures on the hilltop, although a few cut blocks with coats of red stucco and abundant household trash including high-status ceramic fragments were present in the architectural fill. Indeed, construction must have been rapid: the eastern plaza floor extends underneath both Str. M3-1 and the eastern edge of the platform below Str. M3-7. However, the western edge of the floor under the latter platform was never smoothed or finished. The patio platform was therefore built up soon after the plaza floor was laid down, in keeping with a coherent plan for the group's layout. Ik'-style sherds were recovered from the patio fill, indicating a *terminus post quem* for the group of about AD 725.

While the primary tomb in Str. M3-1—if such existed—has so far escaped detection by legitimate and illegitimate excavators alike, an auxiliary burial under the eastern edge of the pyramid platform was disturbed by looters in the 1970s or 1980s. The looters left behind a neat pile of fragmentary long bones and the fragments of a broken but nearly complete orange polychrome bowl decorated with circles and vertical lines. A dedicatory cache discovered in the fill on the structure's axis contained partially burned plant resins, perhaps used as incense, and the disarticulated vertebrae of a big feline.

Both the plaza floors at Las Palmitas were renovated once, as were the upper floors of Strs. M3-5 and M3-9; the western landing of Str. M3-7 was renovated twice during its period of use. Structure M3-3, a low, pyramidal tomb, is stratigraphically subsequent to the second eastern plaza floor. With a vaulted, masonry crypt and thick coats of stucco on its floor and exterior, Str. M3-3 must have been built in the late eighth or early ninth century, before the shortages of labor and materials that characterize Terminal Classic constructions at El Zotz (see Newman et al., chapter 5, this volume). Looters left behind only a few teeth and phalanges, together with some sherds not securely assignable to the tomb's construction, making more precise dating impossible.

BEJUCAL IN THE LATE CLASSIC PERIOD

Bejucal, too, consists of two adjoining architectural groups, although its internal layout differs from that of Las Palmitas (figure 1.3). Bejucal underwent extensive remodeling during the Late Classic period, but, pending detailed ceramic studies and additional carbon dating, it is not yet possible to say when every structure was built (Garrison et al. 2016). Those Late Classic remodeling events which are well dated appear, on the basis of ceramic evidence, to have been roughly contemporaneous with the major construction projects at the Acropolis and Las Palmitas. Late Classic renovations of uncertain date include the final phase of the mortuary pyramid Str. S6-10, in Bejucal's south-eastern courtyard, and the deposition of a second patio floor there. Following the floor renovation, Str. S6-8, across the plaza from Str. S6-10, was erected in a single construction phase.

In the northwestern patio group, Str. S6-4, a low-range building, was probably remodeled around AD 720. The date is based on a Zacatal Cream Polychrome bowl recovered from a cist burial (Bejucal Burial 5) incorporated into the new construction. This vessel, painted with a design reminiscent of jaguar spots, is almost identical to one found in another bedrock cist burial at Tikal (Burial 80) dated to around AD 720 (Becker 1999:99–100; Culbert 1993:figure 60a; Garrison et al. 2016). The final phase of the palatial Str. S6-1 (S6-1-1st) may date to about the same time or later in the eighth century: an Ik'-style polychrome sherd recovered from a looter tunnel and correspond-ing to this phase places the construction after AD 725. Late Classic ampli-fication of Str. S6-2, a platform attached to Str. S6-1, probably belongs to the same construction event. Str. S6-5, another palatial building across the courtyard from those structures, was probably remodeled around the same time, with its new platform covering two earlier buildings. Str. S6-5's inte-rior spaces continued to be modified over the eighth century, with formerly open galleries being divided into smaller, less-accessible rooms (Garrison et al. 2016). In contrast to palatial facilities at Las Palmitas and in the El Zotz site core, Bejucal appears to have been largely abandoned by the end of the Late Classic period.

RURAL POPULATIONS IN THE EL ZOTZ AREA

According to survey work, the commoner population—the great major-ity of people who did not belong to the sociopolitical elite and supported themselves at a household level through subsistence farming and domestic craft production—does not appear to have been densely clustered around the El Zotz site core at any point in the Late Classic period. Instead, while there are some non-elite household groups on the valley floor near the regal-ritual center, Late Classic commoner households appear to have been widely dispersed (Garrison and Garrido López 2012). Rural houselots have been identified in the uplands: in the hills west of Bejucal, and on the slopes and ridges bounding the Buenavista Valley on the north side. Other Late Classic farming households settled the valley floor east of the El Zotz site core, sometimes reoccupying mound groups that had been constructed cen-turies earlier.

Palynological and carbon data from the El Zotz Aguada, analyzed by Timothy Beach, Sheryl Luzzadder-Beach, and Stephen Bozarth Beach et al., chapter 7, this volume; (Bozarth 2010; Luzzadder-Beach et al. 2017) shed light on the environmental history of the site and region. For most of the Early Classic period, the landscape surrounding El Zotz was largely cleared of forest cover and planted in maize, with copal (*Protium*; see Beach et al., chapter 7, this volume) the only trees present in any abundance (Garrison 2012). Forests recovered to an extent around the beginning of the Late Classic period, indicating a decline in cultivation and either a decrease in the Pa'ka'n kingdom's population or an overall shift in settlement far away from the site core. The farming population evidently increased again starting no later than the latter part of the seventh century, coincident with the Caal ceramic phase. Maize and squash were intensively cultivated, while tree species were cleared and burned except for pine and copal. That these trees were managed instead of being cut down can be explained by their economic significance. Fast-growing pine trees would have provided resinous wood for fuel and torches, while more mature timber would have been useful in construction. The ancient Maya used copal resin as an incense in rituals, as an encaustic binder for pigments (Stross 1997), and perhaps in the production of "Maya blue" paint (Arnold et al. 2008).

Excavation data from the intersite zone between El Zotz and El Palmar are consistent with this reconstruction of events. Of the eight rural, presumably commoner houselots in that region probed in 2010, four showed clear ceramic evidence of Caal-phase occupation, three of which had architectural roots in the Late Preclassic or Early Classic period (Garrison, Garrido López et al. 2011; Garrison and Garrido López 2012). No evidence has yet been found for Late Classic occupation at La Avispa. However, a new, non-royal elite residential compound—the La Tortuga Group—was constructed in between Las Palmitas and the El Zotz site core, apparently during the Caal phase.

RELATIONS WITH OTHER POLITIES

While explicit references to an alliance are lacking, epigraphic and material cultural evidence suggests that El Zotz and its neighbor Uaxactun may have been allied with the Snake kingdom at the beginning of the Late Classic period. The king depicted on Lintel 1 from Structure M7-1 was the son of a Pa'ka'n ruler and a lady whose title of *Sak Wayis* ties her to the Mirador Basin (Grube 2008:228–229). As noted above, the *way* theme developed at El Zotz was important to elites in southern Campeche in the eighth century AD. A Late Classic vessel with a hieroglyphic inscription naming a Pa'ka'n king was excavated near El Perú-Waka', an important Calakmul ally and the nearest large site to the west of El Zotz (Fabiola Quiroa, personal communication, 2008).

Connections to El Perú-Waka' may be evident on a more quotidian level. Many of the Late Classic bifacial projectile points excavated at El Zotz were made of chert believed to come from the El Perú-Waka' region (Hruby, chapter 9, this volume). Moreover, at both royal precincts and the non-royal La Tortuga Group, Chaquiste Impressed serving basins are much more common during the Caal ceramic phase than their Chinja Impressed equivalents, placing Caal-phase El Zotz in the "western supercomplex" of Peten ceramic traditions identified by Donald Forsyth (2003:665; Rice and Forsyth 2004:32). The Chaquiste basins from El Zotz are of the same variety typical of Late Classic El Perú-Waka' and La Joyanca, with impressions made in a band of clay applied to the outer surface of the vessel, in contrast to the thickened-band varieties excavated at Zapote Bobal to the south (Forné 2008; see also Czapiewska-Halliday et al., chapter 8, this volume). Since the El Zotz Chaquiste Impressed basins sampled by INAA were produced using the same clay sources as the ash-tempered polychromes and utilitarian redwares excavated from Late Classic contexts at the site, they were likely local manufactures rather than imports (Ronald Bishop, personal communication, 2012). The ceramic and lithic data, then, together suggest a cultural and economic orientation toward the west for both commoners and elites at El Zotz during at least the early and middle parts of the Caal period.

The most convincing clue to friendly relations with Calakmul and its other allies, however, is a polychrome vase, the so-called Vase of the Initial Series (Carter 2015). Now in Guatemala's Museo Nacional de Arqueología y Etnología, this object was excavated in 1931 from a tomb in Pyramid A-1 at Uaxactun and assigned to the Tepeu 1 ceramic phase, corresponding to Mo' at El Zotz (Smith and Morley 1932). The painted scene on the vase depicts a seated ruler, flanked by attendants, receiving tribute from two subordinate lords and an anthropomorphic jaguar. Glyphic captions label the principal actors, and the dedicatory text around the vessel's rim names its original owner: *Bolon Chan K'in*, a name or title also attributed to a Pa'ka'n king in the inscription on an unprovenanced vessel. No Emblem Glyph is present in the Vase of the Initial Series's dedication, but it does feature the typically El Zotz-style substitution of **PA'KA'N-na** for **U**.

A long text in the scene on the vase recounts the celebration of the 7.5.0.0.0 *k'atun* ending (January 2, 255 BC). The name of the agent, apparently the seated king, reads *K'uhul Ajaw Kan*, "Holy Lord Snake." Rather than an Emblem Glyph, this king takes the title *elk'in kaloomte'* ("eastern overlord"), an exceedingly rare title otherwise used once by a Calakmul lady who married into the Yaxchilan dynasty and once by a lord of Lamanai. The captions by the subordinate lords give their names and titles: the one in front, *K'uk' Chan* ("Quetzal Snake"; see Houston 1984), is the *sajal* or local governor of an unspecified territory. Behind him is *Yax Ajaw* ("First Lord"), called *Aj Chiik Nahb*, "he of *Chiik Nahb*." *Chiik Nahb* ("Coati Pool") refers to the city of Calakmul or a precinct thereof (Stuart and Houston 1994). The Snake dynasty appears to have been based at Dzibanche during the Early Classic period, moving its court to Calakmul—previously the capital of another dynasty—during the mid-seventh-century reign of *Yuknoom Ch'e'n* (Martin 2005; Stuart 2012c). The scene on the Vase of the Initial Series could thus present a kind of pseudo-historical charter for the Snake rulers' suzerainty over other Maya lords and a precedent for their relocation to Calakmul.

The very existence of the vase—produced at El Zotz, given to a Uaxactun lord, concerned with Calakmul and the Snake kingdom's hegemony—is hard to explain unless El Zotz and Uaxactun were both part of Calakmul's sphere of influence during the early seventh century. The alliance may date to as early as AD 562, when the Snake king "Sky Witness" decisively defeated Tikal, beginning that site's 130-year monumental hiatus. In the years leading up to the war, some of Tikal's former allies had come under the Snake kingdom's influence (Martin and Grube 2008:104). The royal marriage mentioned on El Zotz Lintel 1 could thus mark the Pa'ka'n lords' entry into that alliance.

Later, in AD 695, a resurgent Tikal inflicted a military defeat on Calakmul, and the Tikal king Jasaw Chan K'awiil I set about restoring his kingdom's regional influence. Texts at Tikal record that Jasaw Chan K'awiil's successor, Yik'in Chan K'awiil, continued his father's conquests, attacking a site in the eastern part of the territory of El Perú-Waka' in AD 743. While there are no clear references to either a war or an alliance between Tikal and El Zotz in the mid-eighth century, effective control of the Buenavista Valley would seem to have been a prerequisite for the El Perú-Waka' campaign. How and when Tikal came to dominate the El Zotz region, however, remains an open question.

There is only one secure reference to El Zotz in the inscriptions of any other site during the Late Classic period. Intriguingly in light of the Vase of the Initial Series, this reference, first noted by Stephen Houston (2008a:3; 2008b:7), appears on Uaxactun Stela 2. Erected in AD 751 to celebrate the 9.16.0.0.0 *k'atun* ending, the monument records a Uaxactun king's visit to

"the Pa'ka'n place" (pa'ka'n nal). The relevant verb is t'abayi, "he goes up."
T'abayi most often refers to the lifting or offering of ceramic vessels, but, as
Houston notes, the verb's second-most common use is to describe flight or
exile in the context of war. Yet there is no indication of military action in
the Stela 2 text, and the reference is probably to the Uaxactun king's ascent
of one of the many hills, temples, or architectural compounds in the El
Zotz territory.

A reference to a place named with the same undeciphered **EARSPOOL**
logogram used by kings of El Zotz appears on Lintel 2 from Temple IV at
Tikal. Two carved wooden lintels from that structure commemorate the military victories of Yik'in Chan K'awiil: Lintel 3 deals with his attack on the
El Perú-Waka' kingdom in 743, while Lintel 2 details an attack on Naranjo's
territory in February of 744. According to its text, Yik'in Chan K'awiil first
"went down from" (ehmey) an unidentified place called Sak Mook? [. . .]
al (**SAK-MOOK?-?-la**) and "arrived" (huli) on the same day at another
unidentified site named Tuubal (**tu-ba-la**). The following day, a place called
EARSPOOL and Wak Kabnal (**6-KAB-NAL-la**) "got brought down" (jubuyi)
at the hands of Yik'in Chan K'awiil's army, "at the cave of" or "in the territory
of" (tu ch'e'n) Naranjo's patron god. Lintel 2 thus sketches out the geography of
the region between Tikal and Naranjo. Sak Mook? [. . .]al is probably a place
at or near Tikal itself, since another monument (Tikal Stela 5) calls the same
place "the cave of" or "the territory of" Tikal's mythic founder. Tuubal would
have been farther east. It can have been no more than a day's rapid march from
Naranjo or Tikal, probably on the frontier between the two larger kingdoms:
Tikal may have controlled the site in this instance, but other inscriptions indicate marriages between Naranjo's kings and ladies from Tuubal.

The paired **EARSPOOL** and Wak Kabnal place names remain to be interpreted. In this context, the former toponym cannot designate El Zotz or a
site close to it. It took Yik'in Chan K'awiil about two days to reach his target,
and his stop at Tuubal confirms that he traveled eastward, whereas El Zotz
would have been about a day's march from Tikal in the opposite direction.
Wak Kabnal names a supernatural place (Tokovinine 2008:179), but, like other
such toponyms, could also apply to a location on the physical landscape. Here,
the reference must be to a real place and not a mythological place or a person, because Wak Kabnal is paired with **EARSPOOL** in a typical "star war"
(jub?) expression (cf. Tokovinine 2008:178). Wak Kabnal, like Wak Minal at La
Corona, could thus have been a shrine or sacred precinct belonging to a patron
deity and named for a mythological site. This explanation is especially plausible in light of Lintel 2's emphasis on the capture and display of enemy gods.

DISCUSSION AND CONCLUSIONS

Data from El Zotz and Bejucal suggest that monumental construction at those sites during the Late Classic period happened mainly, though perhaps not exclusively, in intense, discrete bursts of activity more than through incremental, long-term accretion. Two such construction periods can be identified. The first, focused on the Acropolis, occurred during the Mo' ceramic phase, before AD 650. The second took place sometime after AD 725 and was far more extensive, involving major modifications to two palatial precincts (the Acropolis and Bejucal), the foundation of a new ritual-residential group (Las Palmitas), and the construction of a massive new pyramid (Str. L7-11). Not all elite constructions fit neatly into these two periods—major constructions at the Acropolis and Las Palmitas, for instance, were followed by less ambitious renovations and additions—but the phases appear to be real. On present evidence, only the latter spike in construction corresponds to a clear increase in El Zotz's rural population; during the earlier phase, some previously cultivated areas near the site core may have been abandoned long enough for the forest to partially recover.

Seen in a historical, regional context, the architectural, ceramic, and epigraphic data coincide suggestively with the changing geopolitical situation in the central Maya Lowlands over the course of the Late Classic period. The episodic nature of monumental and commoner household construction in the Pa'ka'n kingdom reflects its perilous position, caught between its massive neighbor Tikal to the east and sites to the north and west allied with the Snake dynasty. When El Zotz was allied with an ascendant Calakmul, from the late AD 500s into the 700s, its rulers had access to the political and economic resources they needed to support ambitious building projects and a thriving ceramic and calligraphic school. On the other hand, events in the late sixth or early seventh century may have motivated some of the dynasty's subjects to relocate, leaving fallow fields behind them.

By contrast, the turn of the eighth century, about the time of Jasaw Chan K'awiil I's revenge on Calakmul, seems to have been a leaner time for the Pa'ka'n lords. Based on the palynological record, commoner population around El Zotz began to grow again, yet construction in royal precincts slowed down considerably. Elites at El Zotz enjoyed another period of good fortune in the mid- to late eighth century AD, reflected in renewed royal construction projects. During this period, the Buenavista Valley's population was growing, fueled in part by personal and/or economic contacts with El Perú-Waka'. Yet by the end of the Late Classic period, either a majority of commoners living at El Zotz and producing ceramic vessels there had cultural ties to the

Uaxactun/Tikal area, or El Zotz obtained most of its serving basins through a Tikal-centered economic network, or (more likely) some combination of both situations was the case.

The major question as regards relations between the Pa'ka'n and Mut kings in the eighth century is when and how El Zotz fell under Tikal's sway. In the absence of historical texts, the archaeological evidence is ambiguous. So far, the ceramic data suggest that El Zotz's rulers built little between about AD 700 and the inception of the Ik'-style polychrome tradition around 725, followed by significant construction activity beginning sometime in the last three quarters of the eighth century. But did the Pa'ka'n court flourish in opposition to Tikal between ca. 725–743, when a drive to the west by Tikal's armies put an end to their independence and building projects? Do the ambitious constructions of the eighth century instead represent wealth newly available to the Pa'ka'n kings, the fruits of peace with Tikal? Or did a ruler of Tikal conquer El Zotz sometime before AD 743, then devote substantial resources to improving his new possession? The absence of surviving Late Classic monumental inscriptions from the El Zotz region might lend support to this last possibility, although it does not mean such monuments never existed: Stela 2 is a good candidate for a Late Classic monument, although whatever inscriptions it may have borne are completely destroyed. Unfortunately, radiocarbon, stratigraphic, and ceramic data are not precise enough to offer any firm clues.

The correspondence presented here among architectural sequence, population, and the epigraphic records at El Zotz and other sites has implications for studies of Classic Maya politics and economics, especially with respect to smaller sites whose rulers were pawns in the geopolitical games of larger polities. The Late Classic rulers of El Zotz claimed sovereignty with the title of *k'uhul pa'ka'n ajaw*, at least during the Mo' ceramic phase, and they glorified themselves and their ancestors with massive building projects during the subsequent Caal phase. Yet it is doubtful whether they ever exercised true autonomy during the Late Classic period. Instead, their moments of greatest material prosperity may have come when one of the central Lowlands' two hegemonic states, Tikal and Calakmul, needed to use El Zotz to attack or contain the other.

5

Collapse, Continuity, Change

El Zotz in the Terminal Classic Period

Sarah Newman, Jose Luis Garrido, and Nicholas P. Carter

The Terminal Classic period in the southern Lowlands may be the most widely known yet poorly understood epoch in ancient Maya archaeology. A long history of both scholarly and popular fascination with the "Classic Maya Collapse" yields a laundry list of proposed causes ranging from deforestation and drought to fatalistic calendrical systems and endemic warfare, yet the potential explanations remain much the same as those initially put forth by Thomas Gann and J. Eric S. Thompson in 1931 (see Webster 2002:217–218). The cessation of certain characteristics of Classic-period courtly life, such as the institution of divine kingship and its associated large-scale construction projects, mass-produced fine polychrome pottery, erected and inscribed monuments, and elaborate tombs and burials (Navarro-Farr 2009:44; Sharer and Golden 2004:41), which once served as identifying markers of the Terminal Classic, have been shown to inaccurately reflect the divergent trajectories of many Maya polities from the eighth and ninth centuries onward. Terminal Classic occupation of the northern Maya Lowlands, particularly the Puuc region, was marked by unparalleled population growth and architectural elaboration (Carmean and Sabloff 1996:317), while many Maya centers in the southern Lowlands that had declined by the end of the Late Classic period (Demarest et al. 1997:247–248) experienced a time of florescence during the Terminal Classic period (Źrałka and Koszkul 2010:23) or witnessed sustained

DOI: 10.5876/9781607327646.c005

occupation into the Postclassic or even colonial periods (Rice et al. 1998:208). In order to draw attention to these complexities characterizing the Maya area during the Terminal Classic period, archaeologists currently emphasize site-specific investigations aimed at identifying variability in regional patterns and local transitions (e.g., Demarest et al. 2004), rather than searching for uniform explanations and ultimate causes. Such case-by-case studies highlight the diverse means by which individual cities or communities responded to sweeping natural and social changes, but can also run the risk of viewing the Maya Collapse as an unrelated mosaic of individual failures, which would be just as misleading as an overly broad description of this time. Examining this tumultuous period requires an investigation into the internal and external pressures faced by the Terminal Classic Maya, as well as an understanding of the cohesive or destabilizing effects of choices and actions at individual, local, and regional scales (Houston and Inomata 2009:295).

Like many other polities in the southern Lowlands, Terminal Classic El Zotz (AD 850–1000) witnessed a sudden and distinctive rupture in sociopolitical organization with the dissolution of divine kingship and its associated royal court. However, this period at El Zotz also served as the eventual nadir of several centuries of gradual decline after the ancient kingdom's Early Classic heyday. Although small-scale artisanal traditions, differences in social status, and trade networks of portable items were maintained into the Early Postclassic period, the intermittent investments in monumental art and architecture that characterized the Late Classic period (see Carter et al., chapter 4, this volume) collapsed entirely. Completed architectural episodes at the site during the Terminal Classic are limited to small platforms and minor residential modifications, while attempts at monumental construction activities were abandoned in an unfinished, interrupted state. The Terminal Classic at El Zotz represents the last gasp of dying traditions—an attempt to hold on to ways of life that eventually broke down and were later reconfigured as the self-sufficient household groups characterizing the Postclassic period at the site (see Kingsley and Gámez, chapter 6, this volume).

THE "TERMINAL CLASSIC": AN INDETERMINATE TERM

In addition to the diversity of social, political, economic, and environmental transformations (whether failures or successes) that characterized the Maya world during the Terminal Classic, one of the major challenges to a better understanding of this epoch is that it remains poorly defined and variably dated. This is perhaps even increasingly the case, as scholars moving away from monolithic causal factors tend to emphasize hyperlocal changes in social, political, and material evidence to identify and describe the Terminal Classic period on a case-by-case basis.

Although it is clear that the drastic variations in Maya society among sites and regions prohibit an overarching definition, the label "Terminal Classic" can refer to a general developmental or devolutionary stage between the Classic and Postclassic periods, a locally significant chronological period, or a regional ceramic horizon. These temporal and culture-historical aspects of the Terminal Classic often overlap (Forsyth 2005:8), despite the fact that each component is further plagued by inexact definitions and characteristics. The date ranges considered as Terminal Classic, derived from dated inscriptions and/or radiocarbon results, can vary widely between AD 750 and 1050 (Aimers 2007:331). Meanwhile, Terminal Classic ceramic phases are often indistinct and site-specific, showing considerable overlap with both Late Classic and Postclassic wares (especially in monochrome groups) and relying heavily on the presence of specific markers of imported or imitated types, such as molded-carved and fine orange pottery (Chase and Chase 2005:73–74; Forsyth 2005:10; Willey et al. 1967:301–303). Finally, correlations among the varied meanings applied to the so-called Terminal Classic are rarely conclusive. At Uaxactun, where the Terminal Classic Tepeu 3 ceramic horizon was originally defined, Smith (1955:106–108) somewhat arbitrarily placed the beginning of Tepeu 3 at the AD 830 (10.0.0.0.0) period ending and its final year at the dedication of Stela 12 in AD 889, the last carved monument known from the site. The dates provided for Tikal's Eznab complex (Culbert 1993:4) are similarly approximate. Stela 24 at Tikal, dedicated in AD 810, was found in association with ceramics of the Late Classic Imix complex (Culbert 1993:figure 112e), meaning that Eznab must have begun some decades later. Culbert (1973:89) then roughly calculated a period of about a century for the duration of the Eznab phase, yielding a chronological range of AD 850–950. These and other examples illustrate how shifts in ceramic styles and/or production techniques, historical dates, and sociopolitical changes are easily and often blurred in discussions of the Terminal Classic period at Maya sites.

Perhaps unsurprisingly, the Terminal Classic shares its problematic character with another key transition: the Protoclassic period (Brady et al. 1998:18). In order to clarify the inconsistencies associated with applications and meanings of the term "Protoclassic," Brady and colleagues (1998:34–35) argued for limiting its use to the description of a ceramic stage distinguishable from either the Preclassic or Classic periods and explicitly defined on the presence or absence of objective, technological criteria. A definition of the Terminal

Classic, however, eludes a clearly delineated set of ceramic attributes. Pottery from this time period is characterized by regionally variable degrees of homogeneity and heterogeneity with respect to not only production technique, form, and surface decoration (Forsyth 2005:10) but also the degree to which the use of certain kinds of vessels varied according to status and location (Chase and Chase 2008:27). The most consistent marker of the Terminal Classic is more basic: it is a time of transitions and transformations (Demarest et al. 2004). It is the period in which we see things change, sometimes rapidly, often drastically. During the Terminal Classic, social organization, material culture, architectural style, and other features of Maya centers can be identified by their distinction from what came before and from what follows. Such changes may signal a period of prosperity, decline, or collapse, but each responds to or impacts broader movements felt throughout the Maya area as a whole. Emphasizing changes at the local level highlights the diverse actions, inactions, and interactions with which the Maya responded to the challenges of the Terminal Classic period.

This chapter reviews the distinctive changes in archaeological patterns that we use to delineate and describe the Terminal Classic period at El Zotz. Specifically, we highlight evidence for an abrupt cessation in monumental construction activities, changes in residential architectural styles and resources, and an emphasis on imported and reworked items to argue for a dissolution of the royal court in the mid-ninth century and an associated decline in the site's ability to procure raw materials, mobilize labor, and create finished products. Contemporaneous modifications made to existing residential structures and high-quality domestic artifacts point toward a continued presence of either local or immigrant elites at the site until approximately the eleventh century, at which point Postclassic El Zotz society shows a complete reorganization of social, ritual, and economic practices (see Kingsley and Gámez, chapter 6, this volume). Finally, we examine the timing of these events with respect to the political histories and material characteristics of other polities in the southern Lowlands and beyond, in order to place El Zotz within the complex processes of changes, interactions, and repercussions that alleviated or contributed to the collapse of defining institutions of Classic Maya society.

THE FALL OF PA'KA'N

Although archaeological evidence at El Zotz points to an abrupt, even interrupted, end to the Pa'ka'n dynasty, we see this sudden downfall as the culmination of a long, gradual decline following the site's heyday during the

Early Classic (see Román et al., chapter 3, this volume). In contrast to early dynasts, Late Classic rulers at El Zotz appear more limited in their capacity to commission monumental art and architecture, in their interactions with other prominent Maya centers, and in the degree of elaboration and continued veneration given to burials and funerary monuments (see Carter et al., chapter 4, this volume). With the kingdom's already sporadic ability to mobilize labor and control resources, the repercussions of dissolving trade networks, collapsing neighboring kingdoms, and migrating populations proved too much for the final ruler of Pa'ka'n. Ultimately, the royal court at El Zotz, as a politically independent institution capable of governing and mobilizing the populations of the Buenavista Valley, disappeared during the late ninth century AD. This end to effective royal authority within the polity constituted a decisive and irreversible break with earlier Classic-period practices.

Evidence for dynastic disruption largely centers on the El Zotz Acropolis (figure 4.1), the palatial complex located at the northern edge of the site core, and its surrounding structures. Three main lines of evidence from these areas support placing the Terminal Classic period at El Zotz between AD 850 and 1000: a reused ninth-century stela, well-preserved ceramics recovered from a massive offering, and overlapping radiocarbon dates associated with this major depositional event.

The reused stela fragment, El Zotz Stela 4, was found intentionally broken and incorporated into the foundation of an elite residence in an area known as the Northwest Courtyard, immediately to the west of the El Zotz Acropolis. The Northwest Courtyard is bordered by structures of the palatial compound on its eastern side, an elevated platform with elite Classic-period structures to the south, and a small limestone quarry to the north. Within the leveled patio of the Northwest Courtyard itself, Strs. L7-19, L7-20, and L7-17 are situated to the west, north, and south, respectively, with the L-shaped Str. L7-18 at its center (figure 5.1). This raised area took shape during the late eighth or early ninth century, toward the end of the Caal ceramic phase (AD 700–850), in one of the episodic construction booms characterizing the architectural history of El Zotz's site center. This was likely the same site-wide building effort responsible for the construction of Strs. L7-8 and L7-9 (figure 4.1), effectively sealing off the eastern edge of the Acropolis; the formation of the site's tallest pyramid, Str. L7-11, in a single construction phase and the creation of Las Palmitas (see Carter et al., chapter 4, this volume).

Although the initial forms of the residential structures of the Northwest Courtyard appeared during the Late Classic period, they underwent several renovations during the Terminal Classic. These buildings were modified not

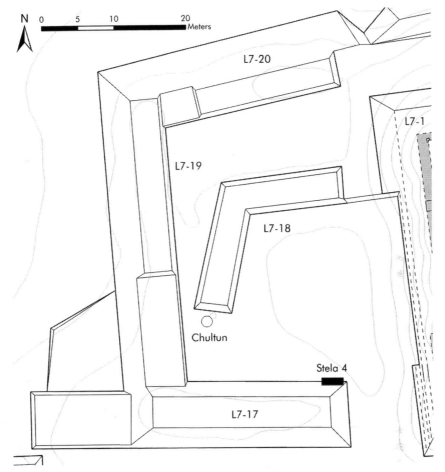

N 0   5   10   20
                        Meters

L7-20

L7-1

L7-19

L7-18

Chultun

Stela 4

L7-17

FIGURE 5.1. *Map of the Northwest Courtyard (map by T. Garrison).*

only in terms of their shape and size, but also with respect to the building materials used for their construction. The first of these Terminal Classic changes to Str. L7-17 buried the existing Late Classic architecture completely and extended its footprint in all directions. Sherds recovered from the construction fill of this phase include both cream-background polychromes with complex designs, characteristic of the Late Classic Caal phase at El Zotz, and high-fired monochromes with thick, durable slips typical of the early Terminal Classic Cucul phase (see Czapiewska-Halliday et al., chapter 8, this volume). These ceramic finds place the first major renovation of Str. L7-17 close to the time of transition between the Caal and Cucul phases, probably around AD 850–900.

The cut piece of El Zotz Stela 4 was reused as the northeast cornerstone in the foundation of Str. L7-17's newly extended platform. The fragment was interred on its side, rotated clockwise 90° from the upright position in which it was meant to be displayed. The text was placed facing inward and somewhat protected from the stone forming the structure's eastern foundations by a loose, sandy fill (figure 5.2). The remaining legible hieroglyphs provide a dedication date reconstructed by Stephen Houston as the *bak'tun* ending 10.0.0.0.0 7 Ajaw 18 Sip (March 12, AD 830) and reveal a hitherto unknown king, *[. . .] Chan Yopaat*, described as a *k'uhul pa'ka'n ajaw*, or "holy Pa'ka'n lord." The Stela 4 fragment thus attests to the existence of divine kingship at El Zotz in AD 830 and marks the site as one of the few Maya kingdoms to record this important *bak'tun* ending, along with Uaxactun, Xultun, and a polity based at Zacpeten (Houston and Inomata 2009:300).

Although few inscribed monuments are known from El Zotz, Stela 4 is typical of the size and style characterizing those of the later years of the Pa'ka'n dynasty. In reviewing the text visible on the Stela 4 fragment, Houston noted both the monument's diminutive size and its stylistic similarities to Stela 2 from El Zotz, found in the site's main plaza. No text is preserved on Stela 2, but Houston identifies it as a Late Classic monument based on its remaining iconographic elements. Like Stela 4, however, the monument was also later reshaped and repurposed, in this case rounded into an altar. The recarving of Stela 2 and its use as an altar may have been related to the celebration of the tenth *bak'tun* ending recorded on Stela 4. The glyph blocks of Stela 4 are carved in relief and heavily eroded, particularly along their upper edges, most likely as a result of the monument's having been displayed for some time in its intended upright position before being cut up and incorporated into Str. L7-17. Although we can only estimate the time frame encompassing the erection and display of Stela 4, the dissolution of the Pa'ka'n dynasty, and the mutilation and reuse of the monument in the Northwest Courtyard, the 10.0.0.0.0 dedication date on the stela fragment provides a *terminus post quem* that aligns roughly with the transitional ceramics recovered from the same phase of Str. L7-17 (AD 850–900).

Contemporaneous, large-scale deposits from within the bounds of the Acropolis further underscore the second half of the ninth century as a period of major transformations at El Zotz. Focused at points of entry into the palace complex, these deposits consist of a variety of broken, burned, and scattered artifacts, distributed across final-phase floors and packed in a layer of dense

(a)

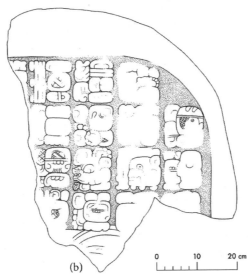

0   10   20 cm

(b)

FIGURE 5.2. *El Zotz Stela 4: (a) Stela 4 in situ (next to the photo scale) as the northeast cornerstone of Str. L7-17 (photo by A. Rubinstein); (b) text of Stela 4 (drawing by S. Houston).*

mud. The deposits were buried beneath thick levels of construction fill—2 m deep in some places—incorporating masonry blocks taken from the partially dismantled superstructures of the Acropolis. Seven targeted test pits (each between 1 and 1.5 m on a side) in Strs. L7-1, L7-8, L7-24, and a restricted patio at the southwest corner of the Acropolis (figure 4.1) recovered 5,842 ceramic sherds (ranging from jars, bowls, and plates to drums and incense burners, as well as several examples of reused or partially reworked sherds); 353 osteological fragments (including 40 worked-bone artifacts and dozens of human remains); 750 chert nodules, flakes, and points; 89 obsidian blade fragments; 41 figurine fragments (including at least one whistle); 78 fragments of marine shell (including four complete rings and pendants); and nine fragments of domestic grinding stones (both manos and metates); burnt residues of tropical hardwoods and flowering plants of the *Bignonia* genus; a small piece of burnt maize cob with two preserved rows of cupules (David Lentz, personal communication, 2010); and modeled stucco fragments. Refit sherds recovered from separate excavation units and differential patterns of burning and weathering observed on these and other artifact and architectural fragments indicate that the objects were used, broken, and scattered before burning took place. Moreover, the variable weathering, rodent gnawing, and dry-burning patterns on bones in these deposits indicate that they represent the redeposition of previously discarded items (Newman 2015b).

These deposits represent a specific type of action within the broad and variable category of ritual burning and censing among the ancient Maya, perhaps associated with the tradition of scattering rites. Scattering rites are widely cited on Classic-period monuments as the paramount ceremony associated with the Maya calendar's period endings (Stuart 1984:9). Understood as a king's active sanctification of time and its passing, and centered on his unique role in the perpetuation and renewal of time, scattering rituals involved casting incense into braziers or onto sacred stone altars (originally interpreted as the scattering of pellets or streams of blood; Love 1987:11). Although scattering rites are often recorded literally as *chok-ch'aaj,* "casting incense" (Stuart 2005:272), an example from Hieroglyphic Stairway 1 at El Reinado is spelled unconventionally as *u chok-ow k'ahk',* "he casts (into?) the fire" (Stuart 2012a:5). The breakage and burning patterns on objects recovered from the deposits in the El Zotz Acropolis are consistent with their having been broken and scattered prior to being burned in place. Although speculative, the relative and absolute dates associated with these deposits and the celebration of the tenth *bak'tun* ending commemorated on Stela 4 lend weight to the idea that this massive depositional event might represent a major scattering rite, with the scale of the ritual reflecting the importance of the Period Ending being celebrated (the ending of a *bak'tun* cycle, an event that occurred only twice in Classic Maya history).

Although these deposits bear certain similarities to pre-abandonment termination rituals (e.g., Garber 1983:802; Yaeger 2010:156–157), the patterns of architectural dismantling and depth of new construction fill at the Acropolis show them to be part of an interrupted process of remodeling. Similar unfinished monumental construction attempts have been documented prior to abandonment at sites such as La Milpa (Zaro and Houk 2012:152), Aguateca (Inomata et al. 2004:798), and Piedras Negras (Fitzsimmons 1999). At El Zotz, the attempted Terminal Classic modifications to the Acropolis follow the trends of earlier Late Classic constructions, continually restricting access to the inner courtyards of the palace and sealing off former points of ingress and egress (see Carter et al., chapter 4, this volume). At the southwestern corner of the Acropolis, a series of low, crudely made retaining walls (roughly 0.80 m high) were erected, made of cut stones placed vertically on their longer sides with little mortar between them to provide support. These walls encircled a restricted patio and sealed off an access stairway to the Northwest Courtyard and a narrow point of entry between Strs. L7-1 and L7-6 (figure 4.1). Over 2 m of construction fill and dismantled architectural elements then buried that space, obscuring the distinction between Strs. L7-1 and L7-6. On the eastern border of the Acropolis, a vaulted passageway running beneath Strs. L7-8 and L7-9 (figures 11.6 and 11.7) was completely buried (although the interior of the tunnel was not filled in). Approximately 2.25 m of construction fill covered the tunnel and the basal platforms of Strs. L7-4 and L7-8, with the thick, ashy matrix and burnt and broken objects of the ritual deposit found just outside the passageway's western entrance.

The abundant ceramics from these deposits in the Acropolis play a major role in defining the Terminal Classic Cucul phase at El Zotz. Due to their rapid deposition and burial, these ceramics are particularly well preserved and often nearly complete, providing excellent examples of unslipped wares, monochrome vessels, and some molded and polychrome vases. They highlight significant changes from the Late Classic Caal phase with regard to production technology, form, and aesthetics. The majority of the vessels represented in the deposit are of the Tinaja group, particularly the Tinaja Red and Cameron Incised types. Unslipped vessels of the Cambio and Encanto groups represent a large portion of the assemblage as well. The most abundant forms of these two main groups are large *ollas* and jars with curved, out-flaring necks, followed by deep bowls, or *tecomates*, with markedly restricted orifices. In smaller quantities, monochrome vessels of the Maquina (brown slip), Infierno (black slip), and Azote (orange slip) groups are present, in the forms of smaller bowls with thin, incurved walls or wide, often footed plates, as well as some cylindrical vases. Polychrome vases and bowls of both the Zacatal (cream slip) and Palmar-Danta (orange slip) groups are rare, present only as small, eroded sherds. There are also examples of a distinctive but unidentified polychrome type, represented in the Acropolis deposits by fragments of barrel vases with modeled collars (a form identical to a whole vessel recovered from a Terminal Classic burial at Las Palmitas, described below). Other less-common forms include incense burners with straight outflaring walls and hollow handles of the Miseria Appliquéd type of the unslipped Cambio group. Fragments of at least one ceramic drum, of the Azote Orange type, have been identified as well. Fine-paste wares are extremely rare in these deposits, with only a handful of small sherds documented (see figure 5.3). The Terminal Classic date assigned to these deposits and their associated ceramics was verified through two radiocarbon samples, from separate excavation units, which returned date ranges of AD 774–978 and AD 776–990 (table 1.1).

Combining radiocarbon, ceramic, and textual dates with archaeological patterns, we see the last kings of Pa'ka'n assembling resources and mobilizing labor forces well into the ninth century, celebrating the tenth *bak'tun* ending with ritual activities, and commemorating that major calendrical event on Stela 4. The subsequent dissolution of effective dynastic power appears to have been relatively rapid. By the beginning of the tenth century, the construction efforts in the Acropolis lay abandoned and Stela 4 had been mutilated and repurposed as raw material by the remaining elites at the site. The failure of the royal court at El Zotz, however, only appears as a significant rupture from within the palace. Although the effects of dynastic downfall were certainly felt, residual elites at El Zotz managed to maintain differences in social status and access to prestige items and imports for at least another century.

HOLDING OUT OR MOVING IN? ELITE CONTINUITIES AT EL ZOTZ

In contrast to the ambitious, punctuated projects undertaken in the Acropolis during the Late and Terminal Classic periods, modifications to residential architecture during the Terminal Classic period were more gradual and consistent. Construction activities concentrated on elite residences of the Northwest Courtyard and the Las Palmitas Group were built upon earlier foundations and focused on maintaining, subdividing, or amplifying

FIGURE 5.3. *Ceramics from the Terminal Classic Acropolis deposit (photo by S. Newman).*

existing spaces. These renovations, however, demonstrate a clear decline from earlier architectural phases in terms of the raw materials used, the sophistication of construction methods, and the complexity of building design (see Mesick, chapter 11, this volume), paralleling the same failure of the royal court to garner the resources and manpower necessary to finish the Acropolis constructions. Yet where organized systems of labor broke down, artifacts recovered from these residences show that the Terminal Classic elites at El Zotz remained involved in networks of contact and exchange, enabling the import of prestigious items. This unidirectional pattern of consumption without production persisted for nearly a century after the dissolution of the Pa'ka'n dynasty before it, too, proved unsustainable and the remaining populations at El Zotz reorganized into independent, self-sufficient household groups (see Kingsley and Gámez, chapter 6, this volume).

Returning to the Northwest Courtyard, three of the four structures composing the group (Strs. L7-17, L7-18, and L7-20) have been investigated through combined horizontal and vertical excavations. As mentioned above, the Northwest Courtyard took its initial form during the late facet of the Late

Classic period, most likely as part of an expansion of the Acropolis as a whole (see Carter et al., chapter 4, this volume). Whereas Strs. L7-17 and L7-20 show significant modifications to their original Late Classic architecture, the initial form of Str. L7-18 appears to have been used continuously throughout the Terminal Classic and Early Postclassic periods without major remodeling.

The Late Classic version of Str. L7-17 was not intensively investigated beyond a single trench, but it is clear that the first Terminal Classic reiteration of the building enlarged the area of the residence by several meters in every direction, though the quality of construction is noticeably poor (figure 5.4). Where the Late Classic platform and wall constructions had been formed from carefully aligned, cut limestone blocks covered by substantial and well-preserved stucco floors, the Terminal Classic phase is constructed of stones of variable sizes and shapes and its floors are thin and required multiple episodes of resurfacing. The Terminal Classic residence also shifted the central axis and orientation of Structure L7-17, breaking with earlier patterns of alignment within the El Zotz site core (Garrison 2012) to orient the structure toward true north (0.44°). This shift, though slight, may be further evidence for the loss of skilled architects and laborers at the site.

Structure L7-17 underwent a series of subsequent modifications through-out the Terminal Classic period. Clear wall foundations and postholes remain as evidence of the final architectural phase, delineating a perishable range structure atop a platform with three distinct terraces. The platform measures approximately 25 m (east–west) long by 8.5 m (north–south) wide, and 1.25 m high at the highest terrace. The superstructure consisted of two rooms of equal size along the northern side of the platform, with the main access from this same side. Cut stones were found positioned vertically along the midline axis of the two rooms. These thin stones were partially held in position by the final stucco floor laid down within the superstructure, suggesting that the two large rooms were subdivided into smaller interior spaces during the structure's final remodeling. The western room had at least one bench tucked along the corner of the front wall, offset from the structure's entryways in order to be hidden from public view.

The building's thin stucco floors appear to have deteriorated quickly and were resurfaced multiple times. Prior to one such repair, the body of an elderly adult male was interred on the structure's axis (El Zotz Burial 12; figure 12.5). The skeleton showed signs of tabular oblique cranial modification, as well as some periostitis and significant tooth loss well before death, indicative of the advanced age of the individual (see Scherer, chapter 12, this volume for details). To inter the body, the existing plaster floor of the first Terminal Classic

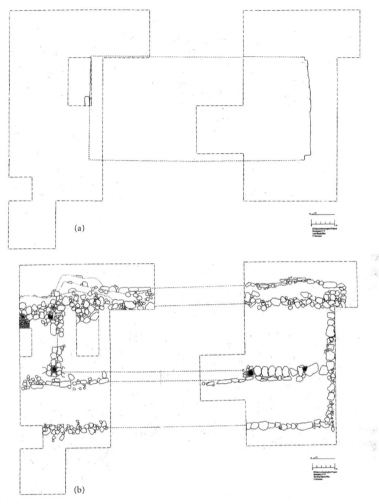

(a)

(b)

Figure 5.4. *(a) Late and (b) Terminal Classic plans of Str. L7-17 (drawings by S. Newman).*

iteration of Str. L7-17 was cut and several of the stones forming the wall foundation below were removed to form a cist 0.45 m long (north–south) by 0.86 m wide (east–west). The body was placed in this cavity in a flexed position on its back, with the head bent forward onto the chest and—unusually for El Zotz—aligned to the west, 0.28 m below the final-phase floor. After the placement of the burial, the floor of the structure was plastered over, combining the interior spaces that had formerly been separated by the wall into which Burial 12 was interred. New internal separations were created along the central east–west axis of the structure's two rooms. Thin stones found standing upright in the final plaster floor probably served as bases to support the interior pole and thatch walls and to protect them from water damage.

Unlike Str. L7-17, the final phase of Str. L7-20 was not exposed horizontally, providing fewer details of its specific architectural forms. However, a trench excavated to bedrock along the central axis of the structure revealed a history of construction similar to that of Str. L7-17, with the bulk of the structure created during the Caal phase of the Late Classic period, then slightly modified throughout the Terminal Classic period. According to the limited data available, the final structure appears to have been more modest than L7-17, most likely a wholly perishable superstructure atop a set of three low platforms. The Late Classic basal platform raised Str. L7-20 roughly 0.40 m above the level of the Northwest Courtyard's patio floor. The two later upper platforms were each another 0.20 m high and inset 0.40 m from the southern edge of the preceding platform, creating a stepped access to the perishable superstructure from the southern side of the building. On the northern side of the structure, however, the three platforms ended abruptly at the same point, forming a drop-off approximately 0.80 m high toward the quarry just beyond. Like Str. L7-17, the basal platform of Str. L7-20 is noticeably better made than the upper, later platforms, which consist of uncut stones covered in multiple applications of thin, deteriorated plaster.

Str. L7-18, the L-shaped building at the center of the Northwest Courtyard, diverges from the rest of the group in both its unique shape and the fact that it shows evidence of only a single episode of construction. As with the rest of the Northwest Courtyard, the structure was first built during the massive Caal-phase investment in the entire area around the Acropolis. Str. L7-18 sits roughly 0.30 m above the leveled patio and is made of large, cut stones held together by thick mortar and covered by a .012-m-thick layer of stucco, most likely representing multiple episodes of resurfacing.

Although only Str. L7-17 was excavated in such a way as to reveal its specific domestic features, such as benches and distinct rooms, the artifacts recovered from all structures investigated in the Northwest Courtyard demonstrate a continuous elite occupation of the group from the Late Classic into the Early Postclassic period. Ceramic artifacts include examples ranging from locally produced Caal-phase polychromes and imported ceramics of the Ik' Emblem Glyph Style (Reents-Budet et al. 2012:68) to Cucul-phase polychromes, molded barrel vases, and fine orange and gray paste wares imported from the

Usumacinta region (Forné et al. 2010:1164), alongside utilitarian and monochrome jars, bowls, and plates (see Czapiewska-Halliday et al., chapter 8, this volume). Nearly all of the obsidian found in the Northwest Courtyard derives from the El Chayal source, the main source of obsidian in the Maya Lowlands throughout the Classic period, with several exhausted obsidian cores and third-series blades indicating local reuse and retouching. This may reflect an inability on the part of the remaining El Zotz elites to maintain far-reaching trade networks into the Postclassic period, when the main font of obsidian shifted to the source at Ixtepeque (Golitko et al. 2012:516). Similarly, chert items typically bear evidence of utilitarian uses and recycling or reworking, but also include large celts, long drills, and imported projectile points and other items of fine El Perú-Waka' flint (see Hruby, chapter 9, this volume). Faunal remains from the Northwest Courtyard reflect a continuation of the patterns and preferences in resource procurement observed for the El Zotz Acropolis during the Classic period. The faunal assemblage also includes several bone tools and adornments, once again pointing to the continued use of the accoutrements of elite life.

Moving north to the hilltop group of Las Palmitas, Terminal Classic construction activities are limited to a single structure atop a preexisting platform at the northern edge of the site's patio group, Str. M3-8 (figure 4.11). Test pits and horizontal excavations focused on this building revealed its changing architectural sequence and forms during its use from the Late Classic period through the late Terminal Classic or Early Postclassic period. Str. M3-8 sits between and perpendicular to a pair of long, elevated range structures (Strs. M3-6 and M3-7), creating a northern barrier to the Las Palmitas palatial complex. The structure's earliest iteration, which dates to the mid-eighth century AD (see Carter et. al, chapter 4, this volume), consisted of a low, narrow bench or parapet that ran the length of the northern side of the palace patio. During the Terminal Classic period, the parapet was covered over by the foundations of a new structure made mostly of perishable materials. All that survives are its masonry components, made of unworked or roughly cut stones, none bearing surviving traces of stucco. These consist of a two-tiered platform, 14 m long, extending east–west along the edge of the patio. The southern, front terrace of the platform is approximately 3.5 m wide and 0.5 m high, while the rear, northern terrace is 2 m wide and 0.8 m high. The building's stone back wall, 1.6 m thick, presently stands only 0.4 m above the upper terrace (1.2 m above the Late Classic patio floor). Given the lack of fallen stones nearby, it is unlikely that the wall was much higher in antiquity. Two short "wings" project outward at right angles from the back wall, enclosing the ends of the upper terrace. These were not later additions but were built together with the back wall as a unit. The masonry wall would have served as the foundation for an upper section made of organic materials, although its considerable width could imply a secondary use as an interior bench. The front of the building was most likely completely open, since no foundation stones were encountered south of the terraces. Presumably, wooden posts would have supported this structure, although no postholes were exposed in the units excavated, and the roof would have been thatched.

Prior to the Terminal Classic remodeling of Str. M3-8, the body of an adult was interred in a cist excavated into the Late Classic patio floor along the building's central axis (El Zotz Burial 7). The body was found in an extended or slightly flexed position, most likely lying on its right side, with the head to the north or slightly northeast in keeping with the general pattern witnessed at El Zotz (Stephen Houston, personal communication, 2010). Unfortunately, the skeleton was badly fragmented and poorly preserved, prohibiting the identification of sex or the observation of cranial modification or potential pathologies (see Scherer, chapter 12, this volume). Three vessels were included as burial offerings: an eroded barrel-shaped vessel of an unidentified polychrome type was placed at the decedent's knees, while a small red bowl or cup of the Tinaja group was placed inside a Maquina Brown tripod plate with rattle feet just north of the head (figure 5.5). The vase had raised, modeled bands below the rim and had once rested on three hollow feet, but these had all been sawn off (perhaps after one of them broke) prior to inclusion in the grave. All three vessels, particularly the polychrome barrel vase, are notably similar in both form and surface treatment to ceramics recovered from the Cucul-phase deposits in the El Zotz Acropolis.

Continuing the pattern observed for the residential structures of the Northwest Courtyard, Str. M3-8's form constitutes a marked departure from the Late Classic architecture of the patio group at Las Palmitas. In contrast to the enclosed, private rooms of earlier structures, Str. M3-8's open front, wide platforms, and possible interior bench suggest that the building may have served as a reception gallery for entrants arriving to the hilltop palace complex from the southern stairway. Although no radiocarbon dates have been obtained for Str. M3-8, contemporaneous deposits from Str. M3-6 (the residential structure forming the western border of the palace group) returned a radiocarbon date range of AD 947–1051 (76.5 percent probability; table 1.1).

Refuse deposits associated with Str. M3-8 and other areas of the Las Palmitas Group contained artifacts similar to those from the Northwest Courtyard: primarily locally produced domestic wares, but also imports and

FIGURE 5.5. *Reconstructed vessels from El Zotz Burial 7 (photo by N. Carter).*

high-quality or finely worked materials. A deep midden immediately north of Str. M3-8, in the corner formed by the platforms of the patio and Str. M3-9, contained abundant fragments of unslipped water jars and Chinja Impressed (Tinaja group) serving bowls, but also of more elaborate containers. These included sherds from Pabellon Molded-carved (Altar group) drinking vessels and a similar local type, Sahcaba Molded-carved, along with a Telchac composite (Chablekal group) dish. Terminal Classic molded-carved sherds (Pabellon and Sahcaba) were also recovered from a midden off the southeast corner of the plaza and from subsurface contexts around Str. M3-7, the range building forming the eastern border of the palace group. The bulk of this material shows steady occupation through the Terminal Classic Cucul phase, but two or three Paxcaman red plates with scroll feet recovered from the upper strata of the Str. M3-8 midden indicate a more limited or perhaps occasional presence at the hilltop site during the Early Postclassic period.

Grinding stones, ceramic spindle whorls, and obsidian blades are also present in these midden deposits, indicating food preparation and other domestic activities during the Terminal Classic occupation of Las Palmitas. In addition to a few worked bone objects and crafting debitage, white-tailed deer represented over 87 percent of the faunal remains recovered from the midden associated with Str. M3-8, highlighting the ability of the group's residents to obtain large, preferred game. Other desirable mammals such as brocket deer, peccary, and tapirs were also included among the faunal refuse, with no evidence of small mammals among the assemblage.

Beyond the boundaries of the royal court, elites remained at El Zotz throughout the Terminal Classic period, holding on to the trappings of noble life as best they could. Although Terminal Classic architecture demonstrates a clear decline in elites' capacity to control labor and resources, imported goods and finely worked objects show that they participated in far-reaching trade networks until the Early Postclassic period. The ability to import desired goods, especially as production at El Zotz waned, may have been what allowed elites of the Northwest Courtyard and Las Palmitas to retain their elevated status. As David Cannadine (1999, quoted in Houston and Inomata 2009:167) writes of the fall of the British aristocracy, "even in decline, nobility serve a role in local society, depending on their ability to retain wealth and dispense assistance." This stands in stark contrast to the rapid dissolution of effective dynastic rule, the interruption of monumental construction activities, and the complete abandonment of the Acropolis, suggesting that economic power and kin-based social rankings far outlasted ideology at El Zotz.

The longevity of elites at El Zotz, however, depended in large part on the circumstances surrounding the polity during the Terminal Classic period. The Pa'ka'n lords may have been major political and economic players in the Peten region during El Zotz's early history, but by the late eighth century their influence had substantially declined from those early days (Carter et al., chapter 4, this volume). The evidence of the nature of the Terminal Classic period at El Zotz detailed thus far must be considered in relation to what we know of the site's contemporaries in order to better understand how these aspects of Classic Maya civilization were maintained and how and why they eventually failed.

BEYOND THE BORDERS: TERMINAL CLASSIC EL ZOTZ IN ITS REGIONAL CONTEXT

The erection of El Zotz Stela 4 and the aborted remodeling project at the Acropolis can be seen as attempts by a local king and his court to bolster their own power and legitimacy during a period marked by serious political disruption at other sites, both far and near. Although those efforts failed, El Zotz's strategic location in the east–west corridor of the Buenavista Valley proved crucial to maintaining what was left of the city's former ways of life. Connections to other polities sustained a social hierarchy, but one that was impoverished and dependent on the fortunes of other sites in the northern

Peten and beyond. Terminal Classic changes at El Zotz, therefore, represent not only the decisions made and actions taken by the inhabitants of that site, but also the repercussions of successes and failures at other polities beyond their control.

At the turn of the ninth century AD, a weakened royal court at El Perú-Waka', to the west of El Zotz, commissioned few final inscriptions and monumental constructions. The absence of any monuments commemorating the tenth *bak'tun* ending and the deliberate destruction of older monuments indicate that the institution of divine kingship ended at El Perú-Waka' some years before dynastic dissolution at El Zotz (Freidel and Escobedo 2005). The ceramic record at El Zotz reflects this loss, with contact on a quotidian, economic level intensified with sites to the east and northeast, especially Uaxactun and Tikal, rather than with the area west of the Buenavista Valley (see Czapiewska-Halliday et al., chapter 8, this volume).

Specific ceramic evidence also confirms continued interaction among elites at El Zotz, Uaxactun, Yaxha, and Tikal. Sherds and partially complete vessels of the Sahcaba Molded-carved type produced using the same mold have been found at all four sites. The first vessels made with this mold to come to archaeologists' attention are a pair of barrel-shaped vases with pedestal bases, excavated at Uaxactun in the 1930s by the Carnegie Institution of Washington project and now in the storeroom of the Museo Nacional de Arqueología y Etnología in Guatemala City (figure 5.6c). The two vases were found under a stucco floor in front of Str. B-12 in Uaxactun's East Patio. At Tikal, another example, again a barrel vase with a pedestal base, was recovered from a midden between Strs. 5D-40 and 5E-30 in the East Plaza (Jones 1996:88). The vases bear two meeting scenes among three supernatural beings. In one scene, an individual wearing a royal "Jester God" diadem and seated on a *K'awiil* head interacts with two other seated personages, one of whom may be the Maize God. The other scene includes a deity with an avian headdress and two older figures with large eyes, perhaps the Paddler Gods. The shared text is recognizably Maya, but it differs from standard Dedicatory Sequences and contains few legible glyphs.

The El Zotz examples consist of two adjoining fragments of the Jester God scene (figure 5.6a), recovered from the domestic midden behind Str. M3-8 at Las Palmitas and another smaller fragment from a midden excavated near Str. L8-22 (figure 5.6b). Based on the curvature of the sherds, they likely came from another barrel-shaped drinking vessel. During the Terminal Classic period, molded-carved vessels of various types played a similar role to Late Classic polychrome vases. High-status, high-prestige objects produced by or

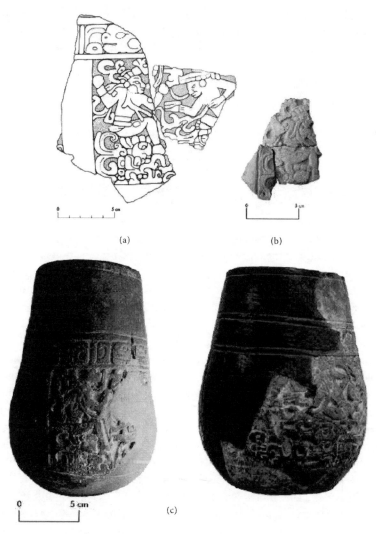

FIGURE 5.6. *Sahcaba Molded-carved vessel fragments from (a and b) El Zotz and (c) Uaxactun (drawings and photos by N. Carter).*

under the supervision of elites, such vessels were circulated among members of that class and displayed in formal settings. While it is not clear at which site the vessels were produced, the presence of these sherds is further evidence that Terminal Classic El Zotz looked eastward for its political and economic networks (Carter 2014).

As during earlier stages of Maya history, the (mis)fortunes of the great behemoth of Tikal continued to shape those of its neighbors during the Terminal Classic period. Serious disruptions to centralized structures of authority at that site are marked not only by the royal court's failure to commission a stela for the tenth *bak'tun* ending, but also by the systematic looting of several royal tombs in mortuary pyramids of the site center. The plunderers evidently knew where to look, digging down into the floors of the shrines atop the pyramids until they reached their targets. Valuable artifacts were removed, undesired objects left behind. Later, the looted tombs were sealed off with construction fill containing Terminal Classic ceramics, the superstructure floors were repaired, and the mortuary shrines continued in use until the center of Tikal was finally abandoned by around AD 1000 (Coe 1990:331–332, 391–392, 400, 416, 432, 459, 495, 500–501, 547–548, 554, 574–575, 582). It remains unclear whether the ancient looters backfilled their own "excavations" or whether the looting took place during a temporary breakdown in royal administration, after which the work of refilling and repairing the shrines was supervised by restored authorities. The fact that Jasaw Chan K'awiil II, a claimant to the Tikal throne, eventually did manage to erect a pair of monuments—Stela 11 and Altar 11—for the 10.2.0.0.0 *k'atun* ending, favors the latter possibility.

This period of instability at Tikal aligns with the rituals and remodeling efforts of the final Pa'ka'n ruler. El Zotz, like several other small royal courts on the periphery of Tikal's probable eighth-century zone of control, asserted its own power as that of Tikal waned. A branch of Tikal's Mut dynasty ruled at the neighboring sites of Ixlu and Zacpeten in the lake district south of Tikal, where they erected monuments between AD 830 and 879 with iconographic ties to late-eighth-century stelae at Tikal. Another ruler, a western *kaloomte'* named 'Olom, established a court at Jimbal, to the north. An inscription at Uaxactun records that 'Olom celebrated the tenth *bak'tun* ending together with a Uaxactun king, who also went by the name of Jasaw Chan K'awiil. Later monuments from Jimbal and Uaxactun suggest that relations between the two courts remained close for at least a generation after 'Olom, until royal monuments ceased to be erected at both sites after AD 889.

Comparatively smaller sites such as El Zotz, Ixlu, and Jimbal were not the only polities to take advantage of the vacuum of power left in the wake of Tikal's downfall, however. In the Triángulo Park area, Terminal Classic architectural booms and demographic increases at Nakum and Yaxha may indicate that those sites served as places of migration for refugee populations as surrounding centers collapsed. Stela D from Nakum, dedicated in AD 849, describes the depicted ruler using the title *elk'in* (?) *kaloomte'*, or "east *kaloomte'*," positioning the local lord as a high, powerful king of the east (Źrałka and Hermes 2012:182). This suggests that the sudden success and political and economic independence gained by Nakum after the collapse of former hegemonies such as Tikal and Naranjo may have positioned that site as an important polity in the eastern part of the southern Lowlands at the end of the Classic period.

Although the evidence is scant, the Terminal Classic presence at El Zotz could represent new groups of elites, perhaps moving in from the east to take advantage of the city's strategic position in the Buenavista Valley. El Zotz's realignment of its trade and exchange relations toward Uaxactun, Tikal, and Yaxha and its unilateral patterns of consumption (without production), the mutilation and reuse of Stela 4 in a residential structure of the Northwest Courtyard, and Burial 12's unusual orientation (with the head to the west) could point to a reoccupation of the site by external elites. Alternatively, local elites, perhaps those who had occupied lower tiers of the dynastic Pa'ka'n hierarchy, could also be responsible for these changes. In either scenario, those who remained at El Zotz represent an active and advantageous response to the changing conditions of the Terminal Classic period. While the sudden decline of nearby major centers and longstanding alliances may have proved too much for the last Pa'ka'n dynast, the emergence of former vassal sites as prominent players in the Peten provided some with an opportunity to capitalize on new political and economic networks and maintain certain social traditions, even as others dissolved.

CONCLUSION

The ups and downs of the Terminal Classic period at El Zotz, as at many other Maya centers, are difficult to describe succinctly. Not long after the successful celebration and commemoration of the tenth *bak'tun* ending and the ambitious program of architectural investment in the Acropolis, the Pa'ka'n dynasty and its associated royal court dissolved abruptly, leaving the palatial complex at El Zotz abandoned in an unfinished state. Elites, whether local or foreign, took advantage of the opportunity to reorganize exchange networks and capitalize on the growth and decline of other centers in the Peten, a strategy that proved successful in maintaining a certain status quo in the short term but tied El Zotz's fate to that of its neighbors and finally led to a more complete collapse of social and political systems. And yet, the volatility of the Terminal Classic period blurs when viewed from a wider perspective, as El Zotz's eventual downfall can also be seen as the endpoint of a long and gradual decline from the site's former apogee during the Early Classic period. The punctuated architectural history of the site and few examples of monumental art of the Late Classic period foreshadow the difficulties in mobilizing labor and obtaining resources observed for the Terminal Classic period, while shifting Late Classic political alliances point to a longer history of opportunistic realignments of economic relationships, maintained through the Terminal Classic period.

El Zotz thus underscores the necessity of understanding Terminal Classic transformations at multiple scales, from minutiae of local changes in social organization and material culture to the repercussions of shifts in larger geopolitical networks. Collapse at El Zotz was neither uniform nor extraordinary, but rather the culmination of specific actions and reactions undertaken over a period of nearly two centuries. Its history aligns with and reflects those of neighboring polities, broadening our understanding of the consequences that individual but interconnected centers still had on one another, and of the larger sociopolitical situation in the southern Lowlands. Simultaneously, however, this history also paints a portrait of the site-specific strategies, successes, and failures orchestrated by the singular responses of El Zotz's remaining inhabitants during turbulent times.

6

In the Wake of "Collapse"

The Post-Dynastic or Early Postclassic Period at El Zotz

Melanie J. Kingsley
and Laura Gámez

The transition from the great cities of the Classic period, such as Tikal, a rival to El Zotz at this time, to the last big Maya kingdoms, like that of the Itza Maya at Tayasal, was previously seen by scholars as one of degradation, demographic abandonment, and cultural collapse. This view can be appreciated in the nomenclature used to describe Maya history: *Preclassic, Classic,* and *Postclassic* are predicated upon notions of birth, florescence, and decay. They also treat the Maya as a large, homogeneous group whose great civilization is laid waste by the Postclassic period. To understand how such a civilization could fail, scholars sought explanations in dramatic variables such as invasion, social revolution, trade failure, subsistence failure, climate change, and drought (e.g., Adams 1973; Culbert 1988; Cowgill 1964; Demarest 1997; Gill et al. 2007; Sabloff 1973; Sabloff and Willey 1967; Thompson 1966; Webster 2002; Yaeger and Hodell 2008).

But much has changed. Scholars now recognize the dynamic cycles of political authority that marked the more-than-two millennia of Maya history and have begun to speak about the tenth century AD as a period of transition and transformation (Aimers 2007; Andrews et al. 2003; Chase and Chase 2004; Demarest 2004; Milbrath and Lope 2009; Rice et al. 2004; Rice and Rice 2004; Schwarz 2009). Recent research suggests that such changes were not caused by external factors, that is, from pressures outside the Maya region, but rather they resulted from multiple

DOI: 10.5876/9781607327646.c006

transformations in sociopolitical life (see Golden and Scherer 2013; Manahan and Canuto 2009; Schwartz and Nichols 2006; and Schwarz 2009 for specific case studies). Part of the difficulty in understanding the complexities of this period is that current views of the Early Postclassic Maya (AD 950–1250) are widely based on archaeological and ethnohistorical data from surrounding regions, such as Belize, the Yucatan Peninsula, and the Highlands of Guatemala, or they come from later time periods, such as the fourteenth to sixteenth-century Itza and Kowoj Maya (e.g., Andrews 2003; Braswell 2003; Chase and Chase 1985; Masson 2002; Milbrath and Lope 2003, 2009; Rice and Rice 1985, 2004, 2009; Stanton and Negrón 2001). Yet scholarly understanding of the Early Postclassic period in the central-southern Maya Lowlands remains incomplete. As a consequence, this chapter focuses on the period following the turmoil of the tenth century AD in the central Maya Lowlands. The immediate postdynastic era is characterized by demographic losses in urban spaces, significant changes in dynastic center political systems, and changes in production, consumption, and distribution choices.

Recent finds at the site of El Zotz give new insight into this turbulent time period. Certain regions experienced extreme to almost complete demographic losses within two or three generations of the demise of their royal courts; other sites continued for three to four centuries (Child and Golden 2008; Demarest et al. 1997; Golden et al. 2010; Inomata 1997; Kingsley et al. 2010, 2012; Webster 2002). Evidence from El Zotz indicates that settlement was not completely abandoned at the end of the Classic period, but that a resilient population managed to reconfigure itself. Archaeological materials indicate that, far from being isolated, this group adopted elements of larger Postclassic Maya traditions from Yucatan to the southern Lowlands and continued to inhabit El Zotz for at least 300–400 years after the departure of its royal court (AD 900–1250/1350). Even after the fourteenth century AD, El Zotz remained a place of importance for some Maya.

This chapter presents a general overview of research conducted from 2008 to 2011 at El Zotz. Postclassic evidence is found in varying quantities across the site, but it is concentrated within a household compound occupying the South Group of El Zotz. For the purposes of this study, households are thought to be multi-sited in their production and consumption practices, involving other individuals outside the household, and are best treated as systems (Wilk 1989:31). Here, a *household compound* is defined as a set of houses—physical structures, readily studied by archaeologists—that are linked socially and economically. The Early Postclassic occupation is conditioned in part by the surrounding topography and the Buenavista Valley more generally (see Houston et al., chapter 1, this volume). Yet, it also hints that such smaller, discrete communities could have existed elsewhere in the southern Maya Lowlands. The near-surface and small-scale nature of the Early Postclassic occupation means that scholars do not yet know its full extent across the Lowland landscape. This finding not only advances our understanding of Postclassic populations in the southern Lowlands but also provides material samples that testify to changes in ritual and economic activities. In our estimation, these shifts likely resulted from the absence of a royal court. The material presented here is only an overview of a larger discussion of this period in Kingsley's (2014) dissertation, which further discusses adaptations to production, consumption, and distribution choices among Early Postclassic households at El Zotz.

POSTCLASSIC OCCUPATION

The material associated with the Postclassic occupation at El Zotz is primarily found within the confines of the South Group (figure 6.1). Two well-provenienced radiocarbon dates for the Postclassic exist outside the South Group, at the Las Palmitas Group and from the summit of the Str. L7-11 pyramid at El Zotz (table 1.1; figure 1.6; Houston et al., chapter 1, this volume). Although neither was found within construction levels, they indicate a Postclassic presence. The former dates to AD 900–1152 (though it is 76.5 percent likely to fall between AD 947 and 1051 in the Terminal Classic) and is associated with the back of Str. M3-6 at Las Palmitas within a mixed context. The Postclassic date at the summit of Str. L7-11 is from AD 1426 to 1632 (with a 71.9 percent probability of falling between AD 1426 and 1524) and is associated with the deposit of two Lacandon-style vessels (figure 13.6; Arredondo Leiva et al. 2008). As at Piedras Negras (Child and Golden 2008.86–87) and other sites, these vessels likely indicate ritual use of the space by visiting Lacandon Maya. Though not radiocarbon dated, there are also a handful of Postclassic-style ceramics marked by the appearance of scroll-style supports in the Northwest Courtyard from Str. L7-17, the Acropolis itself, and the top of a midden at Las Palmitas. Most of these appear in the humus level of excavations and are often mixed with ceramics linked to the Terminal Classic period (see Newman et al., chapter 5, this volume). In all, 313 Postclassic sherds, including Paxcaman and Augustine types, were recovered within the Acropolis and the Northwest Courtyard of El Zotz and 287 from Las Palmitas. This quantity is small relative to the 10,000+ sherds from the South Group of El Zotz. The mixed contexts of the finds also denote that, at least initially, occupation was scattered. By the eleventh century AD, however, these individuals either left or were

FIGURE 6.1. *Map of the South Group and Southern Causeway showing excavations (map by T. Garrison).*

incorporated into the household compound that had begun to coalesce in the South Group. That group contains the longest continuous occupation from this time, extending into the beginning of the Late Postclassic to the end of the thirteenth century AD.

RESEARCH AT THE SOUTH GROUP

Investigations in the South Group began with two test pits in the entrance to the South Group; these were carried out by Varinia Matute in 2008 (Quiroa and Matute 2008). The dense scattering of Postclassic finds led to a more extensive set of vertical and horizontal excavations in three later seasons, directed first by Gámez and then by Kingsley (see Gámez 2009; Kingsley and Cambranes 2011; Kingsley and Rivas 2012 for unit-by-unit descriptions). In total, 76 units of varying sizes, from 1 × 1 m to 2 × 2 m, were placed across the South Group to investigate architectural constructions, activity spaces, middens, and general chronologies (see figure 6.1 for the locations of these units). Three areas, two buildings and one open but terraced space, were extensively examined through horizontal excavation. In addition, middens were found at the northern corners of the platform. Because of topographical constraints only the northwestern unit was extended to include two 1 × 1 m units. Designated as EZ 6K-2 and its extension, EZ 6K-4, this midden is discussed at length later in the chapter as a chronologically controlled, representative sample of the South Group artifacts as a whole. The stratigraphic control presented by these units allowed for a combination of relative dating and absolute dating, relative dating being determined by stylistic changes of ceramic manufacture over time and absolute dating by the AMS samples. Together, these serve to organize material found elsewhere in the site.

GROUP DESCRIPTION

The South Group consists of three nested platforms, an upper 90 × 100 m platform lying on a basal platform, and an additional tertiary platform. Eighteen structures of varying sizes are distributed across the group, with a less-organized dispersal of architecture to the north. An additional six structures are located alongside a walkway or above the terracing that leads north to the main plaza of El Zotz. Ceramic typologies and radiocarbon dating indicate that the secondary platform, along with the five structures it encloses at the south of the group, was built during the Preclassic period, with foundational evidence as early as the Middle Preclassic period (see Doyle and Piedrasanta, chapter 2, this volume). Some modifications occurred in the Early Classic period and again in the Late Classic period. Prior to the Postclassic period, however, the South Group was most active during the Preclassic period and was likely the center of a small community. Some additional constructions were added in the Late Classic, such as Strs. L9–1, L9–17, and L9–19 (no test pits were placed inside these buildings, however, so their dating comes from their similarity to other buildings of the Late Classic period). In addition, the northern half of the platform was likely modified at this time and the beginnings of a walkway created to connect the South Group to the Acropolis lying to the north.

By the Postclassic period, several new houses were built. There is no apparent monumental construction at this time at the site, but other architectural projects were completed, including semi-perishable buildings in previously unused spaces. Terracing too was expanded into defined community activity spaces along the Southern Causeway. This may suggest an active decision to change fully the community dynamics and to redefine previous civic spaces through the creation of domestic architecture in previous monumental settings.

The South Group may have proved an attractive place to establish residences. The topography to the west, east, and south of the group is steeper than any other part of the urban center of El Zotz, while still providing accessibility to the El Zotz Aguada, the site's main water source, which lies northwest of the group (see Beach et al., chapter 7, this volume). This water source would have been central to the longevity of the household compound, and Postclassic materials recovered along its bank indicate its use at this time. This topography perhaps created a naturally controllable area of an otherwise vast landscape. With the building of Str. L8–26 in the Postclassic period, the Maya effectively created a blockage for anyone coming to visit the group.

In all, there are eight buildings that can be attributed to the Postclassic period both on the platform and to the north. The buildings were dispersed and scattered in no apparent pattern, although they did leave open a space between Strs. L8–27 and L8–28, which was used as an extensive activity area. Evidence of food, ceramics, and lithic production and consumption were found here as well as an intentional effort to create the terrace that is Str. L8–27. Because of jungle overgrowth it was difficult to investigate the area to the west of Str. L8–27, but the little architecture reveals its use as an extended activity area—perhaps for a set of gardens. In all, the distributional patterns and quality of the architecture, ceramics, and lithics, which are discussed in more depth later in this chapter, all suggest a residential function. This is not to say that other activities, such as rituals, did not occur here, but rather that these buildings and open spaces consisted of an extended household compound where members interacted on a daily basis.

SOCIAL AND ECONOMIC LIVES OF THE EARLY POSTCLASSIC

The Classic political system consisted of elites attached in hierarchical relationships to a ruling dynasty. This arrangement is reflected in the presence of monumental architecture, exotic raw materials such as jade, and polychrome ceramics. In the absence of the ruling dynasty during the Postclassic period, Kingsley (2014) proposes that heterarchical relationships were more acutely emphasized, though hierarchical relationships would still be active. Evidence from the South Group of El Zotz indicates that these households were non-elite, domestic residences. Investigations into these households illustrate both continuities and divergences from the Classic period. Major artifact classes are each discussed in turn.

MATERIAL CULTURE ANALYSIS OF THE SOUTH GROUP

ARCHITECTURAL CHANGES

Villamil (2007:208) has argued that, in the Postclassic, there was a rejection of the Classic-period spatial order. From the Terminal Classic on, this resulted in a less-organized and less-permanent building program. During the Late Classic period, houses in the central Peten were typically located in formal plaza-centered quadrangles (Ashmore 1981; Schwarz 2009). In the Terminal Classic, domestic architecture became less patterned, with smaller, looser, and scattered groups becoming the norm. According to Schwarz (2009), the apparent change on the Quexil Islands at this time was likely a truncation of earlier, more formal plaza arrangements, reducing the number of structures and the size of the domestic group. By the Postclassic period, building façades became more open (Andres 2005), and isolated single domestic structures more prevalent, a pattern noted across the Peten Lakes region (Rice 1986:310). This led to less-evenly dispersed residential groups (Chase and Chase 2004:25) within densely nucleated communities that were physically and geographically circumscribed (Rice 1988:236).

In addition to the changes in spatial layout, new architectural forms come into existence. Postclassic constructions are often more perishable than in the Classic period. Chase and Chase (2004:19) have proposed that the hallmark of Postclassic architecture consists of perishable edifices with low lines of stones serving as foundational or base walls. This accords with Rice's (1986:304) findings that the principal component of Postclassic constructions is a rect-angular, single-level platform of low height. In the Copan Valley, Manahan and Canuto (2009) have also found wattle-and-daub superstructures from this period whose interior walls were sometimes constructed of reused cut or dressed stones. Not only were stones taken from earlier buildings, but aban-doned Classic structures were also often modified to form household plat-forms. The reuse of stones implies a reduction in the labor capacity of the community to quarry and work new limestone into blocks.

During the Postclassic period, three configurations of the superstructure appear to be prevalent around the Peten Lakes (Rice 1986:307; 1988:234): (1) a single straight wall aligned on the long axis atop a rectangular substructure; (2) an L-shaped construction with the long axis aligned with the back of the structure; and (3) a C-shaped superstructure, whether constructed as walls or benches, with the building front left open. This open area could have had a civic function and served as a reception hall (Rice 1986, 1988). Such buildings served as the center of political life of the Postclassic sites that arose around the Peten Lakes. Perishable structures probably existed around these more permanent foundations.

At El Zotz, we identified the platforms of a minimum of seven Postclassic structures. These constructions follow the loose structural patterning and reuse of Classic-period stones described above. Buildings were constructed in unoccupied spaces both on top of and around preexisting platforms. Foundations were loosely delimited with small walls of often recycled, rarely cut limestone to delineate buildings. Ceramics, lithics, rubble, and even monuments from elsewhere in the site were used as fill for the bases of these structures and then covered with compact dirt. Classic-period monumental construction likely required systematic contributions of labor in the form of corvée. The lack of organized planning and monumentality of the Postclassic buildings suggests that such a labor contribution was no longer imposed on households or that the labor was purely local to that residence. Within horizontal excavations carried out on the western half of Str. L9-11, the largest of the Postclassic buildings, foundational wall stones were often turned with the grain of the stone facing up (figure 6.2); this would have resulted in the faster erosion of the limestone. Perhaps the architects of these buildings were not as knowledgeable in architectural constructions as their Classic predecessors. More likely, permanency of architecture no longer mattered, and these stones, along with the uncut, medium rubble that served as fill, created an even plane on which a compact, dirt floor could be constructed. The Maya also delimited interior living spaces and provided a small wall along which posts could be placed to support a thatched roof, a pattern found on the eastern wall of Str. L9-11. Clearly, investment of labor in construction was quite different and noticeably smaller than during the Late Classic period.

Ultimately, the people who remained at El Zotz modified their built environment. They oriented their households toward an open activity space, and they cut off easy access from the remainder of the site, constructing a physiographic circumscription found naturally at other sites, such as the Quexil Islands or Macanche. They also dispersed their houses away from enclosed, quadrangle, patio groups, the typical layout of the previous period. All told, this resulted in a larger but interrelated household compound.

FIGURE 6.2. *Horizontal excavation of Str. L9-11 with upturned stones identified through hash-marking (drawing by M. Kingsley).*

CERAMIC CHANGES

In addition to demographic and architectural changes, the Classic-to-Postclassic divide is in part defined by dramatic changes in material culture, particularly in ceramics. The chronological divide between these periods relies on the appearance or disappearance of ceramic chronological markers, such as the Saxche and Zacatal polychromes, finewares, and plumbate ceramics, which are associated with the elite. For the Postclassic, the best markers for understanding non-elites in a postdynastic environment are the monochromes and unslipped vessels. In Maya archaeology, ceramics serve as the basis for most chronological interpretations because of the cost of radiocarbon and other absolute dating methods. Scholarly identification of the Early Postclassic period relies heavily on being able to identify the differences between prevalent Late Classic ceramics groups, such as Tinaja and Cambio Unslipped, and Early Postclassic ceramics groups, such as Augustine, Paxcaman, and Pozo Unslipped. Seriation charts of these ceramic groups from the main midden of the South Group can serve as a representative sample of the ceramics in general. The midden holds 4,397 of 22,542 sherds collected in the South Group (19.5 percent), and 355 of 1,930 diagnostic sherds collected (18.4 percent). When attached to absolute dates acquired from radiocarbon testing, the distribution of these ceramic groups through time indicates that, despite the political and demographic ruptures occurring during the tenth century AD, material culture of commoners did not shift radically. The two deepest excavation lots (EZ 6K-2-6 and EZ 6K-4-7) sit above bedrock and date to AD 773–906 (71.8 percent probability; table 1.1). For all sherds, Late Classic markers such as the Cambio, Tinaja, and Encanto groups dominate the data set (figures 6.3a and b). Though this is a wide span of 200 years, it coincides with a time of dynastic turmoil at El Zotz (see Newman et al., chapter 5, this volume). Lots from the middle of the midden (EZ 6K-2-3 and EZ 6K-4-3) continue to have these three "Late Classic" ceramic groups, albeit in lesser numbers, despite a firm Early Postclassic date of AD 1034–1220. Although carbon was not available for the top of the midden, dates acquired from neighboring activity spaces suggest the midden was in use as late as the thirteenth century (table 1.1). At this time, only a handful of these groups are present and the traditional Postclassic markers, and the Paxcaman and Pozo groups, are the most represented.

As expected, Tinaja, Cambio, and Encanto groups dominate during the Postclassic transition, while Pozo and Paxcaman groups dominate the middle of the Postclassic period. A crucial development takes place during the eleventh and twelfth centuries AD. At this time, there is a gradual increase in the popularity and production of Postclassic ceramic types rather than an abrupt change in ceramic types. As a result, ceramic finds alone can no longer be used to make judgments about the presence or absence of Early Postclassic occupation. Ceramic identifications need to be supported by other archaeological finds. More to the point, at El Zotz, then, the gradual transition from Terminal Classic to Postclassic types implies a steady and continuous occupation over the course of more than 300 years. Part of the difficulty with using ceramics alone to determine the existence of Early Postclassic occupation is that this artifact class has been shown to be highly variable. It can be difficult

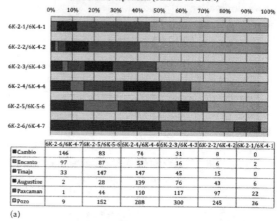

Relative Proportions of Red Monochrome and Unslipped Ceramics in the South Group Midden (Units EZ-6K-2/6K-4)

	6K-2-6/6K-4-7	6K-2-5/6K-5-6	6K-2-4/6K-4-4	6K-2-3/6K-4-3	6K-2-2/6K-4-2	6K-2-1/6K-4-1
▪Cambio	146	83	74	31	8	0
▪Encanto	97	87	53	16	6	2
▪Tinaja	33	147	147	45	15	0
▪Augustine	2	28	139	76	43	6
▪Paxcaman	1	44	110	117	97	22
▫Pozo	9	152	288	300	245	36

(a)

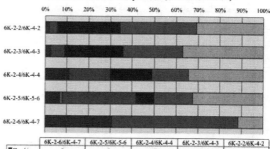

Relative Proportions of Red Monochrome and Unslipped Diagnostic Ceramics in the South Group Midden (Units EZ-6K-2/6K-4)

	6K-2-6/6K-4-7	6K-2-5/6K-5-6	6K-2-4/6K-4-4	6K-2-3/6K-4-3	6K-2-2/6K-4-2
▪Cambio	8	5	12	2	1
▪Encanto	0	1	0	0	0
▪Tinaja	15	25	21	5	2
▪Augustine	0	6	21	21	16
▪Paxcaman	0	13	18	21	19
▫Pozo	3	24	38	29	17

FIGURE 6.3. *Relative proportions of monochrome red and unslipped ceramics from the South Group midden: (a) all sherds; (b) diagnostic sherds (charts by M. Kingsley).*

(b)

to categorize in the absence of a large sample. During the transition to the Early Postclassic period, for example, Classic-period markers were still present, and many of the Postclassic markers, such as scroll supports and snail shell temper, were not yet well established. As a result, smaller samples without radiocarbon dates can lend themselves to temporal confusions.

Rice and Rice (1985:174) have posited that, despite adherence to a common set of rules with respect to design, structure, layout, color, and motif, there were multiple manufacturers and manufacturing loci of ceramics during the Early Postclassic. This diversity of manufacture is attested later in the Middle and Late Postclassic, at least according to D. Chase's (1985) analysis of pottery from Santa Rita. It suggests that potters conformed to form and slip conventions from Mayapan, but that regional differences in paste and firing techniques pointed to local production. After the Classic period, ceramics appear less evenly distributed, with particular ceramic types or groups often restricted to subregions or sites but with high levels of variability within types. Rice (1980:78) proposed that the variability of Postclassic ceramics in terms of paste and slip resulted from a population of experimental potters who lacked technological expertise. More recently, in a follow-up study of some of these ideas, Cecil (2001:271) suggested that the high variability of slip colors, specifically in the Trapeche ceramic group at Ch'ich', Ixlu, and Zacpeten, might result from the same lack of expertise in controlling oxidation during firing.

Through this time, ceramics also appear to be shifting slowly in form and function. Rice (1987b) noted that at Macanche Island the size of vessels, measured through the diameter of rims and thickness of vessel walls, shows a reduction through the Postclassic period in comparison to the Classic period. Schwarz (2009) has concluded that the Classic period's larger vessels were likely necessary because domestic units were larger, a conclusion supported by the architectural changes described above. Since serving vessel size is related to issues of exchange, reciprocity, and feasting (LeCount 1996:242–280; Lucero 2001), decreases in the size of these artifacts would suggest that pots were being used less for social gatherings and more for personal consumption.

In contrast to the data from Macanche Island, vessel size at El Zotz does not change significantly across time periods. Early Postclassic vessels on the whole appear approximately 1 cm smaller in radius than Classic-period vessels, not a substantial change (figure 6.4). By themselves, the major red monochromes, consisting of Tinaja, Augustine, and Paxcaman groups, remain relatively consistent, with radial means of 11.7 cm, 11.2 cm, and 11.4 cm. This underscores the conclusion that changes were slight at best, perhaps the result of the continuity of population noted before. However, the comparison of unslipped wares, which were possibly used for storage purposes, reveals a different pattern. Here, the average Cambio-group vessel has a radius of 14.4 cm while the average Pozo-group vessel has a radius of 11.0 cm. The thickness of vessel walls does decrease, but only slightly. Since the varying households within the South Group's household compound were economically and socially linked, sharing activity spaces and daily practices, it is likely that they also consumed meals together. Perhaps monochrome and unslipped vessels do not change significantly in size because a multitude of individuals outside the nuclear

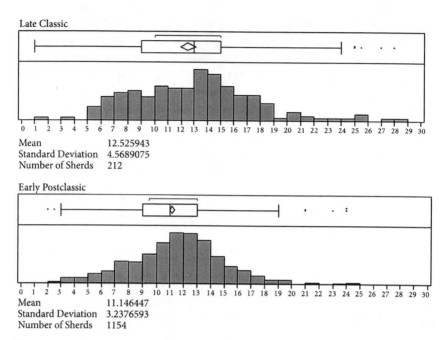

Late Classic

Mean   12.525943
Standard Deviation   4.5689075
Number of Sherds   212

Early Postclassic

Mean   11.146447
Standard Deviation   3.2376593
Number of Sherds   1154

FIGURE 6.4. *Distribution of radii (cm) of vessels in the Late Classic and Early Postclassic periods (charts by M. Kingsley).*

family ate together. Though such an activity would not be a large feasting event, which would require the capacity to store large quantities of water, it affirms that at least within El Zotz the domestic unit remained similar in size from the tenth through thirteenth centuries AD.

The analysis of the everyday wares of commoners, including both monochrome and unslipped vessels, thus indicates that everyday practices remained consistent. (Finewares and polychromes, typically elite markers, are smaller in size because of their fine craftsmanship and were not included in this comparison.) This consistency in vessel size and construction is likely because ceramic production was always conducted at the household level. External turmoil did not affect the manner in which these ceramics continued to be produced. In other words, the ceramics reflect a level of ingrained practice that was not altered or influenced by the departure of the El Zotz dynasty. The transformations that did occur can be more readily attributed to gradual stylistic shifts rather than to any political or economic changes. An analysis of figurines and incensario vessels (figure 6.5), on the other hand, reveals a different pattern of change.

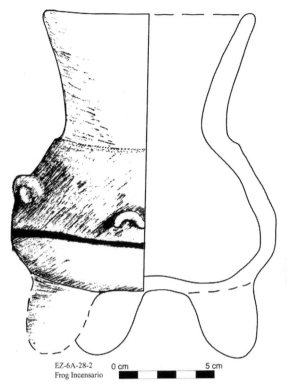

EZ-6A-28-2
Frog Incensario
0 cm   5 cm

FIGURE 6.5. *Frog* incensario *from South Group excavations (drawing by M. Kingsley).*

RITUAL ARTIFACTS: FIGURINES AND *INCENSARIOS*

Christina Halperin (2007) has discussed how the introduction of post-firing perforations in some Terminal Classic figurines from Motul de San José, Peten, illustrates a reformulation of practices in figurine production and consumption, and their social meaning. Perforations in figurines during the Classic period were usually made pre-firing, some examples associated with the manufacture of musical instruments. By the Postclassic period, figurines were often mold-made and characterized by a hole on each side of the figurine, possibly indicating they were meant to be strung and hung or perched on their open bases (Halperin 2010). Halperin goes further, suggesting, "the figures take on the stiff poses, angular and more abstract bodily and facial features and clothing typical of a *localized* interpretation of or interaction with Mesoamerica's Postclassic International style" (Halperin 2010:5, emphasis

0 cm   5 cm

FIGURE 6.6. *Figurine idol from South Group excavations (drawing by M. Ritter-Armour).*

added). We would additionally propose that there is an increase in the manufacture of household idols and that analysis of figurines cannot only indicate localization of production practices but a reorientation of religious priorities in the household.

Within the South Group, 39 figurine fragments were recovered, 36 of them from the Postclassic. Though this may not reflect an increase in manufacturing, the proportional difference is so great as to be statistically significant. Of the half or so that are identifiable, nine form parts of human figurines, seven are zoomorphic in nature, two are human/deity idols (figure 6.6), and two are miniature skeleton masks. The two idols and one owl figure are of particular interest because they follow the pattern described by Halperin: they are mold-made, hollow figures, with holes on the sides for hanging.

The context of these finds provides additional insight into the possible function of the figurines as religious objects. Seven, including one of the idols and the owl figure, come from a single building, Str. L9-11. As the largest of the Postclassic constructions, Str. L9-11 was strategically located to overlook all activity areas in the household compound. Excavations in Str. L9-11 also recovered three jade celts and an obsidian polyhedral core. These appear to be recycled objects, appropriated from the Classic period; their date of manufacture can be surmised from manufacture and wear patterns. Despite this, their discovery in Str. L9-11 suggests that it was the main or "ruling" house of the compound. Its concentration of figurines also implies that it held an important role in the religious life of the community. Although a definitive identification was never possible, Str. L9-11 also had what appeared to be a built-up "altar" in its center. This feature consisted of well-cut stones, stacked four layers deep to create a small bench-like structure. Str. L9-11 was the only building in which a large amount of reconstructible, whole vessels had been left behind upon abandonment of the community in the thirteenth or fourteenth century AD.

The personalization of rituals and emphasis on small group ceremonies may also be reflected by the transposition of two stelae to the base of the South Group platform at some point during the Early Postclassic period (see locations in figure 6.1). Though these stelae are heavily eroded, Houston believes that, to judge from their size, the stelae were in fact plain but cut in Classic-period style (Stephen Houston, personal communication, 2010). They were probably made at the end of the ninth century AD and were moved to their current location during the Postclassic period; excavations at their base uncovered Postclassic ceramics. The fact that other monuments were cut up and used in the fill of new buildings, such as Str. L9-11 (Kingsley and Rivas 2012), implies that a certain amount of selective destruction took place during the Early Postclassic period. This was not a new practice, as is evident from a portion of El Zotz Stela 4 found in an extension to Str. L7-17 added in the Terminal Classic period (see Newman et al., chapter 5, this volume). In the South Group, however, the Maya kept the stelae whole, likely as a statement about the continued social importance of these objects. The carvings were placed in strategic locations in the midst of the household compound, at the base of the platform where anyone walking up to the South Group platform would have seen them.

Lithic Sources and Production Practices

Analysis of obsidian material gathered from Postclassic contexts sharpens our view of shifts in the acquisition, production, and consumption of nonlocal materials. Perhaps because lithic production was a more specialized practice, the Postclassic period heralds changes in both material choices and manufacturing techniques. In the South Group, an increased concentration of Ixtepeque obsidian suggests more limited access or shifting desirability of certain raw materials. In the South Group midden, we can see that, starting in the early eleventh century AD, Ixtepeque obsidian dominates both in frequency and in weight (figure 6.7a,b). El Chayal obsidian, the most popular obsidian in the central Lowlands during the Late Classic, continues to be present, but the upsurge of Ixtepeque is noticeable and differentiates the Postclassic period from earlier periods. The changes in raw material choices and the manufacture of obsidian in the Postclassic illustrate a transformation in or an adjustment to economic practices. This is not surprising, in that scholars believe that obsidian sources were controlled or the exchange of the raw materials themselves mitigated by elites during previous time periods. In the Late Classic, Ixtepeque was relegated to a specific geographic zone. Indeed, the city of Copan may have controlled the source and the distribution of obsidian extracted from it (Braswell 2004; Schortman and Urban 1994).

More generally, qualitative analysis across the Maya area implies that the technologies used to manufacture lithics and obsidian during the Postclassic period shifted from direct production methods common in the Classic period, which required a high degree of skill, to pressure flaking and more indirect-percussion methods. Some tools are actually reused Classic-period tools that were badly reworked during the Postclassic period. This is suggested by pecking on an obsidian polyhedral core and pressure flaking of large chert flakes. As Costin (1991) argues, such evidence of low degrees of skill and labor investment in the final product might be evidence of decentralized production. According to a study of western Mesoamerican obsidian blades by Healan (2009:109), pecked-and-ground platforms, which are common in the Postclassic period, indicate change from full-time core or blade specialists to diversified craft producers; that is, individual producers manufactured flakes and blades from obsidian and other lithics. Healan (2009:109–110) also believes that household members other than the blademaker likely performed the platform grinding. This would imply a change in production strategies from the Classic period. Elite patronage no longer supported craft production, forcing the producers themselves to diversify their production.

Such a change in manufacturing strategy is quite evident among the obsidian blades and flakes in the South Group of El Zotz. Of the 404 obsidian pieces collected, 134 had visible platforms; of these, 102 had platforms designated as pecked and ground. This represented 76 percent of identifiable platforms. As part of an obsidian analysis conducted with Zachary Hruby, platforms were classified as bifacial platforms, bipolar platforms, unmodified platforms, ground platforms (further designated as heavy, medium, or light in its application), pecked and group platforms, and single-facet and multifaced platforms. Such a large percentage would suggest that Healan's conclusions

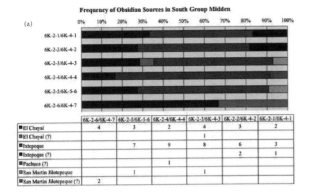

Frequency of Obsidian Sources in South Group Midden

	6K-2-6/6K-4-7	6K-2-5/6K-5-6	6K-2-4/6K-4-4	6K-2-3/6K-4-3	6K-2-2/6K-4-2	6K-2-1/6K-4-1
El Chayal	4	3	2	4	3	2
El Chayal (?)				1		
Ixtepeque		7	9	8	6	3
Ixtepeque (?)					2	1
Pachuca (?)			1			
San Martin Jilotepeque		1		1		
San Martin Jilotepeque (?)	2					

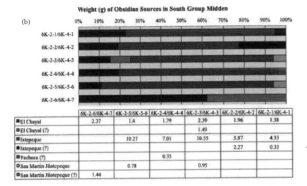

Weight (g) of Obsidian Sources in South Group Midden

	6K-2-6/6K-4-7	6K-2-5/6K-5-6	6K-2-4/6K-4-4	6K-2-3/6K-4-3	6K-2-2/6K-4-2	6K-2-1/6K-4-1
El Chayal	2.37	1.4	1.79	2.39	1.96	1.38
El Chayal (?)				1.49		
Ixtepeque		10.27	7.01	10.55	5.87	4.33
Ixtepeque (?)					2.27	0.33
Pachuca (?)			0.35			
San Martin Jilotepeque		0.78		0.95		
San Martin Jilotepeque (?)	1.44					

FIGURE 6.7. *Obsidian sources from the South Group midden: (a) frequency, (b) weight in grams (charts by M. Kingsley).*

concerning technological shifts in manufacturing techniques in Postclassic western Mexico also apply to the sample from El Zotz, and likely to the general region of the central Maya Lowlands as well.

In general, little primary production evidence is present at El Zotz (e.g., blade cores, exhausted cores, recycled cores, platform rejuvenation flakes, and core fragments). Yet some platform-rejuvenation flakes and a single recycled core were collected. Coupled with the presence of first and second series blades, which are produced through the shaping or maintenance of a core (de Leon et al. 2009:114), this evidence supports the conclusion that some blades were probably being produced locally (Hruby, personal communication, 2010). However, the small number of cores suggests that preparation of raw obsidian either did not happen at El Zotz or happened in rare incidents. As a result, the material could have been imported to the South Group already partially modified. The variability of Postclassic lithic production was perhaps because producers were now free from the structures and limitations that centralized city-states propagated during the Classic period, allowing for increased creativity or variability. It may also indicate a decrease in the ability to stay within the bounds of a single, consistent method of production.

CONCLUSIONS

From the available evidence concerning the Postclassic occupation of El Zotz, two important conclusions emerge. First, that scholarly understanding of the Postclassic period in the central Lowlands has been biased by investigations into Postclassic urban spaces, such as those around Lake Peten Itza. Where topography allowed, occupation continued well into the Postclassic period, as part of distinct communities establishing themselves for generations. What proved central to the survival of the population of El Zotz was the nearby *aguada*, its location within the Buenavista Valley, a possible location for the Camino Real trade route from the southern Lowlands to Yucatan, and proximity to the Lakes region. Not only did they have a water source on which they could depend, but they remained connected to regional networks of communication and trade, giving them access to potential marriage partners and nonlocal goods. In addition, the presence of this community implies that scholars do not yet know the full extent of occupation during this time. Where topographic conditions are favorable we might find more of these small household compounds.

Second, the turmoil of the ninth and tenth centuries in the southern Maya Lowlands did not have a profound impact on daily practice. Although the Postclassic period seems to entail a severe reduction or cessation of some features we now identify with the Classic period, such as monumental architecture and carved-stone monuments, rejection of Classic-period markers on the whole was selective. As Friedman (1992:837) has suggested, "self definition does not occur in a vacuum, but in a world already defined. As such it invariably fragments the larger identity space of which its subjects were previously a part." The result is that certain ideologies and their concurrent materialization are not outwardly rejected but kept or modified.

The nomenclature we continue to use, including "Collapse" and "Postclassic," continues to imply to scholars, particularly those not familiar with the region, a sense of failure and abandonment. To be sure, the demise of the royal dynasty certainly had severe impacts on cultural and economic organizations, but cultural precedence and supraregional sociocultural ties cannot be fully abandoned. Rather, "societies, *even those following state demise,* never discard *all* that had been achieved over centuries of previous state rule" (Graffam 1992:883, emphasis added). Commoner ceramic traditions on the whole seem to have been kept, and changes are likely the result of ordinary stylistic trends rather than a rejection of previous ceramics. This is perhaps the result of continuing occupation by people who had been used to producing their own ceramics even during the Classic period. Architectural conceptions and religious practices, however, do appear to change, with households becoming the central focus of both. Over the course of a century or so, rituals appear to be more evident in household rather than suprahousehold contexts, and there is a reduction in the investment of labor for the construction of households. With the departure of the Classic-period dynastic rule, large community rituals and events in the midst of monumental architecture ceased. Meanwhile, nonlocal raw materials were still accessible, but obsidian production, in particular, shows that full-time specialists were no longer at the forefront of its manufacture.

In the end, the Collapse was very specific in its effects, and the data indicate that the transition to postdynastic Maya society was just as much about continuity as about the cessation of certain ideologies. For the Maya, the Classic-period Collapse prompted a change in sociopolitical organization. It did not, however, generate a disjunction of inter- and intraregional relationships and trade that had produced exchanges of ideas and beliefs for the preceding millennium. Instead, Postclassic Maya occupants of the South Group of El Zotz appear to have maintained many aspects of their larger regional community, even as patterns shifted away from elite-controlled or elite-influenced manufacture.

PART II

Technical Analysis at El Zotz

7

The overarching goal for this study was to begin research on the El Zotz regional environment and its long-term environmental change. We conducted our work along two main lines of inquiry: the major natural resources and proxy evidence for environmental change over the Late Holocene. The natural resources for the El Zotz region are comparable to other parts of the elevated interior region (EIR) of the Maya Lowlands that our teams have studied since the early 1990s around the Petexbatun, Cancuén, and northwestern Belize (Beach et al. 2015). At El Zotz in 2009 and 2010, we did preliminary studies of soils, geomorphology, water quality, water management, and paleoecology. We focused the soil and geomorphology work on the *civales* (large shallow water bodies) at El Palmar and Bejucal, and on the *aguadas* (smaller, shallow depressions and constructed reservoirs) at El Zotz, the El Diablo Group, and near Bejucal, and we conducted the paleoecological work on El Zotz and El Palmar. Our water studies cover a wider region to assess the geography of water chemistry, which should parallel the water chemistry of ancient Maya times because water conforms over time to the rocks through which it flows, especially limestone that imparts components of $CaCO_3$ as well as Mg^+ and SO_4^{+2} because of rapid dissolution. In 2016 we returned to focus on one question that arose after our earlier field seasons: was there a dam that enhanced the reservoir capacity of the *aguada* at El Zotz? Based on a robust range and number of data we present new water

Environments of El Zotz

Water and Soil Chemistry, the El Zotz Dam, and Long-Term Environmental Change

TIMOTHY BEACH,
SHERYL LUZZADDER-BEACH,
COLIN DOYLE,
AND WILLIAM DELGADO

DOI: 10.5876/9781607327646.c007

chemistry findings that outline the water characteristics for this region, new evidence for the El Zotz dam, new estimates of the chronology and capacity of the El Zotz reservoir, and a new synthesis of the environmental history that dates back to the Late Archaic from pollen cores from the El Zotz and El Palmar sediments.

This chapter considers water quality, paleoecology, soils, and water management in the Maya Lowlands. These are all maturing and expanding lines of research for the Maya area, though our work in this chapter and Beach et al. (2011, 2015) and Luzzadder-Beach et al. (2017) are the first on these topics for the El Zotz region. Many additional studies come from the broader region, with the majority around the central Peten lakes and Tikal (Beach et al. 2015). Research on water chemistry for the Maya Lowlands region has lagged behind the other scientific endeavors (Luzzadder-Beach and Beach 2008; Luzzadder-Beach et al. 2017).

ENVIRONMENTS

The El Zotz region lies between the sources of four drainage basins that act as arteries for scores of ancient Maya cities and mosaics of ecotones and natural resources. These drainage basins include the San Pedro Martir River to the west and the Pasión River to the south that flow into the Usumacinta River and the Gulf of Mexico, and the Belize River to the southeast and the Three Rivers basin to the northeast that flow into the Caribbean Sea. The El Zotz region thus sits amidst natural corridors from all directions within a structural valley that bisects the Peten from sea to sea (figure 7.1). This Buenavista Valley, with its prominent Buenavista Escarpment rising to 400 masl (meters above sea level) along its north side, structures many local ecosystems for the El Zotz region. As with much of the Yucatan Peninsula, this area has mostly Cretaceous-Tertiary carbonate rocks, which are faulted into horsts (ridges) and grabens (valleys). This karst region has only seasonal streams, with most of the runoff flowing internally as ground water. The uplands have typical karst features such as *mogotes* (karst hills), as well as little-explored caves (Alvarado and Herrera 2001; Miller 1996). Lowland areas also have a variety of karst landforms, ranging from small dissolution sinks like ponors to larger dolines, uvalas, and poljes. A *cival*, as at El Palmar, is a regional name for non-perennial, grassy, marsh wetlands that form in a wide range of *bajos* and sometimes remain inundated for years at a time. Smaller water bodies called aguadas are common sinks with standing water and occur in this region near El Palmar, El Zotz, the Los Bocutes Aguada near Bejucal, and the El Diablo Group. Many of these

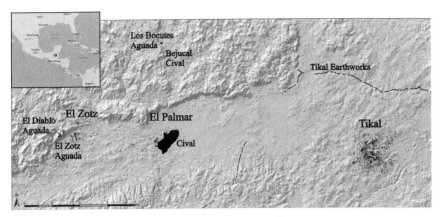

FIGURE 7.1. *Regional map showing sources for paleoenvironmental data (map S. Krause and T. Beach).*

sinks have aggraded with sediment eroded from their watershed as so-called "Maya Clays" deposited from upslope erosion during the ancient Maya period (Anselmetti et al. 2007; Beach et al. 2003, 2018; Dunning et al. 2002).

At El Zotz, the tropical wet and dry climate results from the annual interplay of unstable, rising air from the Intertropical Convergence Zone (ITCZ) and stable, descending air from the Subtropical High Pressure. These conspire to produce about 1,500 mm of rainfall annually, mostly from intense, convective storms during the May-to-December wet season (Luzzadder-Beach et al. 2012). From January through May, the dry season has moisture deficits that grow toward May because soil moisture decreases as temperature increases. Extratropical cyclones sometimes penetrate into the Peten in winter but tropical storms that may reach hurricane force (Boose et al. 2003) produce more rain even though El Zotz lies 160 km from their source in the Caribbean (Luzzadder-Beach et al. 2017).

Many lines of evidence from geochemistry to micropaleontology and modeling indicate substantial climate variations over the Archaic and Maya periods. The Archaic through Preclassic had climatic instability, the Late Preclassic experienced droughts, the Classic-period climate stabilized, but drought returned in the Terminal Classic, Early Postclassic, and Little Ice Age (Luzzadder-Beach et al. 2017). An area of active scientific study is the study of such variation from such global-scale phenomena as the Pacific Decadal Oscillation, the North Atlantic Oscillation, the El Niño Southern Oscillation, and stochastic variation.

Depending on the source, the region's forests are tropical rain forest (Wagner 1964), moist semitropical forest (Holdridge et al. 1971), evergreen tropical forest (Greller 2000; Rzedowski and Huerta 1978), and tropical semi-deciduous forest (Pennington and Sarukhán 1968). The area's vegetation ranges from tall, upland forests, 10–25 m high, to savannas and wetlands. Based on soil and aspect factors, upland forests may be drier *zapotal* forests; drier *ramonales* of *Brosimum alicastrum* (breadnut) on rocky outcrops (Lundell 1937); mesic *caobal* or mahogany *(Swietenia* spp.*)* forests in upland valleys; foot-slope forests, often with sabal palm *(Sabal mauritiiformis)*; deep-soil flats with cohune palm *(Attalea cohune)* copses; wetland interface forests; and scrubby, seasonally dry *bajo* ecosystems with such scrubby trees as logwood (*Haematoxylum campechianum)* (Schulze and Whitacre 1999).

WATER CHEMISTRY METHODS

In the field, we cored and excavated depressions to characterize sediments and sample paleoecological data to study Maya environmental interactions. We discuss methods elsewhere in more detail: for water chemistry see Luzzadder-Beach and Beach (2008, 2009); for phytoliths and pollen see Bozarth and Guderjan (2004) and (Jones 1994); and for soils and stratigraphy see Beach et al. (2002, 2003, 2006, 2008, 2009, 2011, 2015, 2018).

In the 2009 and 2010 field seasons, we monitored available surface water and spring sources in Guatemala's San Miguel la Palotada–El Zotz Biotope. This monitoring occurred at the end of the dry season in each year, representing the region's typical, hydrologically stressed seasonal conditions (Luzzadder-Beach and Beach 2008; Beach et al. 2015). Sample locations and results are indicated in the Water Quality Summary (table 7.1) and discussed below. We used a HACH Conductivity Meter in the field to collect initial field parameters of Total Dissolved Solids (TDS, mg/l), Salinity (Sal, ppt), Electrical Conductivity (EC, μS), and Temperature (°C). These field values assist in monitoring year-to-year variability in water sources, in understanding potential connections between water sources, and for setting up potential sample dilutions and range settings for laboratory analysis and instruments. Water samples were taken in triple-rinsed 500 ml plastic bottles, and then filtered and analyzed for dissolved minerals in the George Mason University Water Quality Lab. The laboratory analyses included post-filtration EC, TDS, Calcium (Ca^{+2}, mg/l), Chloride (Cl^-, mg/l), Magnesium (Mg^{+2}, mg/l), Nitrate (NO_3^-), Sulfate (SO_4^{-2}, mg/l), and Total Hardness (as $CaCO_3$, mg/l), using the HACH Conductivity Meter, wet chemistry titration, and HACH spectrophotometric methods

TABLE 7.1. Water-quality analysis from the San Miguel la Palotada–El Zotz Biotope

Water Sample Site (Year)	Lab EC (μS)	Lab TDS (mg/l)	Lab Salinity (ppt)	NO₃⁻ Nitrate (mg/l)	SO₄⁻² Sulfate (mg/l)	Ca⁺² Calcium (mg/l)	Cl⁻ Chloride (mg/l)
El Palmar Spring (2010)	1691	833	0.8	0.3	483	932	49
El Palmar Cival Shore (2010)	720	346	0.3	0	0	530	31.5
El Palmar Cival (2009)	554	263	0.3	0	0	364	26
El Palmar Cival Water Temple (2009)	570	271	0.3	0.4	0	339	31
El Palmar Aguada Surface (2009)	322	152	0.2	0.4	0	117	26
El Palmar Aguada 5 m depth core (2009)	348	164	0.2	0.5	0	139	23.5
La Cuernavilla Cival, edge (2009)	306	144	0.1	0.2	0	154	19
Aguada Pucte (2010)	568	269	0.3	0.7	72	307	33.25
El Zotz Camp Water (2009)	255F	121F	0.1F	—	—	127	6

F = field values

summarized in Beach et al. (2008) and Luzzadder-Beach and Beach (2009). Values of Na+K are then determined mathematically by totaling and balancing the molecular weights of all other cations and anions. This molecular balancing also cross-checks the water chemistry results (Luzzadder-Beach and Beach 2009).

Water samples came from three kinds of water sources—*civales, aguadas,* and constructed reservoirs—and in one case a perched, confined, and flowing water table in a peat layer at 3 m, that we encountered in an excavation unit near the shore of the Laguna El Palmar (actually a *cival*) in 2010. Surface water is present throughout most years in the *civales* and *aguadas* near the El Palmar site, although it was reported as dry in 2008. There is a constructed *aguada* near the El Zotz site, but it is now filled with sediment; it held no water during our dry season surveys, and we hit no water table in our excavations of the El Zotz Aguada. There is also an *aguada* in a drainage through the escarpment about 4 km north of the El Zotz site, Aguada Pucte, and we were able to obtain a water sample in the dry season of 2010.

REGIONAL WATER CHEMISTRY RESULTS

Field and lab results revealed chemical variations in the regional water supply (table 7.1). In 2009 we sampled six water sites, and three more in 2010. Generally speaking, the *aguadas* below the escarpment showed lower ion water chemistry, and *civales*, with the exception of La Cuernavilla (see Houston et al., this volume, chapter 1 for a site description), showed higher ion concentrations. This is likely due to *aguadas* being smaller and thus more likely to be filled annually with rainwater; *civales* are larger and less likely to go dry annually, so the water in them will undergo repeated annual seasons of evaporation and concentration of their mineral content. Some of the *civales* are also located at an escarpment edge, which may be spring (groundwater) fed, and we have further evidence that some may also be partially fed by perched groundwater, supplementing annual rainfall. Finally, the *aguada* above the escarpment, Pucte, had higher-ion water than the lower-elevation *aguadas*, with a mineral concentration more similar to the spring-fed *civales'* signatures and magnitudes than to the *aguadas'* characteristics, suggesting a hydrogeologic connection between upland drainages and potential lowland seeps and springs. The moderate quality of the *civales*, compared with the perched spring, suggests the *civales* are a combination of emerging groundwater diluted by accumulated rainwater.

SOIL AND PALEOECOLOGY METHODS

We used several physical, stratigraphic, geochemical, and chronological methods to characterize qualities and chronology of sediment layers. Investigations began with field study of soil and sediment sequences, where we characterized Munsell color, HCl reaction, pH, structure, field texture, consistence, preliminary stratigraphy and horizons, magnetic susceptibility, and other physical parameters of soils (Soil Survey Staff 1993, 2003). Every 5–10 cm along soil profiles we recorded magnetic susceptibility with a GF Instruments Magnetic Susceptibility Meter SM-20. Team members also collected artifacts and radiocarbon samples systematically to date sediment sequences. The Soil Laboratory at Brigham Young University (BYU) measured $\delta^{13}C$ (stable carbon isotope ratios) from the humin fraction of the soil organic matter (Beach et al. 2011; Luzzadder-Beach et al. 2016; Sweetwood et al. 2009; Webb et al. 2007; Wright et al. 2009). The BYU Lab also analyzed elements from samples with ICP AES (inductively coupled plasma atomic emission spectrometry) (Johnson et al. 2007). For the AMS dating we sampled young wood or peat or charcoal in distinct layers, and Beta Analytic ran AMS on all samples, which we report as calibrated (by INTCAL13 Radiocarbon Age Calibration) at the two-sigma (95.4 percent probability) level (Reimer et al. 2013) with more specific probabilities offered when available (Bronk Ramsey 2009).

We sampled sequences for pollen, phytoliths, and charcoal at 0.02 m intervals from 0.3 to 3 m from El Palmar. For the El Zotz sediments, we collected six samples from 0.5 to 2.1 m. In both cases, we avoided samples from the topsoils because of the bioturbation associated with topsoil formation. Steven Bozarth of the University of Kansas identified and counted pollen morphs and microscopic charcoal for 22 El Palmar and six El Zotz samples (Luzzadder-Beach et al. 2017).

Soil Humin Carbon Isotopes

Another proxy for long-term impacts on soils are profiles of carbon isotopic ratios through soil horizons because these may show changes of C_4 and C_3 vegetation types (Beach et al. 2011, 2018; Luzzadder-Beach et al. 2017). Several articles detail how soil organic matter and specifically its humin fraction can reflect C_4 and C_3 species, but essentially C_3 species like most tropical trees have carbon isotopic ratios around -30‰, while C_4 species like maize have carbon isotopic ratios around -12‰. Fallout of plant material produces soil organic matter in the root zone and in the surface, and a change between C_4 and C_3 species will change carbon isotopic ratios (Boutton 1996; Boutton et al. 1998; Webb et al. 2004). We need to be mindful that diagenesis will fractionate organic matter and elevate the carbon isotopic ratios by up to 3–4‰ in certain soils in the tropics, meaning that changes of 3–4‰ may result from fractionation and not vegetation change (Ågren et al. 1996; Boutton 1996; Ehleringer 1991; Liu et al. 1997; Martinelli et al. 1996).

SOIL AND PALEOECOLOGY RESULTS

El Palmar

Excavations

El Palmar was mainly a Middle and Late Preclassic city along the edge of the *cival* (Doyle 2013b) between El Zotz and Tikal (figure 1.4). Here we excavated three units and retrieved multiple cores from the *cival* sediments to study environmental resources and paleoecology (figure 7.1). Our three excavations studied soil sequences from the uplands into the Laguna El Palmar, which today is marsh wetland with variably flooded herbaceous plants.

The first soil profile was from a well-drained, upper footslope in a narrow valley near the main site of El Palmar, 4 m above the water table. Our excavation

TABLE 7.2. Elemental analyses (ppm)

Location	Depth	K	Ti	V	Mn	Fe²O₃	Fe	Co
	cm	ppm	ppm	ppm	ppm	ppm	ppm	ppm
El Zotz Aguada	5	3,035	2,915	12,254	49,100	—	24,059	31
2009	20–33	5,330	3,240	0	325	54,900	26,901	35
	50–55	6,230	2,190	0	604	38,200	18,718	24
	90–95	6,810	2,070	1	508	34,400	16,856	18
	105–115	6,830	1,120	12	203	16,100	7,889	9
	115–135	5,720	2,450	19	657	38,500	18,865	21
	155–160	5,730	2,440	19	395	37,800	18,522	19
	200	5,440	1,850	14	518	31,900	15,631	16
	230	5,200	1,910	0	510	30,800	15,092	17
El Diablo Aguada	10	1,470	3,450	29	1090	55,000	26,950	29
2009	25	2,990	3,060	35	940	45,800	22,442	23
	50	3,990	2,220	20	561	32,800	16,072	18
	70	4,860	2,140	26	532	28,900	14,161	15
	90	3,330	1,820	3	429	29,600	14,504	15
	105	4,920	1,430	0	425	19,900	9,751	12
El Palmar Ravine	5	5,470	689	0	470	11,500	5,635	7
2009	30	—	—	—	—	—	—	—
	50	6,130	581	0	247	9,060	4,439	5
	70	6,130	567	0	187	7,540	3,695	6
	100	6,260	636	0	253	9,420	4,616	6
El Zotz Aguada Edge	5–10	3,730	3,160	6	210	52,000	25,480	28
2009	30	5,010	3,390	0	188	54,400	26,656	29
	55–60	5,330	3,470	11	254	55,050	26,975	32
	60–65	5,230	1,820	0	94	27,100	13,279	17
	90–100	5,250	4,180	15	241	64,400	31,556	45
	110–120	4,985	506	0	97	7,910	3,876	4

exposed a 1.3 m soil profile of a Rendoll soil with a mollic A horizon that was thick (0.32 m), organic-rich (5–10 percent organic carbon), and very dark brown (10YR2/1) with well-developed granular structure, and clay texture. Like many young, regional soils formed in limestone, the A horizon was low in Fe, Ti, and Si and high in CaCO₃, N, Ca, K, Mg, and Ba (table 7.2). Below the topsoil

Ni ppm	Cu ppm	Zn ppm	As ppm	Rb ppm	Sr ppm	Zr ppm	Ag ppm	Cd ppm	Sn ppm	Ba ppm	Ce ppm	Pb ppm
51	90	126	4	68	39	102	0	0	0	0	667	12
50	66	108	0	73	71	111	20	0	0	0	287	20
43	53	75	4	42	104	78	18	13	3	222	93	16
36	54	70	4	33	123	82	22	4	7	303	83	0
24	43	53	4	16	197	42	0	3	0	0	0	12
42	54	77	4	41	123	84	0	0	0	0	96	13
39	55	75	2	39	129	101	0	5	12	0	165	17
37	49	67	3	31	149	76	22	6	0	576	0	16
32	45	66	5	28	159	76	0	5	3	214	83	12
30	34	67	7	11	100	109	0	0	0	204	197	15
27	37	64	8	10	105	93	0	0	0	0	314	12
28	39	57	5	7	128	81	20	8	0	213	73	12
23	37	54	7	8	132	74	0	7	0	219	213	0
24	40	54	4	7	134	73	19	7	0	0	45	17
26	46	52	3	7	153	52	20	7	0	267	17	13
25	47	57	2	13	99	35	0	3	0	216	0	0
—	—	—	—	—	—	—	—	—	—	—	—	—
21	48	52	5	11	101	29	0	0	0	251	0	0
19	42	47	6	8	95	26	0	0	0	229	0	0
23	43	56	0	12	108	31	0	8	0	230	0	16
42	64	89	4	80	61	116	0	0	0	0	250	12
43	61	87	2	80	82	122	21	2	0	0	227	17
45	67	91	2	78	70	119	19	0	0	92	232	18
29	50	64	3	37	108	70	0	0	5	0	0	0
58	75	110	4	109	34	163	0	0	0	0	597	16
22	43	44	3	7	159	25	11	7	0	0	0	0

were Bk and Ck horizons and increased higher-energy gravels and cobbles to 0.55 m. From 0.55 to 1.2 m is a boulder line, which was likely a Preclassic terrace, based on the AMS date from this zone (723–236 BC with 541–357 BC as 91.7 percent probable). This one date suggests a young soil that formed after hillslope instability from upslope Middle Preclassic urbanization. Carbon isotopic ratios from the soil profile increase from -28.7‰ at the top to -25.8‰ at ca. 1 m, which is in the range of natural fractionation. These findings parallel those from Early Classic levels at the El Diablo Aguada and the Middle Preclassic levels below *aguada* sediments at El Zotz, discussed below, and all in unlikely agricultural locations (Beach et al. 2011, 2018; Luzzadder-Beach et al. 2017).

At the toeslope next to the water's edge, we excavated an Aquoll soil with the water table at a depth of 1.5 m. The excavation exposed a soil profile with a mollic A horizon, that was thick (0.3 m), organic-rich (6 percent organic carbon), and very dark brown (10YR 2/1) with well-developed granular structure and clay texture. Below the A horizon are Cgk horizons intercalated with very dark gray (10YR 3/1), organic-rich (ca. 10 percent organic carbon) Ab horizons from 0.50 to 0.62 m and 0.83 to 0.90 m. The surface soil down to 1 m formed over 2,000 years, similar to the El Palmar upper footslope, had large quantities of $CaCO_3$, strong HCl reaction, and no argillic horizons. A paleosol with Ab and Cg horizons extended from 1 to 1.55 m and demonstrated a major change in texture, organic matter, and artifacts. In the paleosol Ab horizon, sand increased to 42 percent, organic carbon to 8–12 percent, visible microcharcoal increased, soil color became mostly black (N 2/0), and artifact quantities (lithics, burned ceramics, and obsidian) increased dramatically. The Cg horizon of the paleosol runs from 1.2 to 1.55 m and had gleyed colors of N 5/0 and 4/0 that become faintly laminated, lacustrine sediments below 1.3 m. Near the bottom, analogous to the upper footslope, was another boulder alignment at 1.55 m that may have functioned as a platform or berm at the ancient water's edge. Although we could not identify and date the well-worn artifacts, one AMS date of 88 BC–AD 124 (56 BC–AD 92 is 91 percent probable) at 1.18 m on charred organic material in the Ab horizon and above the rock alignment provides a Late Preclassic date, paralleling El Palmar's occupation (Doyle and Piedrasanta, chapter 2, this volume). Given the evidence for soil erosion and deposition in the upper footslope profile, the sedimentation here probably indicates the sediment cascade from "Maya Clays" and progradation into the *cival*.

Three more lines of evidence help explain this profile. First, the soil and sediment magnetic susceptibility increases by more than two-times in the Ab horizons. Second, the paleosol and modern topsoil have higher trace metals and Fe and Ti. Generally, more metals and increased magnetic susceptibility could indicate a more stable surface (more time for atmospheric deposition), and elevated magnetic susceptibility at the current and former top soil levels may indicate more burned, magnetized metals (Luzzadder-Beach and Beach 2008). Third, we have only spotty pollen evidence (figure 7.2) since this soil

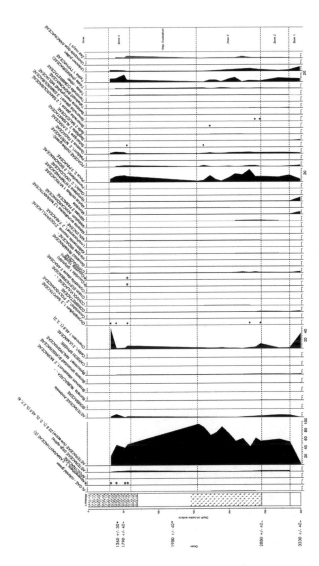

FIGURE 7.2. *Combined pollen profile from El Palmar cores (figure by T. Beach and C. Doyle).*

formed under redox conditions. We recovered the four pollen samples from 0.6, 0.98, 1.46, and 1.55 m in zones of potentially better preservation—that is, these were distinct and highly organic layers. Nonetheless, there were no economic species as well as few pollen (14–90 pollen) dominated by high-spine Asteraceae, more fern pollen, steady amounts of fine charcoal, and charred phytoliths, which may provide little information other than the possible indication of differential pollen preservation, pioneer species in succession, and consistent burning (Luzzadder-Beach et al. 2017).

Carbon isotopic ratio ($\delta^{13}C$) profiles can indicate variations in C_4 and C_3 plants and this profile shows both a significant increase in C_4 species (4.2‰) and variation from the surface to the Late Preclassic. The surface soil reflects the modern tropical forest with -27.7‰ but the paleosol in three assays from 1.1 to 1.34 m ranged from -23.4 to -23.8‰ and the zone through the thin and temporary buried A horizons fluctuated from -23.6 to -27.2‰. This anthropogenic paleosol and one soil layer at 72 cm reflect about 24 percent C_4 species in a region with few such species (Luzzadder-Beach et al. 2017).

El Palmar Core

We obtained the main core from the bottom of the excavation from 1.55 to 3 m from lake and wetland deposits. For comparison, we acquired another short 0.6 m surface core from the *cival* in 2 m of water 20 m east of the excavation. We stopped at 3 m in the core because we hit an artesian aquifer in a peat layer capped by clay under pressure too high to penetrate. We interpreted four stratigraphic zones in the core, and identified three food crops, including arrowroot (*Maranta arundinacea*), squash (*Cucurbita*), and maize (*Zea mays*). The quantity and range of maize pollen indicated both variable intensity and long duration, ranging up to 5.6 percent of total pollen and across a time span from the Late Archaic to the Late Classic from 2.8 to 0.39 m (figure 7.2).

Zone 1 ranges from the bottom at 3 m to about 2.8 m. At 2.95 m, an AMS measure of 1731–1511 BC (1693–1511 BC is 93.6 percent probable) dates generally to the Late Archaic to Early Preclassic, and this narrow zone of peat only extends to 2.8 m. The deepest pollen sample at 3 m had the highest biodiversity and lowest evidence for human alteration with the lowest charcoal counts and sedimentation rate, no *Zea mays*, very low Asteraceae (often disturbance taxa), the highest percentage (9.4) of *Nymphaeae* (waterlily, indicative of a steady water level), and at least 11 different taxa of arboreal pollen. The high frequency (34.8 percent) of cheno-am pollen, which, together with the charcoal, could be evidence of disturbance by humans in Zone 1, still evidence the lowest impacts until the Postclassic.

The fibrous peat layer from 3 to 2.8 m transitions to lacustrine sediments and higher human disturbance below 2.8 m. We interpret that Zone 2 starts below 2.8 m, and between the 3 m date (1731–1511 BC, with 1693–1511 BC as 93.6 percent probable) and up to 2.45 m where an AMS measure of 405–208 BC dates to the early part of the Late Preclassic. The 2.8 m sample (just 0.2 m below the Late Archaic date) has four lines of evidence for human disturbance: charcoal

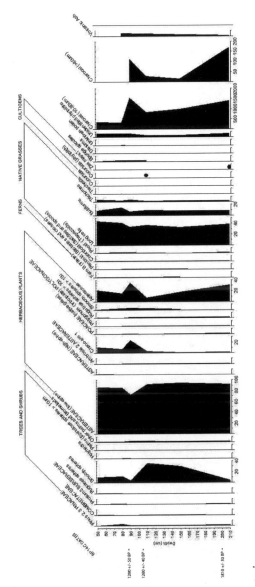

FIGURE 7.3. *Pollen and phytolith data from the El Zotz Aguada (figure by T. Beach and C. Doyle).*

rises (small charcoal increases by 20 times to ca. 300,000, and large charcoal increases to more than 22,000), the disturbance-related species rise (low-spine Asteraceae to 53.5 percent and *Ambrosia* [ragweed] pollen from 0.4 to 5.1 percent of the pollen), and *Zea mays* rises to 0.8–1.4 percent through this zone. For contexts, El Palmar charcoal counts from the Preclassic are one to two orders of magnitude above those from the urban El Zotz Aguada during its highest activity in the Classic period (figure 7.3). Also, *Ambrosia* species (*A. hispida* and *A. peruviana*) from Belize have medicinal values (Balick et al. 2000). Based on the decline of waterlily and pulses in *Typha* (cattails), water levels were probably fluctuating, with clay deposition and nutrients flushed from a rising but still low erosion rate.

The highest human impacts occurred in Zone 3 during the Late Preclassic between 2.45 and 1 m from the 405–208 BC date at 2.45 m to the 88 BC–AD 124 (56 BC–AD 92 is 91 percent probable) date at 1.18 m in the paleosol, which ranges from 1.55 to 1 m (figure 7.2). This zone bridges the Late Preclassic, a key era of building for El Palmar and of climatic variation based on two distant but well-constrained climate records (Beach 2016). The core record reflected city growth because of peak amounts of both small, 80μ or smaller (690,962 counts per sample), and large (131,045 counts per sample) charcoal, increased sedimentation ("Maya Clay" deposition rose by nearly two orders of magnitude), the second-highest levels of *Zea mays* (up to 4.4 percent of all pollen), and the presence of the important cultigen arrowroot (*Maranta arundinacea*). There are also several other fruit and medicinal taxa (Luzzadder-Beach et al. 2017). The Late Preclassic experienced both severe droughts and wet periods that may have contributed to the pulses of erosion, high charcoal from fires, and fluxes of forest taxa.

The toeslope excavation is the upper 1.55 m of this sequence with an anthropogenic paleosol between 1.55 and 1 m in slope and paludal deposition. Pollen preservation was limited in this zone of soil horizons, so we base zone 4 on a 0.6 m core 20 m offshore at a water depth of 2 m. Two AMS dates from this core on discrete, thin peat layers at 0.4 m and 0.55 m were AD 614–763 (AD 614–694 is 92.2 percent probable) dating to the Late Classic, and AD 127–344 from the Late Preclassic to Early Classic transition, respectively. This sequence may cover most of the sequence lost in the terrestrial soil formation because the core's lower date is only slightly later than the 88 BC–AD 124 (56 BC–AD 92 is 91 percent probable) date at 1.18 m in the paleosol (figure 7.2).

In this core at 0.56 m just above the Late Preclassic to Early Classic date is the highest *Zea* pollen level (5.6 percent) as well as other disturbance and economic indicators like *Curcubita* pollen and phyoliths. The high *Zea* pollen continues upward to 2.8 percent at 0.39 m near the Late Classic date. This Late Classic section displays much evidence for economic and disturbance species with the high frequency of low-spine Asteraceae (47.4 percent), cattail (9 percent), and small and large charcoal counts. The uppermost sample at 0.3 m continues to have these disturbance or crop elements such as cheno-am pollen, *Sapotacea*, and high particulate charcoal. Other examples of disturbance taxa decline such as ferns and pine, the latter possibly linked with reforestation that blocked the wafting of distant pine pollen. Moreover, the upper core has increased tree and aquatic plant pollen, and sedimentation declined well below Late Archaic and Late Preclassic rates. These lines of evidence suggest a moderate disturbance despite food and medicinal crop cultivation and burning but higher biodiversity and lower erosion. The El Palmar area, between Tikal and El Zotz, may have become some kind of forest garden even as El Palmar's urban entity had declined (Doyle 2013b; Román et al., chapter 3, this volume).

El Zotz

Excavations

The El Zotz Aguada lies in a cluster of depressions that reach down toward the Buenavista Valley. The main *aguada* is circular with an area of ca. 3 ha and its current floor lies at about 230.5 masl. Our El Zotz excavations provide an overlap with the upper El Palmar record because the El Zotz dates range from the oldest reliable AMS date of AD 128–322 (AD 128–258 is 86.6 percent probable) at 2.1 m to AD 651–869 (AD 651–779 is 83.1 percent probable) at 1.05 m below the surface. We excavated five units from the west side to near the center of the *aguada* to understand the stratigraphy and paleoecology of the sediments. El Zotz units EZ 13A-5, -2, and -3 present a useful record of environmental change in their sediments deposited from the surrounding city over 1,700 years and thus reflect some combination of the soils and land uses of this ancient city (figure 7.3).

The first unit, EZ 13A-2, presents a 2.5 m profile depth with much greater levels of metals (Ti, Fe, Zn, and others) and lower amounts of K than the El Palmar ravine soil (table 7.2). The carbon isotopic ratios from unit EZ 13A-2 rise from -29.1‰ near the surface to -25.4‰ in Late Classic–dated floor sediments and continue near this level (-25.2‰) to just below the Early Classic floor at 2.5 m depth (for graphs see Luzzadder-Beach et al. 2017). Carbon isotopic ratios decline marginally to -26.2‰ from the lower Early Classic floor up to the Late Classic floor. Another 3.6 m deep excavation (EZ13A-3) revealed more change and higher carbon isotopic ratios, increasing near the top from -26.92 to -21.03‰, staying elevated to -23.21‰ at the Late Classic floor and even more so at -22.88‰ just above the Early Classic floor. Based on these measures, the maximum percentage of soil humin from C_4 vegetation, like maize, would be 40 percent but this dropped to as little as 5 percent between floors. Under the lowest floor in unit EZ 13A-3, as much as 22 percent of soil humin derived from C_4 plants, which could mean maize agriculture occurred around or even in the El Zotz Aguada before it became a reservoir.

A third unit in the berm around the *aguada* had very similar elemental chemistry as the *aguada* unit, with high Fe, Ti, and Zn (table 7.2). The carbon isotopic ratio values were also similar but with a significant rise from -30‰ to −22.92‰ down the profile (Luzzadder-Beach et al. 2017). These numbers indicate that up to 27 percent of soil humin derived from C_4 plants.

Overall, the carbon isotopic evidence in dated sequences through the Late Preclassic to present in and around the El Zotz Aguada indicates that most soil humin came from forest or C_3 plants, (Luzzadder-Beach et al. 2017). Some of the highest C_4 vegetation signatures came from near the lowest floor in the Early Classic, which coincides with the *Zea* maize pollen, and in the Late Classic levels (figure 7.3). The Late Classic levels with their elevated C_4 vegetation signatures did not produce maize pollen but did produce *Cucurbita* pollen and phytoliths, which are not C_4 plants but indicate some agriculture even at the height of the upslope city of El Zotz. These zones of increased C_4 vegetation signatures may also correspond to runoff from high maize use and processing near the *aguada*.

Dam and Aguada Water Quantity

We noticed from field survey and AIRSAR remote sensing imagery (Garrison, Chapman, et al. 2011) that the El Zotz Aguada's surrounding ridges met at a natural drainage point where this karst sink would normally drain, possibly as an uvala, an elongate karst depression. The drainage point, however, appeared to have an unnaturally symmetrical berm in the ideal place for a dam, a canyon outlet. We tested this dam hypothesis in May 2016 by placing an excavation unit in the middle of the feature between the two ridges (figure 7.4). We excavated the unit down to 3.5 m below the surface, uncovering the unmistakable stratigraphy of an earthen dam (figure 7.5). The top 0.5 m of the excavation revealed a typical natural soil sequence of 0.2–0.25 m of A horizon of very dark brown clay, lying over gray brown clay down to 0.4–0.5 m. The C1 horizon below this from 0.5 to 1 m was a mélange of brown, pale, and very dark brown clays, which is a common subsoil in the region caused by bio- and argilliturbation (i.e., distortion of horizontal layers by burrowing organisms, roots, and clay expansion and contraction in this wet and dry climate). From 1 to 3.4 m, the strata comprised a series of layers of very dark brown clay, gray clay, and pale clay and *sascab* (weathered limestone), all of which occur in typical *bajo* soil sequences, but not in repeated layers over nearly 2.5 m, as is the case

El Zotz Reservoir and Dam

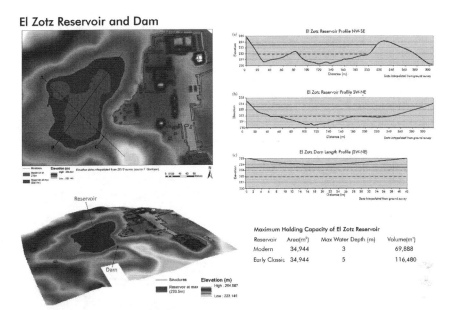

FIGURE 7.4. *El Zotz Aguada (reservoir) and dam (figure by C. Doyle and T. Beach).*

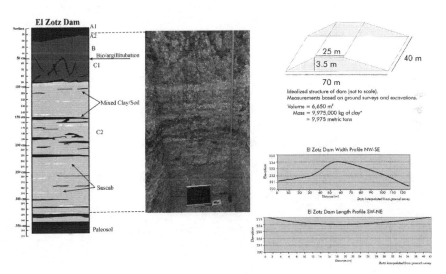

FIGURE 7.5. *El Zotz dam (figure by C. Doyle and T. Beach).*

here. We followed these repeating layers down to a buried topsoil, or paleosol, of black clay and lighter subsoil from 3.4 to 4 m. These strata unambiguously represent a ca. 3.5-m-high dam today, based on the piled layers of clay and *sascab*, and the dam was likely higher at initial construction because of compaction. This excavation indicated the dam would have increased the height of the reservoir by ca. 4 m, given the likely compaction from the time of building. The dam is clearly ancient, given that the El Zotz site is ancient and the dam's surface had a mature soil that took centuries to form. The earliest sediment and floor in the reservoir date to the Early Classic period, but the dam could date later in the city's occupation. The lack of any trace of soil development in the dam fill between the top soil and paleosol indicates a single period of dam construction.

We calculated the size of the dam as the volume of a three-dimensional trapezoid. Our metrics for the calculations came from ground surveys in 2013 and the excavation of the dam in May 2016. The dam's dimensions included a height of 3.5 m based on the excavation, while the topographic surveys suggest a trapezoid with a top width of 25 m and a bottom width of 70 m, and a length of 40 m (figure 7.5). Based on these measurements, the dam at El Zotz has a volume of 6,650 m³. Assuming a bulk density of the packed clay at 1.5 g cm³⁻¹ produces a dam mass of 9,975 metric tonnes (9,975,000 kg). We also compared the ground survey to a 5-m resolution AIRSAR DEM to verify the size of the ancient dam. Although the dimensions of the reservoir were similar between the two data sets, a cross-section of the dam in the AIRSAR data suggests that the bottom of the trapezoid may have been closer to 40 m, rather than 70 m, although the top and lengths were the same. A higher-resolution elevation survey across the entire area will of course improve all estimates. Regardless, these estimates suggest a very large construction effort to manage the natural drainage of the *aguada*. In comparison, the volume of the El Zotz dam is about half of the Palace Dam at Tikal, the largest hydraulic architectural feature known in the Maya area, which is about 14,000 m³ (Scarborough et al. 2012).

Beach et al. (2015) estimated the El Zotz Aguada's reservoir ranged from its present base at ca. 230.5 masl to ca. 234.5 masl, its lowest divide in the southeast, the formerly hypothesized ancient dam discussed above. Based on the Brewer equation with a 4 m maximum depth, 280 m length, and 200 m width, the reservoir could hold 87,920 m³ (87,920,000 liters and 23,226,006.84 gallons). If we use the standard water use per person per day of ca. 2–5 liters (Akpinar-Ferrand et al. 2012; Brewer 2007; McAnany 1990:269), then the full reservoir today could provide enough drinking water for 48,000 to 120,000 people per year. These numbers do not include the balance between precipitation and evaporation, trap efficiency, or water-quality considerations. These estimates are well above the site's estimated populations throughout its period of use. Indeed, the Early Classic's well-made floor lies another 2 m below the present floor, and thus the Early Classic reservoir would have had an even greater storage capacity.

A reanalysis of the topographic data along with the dam excavation, however, reveals that these calculations may overestimate the maximum capacity of the reservoir. A transect across the top of the dam indicates that the lowest part is closer to 234 masl (figure 7.4), though we cannot be sure how much settling occurred in these mounded sediments. Assuming this 234 masl estimate, we recalculated the modern and Early Classic capacity of the dam based on an upper limit of 233.5 masl (3 m of water, which is 1 m below the previous estimates. We used ArcScene 10.2 to calculate the volume of the modern *aguada* from 230.5 to 233.5 masl, resulting in a modern capacity of 50,106 m³ (50,106,000 liters; 13,236,605 gallons).

Another iteration of the calculation assumed the same maximum height of 233.5 masl and then calculated the surface area of the maximum fill in ArcGIS 10.2. We used this surface area at the maximum capacity of the reservoir to estimate what the capacity would have been during the Early Classic, using a modified half ellipsoid-volume formula:

Volume = $(2/3)^*A^*H$

where A = the surface area of the filled reservoir and H = the water depth.

We chose this formula based on the shape and topography of the reservoir, along with the fact that the reservoir's floor was 2 m deeper when built in the Early Classic. Together these produce an ellipsoid shape rather than a cone, and thus we used the half ellipsoid volume formula:

Volume = $(2/3)^*\pi^*a^*b^*c$

where a = half the width of the ellipse, b = half the length of the ellipse, and c = half the height of the ellipsoid.

Since π^*a^*b is the area of the centroid ellipse, the area of the reservoir calculated in ArcGIS replaced this term for the final calculations. The floor of the reservoir was 2 m below the modern surface, and so the filled reservoir height in the Early Classic would have been 5 m of water. Using these parameters with the modified ellipsoid formula, we calculated the Early Classic reservoir capacity to be 116,480 m³ (116,480,000 liters; 30,770,761 gallons).

Based on the new calculations, the reservoir had a total modern volume of 50,106 m³ to 116,480 m³. This range of present to Early Classic volumes of water gives a range of ca. 50–116 million liters of water, enough drinking water for ca. 27,000–64,000 people per year, based on the upper range consumption of 5 liters per person per day. Though our present estimate is lower and does not include precipitation and evaporation, trap efficiency, or water-quality considerations, the reservoir was still very large and could have supported a larger population than the highest estimate for the site. The reservoir was also large compared to others in Maya region; for example, Scarborough et al. (2012) estimated the Palace Reservoir, the largest reservoir at Tikal, to hold a water volume of 74,631 m³. The Palace Reservoir, however, is one of several at Tikal that create greater urban water capacity and distribution.

Paleoecology Record

For the deepest, most central unit (EZ 13A-2) in the El Zotz reservoir we discerned four zones based on a similar series of environmental proxy data as for El Palmar. *Zea mays* occurred only in Zone 1 from the Late Preclassic to Early Classic transition, which may indicate that later urbanization pushed out colonial maize agriculture. In the Early to Late Classic zones above Zone 1, *Cucurbita* was the only clear food taxon. By contrast with El Palmar's record, where no *Protium* (copal) occurred, evidence of this plant appears throughout the El Zotz samples and was the second-most abundant tree taxon after *Pinus* (figure 7.3). We hypothesize the high copal-pollen counts as the result of cultivation, given copal's well-known Maya uses, especially as a source of incense for rituals. High amounts of pine pollen often simply indicate clearing because the far-flying and copiously produced pollen can waft great distances if unimpeded, but there are also sources of pine around 30 km from El Zotz (Beach et al. 2015).

The sediment below the Early Classic floor had a faintly melanized, buried top soil, slightly oxidized colors, and lenticular structured clays with intermittent deposits of gravels. We did not process pollen from these layers because of the oxidized colors. Although evidence for wetland conditions occurs down to 3.6 m in high organic-carbon contents, the floor at ca. 2.2 m evidently changed this environment from a more oxidizing to a more reducing one in the Early Classic, based on the transition from oxidizing to reducing colors above the floor.

Zone 1 starts just above the *aguada's* Early Classic floor at 2.1 m and ranges up to the next pollen sample at 1.5 m. The AMS date of AD 128–322 (AD 128–258 is 86.6 percent probable) just above the floor, Sierra Red ceramics on the floor, and a clear Early Classic jar within the floor date the floor to the Early Classic period. One AMS date of 747–389 BC (556–389 BC is 81.1 percent probable) on charcoal at 2.5 m near the floor is out of line with the other lines of evidence; perhaps this charcoal washed in from excavated sediment used in reservoir construction.

The following lines of evidence for human disturbance peaked at the 2.1 m level. Carbon isotopic ratios were at their farthest from tropical forest, with levels of $\delta^{13}C$ at -22.88‰ and -25.2‰ in EZ 13A-3 and EZ 13A-2, respectively, compared with about −29‰ in tropical forests and the surface average for this region. The small particulate charcoal fractions (< 80 μm) were four times above the levels in the top 0.7 m and peaked for large charcoal (> 80 μm), revealing elevated local and regional fire occurrence. Larger-sized soil particles also increased; sand rose from 0 percent (i.e., ca. 100 percent clay) to 33 percent through this zone, indicating higher energy of deposition. Sand could imply intense runoff or be a clue for water filtration and thus urban hygiene (Scarborough et al. 2012). Lastly, pollen and phytoliths indicate large departures from the tropical forest that occupies the area today. Arboreal species were a small fraction (6.8 percent of phytoliths), while herbaceous taxa like Asteraceae (the sunflower family) and Poaceaea (grasses) dominate. This zone also has the highest amount of economic taxa, including *Zea* and *Protium* (copal) pollen (used for medicine and rituals; Balick et al. 2000) and disturbance indicators such as *Pinus* and volcanic ash.

Zone 2 runs from 1.5 to 1.05 m and dates to the Late Classic, given the AD 651–869 (AD 651–779 is 83.1 percent probable) AMS date at 1.05 m. The proxies for human disturbance are variable through this zone. Although small and large charcoal decline by 30–90 percent, the decrease in $\delta^{13}C$ is minute and high-energy particles range from 5 to 23 percent. Copal and other anthropogenic indicators such as charred phytoliths continue and even increase. One *Cucurbita* (squash) pollen grain occurred at 1.1 m.

We interpret zone 3 based on the upper, Late Classic floor, where two AMS dates—AD 651–869 (AD 651–779 is 83.1 percent probable) at 1.05 m and AD 656–864 (AD 656–778 is 87.4 percent probable) at 0.87 m—bracket the floor and human disturbance indicators peaked again. Most of the phytoliths are native grasses and most of the pollen are Asteraceae and Amarathaceae—disturbance taxa, though they can also be food and medicinal types. The increase in *Pinus* as the most abundant arboreal pollen and relatively high levels of regional and *in situ* charcoal and charred phytoliths also indicate high human disturbance, through no high-energy sand occurs above 1.1 m. Economic pollen include only copal, the possible food-producing or disturbance taxa of cheno-ams, which comprise ~23 percent of the pollen, and three *Cucurbita* phytoliths. Five volcanic ash shards also occur at this level, and like the pine pollen may be indicative of deforestation, because they increase when a watershed is deforested and aerosols can move more freely through landscapes to fall into bodies of water.

Although the highest date in the profile is at 0.9 m, disturbance proxies continue above this to 0.5 m. Indeed, $\delta^{13}C$ reaches its highest level and copal and Asteraceae are still present, but charcoal particles have declined by 80 percent with none larger than 80 µm. This zone probably represents the Terminal to Postclassic, and the upper 0.5 m shows steep decreases to tropical forest levels of $\delta^{13}C$ by 5.89 ppt and 4.3 ppt in the two units.

SOIL EXCAVATIONS NEAR EL DIABLO AND BEJUCAL

Further excavations into the *aguada* at El Diablo and an *aguada* (Los Bocutes Aguada) and a *cival* near Bejucal provide preliminary and regional comparisons (Beach et al. 2015; Luzzadder-Beach et al. 2017). We made one excavation into the margin and another into the center of the small *aguada* at El Diablo. Two lines of evidence indicated quarrying before the *aguada* began to fill: both units had evidence of soil truncation, since they had no buried soil sequence evident in granular structure and increased organic matter, and the margin unit had an abrupt, straight step down by over 1 m in the soft limestone. Moreover, magnetic susceptibility and $\delta^{13}C$ profiles were stable vertically, again contrary to the presence of buried soils. The elemental chemistry data also indicate no evidence of a major horizon change and similar concentrations as El Zotz except more elevated readings in Fe, Mn, and V (table 7.2). In line with the El Diablo Group, all the identifiable artifacts were Early Classic, and two AMS dates from the central unit of the *aguada* gave evidence of rapid Early Classic sedimentation. One Early Classic AMS date at 1.3 m (AD 128–381) in a zone with no evidence for soil formation is roughly the same as a date from 0.95 m (AD 252–530 with AD 242–430 as 90.7 percent probable). Accordingly, at least one-quarter of the soil profile accumulated quickly, probably during and directly after the short site occupation in the Early Classic, thus providing the only evidence of erosion and deposition during Early Classic occupation. The site could have used such a water supply as this *aguada* represents, given its steepness and distance to alternative water sources. Though we found no stone-dressed floor, as at epicentral El Zotz, the clayey *sascab* at the bottom would have impeded percolation and helped water retention. The lowest levels continued to produce artifacts at 1.6 m within layers of indurated *sascab* or plaster.

Two more excavations at the Bejucal Cival and the Los Bocutes Aguada near Bejucal contributed inconclusive evidence for ancient Maya impacts. The Bejucal Cival's Vertisol soil profile demonstrated a maximum carbon isotopic ratio $\delta^{13}C$ of -22.76‰. This would indicate that 27.2 percent of the soil humin derived from C_4 vegetation, which produces a small $\delta^{13}C$ increase in the soil profile of 2‰. This part of the *cival* was unpromising for paleoecological reconstruction because of the strong argilloturbation evident in its slickensides, diagonal horizons, and redox characteristics evident in its orange mottling down to 1.6 m.

The Los Bocutes Aguada provided a more intriguing sediment record with its 2.34 m of sediment deposited above a firm rock surface. The sediment characteristics and the depth of burial were tantalizingly similar to the sequence at the El Zotz Aguada, perhaps including its well-built floor. The Aquoll soil had a dark (10YR 2/1), deep (c. 0.55 m) A horizon that transitioned downward to a very dark gray (7.5YR 3/1) Cg horizon with high organic matter (greater than 6 percent organic carbon down to 2.25 m). The upper 1.65 m of clay lay above 60 cm of laminated clayey sands and silts with visible organics. This sediment sequence has colors and stratigraphy similar to the Early Classic sediments that bury the El Zotz Aguada's floor. But unlike at El Zotz, the $\delta^{13}C$ profile was nearly vertical over its deep profile, ranging up to −22.05‰, which would point to a C_4 vegetation percentage of 28.4 percent. Vigorous bioturbation near the surface may have mixed the profile and subsumed the tropical forest C_3 impacts on soil humin. All of these lines of evidence suggest the value of more study.

DISCUSSION AND CONCLUSIONS

This chapter concludes with five main themes about the environmental findings across the region, the discovery of a major ancient dam at El Zotz, and new calculations for the water storage behind the dam at the El Zotz Aguada. One of the main next steps to understanding the environmental history of the Maya will be to bring enough ecological, climatological, and reservoir studies together to more definitively answer major questions of Maya environmental interactions, such as whether historical trends like reservoir construction and soil erosion coincide with the climatic changes.

First, the water-quality evidence indicates that the natural sources of surface water (*civales*), when seasonally full, were of moderately good quality, but as evaporation reduces the quantity and concentrated ionic content, water would have been less potable later in the dry season. The spring water seeping into the El Palmar Cival was even less potable. Having a large and deep reservoir, such as the El Zotz or El Palmar Aguadas, collecting rainwater runoff is enormously important for a fresh, potable water source that would span the dry season. Perhaps the El Zotz Aguada appears oversized for its projected population for this very reason. A deeper pool of rainwater runoff would not be as affected by evaporation-driven mineral concentration as would a shallower natural source influenced by the local mineral-rich springs elsewhere, such as the El Palmar Cival. The water-quality samples from the El Palmar Aguada, taken late in the dry season of 2009, support this hypothesis with lower conductivity, lower total dissolved solids, and lower calcium, for example, than either the spring or the *cival* in the vicinity. This is not a perfect correlation, because the Aguada Pucte and La Cuernavilla Cival both fall in between these values of other waters of the region, but it is worth exploring with future water-quality studies of *aguadas*, springs, and *civales* of the region.

Second, the environmental history of El Palmar comes from two excavations and two cores into the El Palmar Cival. These provide a 3,600-year record based on six AMS dates, five on a 3 m sequence and one on a soil profile. Overall, pollen from the cores represented three well-known crops—squash (*Cucurbita*), arrowroot (*Maranta arundinacea*), and maize (*Zea mays*)—as well as a number of fruit trees. The lowest levels at a depth of 3 m (the Archaic or Early Preclassic) provide insight into the least human-altered part of the record, when tree diversity was at its highest and cultigens, sedimentation, and charcoal were at their lowest. By 2.8 m, probably still at least as old as the Early Preclassic, multiple lines of human impacts are evident with rising charcoal, cultigens like *Zea mays*, sedimentation, and disturbance taxa. These all continued or expanded through the Preclassic, with *Zea mays* rising from 0.8 to 4.4 percent into the Late Preclassic during the adjacent city of El Palmar's florescence and then peaking during the Late Classic at 5.6 percent, paradoxically when there is little evidence for occupation at El Palmar. Sedimentation followed a similar pattern, but declined in the Classic period even as fruit tree and maize pollen rose and charcoal remained high. The decline in erosion (sedimentation) with continued evidence for agriculture (maize and charcoal) is similar to the finding for Lake Salpeten (Anselmetti et al. 2007), but unlike at Salpeten, settlement had declined in Late Classic El Palmar. The evidence for increased biodiversity of crops and forests and more charcoal but declining sedimentation suggests elements of a sustainable, polycultural forest garden in this zone between El Zotz and Tikal's wall.

Third, the El Zotz Aguada paleoecology record derives from deep excavations, pollen, phytoliths, geochemistry, and charcoal. The first evidence for this sequence is the well-constructed Early Classic floor at 2.2 m depth that changed the *aguada* to a water-storing site. The ecological proxy evidence above the floor indicates a dynamic, humanized landscape. The disturbance taxon Asteraceae dominates throughout, and agricultural evidence is highest at the lowest level near the Early Classic floor with *Zea mays*, copal, and other disturbance pollen and charcoal at high levels. These decline upward to another floor, Late Classic, when copal, squash, pine, palms, herbs, and charcoal peak again before the record ends. The pollen record has steady copal whereas there was none at El Palmar; the other dominant tree pollen at El Zotz was pine, which wafts in from around 30 km. Copal may signal some urban, ritual importance as an incense source or perhaps for use as torchwood.

Fourth, our excavation of May 2016 into the hypothesized dam at the El Zotz Aguada produced clear evidence of a major dam about 3.5 m high, 25–70 m wide, and 40 m long. Volumetrically the dam holds nearly 7,000 m³ and a mass of nearly 10,000 metric tonnes, which is about one-half the largest known Maya dam at Tikal, 20 km east of El Zotz. We do not know the timing of dam construction. It may coincide with the *aguada*'s Early Classic floor and early occupation of the city but it could have been a later add on. This timing is important to compare coincidences of dam construction and drought. If the El Zotz Maya built the dam in the Early Classic or Terminal Classic, those times would coincide with evidence for the end of two deep, severe droughts or the midst of a long drought in multiple Maya records (Luzzadder-Beach et al. 2017).

Fifth, the new evidence for water storage based on the more accurate upper level of the newly discovered dam, produced a maximum depth of 3 m of water and total modern capacity of 50,106 m³. Before the reservoir became aggraded by 2 m of eroded sediment, the reservoir had a total capacity of 116,480 m³, meaning the Early Classic reservoir had more than twice the capacity as today's reservoir and 1.56 times more water storage than Tikal's Palace reservoir, the reservoir with the largest known Maya dam. The range of 50,106–116,480 m³ based on the present and Early Classic volumes of water gives a range of ca. 50–116 million liters of water, enough drinking water for ca. 27,000–64,000 people per year based on 5 liters per person per day consumption. The water-quantity evidence demonstrates the El Zotz Aguada would have provided enough water for a much larger population at even the highest population estimate; by the Postclassic two more meters of sediment lined its floor, yet the reservoir still had high capacity. This would have made persistence through droughts in the Late Classic and Postclassic possible, although, as always, occupants would have needed to maintain quality in an increasingly shallow reservoir.

These conclusions answer some questions such as paleoecological trends, crop types, the discovery of a major dam, water quality, and reservoir water capacities. None of these findings is new for the Peten or the Maya Lowlands. They show the ancient Maya burned and farmed this landscape and made a large investment in water management by building a large dam with a surrounding berm and well-made floor for their large reservoir, which survives to the present as testament to Maya landesque capital. But the research leads to many new questions about Maya adaptation to their environment. One important question to answer will be the presence of terraces or other evidence of farming systems as further evidence of landesque capital. Thus far, we have found little evidence for agricultural terracing in the central Peten but terraces are showing up in more places with the advent of lidar (Beach et al. 2015). Other questions include: Are there indeed holding tanks for water filtration in the El Zotz Aguada? Did the other *aguadas* such as Los Bocutes near Bejucal have engineered floors and dams and water-quality elements? And, can we find additional paleoecological evidence from speleothems in the El Zotz cave and additional cores? This last point underscores the need for more finely resolved climate records near the Maya heartland. Thus far, the best climate records are from southern Belize and northern Yucatan in areas that either have more rainfall or are nearer the freshwater table and thus are less sensitive to droughts (Luzzadder-Beach et al. 2017). Thus the region around El Zotz, with a severe dry season and far from groundwater, is ripe for a finely resolved climate record in the the heart of the Maya Lowlands, in the midst of a growing corpus of reservoir records that could help us test ancient Maya interactions with drought.

8

As at most Lowland Maya sites, the majority of cultural material recovered from excavations at El Zotz and Bejucal by the Proyecto Arqueológico El Zotz (PAEZ) between 2008 and 2011 consists of ceramic vessels and potsherds. This chapter presents a synthesis of the changes in ceramics in the El Zotz region from the Middle Preclassic (~800–300 BC) to the Early Postclassic period (AD 1000–1300). We seek to discern occupational patterns through time and space at El Zotz based on ceramic data collected from seven distinct architectural groups at the site: El Diablo, El Tejón, the Acropolis, the Northwest Courtyard, Las Palmitas, La Tortuga, and the South Group (see Doyle and Piedrasanta, chapter 2, this volume, for ceramics from the site of El Palmar).

The sequential ceramic complexes (Walker 2009) proposed for El Zotz (table 8.1) follow those established for Uaxactun by Robert Smith and James Gifford (1966) and for Tikal by T. Patrick Culbert (1993). Early Middle Preclassic (pre-Mamon or Eb phase at Tikal) ceramics were found in early deposits at El Palmar (Doyle and Piedrasanta 2012:333) but have not been encountered so far at El Zotz. The Ik, Imix, and Eznab phases at Tikal (Tepeu 1, 2, and 3 at Uaxactun) find counterparts in the Mo', Caal, and Cucul phases at El Zotz. Distinct subphases equivalent to Manik/Tzakol 1, 2, and 3 have yet to be defined for the Early Classic Saquij phase at El Zotz, which is thus temporarily divided into an early and a late

Understanding Social, Economic, and Political Change

The Ceramics of El Zotz

Ewa Czapiewska-Halliday, Nicholas P. Carter, Melanie J. Kingsley, Sarah Newman, and Alyce de Carteret

DOI: 10.5876/9781607327646.c008

TABLE 8.1. Ceramic phases at El Zotz, Tikal, and Uaxactun

Approximate dates	Period	El Zotz (provisional)	Tikal	Uaxactun
AD 1000–1300	Early Postclassic	Choc		
			Caban	
AD 850–1000	Terminal Classic	Cucul		
			Eznab	Tepeu 3
AD 700–850	Late Classic	Caal	Imix	Tepeu 2
AD 550–700		Mo'	Ik	Tepeu 1
AD 300–550	Early Classic	Saquij (late)	Manik 3	Tzakol 3
		Saquij (early)	Manik 2	Tzakol 2
AD 200–300		Pop	Manik 1	Tzakol 1
			Cimi	
300 BC–AD 200	Late Preclassic	Chub	Cauac	Chicanel
			Chuen	
600–300 BC		Che		Mamom
	Middle Preclassic		Tzec	
800–600 BC		Unnamed Eb-like complex	Eb	

For Tikal periodization, see Culbert (1993); for Uaxactun, see Smith and Gifford (1966); for El Zotz, see Walker (2009) and Czapiewska (2012).

facet. The great majority of El Zotz's Classic-period ceramics belong to the Peten Gloss and Uaxactun Unslipped wares. In the Early Postclassic period, Monticulo Unslipped, Vitzil Orange-Red, and Volador Dull Slipped wares predominate, equivalent to the Aura complex in the Peten Lakes region (Rice 1987b).

METHOD

All ceramics in the collection were classified according to the type-variety system, applied by Robert Smith, Gordon Willey, and James Gifford (Smith, Willey, and Gifford 1960) to Maya data and widely used to establish occupational chronologies and for intersite comparative studies (e.g., Adams 1971; Ball 1977; Foias 1996; Forsyth 1989; Gifford 1975; Holley 1983; Laporte 2007; López Varela 1989; Sabloff 1975; Smith 1955).

The present study prioritizes modes of form and decoration. Formal modes include vessel types, the shape of vessels of a single type, the forms of rims and lips, and orifice diameter (after Sabloff 1975:22–25). Vessel forms help to suggest their function, in turn hinting at activities possibly carried out in different sectors of the site. Decorative modes considered here include decorative techniques—painting, stamping, incising, and so on—and the structures and varieties of the resulting motifs. As Feinman et al. (1981:872) point out, vessels with complex decorative modes required more labor time to produce than did simpler, more utilitarian ceramics, and were likely more expensive and difficult to obtain. Elsewhere, the abundance or paucity of such modes in physically discrete spaces may reflect the functions of those spaces or the social status of the individuals who used them (Masson 2001:161; P. Rice et al. 1981:219). To explore these issues, spatial and temporal distributions of formal and decorative modes were tracked at El Zotz in order to identify patterns of change over time and to infer the possible functions and relative socioeconomic statuses of different sectors of the site.

THE PRECLASSIC PERIOD: CHE AND CHUB PHASES

Except at El Palmar (see Doyle and Piedrasanta, chapter 2, this volume), ceramics from the Che phase were found in limited numbers. There were 118 Che sherds recovered from the South Group at El Zotz, and no other material from this period was confirmed for the other complexes. Late Preclassic material (Chub phase) occurred more abundantly across a variety of sectors, including El Diablo, El Tejón, the Acropolis, and the South Group (table 8.2). While the 875 mostly Chub-phase sherds from the South Group show a concrete occupational and construction phase in this area, including the construction of the South Group Platform and its main quadrangular plaza group, those found at El Diablo, El Tejón, and the Acropolis of El Zotz come from mixed contexts that also include Saquij-phase sherds. This suggests the presence of just a few small residential groups in those parts of the site, rather than substantial occupation.

Occupation during the Late Preclassic period concentrated at the neighboring site of El Palmar (see Doyle and Piedrasanta, chapter 2, this volume), with the start of a sizeable community in the South Group of El Zotz and limited settlement outside of those two centers. The presence of Preclassic ceramics beneath the Saquij constructions of Str. L7-6 (Meléndez and Houston 2008) might suggest the start of monumental construction in what would become the Acropolis of El Zotz. Yet, as Doyle and Piedrasanta (this volume) point out, the stark contrast in architectural practices between the large civic center

TABLE 8.2. Che- and Chub-phase ceramics at El Zotz

Type: Variety	South Group	El Diablo	El Tejón	Acropolis
CHE PHASE				
CHUNHINTA GROUP				
Black-on-red Bichrome	2			
Centenario Fluted	4			
Chunhinta Black	51			
Deprecio Incised	3			
JOVENTUD GROUP				
Desvario Chamfered	1			
Guitara Incised	6			
Joventud Red	42			
PITAL GROUP				
Muxanal Red-on-cream	1			
Paso Danto Incised	2			
Pital Cream	6			
Che phase total	**118**	**0**	**0**	**0**
% of group's ceramics	**0.78%**			
CHUB PHASE				
DOS HERMANOS GROUP				
Dos Hermanos Red	1			
FLOR GROUP				
Accordion Incised	1			
Flor Cream	15	2		7
IBERIA GROUP				
Iberia Orange	3			
POLVERO GROUP				
Lechugal Incised	3			
Polvero Black	79	2		20
Zelda Incised	1			
Corriental Appliquédd				1
SAVANA GROUP				
Savana Orange	43			

continued on next page

TABLE 8.2.—*continued*

Type: Variety	South Group	El Diablo	El Tejón	Acropolis
SIERRA GROUP				
Alta Mira Fluted	3			
Laguna Verde Incised	10	1		1
Matamoro Bichrome: Red and Black	3			
Repasto Black-on-red	4			1
Sierra Red	268	8		20
Sierra Red: Appliquédd	1			
Sierra Red: Impressed	1			
BOXCAY GROUP				
Boxcay Brown		1		2
UNDETERMINED PRECLASSIC (CHUB CONTEXTS FOR EL DIABLO, EL TEJÓN)				
ACHIOTE GROUP				
Achiotes Unslipped	286	2		
Undetermined	1			
SAPOTE GROUP				
Sapote Striated	151	5		6
SACLUC GROUP				
Caramba Red-on-orange	1			
ERODED				
Eroded: Late Preclassic		1	2	1
Chub phase total	875	22	2	59
% of group's ceramics	5.80%	0.43%	0.40%	0.16%
(n)	15099	5114	494	36854

at El Palmar and the much more modest constructions in the South Group emphasize the centrality of the site of El Palmar in the early history of the Buenavista Valley.

THE EARLY CLASSIC PERIOD: SAQUIJ PHASE

Early Classic occupation at El Zotz can be identified for the hilltop plaza groups of El Diablo and El Tejón, as well as for the site's core area—the Acropolis and the South Group. The East Group also saw significant construction during the Early Classic phase, as established by excavations of Str.

M7-1 from 2012 to the present (Thomas Garrison, personal communication, 2012). However, material recovered from these more recent investigations in the East Group is not included in the present analysis.

As noted above, the Saquij material from El Diablo and El Tejón cannot at present be divided into three phases equivalent to those established at Tikal or Uaxactun. Nonetheless, stratigraphic sequences at Strs. L7-3 and L7-6 at the Acropolis, together with modal changes in the ceramic material, help to distinguish early and late Saquij facets.

El Diablo and El Tejón Groups

Saquij-phase pottery recovered from the El Tejón and El Diablo Groups exhibits characteristics consistent with Uaxactun phases Tzakol 1 through to Tzakol 3: round Z-angles, basal flanges on large bowls, and pedestal bases. At El Diablo, there are a handful ($n = 7$) of sherds with Late Classic (Mo' or Tepeu 1) modes. These come from humic and subhumic contexts above floors in Strs. F8-7, F8-15, and F8-16, and in front of Str. F8-1. With the exception of one sherd from nearby Str. F8-1, the later material seems to appear in the northern section of the group. At both hilltop groups, occasional examples of Chub-phase sherds were found mixed with Saquij-phase ceramics, as outlined above (table 8.2).

Excavations at El Diablo Str. F8-1 recovered 38 complete ceramic vessels and stands from an Early Classic royal tomb (ca. AD 350–400) in the initial phase of the building, along with 17 cache vessels deposited in the architectural fill outside the tomb chamber (Newman 2011a, 2011b). A more detailed description and analysis of these vessels is presented elsewhere (Houston, Newman, Román, and Garrison 2015; Newman et al. 2015). However, it is important to note here several characteristics of the vessels from the first phase of Str. F8-1 and of the rest of the material excavated at El Diablo.

Vessels from the tomb include six bowls (Vessels 1A/B, 15A/B, 17A/B, 18A/B, 19A/B, 20A/B, 22A/B) whose matching lids have central handles with modeled human or animal heads. Three of the bowls are polychromes, with bright red and orange backgrounds and elaborate iconographic motifs (18A/B, 19A/B, 22A/B). The presence of a red background, uncharacteristic of the more "standard" polychrome types found elsewhere in the Maya area, suggests these were probably a local El Zotz variety of high-status, polychrome serving vessels. The tomb assemblage also includes Dos Arroyos Orange and Caldero Buff Polychrome types, which were also recovered from other excavations at El Diablo. All lidded pots from the tomb have basal flanges and annular or support bases, typical of the Tzakol 2 and Manik 2 complexes at Uaxactun and Tikal.

The cache vessels included in the construction fill are smaller bowls and dishes with outflared and outcurved walls (Houston, Newman, Román, and Carter 2015; Newman 2011a). All the complete cache vessels belong to the Aguila Orange type, and numerous additional fragments of the same type and vessel form were recovered from the fill of Str. F8-1 during the cleaning and consolidation of looter tunnels there (Román and Carter 2009:79). The consistency in slip, paste, and vessel form suggests a standardized and intensive production of these kinds of vessels at El Diablo, at least in the historical moment surrounding the construction of Str. F8-1's first phase.

Excavations of later phases of Str. F8-1 and of other structures at El Diablo recovered over 5,000 ceramic sherds (diagnostic assemblage is outlined in table 8.3; analyzed by Ewa Czapiewska-Halliday, Alyce de Carteret, and Joel López Muñoz). Of these, 37.23 percent are eroded and non-diagnostic, making the El Diablo assemblage one of the worst preserved at El Zotz. The material from El Tejón is proportionally more informative (76 percent of sherds are diagnostic), and exhibits characteristics of both the early and late Saquij phases. Still, El Tejón was less extensively excavated than El Diablo (494 sherds were recovered), and future excavations may alter the picture presented here.

Rim sherds from the Quintal and Triunfo groups mainly represent jars and larger *ollas*. At El Diablo and El Tejón, Quintal Unslipped and Triunfo Striated vessels also include large bowls as well as shallow plates. While far simpler in their surface treatment, such vessels formally resemble the cache vessels from Str. F8-1 and certain pieces from the royal tomb: e.g., Cache 3A and 3B; Vessels 12A and 13A/B. The relative abundance of such bowls and plates at El Diablo and El Tejón is unique for El Zotz: they are extremely rare in other Saquij contexts at the site. Out of 488 rim sherds from El Diablo, 67 are Quintal and Triunfo bowls and plates, while out of 764 Early Classic rims from Saquij contexts at the Acropolis, only 18 belong to unslipped and striated bowls and plates.

The diagnostic material also shows additional surface decoration (incision, striation, impression, gouging and incisions, and polychrome painting). Although the majority of such decorations are simple, some of the polychrome bowl fragments bear evidence of elaborate geometric and iconographic motifs. Such fine decoration, however, is rare in preserved contexts outside the Str. F8-1 tomb and in sum constitutes only 0.40 percent of the assemblage at El Diablo. Four Aguila Orange bowl fragments with graffiti-style incisions were also found, two each at El Diablo and El Tejón.

TABLE 8.3. Saquij-phase ceramics from the El Diablo and El Tejón Groups

Type: Variety	El Diablo Early Saquij	El Diablo Late Saquij	El Tejón Early Saquij	El Tejón Late Saquij
QUINTAL GROUP				
Quintal Unslipped	160	645	32	111
Quintal Unslipped: Fluted		1		
Candelario Appliquédd	1	4		
Silvano Incised		5		
Cubierta Impressed	2	6	1	
Alceste Modeled		3		
TRIUNFO GROUP				
Triunfo Striated	253	683	23	75
Triunfo Striated: Impressed	3	1		2
AGUILA GROUP				
Aguila Orange	235	651	13	56
Diego Striated				2
Aguila Orange: Fluted		1		
Pita Incised	2	4		1
BALANZA GROUP				
Balanza Black	44	55	5	4
Lucha Incised	1	11		
Urita Gouged-incised	2	6		
Urita Gouged-incised: Appliquéd	2			
Paradero Fluted	1			
PUCTE GROUP				
Pucte Brown	38	55	2	10
Pluton Striated		1		
Santa Teresa Incised	2	4		
DOS HERMANOS GROUP				
Dos Hermanos Red	31	91	7	25
Dos Hermanos Red: Incised		2		
CARIBAL GROUP				
Caribal Red	8	103		

continued on next page

TABLE 8.3.—*continued*

Type: Variety	El Diablo Early Saquij	El Diablo Late Saquij	El Tejón Early Saquij	El Tejón Late Saquij
DOS ARROYOS GROUP				
Dos Arroyos Orange Polychrome	11	26	2	
Dos Arroyos Orange Polychrome: El Zotz Polychrome		2		
San Blas Red-on-orange	4	10		
Gavilan Black-on-orange				1
YALOCHE GROUP				
Yaloche Cream Polychrome	3	3		
Caldero Buff Polychrome	5	1	1	2
Sub-phase total	808	2374	86	289
% of group's ceramics	15.80%	46.42%	17.41%	58.50%
Saquij phase total	3182		375	
(n)	5114		494	

Two remarkable sherds, one fragment of a Dos Arroyos Orange Polychrome bowl and one of an Aguila Orange jar, were found in a looter tunnel within Str. H6-2 at El Tejón (Piedrasanta 2012:191) and in the context associated with the plaza floor in front of Str. F8-2 at El Diablo (Román and Newman 2011:136). They both have round strap handles that broke in antiquity and were subsequently carved into animal effigies. After the handles and the vessels had broken, leaving the sherds with fragments of the handles attached, some ancient inhabitants of El Zotz made two perforations in each sherd wall for the eyes of the animal and two smaller perforations on the broken handles to suggest nostrils in the beak. The objects are a unique example of the creative reutilization of broken ceramic vessels at El Zotz.

THE ACROPOLIS AND THE SOUTH GROUP

Extensive excavations at the Acropolis and neighboring areas (Marroquín et al. 2011; Meléndez and Houston 2008; Newman and Menéndez 2012; Pérez Robles and Houston 2009) offered a substantial Saquij ceramic assemblage. The Acropolis assemblage derives mainly from Strs. L7-3, L7-6, and L7-8, as well as from excavation lots underneath the plaza floors. The finds correspond to the whole temporal range of Saquij ceramics (table 8.4). Several construction phases were identified for the Saquij occupation of the Acropolis, including sequences of floors (Str. L7-6), which suggests the material found in these deposits probably originated from the middens used by the dwellers of the central precinct at El Zotz, and likely reflects the kinds of objects these groups used and discarded.

To judge from their stratigraphic position, the Early Classic sherds recovered from the earliest phases of Strs. L7-3 and L7-6 substructure belong to the earliest Saquij occupation of the Acropolis (Meléndez and Houston 2008; Pérez Robles and Houston 2009). They display a relatively low variety of ceramic types and a narrow range of vessel forms (table 8.4). Special modes of the early Saquij vessels include basal flanges, Z-angles, and annular and pedestal bases. Vessels with flanges and angles often exhibit additional modes of surface decoration besides slipping (incision, fluting, appliqué, gouging/incision, and painted polychrome designs). Still, only 3.53 percent (n = 65) of all early Saquij sherds (n = 1,843) recovered from the Acropolis and the neighboring Northwest Courtyard show such decorations.

A wide range of vessel sizes (table 8.7), along with the presence of large bowls of various ceramic types, point to different activities in different parts of the Acropolis (figure 8.1). These could have included the domestic use of large, simple, monochrome vessels as well as some social and ritual functions for the larger polychrome vessels. Twenty-two Saquij vessel fragments recovered from the context of a looter tunnel (Newman and Menéndez 2012:141) at Str. L7-8 exhibit a wide range of fine decorative techniques (incised, gouged/incised, and painted) and formal attributes (bowls, plates, vases, and lids). A plate in the Pucte group with three different kinds of surface decorative modes—appliqués, circular tool impressions, and incisions—was recovered from the same context. These 22 sherds contrast with the simpler decorative modes found at Strs. L7-3 and L7-6. Motifs from the Str. L7-8 Saquij collection include complex geometric designs, swirls, step-fret motifs, and figural representations of animals (possibly a dog). From their forms alone—unfortunately, their stratigraphic context does not provide the exact chronological phase—they likely date to the earlier half of the Saquij phase.

The types and varieties represented at L7-3 and L7-6 diversified over successive stratigraphic phases (table 8.4), as did vessel forms and sizes (figure 8.1). While the same ceramic types still dominate the assemblages of later Saquij constructions, types with more varied and complex decorative modes increase in number. Sherds with additional surface decoration constitute 6.10 percent of the later Saquij collections in the Acropolis and the Northwest Courtyard area. It thus appears not only that the proportion of finely decorated ceramics increased by comparison to the earlier Saquij occupation at the Acropolis, but that the ratio of such ceramics to vessels with simple surface treatments

TABLE 8.4. Saquij-phase ceramics from the Acropolis and the South Group

Type: Variety	Acropolis		South Group
	Early Saquij	Late Saquij	Saquij
QUINTAL GROUP			
Quintal Unslipped	147	402	102
Silvano Incised		1	
Cubierta Impressed	3	5	
Candelario Appliquédd	1		
Alceste Modeled		1	
TRIUNFO GROUP			
Triunfo Striated	807	1283	88
Triunfo Striated: Impressed		6	
Triunfo Striated: Incised		1	
Triunfo Striated: Appliquédd	1		
AGUILA GROUP			
Aguila Orange	475	1542	26
Diego Striated	7	25	
Aguila Orange: Fluted		2	
Pita Incised	11	13	
San Clemente Gouged-incised	1	4	
Milpa Impressed		3	
Titiz Bichrome: Orange and Black	3	22	
NESPA GROUP			
Nespa Orange			25
Nespa Orange: Incised			1
BALANZA GROUP			
Balanza Black	78	295	4
Lucha Incised	13	45	1
Urita Gouged-incised	2	10	
Santizo Appliquédd	1	2	
Paradero Fluted		10	
Balanza Black: Impressed	1	1	
Balanza Black: Modeled-incised	1		
PUCTE GROUP			
Pucte Brown	48	182	

continued on next page

TABLE 8.4.—*continued*

Type: Variety	Acropolis		South Group
	Early Saquij	Late Saquij	Saquij
Santa Teresa Incised	4	15	
Pucte Brown: Fluted	1	2	
Pucte Brown: Appliquédd-impressed-incised	1		
BOXCAY GROUP			
Boxcay Brown			19
DOS HERMANOS GROUP			
Dos Hermanos Red	157	134	
Dos Hermanos Red: Incised		2	
CARIBAL GROUP			
Caribal Red	54	116	8
Mahogany Creek Incised			1
DOS ARROYOS GROUP			
Dos Arroyos Orange Polychrome	20	104	17
Dos Arroyos Orange Polychrome: Red Polychrome	1	1	
San Blas Red-on-orange		3	18
Eroded Polychrome		3	12
SACLUC GROUP			
Sacluc Black-on-orange			1
YALOCHE GROUP			
Yaloche Cream Polychrome	2	11	
Caldero Buff Polychrome	3	16	
DIFFERENTIATED COLOR GROUP			
Guachiman Bichrome: Orange Interior		1	
Sub-phase total	1843	4263	323
% of group's ceramics	5.00%	11.57%	2.14%
Saquij phase total		6106	323
(n)		36854	15099

is higher than at El Diablo. The accumulation of vessels with labor-intensive decoration suggests the central precinct at El Zotz on the valley floor might have increased in its economic or social importance during the Saquij phase and the elite activities were no longer centered solely at the hilltop complexes.

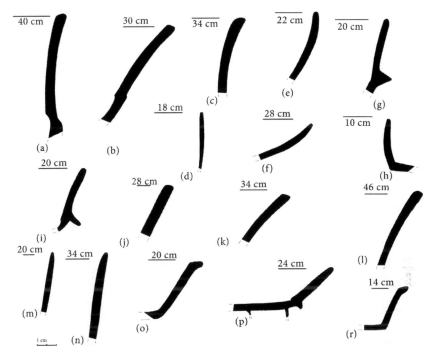

FIGURE 8.1. *Saquij-phase ceramics from the Acropolis Strs. L7-3 and L7-6: Aguila Orange bowls (a–g) and jar (h); Dos Arroyos Orange Polychrome bowls (i–l); Balanza Black bowls (m–o); Lucha Incised plate (p); Pucte Brown plate (r) (drawings by E. Czapiewska-Halliday).*

The frequency of special formal modes such as basal flanges, basal angles, Z-angles, and annular, pedestal, and support bases increases considerably over the Saquij phase. Z-angles on vessel walls are characteristic of Aguila Orange (out of 41 Saquij examples only one was of another type—Balanza Black), while special formal attributes of vessels in the Balanza, Pucte, and polychrome groups tend to concentrate at the bases of vessels (basal flanges, pedestal bases, and basal angles).

Saquij-phase ceramics in the South Group were found in association with modifications to the main platform group, and in particular with the extension of Str. L9-4 by the construction of Str. L9-3. The 323 sherds identified for the Early Classic period show a very low variety of ceramic types (table 8.4), probably linked to the early facet of the Saquij phase at the Acropolis, or preceding it. Some types, like Boxcay Brown, seem modally connected to the previous Che and Chub phases in this area. The implication may be that the Saquij occupation of the South Group continued from the Preclassic period until the fourth century AD, at which point occupation shifted westward and upward to El Diablo and El Tejón.

THE LATE CLASSIC PERIOD: MO' AND CAAL PHASES

The Late Classic Mo' (AD 550–700) and Caal (AD 700–850) phases correspond to significant shifts in the distribution of ceramic material at El Zotz. After the abandonment of the hilltop complexes of the El Diablo and El Tejón Groups in the early sixth century AD (Román et al., chapter 3, this volume), the architectural core of El Zotz on the valley floor expanded. To date, most ceramics belonging to the Mo' phase have been recovered from the architectural fill of these early Late Classic constructions at the Acropolis, Strs. L7-6 and L7-1, and the Restricted Patio, which were later covered over by platforms dating to the Caal phase. A carbon sample from the Mo' phase of Str. L7-1 returned a date of AD 532–650 (88.4 percent probability; table 1.1).

Although there is a relatively small amount of Mo' material in the Late Classic assemblage from the Acropolis (1,761 sherds, or 22.54 percent; Marroquín et al. 2011; Pérez Robles and Houston 2009), sufficient data exist to describe this complex at El Zotz (table 8.5). It is quite similar to Uaxactun Tepeu 1. The Mo'-phase marks the first appearance of typically Late Classic types (Tinaja Red, Infierno Black, Maquina Brown, Cambio Unslipped, and Encanto Striated). Yet fragments of types characteristic of the Saquij phase also appear, constituting approximately 4.29 percent of the material recovered from Mo' phase contexts. Dos Arroyos Orange Polychrome, Aguila, and Balanza vessels are the most common among these, together with occasional Quintal and Triunfo sherds. New polychrome types, Saxche-Palmar and Zacatal types, appear in more significant amounts (17.94 percent of Mo'-phase material) during this phase than the polychromes of the preceding phase (3.26 percent of late Saquij material at the Acropolis). The decoration on the polychrome vessels includes mostly linear and geometric motifs, contrasting with the polychromes recovered from Caal-phase contexts discussed below. The decoration on monochrome vessels is very scarce (0.62 percent) and consists of only basic decorative modes (horizontal incised bands and finger impressions) rather than more elaborate designs. It appears mainly on utilitarian vessels, and includes the first examples of Chaquiste Impressed types (five sherds; see discussion below).

The ceramic assemblages of the Mo'- and Caal-phase construction cores at the Acropolis are similar in nature in many ways. They both include sherds

TABLE 8.5. Mo'- and Caal-phase ceramics from the Acropolis and Las Palmitas

	Acropolis		Las Palmitas
Type: Variety	Mo' phase	Caal phase	Caal phase
CAMBIO GROUP			
Cambio Unslipped	288	1395	1283
Ciro Incised		2	4
Miseria Appliquédd: Miseria	1	2	
Miseria Appliquédd: Cedral	1	3	
Pedregal Modeled	1	7	1
Manteca Impressed	1	8	
ENCANTO GROUP			
Encanto Striated	457	1579	609
Valente Striated-impressed	1	2	
Seferino Striated-incised			1
TINAJA GROUP			
Tinaja Red	544	1784	559
Cameron Incised: Cameron	1	6	7
Cameron Incised: Corozal	1	8	1
Chaquiste Impressed	5	19	4
Chinja Impressed		11	8
Tigran Striated	2		
Tolla Fluted			1
Zelmira Appliquédd		1	
San Julio Modeled			1
INFIERNO GROUP			
Infierno Black	34	105	66
Carmelita Incised		8	
Toro Gouged-incised		1	
Carro Modeled		1	
Chilar Fluted		2	
Infierno Black: Appliquédd			3
Tres Micos Impressed: Sealed	1		
MAQUINA GROUP			
Maquina Brown	60	178	58
Canoa Incised		11	2

continued on next page

TABLE 8.5.—*continued*

Type: Variety	Acropolis Mo' phase	Acropolis Caal phase	Las Palmitas Caal phase
Tenaja Fluted		2	1
Calandria Striated	1		
Calabazo Gouged-incised	1	3	
Maquina Brown: Appliquédd		1	
Maquina Brown: Modeled			1
Azucar Impressed	1	4	
AZOTE GROUP			
Azote Orange	39	108	63
Torres Incised		3	
PAYASO GROUP			
Payaso Orange-brown	4	1	
HARINA GROUP			
Harina Cream	1	6	13
Harina Cream: Modeled			2
SAXCHE-PALMAR GROUP			
Saxche-Palmar Orange Polychrome	262	564	99
Leona Red-on-orange	14	39	16
Chantuori Black-on-orange	10	17	4
Palmar Orange Polychrome		1	
Yuhactal Black-on-red	4	1	1
Saxche-Palmar Orange Polychrome: Incised		1	
ZACATAL GROUP			
Zacatal Cream Polychrome	16	127	13
Chinos Black-on-cream	1	5	3
Juina Red-on-buff			1
Paixban Buff Polychrome	5	23	5
UNIDENTIFIED GROUP			
Unidentified Polychrome	4	16	1
Mo' and Caal phase totals	**1761**	**6055**	**2831**
% of group's ceramics	**4.78%**	**16.43%**	**31.79%**
(n)		36854	8905

from Saquij and even Chub phases, which suggests that the middens that formed the source of material for these substantial construction fills were continuously used by El Zotz inhabitants throughout the occupation of the complex, meaning the content of these contexts is most likely to be mixed.

A group of vessels looted during the 1970s, now located in private collections and museums throughout the world, bear texts and/or iconography that tie them to El Zotz (Carter et al., chapter 4, this volume). They include polychrome bowls and vases depicting deities or *way*, as well as several vessels with dedicatory texts alone, or with texts and geometric designs. The red backgrounds of many of the polychrome vessels link them stylistically and technologically to the Saquij polychromes found in the Str. F8-1 tomb at El Diablo. While no Mo'-phase red polychrome vessels have been excavated from archaeologically controlled contexts at El Zotz, agents of Guatemala's Instituto de Antopología e Historia recovered a fragment of one such vessel from looter spoil at an undetermined location at El Zotz shortly after the site was looted. The sherd, apparently from a vase, depicts the Jaguar God of the Underworld in a style consistent with the looted *way* vessels.

THE ACROPOLIS, STRUCTURE L7-11, AND THE NORTHWEST COURTYARD

The massive construction projects carried out in and near the Acropolis at El Zotz in the eighth century AD provided excellent contexts from which Caal ceramics were retrieved. The most representative collections were recovered from the construction fill of Strs. L7-1, L7-2, L7-3, and L7-6, and from the Restricted Patio in the Acropolis; and from Strs. L7-17 and L7-20 in the Northwest Courtyard. The Caal-phase Acropolis and Northwest Courtyard construction contexts yielded over 6,000 sherds between 2008 and 2011 (77.46 percent of the total Late Classic assemblage from the Acropolis area), (table 8.5), of which over 99 percent are diagnostic of ceramic types consistent with the Tepeu 2 complex at Uaxactun.

Cambio and Encanto jars—the types are often impossible to distinguish from rim and neck sherds, since Encanto jar necks are almost never striated (Foias 1996:187)—along with sherds indicative of other closed-vessel forms appear to abound in the sample (48.46 percent). A few examples were recovered of vessels in the Cambio group with additional surface decoration such as incision, impression, appliqué, and modeling. Unslipped vessels with appliqués and modeled parts are bowl incense burners with outflared or round walls and rows of spike appliqués. These were found exclusively in the massive construction core of Str. L7-1 and probably reflect ritual activities connected to its construction.

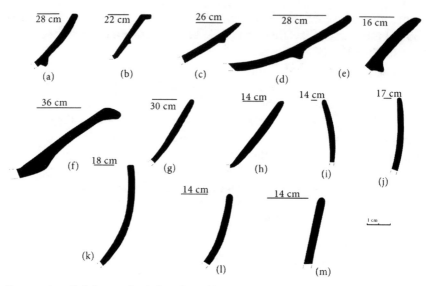

Figure 8.2. *Polychrome sherds from Late Classic Mo' and Caal contexts at the Acropolis: Saxche-Palmar Orange Polychrome plates (a–f), bowls with glyphs (g–h), and bowls (i–k); Zacatal Cream Polychrome bowls (l–m) (drawings by E. Czapiewska-Halliday).*

Caal monochrome vessels are highly variable in shape, with bowls being produced in the full range of shapes (vertical, outflared, outcurved, round, and incurved walls) and a similar diversity of shapes in jars, vases, and plates. Overall, 66.05 percent of the Caal Acropolis vessels (recovered from contexts of the core Acropolis structures—Strs. L7-1, L7-2, L7-3, L7-5, L7-6, L7-7, L7-11, and Courtyard 2) are of closed form, including jars and *ollas*. The closed vessel form is even more prominent in the Northwest Courtyard, where sherds from closed-form vessels constitute as much as 81.60 percent. The open-form vessels, such as bowls and plates, constitute 30.98 percent of the Acropolis core assemblage and 18.08 percent of the Northwest Courtyard ceramics. Compared to other ceramic phases, the Late Classic period is characterized by the highest ratio of bichromes and polychromes relative to other decorative techniques (figure 8.2). These constitute 13.11 percent of the Caal assemblage from the Acropolis area (including Northwest Courtyard structures), which is slightly lower than for the Mo'-phase contexts (17.94 percent).

The orange polychromes were likely produced locally, at El Zotz or in its hinterland, as inferred from their frequent occurrence in Caal-phase contexts at El Zotz. Neutron activation analysis indicates that their pastes were manufactured from the same materials as utilitarian, slipped vessels like

Tinaja-group monochromes (Ronald Bishop, personal communication, 2012). Orange polychromes are relatively uniform in their formal modes, the majority being open serving vessels.

Two complete bowls were found, positioned lip-to-lip, enclosing a dedicatory cache in the construction core of the Str. L7-11 platform (figure 4.10; Arredondo Leiva et al. 2008:77). Both bowls have outflared walls; one is a Saxche-Palmar Orange Polychrome and the other is a Zacatal Cream Polychrome. The design on the bottom vessel (Vessel 1) is almost entirely eroded, and only traces of orange, red, and black paint survive. The polychrome decoration on the top vessel (Vessel 2) is much better preserved: it shows a basketweave design painted in black and red on an orange background. Bowls painted with such design, although on a cream background, were also found at Uaxactun in Tepeu 2 contexts (Smith 1955:figure 60a, 12–17). From the traces of paint on Vessel 1, it can be suggested that the design differed from the one on Vessel 2.

Vases from the Caal phase are in great majority bichrome and polychrome (74.55 percent). They are some of the most highly valued ceramic objects, as evidenced by the numbers of vessels of this form decorated with glyphic inscriptions, as well as courtly and other iconographic scenes found across the Maya area. Zacatal Cream Polychrome vessels are particularly well represented among vases (14 out of 55 confirmed vase fragments). The painted decoration of orange and cream polychrome vessels varies from simple linear and geometric motifs to complex iconographic scenes and hieroglyphic inscriptions.

Modes of decoration were recorded and analyzed within a sample of 267 El Zotz polychrome sherds. Orange polychromes were in majority (64.64 percent) decorated with geometric designs. Complex iconographic designs and glyphic inscriptions appeared on only 35.36 percent of the orange polychrome ceramic types. Polychrome vessels with other, non-orange background colors (cream, buff, black, and other less-common types) showed almost identical proportions of design types: 66.28 percent of sherds were decorated with geometric shapes and 33.72 percent with more complex or textual elements. The largest assemblage of Caal-phase ceramics decorated with figural scenes, iconographic motifs, or hieroglyphs or pseudoglyphs derives from the Acropolis structures, the Northwest Courtyard, and Str. L7-11. Sherds with the El Zotz Emblem Glyph and other texts found in the Acropolis suggest that its inhabitants had the resources and power necessary to commission and obtain objects requiring the skills of specialist calligraphers.

Polychromes of the Caal phase were also found in relatively significant amounts at other locations at El Zotz, including a small residential compound located immediately east from the main *aguada* at El Zotz (see Beach et al., chapter 7, this volume). The high frequency of occurrence of Caal polychromes signals their intensified local production. Their distribution across various architectural compounds suggests the residents outside of the monumental complexes at El Zotz had access to very similar "costly" ceramics (with labor- and skill-intensive surface finish), as did the inhabitants of the palaces during this time period, which is consistent with ceramic studies undertaken at other Maya sites (Beaudry 1984; Foias and Bishop 1997; Fry 1981; Hansen et al. 1991; Hendon 1991). Thus, it is likely the exchange and distribution of luxury and utilitarian, domestic ceramics occurred along the same network, through the same range of craftsmen, and was not controlled by, or restricted to, the high-status groups. Any differences in distribution and frequencies of various ceramic types are more likely to have been caused by the capacity, or lack thereof, to amass luxury items in larger quantities by some households—elite courts—and not by others.

Prudence Rice and Donald Forsyth identified two ceramic "supercomplexes" in the Peten and adjoining areas of Belize and Campeche, distinguished by the presence or absence of certain domestic ceramic types during the Late Classic period (Rice and Forsyth 2004). The eastern supercomplex includes Tikal, Uaxactun, and the sites of the Mirador Basin, while the western stretches from the area around El Perú-Waka' south and west to the Usumacinta and Petexbatun regions (Forné 2006:83–84, 2008:893; Rice and Forsyth 2004:32). Two diagnostic types in the Tinaja group, Chaquiste Impressed and Chinja Impressed, characterize respectively the western and eastern supercomplexes. Chaquiste Impressed vessels can be further divided into two groups, one (well represented at El Perú-Waka' and La Joyanca) with finger impressions made in a band of clay applied to the outside of the vessel, and the other (to the south) with finger or stamp impressions in a band pinched out from the vessel body (Forné 2008). Both types were typically used for incurved-rim bowls, or *tecomates*, and their substitution for one another likely reflects divergent cultural traditions among specialist and non-specialist producers rather than marking ideological or political identity.

El Zotz lies on the border of the eastern and western supercomplexes, and both Chinja Impressed and El Perú-Waka'–style Chaquiste Impressed bowl rims are represented in its ceramic collection (figure 8.3). Both types are rare in the Mo' and Caal phases at the Acropolis (0.45 percent, 35 sherds in total; table 8.5). Of these, however, 24 are Chaquiste Impressed, suggesting a more-intensive cultural interaction with the El Perú-Waka' region during this period. Two of the Chaquiste Impressed sherds were subjected to neutron activation analysis and assigned to the same paste compositional group as Tinaja Red and polychrome sherds believed to have been produced at El Zotz (Ronald

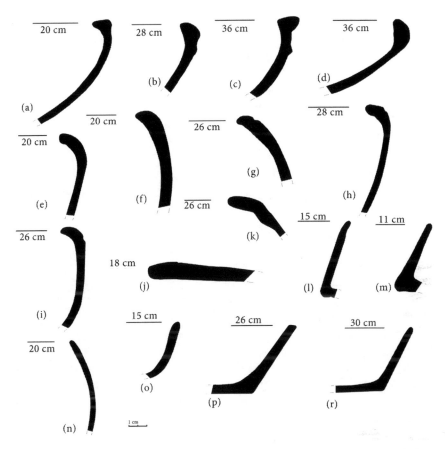

FIGURE 8.3. *Vessels of the Tinaja group from Caal and Cucul contexts of the Acropolis. Caal phase: Tinaja Red basin (a); Chaquiste Impressed basins (b–c). Cucul phase: Tinaja Red basin (d), tecomates (e–f), jars (l–m), and bowls (n–r); Cameron Incised tecomates (g–j); Chinja Impressed tecomate (k) (drawings by E. Czapiewska-Halliday).*

Bishop, personal communication, 2012). The evidence thus suggests that the technique of making appliqué-band Chaquiste Impressed basins, not the finished basins themselves, made its way east from the El Perú-Waka' region during the Mo' and Caal phases.

The Acropolis-area Caal collection contains the largest proportion of nonlocal ceramic types of any of the areas considered, as identified by decorative styles connected to areas outside of El Zotz. These include the polychrome Ik'-style associated with Motul de San José and the resist-reserve Mataculebra type linked to the Usumacinta region. These foreign ceramics are distributed around the core area of El Zotz, although a few Ik'-style sherds were also found at Las Palmitas and at Bejucal (see below). All these examples, predominantly resist-reserve types or polychromes with court scenes or hieroglyphic texts, represent high-value objects. As such, they reflect economic interactions, whether through gift-giving among the aristocracy or through broader trade networks, between El Zotz and other Maya centers.

Las Palmitas and La Tortuga Groups

Ceramic material from the hilltop architectural complex of Las Palmitas, 800 m north of the Acropolis, can be divided into five depositional periods. Two of these correspond to the group's construction and renovation in the Caal phase; two tie to its Terminal Classic construction and use; and a fifth, poorly controlled phase corresponds to its abandonment except—perhaps— for the occasional visit by persons living nearby.

The earliest pottery at Las Palmitas dates to shortly before the group's construction, which took place in a single phase (see Carter et al., chapter 4, this volume). Much of the fill required for the pyramid (Str. M3-1) and raised platforms at the group appears from its contents—isolated fragments of utilitarian and luxury vessels, lithic debitage, and faunal remains including cervid bones and antlers—to have been taken from a midden used by households with access to elaborately decorated vessels. Since there were no earlier constructions at Las Palmitas, this midden was likely associated with elite settlement in the El Zotz site core. Although a few earlier Saquij phase sherds were mixed in with the midden fill, two Ik'-style sherds recovered from the fill under Str. M3-7 indicate that Las Palmitas could not have been constructed before about the second quarter of the eighth century AD, and almost all the ceramic material from the fill is consistent with the Caal phase (table 8.5).

The bulk of the classifiable sherds from the Caal contexts derive from unslipped, utilitarian vessels (67.04 percent of the total). Peten Gloss and related wares make up most of the balance. Water jars are well represented and belong mainly to the unslipped and Tinaja Red types; 239 sherds were identified as pieces of water jars and *ollas*. Closed-form vessel fragments, including jar fragments, constitute as much as 83.33 percent of Las Palmitas Caal assemblage. That is a higher proportion of closed-form vessels than is found at the Northwest Courtyard. As for the remaining sherds, 15.51 percent of the total belong to open forms, including bowls and plates, and 0.42 percent to vases.

Bichromes and polychromes account for 5.02 percent of the Caal-phase collection (table 8.5). The cream polychrome sherds include the two Ik'-style sherds from Str. M3-7. One of four complete vessels excavated at Las Palmitas, a Saxche-Palmar Orange Polychrome bowl, was recovered from a looter tunnel in the base of Str. M3-1 (Carter and Gutiérrez Castillo 2011:94), where it was found in association with disturbed human bones. Decorative techniques, such as incisions, gouging/incisions, fluting, modeling, or appliqué, occur less frequently in the Late Classic Las Palmitas assemblage of monochrome and unslipped ceramics (1.27 percent, n = 36) than at the Acropolis (1.75 percent, n = 106). Thus, the overall frequency of decorated vessels (polychromes combined with decorated monochromes and unslipped vessels) is much lower at the hilltop complex of Las Palmitas (6.32 percent) than it is in the Acropolis area (14.76 percent). This suggests that, at least during the later phase of the Late Classic period, the occupants of Las Palmitas did not have the power to acquire and accumulate the same volumes of labor- and skill-intensive ceramic types as the inhabitants of the Acropolis of El Zotz.

Although not all the sherds recovered from the La Tortuga complex have been analyzed (Belches and Garrido López 2012), the material classified according to type and variety (1,491 sherds) points to the same period of construction and occupation attested for Las Palmitas. The analyzed sample comes from the excavated *chultun* (a bell-shaped storage chamber cut into bedrock) between Strs. N5-1 and N5-2, two units in Strs. N5-2, and six units in Str. N6-4. It represents a mixed collection of Caal and Cucul types. The identifiable material belongs to the Cambio Unslipped and Encanto Striated types (45.67 percent), monochrome slipped wares (16.70 percent), and orange, cream, and buff polychromes (1.95 percent).

The decorated vessels at La Tortuga are mostly domestic in nature, with the exception of a few polychromes. Most of these are painted with simple, geometric motifs, but one sherd decorated with a nonlocal resist-reserve technique was excavated at Str. N6-4. This fragment had been rounded after breaking for reuse. The reutilization of the sherd in the absence of other ceramics of such high quality suggests that the residents of La Tortuga had access to items discarded by a wealthier household—the royal court at the Acropolis being the obvious candidate. Notably, only one Chinja Impressed sherd was included in the sample (found in humus layer of Str. N6-4; Belches and Garrido López 2012:202). Three Chaquiste Impressed and two Pantano Impressed fragments, from the *chultun* and Str. N6-4, might indicate association with the El Perú-Waka' region of the western ceramic supercomplex, consistent with the pattern seen at the Acropolis.

THE TERMINAL CLASSIC PERIOD: CUCUL PHASE

The Terminal Classic Cucul phase (ca. AD 850–1000) was established on the basis of radiocarbon dating, relative stratigraphy, ceramic typology, and the date (March 12, AD 830) on a reused piece of El Zotz Stela 4. The Cucul complex exhibits further changes in formal and decorative modes, reflecting broader trends in the Maya Lowlands as a whole, as well as a shift in the spatial distribution of ceramic material. Terminal Classic pottery was excavated in significant amounts from contexts in the Acropolis, the Northwest Courtyard, Las Palmitas, La Tortuga, and the South Group.

The Acropolis and the Northwest Courtyard

Cucul-phase ceramics in the Acropolis area are associated with minor modifications to palace structures, such as floor or doorjamb remodeling, and, more importantly, with a massive, ritual deposit on top of Str. L7-1 and the Restricted Patio. This deposit appears to correspond to an interrupted construction event near the beginning of the Terminal Classic period (see Newman 2015b; Newman et al., chapter 5, this volume). Out of over 6,000 confirmed Cucul sherds (table 8.6) from the Acropolis structures (not including Strs. L7-8 and L7-24), 78.38 percent (n = 4,720) were retrieved from the ritual deposit. This assemblage is characterized by large vessel fragments and includes several complete and semi-complete vessels (see figure 5.3), especially Infierno Black bowls; Tinaja Red bowls, jars, and vases; and Cameron Incised *tecomates* and basins.

Monochrome slipped vessels are abundant in the ritual deposit, along with Cambio Unslipped and Encanto Striated vessels. Most of them belong to the Tinaja Red type but present highly variable slip colors, ranging from brownish red to dark orange. In some cases, Tinaja group slips tend toward waxiness rather than the standard glossy quality, perhaps indicating experimentation with the production techniques characteristic of the Early Postclassic Choc phase. The pastes of Cucul-phase Tinaja vessels are usually buff in color but tend to appear more orange than those of the Caal phase. Augustine Red, characterized by bright red slip on orange paste, begins to be produced during the Cucul phase but the bulk of the sample was recovered from Early Postclassic Choc contexts. Augustine Red was recovered in greater amounts from the Northwest Courtyard contexts than from the Acropolis, reflecting longer and more continuous occupation of the former group.

As in previous phases, the monochrome types present a great variety of vessel forms and shapes: *tecomates*, basins, bowls, plates, jars, and vases. As used here, the term "basin" refers to bowls with only slightly restricted orifices, "tecomate"

TABLE 8.6. Cucul-phase ceramics from the Acropolis, Las Palmitas, and the South Group

Type: Variety	Acropolis Main	Acropolis NW Courtyard	Las Palmitas	South Group
CAMBIO GROUP				
Cambio Unslipped	1438	1750	1345	
Ciro Incised	2	1		
Miseria Appliquéd: Miseria	5			
Miseria Appliquéd: Cedral	2			
Manteca Impressed		1	2	
Pedregal Modeled		1		
ENCANTO GROUP				
Encanto Striated	1986	1918	1317	
Valente Striated-impressed			3	
TINAJA GROUP				
Tinaja Red	2070	829	964	
Cameron Incised: Cameron	56	19	12	
Cameron Incised: Corozal	4		5	
Chaquiste Impressed	6		2	
Chinja Impressed	8	15	13	
Pantano Impressed			1	
Rosa Punctated	1			
Portia Gouged-incised	5	2		
Tolla Fluted	9		2	
Tinaja Red: Modeled			1	
INFIERNO GROUP				
Infierno Black	159	36	67	
Carmelita Incised	29	5	8	
Toro Gouged-incised	11		1	
Chilar Fluted	5	1	3	
MAQUINA GROUP				
Maquina Brown	46	42	55	
Canoa Incised	3			
Calabazo Gouged-incised	1			
Azucar Impressed	1		2	
Maquina Brown: Modeled	1			

continued on next page

TABLE 8.6.—*continued*

Type: Variety	Acropolis Main	Acropolis NW Courtyard	Las Palmitas	South Group
AZOTE GROUP				
Azote Orange	9	35	65	
Azote Orange: Impressed			1	
Torres Incised	3		3	
PAYASO GROUP				
Payaso Orange-brown	2	68	96	87
Payaso Orange-brown: Fluted				1
Payaso Orange-brown: Incised				1
HARINA GROUP				
Harina Cream		3	13	
Corrales Incised	1	1		
PALMAR-DANTA GROUP				
Saxche-Palmar Orange Polychrome	51	16	83	
Leona Red-on-orange	1	2	5	
Chantuori Black-on-orange	12	1	7	
Palmar Orange Polychrome	33			
Yuhactal Black-on-red	1		1	
Saxche-Palmar Orange Polychrome: Modeled	3			
Leona Red-on-orange: Fluted			1	
ZACATAL GROUP				
Zacatal Cream Polychrome	19	11	22	
Paixban Buff Polychrome	2	3	2	
Chinos Black-on-cream		1	3	
ALTAR GROUP				
Altar Orange	29	4	5	
Altar Orange: Fluted		1		
Pabellon Modeled-carved	1	3	3	3
Pabellon Modeled-carved: Red slip	2			
Tumba Black-on-orange	1			
Islas Gouged-incised			2	1
Trapiche Incised		1	1	1

continued on next page

TABLE 8.6.—*continued*

Type: Variety	Acropolis Main	Acropolis NW Courtyard	Las Palmitas	South Group
TRES NACIONES GROUP				
Tres Naciones Gray			2	1
Carmina Modeled-carved	1		4	
Tres Naciones Gray (Imitation)			2	10
CHABLEKAL GROUP				
Chablekal Fine Gray			1	3
Chicxulub Incised			1	2
Chablekal Fine Gray (Imitation)				2
Chicxulub Incised (Imitation)				7
DAYLIGHT GROUP				
Daylight Orange: Darknight				23
FINE ORANGE GROUP				
Undertermined Fine Orange		3	3	2
Undertermined Fine Orange: Incised			1	2
BALANCAN GROUP				
Provincia Plano-relief				1
MUNA SLATE GROUP				
Tikul Thin				1
SAHCABA GROUP				
Sahcaba Modeled-carved	3		2	
PATOJO GROUP				
Patojo Modeled				10
Cucul phase total	6022	4773	4132	158
% of group's ceramics	16.34%	12.95%	46.40%	1.05%
(n)		36854	8905	15099

to bowls with markedly incurved walls and markedly restricted orifices (figure 8.3, table 8.7), when the angle of the rim is often parallel to the base of the pot. The latter form is most typical of the Cameron Incised, Tolla Fluted, Chinja Impressed, and Chaquiste Impressed types, while the former kind tend not to have any additional surface treatment (figure 8.3).

The quantity of the two impressed Tinaja types—Chinja Impressed and Chaquiste Impressed—during the Cucul phase at the Acropolis is small.

TABLE 8.7. Sizes of Acropolis vessels for Saquij and Cucul phases

Acropolis		Orifice diameter (cm)			
		Range	Mean	σ	Sample size
Early Saquij	Jars	6–28	17.92	5.81	13
	Bowls, plates	7–52	24.56	11.08	34
Late Saquij	Jars	7–36	20.98	7.91	52
	Bowls, plates	6–54	24.07	8.92	137
Cucul	Cambio, Encanto jars	8–38	26.95	8.59	38
	Red monochrome jars	8–48	17	10.18	12
	Bowls, plates	10–50	21.79	7.45	91
	Tecomates, basins	14–34	24.13	4.87	40

There are only 14 such sherds in total, eight of which are Chinja Impressed and six of which are Chaquiste Impressed type. Further, 15 Chinja Impressed fragments and no Chaquiste Impressed fragments were recovered from the Northwest Courtyard. This further widens the difference in occurrence between the two ceramic types. Chinja Impressed *tecomates* and basins, typical of the eastern supercomplex, appear more frequently in the Cucul collection from the Acropolis and might suggest a population transfer or shift in cultural or sociopolitical affiliation. The ceramic type Cameron Incised, represented by the same forms of vessels, is even more common in the Cucul phase (75 sherds from the Acropolis and Northwest Courtyard). The incised band often combined with Chinja Impressed decoration is associated with the Uaxactun and Tikal region (Forsyth 2003:663) and, while it appears in the Acropolis assemblage, it is more frequently found at the Las Palmitas complex.

Closed-form vessels, including a large proportion of jars, constitute 81.14 percent (4,887 sherds) of the Cucul-phase Acropolis sample. Open vessels, bowls, plates, and vases comprise 17.67 percent of the sample (1,064 sherds). These ratios point to a more frequent occurrence of jars and smaller numbers of open serving vessels in the Terminal Classic contexts in comparison to the Caal phase in the Acropolis.

Black-slipped monochrome vessels are more common in the Cucul phase than in the Caal phase. Like the red types, black monochromes are often decorated with incision, gouging/incision, and fluting techniques that recall the importance of blackwares during the Early Classic Tzakol phases at Uaxactun (Smith and Gifford 1966:167–168; figure 8.4). Black-slipped vessels are more likely to have additional techniques of surface decoration applied than the

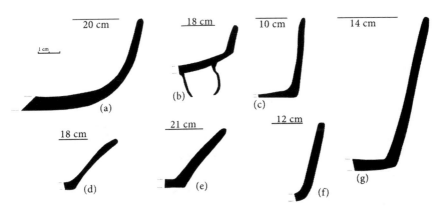

FIGURE 8.4. *Blackwares from the Terminal Classic deposit at the Acropolis: Carmelita Incised bowl (a) and tripod plate (b); Infierno Black bowls (c–f) and vase (g) (drawings by E. Czapiewska-Halliday).*

red-slipped monochromes: 17.48 percent of black-slipped Cucul vessels at El Zotz, and only 4.34 percent of red-slipped ones, showed signs of surface decoration beyond slipping (incision, gouging and incision, and appliqué, among others). Similar proportions of decorated red- and blackwares are recorded for other chronological phases and suggest this was a consistent correlation between color choice and additional surface enhancement.

Polychrome vessels occur in much-reduced amounts during the Cucul phase (1.45 percent of the Cucul assemblages at the Acropolis and the Northwest Courtyard, table 8.6), and the majority of those recovered are eroded. The scarcity of polychromes means that, although surface decoration on monochrome vessels is as scarce as during the Caal phase, there is relatively more decoration on domestic vessels (e.g., bowls and *tecomates*) than on high-value pots. Terminal Classic polychromes at El Zotz include fragments from the Saxche-Palmar group with simple, geometric designs and often—in contrast to Caal-phase polychromes—no visible underslip. Examples of more complex decorative designs or glyphs on Terminal Classic polychromes are extremely scarce in contrast to the Late Classic Caal-phase ceramics. Cylindrical vases with modeled collars around the walls (typological classification pending) were found in the Acropolis deposit and in a Terminal Classic context at Las Palmitas (see below). Vases with these forms include monochromes, bichromes, and polychromes with painted decoration, including glyph bands, although most of their surface treatments are eroded.

Excavations of the ritual deposit at the Acropolis also yielded fragments of drums and incense burners. Fragments of supports were abundant, suggesting that large numbers of tripod vessels were broken and deposited in the proceedings. The ritual deposit shows extensive evidence of post-depositional burning; in several cases, fragments of the same vessels excavated from different parts of the deposit were refitted and found to exhibit different degrees of fire-blackening, indicating intentional breakage of the vessels prior to the burning event.

Although the great majority of Cucul ceramic material is domestic or utilitarian, there are also finely decorated vessels of nonlocal production. These include fine paste types in the Altar Orange group (Pabellon Molded-carved and Tumba Black-on-orange) and the Tres Naciones Fine Gray group (Carmina Molded-carved). In and around the Acropolis, examples of these types were recovered from the ritual deposit at Str. L7-1 and the Restricted Patio, with a few sherds being found in the surface layers of the Northwest Courtyard. Neutron activation analysis suggests that their likely origin was in the upper Usumacinta region, at or near Yaxchilan (Ronald Bishop, personal communication, 2012).

The overall decrease in the consumption of ceramics with labor- and skill-intensive, decorative modes in the Cucul phase, especially the fine polychrome painting characteristic of the Caal phase, might be the result of changing tastes and demands of the consumers, the deliberate rejection of previous Classic ideas, or changes in the ways the elites allocated their resources. It might also signal the diminishing amounts of resources that could have been invested in the luxury ceramics to contrast with the previous abundance of high-end objects at elite courts.

LAS PALMITAS GROUP

Two fairly well-controlled ceramic depositional periods can be distinguished for Las Palmitas during the Terminal Classic period. The first corresponds to the construction of Str. M3-10 in the early ninth century AD; the second corresponds to the subsequent use of Las Palmitas as an elite residence, with domestic refuse piling up in middens behind Strs. M3-6 and M3-10 and off the southeastern corner of the main plaza. A third depositional period corresponds to the group's final occupation and, perhaps, to an occasional visit following abandonment. This material was recovered from humic and sub-humic layers and, with a few exceptions (discussed below), consists mainly of eroded sherds of little or no diagnostic value.

There is only one sealed archaeological context at Las Palmitas dating to the Cucul phase: the earth-and-rubble fill of the Terminal Classic remodeling of

Str. M3-10, together with the cist grave (El Zotz Burial 7) that was excavated in the Late Classic plaza floor just prior to the building's construction (see Carter et al., chapter 4, this volume). Only 30 ceramic objects were recovered from excavations at Str. M3-10, of which 25 could be classified. Three of them are complete vessels, included as offerings in the burial (figure 5.5). Of these, one is a barrel-shaped, polychrome vase of unnamed type, modally similar to vases found in the Acropolis, with modeled, applied bands on its exterior. The other two are a small Tinaja Red bowl and a Maquina Brown tripod plate with rattle feet (Carter and Gutiérrez Castillo 2011).

The Terminal Classic midden deposits (table 8.6) are not sealed and may include some Caal- and Chub-phase material. Nevertheless, their contents contrast with the securely dated Caal-phase ceramics from Las Palmitas. The late date of the Cucul midden deposits is confirmed by the diagnostic Terminal Classic imports and by several Paxcaman Red fragments, especially scroll- and hourglass-shaped supports. Yet these late types were found in the same contexts as orange polychromes, suggesting that the deposits do not, for the most part, date to much later than the early ninth century AD. In addition, the Paxcaman supports differ modally from Paxcaman Red supports recovered from fully Postclassic contexts in the South Group.

Ceramic assemblages recovered from the Terminal Classic middens at Las Palmitas constitute a significant proportion of the diagnostic Cucul material from this architectural complex. Cambio Unslipped and Encanto Striated are by far the most abundant type-varieties in the entire Las Palmitas collection (64.55 percent of the total) followed by Tinaja Red (24.20 percent), and other monochromes as well as Saxche-Palmar Orange Polychrome type (2.01 percent), (table 8.6). A handful of diagnostic Terminal Classic type-varieties— Altar Orange, Pabellon Molded-carved, Tres Naciones Gray, Sahcaba Molded-carved, and a number of other authentic and imitative fine-paste types—were also recovered. Thus, the imports at Las Palmitas come from the same regions as those from the Acropolis and constitute an ever-so-slightly larger proportion of Las Palmitas Cucul assemblage (0.65 percent) than of the Acropolis material (0.45 percent).

Out of the typed sherds from Las Palmitas collections, jar and closed-form sherds occur more than three times as often in the Cucul middens at Las Palmitas (78.21 percent) than in the presumed midden deposits used as construction fill at its foundation during the Caal phase. There are also about twice as many bowl fragments among the typed sherds of identifiably open form from the Cucul middens (102 of 624, 16.35 percent of typed open sherds) than there are among analogous sherds from the foundational deposits (10 of 97, or 10.31 percent). These patterns may highlight differences in depositional activities leading to the formation of Terminal Classic middens at Las Palmitas and Late Classic middens presumably at or near the Acropolis.

Among bowl rim fragments, Tinaja Red and Chinja Impressed predominate and appear in similar proportions to those recovered from the Northwest Courtyard (table 8.6). This signals a shift from the Chaquiste-dominated Caal phase to the Chinja-dominated Cucul phase (see above). The shift might correspond to demographic and/or cultural influence on El Zotz commoner population from sites to the east during the late eighth and ninth centuries AD, as opposed to the western orientation of the earlier Late Classic ceramic tradition.

South Group

Cucul-phase material recovered from the South Group reflects the types found across the site at this time (table 8.6). Foreign ceramics are much fewer in number: there are 14 fineware sherds from the Usumacinta region and a single Muna Slate ware sherd from the northern Yucatan Peninsula. However, 11 sherds produced in central Peten but imitating foreign techniques and styles are also present. These local and nonlocal sherds exhibit fine, elaborate decoration produced using incision, gouging/incision, molding/carving, and plano-relief (Trapiche Incised, Chicxulub Incised, Islas Gouged-incised, Pabellon Molded-carved, imitation of Provincia Plano-Relief).

The majority of the Cucul-phase ceramics, however, are less ornate and come from residential and other domestic contexts, like middens. These include Payaso Orange-brown, Daylight, and Patojo types. In addition, Cambio Unslipped and Encanto Striated types are abundant and extend through the Terminal Classic into the Early Postclassic period. Importantly, the ceramics from the South Group appear to signify the beginning of a new phase of occupation in the South Group that culminates during the Choc phase.

THE POSTCLASSIC PERIOD: CHOC PHASE

Choc-phase ceramics are found in the Acropolis, the Northwest Courtyard, and sectors close to the Acropolis, Las Palmitas, and the South Group. Materials outside of the South Group, however, are limited in number, totaling 600 sherds, while the South Group contains 10,607 sherds (table 8.8). The reason for this stark difference lies in the construction of a new extended household compound in the South Group (see Kingsley and Gámez, chapter

6, this volume). Unlike the mostly unsealed surface contexts of the other El Zotz complexes, the Choc phase in the South Group is found across 10 buildings and two large middens.

The Choc phase was identified through the presence of Augustine, Paxcaman, and Pozo types, as well as by the introduction of new decorative and functional forms including scroll supports and grinding bowls across the site of El Zotz. The more than 300-year Postclassic occupation of the South Group, as identified through several radiocarbon dates from the middens, shows interesting trends in the production of ceramics at this time. It appears that some of the traditional Late Classic–period ceramics, including Cambio, Encanto and Tinaja types, extend into the early part of the Early Postclassic.

In addition, the location of everyday ceramics and the lack of polychromes and other vessels with labor- and skill-intensive decorative techniques during the Choc phase illustrate domestic activities occurring in the midst of earlier monumental zones of the South Group. The presence of two reconstructed incense burners within these contexts might also suggest changes in ritual ideas and practices from earlier phases.

BEJUCAL

While the process of analyzing the ceramics from the site of Bejucal is still ongoing, it is possible to outline several characteristics based on the material classified so far, excavated from 2009 to 2011 (Garrison and Beltrán 2011; Garrison and Del Cid 2012; Garrison and Garrido López 2009b; Garrison et al. 2016). The majority of ceramics recovered to date were collected from looter tunnels and exhibit characteristics typical of the Saquij, Mo', and Caal phases at El Zotz.

Five complete ceramic vessels were recovered in 2010 from looter tunnel 2 in Str. S6-10 (Garrison and Beltrán 2011:295). Two of these are Aguila Orange bowls deposited as a cache in a lip-to-lip position beneath the floor level outside of a looted tomb (Bejucal Burial 2). The remaining complete vessels include a Sierra Red plate with a basal flange and a graffiti-style incised bird on its base, and two ceramic stands of Balanza Black and Lucha Incised types (Czapiewska 2011a). These vessels were broken, probably by the looters, and likely came from the cist tomb (Bejucal Burial 3) at the rear of the tunnel. The modal attributes of these objects are consistent with Uaxactun's Tzakol 1 and Tikal's Manik 1 phases, suggesting that Bejucal was occupied beginning no later than the start of the Early Classic period. Radiocarbon dates indicate

TABLE 8.8. Choc-phase ceramics from the South Group, the Acropolis, and Las Palmitas

Type: Variety	South Group	Acropolis	Las Palmitas
AUGUSTINE GROUP			
Augustine Incised	1		
Augustine Red	1270	198	72
Augustine Red: Cafesoto	124		
Hobomno Incised	42		
Hobomno Incised: Ramsey	2		
Pek Polychrome	19		
Johny Walker Red: Black Label	1		
Augustine Red: Maroon Slip	1		
CHILO GROUP			
Chilo Unslipped	29		
Gotas Composite	1		
FULANO GROUP			
Fulano Black	82		
Fulano Black Incised: Mottled	1		
Fulano Black: Mottled	26		
Menango Incised	6		
Sotano Red-on-paste	2		
PAXCAMAN GROUP			
Undetermined	2		
Ixpop Polychrome	27		
La Justa Composite	1		
Paxcaman Red	2075	20	39
Paxcaman Red: Cafesoto	107		
Paxcaman Red: Escalinata	94		
Picu Incised: Undetermined	1		
Picu Incised: Picu	10		
Picu Incised: Thub	83		
Picu Incised: Cafesoto	1		
Paxcaman Red: Cream Interior	1		
Saca Polychrome	7		
MACCHIATO GROUP			
Macchiato Brown	12		

continued on next page

TABLE 8.8—*continued*

Type: Variety	South Group	Acropolis	Las Palmitas
POSTCLASSIC ORANGE GROUP			
Unnamed	30		
POZO GROUP			
La Justa Composite	13		
Pozo Unslipped	6355	24	133
TOPOXTE GROUP			
Dulces Incised	1		
Topoxte Red	28		
TRAPECHE GROUP			
Picte Red-on-cream	1		
Trapeche Pink	150		
UNDETERMINED			
Red-orange Paste-Light Tan Slip	1		
Choc phase total	10607	242	244
% of group's ceramics	70.25%	0.66%	2.74%

that the first plaza floors were built in the Late Preclassic. The ceramic stands represent two out of only three such objects recovered by PAEZ, the third having been found in the royal tomb at El Diablo.

Excavations at Bejucal in 2011 (Garrison and Del Cid 2012) yielded greater amounts of material dating to the Mo' and Caal phases, including high-quality orange-and-cream polychromes. Unfortunately, the excavations of looter tunnels provided a heavily mixed assemblage, including material from the Early and Late Classic periods. Saxche-Palmar Orange and Zacatal Cream Polychromes are decorated with an array of designs, from simple geometric motifs to complex iconographic scenes. An Ik'-style vase sherd, imported during the Caal phase and recovered from a looter tunnel in Str. S6-1, portrays courtiers wearing elaborate headdresses. A complete Zacatal Cream Polychrome vessel was recovered from Bejucal Burial 5 (Garrison and Del Cid 2012:223). The decoration on this vessel, an abstract design reminiscent of jaguar spots, is consistent with polychrome designs found in Caal contexts at the El Zotz Acropolis and in Tikal Imix complex burials (Culbert 1993).

CONCLUSIONS

The small quantity of Preclassic (Che and Chub phase) sherds recovered at major architectural groups is evidence that, during their early history, there were few inhabitants in what would later be the civic-ceremonial cores of El Zotz. Populations constructed households in the South Group, the Acropolis, and perhaps even the elevated group of El Diablo. The monumental core of the south part of the South Group platform was constructed during the Preclassic period and might be evidence of the formation of a community at El Zotz that may or may not have interacted with the large valley center of El Palmar. Another phase of ceramics notably absent from the El Zotz assemblage is the Pop phase, equivalent to the Cimi phase at Tikal. The lack of these diagnostic ceramics from the Terminal Preclassic or "Protoclassic" phase and little monumental construction dating to the Che and Chub phases support the hypothesis that the first major constructions at El Zotz outside of the South Group date to the onset of the Early Classic period (ca. AD 300–350).

The Saquij-phase material at El Zotz reflects the beginnings of dynastic rule at the site, centered at El Diablo. Constructions at El Tejón and the Acropolis, while mainly associated with utilitarian pottery, also indicate elite activity by the presence of finely decorated ceramics and looted tomb chambers. The increasing accumulation of elite ceramics with labor- and skill-intensive decoration over the late Saquij phase at the Acropolis suggests the Early Classic elites used the central precinct on the valley floor alongside the hilltop locations of El Diablo and El Tejón.

Soon after the onset of the Mo' phase, or the Late Classic period, few major construction events took place at El Zotz. As a result, we have a limited quantity of ceramic material from this phase, often mixed with Saquij-phase diagnostics. Only a few examples suggest a gradual dissemination of Late Classic ceramic types and attributes in the Acropolis area of El Zotz and at El Diablo.

During the Caal phase, sherds in construction fill at the Acropolis of El Zotz and the newly constructed Las Palmitas complex attest to elite power and wealth by the abundance of high-quality vessels, polychromes with iconographic scenes and glyphic inscriptions, and imports. The large amounts of locally produced polychromes, which are also present in smaller amounts in the contexts of smaller household-related complexes—the South Group, La Tortuga, the Northwest Courtyard, the *aguada* residential group, and other residential compounds—highlights their intensified production and distribution at El Zotz during this period. The distribution of high-end pottery likely occurred across the same networks as the utilitarian pottery and, as a result, was accessible to the wider El Zotz community. The presence, albeit in small numbers, of iconographic and glyphic designs on vessels associated with small-scale architecture signals that the access even to the most valuable objects was never constrained. However, the high concentration of texts and the most complex iconographic designs at the Acropolis of El Zotz, on local and nonlocal objects, shows that the power to acquire significant quantities of the most valuable objects remained focused in the hands of the highest elites. It could also indicate the possible distinction, proposed by Ball (1993:259), between a "village-tradition" and a "palace-school" for painted polychrome vessels, in which the latter is characterized by considerable iconographic and epigraphic erudition.

The Cucul-phase ceramics show changes in activity patterns at each of El Zotz's architectural groups. The massive ceramic deposit at the Acropolis gives evidence of large-scale ritual activity, and differs in its content and taphonomy from the Late Classic assemblages found in that group. At the nearby Northwest Courtyard, the ceramic record shows a longer, domestic occupation through the Terminal Classic period. The proportions of vessel types at Las Palmitas may suggest other changes in depositional practices during the ninth century AD.

Las Palmitas did not accumulate the same amounts of "costly" ceramics as the Acropolis during the Caal phase; however, during Cucul phase there were proportionately more vessels with labor-intensive surface finish found at Las Palmitas (3.65 percent) than at the Acropolis and Northwest Courtyard (1.90 percent). These include polychromes from Saxche-Palmar and Zacatal groups, fine-paste ceramics and imitations of fine-paste vessels from Altar, Tres Naciones, and other related ceramic groups. It suggests the two architectural groups—Las Palmitas and the Acropolis—possibly differed in their socioeconomic status or the function of the precincts. The proportions of "costly" ceramics decreased significantly at the Acropolis between the Late and the Terminal Classic periods but remained at similar levels at Las Palmitas. The proportions of these high-value ceramic types at Las Palmitas was much lower than at the Acropolis during the Late Classic Caal period but higher during the Terminal Classic. Thus, it is highly likely that Las Palmitas housed an elite population separate to, and of lower status than, the royal court at the Acropolis of El Zotz and who, in the face of sociopolitical and cultural changes of the Terminal Classic, showed higher level of stability and resilience in maintaining their way of life than the royal courts. An example of a similar pattern was found at the site of Aguateca (Inomata 2003:56–60).

Diminished presence of labor-intensive decoration on Cucul ceramics in general could be the effect of changes in consumers' demands or a decrease in the economic resources necessary for the production of local luxury ceramics (most high-end pottery is of nonlocal origins) and their consumption. The diversity of ceramic types and varieties found at El Zotz is most prominent during the Terminal Classic period. The sociopolitical shifts in the region were accompanied by introduction of new ceramic types, changes to the prevailing aesthetic trends, experimentation with the production and decoration of vessels, and dissemination of new ceramic production techniques from other Maya regions. Thus, the crucial shifts of the Terminal Classic period affected not only the affairs of the ruling elites, but also the domestic, production-based economy of whole communities.

Changes in economic relations with other parts of the Maya world are also evident in the Cucul ceramic record. Imported finewares from the Usumacinta region and from Yucatan are present across all Cucul contexts, including the household middens of the South Group. The evident shift in local production from Chaquiste Impressed to Chinja Impressed basins may signal intensified economic and demographic contact with the Tikal region.

The Early Postclassic Choc phase is characterized at El Zotz by the virtual absence of high-end pottery characteristic of the Classic period. Occupation at this time can only be confirmed for households constructed in the South Group. At Las Palmitas, a few Paxcaman Red plates recovered from one midden may indicate a limited Early Postclassic occupation, or simply the end of Terminal Classic domestic activities. Evidence of the Choc phase at other complexes is limited to humic contexts, suggesting the cessation of occupation outside of the South Group. The production of fine ceramic objects also ceased, and the Postclassic residents at El Zotz focused primarily on domestic activities.

The evidence from Bejucal suggests a continuous and flourishing occupation at this hilltop site spanning from the Early to the Late Classic period, with Saquij, Mo', and Caal ceramics all recovered from the architectural fill of looted buildings. The architectural evidence suggests a change in function for the site: in the Late Preclassic period, Bejucal may have been a relatively publicly accessible ritual center without a permanent population. Beginning in the fourth century AD and continuing into the Late Classic period, it was transformed into a small regal-ritual center with increasingly restricted royal domestic spaces, likely serving as a royal country house for the El Zotz dynasty (Garrison et al. 2016). Substantial further excavation will be required to check and clarify these apparent changes using ceramic evidence. For the present, we can say little more than that the lack of Terminal Classic diagnostics suggests that Bejucal was abandoned by the end of the Caal phase, or at the beginning of the Cucul phase.

The analysis presented here provides some insight into the changing settlement patterns, ritual and hierarchical behavior, and economic activities of El Zotz's inhabitants, from the small-scale Preclassic occupation of the site to the rise and fall of the Pa'ka'n dynasty. Yet ongoing archaeological investigations of the site and analysis of artifacts continue to provide new information about the ancient people of the Buenavista Valley. As this work continues over the coming years, new evidence may clarify, or force the revision of, the foregoing interpretations.

9

Lithic Technologies and Economies at El Zotz

Zachary Hruby

DOI: 10.5876/9781607327646.c009

The economy of the El Zotz region, specifically the procurement, production and consumption of stone tools, is difficult to describe in broad strokes, due to its disjointed history and shifting centers of power. Although the tenuous political position of regional centers through time can be attributed to varying and various masters, many lithic traditions were relatively conservative over hundreds, if not thousands, of years. Local knappers also took part in many lithic traditions that spanned the entirety of the Lowlands, such as the production of celtiform bifaces used for chopping, pecking, and hammering (figure 9.1). However, it is unclear if the continuities in the production of celtiform bifaces justify the view that there was a single constant population serving different governmental bodies over the centuries (see below). In contrast, changes in the style and form of imported and local prestige goods made of stone are good markers of shifts in elite governance and alliance. Other contributors to this volume describe ceramic and architectural evidence of these social changes. Here I focus on the lithic artifacts that mark intersite warfare, transitional economic trade patterns, and everyday social practices. I first describe the morphology and distribution of chert and flint artifacts in the region and continue with a discussion of obsidian goods.

I put special emphasis on chipped-stone artifacts of chert (i.e., chert and its close relatives flint and

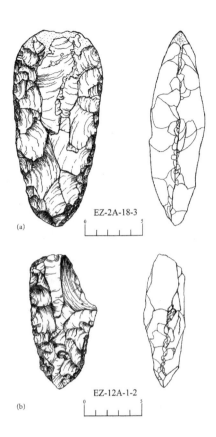

EZ-2A-18-3

(a)

EZ-12A-1-2

(b)

FIGURE 9.1. *Celtiform bifaces of (a) large and (b) medium size; scales in cm (drawings by Z. Hruby).*

chalcedony) and obsidian because they are ubiquitous in the region, either through natural formation or from cultural exchange. Chert formations are common in the Maya Lowlands, although more so in some areas. This distribution creates a patchwork of resource zones that were valuable to the ancient Maya, and to a certain extent guided settlement in the southern Maya Lowlands. As a basic cutting element, chert tools could work for almost any household or ceremonial purpose. Thus, obsidian can be characterized as a luxury item for most of the history of El Zotz, that is, until major stores of local chert and flint were depleted and technologies had shifted, making obsidian blades more available to all social strata. As Barrett (2011) has shown, chert is not an endlessly available resource, even in the chert-rich eastern Lowlands. As local resources became more limited over time, and smaller nodules were collected for use, elaborate means became necessary to bring more material into the polity, or to make lithic technologies more efficient or tool sizes smaller. All of these seem to have taken place in the region of El Zotz.

In summary, not all chipped-stone goods can be described as having the same value over time or even in the same space and time. The primary factors contributing to the value of chipped-stone goods include (1) access to raw materials, (2) skill and labor, and (3) religious belief or political imposition of religious ideologies on the role of craft goods and craft producers in society. At various points in ancient Maya history, these values fluctuated, but they can be partially reconstructed through study of the chipped-stone artifacts themselves. In most cases, El Zotz cannot be described as a major hub of obsidian procurement and distribution or of large-scale chert tool production, but the region nevertheless offers an excellent picture of how these industries change through time in medium-sized polities.

The data collected over a four-year period come from survey and excavations at the main sites investigated by the Proyecto Arqueológico El Zotz (PAEZ), including Bejucal, La Avispa, El Palmar, and primarily El Zotz, including the El Diablo and Las Palmitas Groups. Since this is a broad review of lithic traditions in the region, I focus on time period rather than site-specific analyses. Generally speaking, however, many of the sites and excavations are themselves rather time-specific in the sense that (1) much of the Preclassic material was recovered from the site of El Palmar, (2) Early Classic deposits were found mostly in the El Zotz Acropolis, El Diablo Group, and Bejucal, (3) Late and Terminal Classic artifacts came largely from the El Zotz center and the Las Palmitas Group, and (4) Postclassic habitation appears to have occurred around the South Group, Acropolis, and Northwest Courtyard of El Zotz. There is overlap in most contexts, of course, which is made clear by the many mixed ceramic assemblages found throughout the region (see Czapiewska-Halliday et al., chapter 8, this volume). To clarify matters I have left out most data derived from mixed lots, especially for chert artifacts, and focus on those deposits from a single period. These periods are very broad, however, and for most analyses include Middle Preclassic, Late Preclassic, Early Classic, Late Classic, Terminal Classic, and Postclassic periods. In some cases, where more specificity is granted by the ceramic chronology, I subdivide periods. I also use cases for comparison with other sites, such as El Perú-Waka' and Piedras Negras, where I have worked in the past. I target those sites because I collected information in similar ways. Tikal and Copan may be relevant, but there is less assurance of analytical consistency.

CHERT OVERVIEW

Some archaeologists contend that lithic reduction of chert tools took place primarily in the hinterlands, such as making stone axes for clearing land for planting (e.g., Fedick 1991; Fedick and Ford 1990; King 2000). Those objects were later imported to city centers. Although most of the excavations for this project were carried out in civic centers instead of rural contexts, it is clear that the production of all types of lithic goods took place in areas of denser settlement. In this respect, it resembled El Perú-Waka' and Piedras Negras (Escobedo and Houston 2001, 2002). Specialists likely produced utilitarian goods in centers and the periphery, and ad hoc tools were produced in most household groups. Yet I suggest that much finished work was done in city centers or their near-peripheries. One reason is that so much time and raw material were necessary to master the kinds of stoneworking that produced efficient and effective tools for intensive agricultural work, as well as artisanal activities. The reality is that one does not need fine or even well-constructed bifaces to carry out most agriculture, hunting, or defense. Sharpened hardwood staves as spears or planting sticks and modified cobbles of chert, or multidirectional flake cores used for producing cutting tools, could all have served in transforming wooded lands for less-intensive agriculture. It is possible that bifaces could also fall into the category of "quasi-prestige goods," or at least high-value trade goods, as did obsidian blades. They likely increased efficiency and required a high level of skill to produce.

With lithic goods, we should consider their role in bringing people together to build and use public works. Many stone axes and other bifaces, not to mention jade axes and adzes, were needed to cut and shape the limestone blocks that formed the literal foundation of ancestral legitimacy. To be built, temple groups and royal palaces required chert and jade, and, naturally, raw human labor. This circumstance brings up the issue of forced versus voluntary labor and social cohesion. Although it is clear that chert tools were produced at El Zotz and its hilltop Las Palmitas Group, as well as at El Palmar, there is little evidence of production activities at Bejucal and the El Diablo Group. Relatively few chert artifacts were found at Bejucal, El Diablo, and Las Palmitas, either because of sampling, hilltop discard patterns, or a real dearth of such stone. Larger samples were collected from El Zotz and El Palmar. The artifacts were classified according to size, weight, material, and technology, with special attention to production stage and technological type. The goals of this analysis were to understand the temporal and spatial distribution of biface and uniface tool types, and to identify possible loci of production at both early and late stages. For this study, data on use-wear and material color and quality

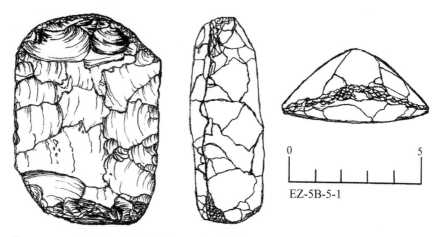

EZ-5B-5-1

FIGURE 9.2. *Thick laurel-leaf biface used as chisel or adze, but repurposed as a pecking or hammering stone; scale in cm (drawings by Z. Hruby).*

were not recorded in a systematic way, but they may prove useful in the future for understanding quarry use and tool use over time.

The most-common biface type in the El Zotz region is the thick celtiform biface of large and medium sizes (for a detailed description, see Hruby 2006; figures 9.1a,b). Commonly referred to as *oval bifaces*, these tools were most often hafted as axeheads and used in chopping activities. When these, and other large bifaces such as adzes were broken, they operated as hammerstones and pecking devices, probably for resurfacing manos and metates (figure 9.2). These exhausted forms usually take on an oval or circular outline. When a celt was broken in use or production, the Maya often resharpened or reworked the broken portion to rejuvenate the biface for further use. Two common flakes came from rejuvenating broken bifaces: alternate flakes from removal of the square edge of the broken end, and resharpening flakes, struck off the dull portion of the bit. The resharpening or retouch flakes were often poorly executed, suggesting that the specialists making the bifaces were not those who resharpened them (Hruby and Rich 2014). Thus, higher levels of axe-reworking flakes and broken bifaces may indicate a household or living area that was more consumer-centric than production-based.

The production debitage in this study consists of earlier- and later-stage production. Nodule-reduction flakes of a partially, mostly, and completely cortical nature were identified in the lithic sample. These types of debitage represent the earliest stages of nodule reduction, probably associated with

TABLE 9.1. Numbers of biface and biface-fragment projectile points found at El Zotz per time period[a]

Time Period	Non-Hunting/ Non-War	Hunting/War	Celt Fragments
Middle Preclassic	18	1	5
Late Preclassic	21	3	17
Early Classic	29	4	18
Late Classic	25	8	17
Terminal Classic	24	25	19
Postclassic	26	8	20

[a] All fragments were divided into hunting/war-related tools versus those unrelated to those functions. A third category represents bifaces and biface fragments from celts, as a subset of the non-hunting/ non-war-related bifaces.

the production of rough bifacial preforms and flake cores. After the preforms were produced, they were then refined into bifaces by the removal of what I term *early-*, *middle-*, and *late-stage biface reduction*, or, in some cases, *thinning flakes*. On the other hand, the flakes removed to produce thick celts are more accurately referred to as *biface-reduction flakes*, which feature a more complex platform, a dorsal surface with flake scars in multiple or opposite directions, and a highly curved ventral surface. The goal in such reduction was not to thin the axe but to maintain a durable, thick cross-section. Nevertheless, a lenticular cross-section likely was desirable for hafting purposes and to form a regular bit for predictable chopping. Consequently, the middle- and late-stage biface-reduction flakes feature more refined curvature, and more complex dorsal morphology and platforms. If the nodule was small, which they often were, then the biface-reduction flake may feature as much cortex as the nodule-reduction flakes.

Unlike Piedras Negras, thin laurel-leaf bifaces of all sizes are uncommon in the El Zotz region. Probable spear, hand spear, and *atl-atl* points used in hunting and warfare are better represented in the Classic period (table 9.1 and figure 9.3), and tend to be of the notched or stemmed varieties (figure 9.4). The biface-thinning flakes removed during the production of these bifaces tend to be made of relatively fine material. They are thinner, too, having an acute platform-to-dorsal surface angle. Projectile points and bifacial knives almost certainly existed for earlier time periods, but there is little evidence for them in our sample. Many of the projectile-point fragments recovered from likely Late Classic contexts may not have been produced at El Zotz. Only a few small bifaces of local material have been recovered, and the majority of

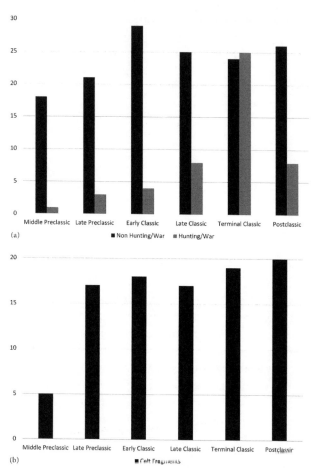

Figure 9.3. *Numbers of biface fragments: (a) hunting/war–related tools versus those unrelated to those functions, and (b) numbers of bifaces and biface fragments from celts, as a subset of the non-hunting/non-war–related bifaces (charts by Z. Hruby).*

them were made of fine brown flint. This material is quite common at El Perú-Waka' (Andrieu 2009, 2014; Barrett 1999, 2004, 2006; Hruby and Rich 2014; Moholy-Nagy 2002). The existence of nodule-reduction flakes and caches of biface-thinning flakes of this material suggest that it was locally available at El Perú-Waka' and then imported into the El Zotz region. The main problem with this interpretation is that the brown flint source has not been located in El Perú-Waka', but points have been identified at Tikal, further complicating

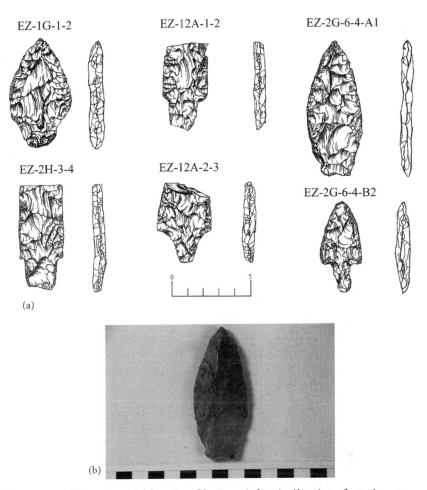

EZ-1G-1-2 EZ-12A-1-2 EZ-2G-6-4-A1

EZ-2H-3-4 EZ-12A-2-3

EZ-2G-6-4-B2

0 5

(a)

(b)

FIGURE 9.4. *Illustrations of (a) various Classic-period projectile points of tapering-stem, laurel-leaf, and straight-stemmed types, and (b) photograph of a broken example of the laurel-leaf type in fine brown flint; scales in cm (drawings and photographs by Z. Hruby).*

the picture. Instead of the laurel-leaf form, which is the typical form at Piedras Negras, the most common type of projectile at El Zotz is the stemmed biface or tapered-stem biface. Stemmed bifaces are also seem to be more common at Yaxchilan than at Piedras Negras, perhaps signifying similar lithic traditions. Pan-Maya biface comparisons are required to clarify these patterns. In contrast, thick laurel-leaf bifaces of small, medium, and large sizes were present in the El Zotz region (see Hruby 2006 for typology). These bifaces were used as chisels and awls, less commonly as pigment grinders. Only 10 of these tools were recovered from the El Zotz region.

As at most Maya sites, the common uniface is a discoidal or circular scraper. Yet some scrapers tend not to have a regular working edge, and biface- and nodule-reduction flakes were commonly transformed into scraping implements. Although there is one possible fragment of a celtiform uniface from the region, they clearly were infrequent tool forms. Uniface-reduction flakes can resemble biface-reduction flakes and flake core flakes, and are thus difficult to identify without a large sample of production debitage for comparison. Unifacial scrapers of various types were relatively frequent in the regional sample, constituting a considerable portion of total stone tools ($n \sim 36$, number based on confirmed and likely fragmentary examples)

The Preclassic Period

As shown in excavations by Doyle and Piedrasanta (chapter 2, this volume; Doyle 2013b), the quantity of chert materials in the regional Preclassic-period sites, and especially in the construction fill of monumental structures, surpasses that of other time periods. Table 9.2 shows that more chert debitage and nodule fragments were systematically and ritually integrated in the construction programs of the Preclassic than at any other period in the El Zotz region. There were, however, no data on the number of artifacts per cubic meter excavated. As a result, this pattern remains unconfirmed. Copious chert nodules and debitage have been noted in other Preclassic structures from Piedras Negras and San Bartolo (Hruby 2006; Kwoka 2014), which indicate that this is not an isolated pattern. Test pits around the El Palmar and La Avispa sites and their vicinities suggest that chert nodules appear intermittently in *bajo* (seasonal swamp) clay, even directly around the civic area of El Palmar. Further geological survey in the area by the author indicates that there is no one chert source or "outcrop." Even local creeks do not provide a reliable stream of chert nodules, and no chert quarry has been identified. These observations suggest that chert nodules at El Zotz came from social or trading networks, not from ease of local supply. High concentrations of chert in Preclassic fill could be interpreted as large-scale production, centralized control of resources, or systematic use of household refuse in construction fill for either practical or ceremonial reasons. All options likely played a role in how debitage came to be included in construction. As Garrison (2012) has noted, the earliest phases of El Zotz and El Palmar contain chert debitage in fill, hinting at a deeply entrenched local pattern.

TABLE 9.2. Debitage types and quantities per time period. Basic chert artifacts categories by count and weight (g) per time period.

Artifact Category	Middle Preclassic		Late Preclassic		Early Classic		Late Classic		Terminal Classic		Postclassic		Total Artifacts	
	Count	Weight	Count	Weight	Count	Weight	Count	Weight	Count	Weight	Count	Weight	Count	Weight
Biface Reduction Flake	256	2412.61	309	3,389.25	460	3,500.45	172	2,112.56	582	4,413.87	566	3,638.99	2,345	19,467.73
Biface/Fragment	28	2266.59	37	3,143.89	61	3948.3	46	2548.1	79	4,319.21	59	3,623.04	310	19,849.13
Flake Core	24	2552.59	54	4,331.5	42	5,302.48	17	1,011.58	11	2,617.05	36	2,854.78	184	18,669.98
Flake Core Flake	54	743.48	26	422.62	28	573.81	8	177.26	2	11.23	110	1,631.43	228	3,559.83
Nodule/Reduction Flake	434	10,570.48	463	14,343.35	515	21,839.52	102	3284.7	184	5,687.26	183	5,614.11	1,881	61,339.42
Production Flake	365	2,430.15	276	2,108.15	360	2,251.45	140	1,009.02	235	1,291.22	299	1,785.00	1,675	10,874.99
Uniface	5	457.29	14	673.71	23	1,663.61	12	724.44	3	114.06	7	823.56	64	4,456.67
Flake Tool	33	886.51	37	1,224.76	52	1,025.65	17	274.83	35	420.45	56	920.12	230	4,752.32
Hammerstone/Fragment	16	5,299.54	7	573.73	9	501.25	8	768.22	16	1,536.61	8	1,852.53	64	10,531.88
Unknown Flake	1,282	10,322.64	1,197	1,4707.73	1,982	15,463.21	416	5,199.86	737	4,605.15	1,306	8,648.58	6,920	58,947.17

The chert debitage and artifacts reflect central Peten patterns of production, with an emphasis on large- and medium-sized biface manufacture (Hruby 2006; Moholy-Nagy 2002). Small biface and macroblade technologies, well known in Belize and the eastern lowlands, are few and far between in the El Zotz region. Secure lithic markers of hunting and warfare are thus not in evidence, although weapons of the Preclassic period may have been of other materials, such as wood, shell, or teeth. But there are telling trends. A comparison between biface fragments of probable agricultural function, such as adzes and axes, and those lithics more suited to aggression hints at heightened warfare in the Late and Terminal Classic periods. The pattern may reflect a shift from organic types of projectile points to those made of stone, yet the overall trajectory is striking. The number of bifaces and biface fragments increases over time, except for a drop in projectile points during the Postclassic. There is also a sharp rise in projectile points from elite contexts during the Late and Terminal Classic (table 9.1 and figure 9.3a). Perhaps, as we shall see, the emphasis on agricultural bifaces in the Postclassic arose from scavenging in earlier deposits.

The majority of lithic items at El Palmar were in construction, usually in its largest structures. As table 9.2 and figure 9.5 indicate, the debitage was not primarily the result of late-stage biface manufacture. Instead, most spall and nodule deposits came from nodule testing, decortication, and early-stage biface-production flakes. Over time, biface debitage becomes more common, while early-stage nodule-reduction flakes decrease. As I have argued elsewhere (Hruby 2007), different kinds of production debitage may have involved metaphors for creation and destruction. Early-stage production debitage was at times cached with world-centering or creation caches. In contrast, building-termination and tomb-closure rituals were marked by the latest stages of production (Hruby and Rich 2014). If this pattern is valid, then the Preclassic debitage ties to creation and the making of temples, not their destruction. Different patterns characterize Late Classic tomb and palatial "decommissioning" at Piedras Negras, and El Perú-Waka' (Hruby and Rich 2014). Similar late-stage debitage was found outside the looted Early Classic tomb (El Zotz Burial 19) in Str. L8-13 (Thomas Garrison, personal communication, 2016).

The proposal that debitage in construction programs simply reflects waste disposal makes little sense, especially given the regional paucity of chert nodules. I also doubt that debitage was a mere byproduct of construction, tossed in after masons had finished their work with blocks of stone. The lack of late-stage biface reduction discounts that possibility, at least in Preclassic structures. In the future, it may be useful to investigate political and religious aspects of debitage deposition in buildings. One scenario is that, while tilling fields,

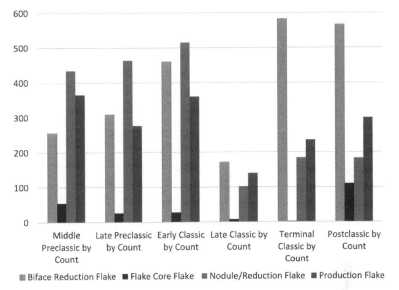

600

500

400

300

200

100

0

| | Middle Preclassic by Count | Late Preclassic by Count | Early Classic by Count | Late Classic by Count | Terminal Classic by Count | Postclassic by Count |

■ Biface Reduction Flake ■ Flake Core Flake ■ Nodule/Reduction Flake ■ Production Flake

FIGURE 9.5. *Basic chert artifact categories by count per time period (charts by Z. Hruby).*

local farmers brought nodules, viable or not, to their elite land owners. At command or on their own account, specialists then transformed that material into bifaces. In either case, the accumulation of raw materials in city centers suggests that nodules were procured, and that some of the initial production activities occurred on site. As table 9.2 and figure 9.5 suggest, this debitage followed a more varied pattern, one according with symbolic ideas about what lithic reduction meant, and for which part of its sequence.

THE CLASSIC PERIOD

After the rise of Early Classic sites, often founded on more defensible positions (see Román et al., chapter 3, this volume), there was a reconfiguration in how chert and obsidian artifacts were discarded, and possibly produced and exchanged. Excavations in Early Classic structures from the El Diablo Group and the El Zotz Acropolis, as well as limited excavations at Bejucal, reveal that debitage ceased to be a ritual or systematic aspect of construction at those sites. This is a puzzle. Early Classic elites had relatively equal access to chipped-stone goods as at other time periods, and there are vast amounts of ceramic artifacts in the fill of their buildings. Yet lithic goods appear to have been discarded or deposited in more discrete ways. El Diablo is a hilltop group, and lithic artifacts may have been thrown over the southern cliff, taken to some other area offsite, or dumped into undiscovered *chultunes* (subterranean cisterns or storage pits). There may also have been a shift in the symbolic use of lithics. During Preclassic times, large deposits of flakes, nodules, and core fragments were associated with apparent burning events and construction phases (Doyle 2013b). At El Palmar this tradition continued into the early years of the Early Classic. The later shift away from this pattern savors of changed meaning. For example, debitage became symbolically connected with burials in some parts of the Maya Lowlands, as well as more or less elaborate uses of lithic items in cache contexts. These are certainly attested in the Acropolis (Courtyard 2) at El Zotz (Meléndez and Houston 2008) and in the Str. M7-1 cache salvaged by Juan Pedro Laporte and his team (Laporte 2006; Ruíz Aguilar 2004).

In contrast to the lack of lithic artifacts on hilltop sites, higher numbers occur in the Preclassic to Early Classic lots at El Palmar and the Early Classic deposits from the El Zotz Acropolis and the South Group. It is unclear whether this pattern expresses continuity with Preclassic debitage or a use of earlier Preclassic fill. Lower-altitude sites appear to feature greater numbers of lithic artifacts in fill. In any case, the debitage in Classic construction derives from later-stage production activities and is not deposited in distinct lenses. The Early Classic sample of finished tools is small, but lithic analysis indicates that finished tools resemble those known for the Late Classic, with medium-sized celtiform bifaces and medium-sized projectile points with shouldered bases (figure 9.4). Also in evidence are fragments of obsidian bifaces from Central Mexico—these are *atl-atl* darts of Pachuca or Otumba obsidian chipped in transverse-parallel flaking style. Ratios of Mexican obsidian also become greater than anything seen in the Preclassic or Postclassic periods (table 9.3). Meanwhile, obsidian from the El Chayal source in Guatemala achieves a near-complete dominance.

The Late and Terminal Classic periods feature greater concentrations of chipped-stone goods in monumental architecture and much richer middens in elite and commoner contexts. However, they differ in significant ways. First, although large quantities of chert artifacts were recovered from construction fill in the palace at El Zotz, they consist more of late-stage biface-production flakes, sometimes burned, and probably associated with ritual termination of earlier structures. This pattern contrasts profoundly with the early-stage debitage in Preclassic structures. Across the site, there are fewer pieces of early-stage debitage, which could indicate that nodule size decreases over time, or that knappers in the city center acquired roughly prepared or decorticated nodules from elsewhere.

TABLE 9.3. Obsidian sources by count and weight (g) per time period, including confirmed source designation and probable source designation.

Source	Middle Preclassic	Late Preclassic	Early Classic	Late Classic	Terminal Classic	Early Postclassic	Middle Postclassic	Unknown Time Period	Total Count and Weight
UNKNOWN									
count		3				1			
weight		7.43				1			
EL CHAYAL									
count	1	57	92	107	141	115	8	95	
weight	0.97	41.11	69.98	38.6	121.55	280.4	6.7	97.5	
PROBABLE EL CHAYAL									
count		8	23	2	7	12	2	9	
weight		8.8	26.08	1.65	7.63	13.22	3.3	11.87	
IXTEPEQUE									
count		1	1	3	3	212	16	5	
weight		1.45	0.6	2.98	3.2	228.53	22.9	2.45	
PROBABLE IXTEPEQUE									
count						15	2	1	
weight						8.14	0.9	0.67	
SAN MARTIN JILOTEPEQUE									
count		11	18	6	2	7		2	
weight		12.98	11.12	6.97	1.94	7.1		1.18	
PROBABLE SAN MARTIN JILOTEPEQUE									
count		5	22		4	6	1	2	
weight		5.01	28.76		1.91	8.72	1.3	1.44	
PACHUCA									
count			5			7		2	
weight			3.37			3.68		2.07	
UCAREO									
count			2	1	1	1		2	
weight			0.81	0.05	0.7	0.8		2.66	

continued on next page

TABLE 9.3—*continued*

Source	Middle Preclassic	Late Preclassic	Early Classic	Late Classic	Terminal Classic	Early Postclassic	Middle Postclassic	Unknown Time Period	Total Count and Weight
OTUMBA									
count				5		2		2	
weight				16.18		4.8		2.36	
ZARAGOZA									
count								1	
weight								0.1	
Total	1	85	163	124	158	378	29	121	1,059
Total Weight	0.97	76.78	140.72	66.43	136.93	556.39	35.1	122.3	1,135.62

The Late Classic also witnesses the introduction of finely flaked caramel-to-brown-colored flint that occurs at other sites across the Maya area. Given the fine, opal-rich nature of this material, I argue that it is a true flint, formed in chalk beds, and deserves special attention. Lithic technologists often refer to this material simply as "fine brown," and it may be the raw material used in the famous eccentrics of Copan as well as the high-quality projectile points discussed here. Since no local source of this fine material is known for the El Zotz region, and few production flakes, it is highly likely that finished lithics were made elsewhere and traded into El Zotz as prestige goods. Since these types of points and production flakes abound at Tikal and El Perú-Waka', it is unclear whether the actual geologic source is to the east or west of El Zotz, or whether it came from multiple sources. Finally, chert and obsidian caches of the Tikal type (Moholy-Nagy 2008) grow in number toward the end of the Early Classic and into the Late Classic, probably associated with the Tikal-style architecture that begins to materialize at El Zotz.

THE POSTCLASSIC PERIOD

With the collapse of large-scale centralized authority at the end of the Classic period (see Newman et al., chapter 5, this volume), there is a massive shift in trade patterns, technology, and style in stone tools. Chert-tool production in general departs from earlier biface traditions. Given the burned, distorted, and often inconsistent nature of Postclassic chert deposits, it is difficult to reconstruct what the Postclassic chipped-stone traditions actually were. It seems evident, however, that there was a disconnection between earlier production systems and what took their place in the Early Postclassic (see Kingsley and Gámez, chapter 6, this volume). Apparently, a combination of scavenging earlier artifacts and a new "minimalist" approach to chert-tool production took place. The predominant form of chipped-stone production manipulated multidirectional flake cores; small points came into existence, too, probably with bow-and-arrow technology (figure 9.6). These small points could also have been used in lightweight *atl-atl* or throwing spears. In either case, the systematic reduction of chert nodules for the production of large- and medium-sized bifaces almost certainly decreased. One problem with determining changes in lithic technology during a rather long Postclassic period is that it is difficult to detect differences in ceramic style over time (Kingsley 2014). The South Group in particular was rich with Postclassic deposits, as has been discussed in detail by Kingsley (2014). However, the obsidian information from this zone revealed much more than chert about culture change (see below).

Chert Discussion and General Temporal Trends

There are nodule-reduction and biface-reduction flakes present throughout the El Zotz region. The frequencies varied, however. In this section I discuss changes in the average sizes and weights of lithic artifacts over time and the implications of these patterns for understanding regional technology and economy. First, I examine the size of biface-reduction flakes over time. This measure reflects the general size of biface being produced, but also of the size of the nodule being reduced. Since lithic technology is subtractive, and not additive like ceramics, knappers can only remove or create flakes smaller than the original blank or nodule. This means that large biface flakes must come from large bifaces and nodules. The lack of large nodules in the region is thus a harbinger for relatively small tools and eccentric flints.

Table 9.4 shows the average weight per biface-reduction flake in unmixed lots. Aside from length and thickness, weight is the most consistent aspect of flake size. Figure 9.7a shows the clearest pattern of flake size over time and suggests that flake size decreases at a constant rate over roughly 2,000 years. Although there is a heightened focus on smaller projectile points (see above), a type associated with hunting or warfare, I argue that the overall trend reflects a reliance on smaller, less-desirable nodules over time. This argument is bolstered by the fact that most projectile points were probably made elsewhere

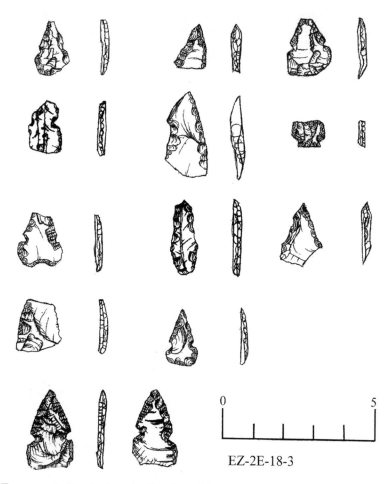

EZ-2E-18-3

FIGURE 9.6. *Postclassic projectile points of chert and obsidian; scale in cm (drawings by Z. Hruby).*

and imported to the site in finished form. In short, this steady decline can be attributed to gradual resource exhaustion. One consequence might have been more complex systems of intersite exchange, as well as multiple sources and trading partners. The decrease in access to viable chert nodules coincides with a striking increase in obsidian cores and blades during the Postclassic period (see below).

According to counts and weights of nodule fragments and nodule-reduction flakes (i.e., the remnants of early-stage tool production), the combined Middle and Late Preclassic artifacts dwarf those of later periods. For the purpose of illustration, lumping all time periods into Preclassic, Classic, and Postclassic periods, a similar pattern arises (table 9.5). Although subtler, a comparison of mixed lots shows a similar pattern of decreased weight-per-artifact percentage, while those artifacts from non-mixed lots shows a more dramatic decrease. These tables confirm that all artifacts become smaller over time, mirroring the resource exhaustion detected among bifaces. The metrics for early-stage reduction evidence indicate that the El Zotz region was exhausting its raw materials over time. These observations were made from a total of 14,909 artifacts in mixed lots (with a total mass of 244.776 kg), and 9,087 artifacts from unmixed lots (with a total mass of 155.406 kg). This sum is unimpressive compared to massive workshops of the eastern Lowlands, but it is quite large compared to the western Peten. Whether these quantities of flakes and other debitage result from access to raw materials or shifting traditions of local waste management remains to be seen.

Separating the basic period designations discloses more diversity. Average biface and biface-fragment sizes decline over time (figure 9.7b), except for a marked increase in the Postclassic period. Whether this spike relates to the scavenging and reuse of bifaces from earlier times is unconfirmed, since very few undamaged and preform specimens were recovered from Postclassic deposits. If, on the other hand, the increase in Postclassic celtiform axe fragments reflects heightened production and not reuse, it follows a more general upward trend from the Preclassic to the Postclassic (table 9.1). This pattern might indicate heightened reliance on stone tools for agricultural purposes. Much depends on the hypothesis of scavenging and reuse.

A study of completely cortical, mostly cortical, and partially cortical nodule-reduction flakes reveals a similar pattern. This may point to the importation of workable blanks from outside the area or the previously discussed case of nodule size decreasing with overexploitation. Table 9.5 shows the variability over time in the size of these types of flakes, but with a general trend of diminished size over time. Completely cortical flakes are relatively static over time, but the average size of mostly cortical and partially cortical flakes may decrease. These data reflect the general trend of resource exhaustion, as was apparently the case in Barrett's study (2006, 2011). Nonetheless, the variation between time periods has yet to be explained.

Small bifaces are less frequent than large bifaces, but they are most common in the Late and Terminal Classic find from the Acropolis (see Carter et al., chapter 4, this volume). The majority of these bifaces consist of fine brown flint, possibly imported from the El Perú-Waka' region. Since there

TABLE 9.4. Average weight (g) per biface-reduction flake and flake core flakes from unmixed lots, as well as a comparison of bifaces and biface fragments to flake cores.

	Middle Preclassic	Late Preclassic	Early Classic	Late Classic	Terminal Classic	Postclassic
Biface-reduction flake	11.86	10.96	9.81	10.11	8.04	6.51
Flake core flake	28.37	16.29	32.41	18.22	3.42	14.50
Biface/fragment	73.87	90.89	72.96	59.88	53.54	66.79
Flake core	101.97	82.29	150.13	57.26	70.78	70.03

TABLE 9.5. Frequency of completely, mostly, and partially cortical nodule reduction flakes, and nodules by count and weight per time period.

	Middle Preclassic			Late Preclassic			Early Classic			Late Classic			Terminal Classic			Postclassic		
	Count	Weight	Average Weight	Count	Weight	Average Weight	Count	Weight	Average Weight	Count	Weight	Average Weight	Count	Weight	Average Weight	Count	Weight	Average Weight
Completely Cortical	37	750	20.27	66	1,443.64	21.87	15	271.08	18.07	8	173.58	21.70	7	95.07	13.58	18	306.75	17.04
Mostly Cortical	140	3554.77	25.39	138	4,111.45	29.79	36	1,008.45	28.01	21	478.76	22.80	45	1,010.12	22.45	46	894.28	19.44
Partially Cortical	101	2063.89	20.43	143	3,043.67	21.28	62	1,477.95	23.84	45	748.28	16.63	90	1,160.16	12.89	62	1,044.49	16.85
Nodule/Fragment	61	3542.21	58.07	56	4,603.48	82.21	59	5,805.52	98.40	3	430.00	143.33	8	2,973.58	371.70	6	2,029.50	338.25
Total	**339**	**9910.87**		**403**	**13,202.24**		**172**	**8,563**		**77**	**1,830.62**		**150**	**5,238.93**		**132**	**4,275.02**	

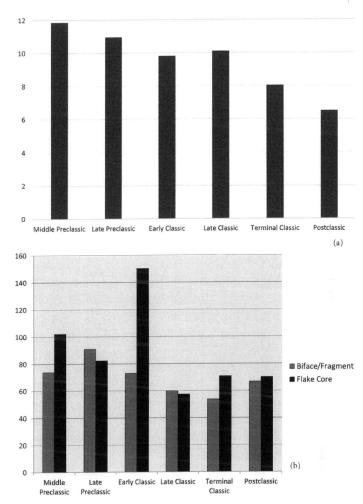

FIGURE 9.7. *(a) Decrease in average weight (g) of biface-reduction flakes over time; (b) average weight (g) per biface and flake core fragments per time period (charts by Z. Hruby).*

are very few biface-thinning flakes and pressure flakes of this material at El Zotz, except for a small deposit in one lot in the Acropolis (EZ 2A-18-3; Pérez Robles et al. 2009:22), the small, fine, usually stemmed, bifaces were probably imported as finished products. The elite context of their recovery intimates that they involved high prestige.

OBSIDIAN OVERVIEW

Like Rice (1987a) and other investigators, I argue that obsidian was a prestige good in some respects up until the Terminal and Early Postclassic periods. Large obsidian nodules became more scarce at most geologic obsidian sources, with implications for core size, which diminished (Braswell 1996; Suyuc-Ley 2011). During the Terminal and Early Postclassic, obsidian was always a restricted resource in the Maya Lowlands, excepting outlier sites in eastern Guatemala and the Baja Verapaz, such as Cancuén and Quirigua. Leading to this restriction was, among other factors, "bottlenecking," the attempted control of riverine, maritime, and terrestrial trade routes during periods of demand and political turmoil, along with the effects of intensive warfare between polities (Golden et al. 2012). There is no direct evidence for the control of an entire obsidian resource zone, only those that chose to control down-the-line trade for more restricted distribution. The other primary factor was the intended control of obsidian blade production within the polities themselves (Hruby 2006, 2007). The Lowland Maya often favored more difficult types of blade production. They drew on relatively low numbers of cores and the expertise of a specialists living in or associated with elite households. My suspicion is that those specialists were highly expert in producing blades. Nevertheless, there exist different blade-core reduction techniques in the Maya Lowlands that reflect regional traditions and access to raw materials.

During Preclassic and Classic times the core platform was modified by lateral and complete platform rejuvenation. This method put all hope of fixing and preparing cores in the lap of the blade maker. While lateral rejuvenation was favored in the Preclassic and Early Classic periods, distal modification appears to have been preferred by the Late Classic Maya. Errors in blade removal were dealt with in distinct ways. There were hinge terminations on the face of the blade core that were either removed by lateral rejuvenation (described by Clark 1997) or from the distal end (described in detail by Hruby 2006). In general, the lateral rejuvenation technique is a marker of the Preclassic and Early Classic periods, while those of the Late Classic relied more on distal rejuvenation and more efficient ways of removing errors from the face of the core. However, there are regional differences in how blade cores were reduced during the Late Classic. These Classic techniques contrast starkly with the pecked-and-ground platforms of the Postclassic, in which many individuals likely handled and prepared cores for blade removal. All modifications could have been done by a single person for the unprepared Preclassic and Classic cores.

The production evidence for obsidian materials in the study area is almost exclusively derived from the reduction of prismatic blade cores. At Piedras Negras and El Perú-Waka', many of the cores were often reduced on one side, which leaves an oval or lenticular cross-section on the exhausted core (Hruby 2006, 2007; Hruby and Rich 2014). This style of core reduction requires a greater degree of distal modification and rejuvenation. Neither is abundantly clear at El Zotz. The "flat core" style of reduction could also indicate that, in general, Piedras Negras received poorer-quality cores that were resistant to reduction. Even and predictable preparation of the macrocore allowed blades to be struck from all sides. The platform angle, if greater than 90 degrees, would not allow for that removal. Although extant cores from the El Zotz region often retained a facet of percussion scarring, the fact that there was an attempt to reduce them in the round suggests a different approach to blade production. This approach recalls Late Classic techniques at Holmul (Hruby et al. 2007) and Quirigua in the eastern Lowlands.

The blade production techniques of the Classic and Preclassic periods were difficult. To a certain extent, they relied on the skills and expertise of one or relatively few individuals. As a whole, these techniques were efficient in the sense that they removed less mass per blade than in the Postclassic. Yet they also required more detailed knowledge of blade detachment. Technological and social changes during the Maya Collapse allowed for a different approach to blade making. The pattern of diminished efficiency in terms of time, rather than wastefulness, ceased with the disintegration of centralized control in the major southern Lowland polities. Blade restriction dropped too. The break in centralized political control led to a breakdown in the domination of obsidian sources and trade routes. This allowed previously inaccessible types of materials and blade-cores to flow into new areas.

Technological evidence of the break consists of more accessible blade-making techniques. These may have required more hours of preparation but less knowledge of esoteric production. Pecked-and-ground platforms made blade making easier for the novice, and the influx of formerly restricted blade cores allowed for households of more varied statuses to produce larger quantities of blades for everyday and specialized uses (Healan 2004, 2006; Rice 1987a). The new platforms did not represent a great discovery, spurred by a need for increased efficiency, but a breakdown of what Inomata (2001) has called "involution" or involutionary ideologies. Earlier production may have been tied to religious ideology and political economy. In the Postclassic, commoners could freely make blades but in a less efficient manner.

Obsidian Sources

The sources in the obsidian sample are quite varied and required visual and chemical testing to substantiate sourcing. Twenty-three artifacts were tested at the X-ray Florescence Spectometry Laboratory in a process outlined by Steven Shackley (2011, 2012). The sample was chosen according to visual characteristics of color and texture. Nine pieces were predicted to come from the El Chayal source, seven pieces from San Martin Jilotepeque, two artifacts from Ixtepeque, three from Otumba, and one each from the Pachuca and Zaragoza sources. After testing by Shackley, two of the Ixtepeque artifacts were shown to be misidentified as El Chayal, yielding an overall accuracy for visual sourcing at roughly 91 percent. These differences were accounted for and hopefully led to more accurate visual sourcing for the remainder of the sample.

Chemical sourcing will be discussed in another publication, especially in comparison to that carried out at other Lowland sites. Nevertheless, preliminary results indicate that the primary sources at El Zotz are typical of Guatemala, heavily reliant on El Chayal in the Guatemala highlands. The role of El Chayal in the Lowlands remains a mystery, but Kaminaljuyu may have played a role in its distribution (Suyuc-Ley 2011). El Chayal obsidian is dominant except for Postclassic deposits in the South Group. There, Ixtepeque abounds by count and weight (table 9.3 and figure 9.8). San Martin Jilotepeque is the third-most common source in the sample, the majority of which came from the El Palmar site. It is a reliable temporal marker for the Preclassic.

The Postclassic shift to Ixtepeque corresponds to a rise in the weight and thickness of blades (table 9.6 and figure 9.9). The shift to household contexts and more wasteful means of producing blades indicates that there was a change in obsidian trade after the Collapse. There is also a higher number of pecked-and-ground platforms from this period, a notable feature of Postclassic obsidian technology (Healan 2004, 2009). The probable increase in Ixtepeque obsidian in the Terminal Classic and its dominance in the Postclassic accompanies the decline of the Copan polity. That kingdom may have been controlling or perhaps hoarding Ixtepeque obsidian in the southeastern periphery. The wider varieties of obsidian in the Postclassic may also arise from a lack of centralized control or attempted control over obsidian sources. However, the El Chayal source retains its significance in the Postclassic (~19 percent of the El Zotz sample). This confirms that, for the Maya, the source was by far the most important, both in terms of large-scale production and distribution. Only in the Preclassic did it seem less popular.

Mexican obsidian is relatively infrequent in the study area, with only a few fragments and possible bifaces. Pachuca is the most common Mexican source,

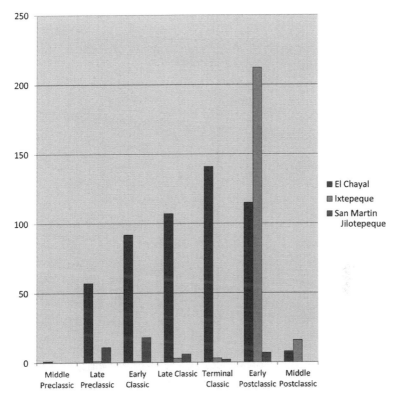

FIGURE 9.8. *Artifact counts of the three most-common Guatemala obsidian sources (El Chayal, San Martin Jilotepeque, and Ixtepeque), based on confirmed source designation (chart by Z. Hruby).*

with Ucareo, Zaragoza, and Otumba obsidian occurring in roughly equal quantities. Obsidian bifaces of both Pachuca and Otumba were found in excavations. Mexican obsidian is relatively rare in the region, but features some notable temporal properties. It was first identified in the Early Classic, which boasts most of the Pachuca green obsidian discovered thus far. Smatterings of Ucareo and Zaragoza appear in the Classic period, but never to the extent attested at Tikal.

CONCLUSIONS

The existence of large celt bifaces in all time periods implies that there is continuity in local chert traditions. Celtiform bifaces were a mainstay of most

TABLE 9.6. Obsidian third-series blade weight (g) and thickness (cm) size per time period and area.

Time Period	Total Count	Total Weight	Average Thickness	Average Weight
Middle Preclassic	N/A	N/A	N/A	N/A
Late Preclassic	36	38.80	0.24	1.08
Early Classic	70	73.20	0.23	1.05
Late Classic	29	32.30	0.24	1.11
Terminal Classic	68	71.35	0.24	1.05
Early Postclassic	280	324.33	0.25	1.16
Middle Postclassic	23	27.25	0.26	1.18
Unknown	89	98.80	0.25	1.11

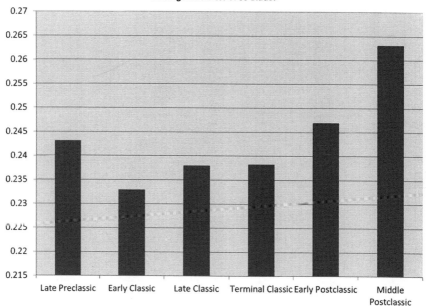

FIGURE 9.9. *Increase of third-series obsidian blade thickness (cm) over time (charts by Z. Hruby).*

Lowland sites, however, and may not make a solid marker of political or social identity in the central Peten. In style and source, celt axes from Yaxchilan differ from those at Piedras Negras or Colha. Such variability does not appear in much of the central Peten, including El Zotz. In other words, celtiform bifaces do not work well as indicators of population changes or replacements. The average size of celts may shift, larger examples occurring earlier, smaller ones later. But the change does not characterize all parts of the Lowlands. Variability is likely from an inconsistent distribution of nodules and nodule sizes in different geologic zones. Resource exhaustion doubtless played a role, too. Indeed, such depletion appears to be at least one of the causes for diminishing sizes of celts in the El Zotz region.

There is little evidence for chert-tool production. What does exist is systematic production of preforms with finished tools varying from area to area. El Palmar was likely producing large-biface preforms and some finished bifaces, yet preform production at El Zotz is weakly attested. So far, large-biface production or finishing seems concentrated around the Acropolis. At present, there is no information about where chert nodules were reduced during the Late and Terminal Classic periods. Houston (personal communication, 2010) has suggested that nodules may have been collected in the hinterland and offered as tribute to El Zotz. It is also possible that rough decortication took place in the hinterland and preforms were offered to the center. Perhaps subsidiary centers were responsible for initial biface production.

Political and economic changes can be best understood through the lens of imported goods. Imported flints, probably originating around the El Perú-Waka' region, Tikal, or points north, seem more frequent in the Late Classic. In the Preclassic and Early Classic periods, there are few small projectile points compared to later times. This can be explained by the use of alternative materials for weaponry, the lower frequency of warfare, variable deposition, or a combination of these. The two known eccentric obsidian and chert caches from the Late Classic greatly resemble those at Tikal. However, if the contact were continuous or closer, one would expect more caches of eccentrics at El Zotz. Terminal Classic deposits are marked by the introduction of small projectile points likely used in local warfare, but imported from far afield. A source for the fine brown flint of this time is needed to discern a strong economic connection with El Perú-Waka'. As for Postclassic deposits, they do not reveal a coherent approach to the production of lithic tools. For daily needs, scavenging may have been the norm. There, bifaces were not produced at any significant scale and local populations seemingly relied on silicified limestone, as well as the reworking of old bifaces and the reduction of multidirectional flake cores.

Obsidian-blade production was focused in the El Zotz region. Our data indicate that blade-core reduction occurred primarily in the Acropolis at El Zotz in the Late Classic and at El Palmar in the Preclassic. Blade production in the Postclassic uncovers one of the most significant and obvious changes in the history of the region, technological shifts that also occur throughout most of Mesoamerica. Increased weight per blade, and perhaps higher frequency of blades in the Postclassic, demonstrates a shift in the way obsidian was perceived and used. With a decline in chert resources, local households may have relied to a greater extent on obsidian as a daily tool for cutting. The obsidian sources represented in the PAEZ sample vary through time, but most follow general patterns for the central Peten. El Chayal is the most common source for most time periods, with Ixtepeque obsidian growing in frequency during the Postclassic period. The future of obsidian studies in the Maya Lowlands must rely on more refined analyses, especially considering material, morphological, and technical traits.

In general, if Tikal was indeed an obsidian hub with greater access to blade cores, then the low numbers of obsidian artifacts at El Zotz would reflect a detachment from that city. El Zotz does not seem to have benefited from the vast quantities of obsidians imported to, and perhaps produced at, its neighbor (Moholy-Nagy 2002). The lack of well-defined lithic traditions at El Zotz points to possible shifts in populations, or more likely, multiple influences from outside forces. There is a long and conservative eccentric-flint and obsidian tradition at Piedras Negras and Tikal. No such tradition occurs at El Zotz—rather, only apparent infrequent dabbling in this type of ceremony. Yet the region was hardly in glorious isolation. El Zotz took part in a range of economic and technological exchanges with other centers over time, two of which must have been Tikal and El Perú-Waka'. It is in its regional setting that El Zotz operates most clearly as a center of lithic conservatism and innovation.

10

Ceramic figurines and figurine-whistles, numbering just over 200, represent a fairly limited artifact class at the site of El Zotz. Albeit small, this collection nonetheless exhibits remarkable diversity in its iconographic representation as well as notable consistency in its manufacture and deposition. With the vast majority of fragments coming from domestic contexts, the study of these figurines complements ongoing research in the site's monumental and civic-ceremonial sectors, providing insights into the lives of the ancient city's residents. This chapter assesses the El Zotz figurine collection recovered during the 2008–2011 field seasons.[1] This is done on three levels. First, an in-depth analysis of the style and iconography of these figurines is provided. Second, the chapter assesses the spatiotemporal contexts from which these figurines were excavated. Finally, it explores in detail aspects of the manufacture and use of these figurines. Because of the fragmentary nature of the collection, this chapter relies on comparisons with other sites in the Maya Lowlands whose collections provide comparable material.

STYLE AND ICONOGRAPHY

The iconography of Maya figurines and figurine-whistles, which has attracted scholarly attention for decades, continues to be a common focus for more recent studies of figurines (e.g., Butler 1935; Halperin 2004; 2007:148–258; Hendon 2003:30–32; Ivic de Monterroso

A Tableau in Clay

Figurines and Figurine-Whistles of El Zotz

Alyce de Carteret
and Jose Luis Garrido

DOI: 10.5876/9781607327646.c010

2002; Joyce 1933; Laporte 2009; Rands and Rands 1965; Robertson 1985; Triadan 2007:275–295; Valdés et al. 2001:656–662; Willey 1972:7–76). Together, these studies have created an extensive corpus, spanning numerous Classic-period sites across the Maya Lowlands, against which the fragmentary El Zotz collection can be compared. Of the 202 figurine and figurine-whistle fragments, only 11 are complete or partially complete, while many (n = 68) are either too small or too eroded to be identified. Nevertheless, the majority (n = 134) can at least be classified as either anthropomorphic or zoomorphic (table 10.1). In a departure from other figurine studies (e.g., Triadan 2014:12), there is no separate category at El Zotz for supernatural figurines. The reasoning for this is twofold: many pieces are too fragmentary to be able to distinguish between a human and a divine personage with any reliability, and many anthropomorphic personages in figurine collections may in fact be deities rather than elite courtiers, the designation often given to them (Stephen Houston, personal communication, 2016). Thus, for the purposes of this chapter, figurines have been classified as either anthropomorphic or zoomorphic in representation, leaving aside the question of the divine nature of some of the anthropomorphic (and likely some of the zoomorphic) personages.

Anthropomorphic Figurines

Three-quarters of the identifiable figurine fragments are anthropomorphic (n = 102, see table 10.2). These fall into one of two categories: either they are modeled in realistic proportions with elegant, if unexpressive, visages, or they take on a more grotesque appearance. This latter category (n = 6), limited to head fragments, corresponds exclusively with representations of dwarfs, discussed below. The former represents an aesthetic category first defined by Mary Butler (1935:641) as *Style X*, noted for its "realistic, finely executed rendering in the round of the human body." This style is most prevalent during the Late and Terminal Classic periods, with evidence for its continued popularity in the Early Postclassic period; it can also be noted in the southern Maya Lowlands and throughout the Yucatan Peninsula (Butler 1935:644). This same aesthetic tradition has been observed by other scholars working with Late Classic collections at Aguateca (Triadan 2007:273; 2014:9), Motul de San José (Halperin 2007:150), Piedras Negras (Ivic de Monterroso 2000:244), Copan (Hendon 2003:30), and Tikal (Laporte 2009:1022). The figurines of El Zotz, dating primarily to the Late and Terminal Classic periods (see below), fit squarely within these regional patterns. At El Zotz, all non-dwarf head fragments (n = 33) fall into this aesthetic category. None of the anthropomorphic body fragments (n =

TABLE 10.1. El Zotz figurine categories.

Category	Figurines (n)
Anthropomorphic	102
Zoomorphic	32
Indeterminate	68
Total	**202**

TABLE 10.2. Anthropomorphic figurines.

Part of Figurine	Count (n)	Class of Figurine	Count (n)
Head	40	Male	18
Body	50	Female	13
Body Ornament	12	Dwarf	6
		Indeterminate	65
Total	**102**	**Total**	**102**

50) exhibit the grotesque proportions characteristic of dwarf figurines, so presumably these can also be classified as part of the Style X tradition. Fragments of body ornamentation, usually consisting of headdresses, earspools, and other headgear, comprise 12 percent of the anthropomorphic sample (*n* = 12). Dwarfs can be depicted wearing the same headdresses as other non-dwarf anthropomorphic figurines (Halperin 2007:196). As a result, fragments of bodily adornment cannot be assigned with confidence to either category.

Although anthropomorphic heads in this style at other sites can represent individuals at numerous stages in life (e.g., Copan, Hendon 2003:30–31), the figurines of El Zotz, as at Aguateca (Triadan 2007:286), primarily depict individuals at the prime of adulthood. Only two examples in the collection represent people of advanced age. A head fragment recovered from a midden in a residential group west of the Five Temples Group could depict an elderly woman (figure 10.1a). A number of features can be distinguished—a veil that covers her head, neck, and part of her shoulders, as well as a necklace of circular beads—though most significant are her sagging jowls and puffy eyes. Once the figurine was fired, a hole was drilled through its head, a feature that would have allowed the item to be suspended. Otherwise, the head fragment is solid.

The other fragment, excavated from a Terminal Classic deposit in the Acropolis's Restricted Patio, pertains to an aged male individual (figure 10.1b). Although the piece is fairly eroded, a number of distinctive features are visible.

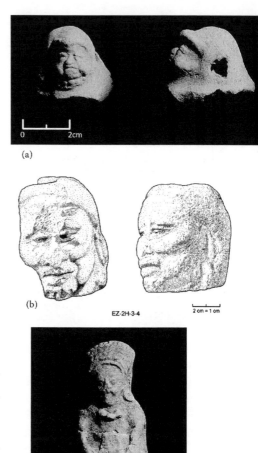

(a)

(b)

EZ-2H-3-4

2 cm = 1 cm

FIGURE 10.1. *Figurines depicting elderly individuals at El Zotz: (a) head fragment of an elderly woman (EZ 10B-2-2) (photo by A. Godoy); (b) head fragment of an elderly man with facial hair (EZ 2H-3-4) (drawing by N. Carter); (c) nearly complete figurine-whistle depicting a seated man with moustache and beard (EZ 10B-12) (photo by A. Godoy).*

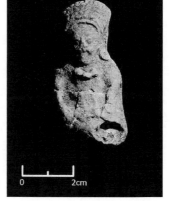

(c)

Stylized wrinkles appear on the man's cheeks, nose, and forehead; a faint beard covers his chin. In other examples of Maya art, beards are almost always associated with elderly individuals. Ancestors, denoted by the *mam* glyph in the ancient inscriptions, are shown with beards in addition to unruly hair and missing teeth (Houston, Stuart, and Taube 2006:49). There are few exceptions. The beard is a noted feature of the young maize god (Taube 1985:179), and the

Terminal Classic rulers of Ceibal often depicted themselves on their monumental stelae with faint beards and other non-Maya characteristics (Houston, Stuart, and Taube 2006:47). One such exception may be present in the El Zotz collection itself (figure 10.1c): a nearly complete figurine-whistle depicts a male individual in a seated position, marked by a full mustache and beard. He wears earspools, a necklace of three beads, and a simple kilt and loincloth wrapped around his waist. A turban, an accessory common in representations of men on figurines from other sites, adorns his head (e.g., Laporte 2009:1024). There is no indication that this individual is of an advanced age, although his seated position with hands over his knees suggests he may be of elite status (see discussion on "ruler" figurines below).

Without lines to cue age or facial hair to show gender, most anthropomorphic faces at El Zotz reveal little else about their identity (see also Hendon 2003:31). Rather, hairstyles, headdresses, other items of adornment, and posture help to distinguish different personages. Gender is one of the primary attributes that can be determined by these characteristics, as a number of other studies have indicated (e.g., Halperin 2007; Hendon 2003; Robertson 1985; Triadan 2007).

Female figurines are often shown wearing simple hair wraps and ties, with hair bound at the top of the head with ribbon, coiled into buns, or left hanging (Robertson 1985:36; Halperin 2007:151). In many examples, women's hair is tied tightly to the head, with one lock left free (Hendon 2003:31). When a woman's hair hangs loose, it is commonly parted at the center, a style associated with female figurines at Palenque (Halperin 2007:179–180; Robertson 1985:33). There are two examples of this central part at El Zotz, both from the Northwest Courtyard (excavation lots EZ 12I-1-1 and EZ 12K-10-3). More common in the El Zotz collection is the *stepped-cut hairstyle* (Halperin 2007:178–179)—defined by Robertson (1985:30–32) as the *type A cut*—in which the figure wears bangs styled in a stepped pattern across the forehead. In one example, the rest of the woman's hair has been wrapped on top of her head in the shape of a cone, a common feature of this hairstyle elsewhere in the Maya world (Halperin 2007:178; Laporte 2009:1024). The stepped-cut hairstyle can appear with a number of steps, as well as with an additional central forelock that extends beyond the highest step of bangs. The forelock that is sometimes present in this hairstyle, associated primarily with women with a few divine exceptions (Halperin 2007:178), is only present at El Zotz in one example (figure 10.2a). At Altar de Sacrificios, the cut adorns female figurines who wear elaborate *huipils*, suggesting the style is associated with elite status (Willey 1972:41). Unfortunately, the fragmentary nature of the El Zotz collection precludes similar observations on the relationship between hairstyle

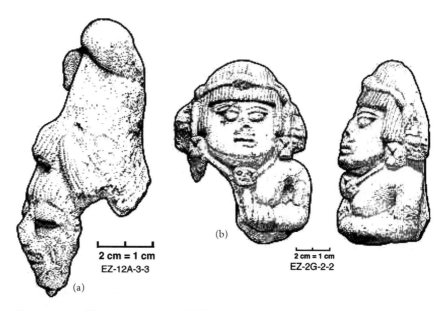

2 cm = 1 cm
EZ-12A-3-3

(b)

2 cm = 1 cm
EZ-2G-2-2

(a)

FIGURE 10.2. *Women's hairstyles on El Zotz figurines: (a) head fragment featuring a central forelock (EZ 12A-3-3) (drawing by N. Carter); (b) woman wearing stepped-cut bangs and elaborate jewelry (EZ 2G-2-2) (drawing by N. Carter).*

and dress from being made. In one example of this hairstyle, the woman's left arm and part of her chest is preserved, yet no clothing is visible (figure 10.2b). Other items of adornment, however, are present: a woven band, embellished in the center, wraps around the head; a pendant depicting an anthropomorphic face hangs around her neck; her flexed arm supports a bracelet with three bands of beads; and, two square-shaped earspools, both inscribed with an "X," hang from each ear. Notably, this is one of the few figurines at the site that has retained traces of pigment. In this case, "Maya blue " (Arnold et al. 2008).

The broad-brimmed hat, nestled on top of the head or perched atop a hair wrap, is a common item of adornment in female figurines during the Late and Terminal Classic periods. The hat, which may have provided protection from sustained exposure to the sun, was emblematic of traveling merchants: the merchant god, God L, is often depicted wearing a broad-brimmed hat made of woven material (Taube 1992:79). Taube (2003:474) also suggests that it might have been part of the costume of the hunting god. The mural paintings associated with Calakmul Str. 1 of the Late Classic Chiik Nahb complex show both male and female figures wearing these broad-brimmed hats, likely woven out of vegetable fiber (Carrasco Vargas et al. 2009:19247). In the murals, all figures wearing the hat—two females and one male—are vendors, each with a caption describing his or her wares: "the person of the vases" (Boucher and Quiñones 2007:45), "the tamale person" (Boucher and Quiñones 2007:43), and "the atole person" (Boucher and Quiñones 2007:41).

Although individuals of both male and female gender are depicted wearing these hats in Maya painting, broad-brimmed hats appear to be associated exclusively with women in other figurine collections (Halperin 2007:156). Many of these women wear the stepped-cut hairstyle discussed previously (Halperin 2007:154; Laporte 2009:1024). As noted, the broad-brimmed hat is typically connected to the top of the head. However, in one example from Lubaantun, Belize, the woman holds the hat in her right hand and carries some sort of cargo in her left (Joyce 1933:Plate I-4). Halperin (2007:155) notes two similar examples of hatted figurines with cargo: in one example from Tikal, the woman carries her cargo with a tumpline, her hat hanging on her back; in another from the northern Altiplano of Guatemala, the cargo sits in front of the hatted individual, who holds what may be a tamale in her hand. The female vendor is one of the most common characters among Late and Terminal Classic figurines (Halperin 2011:131). In fact, more than 50 examples have been recovered from Motul de San José, and they are especially common at Tikal (Halperin 2007:155; Laporte 2009:1024). One instance of this character has been found at El Zotz. Stepped-cut bangs are faintly visible at the top of its forehead. As at Motul de San José (Halperin 2007:154), the El Zotz figurine wears only earspools—featuring a distinctive stippled pattern—and no other jewelry. The piece is solid and the neck is not fragmented, suggesting that the piece may have been attached to a non-ceramic body or served as a removable piece in a hollow ceramic body. In addition to this example, there are two broad-brimmed hats in the collection that have been separated from their figurine bodies. Presumably, given the strong association indicated above, these hats once belonged to female vendors.

Other typically female items of adornment include wraps and skirts in combination with earspools and beaded necklaces, the accessories generally associated with elite women (Morris 1985:246; Valdés et al. 2001:659). The *huipil*, an indigenous women's blouse depicted in exquisite detail on a number of figurines from Lagartero (Morris 1985:246), does not appear at El Zotz. In addition, the fragmentary nature of the collection means that skirts and wraps are either missing or unidentifiable. In some instances, absent distinctive clothing and hair, the female identification of a figurine can be made on the basis of visible breasts, covered or uncovered. In all, 10 anthropomorphic heads and three body fragments can be identified as female according to the traits enumerated above (see table 10.2).

Male personages are most easily identified in figurine collections through specific forms of dress associated with activities and roles commonly performed by Maya men. One of the most common male characters is what Laporte (2009:1023) identifies at Tikal as the *gobernante* or "ruler." These dignitaries, always seated or kneeling with their hands placed over their knees, are often shown wearing a feathered headdress with a supernatural or zoomorphic face at its center (see the H9 headdress in Halperin 2007:162). Although complete versions have not been recovered at El Zotz, four *gobernante* heads and headdress fragments were found in the site's epicenter (excavation lots EZ 2H-5-4, EZ 3B-1-10, EZ 7A-6-3, and EZ v12J-14-2).

Other members of the royal court may be marked by other types of headdress. One of these consists of a large helmet with a rounded opening (see the H10 headdress in Halperin 2007:165–166). Excavations in the Northwest Courtyard produced one example, a probable flute fragment. Halperin (2007:166) notes that these helmets adorn the heads of male palace courtiers in the Early Classic murals of Uaxactun, suggesting that the figurines represented with these items of adornment may have filled similar roles. Another type of headdress takes the form of a cone embellished with hand-modeled, tassel-like elements (see the H7 headdress in Halperin 2007:160–161). One find from Las Palmitas may correspond with this category (figure 10.3a). The enigmatic headdress may be related to the costume worn by sacrificial attendants of the scaffold sacrifice (see Taube 1988:figure 12.3). The round, flowery banners held by attendants in these scenes are also represented in figurine imagery, as seen on a fragment found in the Northwest Courtyard (figure 10.3b). The scaffold sacrifice is associated with rites of political accession, and scaffold imagery is commonly employed as a display of political legitimacy, appearing on the Late Classic niche stelae of Piedras Negras (Taube 1988:figure 12.12), the Late Preclassic murals of San Bartolo (Taube et al. 2010:figure 39), as well as the Early Classic façade of the Temple of the Night Sun at El Diablo (figure 13.4; Román and Gutiérrez 2016:figure 1.15). This imagery in clay suggests that figurines and figurine-whistles at El Zotz depicted elite individuals fulfilling particular roles and duties associated with the ancient city's royal court.

Trophy heads, perhaps belonging to erstwhile captives, comprise another distinctly male personage found among El Zotz figurines. These individuals are marked by free-flowing hair that hangs straight below their suspended, disembodied heads. At Tikal and Lubaantun, they adorn the belts of warriors (Joyce

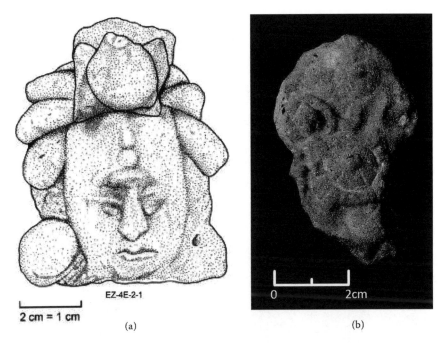

EZ-4E-2-1

2 cm = 1 cm

(a)

0   2cm

(b)

FIGURE 10.3. *Men's headdresses and accessories at El Zotz: (a) head fragment of a man wearing a costume related to the scaffold sacrifice (EZ 4E-2-1) (drawing by N. Carter); (b) fragment of a hand holding a banner similar to those depicted in scenes of the scaffold sacrifice (EZ 12K-3-3) (photo by A. de Carteret).*

1933:Plates V-5, V-11; Laporte 2009:figure 15). One eroded example from El Zotz may be a fragment of a similar figurine (lot EZ 12I-1-1). Another appears on the front of an unusual fragment (figure 10.4). This curious, apple-shaped item consists of two hollow chambers and a hole drilled laterally through its superior portion, suggesting it may have been suspended. The trophy head, in addition to his characteristic free-flowing hair, wears earspools and what may be a cloth binding around the neck. The original function of the item remains enigmatic: if it were suspended, the hair would appear to flow against gravity, and its two chambers have single openings, precluding its use as an instrument.

In addition to the personages described above, some body fragments can be identified as men by the presence of typical male adornment, including loincloths and belts, as well as the marked absence of breasts. Four additional fragments can be identified in this way, with a total of 18 fragments identified as male (see table 10.2).

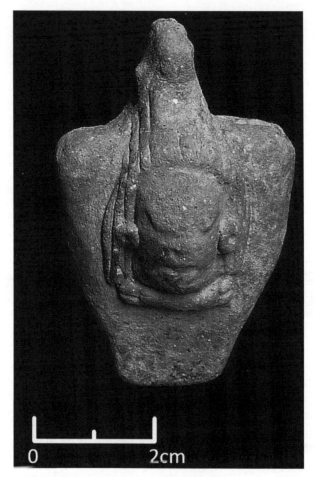

FIGURE 10.4. *Hollow figurine fragment depicting a disembodied trophy head (EZ 12K-6-4) (photo by A. de Carteret).*

Fragments of dwarfs, though scarce (*n* = 6), comprise an important class of anthropomorphic figurines. Like those in other media, dwarf figurines usually display the following attributes: "small stature, abnormally short and fleshy limbs, a protruding abdomen, and a disproportionately large head with prominent forehead, sunken face, and drooping lower lip" (Miller 1985:141). Unfortunately, the El Zotz collection does not contain any complete examples; thus, dwarfs are identified on the basis of their facial characteristics alone.

Body fragments by themselves are not sufficiently diagnostic in their proportions to indicate their belonging to a dwarf.

Dwarfs occupy an important position in ancient and modern Maya thought. Ethnographic evidence indicates that dwarfs are thought to have supernatural abilities and connections with the Underworld (Miller 1985:143). For the Classic Maya, dwarfs may have been part of the royal court, serving as court jesters and holding other roles in political ceremony (Houston 1992:527). This "privileged status" is emphasized by the appearance of dwarfs in monumental sculpture in the Late and Terminal Classic periods, including stelae and lintels at Caracol, Xultun, Tikal, Calakmul, Yaxha, Dos Pilas, Yaxchilan, La Florida, Palenque, and El Perú-Waka' (Miller 1985:148, 152). At El Zotz, representations of dwarfs are limited to six figurine head fragments (see table 10.2), as well as a carved profile noted by Stephen Houston on a jade earspool from the Five Temples Group (Garrido López 2014). Though limited, their presence across media indicates the local importance of dwarfs alongside other elite personages, both male and female.

To review, about one-third (n = 31) of anthropomorphic figurine fragments have an identifiable gender, and of these slightly more (n = 18) can be identified as male rather than female (n = 13). This trend parallels findings at other sites. For instance, male figurines comprise the majority at both Aguateca and Piedras Negras (Ivic de Monterroso 2002:487; Triadan 2014; Valdés et al. 2001:658). Although anthropomorphic figurines can offer scholars insight into personages and labors often unrepresented in other media, especially women and their work (e.g., Joyce 1993:261), most of the identifiable figurines at El Zotz and other sites represent elite individuals or members of the royal court. Even many of the female figurines—with the exception of the hatted merchant class—represent elite, bejeweled women. The fragmentary nature of the collection makes more profound assessments difficult; in most cases, not enough of the figurine fragment remains to evaluate hairstyle, costume, adornment, positions (both bodily and political), and associated activities or duties in conjunction with one another, as has been successfully done for other sites in other studies (e.g., Triadan 2014). What can be said, however, is that the repertoire of individuals represented by El Zotz figurines coalesces around specific characters serving in particular roles, and these same characters appear at coeval sites in the southern Maya Lowlands. It is likely that, across the region, these figurines embodied a shared set of personages with known stories, roles, and duties that could be enacted in play and in domestic ceremony. This suggestion is discussed in greater detail below.

TABLE 10.3. Zoomorphic figurines.

Animal	Count (n)
Bird	5
Owl	5
Monkey	2
Deer	1
Dog	1
Rodent	1
Turtle	1
Snake	1
Indeterminate	15
Total	**32**

ZOOMORPHIC FIGURINES

The zoomorphic figurines of El Zotz (n = 32) are more varied in representation; the ceramic menagerie includes monkeys, deer, and a variety of other mammalian, reptilian, and avian creatures (table 10.3). Of the fragments whose species can be identified (n = 24), a plurality (n = 10) depict birds. Two of these (excavated from lots EZ 8B-1-2 and EZ 2H-5-4) belong to a simple form of whistle commonly found in the central Peten, which have handmade, globular bodies, crude feet as supports, circular eyes applied to either side of the head, and a tail that serves as the whistle's mouthpiece (figure 10.5a, also see Halperin 2007:219; Laporte 2009:1026). Five additional examples of birds can be identified more specifically as owls, based on their well-defined, sometimes slanted eyes, short beaks, and, on occasion, rounded ears (see Laporte 2009:figure 19). In one example from the El Zotz Acropolis, the owl grips prey in its pointed beak (figure 10.5b). A specimen from Motul de San José similarly emphasizes the owl's hunting prowess, depicting the raptor with a snake in its mouth (Halperin 2007:218). Mold-made owls such as these are popular among Late and Terminal Classic zoomorphic figurine assemblages in the central Maya Lowlands (Halperin 2007:218; Laporte 2009:1026). In other Classic Maya media, owls are often associated with warfare, and can be seen accompanying God L, a deity associated with death and the Underworld (Grube and Schele 1994). In contemporary Maya communities, as noted in numerous ethnographic accounts, the nocturnal owl and its screech presages death, illness, or other misfortunes (e.g., Brinton 1890:169). The residents of El

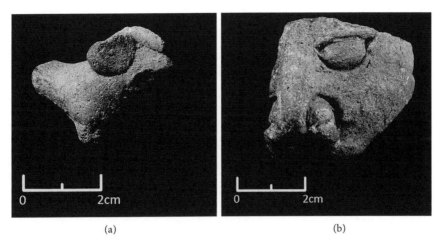

FIGURE 10.5. *Avian figurines at El Zotz: (a) nearly complete globular whistle in the form of a bird (EZ 2H-5-4) (photo by A. de Carteret); (b) fragment of an owl grasping prey in its beak (EZ 2H-3-4) (photo by A. Godoy).*

Zotz may have evoked these associations in using owl-shaped figurines. The attention to birds may also have stemmed from the similarity between their piercing cries and the sound of the clay whistle (see below).

Outside of birds and owls, only one kind of animal is represented by more than one fragment: monkeys (*n* = 2). In one example from the West Patio (excavation lot EZ 8B-1-3), two crude ears have been applied to the back of a hand-modeled head. In the other, recovered from excavations in the Acropolis (lot EZ 2A-5-2), a hollow body with a long, curving tail holds its clasped hands toward the mouth, squatting on two flexed legs. There is as yet no evidence at El Zotz for the human adornment and anthropomorphic poses often sported by monkey figurines at other sites (e.g., Halperin 2007:214; Triadan 2007:288); and, proportionally speaking, there are fewer monkeys at El Zotz than documented elsewhere (e.g., at Aguateca, monkey figurines comprise the majority of zoomorphic representations; see Triadan 2007:278; Valdés et al. 2001:657). These differences suggest that certain animals resonated with some Maya cities more than others. Although the reasoning behind Aguateca's preference for monkeys and El Zotz's preference for birds and owls remains elusive, these choices point to different moods. Monkeys tend to be involved with gaiety, excess, fun, and feasting, owls with prophecy and the dark night (Stephen Houston, personal communication, 2016).

The remaining identifiable zoomorphic figurines are unique examples of distinct animals: a deer, a dog, a rodent, a snake, and a turtle. Fifteen other fragments cannot be identified.

Though there are certainly some standard zoomorphic forms (e.g., the bird whistle), the representation of animals in these figurines is diverse. Compared with anthropomorphic figurines, zoomorphic figurines at El Zotz are more likely to have been made by hand. Out of 32 fragments, 13 are hand-modeled, 12 are mold-made, six exhibit characteristics of both techniques, and one cannot be identified. This suggests greater flexibility in the production of zoomorphic figurines. Workshops, perhaps grouped around families, may have produced certain animals for their own use, and out of the quite particular, idiosyncratic appeal of those creatures.

CONTEXT

As throughout Mesoamerica (see Brumfiel 1996:146; Halperin 2007:286; Hendon 2003:29; Ivic de Monterroso 2002:480; Ruscheinsky 2003:7; Triadan 2007:272), figurines at El Zotz come almost exclusively from residential areas. There are four exceptions to this general trend, all in civic-ceremonial contexts. A fragment of a mold-made dignitary was recovered from the central room on top of Str. L7-11 in a deposit from its time of abandonment (lot EZ 3B-1-10). Another was found on a poorly preserved floor from the final phase of Str. M7-2 in the East Group (lot EZ 7A-6-3); although eroded, it likely represents the headdress of a ruler or dignitary. Two figurines come from the alley of the El Zotz ballcourt, between Strs. L8-2 and L8-3: one is a zoomorphic whistle that may represent a bird (lot EZ 9A-1-3), the other an anthropomorphic fragment in the form of an arm (lot EZ 1C-1-5). The "civic" placement of these figurines, away from domestic contexts, is anomalous.

The rest of the collection shares a number of contextual traits. Almost all can be dated to the Late Classic period or later, with 46 Late Classic fragments, 79 Terminal Classic fragments, and 30 Postclassic fragments. With the exception of three Early Classic (excavated from lots EZ 2B-7-3 and EZ 2F-3-6) and two Late Preclassic fragments (from lots EZ 6F-1-6 and EZ 6J-1-4), some of which may intrude from later deposits, no figurines have been recovered from earlier times. There is no evidence of figurine use at the palatial hilltop groups of El Diablo and El Tejón, both of which had been abandoned by the beginning of the Late Classic period. In terms of context, most figurines at El Zotz occur in middens, construction fill, and general building collapse. This pattern follows observations made elsewhere in the Maya world, where most figurine

TABLE 10.4. El Zotz figurines by architectural group.

Location	Count (n)
Acropolis	63
West Patio	5
Northwest Courtyard	89
Five Temples	22
South Group	12
Las Palmitas	3
La Tortuga	2
East Group	1
Ballcourt	2
Other	3
Total	**202**

fragments are recovered from trash heaps and other contexts of discard (e.g., Hendon 2003:29). Only rarely are they included in ritual deposits or caches—these exceptions, especially two ritual termination deposits from Str. L7-1, are discussed below.

The rest of this section considers the main architectural groups where figurines have been recovered (table 10.4). These include the Acropolis, the West Patio, the Northwest Courtyard, the Five Temples Group, the Las Palmitas Group, and the La Tortuga Group. Some of these groups have only minimal figurine material. Others, such as the Acropolis, made extensive use of figurines.

THE ACROPOLIS

The Acropolis and its environs have the highest concentration of figurines at the site. Of the 202 figurine fragments excavated from El Zotz, 170 (nearly 77 percent) come from the Acropolis and nearby residential groups (including the West Patio and Northwest Courtyard, discussed below). Excavations at the main residential group of the Acropolis yielded 62 figurine fragments, primarily from Strs. L7-1, L7-2, L7-3, and L7-6, which are oriented around the group's West Patio (figure 4.1).

The majority of figurines appear to have been deposited in construction fill or middens. Two notable exceptions include ritual deposits found at the center of Str. L7-1's platform, and on the Restricted Patio located just to the south of Str. L7-1 and west of Str. L7-6. In the former, along with 26 figurine fragments, archaeologists recovered 2,053 fragments of ceramic vessels dating primarily to the Terminal Classic, in addition to pieces of musical instruments, 196 fragments of faunal remains, 150 flakes of worked chert, 14 obsidian blades, three pieces of jade, 55 shell fragments, and grinding stones (*manos* and *metates*) (see Newman 2015b). The figurines include 17 anthropomorphic fragments, among them four that can be identified as male, two as female, a broad-brimmed hat (likely separated from a female vendor, see above), and one representation of a dwarf. Four of the anthropomorphic examples can be identified as whistles. Five figurines from this assemblage are zoomorphic, including two owls, two other birds, and an unidentified body fragment—likely all whistles.

In the latter deposit, the project similarly recovered a wealth of material culture, including an abundance of utilitarian and fine ceramics, faunal remains, chert and obsidian blades, dress items made from shell and jade (such as rings and pendants), and fragments of grinding stones (Marroquín et al. 2011). This assemblage included 20 figurines, both anthropomorphic and zoomorphic, including a dog, owl, bird, and a turtle, two female fragments, a broad-brimmed hat, and a dwarf.

Both of these deposits correlate with the end of occupation at the Acropolis—the materials lay beneath a level of architectural dismantling, probably corresponding with an "interrupted process of remodeling" in the group's final years (Newman 2015b:210). There does not appear to have been a specific order to the deposits; that is, the artifact classes discussed here did not cluster in meaningful ways. Alongside pieces of jade and obsidian were fragments of utilitarian vessels and cooking utensils. Thus, the ritual involved the general and extensive deposition of both rite and quotidian items as a symbolic cessation or transformation of all activity at Str. L7-1 (see Newman et al., chapter 5, this volume). Figurines comprised a significant, although not principal, portion of the building's termination, signifying their importance to domestic activity in the complex.

Figurines from non-ritual deposits at the Acropolis similarly appear in association with a wealth of other items of material culture. Excavations in which figurines were found consistently recovered more than a hundred ceramic sherds in a single lot, often alongside lithic fragments and faunal remains. This trend applies to both middens and layers of construction fill, indicating that general discard piles were exploited for use in the construction of new phases of buildings. What this suggests more broadly, however, is that figurines did not face special treatment as a distinct artifact class when it came to their deposition and discard. The denizens of the Acropolis conceptualized figurines at the moment of their discard as belonging to a broad category of domestic refuse that included ceramics, animal bones, and lithic debitage. The ritual termination assemblages described above emphasize this same point.

The West Patio

Archaeological excavations have recovered five figurines from the West Patio, located just to the southwest of the El Zotz Acropolis. All five of these were found in the uppermost levels of a single unit (EZ 8B-1) near the north façade of Str. L7-16, forming the western margin of the architectural group. The unit corresponds with a midden in use during the final years of the group's occupation; the three lots with figurines all contained a large quantity of material culture, including, in total, 590 ceramic sherds, 72 pieces of flint, four obsidian bladelets, and a number of unworked animal bones. Excavations of the West Patio reveal sustained occupation of the complex from the Early Classic period until the group was abandoned at the beginning of the Terminal Classic period; yet, the figurines recovered from the group are all associated with the final phase of occupation, layers laden with ceramics dating to the Terminal Classic period. Of the figurines that can be identified, one is a mold-made man and two others are zoomorphic: one bird and one monkey.

The Northwest Courtyard

The richest location for figurines is the Northwest Courtyard, a residential group just to the west of the Acropolis, where 89 figurines and figurine fragments were excavated. Twelve of these figurines come from a trench that abuts the western wall of Str. L7-1, the same building with which most of the figurines excavated from the main group of the Acropolis are associated. (Those of the Northwest Courtyard, however, derived primarily from Postclassic rather than Terminal Classic contexts.) The remaining 76 figurines were recovered from horizontal excavations on Strs. L7-17, L7-18, and L7-20, as well as from test pits in the group's central plaza. The patterns evident at the Northwest Courtyard mirror the observations made at the Acropolis and the West Patio. In fact, any pattern previously noted is more pronounced here: figurines are associated with contexts of domestic discard; most lots where figurines were found also contained, on average, hundreds of fragments of ceramic vessels, and in some cases they included upwards of 1,500 vessel fragments; the vast majority of figurines pertain to levels of humus and general building collapse stemming from the final phases of the group's occupation. Notably, the Northwest Courtyard, along with the South Group, comprises the main area of Postclassic occupation at the site, indicating continued and perhaps even amplified use of figurines into this period. Most (n = 24) of the 28 Postclassic figurines come from this architectural group. These include three representations of women, two dwarfs, and one man, most mold made. Although three zoomorphic figurines were recovered from Postclassic contexts, not one could be identified as to its species. The 12 Terminal Classic figurines associated with this group include one man and a number of unidentified body fragments.

The Five Temples Group

Outside of the immediate vicinity of the Acropolis, figurines have been recovered from other architectural groups around the site's civic-ceremonial center. Excavations in a residential group on the west side of the Five Temples Group, just east of the El Zotz Aguada, recovered 20 fragments of figurines. These excavations focused on Strs. K8-1, K8-2, K8-3, and the platform K8-8. Other test pits associated with the group recovered two additional fragments. As in the Acropolis, figurines often appear in dedicated midden deposits associated with large numbers of potsherds. Though excavations suggest that this residence had two distinct periods of occupation, one Early Classic and the other Late Classic, the figurines are associated exclusively with Late Classic material. Fragments include the nearly complete, bearded figurine-whistle discussed earlier along with two other male fragments and another of an elderly woman. Two owls were also recovered.

The South Group

Twelve figurines, including two anthropomorphic and one zoomorphic, have been excavated from the South Group. The patterns observed here mirror those noted elsewhere. The corresponding lots pertain to middens, construction fill, collapse, and general occupational debris. Figurine use at the group appears to be equally divided between the Terminal Classic and Postclassic periods.

The Las Palmitas Group

Three figurines have been recovered from the palatial complex of Las Palmitas, located about 750 m to the north of Str. M7-2 in the East Group. Two of these figurines, including one zoomorphic representation, pertains to the cleaning of a looter tunnel on the northeast corner of Str. M3-7. Associated ceramics date to the Late Classic period. The other fragment was found at the base of the posterior façade of Str. M3-1, to the north of the group, in a Terminal Classic midden. This figurine depicts a man wearing the headdress potentially associated with the scaffold sacrifice (figure 10.4).

THE LA TORTUGA GROUP

Excavations at the small residential complex of La Tortuga, located about a half kilometer to the southeast of Las Palmitas, produced only two Late Classic figurines. Both were recovered from excavations at Str. N6-4, the group's southernmost building. These consist of two poorly preserved anthropomorphic figurine fragments, probably depicting a ruler's headdress.

To reiterate the patterns enumerated above, the following holds true across El Zotz: figurines are generally not in use at El Zotz before the Late Classic period; figurines are, by and large, associated with residential areas; and, finally, figurines are most likely to be found in general, non-ritual discard deposits (e.g., middens and construction fill). No burials or caches at El Zotz have figurines.

MANUFACTURE

In general, figurines at El Zotz have fine pastes of pale beige or reddish hues. If inclusions are visible, they are small and relatively few in number, the most common being calcite, mica, and small ferruginous nodules. These same pastes are frequently observed in the site's ceramics, which are in large part locally manufactured (see Czapiewska-Halliday et al., chapter 8, this volume). The parsimonious explanation would be that the figurines were made locally, too, an observation applicable to other sites in the Maya Lowlands (e.g., Rands and Rands 1965:554; Willey 1972:14).

Figurines are either modeled by hand or formed in a mold. Lumpy shapes and rough seams can often be used to distinguish one technique from the other, although it can sometimes be difficult to tell mold-made faces from the finely crafted originals on which the molds were based (Ivic de Monterroso 2000:244). Many fragments in the El Zotz collection exhibit both techniques (n = 25): headdresses and other items of adornment were often shaped by hand and then adjoined to a mold-made head, and mold-made heads were often attached to (sometimes crudely) hand-modeled bodies. In cases where both techniques are present, the head is most commonly the mold-made element, an observation noted elsewhere (Ivic de Monterroso 2000:245; Laporte 2009:1021). Details of the head, the locus of identity, may have needed more careful crafting, the body constituting a less-identifiable afterthought (Stephen Houston, personal communication, 2016). The sole use of molds is the most prevalent technique (n = 100), although hand-modeled figurines are also common (n = 76). One fragment could not be classified. Despite the ubiquity of mold-made figurines, no molds have been found at El Zotz, though they are known from other sites (see Halperin 2014:174–178).

About two-thirds (n = 167) of all figurine fragments are hollow. Of those that are solid (n = 65), 21 can be identified as anthropomorphic or zoomorphic head fragments that may have been attached to hollow bodies. As has been documented elsewhere (Triadan 2007:271; Valdés et al. 2001:655), the majority of hollow figurines at El Zotz were mold made. As hollow forms, they likely served as whistles and ocarinas; however, fragments have only been categorized as whistles if there is direct evidence of a mouthpiece, finger holes, or a sound hole. In total, 50 whistles have been excavated at El Zotz, of which 20 are anthropomorphic and nine are zoomorphic, three birds and two owls among them.

In a few instances, remnants of paint and slip are visible on the figurines. White paint is observed on a female head fragment from the Northwest Courtyard (lot EZ 12K-3-3), while traces of blue pigment are visible on a zoomorphic fragment from the Acropolis, likely representing a bird's wing (lot EZ 2H-5-4). On some fragments, an eroded red-orange slip is present (lots EZ 12K-2-4 and EZ 7A-6-3). Though these examples are few, they do suggest that many of these artifacts were once adorned in brilliant colors that have since chipped away.

USE

As figurines are often found in contexts of general discard, their function prior to their deposition can be difficult to ascertain and needs to be evaluated closely (Triadan 2007:271). The near-exclusive presence of figurines in middens and construction fill, intermixed with other items of domestic refuse, clarifies little for the El Zotz collection other than a strong connection between figurines and domestic activity. Within the houselot, figurines may have enjoyed a variety of uses.

The rapidly abandoned site of Aguateca provides some insight into what kinds of areas figurines may have been associated with before being discarded. As Triadan (2007:285) notes, "they occur in the side rooms that have storage and cooking vessels, manos and metates, and spindle whorls, artifacts that suggest that the space was used primarily by the women of the household." The association with "female" spaces may indicate their use by both women and children, who are often in the care of women in Maya communities. Ruscheinsky (2003) argues that figurines may have been used by children as toys, a suggestion strengthened by the discovery of complete figurines and figurine-whistles in Terminal Classic child burials at Ceibal (MacLellan and Cordero 2014:78). El Zotz lacks direct evidence for this association, but it seems a strong possibility given the context of the finds.

As children's toys, the personages depicted, both anthropomorphic and zoo-morphic, may allude to known historical and mythic characters whose stories would have been enlivened through child's play. Clay kings, warriors, merchants, and their animal companions became the action figures of the Classic Maya, providing entertainment while teaching young children parables of local importance. That the majority of these items are whistles should not be lost here: sonorous breath, linked to the soul, would have brought the figurines to life (Taube 2004a:74). Similar performances may have been enacted by adults as well. During small-scale domestic rituals and festivals, figurines could have provided music and enlivened tableaus (also see Hendon 2003:30). In such ceremonies, it is possible that the high tone of the figurine-whistle imitated the "creaky speech" associated with deities and oracles in later times (Stephen Houston, personal communication, 2016).

As whistles, the El Zotz figurines likely had other uses. The prevalence of avian iconography suggests they may have been used to summon birds, as suggested by Willey (1972:8). Triadan (2007:287) notes that the sound produced by owl figurines is quite similar to the call of an owl, suggesting that these objects might have caught the attention of wild birds or those tethered within the domestic space. Figurine-whistles may have functioned in a similar way for other animals. In Kantunilkin, Quintana Roo, local groups use whistles to lure deer to the home, as the sound of the whistle imitates the cries of a fawn (Almanza Alcalde, cited in Anderson and Tzuc 2005:75). In addition, the high-pitched sound of Maya figurines may have facilitated communication between humans across long distances or simply across spaces where visibility was limited (e.g., dense jungle vegetation). In an experimental study conducted by King and Sánchez Santiago (2011:397), the authors documented that the sound from clay whistles of similar size and construction could travel at least 350 m. In many Classic Maya cities, this distance could encompass numerous household groups as well as the neighboring forest.

Unfortunately, the evidence from El Zotz eludes concrete conclusions regarding the use of figurine-whistles at the site. There probably was not one "correct" way to engage with the items; rather, there were many functions, both ceremonial and mundane.

CONCLUSION

As mentioned at the beginning of this chapter, the sample of figurine fragments excavated at the site is small. This must be kept in mind when assessing the patterns described above, as continuing research and new evidence could change these observations. Nevertheless, what is evident from these data is that El Zotz fits within broader patterns observed elsewhere in the southern Maya Lowlands. Iconography, context, and manufacture are consistent from site to site, with minor variations. These similarities suggest that, during the Late and Terminal Classic periods, El Zotz participated in a broader tradition of figurine use based in and around the house. Additional excavations will clarify what about figurine use is particular to El Zotz. For now, these finds emphasize the importance of this artifact class for our understanding of quotidian Maya life and foreground the need for further study.

NOTE

1. This analysis does not include figurines from the nearby Preclassic site of El Palmar (for analysis of Preclassic figurines see Doyle 2013b; Doyle and Piedrasanta, chapter 2, this volume).

11

The stone platforms, sprawling plazas, and towering temples of the Classic-period Maya remain iconic symbols of ancient New World civilization. Even the earliest European visitors to these ruined cities marveled at the technical and artistic achievements of the Maya (e.g., Charnay 1888; Stephens 1841, 1843; Waldeck 1838; see also Evans 2004). Today, appreciation for ancient Maya architecture has hardly waned, but much of the mystery once surrounding it has: after more than a century of meticulous study, archaeologists understand a great deal about Maya buildings, including their formal characteristics, stylistic attributes, functional categories, and symbolic meanings. In contrast, far less attention has been paid to how the Maya built these structures (cf. Abrams 1984b, 1987, 1994, 1998, 2000; Carrelli 2000, 2004; Houston, Escobedo, and Mesick 2011; Morris et al. 1931; Roys 1934; Straight 2007). The substantial literature on ancient building practices in the Old World proves that questions about ancient construction processes can hardly be deemed uninteresting, irrelevant, or unknowable (Malacrino 2010). In fact, studies on everything from architectural planning and design (e.g., Arnold 1991; Coulton 1977) to structural engineering (e.g., Landels 2000; Mark 1990, 1993) to the economics of raw material manufacture (DeLaine 1997, 2000) yield surprising insight into not only the techniques laborers used to construct architecture but also how building campaigns affected wider society.

Constructed Landscapes

Architectural Stratigraphy, Behavioral Practices, and Building Technologies at El Zotz

Cassandra Mesick Braun

DOI: 10.5876/9781607327646.c011

As an offshoot of a multi-sited study of construction practices among the Classic-period Maya (Mesick 2012), this chapter presents architectural stratigraphy and behavioral practices discovered at El Zotz. Particular emphasis is placed on strategies archaeologists can use to access and interpret construction technologies during active excavation. More broadly, it highlights how the ability to discern construction techniques can reveal not only stratigraphic sequences, occupation histories, and demographic patterns but also the broader networks of thought and practice, intention and meaning, knowledge and skill that crossed the complex geopolitical landscape of the Classic-period Maya.

RESEARCH FRAMEWORK

Building processes of the Classic period can be productively explored by considering the (1) technical operations and (2) social dimensions of construction in tandem. Investigating the technical aspects entails explaining how structures were created on an ordered, step-by-step basis. Prior studies reveal most building sequences incorporate pre-construction, construction, and post-construction phases (Abrams 1994:43; for Old World examples, see Adam 1994; Arnold 1991; Camp and Dinsmoor 1984; Clarke and Engelbach 1990; Parker 1997; Wright 1985, 1992, 2000a, 2000b). The more specific tasks that take place during each of these phases are highlighted in the ensuing discussion.

If attention to the technical process of construction answers questions of how, consideration of the social dimensions of building addresses questions of why. Adopting an overarching social constructionist approach to understanding technology (Killick 2004), this project attempts to reconstruct a *chaîne opératoire* that crystallized human effort into built form (Leroi-Gourhan 1943, 1945). Methodologically, *chaîne opératoire* research involves examining the decision-making rationale that guided each technical task. Cross-cultural studies consistently demonstrate that the specific choices builders make are influenced by practical and cultural considerations in equal measure, thus demonstrating the inextricability of the technical from the social context (e.g., Dobres 1999, 2000; Lemonnier 1986, 1992, 1993). Cultural beliefs and values differ dramatically from society to society, and if left unacknowledged or unrecognized, these differences can cause misinterpretation of technological practice. Understanding the cultural context of Classic-period construction is arguably of great importance, since ruptures between Western and Maya conceptions of architecture are pronounced.

To begin, Mesoamerican worldview blurs the distinction between nature and culture—a dichotomy that traces its origins back to Classical writers (e.g., Kruft 1994; Morgan 1960) and that has been deeply entrenched in Western thought ever since. For ancient Greek and Roman builders, man-made architecture belonged firmly in the category of culture, while landscape features like the sea or the mountains belonged to the realm of nature; in this paradigm, the very act of building architecture publicly and powerfully demonstrated man's ability to civilize the wild (DeLaine 2002:218–221). Yet, from the origins of Mesoamerican civilizations in the Olmec heartland (Coggins 1982; Schele 1995) through the dissolution of the Aztec Empire (Broda 1987; Townsend 1982), Mesoamerican peoples consistently emphasized the "close relationship, even metaphorical interchangeability, between natural and constructed forms" (Brady and Ashmore 1999:132; see also Ashmore 2009; Guernsey Kappelman 2001; Matos Moctezuma 1992; Staller 2008; Taube 1998:438). In direct opposition to the Classical aversion to linking built architecture with natural topography, the Maya often used the term *witz*, "mountain, hill," to label masonry structures (Stuart and Houston 1994:82–86). Many archaeologists, epigraphers, and art historians argue that these *witz* structures served as the symbolic equivalences of mountains and hills encountered in the natural landscape. Additional topographic features, such as caves and bodies of water, also maintained close ideological and physical links to architecture among the Classic-period Maya (e.g., Ashmore and Knapp 1999; Brady 1991, 1997, 2010; Heyden 1981, 2000; Koontz et al. 2001; Prufer and Brady 2005). Iconography, epigraphy, and ethnography demonstrate that the Maya associated these landscape elements with powerful deities and ancestors; that the semidivine rulers would decide in turn to link the architecture they commissioned and used in public settings with the spiritually charged places of potent supernaturals makes cultural sense.

In a similar vein, the equally fundamental distinction between animate and inanimate collapses when viewed from the perspective of the Classic Maya, since ritual practices reveal that buildings were often conceived as vitalized entities. House dedication rites, for instance, require participants to feed buildings. For the Tzotzil Maya of Zinacantan, this is achieved by enriching the corners, rafters, and center of a newly constructed house with potables such as broth and liquor (Vogt 1976:461–465). Other architectural rituals described in Classic-period inscriptions involved fire and its necessary byproduct, heat. For the ancient and contemporary Maya, a person's vitality, and the power of his soul, is conceptualized as a type of heat (e.g., Gossen 1974; López Austin 1988). "Perhaps," reasons David Stuart (1998:417), "by bringing the heat of fire into a building, the space is vivified and invested with its own soul." Coupled with the pervasive and enduring need to "feed" buildings, these practices exemplify just some of the ways the Maya perceived their architecture as animate (Stuart 1998:395; Taube 1998:446).

It is beyond the purview of the present chapter to elaborate fully on the richly textured worldview that influenced Classic-period conceptions of their landscapes, whether "natural" or "built." This cursory discussion instead aims to provide a sense of how significant a role cultural beliefs play in attempting to reconstruct a holistic system of architectural practice. As is illustrated below, understanding these culturally mediated beliefs is necessary for imputing a decision-making rationale and, ultimately, for reconstructing a uniquely Maya *chaîne opératoire*.

RESEARCH METHODOLOGY

To investigate building at El Zotz, six structures were targeted for detailed stratigraphic analysis: Strs. F8-1, F8-7, and F8-8 at the El Diablo Group (figure 3.3); Strs. L7-6 and L7-11 from the Acropolis of El Zotz (figure 4.1); and Str. M3-7 at the Las Palmitas Group (figure 4.11)—a sample that reflects spatial, chronological, and functional sensitivity to the site. The analysis and interpretation of architectural stratigraphy in these six structures depended largely on Harris Matrices, schematic representations of archaeological deposits that, in this particular case, encode the technical operations of construction (figure 11.1; see also Brown and Harris 1993; Harris 1975, 1989). Although they are standard excavation tools in the Old World and other parts of the Americas, Harris Matrices are not widely used by Mayanists (cf. Hammond 1993). However, they proved invaluable for this project. For instance, as an established method for presenting and interpreting stratigraphic data, these standardized diagrams could be shared with and understood by other project members. Beyond such practical advantages, Harris Matrices also offered conceptual benefits, since creating them provided a direct and constant impetus to view architectural stratigraphy as a manifestation of meaningful cultural behaviors rather than as mere chronological deposits. Put another way, the process of building each matrix translated architectural stratigraphy into behavioral practice. Excavation data from many additional structures at El Zotz supplemented the insight gained from the six case-study structures. This expanded data set revealed further tasks performed during the pre-construction, construction, and post-construction phases. Collectively, information from survey, mapping, and excavation contributed to my results.

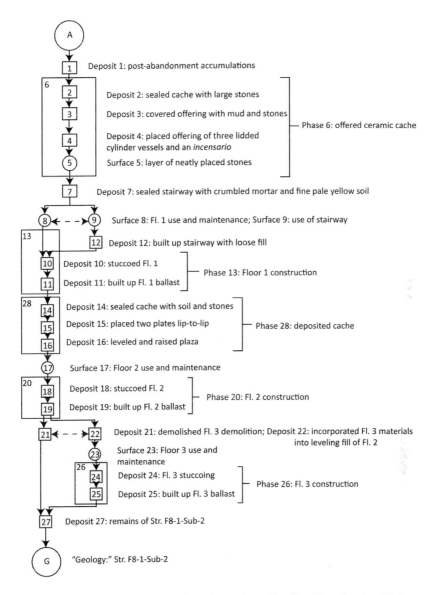

FIGURE II.I. *Harris Matrix created from the south profile of Str. F8-1, based on Unit EZ-5B-3, showing post-abandonment activities that occurred at its summit (drawing by C. Mesick. Braun).*

ARCHITECTURAL PRACTICE AND
TECHNOLOGICAL CHOICE AT EL ZOTZ

This section presents an overview of salient architectural attributes at El Zotz. First to be described are pre-construction activities like site selection, demolition, spatial design, and raw-material procurement and processing. Tasks central to the construction process itself, including nuclear assembly, provisions made for proper use and maintenance, and the installation of masonry, roofing, flooring, and perishable components are described next. The final section summarizes how inhabitants embellished, modified, and repaired architecture as part of the post-construction phase.

Pre-Construction Activities

Identifying pre-construction activities requires both astute observation and reasoned speculation, for during this phase patrons decided where to site a new structure, architects planned spatial layouts, and engineers determined how to make these visions come to life. The sociotechnical rationale guiding these decisions did not always leave overt signatures in the archaeological record.

Site selection

Due to a constellation of factors, data pertaining to when and where the people of El Zotz first began modifying the local landscape are often the most disjointed and partial. First, as elsewhere in Mesoamerica, the inhabitants of El Zotz regularly dismantled unwanted structures and built directly atop their remains. Second, early builders at El Zotz likely created perishable open-air and/or wattle-and-daub structures (see Hill and Clark 2001; Lesure 1997, 1999), which may have been akin to later Postclassic-period pole-and-thatch structures discovered in the South Group (Gámez 2009:133; Kingsley 2014; Kingsley and Gámez, chapter 6, this volume). Left untended, such structures decay and, in the warm, moist climate of northern Guatemala, ultimately leave little more than holes in soil. Finally, archaeologists cannot always safely access early structures, buried as they are under centuries of heavy and unstable overbuilding. These factors diminish the capacity to gain a thorough and accurate understanding of what the original structures looked like—let alone how they were built. Fortunately, specific trends witnessed at El Zotz and its environs permit a few provisional observations.

Recent research at El Palmar offers a useful starting point in this regard: with a significant Middle Preclassic occupation, the site appears to be the earliest node of monumental architecture in the greater El Zotz landscape (Doyle 2012; Doyle and Matute Rodríguez 2009; Doyle and Piedrasanta 2011; chapter 2, this volume; Houston 2007; Matute and Doyle 2008). That the region's original inhabitants chose this site to begin permanent habitation is unsurprising from a practical perspective: El Palmar sits on the shore of a large *cival* (perennial wetland) that is today one of the only sizeable and relatively permanent water sources in the area. In a climatic zone characterized by extreme cycles of rainfall, maintaining a ready water supply for dry months would have been important. This pragmatic appeal appears to have waned by the Early Classic period, when monumental building activity slowed at El Palmar and accelerated at El Zotz (especially in the El Diablo and El Tejón Groups) and Bejucal. The decision to refocus construction efforts at new locales might once again take into account natural features of the landscape. El Zotz is bounded by more impassable terrain to the north, south, and east, possibly indicating that El Palmar's residents sought—maybe even required—a more defensible location (Román et al., chapter 3, this volume). This geographic shift may reflect incipient or escalating tensions between the city and others to its south and east.

Thus far, the decision-making logic for site selection in the broader El Zotz settlement area has focused on practical considerations like access to life-sustaining water and protection from potentially hostile neighbors. Yet it is also feasible to posit more symbolic rationales. First, El Palmar's *cival* might well have served in a dual capacity as a water source and a spiritually charged landscape feature with which rulers wished to associate. Similarly, the position of El Zotz at the foot of an escarpment may have afforded protection while also allowing the site's rulers to link themselves with the large, bat-filled sinkhole and the towering hills that surround it. As hinted above, ample evidence indicates that topographic elements like mountains, caves, and water were crucial to Maya ideology. The proximity between these three features and the original settlements in the area was likely intentional (e.g., Ashmore and Knapp 1999; Brady 1997; Brady and Ashmore 1999; Garrison 2012) and further demonstrates how "geography of the Classic Maya apparently involve[s] a conceit in which there existed substantial overlap between natural and artificial categories" (Stuart and Houston 1994:86).

Demolition events

This section describes the pervasive Maya practice of demolishing buildings once they became obsolete. The most common form of demolition at El Zotz was the deliberate dismantling of buildings or their constituent components; stairways, façades, and roofing were targeted for demolition with greater regularity than platforms, substructures, and interior walls. To this end, such demolition was practical, since it eliminated awkward architectural elements and provided a ready source of raw materials for the superseding entity. For instance, excavations in Str. F8-1 revealed the remains of a structure that predates the El Zotz Burial 9 tomb, which is the oldest intact architecture associated with the building. Remains of this earlier structure are limited to fragments of red-painted stucco and recycled stone blocks that builders later incorporated into the walls and fill of the Burial 9 chamber (Houston, Newman, Román, and Carter 2015). Acropolis Str. L7-6 provides a second example of demolition. Here, to construct a new entryway during the transition between Str. L7-6-Sub.3 and Sub.2, builders reused finished masonry from the obsolete Sub.3; the bulk of Sub.2's structural core likewise came from the rip-out of its architectural predecessor. Eventually, a similar fate befell Sub.2, when its walls and floors were dismantled and used to form the mass of Sub-1 (Meléndez and Houston 2008:47–52, figures 2.3–2.5; Pérez Robles et al. 2009:10–22, figure 1.1). Offering yet another clear example of demolition is the Pyramid of the Wooden Lintel, where Str. M7-1-Sub.1 was partially dismantled in order to make room for a major royal tomb (El Zotz Burial 16) prior to the construction of Str. M7-1-Sub.2 (Thomas Garrison, personal communication, 2013).

Common sense might categorize these destructive, or at least reductive, acts as post-construction tasks. Patterns at El Zotz and nearby sites like Tikal, however, undermine this interpretation, since workers took this step only if they planned to build anew at the same locus. Furthermore, if demolition was a post-construction act signaling the end of a building's use, one would not expect to find intact, albeit naturally decaying, structures all over the Maya world. From this, it can be inferred that when the Maya no longer needed a building and had no plans to reuse its footprint as the location for a new construction, they left the older structure to ruin.

Orientation, spatial layout, and planning

As suggested earlier, it is possible that the founders of El Zotz imbued their nascent city with symbolic import by associating it with landscape features like water, caves, and mountains. Subsequent generations of architects continued to enhance its significance through site orientation, which shows a multi-tiered sensitivity to the cardinal directions. On a broad scale, the site core and its subsidiary settlements maintain an almost precise orientation toward one another, with the urban core of El Zotz occupying a central point—an *axis mundi*—from which the Las Palmitas and El Diablo Groups radiate directly to the north and west, respectively (figure 1.5). On a smaller scale, the arrangement of structures in any one of these three complexes mirrors the emphasis on cardinal directions, since nearly all buildings face north, south, east, or west (figures 3.3 and 4.11).

Buildings in the Las Palmitas Group exemplify this directional sensitivity. There, builders positioned the elevated western patio, bordered on three sides by Strs. M3-6, M3-7, and M3-8, to align almost exactly with the cardinal directions (figure 4.11). The central passageway bisecting Str. M3-7 is positioned opposite two small windows in the eastern façade of Str. M3-6, which initially raised questions about whether these two structures might serve astronomical functions. Project members hypothesized that the sun would pass through the passageway in Structure M3-7 onto the façade of Structure M3-6 (Houston 2007:16). Depending on the time of year and the position of the sun in the sky, the windows of Str. M3-6 would allow the rays to differentially illuminate the interior rooms of the temple, possibly fulfilling calendric purposes and signaling ritual events. Although this conjecture is not without precedent— archaeologists have long posited solar significances associated with "E-Group" complexes at nearby sites such as Uaxactun (see Aimers and Rice 2006 for summary; cf. Doyle 2012)—closer scrutiny has since debunked this proposition. When archaeologists later discovered the doorjambs of the central passageway, they determined that its width (1.68 m) and position vis-à-vis opposite Str. M3-6 had no bearing on movements of the sun (Carter and Gutiérrez Castillo 2011:74). Nevertheless, the ubiquity of directional alignments recorded at El Zotz (whether individual features like the Str. M3-7 passageway or the architectural landscape writ large) suggests that planners paid close attention to orientation when designing and constructing buildings.

Intact interior chambers at El Zotz, especially those associated with mortuary pyramids, also evince unique patterns. Many internally partitioned superstructures were configured with small rooms branching laterally from a central passageway—an atypical layout compared to examples found elsewhere. Notably, however, room layouts in several of Tikal's funerary buildings mirror this arrangement (see Pérez Robles 2011:figures 20.1, 20.6, and 20.8). Since the Tikal structures postdate those at El Zotz, the innovative floor plan may have originated at El Zotz and been subsequently adopted by builders at Tikal. This poses an intriguing possibility about the transmission of architectural knowledge and skill, which many archaeologists believe followed prevailing networks of political and economic power. As a perennially important city, Tikal exercised significant influence, even control, over these networks for centuries; that its architects would embrace spatial layouts from an outlying provincial site hint that dominant centers did not necessarily maintain a monopoly over artisanal talent. Creativity, innovation, and skill may have thus been traveled through the Maya political landscape via channels not yet considered.

Raw materials

Ethnoarchaeological studies among living Maya communities have consistently demonstrated that obtaining and processing architectural raw materials count among the most time- and labor-intensive building tasks (Abrams 1984a; Abrams and Bolland 1999; Erasmus 1965). As a highly visible part of the Mesoamerican archaeological record, stone is perhaps the most obvious raw material laborers used in building endeavors. Stone extraction left overt signs in the archaeological record throughout the area of the biotope surveyed by the project (Garrison, Garrido et al. 2011; Garrison and Kwoka 2012; Knodell and Garrison 2011). During reconnaissance and excavation of newly discovered mounds, Thomas Garrison and his team recorded several quarry sites associated with architecture of all scales (e.g., Aragón 2011:240–243, 247–248; Garrison and Beltrán 2011:302; Garrison, Garrido, et al. 2011:323, 325, 341). Overall, the size of any given quarry paralleled the scale of the masonry architecture in its immediate vicinity.

For instance, approximately 350 m to the south of the East Group at El Zotz, Garrison and his team located a large area of exploited limestone associated with several structures, including a small pyramid and platform complex (Knodell and Garrison 2011:388–389). Closer to the site core, workers created an artificial *aguada* at the El Diablo Group through localized quarrying (Román and Newman 2011:117), and Pedro Aragón noted a sizeable quarry associated with a dense cluster of housemounds near Str. K8–3 (Aragón 2011:240–241). It is impossible, based on current evidence, to confirm that these quarries produced the stone used to build the adjacent building or complex (Aragón 2011:241; Knodell and Garrison 2011:389), but the pairing of masonry architecture with stone exploitation, as well as the parity between the scale of structures and associated quarries, render this a likely possibility.

Archaeologists discovered the most extensively quarried areas along concentrated limestone ridges to the south-southeast of El Zotz (Knodell and Garrison 2011:389). No immediately adjacent architecture was found in association with these expanses of stripped bedrock, suggesting that they comprised a centralized hub of large-scale masonry production. Here, workers could have produced substantial quantities of building stone that they could then transport to construction sites. It is possible that the two distinct patterns of stone extraction described above reflect either a temporal or organizational shift in production techniques. Consider, for instance, that the only quarry directly associated with a major architectural complex appears at the El Diablo Group, which was built during early phases of monumental construction. At this time, the population was probably too small to allow for the centralized mass-production of building stone like that described immediately above. If El Zotz followed the demographic patterns witnessed at other central Peten sites, its population would have peaked during the Late Classic period, when work crews were ample enough to support coordinated labor practices, including the mass production of masonry. Certainly the quality of architectural stonework (a topic addressed below) suggests some measure of craft specialization at this time.

Although masonry is the most visible building material, construction fill was the most plentiful; archaeologists agree that, by volume, the vast majority of Maya architecture is fill, which generally combines two distinct ingredients— (1) a matrix and (2) aggregates or inclusions. At El Zotz, the fill composition varies noticeably through time. The earliest construction fill uncovered at El Zotz Str. M7-1-Sub.1 comprised loose chert without a substantial matrix (Thomas Garrison, personal communication, 2013); these fills were similar to the chert cobbles uncovered at Preclassic El Palmar (Doyle 2013b; Doyle and Piedrasanta, chapter 2, this volume). Later structures, however, revealed fills that relied on denser matrices. During the Early Classic, laborers used glutinous mud extracted from local *bajos*, as evident in the lower strata of Str. F8-1 (e.g., Román and Newman 2011:130–131, figure 3.8). In subsequent centuries, fill matrix increasingly appeared as a nondescript soil that, while still dense, was lighter in color and somewhat less stable than the dark *bajo* muds (Stephen Houston, personal communication, 2013). Perhaps decades of energetic construction activities had divested the local landscape of dense *bajo* soils that provided much-needed structural stability, compelling builders to alter the composition of fill through time.

Structural guidelines

The conclusions presented thus far have been based as much on inference as on direct evidence, largely because pre-construction activities do not always leave discernible material remains. For instance, Mayanists have yet to recover drawn blueprints, measuring systems, or perishable tools such as strings, stakes, or other organic architectural planning aids. In fact, "guidelines" are among the only forms of primary data attesting to the pre-construction phase in the Maya Lowlands. Subtly etched or painted onto floors, guidelines marked the position where architectural elements like walls, interior platforms, retaining walls, doors, or stairways were to be placed (Coe 1990:875–877). The only guidelines discovered by the project appear on the floor of a crypt (Str. M3-3) built into the southeast corner of Str. M3-1, the mortuary pyramid in the Las Palmitas Group (figure 11.2). Compared to examples encountered at other sites, those at Las Palmitas are unique: rather than simply providing a line upon which builders could align the walls, these incisions indicate the placement of individual masonry blocks (Nicholas Carter, personal communication, 2012). This implies one of three possibilities: that all building stones were cut to a standardized size, allowing the planner to measure out the footprint of each block ahead of time; that the stones specifically destined for Str. M3-3 were cut before the guidelines were scratched into the floor plaster, which would also have allowed the lines to be positioned prior to wall assembly; or that planners and masons were in close and continuous contact with one another.

Construction Activities at El Zotz

This section examines activities associated with construction itself, namely those that laborers undertook to erect cores, platforms, walls, and roofing. As in the previous sections, this discussion is organized by major building tasks.

Nuclear assembly

Trenches, test pits, examination of looter tunnels, and excavation at El Zotz indicate that most monumental edifices were erected through the incremental expansion of fill and interior retaining walls. This system, sometimes called *nuclear core assembly* (Coe 1990:878), is widespread throughout the Maya Lowlands. Nuclear assembly entails loading fills into "discrete, progressively expanded and heightened core units, segments, or cells (however termed), whose sum contributes the fundamental mass (as divorced from formal finishing or cladding)" of a given structure (Coe 1990:878). At El Zotz, workers constructed low walls that they then backed with fill and contained with another retaining wall; each wall-fill-wall unit constitutes a discreet core that could be expanded horizontally or vertically to provide the desired dimensions and proportions of the emerging building. For instance, to create height, masons laid down superimposed courses of stone to be backed by upwardly expanding deposits of fill, while a larger footprint was achieved by placing retaining walls in parallel lines in front of one another with intervening fill separating them (Mesick 2012:233).

(a)

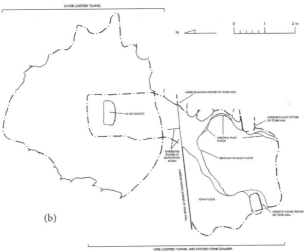

(b)

FIGURE 11.2. *Guidelines etched onto the floor of a crypt located in the southeast corner of Str. M3-1 at Las Palmitas: (a) photograph of guidelines; (b) plan view of the Str. M3-3 crypt at Las Palmitas, indicating the presence and location of etched guidelines (photo and drawing by N. Carter).*

Structure L7-1's Room 3 illustrates nuclear assembly, which is indicative of other structures at El Zotz as well (figure 4.2). Here, workers contained construction fill by building retaining walls of coursed, well-shaped masonry blocks. Instead of using mortar to bind the blocks, small chinking stones were wedged in intervening spaces to provide stability (Marroquín et al. 2011:43). Unfortunately, the lack of horizontal excavation limits more detailed analysis of how nuclear assembly developed and evolved through time at El Zotz.

Perishable building aids

Most discussions of ancient building practices assume that laborers relied on tools crafted from perishable materials to complete their tasks. In the Maya region, where moisture, heat, and soil acidity combine to degrade organics, archaeologists instead rely on indirect evidence to speculate about the use of perishable implements, since the tools themselves do not survive. Iconography on ceramics and other durable media, for instance, portrays wooden scaffolds, ropes, and other objects that would have greatly assisted in construction endeavors. At El Zotz, voids in construction fill and other architectural components also attest to the presence of perishable materials long since decayed.

For example, while working in Str. M3-6, excavators encountered a series of holes in the fill, which also bore impression from wood (Carter and Gutiérrez Castillo 2011:94–95). They interpreted these voids as spaces where workers once positioned logs to help load and distribute fill—a practice with parallels at other Maya sites like Uaxactun (e.g., Smith 1950:39, 47, 70, figure 71b). In addition, excavation in Str. L7-11 revealed X-shaped depressions associated with the deposition of a cache (Arredondo Leiva et al. 2008:77). Archaeologists again interpreted these depressions as voids left behind after crossed vines or ropes—presumably used to lower the cache to its place in construction fill—had disintegrated. Archaeological work at San Bartolo, another site in the Peten, unearthed a fragment of *bajo*-mud-bearing woven imprints on it (figure 11.3), strongly suggesting that laborers relied on baskets to carry loads of fill into the nuclear cores (Karl Taube, personal communication, 2010).

"Invisible" architecture

This section focuses on other aspects of the construction process that leave few material residues for archaeologists to uncover. It focuses first on perishable building materials like thatch and wood before addressing curtains and other interior architectural features intended to enhance the function and comfort of a building for its occupants.

FIGURE 11.3. *Stucco fragment recovered from fill at San Bartolo (Peten, Guatemala). The woven impressions on its surface suggest that perishable baskets may have been used to transport fill into nuclear cores (photo by K. Taube).*

As early as 2009, project archaeologists discovered evidence for pole-and-thatch structures dating to a Postclassic occupation in the South Group (Kingsley and Cambranes 2011:186–189). For example, Laura Gámez (2009:133) encountered an area of bedrock that had been leveled in antiquity to serve as an occupational surface for residents. Although she did not recover evidence for masonry architecture, she did locate four round depressions arranged to form a rectangle. With diameters narrowing from 40 to 20 cm, these holes were dug to a depth of 80 cm, where Gámez discovered decayed organic matter. Together, these features indicate that these depressions were postholes, which once supported upright wooden columns that formed the corners of an open-air building (Gámez 2009:133–134).

Builders also relied on wood to construct roofs—even on monumental structures otherwise made entirely of stone. While working at the summit of Str. L7-11, Caitlin Walker and Stephen Houston unearthed a thick layer of dark organic material mixed with decaying stucco. They interpreted this stratum as the remains of a beam-and-mortar roof because (1) its composition is diagnostic of rotted wood and lime, and (2) the deposit appeared on the summit of

Str. L7-11 (and more specifically atop the walls and floors of its superstructure). Based on careful measurement, excavators calculate that builders would have required approximately 27 m^2 of wood to construct this roof (Arredondo Leiva et al. 2008:88), which represents a significant investment of labor and resources that one could easily miss if not explicitly looking for perishable architecture.

Both direct and indirect evidence attest to the use of wooden beams as vault supports at El Zotz, where several were discovered intact (figure 11.4a). More commonly, beams disintegrated long ago, leaving only sockets like those discovered in the looter trenches that transected Str. M7-2 (figure 11.4b) and the imprint of a discarded beam found in the fill of Str. L7-1 (figure 11.4c). Wooden lintels similarly supported doorways and the load they carried by spanning the distance between the two jambs. Apart from carved lintels once looted from Str. M7-1 (Laporte 2006:figure 11), the only data to suggest their use are traces of decayed wood and lintel beds, which manifest as ledges carved out of stone and often coated in stucco (figure 11.5).

The organic architectural components discussed up to this point were structurally integrated as beams, roofs, and lintels. Other architectural traits, like cord holders, however, speak to the frequent incorporation of less-permanent fixtures—in this case, curtains. Today, cordholders appear as small plaster-coated depressions, holes, or sockets found on doorjambs (Loten and Pendergast 1984:figures 7, 11, pl. 4; Taube 1998:429). Textile panels could then be suspended from rods or dowels inserted into the jamb sockets. Cordholders also appear close to the floor, indicating that curtains could be secured on their bottom borders by a second rod. As a practical exigency, these curtains partitioned space, offered privacy, and kept out some of nature's less desirable elements. The Temple of the Night Sun and the Shrine beneath Str. F8-1 featured these provisions, as did the vaulted passageway that led from off the El Zotz Acropolis (figure 11.6).

Masonry and decorative masonry

Stoneworking technologies are here divided into two categories. The first addresses the masonry used to build foundations, walls, roofs, stairs, and other primary architectural features; the second focuses on superficial elements like stone moldings, outsets, and panels, which routinely graced building façades but served no functional purpose in that structural integrity would not be compromised by their absence. As part of the architectural process, however, such masonry flourishes can hardly be considered adornments in the same way that stucco sculpture or painting would be, since these features were incorporated before walls, vaults, and other vertical elements were fully erected.

FIGURE 11.4. *Incorporation of wood into monumental construction at El Zotz: (a) wood vault beams found intact in Str. M7-1 (photo by S. Houston); (b) postholes in Str. M7-2 (photo by S. Houston); (c) imprint of wooden beam in fill of Str. L7-1 (photo by J. L. Garrido).*

The majority of buildings at El Zotz and its subsidiary settlements boast high-quality masonry. For instance, many walls featured expertly worked stones laid in neat horizontal courses, most of which were later covered with facing stones. Intact cornice stones on several structures, including Str. M7-1 (Pérez Robles 2011:Anexo Fotográfico), exemplify the well-shaped monolithic blocks used in upper-zone construction. Somewhat counterintuitively, much of the completed stonework at El Zotz was later covered with stucco, but it appears that great care and prodigious craftsmanship went into providing a smooth, even surface before plasterers even began their work (e.g., figure 11.7).

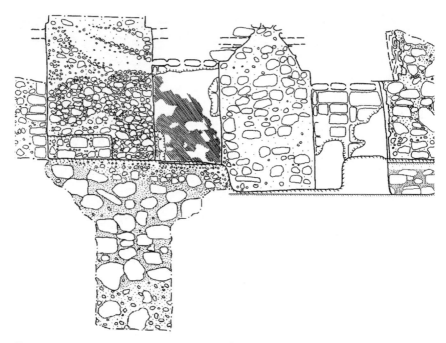

FIGURE 11.5. *Lintel beds found in Str. F8-1 -Sub. 1, seen as rows of flat stones at the tops of stuccoed door jambs (drawing by A. Coronado).*

By 2011, several seasons of excavation allowed the chronological comparison of construction phases across architectural complexes, and an interesting trend emerged with regard to masonry technologies: between the Late and Terminal Classic periods: the quality of stonework declined drastically and abruptly (e.g., Carter and Gutiérrez Castillo 2011:95). Because the years that separate these two cultural-historical periods coincide with the rapid abandonment of the Buenavista Valley as a whole (Garrison, Garrido et al. 2011:354–355), it is possible that that this architectural trend might variously reflect a decline in the population able or willing to serve as masons; a decrease in the technical knowledge and skills required to produce high-quality stonework akin to that created in earlier years; or a combination of these factors. Adobe, tamped mud, or even wattle-and-daub began to supplant the more labor-intensive stonework that flourished during the preceding centuries (Stephen Houston, personal communication, 2011).

As part of the exceptional masonry tradition at El Zotz from the Preclassic through the Late Classic periods, stoneworkers created moldings, cornices,

(a)

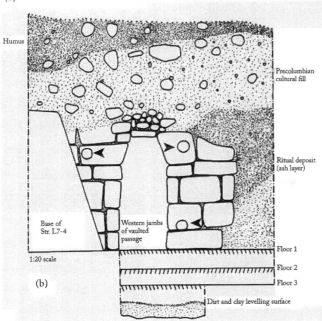

(b)

FIGURE 11.6. *Cordholders in the vaulted passage running underneath Acropolis Strs. L7-4 and L7-8: (a) photograph of the western jambs of the vaulted passage showing the location of cord holders (circles) (photo by A. Godoy); (b) line drawing of the western jamb of the vaulted passageway beneath Strs. L7-4 and L7-8. The cordholders are marked by arrows (drawing by J. L. Garrido).*

FIGURE 11.7. *Passageway under El Zotz Structures L7-8 and L7-4 evidencing expert stonework. The vault here remains intact, and most of its well-cut facing stones retain thick applications of white stucco and red pigment (photo by A. Godoy).*

and panels. Among the most common forms of decorative masonry are basal moldings, which run along the foundations of buildings: Str. L7-6, for instance, featured a basal molding nearly 1 m high (Pérez Robles et al.

2009:17; see also figure 11.5). Other buildings bore *talud*-style moldings, as on the superstructure of the Str. L7-1 pyramid (Marroquín et al. 2011:40–41, 51) or the walls of Str. M7-1 (Pérez Robles 2011:530). The Temple of the Night Sun, associated with early construction episodes of Str. F8-1 in the El Diablo Group, was extraordinarily ornate, featuring large stucco masks created in high relief and connected by a continuous stucco "sky band" decorated with geometric elements and symbols representing Venus (Houston, Newman, Román, and Garrison 2015; Román and Newman 2011:124, figures 3.5, fotos 6–7; Taube and Houston 2015). Structure M7-1, the mortuary pyramid in the East Group, possesses nearly all of these decorative elements (see Pérez Robles 2011:Anexo 1).

Roofing and roofcombs

As mentioned earlier, Str. L7-11 once bore a beam-and-mortar roof. Other buildings at El Zotz attest to more durable roofing made of stone. Unequivocal evidence appears in both the Str. M7-1 pyramid, where archaeologists discovered intact stone vaults in the lower portion of its stone roofcomb (Pérez Robles 2011:fotos 25, 26) and the passageway linking acropolis Strs. L7-4 and L7-8, which is spanned by a standing stone vault (figure 11.7). Elsewhere, the presence of stone vaults and roofing must be inferred. Strs. M3-6 and M3-7 in the Las Palmitas Group were discovered with distinctly shaped blocks resting on top of architectural collapse; from their location and form, they may have originated from a stone roof that crowned both structures (Carter and Gutiérrez Castillo 2011:73–75). As noted in the discussion of architectural demolition, however, roofs were one of the first architectural elements to be dismantled (and are among the first to collapse naturally), which limits the ability to study roofing technologies at El Zotz more comprehensively.

Floors and finished surfaces

During fieldwork, archaeologists encountered dozens of floors and walls, which were often (though not always) coated in a layer of plaster. In fact, the quality and character of finished surfaces at El Zotz—whether walls or floors—varies quite dramatically. Data from the El Diablo Group, for instance, indicate that builders covered constructed features with substantial applications of fine gray or white stucco. There, most Early Classic-period plastered floors were several centimeters thick, some structures featured elaborate stucco façade masks (see figure 3.5), and chunks of the material itself were used as ritual offerings in Str. F8-1. Renovative replastering, a topic discussed below, also relied on thick stucco finishes.

The striking absence of stucco floors in many phases of the architecture of the Las Palmitas Group, however, hints that its popularity as a building material and decorative medium may have declined during the Late Classic period. This pattern may be explained by practical concerns of the time, since manufacturing lime-based stucco and mortar is a long, labor-intensive process involving considerable quantities of raw materials: lime must be created by pulverizing seashells or limestone, into which large volumes of water must be mixed; kindling must be collected to create high-temperature fires; and the resulting slurry must be heated over long-burning fires (Abrams 1994:49; see also Erasmus 1965:290; Hyman 1970; Morris et al. 1931; Roys 1934). Thus, one possible cause for a decreasing dependence on stucco is the eventual exhaustion of necessary resources. In fact, paleoenvironmental data suggest heavy reductions in arboreal species in both the Early and Late Classic, with a brief recovery in the seventh century AD (Beach et al., chapter 7, this volume). Perhaps irrigating crops and maintaining a drinking supply outweighed the need or desire to produce stucco. Even today, the lack of surface water at El Zotz and the seasonality of rains can create temporary water shortages. Although a reasonable explanation, other data reveal a parallel decline in stucco at other Late Classic cities, suggesting a possible aesthetic component to this decision; irrespective of the guiding rationale, the decreasing use of this material was pervasive throughout the Maya Lowlands and hardly limited to El Zotz.

Building pauses

At the El Diablo Group, patterns in plastering practices suggest that builders occasionally halted their construction activities. While constructing Str. F8-1-Sub.2, for instance, builders laid thick strata of stucco over flooring ballast and wall tops. Because wet laid stucco requires time to dry before reaching the strength required to support overlying structures, these stucco layers (or pauselines) may represent a "curing interval" during which the stucco surfaces would have been allowed to harden (Coe 1990:883). During these periods workers could have engaged in other tasks, so pauselines do not necessarily imply a full cessation of work. In fact, this type of construction halt could be a signal of synchronicity in the building process rather than indecision, uncertainty, or unintended inactivity. In this way, pauselines must be distinguished from stoppages that result from an abrupt or otherwise unplanned cessation of work (Houston, Escobedo, and Mesick 2011; Inomata et al. 2004; Proskouriakoff 1950:111; Willey 1974).

Intentional pauses at other central Peten sites exhibit traits markedly similar to those observed at El Zotz, such as stucco levels that continue under walls and upper-zone masses. These examples further reveal a chronological pattern, in that pauselines appear commonly during earlier years of architectural development but are rarely observed in Late Classic–period stratigraphy. That pauselines occur at El Diablo, the hub of Early Classic–period construction at El Zotz, fits this pattern and supports the idea that this may have been a locally shared practice among early builders in the central Peten.

Post-Construction Activities at El Zotz

For Maya architects, engineers, and laborers, the building process hardly ended when major architectural elements had been successfully erected. Instead, buildings at El Zotz illustrate how work continued well past this point, first through processes of decorative elaboration, then through ongoing maintenance and occasional repairs.

Architectural embellishment

After erecting walls and floors, stairways and roofs, Maya artisans often adorned architectural façades with sculpture and paint. Structure F8-1 and its associated predecessors offer robust evidence about these post-construction acts. Based on fragments of stucco incorporated into the construction of the Burial 9 tomb, it appears that Str. F8-1 bore a painted and plastered façade, even in its earliest-known iterations (Houston, Newman, Román, and Carter 2015). Subsequent versions of the building were indeed saturated by stucco, from the elaborately modeled masks on the cornice frieze of the Temple of the Night Sun to the megalithic façade sculptures of Str. F8-1-Sub.1 (figure 3.5; see also Houston, Newman, Román, and Garrison 2015; Román and Carter 2009:figure 3.15; Román and Newman 2011:figure 5; Taube and Houston 2015).

Comparative data imply that such sculptures were often painted as well. However, very little pigment was discovered directly on the decorations themselves. The beautiful sculptures of the Temple of the Night Sun, for example, bore traces of red pigment only on their undersides and in areas protected by the overhanging cornice. Additional data for painting activities come from architectural fill, where painted stucco fragments were occasionally recovered, most often in shades of black and red (e.g., Marroquín et al. 2011:87–88).

Secondary adjustments

After a building was originally erected, architects could call for modifications to its form or arrangement. At El Zotz, these secondary adjustments can be identified in the stratigraphic sequences interpreted through the creation of Harris Matrices. For example, excavation in the superstructure of Str. L7-11 revealed a sequence of alterations made after the original version of the building had been used for some time: the room was divided into two by the addition of a first wall, which was later complemented by a second; builders eventually added two benches and a third wall that contained a niche (Arredondo Leiva et al. 2008:83–89). Similarly, incremental adjustments also transformed Str. L7-6, even if the stratigraphy there is less conducive to reconstructing a clear, sequential chain of events (Mesick 2012:145–153, figure 3.23a).

However, with the exception of the royal Acropolis, the buildings of El Zotz were used for comparatively short stretches of time; the entire complex at El Diablo seems to have been initiated, used, terminated, and abandoned in the span of a century. In contrast, at places like Tikal, architecture was used continuously for a millennium, sometimes longer. Structures with such long occupation spans generally provide richer details concerning subtle changes in form and layout through time.

Repair and maintenance

The environment, landscape, and climatic patterns in the Maya world make it difficult to maintain structurally stable and visually appealing buildings. Even among indigenous communities living in the area today, seasonal flooding can lead to the erosion of floors and contribute to mold and fungal growth (Abrams 1994:31–36). Insects, bats, and other animals could easily infest buildings (especially those that incorporated significant perishable components), becoming not only a nuisance to human occupants but also an accelerant for decay. Stucco was easily prone to wear and weakening through exposure to the sun and other elements. As a result, the Maya often continued building pursuits after initial construction by way of maintenance and repair.

In the Shrine and the Temple of the Night Sun found below Str. F8-1, archaeologists discovered evidence that builders repeatedly attempted to correct failing designs: berms were added to the Shrine to keep water from flooding in, while the vault of the temple was rebuilt on more than one occasion (Stephen Houston, personal communication, 2012). Sculpted portions of the façade were not strongly adhered to wall surfaces, while the poor preservation of paint on the sculpted cornice suggests that the structure had been long exposed to sunlight, leading to the decay of pigment. The substandard craftsmanship provides unparalleled insight into the measures later builders took to allay some of the structures' deficiencies.

Other archaeological signs of renovation and repair come through replastering. Behavioral patterns at El Zotz are unique in this regard: at many other sites, resurfacing activities tended to involve, at most, depositing a thin layer of sand, gravel, or small particulates over a used floor, tamping them down, and washing the new surface with a thin coat of plaster. At El Zotz, these routine resurfacings involved far more materials and labor. In fact, residents at the site seemed to require carefully releveled floors and disproportionately thick (ca. 10 cm or more) applications of plaster. Such signatures suggest that these activities were significant undertakings and may have been linked to a ritual cycle of building renewal rather than simple renovations to old or damaged surfaces.

A consideration of Maya architectural ritual (e.g., Miller 1998; Mock and Walker 1998; Stuart 1998; Tozzer 1941:161) suggests that not all maintenance stemmed from a need for remediation: proper building maintenance also required periodic ritual renewals. Indeed, the consistent discovery of caches within building fill reveals that the building process at El Zotz was not merely a technical one, it was also marked by purposeful symbolic behaviors. Compared to ritual deposits at other sites, caches at El Zotz show interesting patterns. First, nearly all were placed on top of intentionally prepared surfaces and carefully sealed using either large stones or clean fill. In at least two instances—the termination of Str. F8-8 and the abandoned final building phase of Str. L7-6—this ritual sealing used alluvial mud from nearby *bajos*. It is possible that ritual participants took deliberate pains to collect "special" materials specifically for these purposes. Still, caches decline toward the later years of occupation. In Preclassic and Early Classic contexts, buildings were systematically and formally terminated by their patrons and, presumably, the larger population as a whole. This suggests intentionality—that people had planned to move elsewhere or to erect a brand new structure, instead of reusing or burying an existing one. The general lack of cache deposits in those areas occupied later in the site's history (e.g., the Las Palmitas Group and areas of the royal Acropolis at El Zotz) hints that abandonment might have occurred far more rapidly, perhaps even unexpectedly.

SUMMARY AND CONCLUSION

This chapter reinforces occupation histories and construction phases outlined elsewhere in this volume. However, it can also provide some unexpected and surprising insight—especially with regard to how we design excavation strategies and approach stratigraphic interpretation. Perhaps more so than anything else, examining building practices through the lens of technological decision-making provides a new way of seeing architectural stratigraphy. One the one hand, it compels excavators to look critically and deliberately for physical signatures that could be easily missed: even keen-eyed excavators note that uncovering certain features is no straightforward task (Coe 1990:877). Consider the difficulty entailed in discovering and recording guidelines like those described above. This requires, first and foremost, horizontal excavation of sufficient scope to expose broad expanses of the floors where they would have been painted or etched. Yet time constraints, permit restrictions, safety concerns, and differing excavation techniques often restrict the extent of horizontal stripping archaeologists can achieve at Maya sites. Even if guidelines are exposed, damage from the weight of overlying construction, ancient demolition, or even the excavation process itself often damages or erases the lines and makes them difficult to detect. Overlooking such subtle features can lead to underreporting of certain practices or even architectural forms, which in turn can have ramifications for how we understand and interpret the development of Maya society.

In addition to skewing perceptions of what was typical or atypical, common or unique, conventional or innovative in Maya architecture, this study also forces a reconsideration of the overall utility of certain categories of data. For example, few archaeologists consider fill a particularly rich source of information, apart from diagnostic ceramics and other datable materials it might contain (cf. Deetz 1977:14–16; Rubertone 1989:51–52). At El Zotz, however, fill composition reveals temporal patterns and hints about changing interactions between human populations and the natural resources of the landscape.

On an even broader conceptual level, this study demonstrates one means to shift the way we conceptualize architectural landscapes. By affording interpretive primacy to the process of building rather than to the already-finished product that constitutes the unit of analysis in conventional work on Maya architecture, this approach challenges an increasingly discredited notion of material culture as static. Instead, it underscores human agency and practice as the social vehicles through which buildings become materialized. This emphasis takes us one step further toward repeopling ancient sites and landscapes with the architects, laborers, and patrons so often eclipsed in archaeological accounts of Maya buildings.

12

Of late, Maya archaeology has seldom had the time or investment to assemble the large samples of human remains that earlier projects took for granted (Scherer 2017). These problems are compounded by perennially poor preservation and a high intensity of looting. This is not, however, to say that Mayanist bioarchaeology works under impossible conditions. Rather, this changed landscape of field and laboratory work requires us to develop new research questions and methodology. What, above all, can we learn from small, poorly preserved skeletal samples? As I will demonstrate over the course of this chapter, there is in fact considerable information in relatively small skeletal samples, even when some of our data come from looted contexts. After a brief overview of the state of the field in Mayanist bioarchaeology, this chapter presents a detailed summary of the burials and skeletons of El Zotz, Bejucal, and El Palmar that were studied from 2008 to 2016. The chapter concludes with a brief synthesis, illustrating how data from human skeletons and burials can illuminate aspects of Classic Maya mortuary practice, highlighting especially the distinct role of fire in funerary rites at El Zotz and Bejucal.

LOOKING BACK, MOVING FORWARD

Throughout much of the twentieth century, the archaeology of the Lowland Maya, particularly as practiced in Guatemala, was characterized by large-

Grave Matters

Bioarchaeology and Mortuary Archaeology at El Zotz, Bejucal, and El Palmar

ANDREW K. SCHERER

DOI: 10.5876/9781607327646.c012

scale, multiyear projects with heavy investiture in long-term excavation programs (e.g., Black 1990; Smith 1950; Weeks et al. 2005). The apogee was arguably the work at Tikal, first under the auspices of the University Museum of the University of Pennsylvania in the 1950s and 1960s and later by the Proyecto Nacional Tikal in the late 1970s and early 1980s (Coe 1967; Laporte and Fialko 1985, 1995; Sabloff 2003). Contemporary projects of lesser scale were executed at Altar de Sacrificios (Willey 1973), and in Belize at Lamanai (Pendergast 1981), Lubaantun (Hammond 1975), and Altun Ha (Pendergast 1979, 1982, 1990). Inspired by theoretical trends that were shaping archaeology in the 1960s and 1970s, archaeologists turned their attention to the problem of the "house," excavating well over a thousand Classic Maya burials in a matter of decades at these and other sites (Becker 1999; Haviland 1985). For the first time, osteologists had the sample sizes necessary to explore complex questions with Classic Maya skeletal data (Haviland 1967; Saul 1972).

By the late 1970s, the field of bioarchaeology coalesced as a methodological and theoretical approach to ancient human skeletons, heavily influenced by the adaptivist paradigm advocated by practitioners of the "New Archaeology" (Buikstra 1976, 1977). For much of the two decades that followed, bioarchaeologists were primarily invested in questions of adaptation, health, and subsistence (e.g., Cohen and Armelagos 1984; Larsen et al. 2002; Larsen 2002, 2006). In the Maya area, bioarchaeologists found a calling as specialists well positioned to comment on hypotheses pertaining to the "rise and fall" of the Classic Maya (e.g., White 1988; Whittington 1989; Wright 2006; Wright and White 1996). By the 1990s, projects such as the Vanderbilt Petexbatun Project (Demarest 1997) and the Brigham Young–del Valle Piedras Negras Project were conceived with bioarchaeology as an integral component of the research design (Houston et al. 1998).

The turn of the millennium, however, has marked an important shift in the structure and organization of Mayanist archaeology, especially as practiced in Guatemala. The available level of private funding that is necessary to run large-scale, long-term projects has declined precipitously. It is now increasingly difficult for faculty to secure repeated long-term leaves from the university in order to oversee months of field and laboratory work on an annual basis. Although there are some exceptions, most Mayanist projects have become more limited in size and scale, organized strategically to answer key theoretical and culture historical questions that can be addressed with less financial and infrastructural investment (e.g., Foias and Emery 2012; Golden and Scherer 2006; Inomata et al. 2013; Scherer and Golden

2012; Webster et al. 2007). As a result, the number of burials excavated has substantially diminished. We likely will never see future Maya burial sample sizes comparable to those produced at Tikal, Altar de Sacrificios, Piedras Negras, and similar large-scale projects of the twentieth century.[1] Writing about the state of Mayanist bioarchaeology over a decade ago, Lori Wright predicted that these diminishing sample sizes would prompt bioarchaeologists to focus increasingly on "life history approaches" that "combine chemical and pathological data into a sensitive reconstruction of individual health and illness" (Wright 2004:211). She correctly cautioned, however, that "past behavior and biology can only be truly understood through a population approach," the sort of analysis that requires sample sizes of hundreds of skeletons, more characteristic of the large field projects of decades past (Wright 2004:211). Indeed, those older skeletal collections should be revisited to refine the methods and approaches available for understanding ancient Maya subsistence, health, and population structure (e.g., Cucina et al. 2011; Cucina and Tiesler 2003; Saul 1972; Scherer 2007; Scherer et al. 2007; White et al. 1993; White et al. 2001; Wright 2005, 2006; Wright and White 1996). Yet Wright did not acknowledge in her review that the study of human skeletons can tell us much more than what people ate, what diseases they had, or where they came from. In recent years, bioarchaeologists have begun to explore more deeply problems related to ritual practice, belief, and ideology (e.g., Duncan 2006, 2011; Duncan and Hofling 2011; Scherer 2015a; Scherer et al. 2014; Tiesler 2007, 2012; Tiesler et al. 2004). These recent studies have grappled with small sample sizes of recent excavations yet have managed to produce valuable results. Their success owes in no small part to the close linkage between field archaeology and bioarchaeology, something that was typically lacking in studies of human skeletons in decades past.

As an additional obstacle facing Mayanist bioarchaeology, rampant looting continues to ravage the region. El Zotz and Bejucal have been heavily targeted by looters, producing unknown (but apparently sizable) quantities of fine mortuary objects for art museums and private collectors around the world, resulting in significant destruction of both architecture and archaeological context at the site. At El Zotz and Bejucal, the archaeologists wisely chose to capitalize on this tragic situation and conducted extensive studies of the looter tunnels and the burial chambers they exposed. As part of this work, they recovered both the human remains and fragments of the mortuary objects overlooked or left behind by the looters. As is explored later in this chapter, even these disturbed fragments, if properly documented and recovered, can still yield useful data.

RESEARCH DESIGN

Ideally, the bioarchaeologist is in the field and oversees the excavation of all of the burials. Recent research by Vera Tiesler, Andrea Cucina, and colleagues, whose fieldwork is influenced by the archaeothanatological approach advocated by Henri Duday (2009), highlights the importance of bioarchaeology as an integrated field and laboratory endeavor (Tiesler 2007; Tiesler et al. 2010). As their work demonstrates, proper identification and location of the skeleton can yield useful information regarding the postmortem manipulation of the body, among other factors. Further, the presence of the bioarchaeologist in the field ensures that the skeletons are properly handled and excavated. This is important even for human remains recovered from looted burials where some evidence of the original archaeological context may still be preserved.

Bioarchaeology has been an integral component of the field and laboratory work by the El Zotz Project since its inception. However, professional obligations on other field projects and the remoteness of El Zotz made it impossible for me to participate directly in the excavations. Nevertheless, I implemented the excavation and documentation protocols at El Zotz based on the approach used on my own field project. Each burial was pedestaled and documented by a field plan and photography. The excavators filled out burial forms and took extensive notes for each burial, recording information regarding burial location, burial architecture, the general state of preservation, and especially the disposition of the bones. Rather than attempting field identification, excavators assigned each bone (or bone fragment) a unique number, noted that number on the burial plan, and then worked with me in the laboratory to reconstruct the position of the skeleton and ultimately the position of the body at the time of interment.

I undertook the laboratory analysis of each skeleton with the goal of obtaining a full complement of osteological data: inventory, age, sex, stature, skeletal and dental pathology, cranial metrics, postcranial metrics, dental metrics, dental nonmetrics, cranial and dental modification, and taphonomy. A general overview of these data is reported here. I employed standard osteological methods (Buikstra and Ubelaker 1994; White et al. 2011). When possible, I estimated age by Transition Analysis (Boldsen et al. 2002; Milner and Boldsen 2012). I evaluated stature using the formulae of Santiago Genovés (1967) as corrected by Andrés del Ángel and Hector Cisneros (del Ángel and Cisneros 2004). I also recorded cranial and dental modification following standard approaches for Mesoamerican populations (Romero Molina 1986; Tiesler 2012). Macroscropic analyses were complemented by dietary stable isotope analysis, the results of which are still forthcoming. We are considering migratory stable isotopic research but will defer that for a future publication.

From 2009 to 2016, 32 burials have been designated for El Zotz, seven burials at Bejucal, and four burials from El Palmar (tables 12.1 and 12.2). At least three of the deposits designated as burials are sacrificial deposits (El Zotz Burials 6, 15, and El Palmar Burial 4) and one of the burial designations is for a deposit that does not in fact exist (El Zotz Burial 21). This tally of burials includes both disturbed and undisturbed mortuary contexts investigated by the team. Additional information regarding the osteology and archaeology of the burials from El Zotz, Bejucal, and El Palmar are available in the project interim reports for the 2008–2016 field seasons (Arredando Leiva and Houston 2008; Garrido López, Garrison, et al. 2012; Garrido López et al. 2011; Garrido López, Houston, et al. 2012; Garrido López et al. 2014; Garrido López et al. 2015a; Garrido López et al. 2016; Gutiérrez Castillo et al. 2017; Pérez Robles, Román, and Houston 2009).

The role of bioarchaeology on the El Zotz project was originally envisioned as pertaining primarily to issues related to human-landscape interaction in diachronic perspective. We had anticipated a skeletal sample size sufficient to explore chronological changes in health, diet, and population structure. However, because of a variety of factors, including those noted earlier, a large-scale program of household archaeology was ultimately not realized at El Zotz and the burial sample is, at the time of writing, substantially smaller than we had anticipated. On the other hand, detailed studies of the surprising number of major and minor civic-ceremonial centers shared among El Zotz (the epicenter, El Diablo, and El Tejón), Bejucal, and El Palmar provide critical new data on the evolution of elite ritual life in the central Peten (Doyle 2013b; Garrison et al. 2016). It is within this framework of research that bioarchaeology has proven most valuable at El Zotz.

What follows are the results of these analyses. Burials 6 and 15 are discussed in the context of Burial 9. In describing funerary architecture, I use a modified version of Ledyard Smith's (1972:212) typology from Uaxactun, which has been widely adopted by Mayanists (Scherer 2015a; Welsh 1988). *Simple burials* are graves with no formal burial architecture. *Cists* are inhumations with only minor elaboration to delimit the mortuary space from the surrounding architecture or soil, such as rocks placed around the body. *Simple crypts* are formal masonry-walled containers, complete with a lid that was often made of large, flat limestone slabs. Their internal height is less than 0.5 m. *Elaborate crypts* are larger, more complex versions of the former and have internal heights of 0.5 m to 1.0 m. *Tombs* are vaulted burial chambers with an interior height greater

TABLE 12.1. Mortuary archaeological summary for burials from El Zotz (EZ), Bejucal (BL), and El Palmar (EP)ᵃ.

Burial	Structure	Chronology	Burial Facility	Orientation	Body Position	Mortuary Artifacts	Thermal exposure of human remains
EZ Burial 1	F8-14	Early Classic	Tomb	N	?	extensive, looted	Yes
EZ Burial 2	L7-6	Early Classic	Cist	N	extended, ventral	shell pendent	No
EZ Burial 3	K8-2	Early Classic	Cist	N	flexed, right side	four ceramic vessels	No
EZ Burial 4	L7-3	Late Classic	Cist	N	extended, supine	two ceramic vessels	No
EZ Burial 5	L7-1	Late Classic	Cist	N	flexed, supine	one ceramic vessel	No
EZ Burial 6	F8-1	Sacrificial depos t associated with Burial 9					
EZ Burial 7	M3-8	Terminal Classic	Cist	N	extended, supine	three ceramic vessels	No
EZ Burial 8	L7-2	Late Classic	Cist	N	flexed, supine	three ceramic vessel	Yes
EZ Burial 9	F8-1	Early Classic	Tomb	N	extended, supine	extensive	Yes1
EZ Burial 10	M3-3	Late Classic	Tomb	N	?	looted	?
EZ Burial 11	L7-8	Late Classic	Tomb	N	?	looted	?
EZ Burial 12	L7-17	Terminal Classic	Simple	E	flexed, supine-inclined	none	No
EZ Burial 13	H6-2	Early Classic	Tomb	N	?	looted	?
EZ Burial 14	H6-2	Early Classic	Tomb	N	?	looted	?
EZ Burial 15	F8-1	Sacrificial deposit associated with Burial 9					
EZ Burial 16	M7-1	Early Classic	Tomb	N	?	looted	?
EZ Burial 17	M7-1	Early Classic	Simple	?	?	looted	?
EZ Burial 18	H6-2	Early Classic	Tomb	N	?	looted	?

continued on next page

TABLE 12.1.—continued

Burial	Structure	Chronology	Burial Facility	Orientation	Body Position	Mortuary Artifacts	Thermal exposure of human remains
EZ Burial 19	L8-13	Early Classic	Tomb	?	?	looted	?
EZ Burial 20	L8-9	Early Classic	Cist or Crypt	?	?	looted, 126 jade and shell beads, worked bone, obsidian blades (Pachuca?)	Yes
EZ Burial 21	L8-9	Burial created in error—Burial 21 is the same deposit as Burial 20.					
EZ Burial 22	L8-11	Late Classic?	Tomb	?	?	looted, worked shell	?
EZ Burial 23	L8-10	Late Classic?	Tomb	?	?	looted, jade beads, jade mask tesserae, shell fragment	Yes
EZ Burial 24	L8-19	Early to Late Classic	?	?	?	looted, jade bead, vase	?
EZ Burial 25	M7-1	Early Classic	Elaborate crypt	N	extended, supine	four vases, three jade beads, one shell bead, stingray spine	Yes
EZ Burial 26	L8-17	Late Classic	Tomb	?	?	looted, 3 jade beads	Yes
EZ Burial 27	Midden	Early Classic	Simple	—	isolated head and long bones	none	No
EZ Burial 28	I10-4	Terminal Classic	Cist	N	extended, supine	plate, vase, bowl	No
EZ Burial 29	L8-20	Early Classic	Tomb	N	?	looted, obsidian, jade, bone, ceramics	Yes?

continued on next page

TABLE 12.1.—continued

Burial	Structure	Chronology	Burial Facility	Orientation	Body Position	Mortuary Artifacts	Thermal exposure of human remains
EZ Burial 30	L8-13	Late Classic	Tomb	N	extended, supine	two bowls, plate, shell bead, jade beads, jade ear ornaments	No
EZ Burial 31	I10-3	Terminal Classic	Cist	S	flexed, right side	plate	No
EZ Burial 32	I10-3	Terminal Classic	Cist	N	flexed, right side	none	No
BL Burial 1	Southeast Courtyard	Early Classic	Simple	S	extended, supine	?	No
BL Burial 2	S6-10	Early Classic	Tomb	N	?	looted	Yes
BL Burial 3	S6-10	Late Preclassic	Crypt	N	?	looted	Yes
BL Burial 4A	S6-4	Classic	?	?	?	looted	No
BL Burial 4B	S6-4	Classic	?	?	?	looted	No
BL Burial 5	S6-4	Late Classic	Cist	N	flexed, right	ceramic vessel	No
BL Burial 6	S6-10	Early Classic	Cist	NE	extended, supine	none	No
BL Burial 7	S6-8	Late Classic	?	?	?	looted	No
EP Burial 1	E4-4	Early Classic	Simple		disarticulated	none	No
EP Burial 2	E5-7, Str. 4	Early Classic	Cist	N	extended, supine	shell, chert, crystal	No
EP Burial 3	E5-1	Early Classic	Tomb	N	?	looted, jade mask	?
EP Burial 4	D5-1	Late Preclassic	Cache	W, ?	two individuals: seated and unknown	fragment of jade and obsidian (Burial 4A)	No

ᵃ Refers to the secondary occupants within the burial chamber. The primary occupant was unaffected.

TABLE 12.2. Osteological summary for skeletons from burials from El Zotz (EZ), Bejucal (BL), and El Palmar (EP)[a].

Burial	Minimum Number of Individuals	Sex	Age	Stature	Cranial Modification	Dental Modification	Pathology
EZ Burial 1	2	Male?	Old adult (> 50 years)		?	?	
EZ Burial 2	1	?	6–12 months		Yes	No	porotic hyperostosis and cribra orbitalia
EZ Burial 3	1	Male?	Old Adult (> 50 years)		?	No	
EZ Burial 4	1	Female	20–35 years	157.58 cm	Yes	No	occupational changes of pectoral girdle, periostitis
EZ Burial 5	1	Male	Adult		Yes	Yes	periostitis
EZ Burial 6	Sacrificial deposit associated with Burial 9.						
EZ Burial 7	1	?	Adult			No	
EZ Burial 8	1	Male	Old Adult (> 55 years)		Yes		
EZ Burial 9	7	Male?	Old adult (> 50 years)		?	Yes	osteoarthritis
EZ Burial 10	1	?	Adult		?	?	
EZ Burial 11	2	?	Adult		?	Yes	
EZ Burial 12	1	Male	Old Adult (> 65 years)	162.5 cm	Yes	Yes	periostitis, osteoarthritis

continued on next page

TABLE 12.2.—continued

Burial	Minimum Number of Individuals	Sex	Age	Stature	Cranial Modification	Dental Modification	Pathology
EZ Burial 13	Looted burial from Structure H6-2. No human remains.						
EZ Burial 14	Looted burial from Structure H6-2. No human remains.						
EZ Burial 15	Sacrificial deposit associated with Burial 9						
EZ Burial 16	Looted Burial from Structure M7-1. No human remains.						
EZ Burial 17	Looted burial in front of Structure M7-1—inside of a stuccoed masonry altar.						
EZ Burial 18	Looted burial from Structure H6-2. No human remains.						
EZ Burial 19	Looted burial from Structure L8-13. No human remains.						
EZ Burial 20	1?	?	?		?	?	
EZ Burial 21	Burial created in error—Burial 21 is the same deposit as Burial 20.						

continued on next page

TABLE 12.2.—continued

Burial	Minimum Number of Individuals	Sex	Age	Stature	Cranial Modification	Dental Modification	Pathology
EZ Burial 22	Looted burial from Structure L8–11. No human remains.						
EZ Burial 23	2	?, ?	Adult, 5–10 years			?	
EZ Burial 24	3	?, ?, ?	Adolescent or Adult, Adolescent or Adult, 5–10 years		?, ?, ?	Yes, of at least 1 individual	
EZ Burial 25	1	Male	Adult		Yes	Yes	osteoarthritis
EZ Burial 26	Looted burial from Structure L8–17.						
EZ Burial 27	1	?	3–5 years		Yes	No	
EZ Burial 28	2	Male?, ?	Adult, 5 years (± 16 mos.)		Yes, Yes	Yes, No	The child demonstrates porotic hyperostosis.
EZ Burial 29	Looted burial from L8–20. No bone recovered or possibly misinterpreted as burned shell. Not subject to osteological analysis.						
EZ Burial 30	1	?	Adolescent or Adult		Yes	?	
EZ Burial 31	1	?	Adolescent of Adult		?	?	
EZ Burial 32	1	Male	Adult		Yes	Yes	osteoarthritis, ante-mortem fracture

continued on next page

TABLE 12.2.—*continued*

Burial	Minimum Number of Individuals	Sex	Age	Stature	Cranial Modification	Dental Modification	Pathology
BL Burial 1	1	?	Adult		?	?	
BL Burial 2	1	?	Late Adolescent or Adult (> 16 years)		?	?	trauma
BL Burial 3	1	?	Adult		?	Yes	
BL Burial 4A	1	Male	20–27 years			Yes	
BL Burial 4B	1	Female	20–26 years		?	No	fractured foot
BL Burial 5	1	Male	26–50 years		Yes	Yes	hand and foot fractures
BL Burial 6	1	?	3–9 months		?	No	
BL Burial 7	1	Male?	Adult		?	?	
EP Burial 1	1	?	Late Adolescent or Adult		?	No	
EP Burial 2A	1	?	Adult		?	?	
EP Burial 2B	1	?	16—32 months		?	No	
EP Burial 3	Looted burial from El Palmar Structure E5–1.						
EP Burial 4	2	?, ?	2–4 years, 2 months		Yes, ?	No, No	The first individual demonstrates a possible perimortem fracture.

[a] Osteological information refers to the primary occupant of the burial chamber. Sacrificial mortuary deposits, including Burial 6, are detailed in the text but not included here. Blank spaces in the table indicate missing data

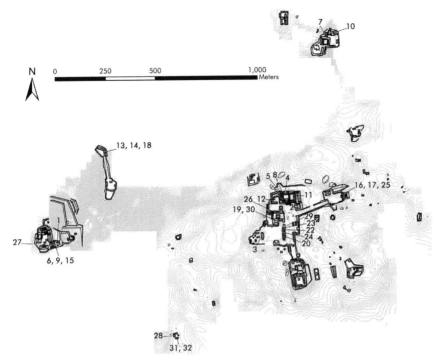

FIGURE 12.1. *Map showing locations of El Zotz burials (map by T. Garrison).*

than 1.0 m. Obviously, this is an etic typology, though one that nevertheless accords roughly with distinctions that would have been understood by the Maya. For example, no burial of a known Maya king that I am aware of, where *ajaw* status can be independently confirmed with textual evidence, is anything smaller than a tomb.

EL ZOTZ BURIAL 1

Burial 1 is a looted tomb of the Early Classic period in Str. F8-14, a building in the El Diablo complex, cleared by Alejandro Gillot Vassaux in 2008 (figure 12.1). The tomb measures 3.60 m (length) × 1.10 m (width) × 1.80 m (height) and was oriented on a north-northwest axis (348° east of north), perpendicular to the long axis of the structure.[2] When excavating the tomb, Gillot recovered a variety of objects, including three fragments of shell, seven animal bones, three fragments of red specular hematite, two fragments of jade, three other necklace beads, a piece of quartz, fragments of a pyrite

TABLE 12.3. Excavation contexts for burials from El Zotz (EZ), Bejucal (BL), and El Palmar (EP).

Burial #	Structure	Operation	Year	Looted?	Context citation	Preliminary osteology	Notes	Final publication
BL Burial 1	SE Courtyard	BL 1A-1-8	2009	No	Garrison and Garrido López 2009b:252	Scherer 2009:327–328		Garrison et al. 2016; Scherer, chapter 12, this volume
BL Burial 2	S6-10	BL 1B-2-4	2010	Yes	Garrison and Beltrán 2011:294	Scherer 2012:275		Garrison et al. 2016; Scherer, chapter 12, this volume
BL Burial 3	S6-10	BL 1B-6-5	2010	Yes	Garrison and Beltrán 2011:301	Scherer 2012:275–276		Garrison et al. 2016; Scherer, chapter 12, this volume
BL Burial 4	S6-4	BL 2F-1-1	2011	Yes	Garrison and Del Cid 2012:222–223	Scherer 2012:277–279		Garrison et al. 2016; Scherer, chapter 12, this volume
BL Burial 5	S6-4	BL 2F-2-1	2011	No	Garrison and Del Cid 2012:223	Scherer 2012:279		Garrison et al. 2016; Scherer, chapter 12, this volume
BL Burial 6	S6-10	BL 1B-6-10	2011	No	Garrison and Del Cid 2012:225	Scherer 2012:279		Garrison et al. 2016; Scherer, chapter 12, this volume
BL Burial 7	S6-8	BL 1F-1-1	2011	Yes	Garrison and Del Cid 2012:219–220	Scherer 2012:280		Garrison et al. 2016; Scherer, chapter 12, this volume
EP Burial 1	E4-4	EP 1B-2-14	2009	No	Doyle and Matute Rodríguez 2009:214	Scherer 2009:328–329		Doyle 2013a; Scherer, chapter 12, this volume

continued on next page

TABLE 12.3.—continued

Burial #	Structure	Operation	Year	Looted?	Context citation	Preliminary osteology	Notes	Final publication
EP Burial 2	E5-7 Str. 4	EP 5C-1-2	2011	No	Doyle and Piedrasanta 2012:211–212	Scherer 2012:280		Doyle 2013a; Scherer, chapter 12, this volume
EP Burial 3	E5-1	EP 9B-1-2	2011	Yes	Doyle and Piedrasanta 2012:213–214	No bones recovered		Doyle 2013a; Scherer, chapter 12, this volume
EP Burial 4	D5-1	EP 10A-1-14	2016	No	Garrison et al. 2017:114–117	Garrison et al. 2017:114–117		Scherer, chapter 12, this volume
EZ Burial 1	F8-14	EZ 5X-2-1	2008	Yes	Gillot Vassaux 2008a:126–131	Scherer 2009:321–322		Scherer, chapter 12, this volume
EZ Burial 2	L7-6	EZ 2A-10-5	2009	No	Peréz Robles et al. 2009:15	Scherer 2009:323–324		Scherer, chapter 12, this volume
EZ Burial 3	K8-2	EZ 10B-2-5	2009	No	Cambranes 2009:175–176	Scherer 2009:324–325		Scherer, chapter 12, this volume
EZ Burial 4	L7-3	EZ 2F-2-8	2009	No	Peréz et al. 2009:33–34	Scherer 2009:325–327		Scherer, chapter 12, this volume
EZ Burial 5	L7-1	EZ 2G-7-8	2010	No	Marroquín et al. 2011:20–21	Scherer and Garrett 2011a:413–414; Scherer 2012:269–273		Scherer, chapter 12, this volume
EZ Burial 6	F8-1	EZ 5B-28-9	2010	No	Román and Newman 2011:130	Scherer and Garrett 2011b:426–427		Scherer 2015b; chapter 12, this volume

continued on next page

Table 12.3.—continued

Burial #	Structure	Operation	Year	Looted?	Context citation	Preliminary osteology	Notes	Final publication
EZ Burial 7	M3-8	EZ 4G-1-6	2010	No	Carter and Gutiérrez Castillo 2011:89-90	Scherer 2012:273		Carter 2014; Scherer, chapter 12, this volume
EZ Burial 8	L7-2	EZ 2B-10-7	2010	No	Marroquín et al. 2011:17	Scherer and Garrett 2011a:414; Scherer 2012:273-274		Scherer, chapter 12, this volume
EZ Burial 9	F8-1	EZ 5B-29-1	2010	No	Román and Newman 2011:132-133	Scherer and Garrett 2011b:427-441		Houston et al. 2015; Scherer 2015
EZ Burial 10	M3-3	EZ 4X-13-1	2011	Yes	Carter and Gutiérrez Castillo 2012b:39-40	Scherer 2012:275		Carter 2014; Scherer, chapter 12, this volume
EZ Burial 11	L7-8	EZ 2J-3-5	2011	Yes	Newman and Menéndez 2012:142	Scherer 2012:275		Scherer, chapter 12, this volume
EZ Burial 12	L7-17	EZ 12J-6-4	2011	No	Newman and Menéndez 2012:149	Scherer 2012:274		Scherer, chapter 12, this volume
EZ Burial 13	H6-2	EZ 17B-4-X	2011	Yes	Piedrasanta 2012:191	No bones recovered		Scherer, chapter 12, this volume
EZ Burial 14	H6-2	EZ 17B-4-X	2011	Yes	Piedrasanta 2012:191	No bones recovered		Scherer, chapter 12m this volume
EZ Burial 15	F8-1	EZ 19A-10-4	2012	No	Gutiérrez et al. 2012:22-23	Scherer 2014:159-160		Scherer 2015b; chapter 12, this volume

continued on next page

TABLE 12.3.—*continued*

Burial #	Structure	Operation	Year	Looted?	Context citation	Preliminary osteology	Notes	Final publication
EZ Burial 16	M7-1	EZ 21C-2-1	2012	Yes	Garrison et al. 2012:67	Scherer 2014:159–160		Scherer, chapter 12, this volume
EZ Burial 17	M7-1	EZ 21A-1-2	2012	Yes	Garrison et al. 2012:60–61	Scherer 2014:159–160		Scherer, chapter 12m this volume
EZ Burial 18	H6-2	EZ 20D-1-1	2012	Yes	Piedrasanta and Hernández 2012:50	Scherer 2014:159–160		Scherer, chapter 12, this volume
EZ Burial 19	L8-13	EZ 23G-18-1	2006/2015	Yes	Hernández and Garrido 2016:50; Houston, Nelson, et al. 2006:8–9	No bones recovered	Listed as Burial 29 in Hernández and Garrido 2016	Scherer, chapter 12, this volume
EZ Burial 20	L8-9	EZ 23A-2-1	2013	Yes	Excavated as Burial 21	Scherer 2014:160–161	Burial 21 in the field	Scherer, chapter 12, this volume
EZ Burial 21	L8-9	EZ 23A-2-1	2013	Yes	Garrido López 2014:95	Analyzed as Burial 20	Burial 20 in analysis	Scherer, chapter 12, this volume
EZ Burial 22	L8-11	EZ 23B-2-1	2013	Yes	Garrido López 2014:96–97	No bones recovered		Scherer, chapter 12, this volume
EZ Burial 23	L8-10	EZ 23C-3-1	2013	Yes	Garrido López 2014:98	Scherer 2014:161		Scherer, chapter 12, this volume
EZ Burial 24	L8-19	EZ 23D-1-1	2014	Yes	Garrido López 2015:77–78	Scherer and de Carteret 2016:157–158		Scherer, chapter 12, this volume

continued on next page

TABLE 12.3.—*continued*

Burial #	Structure	Operation	Year	Looted?	Context citation	Preliminary osteology	Notes	Final publication
EZ Burial 25	M7-1	EZ 21E-1-5	2012	No	Garrison 2015:60-62	Scherer and de Carteret 2016:158-160		Scherer, chapter 12, this volume
EZ Burial 26	L8-17	EZ 26A-1-7	2012	Yes	Newman 2015a:96-97	Scherer and de Carteret 2016:165-166		Scherer, chapter 12, this volume
EZ Burial 27	Midden	EZ 19E-2-4	2014	No	Gutiérrez and Román 2015:30	Scherer and de Carteret 2016:160-161		Scherer, chapter 12, this volume
EZ Burial 28	I10-4	EZ 25C-17-11	2015	No	de Carteret 2016:67-68	Scherer and de Carteret 2016:161-163		de Carteret 2017; Scherer, chapter 12, this volume
EZ Burial 29	L8-20	EZ 23F-1-1	2015	Yes	Hernández and Garrido 2016:38	No bones recovered		Scherer, chapter 12, this volume
EZ Burial 30	L8-13	EZ 23G-16-5	2015	No	Hernández and Garrido 2016:47-49	Scherer and de Carteret 2016:163		Scherer, chapter 12, this volume
EZ Burial 31	I10-3	EZ 25D-4-6	2015	No	de Carteret 2016:70-71	Scherer and de Carteret 2016:164		de Carteret 2017; Scherer, chapter 12, this volume
EZ Burial 32	I10-3	EZ 25D-7-7	2015	No	de Carteret 2016:74-75	Scherer and de Carteret 2016:164		de Carteret 2017; Scherer, chapter 12, this volume

and hematite mirror, a shell disc in the form of a flower, four shell rings, a nacreous bead, fragments of an 11-cm ceramic disc, and a fragment of a thin charred-wood panel. Gillot also noted that some of the fragments of the tomb wall exhibited burning and others showed red paint. Pottery fragments recovered by Gillot are likely the remains of what were once complete vessels placed within the tomb, including an incised Balanza Black dish similar to pots recovered in Burial 9.

Human remains were scattered throughout the tomb, disturbed by the looters. These fragments correspond to at least two individuals: an adult (Skeleton A) and a subadult (Skeleton B). In view of the Maya tendency to place multiple sacrificial offerings within Early Classic tombs, the subadult remains may include multiple individuals of similar age.

Skeleton A

Skeleton A represents all of the human bone fragments that are attributable to an adult individual, presumably the primary occupant of the tomb. Although no cranial fragments could be definitively linked to the adult, a right mandibular canine likely belongs to this person. The postcranial skeleton includes fragments of a radius, first metatarsal, distal pedal phalanx, the left scapula, fragments of at least two lower thoracic or upper lumbar vertebrae, one proximal hand phalanx, and 91 long-bone diaphysis fragments. Approximately 100 other postcranial fragments could either belong to Skeleton A or Skeleton B.

The long-bone fragments are large and quite robust, suggesting Skeleton A is probably male, though the os coxae and skull are unobservable, making a definitive identification of sex impossible. Skeletal development indicates an adult individual. The skeleton is otherwise too poorly preserved and fragmented to observe for pathology or body modification.

Some fragments exhibit flecks of red cinnabar. This was most apparent on two vertebral fragments (one body, one superior articular process) and a rib fragment. Other fragments have a faint reddish hue that may also be from pigment. Because of the poor preservation and fragmentary nature of the skeleton, it is not clear if the pigment was applied directly to the skeleton or if the bone was simply in contact with funerary goods that were covered in red pigment.

Six vertebral fragments and the proximal hand phalanx are discolored as a result of thermal exposure. These fragments are blackened but not calcined. The burning within the tomb noted by Gillot suggests that the skeleton was exposed to fire within the burial chamber, though not enough of the skeleton is present to determine if the body was burned while it was fleshed or if the tomb was reentered and burned after decomposition had occurred.

Skeleton B

Skeleton B is a partially complete subadult skeleton. Skeleton B is generally better preserved than Skeleton A. The skull is represented by the left frontal squama, the anterior half of the right mandible, and five other cranial fragments. The postcranial skeleton includes fragments of both humeri, both radii, both ulnae, the right femur, left tibia, and both fibulae. Other postcranial remains include a metacarpal diaphysis fragment, a proximal manual phalanx (epiphysis unfused), the lateral border of an unsidable scapula, and 10 rib fragments. Thirteen other long-bone fragments are also present.

Sex is indeterminate. Dental development indicates an age at death of 5–9 years. No skeletal pathology was observed. The frontal is flattened, though the cranium is too incomplete to determine the type of cranial modification. None of the teeth was artificially modified, though no anterior teeth are present. None of the subadult remains exhibit pigmentation.

EL ZOTZ BURIAL 2

Burial 2, excavated by Stephen Houston, was located in the fill of the substructure of L7-6 (figure 12.2). The burial chamber consisted of a cist cleared in the fill, 0.5 m long and 0.3 m wide, and was capped by a series of *lajas* (flat limestone slabs). The body lay in an extended ventral position, the head oriented to the north, arms and legs extended. The only object found within the grave was a pendant of five tiny shells, unworked.

The skeleton is mostly complete, though poorly preserved. Sex is indeterminate. Skeletal development is consistent with someone who died around his first year of life. Cribra orbitalia is evident in the right eye orbit and the superior squama of the occipital and fragments of the parietal demonstrate active porotic hyperostosis. Porosity is also visible on both temporal squamae near the root of the temporal process and on the ala of the greater wings of the sphenoid. Combined, these lesions suggest either anemia or scurvy. No postcranial pathology was observed, though nearly all bone surfaces are too eroded to observe the presence/absence of pathology. The cranium exhibits flattening of the frontal bone although the type of cranial modification is unknown.

FIGURE 12.2. *Photo of Burial 2 (photo by S. Houston).*

EL ZOTZ BURIAL 3

Burial 3 was excavated by Rafael Cambranes along the western façade of Str. K8-2, west of the Five Temples Group (figure 4.4). The burial cist was intruded into the floor and consisted of an oval space measuring 0.90 m in length, 0.65m in width, and 0.45m in height. The cist was covered by three *lajas*. The body was placed on its right side, its legs tightly flexed with the ankles at the pelvis, and was oriented with the head toward the north. The head rested on a large perforated dish and the corpse was accompanied by two bowls (polychrome and monochrome) and a polychrome cylinder vase, all dating to the Early Classic period.

The skeleton is poorly preserved and extremely fragmented. The skull is partially complete but heavily shattered and badly eroded. The dentition is represented by only the left central maxillary incisor. The diaphyses of all of the long bones are present though poorly preserved and in many unreconstructable pieces. Other postcranial remains include an unsidable fragment of a scapula and fragments of ribs. The incompleteness of the skeleton reflects poor preservation, not prior removal of bones from the burial chamber.

Although incomplete, morphology of the skull and the general size and robusticity of the postcranial remains indicates a probable male individual. The individual had reached an advanced age (> 50 years) at the time of death.

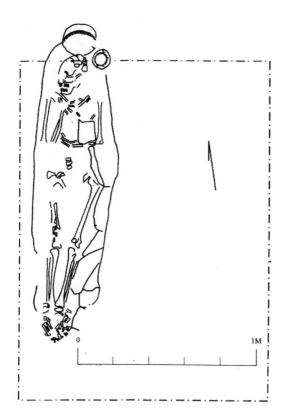

FIGURE 12.3. *Plan of Burial 4 (drawing by F. Quiroa).*

The mandible, consisting of an anterior fragment of the body, is edentulous. The individual also exhibits advanced osteoporosis. The cortical bones of the long-bone diaphyses are all extremely thin and fragile. Rugged muscle attachments indicate the individual lived an active life, yet was likely debilitated later in life by the weakening of his bones. The surface of the skeleton is too poorly preserved to observe for other pathology.

The cranium is too fragmentary to determine if it was modified. The single maxillary incisor was not artificially modified. Dental wear is also quite minimal, considering the advanced age of the individual.

EL ZOTZ BURIAL 4

Burial 4 was excavated by Fabiola Quiroa within Str. L7-3 (figure 12.3). The feature consisted of a cist intruded into the floor of the structure, measuring 1.9 m in length, 0.5 m in width, and 0.3 m in height. The body was interred in an extended supine position with the head to the north and the arms flexed over the thorax. Located above the head of the deceased were a Tinaja Red bowl and a smaller bowl of an uncertain type. These vessels date the burial to the Late Classic period (Tepeu 1).

The skeleton is mostly complete but quite fragmentary, and much of the bone surface is quite eroded. The cranium is fragmentary and partially complete. All of the teeth are present. The postcranial skeleton is fragmentary and includes fragments of all long bones, the left patella, the hands and feet, both clavicles, both scapulae, both os coxae, much of the vertebral column, the sacrum, the first segment of the coccyx, and 125 rib fragments. The sex of the individual is female. The individual is a young adult (20 to 35 years of age) based on sternal rib end morphology, lack of suture closure, and lack of dental wear.

There is slight arthritic lipping of the glenoid fossa of the left scapula (the right scapula is missing). The right clavicle exhibits a well-developed costal tuberosity, the attachment site for the costoclavicular ligament. The corresponding portion of the left clavicle is missing. This bony remodeling may be a reflection of repetitive, strenuous use of the pectoral girdle, perhaps in grinding maize.

Most bone surfaces were too eroded to reliably observe pathology. Nevertheless, both tibiae exhibit periostitis.

Although fragmentary, the cranium clearly exhibits tabular oblique deformation. Both the frontal and occipital are flattened and a slight postcoronal sulcus is present. The teeth do not show artificial modification. The left tibia measures 35.4 cm (34.3 cm without the medial malleolus) corresponding to an estimated living stature of 157.58 cm.

EL ZOTZ BURIAL 5

Burial 5, excavated by Jose Luis Garrido and Stephen Houston, consists of a cist intruded along the eastern façade of Str. L7-1, below the final stairway of the structure (figure 4.6). The burial facility consisted of a small space (0.85 m in length and 0.49 m in width), excavated into the fill and capped by irregular stone. The body was tightly wrapped in a bundle, knees and arms over the chest, and placed supine, head to the north. A small ceramic vessel was located northwest of the head.

The skeleton is partially complete, fragmentary, and poorly preserved. The skull is fragmentary and includes most of the dentition, lacking only LM_2 and RM_3. The postcranial skeleton includes fragments of both humeri, both radii, both ulnae, both femora, both tibiae, both fibulae, the left clavicle, the left scapula, two cervical vertebrae, 15 rib fragments, eight unidentifiable metacarpal diaphyses, and nine phalanges of the hand. According to the morphology of the skull and the robusticity of the postcranial skeleton, the individual is male. The midshaft circumference of the right femur is 90 mm, well within Wrobel et al.'s (2002) sectioning point for male Maya individuals. Skeletal development indicates the individual is an adult.

Although the majority of the bone surfaces are eroded, sclerotic periostitis was noted on the right femoral and tibial diaphyses. The frontal bone is flattened, likely corresponding to tabular oblique modification. The anterior dentition demonstrate artificial modification: LI^1 (A2), RI^1 (A2), LI^2 (A2), RI^2 (A2), LC^1 (A1), RC^1 (A2), LI_1 (A2), RI_1 (A2), LI_2 (A2), RI_2 (A2), LC_1 (A2), and RC_1(A2).

EL ZOTZ BURIAL 7

Burial 7, excavated by Nick Carter, is a shallow intrusive cist, located below Str. M3-8, and dating to the Terminal Classic period. The mortuary space was covered by a series of irregular stones. The body appears to have been interred in an extended supine position, head to the north. A tripod plate was located to the northeast of the individual and contained a small bowl. A cylinder vase was placed to the west of the skeleton. Carter also found five fragments of chert within the burial chamber, including two nodules that may have formed part of the offering.

The skeleton is incomplete, fragmentary, and poorly preserved. The cranium is partially complete, though the majority of teeth are present. The postcranial skeleton consists of fragments of the long bones, hands, scapulae, ribs, and a single thoracic vertebra fragment. Sex is indeterminate. Dental and skeletal development indicates the individual is an adult. The bone surfaces are too eroded to observe pathology. The cranium is too incomplete to determine if it was modified. None of the teeth was artificially modified.

EL ZOTZ BURIAL 8

Burial 8, excavated by Elizabeth Marroquín, was located to the southwest of Str. L7-2 (figure 4.7). The burial consisted of a cist, 1.0 m in length and 0.7 m in width, and covered by two layers of stone. The body was tightly flexed in a bundle, hands and knees brought up to the chest, and resting supine, head to the north. Remnants of the body wrap were evident as textile impregnated with stucco.

The bundled corpse was accompanied by a small bowl placed within a tripod plate to the east of the body (as observed for Burial 7) and a cylinder vase placed to the west of the corpse. The ceramics date to the Late Classic period (Tepeu 2).

The skeleton is partially complete, poorly preserved, and badly fragmented. The skull is represented by the frontal bone, both parietals, fragments of both temporals, the sphenoid, both maxillae, and the mandible. The postcranial skeleton includes fragments of all of the long bones, the os coxae, the hands, the pectoral girdle, the feet, the sternum, the hyoid, the vertebral column, sacrum, and ribs. The morphology of both the os coxae and cranium indicate the individual is a male. Overall, the skeleton is large and robust. All evidence, including an edentulous maxilla and mandible, indicate the skeleton is that of an old adult, 55 years old or greater.

The majority of the bone surfaces are unobservable for pathology. Nevertheless, a small area of woven persiostitis is located on the distal end of the left tibial diaphysis. The cervical vertebral bodies exhibit minor osteophytic lipping and porosity consistent with osteoarthritis. The cranium demonstrates tabular oblique deformation. The frontal is flattened and there is a slight post-coronal sulcus and a slight sagittal sulcus.

Portions of the skeleton demonstrate thermal alteration. The frontal is the most severely affected (figure 12.4). The entire squama is dark brown with shrinkage and flaking of the ectocranial surface. Both parietals are also affected, exhibiting brown discoloration that gradually dissipates posteriorly near the lambdoidal suture. Unfortunately, the corresponding fragments of the occipital are missing. The discoloration is continuous across the coronal suture and the endocranial surface is unaffected, indicating the cranium was articulated at the time of the heat exposure. There is an isolated area of blackening on the posterior aspect of the right temporal. The maxillae are light brown in coloration and the right mandible exhibits an isolated area of dark brown coloration on the external surface of the body and ascending ramus.

The postcranial skeleton is also affected. An isolated area of dark brown coloration is located on the right humerus with significant periosteal destruction on the distal third of the anterior-lateral diaphysis. The right clavicle, ulna, radius, metacarpals, and phalanges exhibit isolated areas of brown discoloration. Dark brown discoloration and superficial shrinkage are evident on the lateral aspect of the left humerus exhibits. The left clavicle, radius, and ulna fragments demonstrate isolated areas of brown discoloration and shrinkage. Some of the iliac fragments are discolored brown and black with shrinkage. Unfortunately, the vertebral column, ribs, and legs are too fragmentary and poorly preserved to reconstruct the pattern of burning.

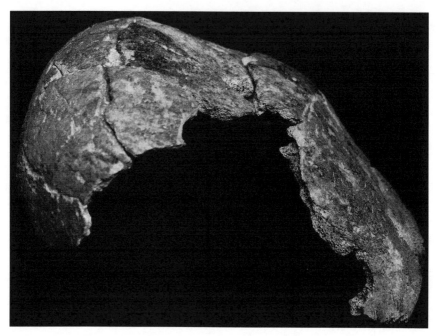

FIGURE 12.4. *Cranium from Burial 8, right lateral view (photo by A. Scherer).*

As demonstrated by the frontal bone, maxilla, and mandible, the upper portion of the face was the focal area of burning. After the face, the arms and hands, which were flexed across the chest, are the most affected bone. This suggests that the body was burned more or less in the position that it was found. However, there was no burning evident in the surrounding matrix. Thus, it seems the body was first wrapped and then burned, with flame directed primarily against the face. It may be that the stucco wrap partly protected the body. Alternatively (or additionally), a mask or some other combustible material may have covered the face when it was exposed to fire.

The right frontal demonstrates an irregular, curving fracture pattern that is inconsistent with the other cranial fractures, which are angular (as is typical of postmortem damage). It is difficult to say whether the irregular fracture margin is simply due to the significant damage caused to the frontal by thermal alteration, or if it was the result of perimortem trauma. The corresponding bone that comprised the opposing edge of the fracture margin is missing.

EL ZOTZ BURIAL 9

The details of the archaeology and osteology of Burial 9 are fully reported elsewhere (Scherer 2015b). What follows is a brief summary of the osteological findings. The tomb contained the remains of seven individuals, an adult probable male (Skeleton A) and six children of indeterminate sex (Skeletons B–G). The children range in age from a few months to about five years old. Each of the children was placed in a lip-to-lip cache vessel assemblage. The primary occupant was laid in a supine position on a bier made of a wood or some other perishable material. Unfortunately, because of poor preservation and the fragmentary nature of the skeleton, the only conclusions that can be drawn is that the remains derive from a probable male, middle to old age. The body was wrapped in a textile that was impregnated in a hardening resin. There is no indication of the cause of death for the primary occupant of the tomb.

As for the other six individuals, it is clear that these children were sacrificed as part of the funerary rites for the primary tomb occupant. The two oldest individuals (four to five years) are represented only by teeth—all that remained of what were probably severed heads. Their lack of bodies may simply be a practicality; an intact five-year-old would not fit inside of one of these vessels. Whatever the case, the significance of these paired, severed heads remains to be discerned. The very young age of these child sacrifices is in marked contrast to the "typical" pattern at other Maya sites, where the sacrificed youths tend to be older, around eight to twelve years of age (Houston and Scherer 2010). Two other sacrificed youths were encountered in lidded cache vessels placed outside of the tomb and were designated Burials 6 and 15. The child in Burial 6 was two to four years old when it was killed. The infant in Burial 15 was only four to eight months old and was decapitated, placed in the bowl in a flexed supine position with the head located over the lower back.

Heat exposure is evident on the remains of each one of the children, including the two located outside of the tomb. In all cases, it appears that the children lay within the vessels (in two instances as heads only) and some sort of burning material was placed within the vessel assemblage. None of the remains are calcined and instead demonstrate only discoloration and some surficial cracking. This is consistent with fleshed bodies that were exposed to flame or a smoldering material for a time insufficient to result in complete destruction of the soft tissue. In other words, these children were not immolated with the intent to cremate their bodies. A further consistency is that Burial 6, Skeleton E, and Skeleton G all demonstrate heat exposure that targeted the face and lower body. As noted with Burial 8, it may be that either their faces were covered in a combustible material, such as a mask, or their bodies were differentially protected from heat. There is a blackened substance attached to the bones of both Skeleton E and Skeleton G that may be carbonized copal or some other resinous material burned within the vessels.

Finally, red pigment was noted on some skeletal elements from nearly all of the individuals. Specular red hematite was applied directly to the body of Skeleton A, presumably as a viscous paint. With the decomposition of the body, the hematite appears to have transferred to the bone, where it still adheres. None of the children's skeletal remains demonstrate traces of specular hematite. In the case of Skeleton A, a layer of red cinnabar was applied over a layer of hematite. Unlike the hematite, the cinnabar is quite loose and can easily be brushed off the bone without careful handling. Cinnabar was detected on the remains of Skeletons D, E, and G and also within the vessel that contained Skeleton F. However, in the case of the children's skeletons, the cinnabar is present only in trace amounts and appears to have fallen onto the remains following the collapse of the funerary bier that held Skeleton A.

EL ZOTZ BURIAL 10

Burial 10, investigated by Nicholas Carter, pertains to a tomb located in Str. M3-3 that was completed destroyed by looters. The long axis of the burial chamber was oriented north–south and was not fully cleared by Carter because of the risk of roof collapse. The chamber measured 1.02 m wide and 1.80 m high. Only a few skeletal elements were recovered, including two metacarpal fragments, a right maxillary canine, a right maxillary first molar, and 11 other postcranial fragments. The remains pertain to an adult of indeterminate sex.

EL ZOTZ BURIAL 11

Burial 11 was identified by Sarah Newman during her investigation of a looter trench that perforated Str. L7-8 of the Acropolis. The chamber was intrusive into the structure, dates to the Late Classic period, and measures 1.1 m in height and 1.25 m in width. Length was unobtainable as the northern end of the tomb was destroyed by the looter tunnel. A small opening perforated one wall, perhaps functioning as a "psychoduct," though it only continues for only about 20 cm. Such features have been noted at other Maya sites, the most famous being the long tube that winds from Pakal's tomb along the staircase in the Temple of the Inscriptions (Ruz Lhuillier 1973). Such devices may have been used to communicate with the dead or to facilitate the departure of souls

(Fitzsimmons 2009:130; Scherer 2015a). In Burial 11, Newman also recovered a variety of artifacts, including an earplug made from *Spondylus* shell.

The human remains come primarily from a single, heavily fragmented, incomplete subadult skeleton. Fragments include the cranial vault, a sacral body, bones of the hand, bones of the feet, a fragment of the first cervical vertebra, and 46 other postcranial fragments. Also present is a deciduous right first molar. Sex is indeterminate. Dental development and the length of the first metatarsal (34.4 mm) indicate an age at death between three and seven years. The cranium is too fragmentary to determine if it was modified. Newman also recovered a modified incisor from an adult, indicating the presence of a second individual, presumably the tomb's primary occupant.

EL ZOTZ BURIAL 12

Burial 12 was excavated by Sarah Newman in Str. L7-17 and dates to the Terminal Classic period (figure 12.5). This simple inhumation had no formal burial facility and consisted of a hole 0.86 m long by 0.45 m wide, excavated into the fill of the structure. The body was tightly bundled and lay supine, with the knees brought up to the chest and the head pointing to the east.

The skeleton is generally well preserved, complete but fragmentary. The majority of the teeth were lost antemortem and only eight remain. The individual is an old adult male. Age was estimated based on pubic symphysis and auricular surface morphology using Transition Analysis and based on the Danish archaeological prior distribution, as was done in the recent re-aging of Pakal's remains (Buikstra et al. 2006). The result for the Burial 12 skeleton is a maximum likelihood of 82.4 years with a 95 percent probability that the individual died between the ages of 65.2 and 93.8 years. The elderly age of the individual is reaffirmed by the extensive antemortem tooth loss and osteoarthritis of the cervical vertebrae.

The surfaces of the majority of the long bones are too eroded to identify pathology. Nevertheless, mixed woven and striate-sclerotic periostitis covers much of the lengths of the diaphysis of both ulnae. Both radii also demonstrate mixed woven and striate-sclerotic periostitis and are noticeably swollen on their distal extremities. Of the bones of the leg, the fibulae are the best preserved and exhibit extensive woven and striate-sclerotic periostitis along most of the lengths of their diaphysis, including noticeable thickening of the distal ends. Periostitis is also present on the left tibia, though its surface is badly eroded. Combined, these lesions are evidence of an active systemic infection at the time of death.

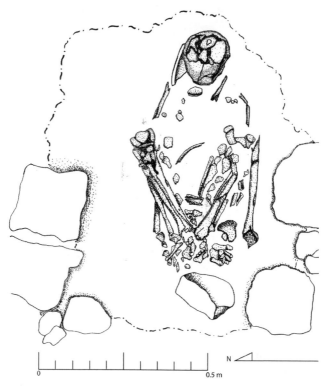

FIGURE 12.5. *Plan of Burial 12 (drawing by S. Newman).*

The cranium was modified in the tabular oblique form. The frontal is obliquely flattened; there is a very slight postcoronal sulcus, bilateral expansion of the cranial vault, and a very slight sagittal sulcus. Unfortunately, the basilar portion of the cranium is absent, and it is not possible to determine if it too was flattened. Of the anterior teeth, three teeth are present and demonstrate modification: LC^1(B5), LI$_2$ (B2), LC$_1$ (B2). The maximum length of the ulna is 25.9 cm, corresponding to an estimated stature of 162.5 cm.

Focal areas of rodent gnawing are evident along the bones of the left leg and the cranium (figure 12.6). Newman reports that the burial was riddled with rodent tunnels and that a nest of rats was found adjacent to the burial chamber. An unusual circular defect of the cranium was also gnawed. The defect is located at lambda and is associated with a perimortmem fracture that radiates from the site of the defect. It is unclear what initiated the fracture. It may have been caused by a violent blow to the cranium, either an accident or

FIGURE 12.6. *Rodent gnawing, left femur, Burial 12 (photo by A. Scherer).*

homicide. Alternatively, the hole may have been created following his death, damage that was done intentionally or accidentally during the bundling or display of the body. Whatever the case, the defect seems to have attracted rodents that enlarged the inferior aspect of the perforation. Recall that the skeleton from Burial 8, also an old adult male, demonstrated possible evidence of cranial trauma.

EL ZOTZ BURIALS 13–14 AND 16–19

Burials 13, 14, and 18 are small tomb chambers located within Str. H6-2. All three chambers were exposed by looters and documented by Rony Piedrasanta. They date to the Early Classic period.

Burial 16, documented by Thomas Garrison, is a massive looted tomb located within Str. M7-1. The chamber measures 2.83 m in length, 1.43 m in width, and almost 2.00 m in height and dates to the Early Classic period. A notable feature of the tomb is that a vaulted stairway led into the eastern wall of the tomb, presumably to facilitate post-interment rites within the chamber.

Burial 17, another looted chamber, was also investigated by Garrison. The burial was located within a stucco altar in front of Str. M7-1.

Burial 19 is a looted tomb in Str. L8-13 that was documented in 2006. The form of the tomb is square with rounded edges, and with lateral benches and a small opening in the wall that may have served as a "psychoduct."

EL ZOTZ BURIAL 20

Burial 20, documented by Jose Luis Garrido López, designates a looted burial located within Str. L8-9 of the Five Temples Group. Although dimensions of the burial chamber are not given, the grave appears to have been a cist or simple crypt. The burial dates to the Early Classic period and among the objects recovered by archaeologists from this previously looted interment were 126 small beads of jade and shell, worked bone (including at least one needle, perhaps the pin of a burial shroud), and blades of green obsidian (perhaps from the Pachuca source in Central Mexico).

Human remains were also recovered, including 16 cranial-vault fragments, three mandible fragments, 73 postcranial fragments, a right maxillary canine, a left mandibular incisor (artificially modified but now heavily worn), and a left mandibular second premolar. It is unclear if the cranium was artificially modified. The majority of the bones show thermal alteration. The ectocranial surface of at least five of the cranial fragments are blackened (carbonized), whereas the endocranial surfaces are only light brown. Tooth roots also show light brown discoloration, suggesting they had fallen outside of the alveolus prior to or during the burning episode. From these fragmentary remains it is impossible to determine if the burning event occurred while the body was still fleshed or after skeletonization.

EL ZOTZ BURIAL 21

Burial 21 was designated by mistake and is the same deposit as that identified as Burial 20.

EL ZOTZ BURIAL 22

Burial 22 is a looted tomb documented by Garrido López in Str. L8-10 of the Five Temples Group. Among the artifacts recovered was a worked *Spondylus*-shell object. No human remains were recovered.

EL ZOTZ BURIAL 23

Burial 23 is a looted tomb documented by Jose Luis Garrido López in Str. L8-10 of the Five Temples Group. Objects recovered include jade beads, jade tesserae for a mask, a grinding stone, and a shell fragment.

At least two individuals are represented among the collected human remains. Skeleton A, an adult of unknown sex, consists of 13 cranial-vault fragments, a femur head, a proximal third diaphysis of a right humerus, a fibula-shaft fragment, an ulna-shaft fragment, two metatarsals, one pedal phalanx (probably proximal), and approximately 100 other unidentifiable postcranial fragments.

Skeleton B, a child of five to ten years of age, is represented by two cranial-vault fragments, three deciduous teeth (a left maxillary canine, a right first maxillary molar, and a right first mandibular molar), and four permanent teeth (a left maxillary first molar, a second right mandibular incisor, a right mandibular canine, and a right second mandibular premolar). The postcranial skeleton includes a proximal humerus epiphysis (unfused), an unidentifiable metacarpal, a proximal hand phalanx (epiphysis unfused), an unfused left pubis, an unfused first segment of the coccyx, a proximal pedal phalanx (epiphysis unfused), seven long-bone fragments, and 13 rib fragments. None of the teeth are modified and the cranium is too incomplete to determine if it was modified.

A number of Skeleton A's long-bone fragments demonstrate brown to black discoloration with longitudinal cracking on the periosteal surfaces. Corresponding endosteal surfaces are unaffected, suggesting burning of fleshed bone and/or complete bone. The metatarsals, pedal phalanx, and the cranial-vault fragments are unaffected. Two long-bone fragments show traces of red pigment, possibly cinnabar. All surfaces are too poorly preserved to observe pathology. None of the subadult remains show thermal alteration.

EL ZOTZ BURIAL 24

Burial 24 is a looted tomb documented by Jose Luis Garrido López in Str. L8-19 of the Five Temples Group. Among the artifacts recovered from the looter tunnel were fragments of a polychrome vase and a jade bead.

At least three individuals could be identified among the commingled human remains recovered by the archaeologists. This minimum number of individuals is based on the duplication of skeletal elements, size, and age differences among the femoral remains.

Skeleton A is represented by a poorly preserved, relatively large and robust femoral diaphysis. The size of the bone is consistent with that of an older adolescent or adult. Sex is indeterminate.

Skeleton B is represented by left and right femoral diaphyses. Both diaphyses are from the subtrochanteric region. This individual is notably smaller than Skeleton A and is much better preserved. Based on size and the development of the muscle attachment sites the individual is an older adolescent or adult. Sex is indeterminate.

Skeleton C is represented by an unfused femoral diaphysis of an approximately five-to-ten-year-old child. Sex is indeterminate.

The majority of the other skeletal elements cannot be identified to an individual. These include 23 cranial-vault fragments that appear to come from the same individual, 15 rib fragments, 280 unidentifiable postcranial fragments, a right capitate, left third metacarpal, two unidentifiable metacarpals, three proximal manual phalanges, three intermediate manual phalanges, one distal manual phalanx, two mandible fragments, five vertebral fragments, 11 scapula fragments, three os coxae fragments, a patella fragment, one left first metatarsal, an unsided pedal navicular fragment, six unidentifiable metatarsals, three proximal pedal phalanges, and one distal pedal phalanx. Teeth include LI^1, RI^1, RI^2, RC^1, LM^1, LM^2, LM^3, LI_1, RI_1, RP_4, RM_1, RM_3, LP_4, and LM_2. The superior incisors were inlayed with pyrite or hematite and RI^1 was perforated by two incrustations, although the material had been lost prior to recovery of the tooth (figure 12.7). Although very few Maya teeth contain multiple inlays, notable exceptions at El Zotz include a lateral incisor from the primary occupant of the royal tomb excavated at the El Diablo Complex and also from Burial 25 (compare with figure 12.8 and Scherer 2015b:figure 4.19). This pattern may reflect particular style or tradition at El Zotz. The lower incisors were not modified.

No pathology was observed on any of the fragments. Although no diagnostic age or sex element is present, most if not all of the fragments are from adult individuals. However there does seem to be some size difference, especially among the manual phalanges, corresponding to the larger (Skeleton A) and smaller (Skeleton B) adult individuals.

EL ZOTZ BURIAL 25

Burial 25 is an elaborate crypt excavated by Thomas Garrison and Sarah Newman within Str. M7-1. The burial chamber was intrusive in the first version of the *adosada* platform of the pyramid. The burial chamber measured 2.15 m in length (north–south) and 0.5 m in width (east–west). A single individual was encountered in a supine extended position with the arms crossed over the chest. Considering the positioning of the arm bones and the relatively tight constriction of the legs, it is likely the body was wrapped in a burial shroud. Some of the skeletal elements were disturbed, apparently by rodents who left gnawing marks on the bones and whose remains were also recovered within the chamber. Four ceramic vessesls were placed to the north of the cranium. Other funerary goods include three jade beads, a burned-shell bead, and a

Figure 12.7. *Dental modification from El Zotz Burial 24 (photo by A. Scherer).*

fragmentary stingray spine. One of the jade beads is larger than the others and was possibly originally placed in the mouth of the decedent.

The skeleton of Burial 25 is largely complete and is of an adult male individual. The skull is partially complete and fragmentary and the dental remains includes RI^2, RP^3, LP^4, LM^1, LI_1, RI_1, LI_2, RI_2, LP_3, RP_3, RP_4, LM_1, RM_2, and LM_2. The postcranial skeleton is for the most part complete and is only missing the hyoid, the majority of the left scapula, the left clavicle, the os coxae, and part of the vertebral column and some of the bones of the hands and feet. Although no pathology was observed the bone surfaces were generally poorly preserved. The cranium was artificially modified although it is too fragmentary to determine the exact shape. The teeth are artificially modified and three jade inlays were found during excavation (figure 12.8).

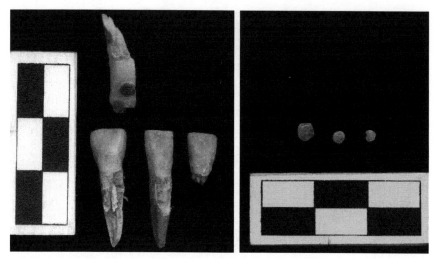

FIGURE 12.8. *(left) Dental modification from El Zotz Burial 25 and (right) loose jade dental inlays recovered from the burial (photos by A. Scherer).*

The skeletal remains exhibit discoloration and fragmentation due to exposure to heat or flame. The frontal bone is especially blackened and the other bones of the face show brown discoloration, suggesting the head or face was targeted with fire. Likely the burning was focused largely on the facial region. Indeed, the orbital region is largely destroyed, perhaps as a result of the burning, although rodent gnawing is also evident on the frontal bone. Unfortunately the posterior portion of the cranium is largely missing. Most of the thermal discoloration is limited to the ectocranial surface, suggesting the burning event happened while the body was still fleshed. However, there is a fragment at lambda that includes portions of both parietals that show thermal alteration of both the ectocranial and endocranial surfaces, suggesting that some fragmentation of the skull may have occurred during the burning event.

A significant portion of the postcranial skeleton also demonstrates thermal discoloration. Although the details are beyond the scope of this chapter, the pattern of burning, when compared with the disposition of the skeletal remains at the time of excavation, is consistent with the burning of a wrapped body with a focal area of destruction concentrated on the face as well as lateral aspects of the long bones, indicating sources of heat or flame placed along the length of the body, which is especially evident in the pattern of thermal alteration of the right humerus. As with all fire events at El Zotz, the burning is consistent with brief exposure to a relatively low-temperature fire and not full-body cremation. Disturbance by rodents likely occurred sometime after that burning event.

EL ZOTZ BURIAL 26

Burial 26, investigated by Sarah Newman, was a large looted tomb located in Str. L8-17. The tomb measured 2.20 m in length (north–south) and 0.80 m in width (east–west). Among the materials recovered from the looter tunnel were three jade beads, nine felid distal phalanges, and two fragments of a bone needle or pin.

A partially complete skeleton from a single individual of indeterminate sex was recovered. The skull includes fragments of the frontal bone, the right temporal, the mandible, and another 15 unidentifiable fragments. The teeth include the RC^1, RP^4, LP_4, RM_1, LM_2, and LM_3. The postcranial skeleton is represented by fragments of both scapulae, the left humerus, the right radius, both ulnae, both femora, both tibiae, the right fibula, vertebrae, the sacrum, ribs, hands, and feet.

All evidence suggests the individual was of a relatively advanced age (> 50 years) at the time of death. A left mandible fragment includes an alveolar canal that was in the process of closing, evidence of healing after tooth loss. Moreover, the height of the mandibular body is noticeably reduced, further evidence of antemortem tooth loss and suggestive of an older age for this individual.

Mild to extensive osteophytic development and porosity is evident on three lower thoracic or lumbar body fragments and the radial head on the articular circumference, consistent with age-related degenerative joint disease. The visible articular surfaces of the carpals, metacarpals, and phalanges are unaffected by degenerative joint disease. No other articular surfaces are visible.

The cranium is too fragmentary to determine if it was artificially modified. Of the anterior teeth only the RC^1 demonstrates modification, consistent with Romero's type A4. Much of the skeleton demonstrates evidence of thermal alteration. All cranial-vault fragments exhibit brown and black discoloration of their ectocranial surfaces yet the endocranial surfaces are largely unaffected. Brown discoloration and surficial cracking is evident on much of the postcranial skeleton, including the diaphysis of the left humerus, the anterior surface of the left ulna, the anterior and posterior surfaces of the right ulna and radius, the right femoral diaphysis (the left femur is unaffected), the left tibial fragment (the right tibia is absent), and the dorsal and ventral surfaces of some rib fragments. The bones of the hand appear largely unaffected aside from some light brown discoloration. Overall the thermal alteration appears focused on the anterior surfaces of the skeleton. The pattern of burning on the cranial vault would suggest burning of a fleshed body. Similarly only the periosteal surfaces of the long bones are affected (not the endosteal surfaces) which would indicate burning of either a fleshed body or at least non-fragmented bone.

EL ZOTZ BURIAL 27

Burial 27, excavated by Yeny Gutiérrez Castillo and Edwin Román, was a simple burial found within a midden and dating to the Early Classic period. The body was interred flexed, apparently on its left side. There were no burial goods.

The child's skeleton (three to five years, indeterminate sex) is poorly preserved, fragmentary, and largely incomplete. The skull is represented by fragments of the frontal, both parietals, occipital, petrous portions of both temporal bones, and the mandible. The dention is nearly complete and includes li^1, li^2, lm^2, rm^1, rm^2, ri_2, lc_1, rc_1, rm_1, lm_2, rm_2, LI^1, RI^1, RI^2, RP^3, LP^4, RP^4, LM^1, RM^1, LM^2, RM^2, RI_1, RI_2, LC_1, RC_1, LP_3, LP_4, LM_1, RM_1, and LM_2. The postcranial skeleton includes fragments of both humeri, the diaphyses of both femora, the right tibia, the left fibula, the left clavicle, three neural-arch fragments of cervical vertebra, the right first rib, and about 50 other unidentifiable fragments. The surfaces of all bone are covered in a layer of lime that canot be removed, making the observation of pathology impossible. The cranium demonstrates oblique mimetic deformation. The teeth are unmodified.

EL ZOTZ BURIAL 28

Burial 28, excavated by Alyce de Carteret, designates the remains of two individuals buried on the central axis of Str. I10-4. Skeleton A was buried in a cist excavated into the bedrock and covered by *lajas*. The burial chamber measured 2.0 m in length and 0.54 m in width. The body was deposited in an extended supine position with the head oriented to the north. The arms were crossed over the chest and judging from the tight placement of the legs the body was perhaps wrapped in a burial shroud. The decedent's head rested on a plate and a cylinder vessel and bowl were located at the individual's feet. Worked bone was found between the individual's legs.

Skeleton A is the largely complete but quite fragmentary skeleton of a probable male adult. The cranium is represented by fragments of the frontal, both parietals, and very fragmentary maxillae and mandible. All of the teeth are present with the exception of LP_3, RP_3, LP_4, RP_4, and LM_1. The postcranial skeleton includes fragmentary diaphyses of all of the long bones, fragmentary os coxae, a fragmentary vertebral column, rib fragments, fragments of both scapulae, a fragmentary right clavicle, and elements of the hands and feet. Dental wear is relatively significant, suggesting the individual is at least 30 years old, if not older. For the most part the bone surfaces are too poorly preserved to observe for pathology. The cranium is modified, but is too fragmentary to determine the type of modification. The maxillary incisors and canines are modified, corresponding to Romero's type A4 (the central incisors may have been modified in the *ik'* style, Romero type A4, but the form was obliterated due to dental wear). The lower incisors and canines are modified in the *ik'* fashion (Romero type C3).

Skeleton B is a five-year-old child (± 16 months) that was buried to the west of Skeleton A in a cist excavated into the bedrock that measured 0.88 m in length and 0.70 m in width. The body was placed on its right side in a flexed position with the head oriented to the south and the face looking to the east. There were no associated burial goods. The skeleton is partially complete, fragmentary, and poorly preserved. The skull consists of fragments of the frontal, both parietals, the occipital, petrous portions of the temporals, an unsided incus, and the mandible. All of the deciduous and permanent teeth are present except for ri^1, li^2, and the permanent third molars, which are not developed at that age. The postcranial skeleton includes fragments of all long diaphyses, much of the vertebral column, much of the ribs, both scapulae, both clavicles, an unfused body segment of the sternum, the body of the hyoid, two proximal manual phalanges, four intermediate manual phalanges, six distal manual phalanges, and an unidentifiable metatarsal diaphysis.

Although the cranium of Skeleton B was largely unobservable for pathology, a fragment of the occipital near lambda demonstrates active porotic hyperostosis. The postcranial skeleton was for the most part too poorly preserved to observe for pathology. The cranium was artificially modified and, although it is fragmentary, the shape likely corresponds to the tabular oblique form. None of the teeth are modified.

EL ZOTZ BURIAL 29

Burial 29 is a looted Early Classic tomb located in Str. L8-20. Among the materials recovered from the looter tunnel were obsidian, jade, animal bone, ceramics, and burned-shell tubes. Although no human bone was reported

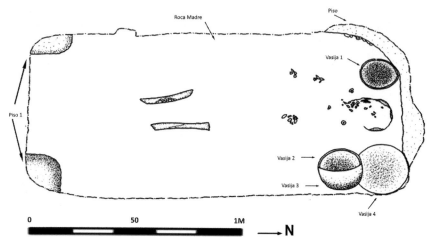

FIGURE 12.9. *Plan of El Zotz Burial 30 (drawing by D. Hernández).*

or analyzed in the laboratory, it is possible that some of the animal bone or burned-shell tubes were in fact human remains.

EL ZOTZ BURIAL 30

Burial 30 is a Late Classic tomb located in the *adosado* platform of Str. L8-13 (figure 12.9). The chamber measures 1.80 m in length (north–south) and 0.80 m (east–west) and more or less set on the north–south axis of the structure. The burial chamber was disturbed by extensive rodent activity. A single occupant was placed in an extended supine position. Four ceramic vessels (three bowls and a plate) were placed around the decedent's head. One of these vessels contains a text pertaining to the royal dynasty of El Zotz (figure 1.10). Other recovered materials include a shell bead, jade beads, and jade ear ornaments. The absence of sacrificial victims within the tomb is in contrast to those of Early Classic El Zotz, but is in parallel to the Late Classic tombs of Tikal, which also are largely void of the remains of children who were ritually killed.

The skeleton is very poorly preserved, incomplete, and fragmentary. The cranium consists of approximately 50 fragments, including fragments of the frontal, anterior left parietal, the petrous portion of the left temporal, and the sphenoid. The postcranial skeleton includes various unidentifiable long-bone fragments, a fragment of the os coxae, vertebral fragments, a rib fragment, and various other fragments. Due to the poor skeletal preservation, sex is unknown. Judging by the size of the bone, the individual was an adolescent or adult (though almost certainly an adult, considering the context). All bone surfaces are too badly eroded to observe for pathology. The cranium was artificially modified but is too incomplete to determine the form. Traces of red pigment (either cinnabar or red hematite) were noted on two cranial-vault fragments.

EL ZOTZ BURIAL 31

Burial 31, excavated by Omar Alcover Firpi and Alyce de Carteret, was a Terminal Classic cist excavated into the bedrock beneath Str. I10-3 that measured 0.86 m in length (north–south) and 0.53 m in breadth (east–west) and was covered by a series of *lajas*. The body was placed in a flexed position on its right side with the head oriented to the south and the face looking east. A single plate was located in the east side of the cist.

The skeleton is largely incomplete and poorly preserved and consists of two manual phalanges (diaphyses only) and 33 unidentifiable postcranial fragments. Sex is indeterminate. Based on the size of the phalanges, the individual was an older adolescent or adult. Little else can be said about this individual.

EL ZOTZ BURIAL 32

Burial 32, excavated by Alcover Firpi, Danilo Hernández, Rony Piedrasanta, and Alyce de Carteret, consisted of a flexed body placed directly on the floor of Str. I10-3, and covered by *lajas*. The head was oriented to the east with the face oriented to the north. The burial was disturbed by rodents after the initial interment and many of the bones show signs of gnawing. There were no associated grave goods.

The skeleton is of an incomplete and fragmentary adult male. The skull is represented by a fragment of right frontal, the right occipital, the right temporal, fragments of the parietals, the mandible, and other miscellaneous fragments. Teeth include RI^2, RC^1, RP^4, RM^1, LM^1, and RM^3. The postcranial skeleton includes fragments of both clavicles, the right humerus, both radii, both ulnae, both femora, eight manual phalanges, two pedal phalanges, and numerous other fragments. The right side is notably better preserved than the left (especially the cranium), which may be due to the burial position (the decedent was laid on his right side) and subsequent disturbance.

The linea aspera of both femora demonstrate slight enthesophyte development and the temporal mandibular joint of the right temporal has some porosity of its surface consistent with slight osteoarthritis. The right frontal fragment exhibits a well-healed depressed fracture. Three small bony nodules are evident on the endocranial surface of the lesion. No other notable pathology is evident on the bone surfaces, which are generally well preserved. The cranium is artificially modified, although the type is uncertain due to incomplete preservation. Of the two maxillary teeth that are present, both are modified: RI^2 (Romero type A4) and RC^1 (Romero type B5)

BEJUCAL BURIAL 1

Burial 1 was excavated by Jose Luis Garrido within Plaza A of Bejucal. This Classic-period grave intruded into the fill of the plaza; the body was placed directly on bedrock, apparently in an extended supine position with the head oriented to the south. Recovered remains include portions of the cranium, five teeth, an unsidable scapula fragment, 31 long-bone fragments, and 29 miscellaneous fragments. All of the remains are badly eroded and poorly preserved. The skeleton is too incomplete to determine sex. The development and wear of the teeth indicate an adult individual. Pathology is unobservable. The anterior teeth are too heavily worn to determine if they were artificially modified.

BEJUCAL BURIAL 2

Burial 2 of Bejucal is an Early Classic–period looted tomb located in Str. S6-10, investigated by Thomas Garrison. The long axis of the tomb is north–south, and Garrison noted a perforation in one of the tomb walls that may have served as a "psychoduct." The excavator found human remains located inside and outside of the burial chamber that appear to pertain to the same individual. The recovered skeletal remains include a pedal phalanx, a femur fragment, and 39 other unidentifiable long-bone fragments. The epiphysis of the phalanx is fused, indicating the individual is a late adolescent or adult (> 16 years). Sex is indeterminate. The anterior aspect of the femur fragment is discolored brown and black consistent with thermal exposure. No skeletal pathology was observed. Rodent gnawing was evident on one of the fragments.

BEJUCAL BURIAL 3

Burial 3 is a Late Preclassic–period looted crypt investigated by Thomas Garrison within Str. S6-10. The crypt chamber was excavated into bedrock, capped by *lajas*, and oriented north–south. The skeleton is largely incomplete, fragmentary, and poorly preserved. The skull is partially complete and includes 15 teeth. The postcranial skeleton consists of isolated fragments of the right ulna, the left and right scapula, the atlas, two thoracic vertebrae, two lumbar vertebrae, a rib fragment, a fragment of the right innominate, fragments of both femora, fragments of both tibiae, three fibula fragments, four metacarpal fragments, two metatarsal fragments, and two proximal pedal phalanges. Numerous other cranial and postcranial fragments are present. I noted no duplicate elements and so it is likely, though not certain, that these skeletal elements come from the same individual. Sex is indeterminate. Epiphyseal union and dental development indicate the remains are from an adult individual. Periostitis is evident on fragments of the right femur and unsided tibial fragments. The cranium is too incomplete to determine if it was modified. LI^2 exhibits a pyrite inlay; LI^1 and RI^1 are not modified. No other anterior teeth are present.

There is abundant evidence of perimortem trauma. There is a 15.2 mm long, 1.3 mm wide, and 1.5 mm deep cut on one of the left parietal fragments. The cut is located near the coronal suture. The cut is deepest anteriorly and proceeds posterior–superiorly. The cut sliced through the outer table to the depth of the diploe. A fragment of the right temporal near the mastoid process exhibits three cuts. The first consists of very slight scraping, 6.4 mm long. The other cuts, 3.3 and 4.5 mm long, are also slight, though these latter two defects may be postmortem damage caused during looting. The right mandible fragment demonstrates a perimortem fracture of the body near the ascending ramus. The fracture margin is characterized by linear splitting, caused either by thermal alteration (see below) or postmortem decay. Whatever the case, the absence of irregular fraying indicates the bone was fractured prior to the surficial cracking. The axis (second cervical vertebrae) was chopped, completely bisecting the centrum. The inferior aspects of the centrum, the right inferior articular facet, the left superior and inferior articular facets, and the neural arch are missing. There is a tiny (2 mm) fracture that extends superiorly from the lesion on the posterior aspect of the centrum. There is hinging of the anterior aspect of the vertebra, exposing trabecular bone on the anterior aspects of the centrum and articular facets. The damage is quite similar to trauma reported by Andrea Cucina and Vera Tiesler for the third cervical vertebrae of one of the sacrificial victims from Pakal's tomb (Cucina and Tiesler 2006:114). In both cases, the blow that fractured the vertebrae proceeded posterior–anteriorly, likely an intent to decapitate by chopping posteriorly at the base of the head. Two unsided tibia fragments exhibit spiral fractures along conjoining edges consistent with perimortem trauma. All other tibial fractures are postmortem. The combined evidence for perimortem trauma may relate to human sacrifice. If so, Bejucal Burial 3 presents some of the earliest evidence for ritual violence among the Lowland Maya (see also Inomata 2014).

Many of the skeletal fragments are thermally altered. The external tables of the frontal and left parietal are completely browned with isolated areas of black and gray discoloration. Notably, the endocranial surface does not exhibit discoloration and the margin between the thermally altered external surface and the unaltered internal table is visible along the edges of the broken fragments. Thus, the skull was burned while it was still articulated, perhaps while still covered by flesh. The petrous portion of the right temporal is unaffected, and the other two fragments exhibit only a few spots of gray discoloration.

The right ilium fragment exhibits light brown-black discoloration on the interior aspect, above the greater sciatic notch. Unsided proximal femur fragments exhibit brown-black discoloration and splitting of the periosteal surface because of shrinkage. A left femoral diaphysis fragment is discolored brown and gray and the entire visible periosteal surface shows significant cracking. Right femoral fragments are discolored brown-black and demonstrate surficial cracking along the anterior aspect of the bone. The posterior aspect is largely unaffected. Left and right tibial fragments also show brown and black discoloration and surface shrinkage, though both bones are too fragmented to determine the location of the discoloration. Some fibula fragments are discolored gray and brown. The four lumbar vertebra fragments demonstrate isolated areas of brown, black, and gray discoloration. The acromion process of the right scapula exhibits a few isolated areas of black-gray discoloration; otherwise the bone is largely unaffected. The metacarpals also show a few areas of gray discoloration. The left ulna fragment has a few areas of brown and gray discoloration.

In sum, the majority of the skeleton exhibits light thermal alteration. The pattern of thermal alteration is most consistent with heat exposure of a fleshed body. None of the endocranial or endosteal surfaces were affected and there were no discontinuities in thermal alteration across fracture sites. The focus on the head, abdomen, and anterior surfaces of the legs is similar to that observed on the children's skeletons from Burial 9 and may indicate the placement of burning material on the face and abdomen. Notably, the thermal discoloration within the cut on the parietal is the same as that of the surrounding bone, indicating that the trauma preceded the thermal alteration.

There is red pigment (specular hematite and cinnabar) on a fragment of the right frontal (brow ridge), the right mandible fragment, an unidentified metacarpal, and a tibia fragment. Presumably the body was painted prior to heat exposure. As areas of the flesh burned away, the pigmentation transferred to the bone below. Alternatively, the bone may have become impregnated with pigment as a result of disturbance in the tomb caused by natural collapse or the activities of looters. This had also occurred in Burial 9: the children were not painted red but nevertheless demonstrated traces of red pigment as a result of tomb collapse and scattering of cinnabar from painted materials. If this interpretation is correct, it may be that the individual represented by these skeletal remains was not the primary occupant of the tomb chamber. Instead, the skeleton may be from someone who was ritually killed in activities related to the funerary or post-funerary rites performed at Bejucal Burial 3.

Nine human skeletal fragments were recovered from a lot located in the looter tunnel connecting Burials 2 and 3 (BL 1B-2-5). At least three of the fragments are from a left humerus of what was likely an adult individual. It is unclear to which burial these fragments originally belonged.

BEJUCAL BURIAL 4

Burial 4 is a collection of human remains found by Thomas Garrison and David Del Cid on the floor of a looter tunnel within Str. S6-4. The original burial context was destroyed. The bones were commingled with ceramics from both the Early and Late Classic periods. Two individuals are present, presumably disturbed from two different burials. The remains are generally well preserved but fragmentary. All elements correspond to adult individuals. One of the two individuals is larger than the other. The larger of the two individuals was identified as Skeleton A and the other as Skeleton B. The bones of the cranial vault and legs were generally too fragmentary to sort between the two individuals. However, it was possible to isolate the two individuals in the maxillary, mandibular, and dental remains.

SKELETON A

Skeleton A is represented by fragments of both humeri, the right ulna, the right radius, the left os coxae, and bones of both feet. The individual is male based on the morphology of the os coxae. Transition Analysis of the auricular surface produced a maximum likelihood estimate of 15 years old at death (with a 95 percent likelihood range of 15 to 26.9 years). However, all visible epiphyses are fused, suggesting that 20 to 26.9 years is a more accurate estimate of the age at death. Thirteen teeth are present. Some of the anterior teeth demonstrate modification: LI^1 (B5), LC^1 (B5), and LI$_1$ (unmodified).

Skeleton B

Skeleton B is represented by fragments of the left humerus, both ulnae, both radii, both os coxae, both feet, and the right fibula. The individual is female based on the morphology of the os coxae. Transition Analysis of the auricular surface produced a maximum likelihood estimate of 15 years old at death (with a 95 percent likelihood range of 15 to 26.4 years). However, all visible epiphyses are fused, suggesting that 20 to 26.4 years is a more accurate estimate of the age at death. Twenty teeth are present and none are modified.

Skeleton 4B's right ankle was broken antemortem. The right ankle and foot are represented by the right distal fibula, the talus, calcaneous, navicular, all three cuneiforms, the third metatarsal, and an unidentified metatarsal. Of the bones present, the fibula and talus were affected. The distal fibula is crushed and the articular surface is obliterated by new bone growth. There is a mix of woven-sclerotic periostitis overlying the majority of the distal extremity of the bone. Perforations (cloaca) in the medial aspect of the distal epiphysis indicate drainage through the bone, although the perforation appears to have been closing at the time of death. The talus is severely deformed. The head is significantly misaligned and is reoriented approximately 20 degrees medial from its original location. There is extensive osteophyte growth on the medial aspect of the neck and head of the talus and sclerotic bone over the entire trochlea. The sustentaculum tali of the calcaneus is reduced in size, and porosity of the talar and cuboid articular facets is evident. Unfortunately, the distal tibia, cuboid, and majority of metatarsals are absent. Likely, Skeleton B's foot was crushed at least a year or more prior to her death. The distal fibula and talus appear to have no longer articulated (or articulated poorly) and judging by the extensive osteophyte development of the trochlea, mobility of the ankle joint was severely compromised. Infection is evident in the fibula, though it appears to have been well-healed by the time of death. The displacement of the head of the talus likely caused misalignment of the foot and it may not have been able to bear weight.

Skeleton A or B

Much of the remaining cranial and postcranial skeleton of Skeletons A and B are present but cannot be sorted definitively to either individual. Some of the cranial fragments are flattened, consistent with artificial modification. A fragment of the left occipital squama exhibits compression near the external protuberance that may be trauma sustained in infancy during the modeling of the cranium.

BEJUCAL BURIAL 5

Burial 5 was discovered by Stephen Houston in Str. S6-4, and excavated by Thomas Garrison and Nicholas Carter. The burial consists of a cist dug into bedrock and covered by two *lajas* (Garrison et al. 2016:figure 10). The body was placed in the ground flexed on the right side, ankles brought up to the hips and arms folded in front. The head was oriented to the north, the face looking west. A Zacatal Cream Polychrome vessel was located in front of the individual, providing a Late Classic–period (Tepeu 2) date for the burial. The skeleton is nearly complete, though fragmentary, and much of the bone surfaces are eroded. The skull is nearly complete and the vault is partially articulated. All of the teeth are present. Morphology of the os coxae and skull indicate the individual is male. Overall, the skeleton is large and robust. Transition Analysis of the pubic symphysis morphology yielded a maximum likelihood estimate of 37.2 years old at death (with a 95 percent likelihood range of 26.4 to 60 years). The lack of degenerative pathology and dental wear suggests an estimate of 26 to 50 years is reasonable.

The right fifth metacarpal exhibits a well-healed antemortem spiral fracture of its medial-palmar aspect, a so-called boxer's fracture. The left fifth metatarsal and corresponding proximal phalanx exhibit well-healed antemortem fractures. The metacarpal is fractured on the superior-distal end. The phalanx is fractured on the distal end. Although it is enticing to consider these hand and foot trauma as sustained in the ball game or at war, it is just as likely that these injuries occurred during more mundane tasks, such as masonry work.

The cranium is artificially modified. The frontal is flattened and there is a postcoronal sulcus, indicative of tabular oblique modification. Though damaged, it does not appear that there is corresponding flattening of the occipital. The anterior maxillary teeth are modified corresponding to the *ik'* pattern: LI^1 (B4), RI^1 (B4), LI^2 (A4), RI^2 (A4), LC^X (A4), RC^X(A4). All of the mandibular teeth are filed, corresponding to Romero's B1 type.

BEJUCAL BURIAL 6

Burial 6 was excavated by Thomas Garrison and David Del Cid within the fill of Str. S6-10 and dates to the Early Classic period (Garrison et al.

2016:figure 7). The cist consisted of a ring of stones delineating the burial space, 0.63 m in length and 0.43 m in width. The body was placed in an extended supine position with the head to the northeast. There were no burial goods. The skeleton is largely complete, well preserved, but extremely fragmented. All deciduous teeth are present and unerupted. Sex is indeterminate. Dental development indicates the individual was three to nine months old at the time of death. No pathology was observed. The cranium is too fragmentary to determine if it was modified. None of the teeth are modified. There is significant rodent gnawing on both femoral fragments.

BEJUCAL BURIAL 7

Thomas Garrison and David Del Cid detected Burial 7 within a looter tunnel in Str. S6-8 by the presence of human remains. Unfortunately, architectural destruction was so complete they were unable to identify the burial chamber. The burial dates to the Late Classic period based on its stratigraphy. The skeleton is incomplete, badly fragmented, and poorly preserved and includes fragments of the cranium, a right mandibular canine, the humeri, the left radius, the right ulna, the right scapula, one unidentifiable metacarpal fragment, two unidentifiable metatarsal fragments, an unsided femur fragment, and an unsided tibia fragment. There are approximately 50 other unidentifiable postcranial fragments present. The skeleton is a probable male, based on the morphology of the cranium. The individual is an adult based on skeletal development. None of the skeletal surfaces are observable for pathology. The cranium is too incomplete to determine if it was modified. The canine does not exhibit artificial modification.

EL PALMAR BURIAL 1

The skeleton was found by James Doyle, disarticulated and spread throughout the structural fill within Str. E4-4. He dates the deposit to the Early Classic period. The skeleton is partially complete and poorly preserved. Bones of the hands, feet, and vertebral column are notably absent among the fragments, suggesting the remains may be from a secondary inhumation. The burial may have been disturbed during construction activities. Sex is indeterminate. The size of the long bones and dental development indicate the individual is a late adolescent or adult. Bone surfaces are too badly eroded to observe for pathology. The cranium is too incomplete to observe cranial modification. Eighteen teeth are present, including most of the anterior maxillary dentition. None of the teeth are artificially modified.

A possible second individual is represented by a deciduous right mandibular second molar. No corresponding juvenile remains were recovered. Although deciduous teeth are occasionally retained into adulthood, it is unlikely this tooth is from the same individual as the others, considering its minimal wear.

EL PALMAR BURIAL 2

Burial 2, investigated by James Doyle, was an Early Classic burial intruded into the Preclassic Platform E5-7 (Doyle 2013b:figure 47). The cist consisted of a series of irregular rocks arranged to create a space 1.62 m in length, 0.30 m in width, and 0.20 m in height. Burial 2 contained the remains of two individuals. It appears that the excavators encountered a primary extended burial (Skeleton A) and, in the process of excavation, found a second set of remains nearby (Skeleton B). Skeleton B may have been disturbed when Skeleton A was interred or may simply represent a second individual that was buried nearby. Skeleton A lay in an extended supine position with the head to the north. Funerary goods included several fragments of marine bivalve, worked chert, and mineral crystals.

Skeleton A

Skeleton A is mostly incomplete, fragmentary, and poorly preserved. The skeleton consists of the diaphyses of both humeri, radii, ulnae, femora, tibiae, fibulae, one unidentifiable metacarpal fragment, and two proximal manual phalanges. Other small, unidentifiable fragments are present that likely represent other aspects of the skeleton. The only element of the skull that is present is a right maxillary central incisor. The incisor exhibits substantial wear and a massive caries on the labial aspect at the cemento-enamel junction. Sex is indeterminate. Extensive wear of the central incisor and the size of the remains indicate the individual is an adult. The incisor is too worn to determine if it was artificially modified.

Skeleton B

Skeleton B is represented by approximately 20 small cranial-vault fragments and a nearly complete set of deciduous teeth, along with a few developing permanent teeth. Sex is indeterminate.

Based on dental development, the individual was 16 to 32 months old at the time of death.

EL PALMAR BURIAL 3

James Doyle excavated Burial 3 within Str. E5-1 (Doyle 2013b:figure 66). This looted burial dates to the Early Classic period; the chamber's long axis runs north–south. The tomb measures 2.80 m in length, 0.80 m wide, and 1.10 m in height. Doyle recovered chert, worked shell, and pieces of a jade mosaic mask.

EL PALMAR BURIAL 4

El Palmar Burial 4 is a Late Preclassic–period deposit of cache vessels excavated by Thomas Garrison from El Palmar Str. D5-1 (figure 13.1). Two of the vessels contained the remains of a single child, respectively. One of the vessels was a large, lidded, cylindrical urn (Burial 4A) and the other was a more typical cache-size vessel (Burial 4B).

The Burial 4A vessel was filled with sediment. The upper layer consisted of loose silt whereas the majority of the fill was a hard, dense matrix. At the transition from the loose sediment to dense fill, a tooth was encountered, followed thereafter by cranial fragments in all locations of the pot. The matrix also included some ceramic sherds, some of which are likely from the lid above, which had collapsed. However, there are also fragments of other vessels, including a small black bowl and a red plate, that were likely placed into the offering vessel after the child's body was interred. Charcoal was also mixed within the matrix.

About 5 cm from the base of the vessel the sediment was looser, less dense, and browner in color. Within this matrix the majority of the postcranial skeleton was encountered. The legs were articulated on the floor of the vessel and consistent with a seated position. The bones of the arms were less articulated but located as one would expect on either side of the body. The thorax and cranium were largely disarticulated. From the position of the bones of the legs it is clear that the child was sitting on the eastern side of the pot, feet touching in front of the body. Judging from the positioning of the legs, the child was facing west when deposited. The child's knees were pointed to either side. It is possible that the child may have been originally set with legs set in front of the chest, knees pointing up, and that following decay the knees fell to either side of the body. However, considering the complete articulation of the bones of the legs, it is more likely that the position found during excavation was the original position of the legs at the time of interment.

A tiny obsidian fragment was found on the left side of the body, near the left arm. A tiny jade fragment was found near the right arm. Perhaps both elements were intentionally placed on either side of the body. Also found was a small fragment of a shiny material, perhaps pyrite.

It is likely that the child was placed first, and the vessels (or vessel fragments) and charcoal matrix was placed over the child. The cranial remains and teeth (particularly the permanent teeth) were found throughout the vessel. Presumably once the head decomposed (note that the sutures of the cranium are fully open at this age and so will not stay articulated, as an adult cranium would) the cranial elements spread throughout the vessel, likely aided by the process of putrefaction or water moving through the vessel contents.

The skeleton from Burial 4A is that of a poorly preserved and highly fragmented two- to four-year-old child of indeterminate sex. The skull is represented by fragments of the frontal bone, both parietals, the occipital, both temporal bones, and both zygomatic bones. Both the maxilla and mandible are absent, although a complete set of deciduous dentition and many of the permanent teeth (RI^1, RI^2, RC^1, RP^4, LM^1, RI_1, LI_2, RI_2, RC_1, LM_1, and RM_1) are present. The postcranial skeleton includes the left clavicle, both humeri, both radii, both ulnae, both femora, both tibia, both fibula, and rib and vertebral fragments. The skeleton was generally too poorly preserved to observe for antemortem pathology. Damage to the right neural arch of the second cervical vertebra was possibly caused at the time of death, perhaps as a result of decapitation. The cranium was artificially modified, likely in the tabular oblique form, although the cranium is overall too incomplete to determine the form with certainty. The teeth are not modified.

Burial 4B was a cache vessel that fractured into multiple fragments upon being lifted from the ground, disturbing the original location of the skeletal remains. As a result it is impossible to determine the original position of the child's body. The skeleton is that of a neonate, no more than four months old. The cranium is represented by 34 vault fragments and the right petrous portion of the temporal. Teeth include li^1, ri^1, lm^1, and lm_1. The postcranial skeleton includes fragments of both scapulae, the right clavicle, both humeri, both radii, both ulnae, both femora, both fibulae, seven ribs, and two proximal hand phalanges. The skeleton is too poorly preserved and incomplete to observe for pathology and cranial modification. None of the teeth are modified.

DISCUSSION

From the combined 42 burials excavated from El Zotz, Bejucal, and El Palmar, it is difficult to draw any conclusions regarding diet, health, or population structure, topics often considered in bioarchaeological studies of the

Maya. This is especially the case as the publication of dietary stable isotope analyses is forthcoming and roughly half of those 42 burials are from looted contexts. Moreover, the vast majority of those interments are from high-status contexts, offering little opportunity to explore social difference in diet, health, and ritual practice. However, considering the sizable quantity of elite and royal burials in the sample, the El Zotz burial series provides an excellent opportunity to comment on high-status ritual practice at this Maya regal center, including corpse placement, ritual violence, and exposure to heat and flame.

The burial sample spans the Late Preclassic through Terminal Classic periods. Of the 29 cases where body position could be observed, 24 (82.8 percent) were oriented to the north. A northward orientation is also the dominant burial axis at Tikal, Uaxactun, and other central Peten sites (Welsh 1988:59). However, northerly oriented burials at these sites tend to be closer to 10° east of north, reflecting the general orientation of the architecture at these centers. At El Zotz, much of the architecture is oriented towards true north with an important exception: the first westward facing pyramids and their substructures. These are the principal ritual structures of the site, built during the Early Classic period, and are oriented 9° west of north, a pattern quite particular to El Zotz. The burial sample reflects both of these orientations, with many oriented to true north whereas others, including the tomb of the probable founder of the dynasty, are oriented to 9° west of north. In contrast, buildings at Tikal, like the burials, tend to be oriented 10–12° east of north (and its perpendiculars). Elsewhere in the Maya area other orientations are favored. For example, at Piedras Negras, northeast (30° east of north) is preferred and at Yaxchilan 120° east of north is the mortuary axis (Golden et al. 2008). Unlike modern, Western views of geographic space, north was not the principal cardinal direction for the Maya. Instead, east, the direction of the rising sun, was the principal direction and east–west was the primary axis. For example, early colonial indigenous maps invariably place east at the top of the paper, in contrast to the western convention of situating north at the top (Becker 2004:131; Solari 2013:66, 107).

A number of possibilities may explain the preference for north in the orientation of bodies at El Zotz, Bejucal, and El Palmar. Today, the Tzeltal and other contemporary Maya conceptualize north as up, conflating north with the sun at zenith (Gossen 1974:33). In Classic-period iconography, souls and ancestors are often rendered as solar bodies, seated in mirror-like cartouches as evident, for example, on the Berlin Vase (K6547). Therefore, the preference for north in the burials of central Peten may instead suggest solar ascent of the soul, especially when we consider that souls entered and exited the body via the orifices of the head (Houston and Taube 2000:267–273). As Karl Taube (2004b) shows, the path of the sun is the route to Flower Mountain, the celestial home of ancestors and other supernatural beings. Clemency Coggins (1980) was among the first to suggest that the Maya referenced the cosmos in their settlement design, pointing especially to the twin-pyramid complexes at Tikal. Coggins and others suggest that at Tikal and other central Peten sites, south related to the underworld, and north was symbolically linked to the celestial heavens, ancestors, and kingly power (Ashmore 1991, 2005; Ashmore and Geller 2005; Ashmore and Sabloff 2002; Weiss-Krejci 2011).

At El Zotz and Bejucal nine of the 30 burial deposits to produce human bone show evidence of exposure of human remains to heat or flame (Burial 9 and its associated sacrificial offerings are treated here as a single deposit). No burning was evident on human remains from El Palmar, although ash does seem to have been spread over the remains of the child's body in the offering designated Burial 4A. The remarkable evidence for thermal exposure of so many skeletons at El Zotz and Bejucal underscores the importance of fire in the mortuary rituals of these sites, suggesting a shared royal mortuary tradition among these two centers. Although the sample size is small, none of the burials excavated from outside of the royal precinct (Burials 28, 31, 32) show evidence of burning (see figure 12.1).

For the Maya, fire and heat are understood to derive from the sun. In contemporary thought, heat is associated with good health, and powerful individuals are said to be particularly hot (Gossen 1974:449). Fire is also transformative: it converts earthly matter into smoke and vapor, a substance that can travel to celestial and otherworldly places where it can be consumed by ancestors and other supernaturals (Christenson 2007:188). Presumably, the localized burning we see on the victims of human sacrifice at El Zotz and Bejucal relates to the placement of copal and other burning objects in direct contact with the bodies of the dead.

Six looted burials—El Zotz Burials 1, 20, 23, and 26 and Bejucal Burials 2 and 3—contained fragmentary skeletal remains with evidence for thermal exposure. These may have been the remains of sacrificial victims, similar to the burned children found associated with El Zotz Burial 9. The trauma evident on the remains from Bejucal Burial 3 would suggest as much. Another body, the bundled old man from Burial 8, was unambiguously burned while he was still a fleshed corpse, prior to his inhumation. As noted in the burial description, the face was the most significantly affected. Fire may have been directed at his face, perhaps he even wore a mask or some other combustible material, or it may simply be that the rest of his body was better protected by a funerary wrap. As a bundled body in a cist, his burial paralleled the bundled men placed in El Zotz Burials 5 (adult) and 12 (old adult). The skeleton in Burial 8 demonstrates an irregular fracture of the frontal that may be either trauma or simply irregular postmortem damage of bone that was already weakened by thermal alternation. A perimortem or early postmortem fracture is also evident on the cranium from Burial 12. The fracture may be traumatic in origin, or could relate to the burial environment, the head placed immediately below a surface with substantial stone overburden.

Are these bundled bodies the remains of old men who were ritually killed? There are numerous references to *puluyi*, "it burns," in Classic-period inscriptions, and a range of monuments and polychrome vessels show the burning of captives and other beings (Houston and Scherer 2010:170; Stone and Zender 2011:161; K278, K4118). Perhaps these men were offered as sacrifice within the Acropolis to activate or energize the space. Today, the Tzotzil and other Maya groups sacrifice chickens in a variety of contexts, including new house construction. As Evon Vogt reports, a black rooster is killed and buried in the center of a new house as part the *ch'ul kantela*, "holy candle," ceremony to give the house its soul (Vogt 1969:461–463).

Unfortunately, the origins of the cranial fractures in Burials 8 and 12 are ambiguous and old men seem an unusual sacrificial offering. Adult sacrifice as mortuary ritual is remarkably rare in the Maya area (Houston and Scherer 2010). Tikal Burial 10, the presumed tomb of the Early Classic–period king Yax Nuun Ahiin, and the tombs of K'inich Janaab Pakal and the so-called Red Queen of Palenque are notable exceptions (Coe 1990:479–490; Cucina and Tiesler 2006; Tiesler and Cucina 2006). Generally in Mesoamerica, we envision the bundling of corpses as a means to display the bodies and later their transport to the grave, as is reported for highland lords of the conquest era (Miles 1957:749). Though not kings, these El Zotz men may nevertheless have been important members of the royal court, explaining their interment within the Acropolis.

Further, the burning of bodies does not necessarily imply desecration of a sacrificial victim. The burned bones of the adult individual from Burial 1 show red pigment, marking him as a likely member of the royal family, not a sacrificial victim. Moreover, there is evidence for burning of royal bodies at other Maya sites. At Piedras Negras, Burial 13 was reentered with smoke and fire, presumably to reactivate the sacred space or conjure the dead king decades after his death (Escobedo 2004; Scherer 2015a). The burning within the burial chamber of El Zotz Burial 1 suggests it was the site of the fire. In contrast, the absence of fire exposure in Burial 8 indicates the burning happened elsewhere.

In general, the Maya use of fire on bodies should not be understood in a binary of *veneration* or *desecration*, but more accurately in a continuum of *transformation*—a practice that facilitated the departure of the spirits of the dead and the sacrificed alike. What is remarkable is that evidence for the use of heat and fire in mortuary rites at El Zotz, Bejucal, and El Palmar (the child sacrifice) is evident from the Late Preclassic through the Late Classic period, suggesting some continuity in this ritual practice.

Demographically, the combined skeletal sample from El Zotz, Bejucal, and El Palmar is unusual. If we exclude the sacrificed children, the burial sample is remarkably lopsided for adults (27/30; 90.0 percent). Normally, roughly a third of the mortuary sample should be children and adolescents. Of the eight adults that could be more narrowly aged in this burial sample, half of them were 50 years or older at the time of death. Obviously, the skewed age-at-death profile is partly sample bias; the majority of the skeletons come from burials within pyramids or the Acropolis. Nevertheless, the demographic data are striking in that they demonstrate that at least for the privileged, the "golden years" were achievable for quite a few of the El Zotz nobility, contradicting claims that old age was often rhetorically faked by Maya nobility (Hernández and Márquez 2006; Marcus 1992:235).

Three observations can be made of the tombs as mortuary facilities at El Zotz, Bejucal, and El Palmar: there are a remarkably large number of them, most date to the Early Classic period, and they are dispersed across the land-scape. If we include a looted tomb that was found on reconnaissance and reported in Garrison, Garrido et al. (2011), of the 37 burials from the El Zotz region for which the original architecture is understood, 17 (45.9 percent) are tombs. Obviously, that number reflects in part the vigorous looting of El Zotz and the equally focused attentions of the archaeologists on document-ing those deposits. Yet, as a point of comparison, of a sample of 311 buri-als excavated at Tikal by the University Museum and Guatemalan National projects, only 20 of those burials were tombs (6.4 percent). In other words, Tikal has produced only twice as many tombs as the El Zotz region, despite having a burial sample size 12 times greater. At Caracol, tombs functioned as ossuaries, housing multiple individuals (Chase and Chase 1996, 1998). Although our understanding of the demography of the tombs reviewed here is complicated by looting, there is no evidence to indicate the inhumation of many individuals of equivalent age or social status within a single tomb at El Zotz and neighboring sites. Rather, the pattern at El Zotz seems more akin to that at Tikal and other Maya sites: a primary occupant accompanied by sacrificed "attendants."

Patricia McAnany (1998, 2013; McAnany et al. 1999) calls attention to the role of funerary rites in place-making and claims to resources and authority among the ancient Maya. At Tikal, 17 of the 20 tombs for which locational data are available were found in the site epicenter; the other three (Burials 159, 160, and 162) were excavated by William Haviland and others in Group 7F, located 1.25 km from the Great Plaza (Haviland 1981). Spatially, there was a close linkage between the tombs of the dead (in the North Acropolis, Great Plaza, and Mundo Perdido) and the day-to-day performance of the court in the Central Acropolis of Tikal. In contrast, the tombs reported here were found scattered across the landscape, at the epicenter of El Zotz as well as at El Diablo and satellite groups and sites such as El Tejón, Las Palmitas, Bejucal, and El Palmar. It may be that the dispersion of tombs on the El Zotz landscape was an attempt by the court to spread its ritual authority by placing its dead throughout the domain. Yet it is unlikely that all of these tombs were used to house the remains of kings and queens or even the royal family. There may simply have been a local preference for ostentatious interments. On the other hand, the many elaborate tombs in the vicinity of El Zotz may be the most salient example of a more complex sociopolitical situation where authority never fully coalesced around the royal court. This may explain, for example, why a tomb was placed at El Palmar during the Early Classic period, the most important site in the region during the Late Preclassic period. The placement of the tomb may have been meant to draw connection to the ancestral ritual center as opposed to the court at El Zotz.

We must also consider the curious polarity of mortuary space and architecture at El Zotz, where most burials either were large tombs with extended bodies or cramped cists for flexed and bundled corpses. The lack of crypts in this burial sample is striking and one of the two known crypts, Bejucal Burial 3, may have been a container for the remains of a Late Preclassic sacrificial victim. In contrast, 61 of the 311 burials (19.6 percent) from Tikal are crypts. The issue is compounded by the identities of the two old men (Burial 8 and 12) that were bundled within cists inside of the Acropolis. They may have been sacrificial offerings, as noted earlier. However, the evidence is ambiguous, and their age and burial location may identify them instead as important courtiers at El Zotz. The recovery of ceramic vessels near the body in Burial 8 further diminishes the likelihood that this man was ritually killed. As courtiers, these old men may not have been important enough to warrant monumental veneration, but in death continued to serve the court. The study of future burials excavated away from the elite center of El Zotz may clarify some of these issues.

CONCLUDING REMARKS

No amount of planning can eliminate uncertainty and chance from archaeology. When the El Zotz archaeological project began there was a reasonable expectation of uncovering a large burial sample, one suitable for exploring questions of diet, health, and population structure. What was not anticipated was the unusual settlement pattern and sociopolitical history at El Zotz, including an unexpectedly high number of monumental constructions dispersed over the landscape, many of which seem to date to the Early Classic period. Unfortunately, most of these structures have been subject to intensive looting. A significant amount of the project's time and energies were diverted to documenting these features before further damage was done. Although a large osteological sample never materialized, the efforts of the El Zotz Project have produced a small and distinct mortuary sample that, while unsuitable for testing the original research hypotheses, affords an unprecedented glimpse at elite mortuary ritual, especially as practiced in the Early Classic period. A careful marriage of bioarchaeology and mortuary archaeology has shown that much useful information can be gleaned from these scant remains.

When viewed in comparative light, the El Zotz data provide good evidence for both commonality and diversity in Classic period (especially Early Classic period) funerary rites. The El Zotz and Bejucal mortuary sample is especially distinct for the large number of tombs, comprising almost half of the mortuary sample. In nearly all of these contexts, there is good evidence for the ritual use of fire throughout the Classic period. At Tikal, Oswaldo Chinchilla, Oswaldo Gómez, and Vera Tiesler (Chinchilla Mazariegos and Gómez 2010; Chinchilla Mazariegos et al. 2015) have recently reported on a deposit of what appears to be burned sacrificial victims from a non-mortuary context in the Plaza of the Seven Temples, which they interpret as related to the birth of the sun. Indeed, the burning of bodies at El Zotz is undoubtedly linked to the solar imagery at El Diablo, and ultimately Classic-period beliefs regarding both kingship and the postmortem status of souls. Careful consideration of the skeletal evidence also points to the importance of ritual violence in elite mortuary rites. Future discovery and careful documentation of intact tombs at El Zotz may help better understand the many looted burial chambers in the region. Further work at El Zotz will also increase the non-elite mortuary sample, which will facilitate better understanding of the region's burial practices as a whole.

The research at El Zotz highlights future directions in Mayanist bioarchaeology. Despite the obstacles of small sample size, poor preservation, and rampant looting, the study of the bones and burials must remain an important part of research design. Certain bioarchaeological questions are only appropriate for sites with large burial sample sizes, including research pertaining to demography, morbidity, mortality, and population structure. Yet we should not dismiss the value of small sample sizes or skeletal remains from looted contexts. Although much is tragically lost to looting, careful documentation and collaboration among field and laboratory specialists can tease useful data from these seemingly destroyed contexts, allowing us to forge ahead and ask new questions of ancient Maya bones and burials.

NOTES

1. Of field projects in Guatemala, the El Perú-Waka' Archaeological Project is the notable exception, having produced over 60 burials over the last decade (Pérez Calderón 2013; Rich 2011). The Holmul Archaeological Project has also produced a relatively large sample of burials. The San Bartolo Project and the subsequent project at Xultun maintained heavy investment and numerous field seasons, but much of those energies were devoted to investigation of the murals and the epicenter of the site (Garrison 2007; Runggaldier 2009; Saturno et al. 2005; Taube et al. 2010). Throughout this period, the El Mirador Project has maintained a massive infrastructure and has conducted many field seasons of work. However, bioarchaeological data from this research have never been reported.

2. Figure 12.1 shows the location of all of the El Zotz burials. Table 12.3 provides references for the excavation context of each burial as well as the references for the preliminary osteological analysis. Note that, due to a documentation error, El Zotz Burials 20 (lab analysis) and 21 (excavation) are the same interment.

13

Landscapes are the settings where human drama unfolds over time. Interactions, whether political, economic, social, ideological, or environmental, leave their traces in the ground for scholars to recover. The research reported in this volume opens a temporal perspective on how the Pa'ka'n dynasty, along with its antecedent and descendant populations, settled, inhabited, and abandoned the landscape of the Buenavista Valley, all in the shadow of Tikal, one of the greatest Precolumbian polities. Over the course of approximately 2,500 years, residents of this important geographical corridor made settlement decisions and participated in cultural behaviors and interactions that were dictated, or at least impacted, by broader political and environmental patterns in the Maya Lowlands. A review of this cultural history detects no consistent rhythm. There are periods of frenzied activity, movement, and growth, interspersed between extended periods of either reclusiveness or stability, depending on the segment of society being examined. Adaptation to changing landscapes was the key to long-term survival in the region, and these adaptive strategies are best understood within a broader context.

A CULTURAL SYNTHESIS OF THE BUENAVISTA VALLEY

First Settlers (~1300 BC–~800 BC)

The Archaic and Early Preclassic populations of the Maya Lowlands were extremely low, with the Peten

An Inconstant Landscape

Pa'ka'n in Regional View

Thomas G. Garrison
and Stephen Houston

DOI: 10.5876/9781607327646.c013

likely being the last major region of Mesoamerica to receive extensive occupation. The Buenavista Valley is an area that would have been particularly appealing to early settlers. The large wetland *cival*, referred to as the Laguna El Palmar today, would have been even more extensive in the time when early colonists arrived, providing an array of subsistence and utilitarian resources. Agriculture had reached the Mesoamerica Lowlands thousands of years earlier (Pope et al. 2001), but these first populations were likely still preceramic, similar to other early communities detected in the Maya area (Doyle and Piedrasanta, chapter 2, this volume; Lohse 2010). By no later than 1300 BC, land clearings for maize agriculture reached a scale detectable in sedimentary records (Beach et al., chapter 7, this volume). We are uncertain what this first community looked like, but a heat-treated chert biface, found at the bottom of a 7-m-deep excavation unit, may be a vestige of that time.

MIDDLE PRECLASSIC (~800 BC–300 BC)

The exact beginning of Middle Preclassic settlement is not totally clear but, by comparison with other regions of the Lowlands, it was probably as early as 1000 BC and included an increased population that adopted early pre-Mamom ceramic traditions. Doyle and Piedrasanta (chapter 2, this volume) note that, sometime between 800 and 500 BC, people living on the western edge of the Laguna El Palmar built a large elevated plaza that would eventually grow into the largest Preclassic settlement in the valley. Residents living near the El Zotz Aguada, likely a natural wetland depression at this time, also constructed a residential platform that housed the earliest population known in that area. Eventually, this sector would grow into the El Zotz South Group. Ceramic evidence hints that La Avispa may have been a third area of Middle Preclassic occupation, though excavations have not been extensive enough to confirm this surmise. Regardless, El Palmar was the preeminent Preclassic site at this time, with the new plaza surface covering 16 times the area of the South Group.

Monumental architecture in the valley has its origins at El Palmar with the first of three Middle Preclassic construction phases of an E-Group coinciding with the plaza construction (figures 2.3 and 2.5). For Doyle (2013a), E-Groups and their associated plazas provided the frameworks for early Maya urban planning, a suggestion further evidenced by their presence as foundational structures at many Lowland sites (Clark and Hansen 2001; Doyle 2012). Functioning as a solar observatory, or at least as an architectural complex oriented to the sun and world directions, the E-Group highlights an institutionalized emphasis on the solar cycle. The ordered space defined by the architectural complex replicates the laying out of a *milpa*, or cornfield, a metaphor for the construction of the universe in the K'ichee' Maya creation myth, the *Popol Vuh* (Christenson 2007; Doyle 2013a:797). Estrada-Belli (2006) has convincingly linked offerings in E-Groups to water and maize, with blue-green jade fetishes having direct connections to the Maize God himself (Taube 2000:300–303). Indeed, an E-Group offering of jades from Ceibal (CB118; Inomata et al. 2010:figures 6, 7) has the appearance of a mythical maize field if the dozen celts are considered as sacred corn. At El Palmar, the foundational E-Group structure (Str. E4-1-6th) contained a polished biface-reduction flake of blue-green jade (figure 2.4a) at its core, linking it to similar offerings, albeit less formally.

Despite such public architecture, and its seeming link to cosmology and agriculture, there is no clear evidence for socioeconomic inequality in the material culture from the early centuries of this period. Compositional analysis of pottery throughout the Preclassic indicates the exploitation of a wide variety of clay sources, suggesting that there was broad access to ceramics, from multiple sources. Construction fill is predominately discarded material from chert production, which Hruby (chapter 9, this volume) believes was deposited ritually. As the Middle Preclassic continued, the E-Group was expanded two more times. We cannot say to what degree inequality emerged during these centuries. But, at a certain point, monumentality reached a scale that required organization of the labor force above a communal level. Could this have occurred at El Palmar by the end of the Middle Preclassic? The pattern noted at Ceibal, Guatemala, which hints at large-scale construction in the absence of settled populations, may not apply at El Palmar, which first flourished some centuries after the earliest building at Ceibal (Inomata, MacLellan, and Burham 2015; Inomata, MacLellan, Triadan et al. 2015).

LATE PRECLASSIC (300 BC–AD 200)

The Late Preclassic is a time of population expansion throughout the Maya Lowlands (Culbert and Rice 1990). Not only did El Palmar continue to grow at this time, but the presumably rural settlement detected in the uplands surrounding the site—as well as at the base of the Buenavista Valley northern escarpment and the area immediately east of El Zotz—indicates a general increase in regional population. Paleoenvironmental data from the El Zotz Aguada show increased maize agriculture around that feature, while additional cultigens like arrowroot and squash appear in contexts around El

Palmar (Beach et al., chapter 7, this volume). Traditional models of emergent complexity (Service 1962) argue that increased population generally leads to more complex forms of social organization (though the opposite could likely be true as well). That appears to be reflected in the Buenavista Valley record, particularly at the site of El Palmar. To be sure, as noted above, developments in the Pasión River drainage to the south hint that local "complexity" in the Buenavista Valley only took place against a backdrop of prior shifts elsewhere.

At El Palmar (Doyle and Piedrasanta, chapter 2, this volume), the E-Group complex continued to expand, going through a further three phases during the Late Preclassic period. In addition, the site core expanded to its present extent over the course of these centuries (figure 1.4). Notable in this growth is the construction of a Triadic Group immediately south of the E-Group (figure 2.9a). Fragments of modeled stucco recovered from looter excavations show that monumental art programs were implemented at the Triadic Group, and it is likely that the later versions of the main E-Group pyramid were decorated with monumental masks as well. The exact function of Triadic Groups is uncertain, but they are ubiquitous in Late Preclassic site cores. Indeed, they may even have functioned as mortuary pyramids associated with the rise of dynastic kingship (Hansen 1998:77–81).

Excavations into the largest triadic pyramid at El Palmar (Str. D5–1) in 2016 revealed a massive dedicatory offering at its base, consisting of seven vessels, an obsidian core, two *Spondylus* shells, and a jade bead (figure 13.1). Four of the vessels were lip-to-lip caches containing the remains of children (Scherer, chapter 12, this volume). The caching of (presumably sacrificed) children is a practice commonly seen at El Zotz from the Early Classic on. It forms one line of evidence that helps to secure a link between these two successive settlements. Immediately above the level of the main offering, excavators encountered at least two separate offerings of dog skeletons associated with three more ceramic vessels. Dogs are linked with the Underworld in Maya religion, serving as guides for the dead, evidenced in multiple burial contexts and iconographic examples dating back to the Preclassic (Miller and Taube 1993:80; Thompson 1970:300–301). Seemingly hinting at a mortuary function for the structure, future excavations may clarify what role the Triadic Group played at Late Preclassic El Palmar.

Other evidence that El Palmar was expanding its influence throughout the Buenavista Valley during the Late Preclassic comes from the minor site of La Avispa (figure 1.7), which may in fact have been just an outlying group of El Palmar (see Epilogue below). Most of the site appears to date to this time and consists mainly of residential mounds. The lone exception is a single

FIGURE 13.1. *Offering 1 from El Palmar, Str. D5-1 (photo by T. Garrison).*

monumental complex on top of a large platform (Str. P8–3) at the eastern edge of the site. A miniature Triadic Group in its own right, the plaza of this group mimics the ratios that Doyle (2013a) identified for the El Palmar urban plan. While inconclusive, this pattern could indicate a more regional administrative authority for the emerging polity at El Palmar. There is also evidence of early activity at Bejucal, as seen in the leveling of bedrock and the construction of two early round temples of the sort recovered at Uaxactun, Guatemala (Laporte and Valdés 1993:71, 102, figures 33, 48). Consecrating the hilltop, the buildings at Bejucal rested on three natural limestone apertures at its peak. One of the temples covered the burial of a woman interred with transitional ceramics taking on Early Classic forms, while still maintaining Late Preclassic slips (Garrison et al. 2016:538–540).

LATE PRECLASSIC TO EARLY CLASSIC TRANSITION (AD 200–~300)

One of the biggest ruptures in the occupation of the Buenavista Valley and its surroundings occurred during the transition between the Preclassic and Classic periods. This approximately 100-year period is characterized by a major shift in the center of authority in the valley. A new, or perhaps renewed, dynast constructed a royal palace at the El Diablo Group, on the edge of a steep escarpment west of El Zotz. This relatively sudden rearrangement of a Preclassic pattern that had grown organically over a period of 1,500 years signals that there must have been novel forces of change in play. The Laguna El Palmar is a significant area of resources in the valley. The decision to move away would not have been taken lightly.

As with many complex changes, a variety of factors doubtless contributed to the shift in settlement. First, a general drying trend occurred around this time, expressed in the sedimentary records from El Palmar and the lagoon itself (Beach et al., chapter 7, this volume). Although the El Palmar wetland may have been more extensive than it is at present, it never fully underwent the transformation to a seasonal swamp or *bajo*, a process clearly documented in other early Lowland environs, including near El Mirador (Dunning et al. 2002). Investigations in the area between El Zotz and El Palmar show that the rural population continued to grow steadily but gradually shifted away from El Palmar toward El Zotz.

Mild environmental strain may have been present, but other factors must have also been responsible for the dramatic shift in settlement. Major sites to the north, like El Mirador, Nakbe, Tintal, and San Bartolo collapsed during this period. At some sites, like Cival in the eastern Peten, defensive walls were constructed around the settlement, indicating a perceived need for defense (Estrada-Belli 2011). Perhaps areas like the Buenavista Valley were appealing places for populations fleeing their degraded homelands; rather than trying to defend the wide-open valley floor, elites relocated to the escarpment edge. Lidar evidence also demonstrates that there was a preoccupation with defense along the escarpment (see Epilogue).

The monumental precinct of El Palmar was all but abandoned. There were minor modifications to some structures at the site (Doyle and Piedrasanta, chapter 2, this volume), but, for the most part, the population left. There are a few lines of evidence that support the idea that the elites who established the hilltop palace at El Diablo had come directly from El Palmar, rather than being an immigrant population. First, as mentioned earlier, the practice of offering infants in lip-to-lip caches is clearly established in the Late Preclassic at El Palmar; this type of ritual continued at El Diablo, especially in Str. F8-1 (Houston, Newman, Román, and Garrison 2015; Román et al., chapter 3, this volume; Scherer, chapter 12, this volume). Second, the ceramic paste at El Palmar and El Diablo is identical in some cases, indicating the long-term, continuous exploitation of known local clays (Doyle and Piedrasanta, chapter 2, this volume). Finally, during an expanded mapping program at El Palmar in 2016, Alcover Firpi discovered a causeway extending east-northeast from the

E-Group and ending in a residential platform (figure 1.4). When compared with the valley epicenter of El Zotz (figure 1.5), the similarities are striking, with both sites taking the unusual form of an inverted L. (Nonetheless, as discussed below, the discovery by lidar of other causeways may muddy this picture, at least for outliers of El Palmar.) Houk (2003:63) argues that the sites of La Milpa and La Honradez established descendant communities in the Three Rivers region through the use of site-plan replication during a period of political instability (in that case, the collapse of the Río Azul polity). The case of the Buenavista Valley may represent an earlier example of a similar process (see the Epilogue for an alternative scenario).

EARLY CLASSIC (AD ~300–562)

A refined chronology of the sequence of events at the beginning of the Early Classic period has been complicated by a plateau in the radiocarbon calibration curve at this critical juncture. However, a combination of radiocarbon (AD 137–334; table 1.1), stratigraphic, and ceramic analysis suggests that there was a palace structure built at El Diablo in the early fourth century AD. This large construction was built over earlier architecture whose function is unclear. The establishment of the palace here meets most of the criteria of a "disembedded" or "reembedded capital" (Houston et al., chapter 1, this volume; Joffe 1998). A new seat of authority was established at a somewhat abrupt pace, involving a palace with considerable visibility over the surrounding landscape (Doyle et al. 2012).

The desire to be situated in a naturally defensible location, one that had clear views of the intersection of the Buenavista Valley and the north–south drainage that bisects its northern edge, must have had benefits. Clearly, it outweighed the merits of being situated, as before, on the fertile valley bottom adjacent to the abundant resources of the El Palmar wetland. Tikal was growing rapidly at this time. The thirteenth king of their dynasty likely died in AD 359 (Martin and Grube 2008:27), and the power of the site was probably starting to cast a shadow westward toward the occupants of the Buenavista Valley. Perhaps not wanting to submit to this emerging regional power, the decision was made to start anew at El Diablo. An alternative view, that Tikal embedded the new palace, cannot be discounted either—elites seem to have drawn on the same ateliers for their finer ceramics. The only transparent way to clarify these relations would be textual. The possible mention of El Diablo on Tikal Stela 31 hints that such data exist but not, alas, on that particular monument: the relevant date occurred on a now-missing base of the stela (Houston, Newman, Román, and Garrison 2015:231–232, figure 6.3).

Modeled stucco fragments from the El Diablo palace show that this was a truly elite construction and that whoever commissioned the building had access to master craftsmen. The culmination of this innovative architectural decoration is expressed in the construction of the Temple of the Night Sun, the funerary monument above the tomb (El Zotz Burial 9) of the probable dynastic founder of Pa'ka'n (Houston, Newman, Román, and Garrison 2015; Román et al., chapter 3, this volume). The dating of the tomb is difficult. The tightest radiocarbon assay (AD 256–400 , with a 74.8 percent probability of falling within AD 316–400; table 1.1) comes from a columnar altar outside the tomb used for making offerings during the interment. Another date from inside a vessel in the tomb has a wider range, between AD 240 to 410. Bejucal Stela 2 is explicit in the royal accession of someone with a known Pa'ka'n name in AD 381, in fact, a subordinate to the great central Mexican invader Sihyaj K'ahk', who entered the Maya Lowlands three years before. A vessel lid from within Burial 9 displays the Teotihuacan *ojo de reptil* motif, raising a number of possibilities (Newman et al. 2015:103–105).

First, the occupant of Burial 9 may be the king mentioned on the Bejucal stela, a figure reigning for no more than 14 years. This raises the question of who is buried in Bejucal Burial 2, a looted royal tomb in line with Stela 2 from that site. Also, who was using the early-fourth-century AD palace at El Diablo if this was the first king? A second possibility is that the occupant of Burial 9 was the ruler who commissioned the early palace; he died at an old age in the three-year window between the entry of Sihyaj K'ahk' into the Maya Lowlands and the accession of the ruler on Bejucal Stela 2. Osteological analysis shows that the king was over 50 years old at the time of his death and was suffering from osteoarthritis (Scherer, chapter 12, this volume; table 12.2). The combination of the dating of the palace architecture, radiocarbon assays associated with Burial 9, the archaeological context of Bejucal Stela 2, and the osteological analysis of the king's remains all suggest that the El Diablo royal tomb housed a dynastic founder. He established and ruled Pa'ka'n from a hilltop palace during much of the fourth century AD, before passing away as major changes started to unfold in the Maya Lowlands with the arrival of Sihyaj K'ahk'. The Temple of the Night Sun, covering the founder's tomb, is decorated with 14 masks emphasizing solar and rain-related themes (Taube and Houston 2015). The same seasonal and even agricultural forces harnessed through the construction and dedication of the El Palmar E-Group are tied explicitly to royal authority at El Diablo.

Bejucal became more important to the new dynasty at El Zotz during the Early Classic. Perhaps at the impetus of the king named on the stela at the site,

FIGURE 13.2. *Modeled stucco in situ at Bejucal (photo by A. Godoy).*

a royal residence was established to the northwest of the early temples. This king, whose name eludes complete decipherment, may be the same one who received a gift from K'inich Bahlam I of El Perú-Waka', a ruler who also acknowledged subordination to Sihyaj K'ahk' (Guenter 2014:150–154). At some point in the Early Classic an important individual died, perhaps the king named on Stela 2, and was interred at the site of the earlier temples, fully appropriating the sacred hilltop for the dynasty. In addition to the epigraphy, the modeled stucco that decorates the building covering the tomb has clear links to the architectural craftsmanship and celestial themes at El Diablo (figure 13.2). Over time, Bejucal became a royal country house, perhaps situated among favored hunting grounds or agricultural plots of the elites (Garrison et al. 2016).

At El Zotz itself, the population grew during the fifth century A D. Additional elite housing was established at the El Tejón Group on a hilltop adjacent to El Diablo. In the valley lowlands, probably in the late fourth century A D, a ruler commissioned an elaborately decorated platform (Str. M7-1-Sub. 1-1st) oriented to the east, toward El Palmar, at the location that would eventually become the East Group. El Palmar still held importance in the landscape as evidenced by ritual offerings at a temple (Str. F5-1) on the edge of the lagoon and the burial of an important individual (El Palmar Burial 3) in Str. E5-1, directly in front of the main pyramid of the Triadic Group.

Environmental evidence from El Palmar shows that maize farmers occupied the immediate area in pulses during this time, interspersed with intervals of forest regeneration (Beach et al., chapter 7, this volume; Luzzadder-Beach et al. 2017). The rural settlement between El Zotz and El Palmar reached its maximum extent during the Early Classic. Pollen data from the El Zotz Aguada, which by this time had likely been dammed and grown into a massive reservoir, contain no maize pollen at this interval. This means that, as the city grew, agriculture had moved well outside the limits of urban settlement. Indeed, so much forest had been cleared around the *aguada* that the only arboreal species represented is copal, a tree whose resin was an important source for ritual incense.

One of the areas that likely began to grow while Pa'ka'n kings still ruled from El Diablo is the Five Temples Group, immediately east of the *aguada*. Operations by Jose Luis Garrido López revealed a series of looted tombs (Burials 19, 20, 22–24, and 29 in figure 12.1) dating to the Early Classic. Unfortunately, the damage done to these interments makes it impossible to pin down their chronology, but it seems that, with space at a premium at El Diablo, the dynasty established a royal necropolis on the valley floor. The royal nature of these tombs is indicated by the tomb architecture itself (vaults, painted walls), as well as a handful of precious objects left behind by looters: these include a large jade earflare (figure 13.3), a pair of carved-jade earflares, pieces of jade mosaics, and green obsidian that probably originated in the Teotihuacan-controlled Pachuca source of central Mexico (Garrido López et al. 2015b).

Sometime in the late fifth or early sixth century AD, the El Diablo Group was abandoned and the local seat of authority shifted to the valley floor, or at least to a less elevated, flatter area adjacent to it. Oddly this occurred in the midst of a major, seemingly abortive renovation effort at El Diablo (Houston, Newman, Román, and Carter 2015). There is evidence for elite residential activity in platforms beneath the El Zotz Acropolis that date to this time (Newman 2015b:197). A painted masonry structure beneath Str. L7-6 may represent one of the early administrative buildings for the relocated dynasty. The site's ritual core also migrated. Builders covered the decorated platforms in the East Group with a new monumental platform, this time placed in direct alignment with the Temple of the Night Sun and facing west toward El Diablo. This feature, which we call the "Accession Platform" (Str. M7-1-Sub. 2), was the funerary monument for a pivotal king whose tomb, a massive one (El Zotz Burial 16), was unfortunately looted.

FIGURE 13.3. *Jade earflare from El Zotz Burial 23 (9 cm in diameter; photo by T. Garrison).*

The platform itself is decorated with monumental masks of the god *Ux Yop Huun*, linking the structure to the diadem of royal accession (Stuart 2012b), as well as the cosmological center of the universe as a rollout representation of the jade hearth (Taube 1998). This platform was likely the site of royal accession ceremonies for at least part of the Early Classic (Taube et al. 2010:60–69). Recently uncovered iconography from the north wall of the Temple of the Night Sun depicts scaffolding (figure 13.4) beneath a seated king, interrupted by the frieze containing the masks of gods. This may be linked to accession ceremonies in the temple or to the first *k'atun* (~20-year) celebration after such accessions.

Over the course of the sixth century AD, a pyramid (Str. M7-1-3rd) was built to cover the Accession Platform, though not before the king in Burial

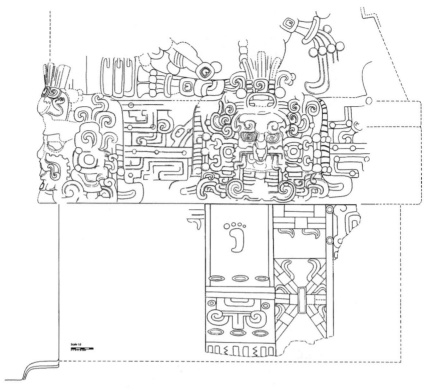

FIGURE 13.4. *Iconography of scaffolding, Temple of the Night Sun (scaffold drawing by D. Hernández; temple drawing by S. Houston and M. Clarke)*

16 was revisited via a vaulted access tunnel. This passageway, built during the original construction of the platform, was reopened via the destruction of the upper portion of the central *Ux Yop Huun* mask. Sometime before AD 550 a royal individual was buried in a remodeling of a central addition, or *adosado*, that had been placed at the front of the pyramid. This person was interred with four vessels, including a tripod plate with a Waterlily Monster motif, acting as a head variant glyph for **NAHB**, serving as a metaphor for a primordial pool. Combined with the earth symbols around the rim, the vessel has cosmological connotations (figure 13.5). Finally, the pyramid was twice amplified, resulting in the building seen on the surface today, nicknamed the Pyramid of the Wooden Lintel (Str. M7-1-1st).

The pyramid's eponymous carved lintel (figure 3.4) dates stylistically to the early sixth century AD, which means that it was either an heirloom from an

FIGURE 13.5. *Waterlily Monster pot from El Zotz Burial 25 (drawing by M. Clarke).*

earlier version of the pyramid or carved in a deliberately archaic style. The sculpture depicts a Pa'ka'n ruler and names his parentage, including his mother who carries the *Sak Wayis* title associated with the Snake kings of Dzibanche, and later Calakmul. This is important in that it shows a clear connection to Tikal's rival, suggesting that not all was well in the relationship between El Zotz and its enormous neighbor to the east. Tikal was defeated by the Snake dynasty in AD 562 (Martin and Grube 2008:38–40), and this presented renewed opportunities for the kings of Pa'ka'n.

LATE CLASSIC (AD 550–850)

By the end of the Early Classic period, growth stagnated at El Zotz. The dynasty had moved to the valley floor, but it had not created a substantial palace befitting a royal dynasty. The most significant investment took place through constant amplification of Str. M7-1 and perhaps some of the funerary structures in the Five Temples Group. With the defeat of Tikal it appears that the Pa'ka'n dynasty finally had some breathing room. This is reflected in a burst of cultural innovation and, eventually, architectural expansion not seen since the late fourth to early fifth centuries AD.

In AD 573, El Zotz Stela 1 was erected. This badly damaged monument depicts a ruler in full regalia, underscoring the health of the royal line. On the side of the monument is the first datable example of a sculptor's signature from the Maya Lowlands (Houston et al., chapter 1, this volume). Further artistic innovation is seen in ceramics from this time. A series of red-background pots represent the earliest examples of supernatural creatures called *way*. Many of these pots name Pa'ka'n lords as owners, including three examples using the *k'uhul ajaw*, "holy lord," title, reflecting rulership status (Carter et al., chapter 4, this volume). During this period, El Zotz also maintained close ties with its long-time ally, El Perú-Waka'. A vessel from the minor center of Chakah, just south of El Perú-Waka', is labeled with the name of an El Zotz ruler (Freidel and Escobedo 2014:32–33). The more recent examination of a bowl in the San Diego Museum of Man hints that this relationship may have been closer still, with the possibility of an El Perú-Waka' prince coming to power at El Zotz (Houston et al., chapter 1, this volume; Looper and Polyukhovych 2016). The San Diego bowl, the ex–Museu Barbier-Mueller pot (figure 1.9), and a vessel from El Zotz Burial 30 in the Five Temples Group (figure 1.10) all have texts that connect lords through their maternal lines, usually a sign of dynastic unrest. What this unrest might have entailed is unclear: did the Pa'ka'n dynasts begin to connect themselves with a growing hegemony led by the Snake dynasty? Guenter (2014:154) argues for a similarly disruptive time at El Perú-Waka', during which there was a hiatus in monument erection that, when resumed, revealed that the local kings had firmly allied themselves with the Snake kings. As noted elsewhere (Houston et al., chapter 1, this volume), there is another, unresolved question at El Zotz: the concentration of so many lords with the title within a relatively short amount of time raises the possibility of concurrent lords. The epigraphic record is insufficient to clarify this matter, and there is an alternative explanation of short reigns for successive kings.

There was some architectural growth at El Zotz in the seventh century AD. The Acropolis, especially Str. L7-1, underwent a massive renovation, the fill of which included a sherd referring to a *k'uhul Pa'ka'n ajaw* (figure 4.3). The five burial temples on the east side of the Five Temples Group were united under a single, long platform with five "false" temples on top. The layout is reminiscent of the Las Coronitas Group at La Corona (Baron 2013:figures 6.1, 6.2), another site closely linked to the Snake dynasty during this period. The exact timing of this renovation is unclear, so it is possible that, after a brief period of independence, El Zotz was now subordinating itself to the ideological canons of the Snake lords, just as it had under Early Classic Tikal.

In AD 695, Jasaw Chan K'awiil I of Tikal brought the Snake Kingdom's expanding hegemony crashing down with a decisive military defeat (Martin and Grube 2008:44–47). With that influence removed, the Pa'ka'n dynasty embarked on its most ambitious program of expansion to date. The Acropolis was amplified on all sides, being built up around three patios. The first version of the Northwest Courtyard was devised just to the west. Newman (2015b:201–204) notes that, in many cases, these Late Classic expansions were also focused on the restriction of space in elite contexts. The largest pyramid (Str. L7-11) at the site was built just southeast of the Acropolis, indicating dynastic investments and corresponding rituals into the eighth century AD (Blankenship 2012; Carter et al., chapter 4, this volume). Sometime after AD 725, the Las Palmitas Group was built on a hilltop north of the site center in what was largely a single construction episode.

Outside the site core, the rural area of the Buenavista Valley still saw substantial populations, though they were now more centered on El Zotz than ever before. There was renewed activity at La Avispa, according to a radiocarbon date (AD 648–770; table 1.1) found beneath a final, preserved plaster floor. Bejucal also reached its maximal extent during this period, being built up over two substantial courtyards. A ceramic vessel from Bejucal Burial 5 securely dates to the first half of the eighth century AD (Garrison et al. 2016:543, figure 10).

It is unclear what the relationship between El Zotz and Tikal was like during this period of renewal. Tikal had embarked on an evident campaign of revenge against those who supported Calakmul in the seventh century AD (Martin and Grube 2008:48–50). Carter et al. (chapter 4, this volume) argue that, by the end of the eighth century, most of El Zotz's interactions, at both the elite and commoner levels, were oriented toward Tikal and sites east, with no trace of the previously strong relationship with El Perú-Waka'. These bonds were reflected in a possible royal visit, perhaps involving exile, from a king of Uaxactun in AD 751. Even as dynastic kingship began to collapse across the Maya Lowlands at the beginning of the ninth century AD, El Zotz appears to have remained robust. El Zotz Stela 4, found broken and used as a cornerstone in a Terminal Classic platform, shows that a Pa'ka'n lord celebrated the all-important completion of the 10th bak'tun in AD 830, an event that went unrecorded at Tikal (Martin and Grube 2008:53). Perhaps the collapse of Tikal gave El Zotz space for sustained, more autonomous activity. To the west of El Zotz lay the considerable site of La Brisanta, at the intersection of the Buenavista Valley and a north–south opening leading toward Tikalito, another substantial center briefly explored by our team. Although not yet excavated, La Brisanta had ceramics from the late eighth century AD spilling out of looter pits on one substantial pyramid, as well as at least two palaces, plain altars, and stelae.

TERMINAL CLASSIC (AD 850–1000)

The Terminal Classic at El Zotz saw the probable collapse of the Pa'ka'n dynasty, but not the end of the settlement itself, or even of elite culture (Newman et al., chapter 5, this volume). The decay of the dynasty is expressed overtly by the active destruction and repurposing of monuments at the site. This included the cutting up of Stela 4, used as an architectural cornerstone in Str. L7-17 of the Northwest Courtyard, and the mutilation of Stela 2, reshaped into a Terminal Classic altar. A massive deposit of smashed, burned, and scattered artifacts placed over various portions of the Acropolis may be interpreted as a scattering ritual in preparation for a major remodeling program, perhaps as early as the AD 830 *bak'tun* ending (Newman 2015b; Newman et al., chapter 5, this volume). However, the remodeling was never realized, and dynastic kingship came to a rapid end.

Despite this change, a substantial population endured at El Zotz throughout the Terminal Classic. Elites are clearly identified in the Northwest Courtyard and Las Palmitas Group, where minor architectural renovations continued throughout the period, though not with the same skill of construction exhibited in earlier periods. These elites attempted to maintain connections with other surviving Lowland populations through exchange, best exemplified by the presence of molded-carved ceramics at multiple sites in the central Peten (Newman et al., chapter 5, this volume).

The collapse of the local dynasty provided more opportunities for lower-status people as well. The intersite area between El Zotz and El Palmar was mostly abandoned. However, recent residential test-pitting at El Zotz and horizontal excavations by de Carteret (2016, 2017) in the I10 Group, west-southwest of the site core, show that substantial Terminal Classic platforms were being built around courtyards and in support of household populations. Perhaps the people not allowed to reside so close to the city center now had that opportunity. By AD 1000, most of the residents of El Zotz, elite and non-elite alike, had abandoned the region. The collapse of surrounding centers likely played a contributing factor, and the dissolution of exchange networks would have interrupted people's ability to harness resources.

Early Postclassic (AD 1000–~1300)

The paleoenvironmental record from the El Zotz Aguada shows an 80 percent reduction in carbon in the centuries following the Late Classic period. This is a proxy data set for a vast reduction in the clearance of agricultural lands, reflecting, too, a large-scale reduction in population (Beach et al., chapter 7, this volume). Yet, a small population did survive at El Zotz, mostly centered around the South Group, with other possible occupations in the Northwest Courtyard and Las Palmitas (Kingsley and Gámez, chapter 6, this volume). Undoubtedly the sophisticated, engineered dam that created the voluminous El Zotz Aguada (Beach et al., chapter 7, this volume) was still functioning. This attracted inhabitants who could have chosen other locations in the landscape.

The surviving groups were organized into households that engaged in diverse exchange networks (Kingsley 2014; Kingsley and Gámez, chapter 6, this volume). In this regard, the turmoil of dynastic collapse did not have a notable effect on the day-to-day existence of those who chose to stay around El Zotz and maintain their agricultural way of life. Economic exchange was renegotiated, the available resources shifted to some extent, and there was a clear loss of some craft specialization, but these were mostly farmers going about their daily business. A carbon sample associated with a Postclassic toad-effigy pot dates to AD 1265 to 1388 (table 1.1), which means that there were people living at El Zotz well into the thirteenth century AD, and possibly into the fourteenth. Eventually, as in most other areas of the Maya Lowlands, this small population vanished, leaving the city to be reclaimed by the jungle.

Late Postclassic (AD ~1300–1519)

On its final floor, the summit of Str. L7-11 supported a pair of pots with crude faces, including ears and earspools, both enveloped by a thick lens of ash (figure 13.6); a short distance below lay the head of a broken figurine of far earlier date, facing upwards. Carbon located just above the pots returned a date of AD 1426 to 1632 (with a 71.9 percent probability of dating before Spanish contact; table 1.1). These vessels were offerings from late Maya, the so-called Lacandon (but probably not speaking that Mayan language) who continued to live in the area and, near the Usumacinta region, performing rituals at ruined sites into the twentieth century (see also Moholy-Nagy 2012). The presence of these offerings reinforces the idea that El Zotz was located near a major Precolumbian transportation corridor, perhaps the one that eventually became the *camino real* connecting Flores, Guatemala, with Mérida, Yucatan

FIGURE 13.6. *Lacandon god pots from Str. L7-11 (photo by S. Houston).*

(Houston et al., chapter 1, this volume). Such relative accessibility may explain the prolonged occupation of El Zotz compared to other central Peten centers. The late occupants of the *aguada* edge, closely tied to Lake Peten Itza and beyond, were unlikely to have been isolated from other populations.

CONCLUSIONS

This cultural synthesis of Maya people in the Buenavista Valley tells the story of an adaptive population that was alive to opportunity. When environmental abundance was available, such as for the first settlers of El Palmar and the final occupants of El Zotz, people readily took advantage of it by optimizing accessibility. When it was more prudent to align with a larger power in the interest of political survival, local rulers entered into alliances, usually as subordinates. An agile opportunism characterizes El Zotz's relationship with both Early Classic Tikal and the seventh-century-AD Snake dynasty. However, when possible, the kingdom of Pa'ka'n expressed itself in distinctive ways. Boldy decorated buildings of the fourth century AD, sculptural and ceramic innovation in the sixth and seventh centuries AD, and a flurry of architectural expansion in the eighth century AD are all examples of relatively brief moments when El Zotz found a cultural, aesthetic, and perhaps political autonomy.

The lacuna of textual data from El Zotz is frustrating compared to other major sites of the Peten. However, a landscape approach to the archaeology of

Pa'ka'n allows us to present a relatively clear picture of unfolding events. The more recent investigations from 2012 to the present, from which some results are presented in this chapter, have focused more on the earliest phases of El Zotz, when we know that local exertions were at a peak. But, for archaeologists, there is much to be done. Further exploration of El Palmar and other Preclassic sites will reveal more about the emergence of sociopolitical complexity in the region. Sites such as La Brisanta and Tikalito remain little known, yet ripe for study. A lidar survey flown in the summer of 2016 is already changing our understanding of ancient Pa'ka'n, as detailed in the Epilogue below. The landscape of El Zotz may have been inconstant, our crafting of explanation a challenge. Yet the promise is great that future evidence will intrigue and, beyond that, surprise.

EPILOGUE

In April 2009, a new Light Detection and Ranging (lidar) sensor was flown over the ancient Maya city of Caracol, Belize, in a collaboration between the archaeological project directors, Arlen and Diane Chase, and the National Center for Airborne Laser Mapping (NCALM) (Chase et al. 2010, 2011). In lidar, a sensor blasts the jungle canopy with laser beams from an airplane, recording x,y,z coordinates when an individual laser encounters a point of resistance. The vast majority of these beams hit jungle foliage, but a percentage penetrate to the forest floor. By manipulating the resultant point cloud in spatial software, one may digitally remove the forest overburden, revealing the landscape of the ancient Maya in ways never before seen. The revolutionary work at Caracol has inspired a strong investment in lidar technology throughout the Maya area.

In 2016, the Fundación Patrimonio Cultural y Natural Maya (PACUNAM) raised funding for and designed a large-scale project mission, with data collection by NCALM over approximately 2,100 km², from 10 discrete polygonal areas in the Maya Biosphere Reserve of northern Guatemala. This survey included 105 km² of data over the San Miguel la Palotada-El Zotz Biotope and an additional 40 km² of data in a narrow band linking PAEZ's study area to the western outskirts of Tikal. At the time of this writing, early ground-truthing results indicate substantial changes in our preconceptions about ancient Maya settlement density, agriculture, and defensive works. These are the subject of publications in preparation. But there are already important implications for the results in this volume, as summarized in this chapter.

The site of El Palmar now has a footprint approximately 40 times larger than the known site core. This estimate not only includes a vast number of Preclassic-period house platforms but also numerous causeways and elaborate hydrological features. The area is so large that it appears the minor center of La Avispa is, in fact, a western architectural group within greater El Palmar. The alteration of drainages, possibly directing water toward raised field systems, also stand out in the lidar data, though the dating of these features will need confirmation by excavation. The implications of a larger El Palmar are momentous, particularly when considering the critical Late Preclassic to Early Classic transition period discussed above. El Palmar would have been *the* major Late Preclassic rival to Tikal, and the likelihood of a violent, decisive conflict between the two has increased.

Perhaps corroborating the bellicose nature of the Buenavista landscape, lidar data reveal a number of apparent linear, defensive features. In addition to the well-known Tikal earthworks, the Maya of the Pa'ka'n dynasty were preoccupied with fortifying positions along the edge of the escarpment to the northern side of the Buenavista Valley. This is seen around the El Diablo hilltop, where massive terraces and walls provided checkpoints for those wishing to ascend to the Early Classic palace. Smaller groups along the escarpment edge exhibit similar protective measures with semi-circular contouring protecting the exposed northern access points to groups. At the base of one of these, just east of the La Curenavilla Cival, a large redoubt, protected by a wall and canal system, looks to be paired with the elevated, defended groups above. An east–west wall appears to block a valley leading north from this sector of contoured walls to Bejucal. The small, encircled tower of El Fortín, discovered by Alcover in 2015, links to a possible ridgeline road linking other architectural groups with broad views of the surrounding landscape. The date of all of these features is unclear, but it is tempting to place them in the Early Classic, analogous to the well-established chronology of the El Diablo Group. This again raises the question of what really happened at the collapse of El Palmar. Are we seeing a terrified, surviving population simply trying to persevere in the naturally defensible uplands? Or was this, in effect, a landscape tied to the celebrated *entrada* by which Teotihuacan made its presence felt in the Maya Lowlands? The highly regimented nature of buildings in the moated redoubt do not resemble features seen elsewhere. Testing awaits.

Other details in the lidar data indicate that there is much work to be done to understand ancient Pa'ka'n. To the north of the Las Palmitas Group at El Zotz is a large elevated compound, perhaps originally an E-Group, that was almost certainly an immediate part of the polity center. The royal country house of Bejucal also appears larger than what we knew, with a large platform to the south containing visibly looted structures. Other possible minor centers exist just east of the Pucte Aguada, located within the north–south drainage that divides the escarpment, and in the *bajos* east of El Palmar, possibly in connection with vast relic field systems. These sites are in addition to the thousands of house mounds located throughout the rolling hills north of the Buenavista Valley.

These new lidar data, though still unprobed, pose tantalizing questions that only future field research can answer. Refining temporal resolution at a regional scale must be a high priority. As it stands, we can see the total impact the Maya had on this landscape, but it is not completely clear in what order events unfolded. We must also devise survey and reconnaissance strategies that maximize the value of lidar while recognizing that there are features not yet detected. Where, for example, are the *chultunes*? As more regions are covered by lidar surveys, Mayanists must begin to question all previous interpretations of ancient settlement. Never before have we been able to perceive in totality how the Maya affected the Lowland landscape. Earlier phases of our project offered valuable evidence, but they must now be complemented by thrilling and surprising leads from lidar.

Abrams, Elliot. 1984a. "Replicative Experimentation at
  Copan, Honduras: Implications for Ancient Eco-
  nomic Specialization." *Journal of New World Archaeology*
  6(2):39–48.
Abrams, Elliot. 1984b. "Systems of Labor Organization
  in Late Classic Copan, Honduras: The Energetics
  of Construction." PhD dissertation, Department of
  Anthropology, Pennsylvania State University, University
  Park, PA.
Abrams, Elliot. 1987. "Economic Specialization and Con-
  struction Personnel in Classic Period Copan, Honduras."
  American Antiquity 52(03):485–499. https://doi.org/10
  .2307/281595.
Abrams, Elliot. 1994. *How the Maya Built their World: Ener-
  getics and Ancient Architecture*. Austin: University of Texas
  Press.
Abrams, Elliot. 1998. "Structures as Sites: The Construction
  Process and Maya Architecture." In *Function and Mean-
  ing in Classic Maya Architecture*, ed. Stephen D. Houston,
  123–140. Washington, DC: Dumbarton Oaks Research
  Library and Collection.
Abrams, Elliot. 2000. "Observaciones preliminares sobre el
  proceso de construcción en Piedras Negras." In *Proyecto
  Arqueológico Piedras Negras: Informe Preliminar 4*, ed.
  Stephen D. Houston and Héctor L. Escobedo, 587–592.
  Report submitted to the Guatemala Instituto de Antrop-
  ología e Historia.
Abrams, Elliot, and Thomas W. Bolland. 1999. "Architec-
  tural Energetics, Ancient Monuments, and Operations

DOI: 10.5876/9781607327646.c014

Management." *Journal of Archaeological Method and Theory* 6(4):263–291. https://doi.org/10.1023/A:1021921513937.

Adam, Jean-Pierre. 1994. *Roman Building: Materials and Techniques.* Trans. Anthony Mathews. Bloomington, IN: Indianapolis University Press.

Adams, Richard E. W. 1971. *The Ceramics of Altar de Sacrificios.* Papers of the Peabody Museum of Archaeology and Ethnology 63(1). Cambridge, MA: Peabody Museum.

Adams, Richard E. W. 1973. "The Collapse of Maya Civilization: A Review of Previous Theories." In *The Classic Maya Collapse*, ed. T. Patrick Culbert, 21–34. Albuquerque: University of New Mexico.

Adams, Richard E. W. 1990. "Archaeological Research at the Lowland Maya City of Río Azul." *Latin American Antiquity* 1(1):23–41. https://doi.org/10.2307/971708.

Adams, Richard E. W. 1999. *Rio Azul: An Ancient City.* Norman: University of Oklahoma Press.

Ågren, Göran I., Ernesto Bosatta, and Jerome Balesdent. 1996. "Isotope Discriminationd during Decomposition of Organic Matter: A Theoretical Analysis." *Soil Science Society of America Journal* 60(4):1121–1126. https://doi.org/10.2136/sssaj1996.03615995006000040023x.

Agurcia Fasquelle, Ricardo, and Barbara W. Fash. 2005. "The Evolution of Structure 10L-16, Heart of the Copán Acropolis." In *Copan: The History of an Ancient Maya Kingdom*, ed. E. Wyllys Andrews and William L. Fash, 201–237. Santa Fe, NM: School of American Research Press.

Aimers, James J. 2007. "What Maya Collapse? Terminal Classic Variation in the Maya Lowlands." *Journal of Archaeological Research* 15(4):329–377. https://doi.org/10.1007/s10814-007-9015-x.

Aimers, James J., and Prudence M. Rice. 2006. "Astronomy, Ritual, and the Interpretation of Maya 'E-Group' Architectural Assemblages." *Ancient Mesoamerica* 17(01):79–96. https://doi.org/10.1017/S0956536106060056.

Akpinar-Ferrand, Ezgi, Nicholas P. Dunning, David L. Lentz, and John G. Jones. 2012. "Use of Aguadas as Water Management Sources in Two Southern Maya Lowland Sites." *Ancient Mesoamerica* 23(01):85–101. https://doi.org/10.1017/S0956536112000065.

Alcover Firpi, Omar. 2016. Landscapes of War, Landscapes of Cooperation: Regional Settlement at El Zotz, Guatemala. MA thesis, Brown University, Providence, RI.

Aldenderfer, Mark, and Herbert D. G. Maschner. 1996. *Anthropology, Space, and Geographic Information Systems.* New York: Oxford University Press.

Alvarado, Gilberto Daniel, and Isaac Rodolfo Herrera. 2001. *Mapa Fisiográfico-Geomorfológico de la República de Guatemala a escala 1:250,00.* Memoria Técnica: Ministerio de Agricultura, Ganadería, y Alimentación. Guatemala City: Programa de Emergencia por Desastres Naturales.

Anderson, Eugene N., and Felix Medina Tzuc. 2005. *Animals and the Maya in Southeast Mexico.* Tucson: University of Arizona Press.

Andres, Christopher R. 2005. "Building Negotiation: Architecture and Sociopolitical Transformation at Chau Hiix, Lamanai, and Altun Ha, Belize." PhD dissertation, Department of Anthropology, Indiana University. Bloomington, IN.

Andrews, Anthony P., E. Wyllys Andrews, and Fernando Robles Castellanos. 2003. "The Northern Maya Collapse and Its Aftermath." *Ancient Mesoamerica* 14(01):151–156. https://doi.org/10.1017/S095653610314103X.

Andrews, George F. 1986. "Notes on El Zotz: A Little-Known Site in Petén, Guatemala." *Mexicon* 8(6):123–125.

Andrieu, Chloé. 2009. "Los talleres de jade de Cancuen, Guatemal, en su contexto regional: Producción y distribución del jade en el área maya." Paper Presented at the 53rd International Congress of Americanists, Mexico City.

Anselmetti, Flavio S., David A. Hodell, Daniel Ariztegui, Mark Brenner, and Michael F. Rosenmeier. 2007. "Quantification of Soil Erosion Rates Related to Ancient Maya Deforestation." *Geology* 35(10):915–918. https://doi.org/10.1130/G23834A.1.

Aoyama, Kazuo. 2011. "Análisis de microuso en la macronavaja asociada con la tumba real del Clásico Temprano de El Zotz, Guatemala." In *Proyecto Arqueológico "El Zotz" Informe No. 5: Temporada de Campo 2010,* ed. Jose Luis Garrido López, Stephen Houston, and Edwin Román, 467–469. Report submitted to the Guatemala Instituto de Antropología e Historia.

Aoyama, Kazuo. 2015. "Microwear Analysis of the Obsidian Macroblade." In *Temple of the Night Sun: A Royal Tomb at El Diablo, Guatemala,* by Stephen Houston, Sarah Newman, Edwin Román, and Thomas Garrison, 240–242. San Francisco, CA: Precolumbia Mesoweb Press.

Aragón, Pedro. 2011. "Pozos de sondeo en áreas habitacionales (Operaciones 10, 12, 15 y 16)." In *Proyecto Arqueológico "El Zotz" Informe No. 5: Temporada de Campo 2010,* ed. Jose Luis Garrido López, Stephen Houston, and Edwin Román, 233–254. Report submitted to the Guatemala Instituto de Antropología e Historia.

Aretxaga, Begoña. 2003. "Maddening States." *Annual Review of Anthropology* 32(1):393–410. https://doi.org/10.1146/annurev.anthro.32.061002.093341.

Arnold, Dean E., Jason R. Branden, Patrick Ryan Williams, Gary M. Feinman, and J. P. Brown. 2008. "The First Direct Evidence for the Production of Maya Blue: Rediscovery of a Technology." *Antiquity* 8(315):151–164. https://doi.org/10.1017/S0003598X00096514.

Arnold, Dieter. 1991. *Building in Egypt: Pharaonic Stone Masonry.* Oxford: Oxford University Press.

Arredondo Leiva, Ernesto, and Stephen Houston, eds. 2008. *Proyecto Arqueológico "El Zotz" Informe No. 1: Temporada de Campo 2008*. Report submitted to the Guatemala Instituto de Antropología e Historia.

Arredondo Leiva, Ernesto, Stephen Houston, and Caitlin Walker. 2008. "Edificios piramidales (Operación 3)." In *Proyecto Arqueológico "El Zotz" Informe No. 1: Temporada de Campo 2008*, ed. Ernesto Arredondo Leiva and Stephen Houston, 71–94. Report submitted to the Guatemala Instituto de Antropología e Historia.

Ashmore, Wendy. 1981. *Lowland Maya Settlement Patterns*. Albuquerque: University of New Mexico Press.

Ashmore, Wendy. 1991. "Site-Planning Principles and Concepts of Directionality among the Ancient Maya." *Latin American Antiquity* 2(3):199–226. https://doi.org /10.2307/972169.

Ashmore, Wendy. 2005. "The Idea of a Maya Town." In *Structure and Meaning in Human Settlements*, ed. T. Atkin and J. Rykwert, 35–54. Philadelphia: University of Pennsylvania Museum of Archaeology and Anthropology.

Ashmore, Wendy. 2009. "Mesoamerican Landscape Archaeologies." *Ancient Mesoamerica* 20(2):183–187. https://doi.org/10.1017/S0956536109990058.

Ashmore, Wendy, and Pamela L. Geller. 2005. "Social Dimensions of Mortuary Space." In *Interacting with the Dead: Perspectives on Mortuary Archaeology for the New Millennium*, ed. G.F.M. Rakita, J. E. Buikstra, L. A. Beck, and S. R. Williams, 81–92. Gainesville: University Press of Florida.

Ashmore, Wendy, and A. Bernard Knapp, eds. 1999. *Archaeologies of Landscape: Contemporary Perspectives*. Malden, MA: Blackwell.

Ashmore, Wendy, and Jeremy A. Sabloff. 2002. "Spatial Orders in Maya Civic Plans." *Latin American Antiquity* 13(2):201–215. https://doi.org/10.2307/971914.

Aulie, H. Wilbur, and Evelyn W. de Aulie. 1978. *Diccionario Ch'ol de Tumbalá, Chiapas, con Variaciones Dialectales de Tila y Sabanilla*. DF, México: Instituto Lingüístico de Verano.

Balick, Michael J., Michael Nee, and Daniel E. Atha. 2000. "Checklist of the Vascular Plants of Belize with Common Names and Uses." New York. *Memoirs of the New York Botanical Garden* 85.

Ball, Joseph W. 1977. *The Archaeological Ceramics of Becan, Campeche, Mexico*. Middle American Research Institute, Pub. 43. New Orleans: Tulane University.

Ball, Joseph W. 1993. "Pottery, Potters, Palaces and Polities: Some Socioeconomic and Political Implications of Late Classic Maya Ceramic Industries." In *Lowland Maya Civilization in the 8th Century*, ed. Jeremy A. Sabloff and John F. Henderson, 243–272. Washington, DC: Dumbarton Oaks Research Library and Collection.

Barbier, Jean Paul, Laurence Martet, and Eric Ghysels, eds. 1997. *Artes rituals del Nuevo Continente: América Precolombina*. Milan, Italy: Skira Editores.

Baron, Joanne P. 2013. "Patrons of La Corona: Deities and Power in a Classic Maya Community." PhD dissertation, Department of Anthropology, University of Pennsylvania, Philadelphia.

Barrett, Jason W. 1999. "The Interpretation of Postclassic Lithic Production Patterns at Colha, Belize, through a Synthetic Analysis of Archaeological Data." Master's thesis, Department of Anthropology, Texas A&M University, College Station.

Barrett, Jason W. 2004. "Constructing Hierarchy through Entitlement: Inequality in Lithic Resource Access among the Ancient Maya of Blue Creek, Belize." PhD dissertation, Department of Anthropology, Texas A&M University, College Station.

Barrett, Jason W. 2006. "Rethinking Long-Distance Exchange and the Economic Interdependence of Maya Sites during the Late Preclassic Period: The View from Northern Belize." In *Archaeological Investigations in the Eastern Maya Lowlands: Papers of the 2005 Belize Archaeological Symposium*, ed. John Morris, Sheryline Jones, Jaime Awe, and Christophe Helmke, 113–128. Research Reports in Belizean Archaeology Vol. 3. Belmopan, Belize: Institute of Archaeology, National Institute of Culture and History.

Barrett, Jason W. 2011. "Ancient Maya Exploitation of Non-Renewable Resources in the Eastern Maya Lowlands." In *The Technology of Maya Civilization: Political Economy and Beyond in Lithic Studies*, ed. Zachary X. Hruby, Geoffrey Braswell, and Oswaldo Chinchilla, 57–68. Sheffield: Equinox Publishing.

Bauer, Andrew M., Peter G. Johansen, and Radhika L. Bauer. 2007. "Toward a Political Ecology in Early South India: Preliminary Considerations of the Sociopolitics of Land and Animal Use in the Southern Deccan, Neolithic through Early Historic Periods." *Asian Perspectives* 46(1):3–35. https://doi.org/10.1353/asi.2007.0001.

Beach, Timothy. 2016. "Climate Change and Archaeology in Mesoamerica." *Global and Planetary Change* 138:1–2. https://doi.org/10.1016/j.gloplacha.2016.02.004.

Beach, Timothy, Nicholas Dunning, Sheryl Luzzadder-Beach, Duncan E. Cook, and Jon C. Lohse. 2006. "Impacts of the Ancient Maya on Soils and Soil Erosion in the Central Maya Lowlands." *Catena* 65(2):166–178. https://doi.org/10.1016/j.catena.2005.11.007.

Beach, Timothy, Nicholas Dunning, Sheryl Luzzadder-Beach, and Vernon L. Scarborough. 2003. "Depression Soils in the Lowland Tropics of Northwestern Belize: Anthropogenic and Natural Origins." In *The Lowland Maya Area: Three Millennia at the Human-Wildland Interface*, ed. Arturo Gómez-Pompa, Michael Allen, Scott L. Fedick, and Juan J. Jiménez-Osornio, 139–174. Binghamton, NY: The Haworth Press.

Beach, Timothy, and Sheryl Luzzadder-Beach. 2009. "Investigaciones Paleoambientales en El Zotz, Temporada 2009." In *Proyecto Arqueológico "El Zotz" Informe*

No. 4: Temporada 2009, ed. Griselda Pérez Robles, Edwin Román, and Stephen Houston, 289–294. Report submitted to the Guatemala Instituto de Antropología e Historia.

Beach, Timothy, Sheryl Luzzadder-Beach, Duncan Cook, Samantha Krause, Colin Doyle, Sara Eshleman, Greta Wells, Nicholas Dunning, Michael Brennan, Nicholas Brokaw, Marisol Cortes-Rincon, Gail Hammond, Richard Terry, Debora Trein, and Sheila Ward. 2018. "Stability and Instability on Maya Lowlands Tropical Hillslope Soils." Geomorphology 305, 185–208.

Beach, Timothy, Sheryl Luzzadder-Beach, Nicholas Dunning, and Duncan Cook. 2008. "Human and Natural Impacts on Fluvial and Karst Depressions of the Maya Lowlands." *Geomorphology* 101(1–2):301–331.

Beach, Timothy, Sheryl Luzzadder-Beach, Nicholas Dunning, Jon Hageman, and Jon C. Lohse. 2002. "Upland Agriculture in the Maya Lowlands: Ancient Maya Soil Conservation in Northwestern Belize." *Geographical Review* 92(3):372–397. https://doi.org/10.2307/4140916.

Beach, Timothy, Sheryl Luzzadder-Beach, Nichoas Dunning, John G. Jones, Jon C. Lohse, Thomas H. Guderjan, Steven Bozarth, Sarah Millspaugh, and Tripti Bhattacharya. 2009. "A Review of Human and Natural Changes in Maya Lowlands Wetlands over the Holocene." *Quaternary Science Reviews* 28(17-18):1710–1724. https://doi.org/10.1016/j.quascirev.2009.02.004.

Beach, Timothy, Sheryl Luzzadder-Beach, Jonathan Flood, Stephen Houston, Thomas Garrison, Edwin Román, Steven Bozarth, and James Doyle. 2015. "A Neighborly View: Water and Environmental History of the El Zotz Region." In *Tikal: Paleoecology of an Ancient Maya City*, ed. David L. Lentz, Nicholas P. Dunning, and Vernon L. Scarborough, 258–279. Cambridge, UK: Cambridge University Press. https://doi.org/10.1017/CBO9781139227209.013.

Beach, Timothy, Sheryl Luzzadder-Beach, Richard Terry, Nicholas Dunning, Stephen Houston, and Thomas Garrison. 2011. "Carbon Isotopic Ratios of Wetland and Terrace Soil Sequences in the Maya Lowlands of Belize and Guatemala." *Catena* 85(2):109–118. https://doi.org/10.1016/j.catena.2010.08.014.

Beaudry, Mary. 1984. *Ceramic Production and Distribution in the Southeastern Maya Periphery: Late Classic Painted Serving Vessels*. BAR International Series, Vol. 203. Oxford, UK: Archaeopress.

Becker, Marshall J. 1999. *Excavations in Residential Groups at Tikal: Groups with Shrines. Tikal Report 21*. Philadelphia: University Museum, University of Pennsylvania.

Becker, Marshall J. 2004. "Maya Heterarchy as Inferred from Classic Period Plaza Plans." *Ancient Mesoamerica* 15(1):127–138. https://doi.org/10.1017/S0956536104151079.

Belches, Diana, and Jose Luis Garrido López. 2012. "Operación 18: Investigaciones en el Grupo La Tortuga (Operación 18)." In *Proyecto Arqueológico El Zotz Informe No.*

6: Temporada 2011, ed. Jose Luis Garrido López, Stephen Houston, Edwin Román, and Thomas Garrison, 197–206. Report submitted to the Guatemala Instituto de Antropología e Historia.

Beltrán, Boris, and Edwin Román. 2012. "Investigaciones en el Grupo El Diablo." In *Proyecto Arqueológico "El Zotz" Informe No. 6: Temporada 2011*, ed. Jose Luis Garrido López, Stephen Houston, Edwin Román, and Thomas Garrison, 71–106. Report submitted to the Guatemala Instituto de Antropología e Historia.

Berjonneau, Gerarld, and Jean-Luc Sonnery. 1985. *Rediscovered Masterpieces of Mesoamerica: Mexico–Guatemala–Honduras*. Boulogne, France: Editions Art 135.

Black, Stephen L. 1990. "The Carnegie Uaxactun Project and the Development of Maya Archaeology." *Ancient Mesoamerica* 1(02):257–276. https://doi.org/10.1017/S0956536100000298.

Blankenship, Kate. 2012. "A Pyramid Out of Place?: An Analysis of Structure L7-11 at the Classic Maya Site of El Zotz, Guatemala." Master's thesis, Department of Anthropology, Brown University, Providence, RI.

Blanton, Richard E. 1998. "Beyond Centralization: Steps Toward a Theory of Egalitarian Behavior in Archaic States." In *Archaic States*, ed. Gary M. Feinman and Joyce Marcus, 135–172. Santa Fe, NM: School of American Research.

Boldsen, Jesper L., George R. Milner, Lyle W. Konigsberg, and James W. Wood. 2002. "Transition Analysis: A New Method for Estimating Age from Skeletons." In *Paleodemography: Age Distributions from Skeletal Samples*, ed. R. D. Hoppa and J. W. Vaupel, 73–106. Cambridge, UK: Cambridge University Press. https://doi.org/10.1017/CBO9780511542428.005.

Boose, Emery R., David R. Foster, Audrey Barker Plotkin, and Brian Hall. 2003. "Geographical and Historical Variation in Hurricanes Across the Yucatán Peninsula." In *The Lowland Maya Area: Three Millennia at the Human-Wildland Interface*, ed. Arturo Gómez-Pompa, Michael Allen, Scott L. Fedick, and Juan J. Jiménez-Osornio, 495–516. Binghamton, NY: The Haworth Press.

Boucher, Sylviane, and Lucía Quiñones. 2007. "Entre mercados, ferias y festines: los murales de la Sub 1-4 de Chiik Nahb, Calakmul." *Mayab* 19:27–50.

Boutton, Thomas W. 1996. "Stable Carbon Isotope Ratios of Soil Organic Matter and Their Use as Indicators of Vegetation and Climate Change." In *Mass Spectrometry of Soils*, ed. Thomas W. Boutton and Yamasaki Shin-ichi, 47–82. New York: Marcel Dekker.

Boutton, Thomas W., Steven R. Archer, Andrew J. Midwood, Stephen F. Zitzer, and Roland Bol. 1998. "$\delta 13C$ Values of Soil Organic Carbon and Their Use in Documenting Vegetation Change in a Subtropical Savanna Ecosystem." *Geoderma* 82(1):5–41. https://doi.org/10.1016/S0016-7061(97)00095-5.

Bozarth, Steven R. 2010. "Analysis of Pollen, Biosilicates, Charred Phytoliths, and Concentrations of Particulate Charcoal at El Zotz, Guatemala." Report circulated to the Proyecto Arqueológico El Zotz.

Bozarth, Steven R., and Thomas H. Guderjan. 2004. "Biosilicate Analysis of Residue in Maya Dedicatory Cache Vessels from Blue Creek, Belize." *Journal of Archaeological Science* 31(2):205–215. https://doi.org/10.1016/j.jas.2003.08.002.

Brady, James E. 1991. "Caves and Cosmovision at Utatlan." *California Anthropologist* 18:1–10.

Brady, James E. 1997. "Settlement Configuration and Cosmology: The Role of Caves at Dos Pilas." *American Anthropologist* 99(3):602–618. https://doi.org/10.1525/aa .1997.99.3.602.

Brady, James E. 2010. "Offerings to the Rain Gods: The Archaeology of Maya Caves." In *Fiery Pool: The Maya and the Mythic Sea*, ed. Daniel Finamore and Stephen D. Houston, 223–225. New Haven, CT: Yale University Press; Salem, MA: Peabody Essex Museum.

Brady, James E., and Wendy Ashmore. 1999. "Mountains, Caves, Water: Ideational Landscapes of the Ancient Maya." In *Archaeologies of Landscape: Contemporary Perspectives*, ed. Wendy Ashmore and A. Bernard Knapp, 124–145. Malden, MA: Blackwell.

Brady, James E., Joseph W. Ball, Ronald L. Bishop, Duncan C. Pring, Norman Hammond, and Rupert A. Housley. 1998. "The Lowland Maya 'ProtoClassic': A Reconsideration of Its Nature and Significance." *Ancient Mesoamerica* 9(01):17–38. https://doi.org/10.1017/S0956536100001826.

Braswell, Geoffrey E. 1996. "A Maya Obsidian Source: The Geoarchaeology, Settlement History, and Ancient Economy of San Martín Jilotepeque, Guatemala." PhD dissertation, Department of Anthropology, Tulane University, New Orleans, LA.

Braswell, Geoffrey E. 2003. "Highland Maya Polities." In *The Postclassic Mesoamerican World*, ed. Michael E. Smith and Frances F. Berdan, 45–49. Salt Lake City: University of Utah Press.

Braswell, Geoffrey E. 2004. "Lithic Analysis in the Maya Area." In *Continuities and Changes in Maya Archaeology: Perspectives at the Millennium*, ed. Charles W. Golden and Greg Borgstede, 177–199. New York: Routledge.

Brewer, Jeffrey L. 2007. "Understanding the Role of a Small Depression in Ancient Maya Water Management at the Medicinal Trail Site, Northwest Belize." Master's thesis, Department of Geography, University of Cincinnati. Cincinnati, OH.

Brinton, Daniel G. 1890. *Essays of an Americanist*. Philadelphia: Porter & Coates.

Broda, Johanna. 1987. "The Provenience of the Offering: Tribute and *Cosmovisión*." In *The Aztec Templo Mayor*, ed. Elizabeth Boone Hill, 211–256. Washington, DC: Dumbarton Oaks Research Library and Collection.

Bronk Ramsey, Christopher. 2009. "Bayesian Analysis of Radiocarbon Dates." *Radiocarbon* 51(1):337–360. https://doi.org/10.1017/S0033822200033865.

Brown, Marley R., and Edward C. Harris. 1993. "Interfaces in Archaeological Stratigraphy." In *Practices of Archaeological Stratigraphy*, ed. Edward C. Harris, Marley R. Brown, and Gregory J. Brown, 7–20. London: Academic Press. https://doi.org/10.1016/B978-0-12-326445-9.50006-X.

Brumfiel, Elizabeth M. 1996. "Figurines and the Aztec State: Testing the Effectiveness of Ideological Domination." In *Gender and Archaeology*, ed. Rita P. Wright, 144–166. Philadelphia: University of Pennsylvania Press.

Buikstra, Jane E. 1976. *Hopewell in the Lower Illinois River Valley: A Regional Study of Human Biological Variability and Prehistoric Mortuary Behavior*. Archaeological Program Scientific Papers, No. 2. Evanston, IL: Northwestern University Press.

Buikstra, Jane E. 1977. "Biocultural Dimensions of Archaeological Study: A Regional Perspective." In *Biocultural Adaptation in Prehistoric America*, ed. R. L. Blakely, 67–84. Southern Anthropological Society Proceedings No. 11. Athens: University of Georgia Press.

Buikstra, Jane E., George R. Milner, and Jesper L. Boldsen. 2006. "Janaab' Pakal of Palenque." In *Janaab' Pakal of Palenque*, ed. V. Tiesler and A. Cucina, 48–59. Tucson: The University of Arizona Press.

Buikstra, Jane E., and Douglas H. Ubelaker. 1994. *Standards for Data Collection from Human Skeletal Remains*. Arkansas Archeological Survey Research Series No. 44. Fayetteville: Arkansas Archeological Survey.

Butler, Mary. 1935. "A Study of Maya Mouldmade Figurines." *American Anthropologist* 37(4):636–672. https://doi.org/10.1525/aa.1935.37.4.02a00080.

Cambranes, Rafael. 2009. "Operaciones 8, 9, 10 y 11: Programa de Pozos de Sondeo." In *Proyecto Arqueológico "El Zotz" Informe No. 4: Temporada 2009*, edited by Griselda Pérez Robles, Edwin Román, and Stephen Houston, 167–198. Report submitted to the Guatemala Instituto de Antropología e Historia.

Camp, John McKay, II, and William B. Dinsmoor Jr. 1984. *Ancient Athenian Building Methods*. Excavations of the Athenian Agora Picture Book No. 21. Athens, Greece: American School of Classical Studies at Athens.

Cannadine, David. 1999. *The Decline and Fall of the British Aristocracy*. New York: Vintage.

Carmean, Kelli, and Jeremy A. Sabloff. 1996. "Political Decentralization in the Puuc Region, Yucatán, Mexico." *Journal of Anthropological Research* 52(3):317–330. https://doi.org/10.1086/jar.52.3.3630087.

Carrasco Vargas, Ramón, and María Cordeiro Baqueiro. 2012. "The Murals of Chiik Nahb Structure Sub 1-4, Calakmul, Mexico." In *Maya Archaeology 2*, edited by

Charles Golden, Stephen Houston, and Joel Skidmore, 8–59. San Francisco, CA: Precolumbia Mesoweb Press.

Carrasco Vargas, Ramón, Verónica A. Vázquez López, and Simon Martin. 2009. "Daily Life of the Ancient Maya Recorded on Murals at Calakmul, Mexico." *Proceedings of the National Academy of Sciences of the United States of America* 106(46):19245–19249. https://doi.org/10.1073/pnas.0904374106.

Carrelli, Christine W. 2000. "Masonry Construction Systems at the Acropolis, Copan, Honduras." Research Report submitted to the Foundation for the Advancement of Mesoamerican Studies. Accessed June 27, 2016. http://www.famsi.org/reports/94036/index.html.

Carrelli, Christine W. 2004. "Measures of Power: The Energetics of Royal Construction at Early Classic Copan." In *Understanding Early Classic Copan*, ed. Ellen E. Bell, Marcello A. Canuto, and Robert J. Sharer, 113–127. Philadelphia: University of Pennsylvania Museum of Archaeology and Anthropology.

Carter, Nicholas P. 2014. "Kingship and Collapse: Inequality and Identity in the Terminal Classic Southern Maya Lowlands." PhD dissertation, Department of Anthropology, Brown University, Providence, RI.

Carter, Nicholas P. 2015. "Once and Future Kings: Classic Maya Geopolitics and Mythic History on the Vase of the Initial Series from Uaxactun." *The PARI Journal* 5(4):1–15.

Carter, Nicholas P., and Yeny M. Gutiérrez Castillo. 2011. "Excavaciones en el Grupo Norte o Las Palmitas (Operación 4)." In *Proyecto Arqueológico "El Zotz" Informe No. 5: Temporada de Campo 2010*, ed. Jose Luis Garrido López, Stephen Houston, and Edwin Román, 67–116. Report submitted to the Guatemala Instituto de Antropología e Historia.

Carter, Nicholas P., and Yeny M. Gutiérrez Castillo. 2012a. "El cambio interregional y la continuidad social en el Grupo Las Palmitas." In *XXV Simposio de Investigaciones Arqueológicas en Guatemala, 2011*, ed. Bárbara Arroyo, Lorena Paiz, and Héctor Mejía, 307–315. Guatemala City: Ministerio de Cultura y Deportes, Instituto de Antropologías e Historia, Asociación Tikal.

Carter, Nicholas P., and Yeny M. Gutiérrez Castillo. 2012b. "Investigaciones en el Grupo Norte o Las Palmitas (Operación 4)." In *Proyecto Arqueológico El Zotz Informe No. 6: Temporada 2011*, ed. Jose Luis Garrido López, Stephen Houston, Edwin Román, and Thomas Garrison, 19–70. Report submitted to the Guatemala Instituto de Antropología e Historia.

Carter, Nicholas P., Rony E. Piedrasanta, Stephen D. Houston, and Zachary Hruby. 2012. "Signs of Supplication: Two Mosaic Earflare Plaques from El Zotz, Guatemala." *Antiquity* 86(333). Project Gallery. Accessed May 21, 2016. http://antiquity.ac.uk/projgall/carter333/.

Castañeda Tobar, José Francisco. 2013. "Monumentos de El Perú-Waka': Nuevos
hallazgos." In *Proyecto Regional Arqueológico El Perú-Waka', Informe No. 11, Tempo-rada 2013*, ed. Juan Carlos Pérez Calderón and David A. Freidel, 192–207. Report
submitted to the Guatemala Instituto de Antropología e Historia.

Cecil, Leslie G. 2001. "Technological Styles of Late Postclassic Slipped Pottery from
the Central Peten Lakes Region, El Peten, Guatemala." PhD dissertation, Depart-ment of Anthropology, Southern Illinois University, Carbondale, IL.

Charnay, Désiré. 1888. *The Ancient Cities of the New World: Being Voyages and Explora-tions in Mexico and Central America from 1857–1882*. Trans. J. Gonino and Helen S.
Contant. New York: Harper & Brothers.

Chase, Arlen F., and Diane Z. Chase. 1985. "Postclassic Temporal and Spatial Frames
for the Lowland Maya: A Background." In *The Lowland Maya Postclassic*, ed.
Arlen F. Chase and Prudence M. Rice, 9–22. Austin: University of Texas Press.

Chase, Arlen F., and Diane Z. Chase. 1995. "External Impetus, Internal Synthesis,
and Standardization: E-Group Assemblages and the Crystallization of Classic
Maya Society in the Southern Lowlands." In *Emergence of Maya Civilization: The
Transition from the Preclassic to the Early Classic*, ed. Nikolai Grube, 87–101. Schwa-ben, Germany: Saurwein, Mark.

Chase, Arlen F., and Diane Z. Chase. 2005. "Contextualizing the Collapse: Hege-mony and Terminal Classic Ceramics from Caracol, Belize." In *Geographies of
Power: Understanding the Nature of Terminal Classic Pottery in the Maya Lowlands*,
edited by Sandra L. López Varela and Antonia E. Foias, 73–91. BAR International
Series 1447. Oxford, UK: Archaeopress.

Chase, Arlen F., and Diane Z. Chase. 2008. "Methodological Issues in the Archaeo-logical Identification of the Terminal Classic and Postclassic Transition in the
Maya Area." *Research Reports in Belizean Archaeology* 5:23–36.

Chase, Arlen F., Diane Z. Chase, and John F. Weishampel. 2010. "Lasers in
the Jungle: Airborne Sensors Reveal a Vast Maya Landscape." *Archaeology*
64(4):29–31.

Chase, Arlen F., Diane Z. Chase, John F. Weishampel, Jason B. Drake, Ramesh L.
Shrestha, K. Clint Slatton, Jaime J. Awe, and William E. Carter. 2011. "Airborne
LiDAR, Archaeology, and the Ancient Maya Landscape at Caracol, Belize." *Jour-nal of Archaeological Science* 38(2):387–398. https://doi.org/10.1016/j.jas.2010.09.018.

Chase, Diane Z. 1985. "Ganned but Not Forgotten: Late Postclassic Archaeology and
Ritual at Santa Rita Corozal, Belize." In *The Lowland Maya Postclassic*, ed. Arlen F.
Chase and Prudence M. Rice, 104–125. Austin: University of Texas Press.

Chase, Diane Z., and Arlen F. Chase. 1996. "Maya Multiples: Individuals, Entries,
and Tombs in Structure A34 of Caracol, Belize." *Latin American Antiquity*
7(1):61–79. https://doi.org/10.2307/3537015.

Chase, Diane Z., and Arlen F. Chase. 1998. "The Archaeological Context of Caches, Burials, and Other Ritual Activities for the Classic Period (as Reflected at Caracol, Belize)." In *Function and Meaning in Classic Maya Architecture*, ed. Stephen D. Houston, 299–332. Washington, DC: Dumbarton Oaks.

Chase, Diane Z., and Arlen F. Chase. 2004. "Hermeneutics, Transitions, and Transformations in Classic to Postclassic Maya Society." In *The Terminal Classic in the Maya Lowlands: Collapse, Transition, and Transformation*, ed. Arthur A. Demarest, Prudence M. Rice, and Don S. Rice, 12–27. Boulder: University of Colorado Press.

Cheetham, David. 2005. "Cunil: A Pre-Mamom Horizon in the Southern Maya Lowlands." In *New Perspectives on Formative Mesoamerican Cultures*, ed. Terry Powis, 1–14. BAR International Series, Vol. 1377. Oxford, UK: Archaeopress.

Cheung, Kristina Alyssa. 2014. "Inferring Ancient Technology and Practices of the Elite Maya Kingship through the Application of Materials Engineering Characterization Modalities." Master's thesis, Department of Materials Science and Engineering, University of California, Los Angeles.

Child, Mark, and Charles W. Golden. 2008. "The Transformation of Abandoned Architecture at Piedras Negras." In *Ruins of the Past: The Use and Perception of Abandoned Structures in the Maya Lowlands*, ed. Travis W. Stanton and Aline Magnoni, 65–89. Boulder: University of Colorado Press.

Chinchilla Mazariegos, Oswaldo, and Oswaldo Gómez. 2010. "El Nacimiento del Sol en Tikal: Interpretación de un Entierro Asociado al Conjunto de Tipo Grupo 'E' de Mundo Perdido." In *XXIII Simposio de Investigaciones Arqueológicas en Guatemala, 2009*, ed. Bárbara Arroyo, Adriana Linares Palma, and Lorena Paiz Aragon, 1193–1201. Guatemala City: Museo Nacional de Arqueología y Etnología.

Chinchilla Mazariegos, Oswaldo, Vera Tiesler, Oswaldo Gómez, and T. Douglas Price. 2015. "Myth, Ritual, and Human Sacrifice in Early Classic Mesoamerica: Interpreting a Cremated Double Burial from Tikal, Guatemala." *Cambridge Archaeological Journal* 25(1):187–210. https://doi.org/10.1017/S0959774314000638.

Christenson, Allen J. 2007. *Popol Vuh: The Sacred Book of the Maya. The Great Classic of Central American Spirituality, Translated from the Original Maya Text*. Norman: University of Oklahoma Press.

Clark, John E. 1997. "Prismatic Blade-making, Craftsmanship, and Production: An Analysis of Obsidian Refuse from Ojo de Agua, Chiapas, Mexico." *Ancient Mesoamerica* 8:137–159. https://doi.org/10.1017/S0956536100001620.

Clark, John E., and David Cheetham. 2002. "Mesoamerica's Tribal Foundations." In *The Archaeology of Tribal Societies*, ed. William Parkinson, 278–339. Ann Arbor, MI: International Monographs in Prehistory.

Clark, John E., and Richard D. Hansen. 2001. "Architecture of Early Kingship: Comparative Perspectives on the Origin of the Maya Royal Court." In *Royal Courts of the Ancient Maya,* Volume 2: *Data and Case Studies,* ed. Takeshi Inomata and Stephen D. Houston, 1–45. Boulder: Westview Press.

Clarke, Somers, and R. Engelbach. 1990. *Ancient Egyptian Construction and Architecture.* New York: Dover.

Coe, Michael D. 1973. *The Maya Scribe and His World.* New York: The Grolier Club.

Coe, William R. 1967. *Tikal: A Handbook of the Maya Ruins.* Philadelphia: University Museum, University of Pennsylvania.

Coe, William R. 1990. *Excavations in the Great Plaza, North Terrace, and North Acropolis of Tikal.* 6 vols. Tikal Report 14. Philadelphia: University Museum, University of Pennsylvania.

Coggins, Clemency Chase. 1980. "The Shape of Time: Some Political Implications of a Fourt-Part Figure." *American Antiquity* 45(04):727–739. https://doi.org/10.2307/280144.

Coggins, Clemency Chase. 1982. "The Zenith, the Mountain, the Center, and the Sea." In *Ethnoastronomy and Archaeoastronomy in the American Tropics,* ed. Anthony F. Aveni and Gary Urton, 111–123. Annals of the New York Academy of Sciences No. 385. New York: New York Academy of Sciences. https://doi.org/10.1111/j.1749-6632.1982.tb34261.x.

Cohen, Mark N., and George J. Armelagos, eds. 1984. *Paleopathology at the Origins of Agriculture.* New York: Academic Press.

Costin, Cathy L. 1991. "Craft Specialization: Issues in Defining, Documenting, and Explaining the Organization of Production." In *Archaeological Method and Theory,* vol. 3. ed. Michael Schiffer, 1–56. Tucson: University of Arizona Press.

Coulton, John J. 1977. *Ancient Greek Architects at Work: Problems of Structure and Design.* Ithaca, NY: Cornell University Press.

Cowgill, George. 1964. "The End of Classic Maya Culture: A Review of Recent Evidence." *Southwestern Journal of Anthropology* 20(2):145–159. https://doi.org/10.1086/soutjanth.20.2.3629323.

Crumley, Carole L. 1995. "Heterarchy and the Analysis of Complex Societies." In *Heterarchy and the Analysis of Complex Societies,* ed. Robert M. Ehrenreich, Carole L. Crumley, and Janet E. Levy, 1–5. Archaeological Papers of the American Anthropological Association no. 6. Washington, DC: American Anthropological Association. https://doi.org/10.1525/ap3a.1995.6.1.1.

Crumley, Carole L. 2003. "Alternative Forms of Societal Order." In *Heterarchy, Political Economy, and the Ancient Maya: The Three Rivers Region of the East-Central Yucatan Peninsula,* ed. Vernon L. Scarborough, Fred Valdez Jr., and Nicholas Dunning, 136–145. Tucson: University of Arizona Press.

Crumley, Carole L., and William H. Marquardt. 1987. "Regional Dynamics in Burgundy." In *Regional Dynamics: Burgundian Landscapes in Historical Perspective,* ed.

Carole Crumley and William H. Marquardt, 609–623. San Diego, CA: Academic Press.

Cucina, Andrea, Cristina Perera Cantillo, Thelma Sierra Sosa, and Vera Tiesler. 2011. "Carious Lesions and Maize Consumption among the Prehispanic Maya: An Analysis of a Coastal Community in Northern Yucatan." *American Journal of Physical Anthropology* 145(4):560–567. https://doi.org/10.1002/ajpa.21534.

Cucina, Andrea, and Vera Tiesler. 2003. "Dental Caries and Antemortem Tooth Loss in the Northern Peten Area, Mexico: A Biocultural Perspective on Social Status Differences among the Classic Maya." *American Journal of Physical Anthropology* 122(1):1–10. https://doi.org/10.1002/ajpa.10267.

Cucina, Andrea, and Vera Tiesler. 2006. "The Companions of Janaab' Pakal and the 'Red Queen' from Palenque, Chiapas: Meanings of Human Companion Sacrifice in Classic Maya Society." In *Janaab' Pakal of Palenque: Reconstructing the Life and Death of a Maya Ruler*, ed. Vera Tiesler and Andrea Cucina, 102–125. Tucson: University of Arizona Press.

Culbert, T. Patrick. 1973. "The Maya Downfall at Tikal." In *The Classic Maya Collapse*, ed. T. Patrick Culbert, 63–92. Albuquerque: University of New Mexico Press.

Culbert, T. Patrick. 1988. "The Collapse of Classic Maya Civilization." In *The Collapse of Ancient States and Civilizations*, ed. Norman Yoffee and George Cowgill, 69–101. Tucson: University of Arizona Press.

Culbert, T. Patrick. 1991. *Classic Maya Political History: Hieroglyphic and Archaeological Evidence*. Cambridge, UK: Cambridge University Press.

Culbert, T. Patrick. 1993. *The Ceramics of Tikal*. Tikal Report 25A. Philadelphia: University Museum, University of Pennsylvania.

Culbert, T. Patrick. 1999. "La secuencia cerámica Preclásica en Tikal y la Acrópolis del Norte." In *XII Simposio de Investigaciones Arqueológicals en Guatemala, 1998*, ed. Juan Pedro Laporte and Héctor L. Escobedo, 64–74. Guatemala: Ministerio de Cultura y Deportes, Instituto de Antropología e Historia, Asociación Tikal.

Culbert, T. Patrick. 2003. "The Ceramics of Tikal." In *Tikal: Dynasties, Foreigners, and Affairs of State*, ed. Jeremy A. Sabloff, 47–82. Santa Fe, NM: School of American Research Press.

Culbert, T. Patrick, and Don S. Rice, eds. 1990. *Precolumbian Population History in the Maya Lowlands*. Albuquerque: University of New Mexico Press.

Czapiewska, Ewa. 2011a. "Análisis Preliminar de la cerámica de El Zotz, Temporada 2010." In *Proyecto Arqueológico "El Zotz" Informe No. 5: Temporada de Campo 2010*, ed. Jose Luis Garrido López, Stephen Houston, and Edwin Román, 395–412. Report submitted to the Guatemala Instituto de Antropología e Historia.

Czapiewska, Ewa. 2011b. "Social, Economic and Political Transformation in the Acropolis Group at El Zotz, Guatemala." Master's thesis, University College London.

Czapiewska, Ewa. 2012. "Análisis cerámico de la temporada 2011 del Proyecto Arqueológico El Zotz." In *Proyecto Arqueológico El Zotz Informe No. 6: Temporada 2011*, ed. Jose Luis Garrido López, Stephen Houston, Edwin Román, and Thomas Garrison, 255–267. Report submitted to the Guatemala Instituto de Antropología e Historia.

Czapiewska-Halliday, Ewa. 2018. "The Study of Value: Social, Economic and Political Dimensions of Palace Complexes at El Zotz." PhD dissertation, Institute of Archaeology, University College London. London, UK.

de Carteret, Alyce M. 2013. "The Red Shift: Changing Tastes and Their Implications at the Elite Maya Residence of El Diablo, Guatemala." Master's thesis, Department of Anthropology, Brown University, Providence, RI.

de Carteret, Alyce. 2015. "Ceramics from the El Diablo Fill." In *Temple of the Night Sun: A Royal Tomb at El Diablo, Guatemala*, by Stephen Houston, Sarah Newman, Edwin Román, and Thomas Garrison, 82–83. San Francisco: Precolumbia Mesoweb Press.

de Carteret, Alyce M. 2016. "Excavaciones en el Grupo I10 (Operación 25)." In *Proyecto Arqueológico El Zotz Informe Final: 10ma Temporada de Campo*, ed. Jose Luis Garrido López, Yeny Myshell Gutiérrez Castillo, Edwin René Román Ramirez, Thomas Garrison, and Stephen Houston, 61–84. Report submitted to the Guatemala Instituto de Antropología e Historia.

de Carteret, Alyce M. 2017. "Building Communities: The Craft of Housebuilding among the Classic Maya." PhD dissertation, Department of Anthropology, Brown University. Providence, RI.

Deetz, James. 1977. *In Small Things Forgotten: The Archaeology of Early American Life.* Garden City, NY: Anchor Banks.

del Ángel, Andrés, and Hector B. Cisneros. 2004. "Technical Note: Modification of Regression Equations Used to Estimate Stature in Mesoamerican Skeletal Remains." *American Journal of Physical Anthropology* 125(3):264–265. https://doi.org/10.1002/ajpa.10385.

DeLaine, Janet. 1997. "The Baths of Caracalla in Rome: A Study in the Design, Construction, and Economics of Large-Scale Building Projects in Imperial Rome." *Journal of Roman Archaeology,* Supplement No. 25. Portsmouth, RI: Journal of Roman Archaeology.

DeLaine, Janet. 2000. "Bricks and Mortar: Exploring the Economics of Building Techniques at Rome and Ostia." In *Economies Beyond Agriculture in the Classical World*, ed. David J. Mattingly and John Salmon, 230–268. New York: Routledge.

DeLaine, Janet. 2002. "The Temple of Hadrian at Cyzicus and Roman Attitudes to Exceptional Construction." *Papers of the British School at Rome* 70:205–230. https://doi.org/10.1017/S0068246200002154.

de León, Jason P., Kenneth. G. Hirth, and David M. Carballo. 2009. "Exploring Formative Period Obsidian Blade Trade: Three Distribution Models." *Ancient Mesoamerica* 20: 113–128.

Demarest, Arthur. 1997. "The Vanderbilt Petexbatún Regional Archaeological Project 1989–1994: Overview, History, and Major Results of a Multidisciplinary Study of the Classic Maya Collapse." *Ancient Mesoamerica* 8(02):209–227. https://doi.org/10.1017/S0956536100001693.

Demarest, Arthur. 2004. "After the Maelstrom: Collapse of the Classic Maya Kingdoms and the Terminal Classic in Western Peten." In *The Terminal Classic in the Maya Lowlands: Collapse, Transition, and Transformation*, ed. Arthur A. Demarest, Prudence M. Rice, and Don S. Rice, 102–125. Boulder: University Press of Colorado.

Demarest, Arthur A., Chloé Andrieu, Paola Torres, Mélanie Forné, Tomás Barrientos, and Marc Wolf. 2014. "Economy, Exchange, and Power: New Evidence from the Late Classic Maya Port City of Cancuen." *Ancient Mesoamerica* 25(01):187–219. https://doi.org/10.1017/S0956536114000121.

Demarest, Arthur A., Matt O'Mansky, Claudia Wolley, Dirk Van Tuerenhout, Takeshi Inomata, Joel Palka, and Héctor Escobedo. 1997. "Classic Maya Defensible Systems and Warfare in the Petexbatun Region: Archaeological Evidence and Interpretations." *Ancient Mesoamerica* 8(02):229–253. https://doi.org/10.1017/S095653610000170X.

Demarest, Arthur A., Prudence M. Rice, and Don S. Rice, eds. 2004. *The Terminal Classic in the Maya Lowlands: Collapse, Transition, and Transformation*. Boulder: University Press of Colorado.

Dobres, Marcia-Anne. 1999. "Technology's Links and *Chaînes*: The Processual Unfolding of Technique and Technician." In *The Social Dynamics of Technology: Practice, Politics, and World Views*, ed. Marcia-Anne Dobres and Christopher R. Hoffman, 124–146. Washington, DC: Smithsonian Institution Press.

Dobres, Marcia-Anne. 2000. *Technology and Social Agency: Outlining a Practice Framework for Archaeology*. Oxford, UK: Blackwell Publishers.

Doyle, James A. 2012. "Re-Group on 'E-Groups': Monumentality and Early Centers in the Middle Preclassic Maya Lowlands." *Latin American Antiquity* 23: 355–379. https://doi.org/10.7183/1045-6635.23.4.355.

Doyle, James A. 2013a. "Early Maya Geometric Planning Conventions at El Palmar, Guatemala." *Journal of Archaeological Science* 40(2):793–798. https://doi.org/10.1016/j.jas.2012.08.006.

Doyle, James A. 2013b. "The First Maya 'Collapse': The End of the Preclassic Period at El Palmar, Peten, Guatemala." PhD dissertation, Department of Anthropology, Brown University, Providence, RI.

Doyle, James A. 2017. *Architecture and the Origins of Preclassic Maya Politics*. Cambridge, UK: Cambridge University Press. https://doi.org/10.1017/9781316535684.

Doyle, James A., Thomas G. Garrison, and Stephen D. Houston. 2012. "Watchful Realms: Integrating GIS Analysis and Political History in the Southern Maya Lowlands." *Antiquity* 86(333):792–807. https://doi.org/10.1017/S0003598X0004792X.

Doyle, James A., and Stephen D. Houston. 2012. "A Watery Tableau at El Mirador, Guatemala." Accessed May 21, 2016. https://decipherment.wordpress.com/2012/04/09/a-watery-tableau-at-el-mirador-guatemala/.

Doyle, James A., Stephen D. Houston, Thomas G. Garrison, and Edwin Román. 2011. "¿Al alcance de la vista de Mundo Perdido? La planificación urbana y el abandono abrupto de El Palmar, Petén, Guatemala." In *XXIV Simposio de Investigaciones Arqueológicas en Guatemala, 2010*, ed. Bárbara Arroyo, Lorena Pais Aragón, Adriana Linares Palma, and Ana Lucía Arroyave, 45–56. Guatemala: Ministerio de Cultura y Deportes, Instituto de Antropología e Historia, Asociación Tikal.

Doyle, James A., and Varinia Matute Rodríguez. 2009. "Operaciones 1, 2, 3, 4 y 7: Excavaciones y Levantamiento Topográfico de la Temporada 2009 en El Palmar." In *Proyecto Arqueológico "El Zotz" Informe No. 4: Temporada 2009*, ed. Griselda Pérez Robles, Edwin Román, and Stephen Houston, 209–248. Report submitted to the Guatemala Instituto de Antropología e Historia.

Doyle, James A., and Rony Piedrasanta. 2011. "Excavaciones en El Palmar (Operación 8)." In *Proyecto Arqueológico "El Zotz" Informe No. 5: Temporada de Campo 2010*, ed. Jose Luis Garrido López, Stephen Houston, and Edwin Román, 265–292. Report submitted to the Guatemala Instituto de Antropología e Historia.

Doyle, James A., and Rony Piedrasanta. 2012. "Excavaciones y Reconocimiento en el sitio El Palmar." In *Proyecto Arqueológico El Zotz Informe No. 6: Temporada 2011*, ed. Jose Luis Garrido López, Stephen Houston, Edwin Román, and Thomas Garrison, 207–218. Report submitted to the Guatemala Instituto de Antropología e Historia.

Duday, Henri. 2009. *The Archaeology of the Dead: Lectures in Archaeothanatology*. Oxford, UK: Oxbow Books.

Duncan, William N. 2006. "Understanding Veneration and Violation in the Archaeological Record." In *Interacting with the Dead: Perspectives on Mortuary Archaeology for the New Millenium*, ed. G.F.M. Rakita, J. E. Buikstra, L. A. Beck, and S. R. Williams, 207–227. Gainesville: University of Florida.

Duncan, William N. 2011. "A Bioarchaeological Analysis of Sacrificial Victims from a Postclassic Maya Temple from Ixlú, Petén, Guatemala." *Latin American Antiquity* 22(4):549–572. https://doi.org/10.7183/1045-6635.22.4.549.

Duncan, William N., and Charles Andrew Hofling. 2011. "Why the Head? Cranial Modification as Protection and Ensoulment among the Maya." *Ancient Mesoamerica* 22(01):199–210. https://doi.org/10.1017/S0956536111000162.

Dunning, Nicholas P. 1995. "Coming Together at the Temple Mountain: Environment, Subsistence and the Emergence of Lowland Maya Segmentary States." In
*The Emergence of Lowland Maya Civilization: The Transition from the Preclassic to
the Early Classic*, ed. Nikolai Grube, 61–70. Acta Mesoamericana, Vol. 8. Markt
Schwaben, Germany: Verlag Anton Saurwein.

Dunning, Nicholas P., Timothy Beach, and Sheryl Luzzadder-Beach. 2006. "Envi-
ronmental Variability among the Bajos in the Southern Maya Lowlands and Its
Implications for Ancient Maya Civilization and Archaeology." In *Pre-Columbian
Water Management: Ideology, Ritual, and Power*, ed. Barbara W. Fash and Lisa
Lucero, 81–99. Tucson: University of Arizona Press.

Dunning, Nicholas, Sheryl Luzzadder-Beach, Timothy Beach, John G. Jones,
Vernon Scarborough, and T. Patrick Culbert. 2002. "Arising from the *Bajos*: The
Evolution of a Neotropical Landscape and the Rise of Maya Civilization." *Annals
of the Association of American Geographers* 92(2):267–283. https://doi.org/10.1111
/1467-8306.00290.

Ehleringer, James R. 1991. "13C/12C Fractionation and Its Utility in Terrestrial
Plant Studies." In *Carbon Isotope Techniques*, ed. David C. Coleman and Brian Fry,
187–200. San Diego, CA: Academic Press. https://doi.org/10.1016/B978-0-12
-179730-0.50017-5.

Elisséeff, Nikita. 1983. "Urbanisme et urbanization des amṣār." In *La ville dans le
proche-orient ancien: Actes du Colloque de Cartigny 1970*, ed. Françoise Brüschwei-
ler, Yves Christe, Robert Martin-Achad, Bruno Urio, and Jacques Vicari, 151–160.
Leuven, Belgium: Editions Peeters.

Erasmus, J. Charles. 1965. "Monument Building: Some Field Experiments." *Southwestern Journal of Anthropology* 21(4):277–301. https://doi.org/10.1086/soutjanth
.21.4.3629433.

Escobedo, Héctor L. 2004. "Tales from the Crypt: The Burial Place of Ruler 4,
Piedras Negras." In *Courtly Art of the Ancient Maya*, ed. M. Miller and S. Martin,
277–280. New York: Thames and Hudson.

Escobedo, Héctor, and Stephen Houston. 2001. "Reporte de la cuarta temporada
de campo del proyecto Piedras Negras, Peten." In *XIV Simposio de Investigaciones
Arqueológicas en Guatemala, 2000*, ed. Juan Pedro Laporte, Ana Claudia de Suasnávar, and Bárbara Arroyo, 537–553. Guatemala: Ministerio de Cultura y Deportes,
Instituto de Antropología e Historia, Asociación Tikal.

Escobedo, Héctor, and Stephen Houston. 2002. "Arqueología e historia en Piedras
Negras, Guatemala: Síntesis de las temporadas de campo de 1997–2000." In *XV
Simposio de Investigaciones Arqueológicas en Guatemala, 2001*, ed. Juan Pedro Laporte,
Héctor Escobedo, and Bárbara Arroyo, 151–160. Guatemala: Ministerio de Cultura
y Deportes, Instituto de Antropología e Historia, Asociación Tikal.

Estrada-Belli, Francisco. 2006. "Lightning Sky, Rain, and the Maize God: The Ideology of Preclassic Maya Rulers at Cival, Peten, Guatemala." *Ancient Mesoamerica* 17(01):57–78. https://doi.org/10.1017/S0956536106060068.

Estrada-Belli, Francisco. 2011. *The First Maya Civilization: Ritual and Power before the Classic Period.* New York: Routledge.

Estrada-Belli, Francisco, Alexandre Tokovinine, Jennifer M. Foley, Heather Hurst, Gene A. Ware, David Stuart, and Nikolai Grube. 2009. "A Maya Palace at Holmul, Peten, Guatemala and the Teotihuacan 'Entrada': Evidence from Murals 7 and 9." *Latin American Antiquity* 20(01):228–259. https://doi.org/10.1017/S1045663500002595.

Estrada-Belli, Francisco, and David Brent Wahl. 2010. "Prehistoric Human-Environment Interactions in the Southern Maya Lowlands: The Holmul Region Case." Report submitted to the National Science Foundation.

Evans, R. Tripp. 2004. *Romancing the Maya: Mexican Antiquity in the American Imagination, 1820–1915.* Austin: University of Texas Press.

Fedick, Scott. 1991. "Chert Tool Production and Consumption among Classic Period Maya Households." In *Maya Stone Tools: Selected Papers from the Second Maya Lithic Conference,* ed. Thomas Hester and Harry Shafer, 251–265. Monographs in World Archaeology No. 1. Madison, WI: Prehistory Press.

Fedick, Scott, and Anabel Ford. 1990. "The Prehistoric Agricultural Landscape of the Central Maya Lowlands: An Examination of Local Variability in a Regional Context." *World Archaeology* 22(1):18–33. https://doi.org/10.1080/00438243.1990.9980126.

Feinman, Gary M., S. Upham, K. G. Lightfoot. 1981. "The Production Step Measure: An Ordinal Index of Labor Input in Ceramic Manufacture." *American Antiquity* 46:871–884.

Fields, Virginia M., and Alexandre Tokovinine. 2012. "Belt Plaque." In *Ancient Maya Art at Dumbarton Oaks,* ed. Joanne Pillsbury, Miriam Doutriaux, Reiko Ishihara-Brito, and Alexandre Tokovinine, 178–183. Pre-Columbian Art at Dumbarton Oaks, Number 4. Washington, DC: Dumbarton Oaks Research Library and Collection.

Fitzsimmons, James L. 1999. "PN 51: Excavaciones en la Estructura O-17." In *Proyecto Arqueológico Piedras Negras, Informe Preliminar No. 3: Tercera Temporada, 1999,* ed. Héctor L. Escobedo and Stephen D. Houston, 285–297. Report presented to the Guatemala Instituto de Antropología e Historia.

Fitzsimmons, James L. 2009. *Death and the Classic Maya Kings.* Austin: University of Texas Press.

Foias, Antonia E. 1996. "Changing Ceramic Production and Exchange Systems and the Classic Maya Collapse in the Petexbatun Region." PhD dissertation, Department of Anthropology, Vanderbilt University, Nashville, TN.

Foias, Antonia E. 2013. *Ancient Maya Political Dynamics*. Gainesville: University Press of Florida. https://doi.org/10.5744/florida/9780813044224.001.0001.

Foias, Antonia E., and Ronald L. Bishop. 1997. "Changing Ceramic Production and Exchange in the Petexbatun Region, Guatemala: Reconsidering the Classic Maya Collapse." *Ancient Mesoamerica* 8(02):275–291. https://doi.org/10.1017/S0956536 100001735.

Foias, Antonia E., and Kitty F. Emery, eds. 2012. *Motul de San José: Politics, History, and Economy in a Classic Maya Polity*. Gainesville: University Press of Florida. https://doi.org/10.5744/florida/9780813041902.001.0001.

Forné, Mélanie. 2006. *La cronología de La Joyanca, Petén Noroccidente, Guatemala*. BAR International Series, Vol. 1572. Oxford, UK: British Archaeological Reports.

Forné, Mélanie. 2008. "Unidad Cultural y Estudio Cerámico: Un Punto de Vista desde Zapote Bobal, Noreste de Petén." In *XXI Simposio de Investigaciones Arqueológicas en Guatemala, 2007*, ed. Juan Pedro Laporte, Bárbara Arroyo, and Héctor Mejía, 892–908. Guatemala: Ministerio de Cultura y Deportes, Instituto de Antropología e Historia, Asociación Tikal, Fundación Arqueológica del Nuevo Mundo.

Forné, Mélanie, Ronald L. Bishop, Arthur A. Demarest, M. James Blackman, and Erin L. Sears. 2010. "Gris Fino, Naranja Fino: Presencia Temprana y Fuentes de Producción, El Caso de Cancuen." In *XXIII Simposio de Investigaciones Arqueológicas en Guatemala, 2009*, ed. Bárbara Arroyo, Adriana Linares, and Lorena Paiz, 1150–1169. Guatemala: Ministerio de Cultura y Deportes, Instituto de Antropología e Historia, Asociación Tikal.

Forsyth, Donald W. 1989. *The Ceramics of El Mirador, Petén, Guatemala: El Mirador Series, Part 4*. Papers of the New World Archaeological Foundation 63. Provo, UT: Brigham University.

Forsyth, Donald W. 2003. "La Cerámica del Clásico Tardío de la Cuenca Mirador." In *XVI Simposio de Investigaciones Arqueológicas en Guatemala, 2002*, ed. Juan Pedro Laporte, Bárbara Arroyo, Héctor Escobedo, and Héctor Mejía, 657–671. Guatemala: Ministerio de Cultura y Deportes, Instituto de Antropología e Historia, Asociación Tikal.

Forsyth, Donald W. 2005. "A Survey of Terminal Classic Ceramic Complexes and their Socioeconomic Implications." In *Geographies of Power: Understanding the Nature of Terminal Classic Pottery in the Maya Lowlands*, edited by Sandra L. López Varela and Antonia E. Foias, 7–22. BAR International Series 1447. Oxford: Archaeopress.

Fox, John W., Garrett W. Cook, Arlen F. Chase, and Diane Z. Chase. 1996. "Questions of Political and Economic Integration: Segmentary versus Centralized States among the Ancient Maya." *Current Anthropology* 37(5):795–801. https://doi.org/10 .1086/204563.

Freidel, David A. 1992. "Ahau as Idea and Artifacts in Classic Lowland Maya Civilization." In *Ideology and Pre-Columbian Civilization*, ed. Arthur A. Demarest and Geoffrey W. Conrad, 115–153. Santa Fe, NM: School of American Research Press.

Freidel, David A., and Héctor L. Escobedo. 2005. "Eliminando a los reyes sagrados y restableciendo a los dioses: Algunas consideraciones generals de la segunda temporada de campo en El Perú-*Waka*." In *XVIII Simposio de Investigaciones Arqueológicas en Guatemala, 2004*, ed. Juan Pedro Laporte, Bárbara Arroyo, and Héctor Mejía, 333–338. Guatemala: Ministerio de Cultura y Deportes, Instituto de Antropología e Historia, Asociación Tikal, Foundation for the Advancement of Mesoamerican Studies.

Freidel, David A., and Héctor L. Escobedo. 2014. "Stelae, Buildings, and People: Reflections on Ritual in the Archaeological Record at El Perú-Waka." In *Archaeology at El Perú-Waka': Ancient Maya Performances of Ritual, Memory, and Power*, ed. Olivia C. Navarro-Farr and Michelle Rich, 18–33. Tucson: University of Arizona Press.

Freidel, David A., and Linda Schele. 1988. "Kingship in the Late Preclassic Maya Lowlands: The Instruments and Places of Ritual Power." *American Anthropologist* 90(3):547–567. https://doi.org/10.1525/aa.1988.90.3.02a00020.

Friedman, Jonathan. 1992. "The Past in the Future: History and the Politics of Identity." *American Anthropologist* 94(4):837–859. https://doi.org/10.1525/aa.1992.94.4.02a00040.

Fry, Robert E. 1981. "Pottery Production-Distribution Systems in the Southern Maya Lowlands." In *Production and Distribution: A Ceramic Viewpoint*, ed. Hilary Howard and Elaine L. Morris, 145–168. BAR International Series, Vol. 120. Oxford, UK: Archaeopress.

Gámez, Laura L. 2009. "Operación 6, Excavaciones en el Grupo Sur." In *Proyecto Arqueológico "El Zotz" Informe No. 4: Temporada 2009*, ed. Griselda Pérez Robles, Edwin Román, and Stephen Houston, 121–154. Report submitted to the Guatemala Instituto de Antropología e Historia.

Gámez, Laura L. 2013. "Cosmology and Society: Household Ritual among the Terminal Classic (A.D. 850–950) Maya People of Yaxha, Guatemala." PhD dissertation, Department of Anthropology, University of Pittsburgh, PA.

Garber, James F. 1983. "Patterns of Jade Consumption and Disposal at Cerros, Northern Belize." *American Antiquity* 48(4):800–807. https://doi.org/10.2307/279780.

Garrido López, Jose Luis. 2014. "Excavaciones en el Grupo de los Cinco Templos (Operación 23)." In *Proyecto Arqueológico El Zotz Informe Final 2013, Temporada de Campo #8*, ed. Jose Luis Garrido López, Thomas G. Garrison, Edwin R. Román, and Stephen D. Houston, 93–102. Report submitted to the Guatemala Instituto de Antropología e Historia.

Garrido López, Jose Luis. 2015. "El Grupo de los Cinco Templos (Operación 23): Excavaciones en la Estructura L8-19 y L8-20." In *Proyecto Arqueológico El Zotz Informe Final 2014, Temporada de Campo #9*, ed. Jose Luis Garrido López, Edwin R. Román, Thomas G. Garrison, and Stephen D. Houston, 77–91. Report submitted to the Guatemala Instituto de Antropología e Historia.

Garrido López, Jose Luis, Thomas G. Garrison, Edwin R. Román, and Stephen Houston, eds. 2012. *Proyecto Arqueológico El Zotz Informe No. 7: Temporada 2012.* Report submitted to the Guatemala Instituto de Antropología e Historia.

Garrido López, Jose Luis, Thomas G. Garrison, Edwin R. Román, and Stephen Houston, eds. 2014. *Proyecto Arqueológico El Zotz, Informe Final 2013, Temporada de Campo #8.* Report submitted to the Guatemala Instituto de Antropología e Historia.

Garrido López, Jose Luis, Yeny Myshell Gutiérrez Castillo, Edwin René Román Ramirez, Thomas Garrison, and Stephen Houston, eds. 2016. *Proyecto Arqueológico El Zotz, Informe Final, 10ma Temporada de Campo.* Report submitted to the Guatemala Instituto de Antropología e Historia.

Garrido López, Jose Luis, Stephen Houston, and Edwin Román, eds. 2011. *Proyecto Arqueológico "El Zotz" Informe No. 5: Temporada 2010.* Report submitted to the Guatemala Instituto de Antropología e Historia.

Garrido López, Jose Luis, Stephen Houston, and Edwin Román, eds. 2012. *Proyecto Arqueológico El Zotz Informe No. 6: Temporada 2011.* Report submitted to the Guatemala Instituto de Antropología e Historia.

Garrido López, Jose Luis, Edwin R. Román, Thomas G. Garrison, and Stephen Houston, eds. 2015a. *Proyecto Arqueológico El Zotz, Informe Final 2014, Temporada de Campo #9.* Report submitted to the Guatemala Instituto de Antropología e Historia.

Garrido López, Jose Luis, Edwin Román, Thomas Garrison, and Stephen Houston. 2015b. "El Grupo de los Cinco Templos: La Necrópolis Real de El Zotz." In *XXVIII Simposio de Investigaciones Arqueológicas en Guatemala, 2009,* ed. Bárbara Arroyo, Luis Méndez Salinas, and Lorena Paiz, 191–196. Guatemala City: Museo Nacional de Arqueología y Etnología.

Garrison, Thomas G. 2007. "Ancient Maya Territories, Adaptive Regions, and Alliances: Contextualizing the San Bartolo-Xultun Intersite Survey." PhD dissertation, Department of Anthropology, Harvard University. Cambridge, MA.

Garrison, Thomas G. 2012. "El paisaje natural, politico, y urbano de El Zotz." Paper presented at the Museo Popol Vuh, Universidad Francisco Marroquín, Guatemala. Accessed May 21, 2016. https://newmedia.ufm.edu/gsm/index.php/Garrisonpaisajedelzotz.

Garrison, Thomas G. 2015. "Investigaciones en el Grupo Este de El Zotz." In *Proyecto Arqueológico El Zotz Informe Final 2014, Temporada de Campo #9,* ed. Jose Luis Garrido López, Edwin R. Román, Thomas G. Garrison, and

Stephen D. Houston, 59–76. Report submitted to the Guatemala Instituto de Antropología e Historia.

Garrison, Thomas G., Omar Alcover Firpi, Henry Pérez, and Andrew K. Scherer. 2017. "Investigaciones en el sitio El Palmar (Operación 10)." In *Proyecto Arqueológico El Zotz, Informe Final 2016, Temporada de Campo #11*, ed. Yeny Myshell Gutierrez Castillo, Jose Luis Garrido López, Thomas G. Garrison, Stephen Houston, and Edwin Román, 109–142. Report submitted to the Guatemala Instituto de Antropología e Historia.

Garrison, Thomas G., and Fernando Beltrán. 2011. "Investigaciones en Bejucal (Operación 1)." In *Proyecto Arqueológico "El Zotz" Informe No. 5: Temporada de Campo 2010*, ed. Jose Luis Garrido López, Stephen Houston, and Edwin Román, 293–319. Report submitted to the Guatemala Instituto de Antropología e Historia.

Garrison, Thomas G., Bruce Chapman, Stephen Houston, Edwin Román, and Jose Luis Garrido López. 2011. "Discovering Ancient Maya Settlements Using Airborne Radar Elevation Data." *Journal of Archaeological Science* 38(7):1655–1662. https://doi.org/10.1016/j.jas.2011.02.031.

Garrison, Thomas G., and David Del Cid. 2012. "Investigaciones de Rescate en Bejucal." In *Proyecto Arqueológico El Zotz Informe No. 6: Temporada 2011*, ed. Jose Luis Garrido López, Stephen Houston, Edwin Román, and Thomas Garrison, 241–254. Report submitted to the Guatemala Instituto de Antropología e Historia.

Garrison, Thomas G., and Nicholas P. Dunning. 2009. "Settlement, Environment, and Politics in the San Bartolo-Xultun Territory, El Peten, Guatemala." *Latin American Antiquity* 20(04):525–552. https://doi.org/10.1017/S1045663500002868.

Garrison, Thomas G., and Jose Luis Garrido López. 2009a. "Operaciones IR 8A, Programa de Investigaciones Regionales: Excavaciones de sondeo en el sitio La Avispa, (Cuadrantes O9 y P8)." In *Proyecto Arqueológico "El Zotz" Informe No. 4: Temporada 2009*, ed. Griselda Pérez Robles, Edwin Román, and Stephen Houston, 265–280. Report submitted to the Guatemala Instituto de Antropología e Historia.

Garrison, Thomas G., and Jose Luis Garrido López. 2009b. "Operación 1, Investigaciones en Bejucal." In *Proyecto Arqueológico "El Zotz" Informe No. 4: Temporada 2009*, ed. Griselda Pérez Robles, Edwin Román, and Stephen Houston, 249–264. Report submitted to the Guatemala Instituto de Antropología e Historia.

Garrison, Thomas G., and Jose Luis Garrido López. 2012. "Investigaciones intersitios en el reconocimiento de las Tierras Bajas." In *XXV Simposio de Investigaciones Arqueolóogicas en Guatemala, 2011*, ed. Bárbara Arroyo, Lorena Paiz, and Héctor Mejía, 1029–1044. Guatemala City: Ministerio de Cultura y Deportes, Instituto de Antropologías e Historia, Asociación Tikal.

Garrison, Thomas G., Jose Luis Garrido López, Octavio Axpuac, Alexander Smith, Timothy Beach, Sheryl Luzzadder-Beach, and Fernando Beltrán.

2011. "Investigaciones regionales en el Biotopo San Miguel la Palotada." In *Proyecto Arqueológico "El Zotz" Informe No. 5: Temporada de Campo 2010*, ed. Jose Luis Garrido López, Stephen Houston, and Edwin Román, 321–386. Report submitted to the Guatemala Instituto de Antropología e Historia.

Garrison, Thomas G., Jose Luis Garrido López, and Alyce M. de Carteret. 2012. "Investigaciones en la Estructura M7-1 (Operación 21)." In *Proyecto Arqueológico El Zotz Informe No. 7: Temporada 2012*, ed. Jose Luis Garrido López, Thomas Garrison, Edwin Román, and Stephen Houston, 59–98. Report submitted to the Guatemala Instituto de Antropología e Historia.

Garrison, Thomas G., Stephen D. Houston, Andrew K. Scherer, David Del Cid, Jose Luis Garrido López, Ewa Czapiewska-Halliday, and Edwin Román. 2016. "A Royal Maya Country House: Archaeology at Bejucal, Guatemala." *Journal of Field Archaeology* 41(5):532–549. https://doi.org/10.1080/00934690.2016.1219213.

Garrison, Thomas G., and Joshua J. Kwoka. 2012. "Programa de mapeo y reconocimiento en El Zotz y el Biótopo San Miguel la Palotada." In *Proyecto Arqueológico El Zotz Informe No. 6: Temporada 2011*, ed. Jose Luis Garrido López, Stephen Houston, Edwin Román, and Thomas Garrison, 241–254. Report submitted to the Guatemala Instituto de Antropología e Historia.

Geertz, Clifford. 2004. "What Is a State if It Is Not Sovereign? Reflections on Politics in Complicated Places." *Current Anthropology* 45(5):577–593. https://doi.org/10.1086/423972.

Genovés, Santiago. 1967. "Proportionality of Long Bones and Their Relation to Stature among Mesoamericans." *American Journal of Physical Anthropology* 26(1):67–77. https://doi.org/10.1002/ajpa.1330260109.

Gifford, James C. 1975. *Prehistoric Pottery Analysis and the Ceramics of Barton Ramie in the Belize Valley*. Memoirs of the Peabody Museum of Archaeology and Ethnology, Vol. 18. Cambridge, MA: Harvard University.

Gill, Richardson B., Paul A. Mayewski, Johan Nyberg, Gerald H. Haug, and Larry C. Peterson. 2007. "Drought and the Maya Collapse." *Ancient Mesoamerica* 18(02):283–302. https://doi.org/10.1017/S0956536107000193.

Gillot Vassaux, Alejandro. 2008a. "Grupo El Diablo (Operacion 5)." In *Proyecto Arqueológico "El Zotz" Informe No. 1: Temporada de Campo 2008*, ed. Ernesto Arredondo Leiva and Stephen Houston, 115–134. Report submitted to the Guatemala Instituto de Antropología e Historia.

Gillot Vassaux, Alejandro. 2008b. Grupo Las Palmitas (Operación 4). In *Proyecto Arqueológico "El Zotz" Informe No. 1: Temporada de Campo 2008*, ed. Ernesto Arredondo Leiva and Stephen Houston, 95–114. Report submitted to the Guatemala Instituto de Antropología e Historia.

Golden, Charles W. 2002. "Bridging the Gap between Archaeological and Indigenous Chronologies: An Investigation of the Early Classic /Late Classic Divide at Piedras Negras, Guatemala." PhD dissertation, University of Pennsylvania, Philadelphia, PA.

Golden, Charles, and Andrew K. Scherer. 2006. "Border Problems: Recent Archaeological Research along the Usumacinta River." *PARI Journal* 7(2):1–16.

Golden, Charles, and Andrew Scherer. 2013. "Territory, Trust, Growth and Collapse in Classic period Maya Kingdoms." *Current Anthropology* 54(4) 397–435.

Golden, Charles, Andrew K. Scherer, Ana Lucia Arroyave, Melanie Kingsley, Alejandro Gillot Vassaux, Rony Piedrasanta, and Gendry Valle. 2010. "Sitios desconocidos, perdidos y olvidados: Reconocimiento en el Parque Nacional Sierra del Lacandón." *XXIII Simposio de Investigaciones Arqueológicas en Guatemala, 2009*, ed. Bárbara Arroyo, Adriana Linares Palma, and Lorena Paiz Aragon, 62–74. Guatemala City: Ministerio de Cultura y Deportes, Instituto de Antropología e Historia, and Asociación Tikal.

Golden, Charles, Andrew Scherer, A. René Muñoz, and Zachary Hruby. 2012. "Polities, Boundaries, and Trade in the Classic Period Usumacinta River Basin." *Mexicon* 34:11–19.

Golden, Charles, Andrew K. Scherer, A. René Muñoz, and Rosaura Vásquez. 2008. "Piedras Negras and Yaxchilan: Divergent Political Trajectories in Adjacent Maya Polities." *Latin American Antiquity* 19(3):249–274. https://doi.org/10.1017/S104566 350000794X.

Golitko, Mark, James Meierhoff, Gary M. Feinman, and Patrick Ryan Williams. 2012. "Complexities of Collapse: The Evidence of Maya Obsidian as Revealed by Social Network Graphical Analysis." *Antiquity* 86(332):507–523. https://doi.org/10.1017 /S0003598X00062906.

Gossen, Gary H. 1974. *Chamulas in the World of the Sun: Time and Space in Maya Oral Tradition*. Cambridge, MA: Harvard University Press.

Graffam, Gray. 1992. "Beyond State Collapse: Rural History, Raised Fields, and Pastoralism in the South Andes." *American Anthropologist* 94(4):882–904. https://doi.org/10.1525/aa.1992.94.4.02a00060.

Greller, Andrew M. 2000. "Vegetation in the Floristic Regions of North and Central America." In *Imperfect Balance: Landscape Transformations in the Precolumbian Americas*, ed. David L. Lentz, 39–87. New York: Columbia University Press. https://doi.org/10.7312/lent11156-006.

Grube, Nikolai. 1992. "Classic Maya Dance: Evidence from Hieroglyphs and Iconography." *Ancient Mesoamerica* 3(2):201–218. https://doi.org/10.1017/S0956536100 00064X.

Grube, Nikolai. 2008. "Monumentos Esculpidos: Epigrafía e iconografía." In *Reconocimiento Arqueológico en el Sureste del Estado de Campeche, México: 1996—2005*, ed. Ivan Šprajc, 177–231. BAR International Series, Vol. 1742. Oxford, UK: Archaeopress.

Grube, Nikolai, and Linda Schele. 1994. "Kuy, the Owl of Omen and War." *Mexicon* 16(1):10–17.

Guenter, Stanley P. 2007. "The Emblem Glyph of El Peru." *The PARI Journal* 8(2):20–23.

Guenter, Stanley P. 2014. "The Epigraphy of El Perú-Waka'." In *Archaeology at El Perú-Waka': Ancient Maya Performances of Ritual, Memory, and Power*, ed. Olivia C. Navarro-Farr and Michelle Rich, 147–166. Tucson: University of Arizona Press.

Guernsey Kappelman, Julia. 2001. "Sacred Geography at Izapa and the Performance of Rulership." In *Landscape and Power in Ancient Mesoamerica*, ed. Rex Koontz, Kathryn Reese-Taylor, and Annabeth Headrick, 81–111. Boulder, CO: Westview Press.

Gutiérrez Castillo, Yeny M. 2015. "Análisis de artefactos malacológicos provenientes del sitio arqueológico El Zotz, Guatemala." Licenciatura tesis, Universidad de San Carlos de Guatemala.

Gutiérrez, Yeny Myshell, Alyce de Carteret, and Edwin Román. 2012. "Excavaciones en el Grupo El Diablo (Operación 19)." In *Proyecto Arqueológico El Zotz Informe No. 7: Temporada 2012*, ed. Jose Luis Garrido López, Thomas Garrison, Edwin Román, and Stephen Houston, 17–46. Report submitted to the Guatemala Instituto de Antropología e Historia.

Gutiérrez, Yeny Myshell, and Edwin Román. 2015. "Excavaciones en el Grupo El Diablo (Operación 19)." In *Proyecto Arqueológico El Zotz Informe Final 2014, Temporada de Campo #9*, ed. Jose Luis Garrido López, Edwin R. Román, Thomas G. Garrison, and Stephen D. Houston, 19–43. Report submitted to the Guatemala Instituto de Antropología e Historia.

Gutiérrez, Yeny Myshell, and Edwin Román. 2014. "Excavaciones en el Grupo El Diablo (Operación 19)." In *Proyecto Arqueológico El Zotz Informe Final 2013, Temporada de Campo #8*, ed. Jose Luis Garrido López, Thomas G. Garrison, Edwin R. Román, and Stephen D. Houston, 15–42. Report submitted to the Guatemala Instituto de Antropología e Historia.

Gutiérrez Castillo, Yeny Myshell, Jose Luis Garrido López, Thomas G. Garrison, Stephen Houston, and Edwin Román, eds. 2017. *Proyecto Arqueológico El Zotz, Informe Final, 11 Temporada de Campo*. Report submitted to the Guatemala Instituto de Antropología e Historia.

Halperin, Christina T. 2004. "Realeza maya y figurillas con tocados de la Serpiente de Guerra de Motul de San José, Guatemala." *Mayab* 17:45–60.

Halperin, Christina T. 2007. "Materiality, Bodies, and Practice: The Political Economy of Late Classic Maya Figurines from Motul de San José, Petén, Guatemala." PhD dissertation, Department of Anthropology, University of California at Riverside.

Halperin, Christina T. 2010. "Maya State Collapse and Changes in Household Ritual: History-Making from a Microscale Perspective." Paper Presented at the 75th Annual Meeting of the Society for American Archaeology, St. Louis, MO.

Halperin, Christina T. 2011. "Late Classic Maya Textile Economies: An Object History Approach." In *Textile Economies: Power and Value from the Local to the Transnational*, ed. Walter E. Little and Patricia A. McAnany, 125–145. Lanham, MD: Altamira Press.

Halperin, Christina T. 2014. *Maya Figurines: Intersections between State and Household.* Austin: University of Texas Press.

Halperin, Christina T., and Antonia E. Foias. 2010. "Pottery Politics: Late Classic Maya Palace Production at Motul de San José, Petén, Guatemala." *Journal of Anthropological Archaeology* 29(3):392–411. https://doi.org/10.1016/j.jaa.2010.06.001.

Hammond, Norman. 1975. *Lubaantun: A Classic Maya Realm.* Cambridge, MA: Peabody Museum of Archaeology and Ethnology, Harvard University.

Hammond, Norman. 1993. "Matrices and Maya Archaeology." In *Practices of Archaeological Stratigraphy*, ed. Edward C. Harris, Marley R. Brown, and Gregory J. Brown, 139–152. London: Academic Press. https://doi.org/10.1016/B978-0-12-326445-9.50016-2.

Hansen, Richard D. 1998. "Continuity and Disjunction: The Pre-Classic Antecedents of Classic Maya Architecture." In *Function and Meaning in Classic Maya Architecture*, ed. Stephen D. Houston, 49–122. Washington, DC: Dumbarton Oaks Research Library and Collection.

Hansen, Richard D., Ronald L. Bishop, and Federico Fahsen. 1991. "Notes on Codex-Style Ceramics from Nakbe, Peten, Guatemala." *Ancient Mesoamerica* 2(02):225–243. https://doi.org/10.1017/S0956536100000547.

Hansen, Richard D., Stephen Bozarth, John Jacob, David Wahl, and Thomas Schreiner. 2002. "Climatic and Environmental Variability in the Rise of Maya Civilization: A Preliminary Perspective from Northern Peten." *Ancient Mesoamerica* 13(02):273–295. https://doi.org/10.1017/S0956536102132093.

Hansen, Richard D., Wayne K. Howell, and Stanley P. Guenter. 2008. "Forgotten Structures, Haunted Houses, and Occupied Hearts: Ancient Perspectives and Contemporary Interpretations of Abandoned Sites and Buildings in the Mirador Basin, Guatemala." In *Ruins of the Past: The Use and Perception of Abandoned Structures in the Maya Lowlands*, ed. Travis W. Stanton and Aline Magnoni, 25–64. Boulder: University Press of Colorado.

Hansen, Richard D., Edgar Suyuc Ley, and Héctor Mejía. 2011. "Resultados de la temporada de investigaciones 2009: Proyecto Cuenca Mirador." In *XXIV Simposio de Investigaciones Arqueológicas en Guatemala, 2010*, ed. Bárbara Arroyo, Lorena Pais Aragón, Adriana Linares Palma, and Ana Lucía Arroyave, 187–204. Guatemala: Ministerio de Cultura y Deportes, Instituto de Antropología e Historia, Asociación Tikal.

Hansen, Thomas Blom, and Finn Stepputat. 2006. "Sovereignty Revisited." *Annual Review of Anthropology* 35(1):295–315. https://doi.org/10.1146/annurev.anthro.35.081705.123317.

Harris, Edward C. 1975. "The Stratigraphic Sequence: A Question of Time." *World Archaeology* 7(1):109–121. https://doi.org/10.1080/00438243.1975.9979624.

Harris, Edward C. 1989. *Principles of Archaeological Stratigraphy*. 2nd ed. London: Academic Press.

Haviland, William A. 1967. "Stature at Tikal, Guatemala: Implications for Ancient Maya Demography and Social Organization." *American Antiquity* 32(03):316–325. https://doi.org/10.2307/2694660.

Haviland, William A. 1981. "Dower Houses and Minor Centers at Tikal, Guatemala: An Investigation into the Identification of Valid Units in Settlement Hierarchies." In *Lowland Maya Settlement Patterns*, ed. Wendy Ashmore, 89–120. Albuquerque: University of New Mexico Press.

Haviland, William A. 1985. *Excavations in Small Residential Groups of Tikal: Groups 4F-1 and 4F-2 Tikal Reports No. 19*. Philadelphia: University Museum Publications, University of Pennsylvania.

Haviland, William A. 2014. *Excavations in Residential Areas of Tikal: Non-Elite Groups without Shrines: The Excavations*. Tikal Reports 20. Philadelphia: University Museum, University of Pennsylvania.

Healan, Daniel M. 2004. "Extracción prehispanica de obsidiana en el área de Ucareo-Zinapecuaro, Michoacán." In *Bienes Estratégicos del Antiguo Occidente de México*, ed. Eduardo Williams, 33–76. Zamora: Colegio de Michoacán.

Healan, Daniel M. 2006. "The Long and Short of Prismatic Blades." *Human Mosaic* 36:29–36.

Healan, Daniel M. 2009. "Ground Platform Preparation and the 'Banalization' of the Prismatic Blade in Western Mesoamerica." *Ancient Mesoamerica* 20(01):103–111. https://doi.org/10.1017/S0956536109000108.

Hendon, Julia A. 1991. "Status and Power in Classic Maya Society: An Archaeological Study." *American Anthropologist* 93(4):894–918. https://doi.org/10.1525/aa.1991.93.4.02a00070.

Hendon, Julia A. 2003. "In the House: Maya Nobility and Their Figurine-Whistles." *Expedition* 45(3):28–33.

Hernández, Danilo, and Jose Garrido. 2016. "Excavaciones en el Grupo de Los Cinco Templos: Operación 23." In *Proyecto Arqueológico El Zotz Informe Final: 10ma Temporada de Campo*, ed. Jose Luis Garrido López, Yeny Myshell Gutiérrez Castillo, Edwin René Román Ramirez, Thomas Garrison, and Stephen Houston, 37–60. Report submitted to the Guatemala Instituto de Antropología e Historia.

Hernández, Patricia, and Lourdes Márquez. 2006. "Longevity of Maya Rulers of Yaxchilán." In *Janaab' Pakal of Palenque: Reconstructing the Life and Death of a Maya Ruler*, ed. V. Tiesler and A. Cucina, 126–145. Tucson: University of Arizona Press.

Heyden, Doris. 1981. "Caves, Gods, and Myths: World-View and Planning in Teotihuacan." In *Mesoamerican Sites and World Views*, ed. Elizabeth P. Benson, 1–39. Washington, DC: Dumbarton Oaks Research Library and Collection.

Heyden, Doris. 2000. "From Teotihuacan to Tenochtitlan: City Planning, Caves, and Streams of Red and Blue Waters." In *Mesoamerica's Classic Heritage from Teotihuacan to the Aztecs*, ed. Davíd Carrasco, Lindsay Jones, and Scott Sessions, 165–184. Boulder: University Press of Colorado.

Hill, Warren D., and John Clark. 2001. "Sports, Gambling, and Government: America's First Social Compact?" *American Anthropologist* 102:467–484.

Holdridge, Leslie R., and William C. Grenke, W. H. Hatheway, T. Liang, and J. A. Tosi Jr. 1971. *Forest Environments in Tropical Life Zones: A Pilot Study*. Oxford, UK: Pergamon Press.

Holley, George. 1983. "Ceramic Change at Piedras Negras, Guatemala." PhD dissertation, Department of Anthropology, Southern Illinois University, Carbondale, IL.

Houk, Brett A. 2003. "The Ties that Bind: Site Planning in the Three Rivers Region." In *Heterarchy, Political Economy, and the Ancient Maya: The Three Rivers Region of the East-Central Yucatan Peninsula*, ed. Vernon L. Scarborough, Fred Valdez, Jr., and Nicholas Dunning, 52–63. Tucson: University of Arizona Press.

Houston, Stephen D. 1984. "An Example of Homophony in the Maya Script." *American Antiquity* 49(04):790–805. https://doi.org/10.2307/279744.

Houston, Stephen D. 1987. "The Inscriptions and Monumental Art of Dos Pilas, Guatemala: A Study of Classic Maya History and Politics." PhD dissertation, Department of Anthropology, Yale University, New Haven, CT.

Houston, Stephen D. 1992. "A Name Glyph for Classic Maya Dwarfs." In *The Maya Vase Book: A Corpus of Rollout Photographs of Maya Vases 3*, ed. Justin Kerr, 526–531. New York: Kerr Associates.

Houston, Stephen D. 2007. "Interpretaciones acerca del sitio El Palmar y el grupo de Las Palmitas." In *Proyecto Arqueológico El Zotz Informe no. 2: Temporada 2007*, ed. Stephen D. Houston and Héctor L. Escobedo, 15–18. Report submitted to the Guatemala Instituto de Antropología e Historia.

Houston, Stephen D. 2008a. "The Epigraphy of El Zotz." Accessed May 21, 2016. www.mesoweb.com/zotz/articles/ZotzEpigraphy.pdf.

Houston, Stephen D. 2008b. "In the Shadow of a Giant." Accessed May 21, 2016. http://www.mesoweb.com/zotz/articles/Shadow-of-a-Giant.pdf.

Houston, Stephen D. 2009. "A Splendid Predicament: Young Men in Classic Maya Society." *Cambridge Archaeological Journal* 19(2):149–178. https://doi.org/10.1017/S0959774309000250.

Houston, Stephen D. 2014. "Deathly Sport." *Maya Decipherment: Ideas on Ancient Maya Writing and Iconography.* Accessed July 19, 2016. https://decipherment.wordpress.com/2014/07/29/deathly-sport/.

Houston, Stephen D. 2016. "Recrowned Kingdoms." *Maya Decipherment: Ideas on Ancient Maya Writing and Iconography.* Accessed February 1, 2017. https://decipherment.wordpress.com/2016/12/21/recrowned-kingdoms/.

Houston, Stephen D., Héctor Escobedo, Donald Forsyth, Perry Hardin, David L. Webster, and Lori E. Wright. 1998. "On the River of Ruins: Explorations at Piedras Negras, Guatemala, 1997." *Mexicon* XX:16–21.

Houston, Stephen, Hector L. Escobedo, and Cassandra L. Mesick. 2011. "Creating a Cityscape: Construction Technology at Piedras Negras, Guatemala." In *Representaciones y espacios públicos en el area maya: Un estudio interdisciplinario,* ed. Rodrigo Liendo Stuardo and Francisca Zalacquett Rock, 23–36. DF, Mexico: Universidad Nacional Autónoma de México.

Houston, Stephen D., and Takeshi Inomata. 2009. *The Classic Maya.* New York: Cambridge University Press.

Houston, Stephen, and Simon Martin. 2016. "Through Seeing Stones: Maya Epigraphy as a Mature Discipline." *Antiquity* 90(350):443–455. https://doi.org/10.15184/aqy.2016.33

Houston, Stephen D., Zachary Nelson, Héctor L. Escobedo, Juan Carlos Meléndez, Ana Lucía Arroyave, Fabiola Quiroa, and Rafael Cambranes, eds. 2006. *Levantamiento Preliminar y Actividades de Registro en El Zotz, Biotopo San Miguel la Palotada, Petén.* Report submitted to the Guatemala Instituto de Antropología e Historia.

Houston, Stephen, Sarah Newman, Edwin Román, and Nicholas Carter. 2015. "A Temple over Time." In *Temple of the Night Sun: A Royal Tomb at El Diablo, Guatemala,* by Stephen Houston, Sarah Newman, Edwin Román, and Thomas Garrison, 30–83. San Francisco, CA: Precolumbia Mesoweb Press.

Houston, Stephen, Sarah Newman, Edwin Román, and Thomas Garrison. 2015. *Temple of the Night Sun: A Royal Tomb at El Diablo, Guatemala.* San Francisco, CA: Precolumbia Mesoweb Press.

Houston, Stephen, Edwin Román, Thomas Garrison, Timothy Beach, Sheryl Luzzadder-Beach, Zachary Hruby, Nicholas Carter, James Doyle, Jose Luis Garrido, Arturo Godoy, et al. 2011. "Al Valle de Buenavista: Investigaciones Recientes en el Centro Dinástico de El Zotz y sus Cercanias." In *XXIV Simposio de Investigaciones Arqueologicas en Guatemala, 2010*, ed. Bárbara Arroyo, Lorena Pais Aragón, Adriana Linares Palma, and Ana Lucía Arroyave, 227–236. Guatemala: Ministerio de Cultura y Deportes, Instituto de Antropología e Historia, Asociación Tikal.

Houston, Stephen D., Edwin Román, Thomas Garrison, Jose Luis Garrido, Nicholas Carter, James Doyle, Elsa Dámaris Menéndez, Sarah Newman, and Melanie Kingsley. 2012. "En la vista de P*a' Chan*: Procesos dinámicos en El Zotz, Peten y sus cercanías." In *XXV Simposio de Investigaciones Arqueológicas en Guatemala, 2011*, ed. Bárbara Arroyo, Lorena Paiz, and Héctor Mejía, 181–192. Guatemala City: Ministerio de Cultura y Deportes, Instituto de Antropologías e Historia, Asociación Tikal.

Houston, Stephen D., and Andrew K. Scherer. 2010. "La Ofrenda Máxima: El Sacrificio Humano en la Parte Central del Área Maya." In *Nuevas Perspectivas Sobre el Sacrificio Humano entre los Mexicas*, ed. Leonardo López Luján and Guilhem Olivier, 167–191. Mexico City: Instituto Nacional de Antropología e Historia, Mexico.

Houston, Stephen D., and David Stuart. 1989. *The Way Glyph: Evidence for 'Co-Essences' among the Classic Maya*. Research Reports on Ancient Maya Writing 30. Washington, DC: Center for Maya Research.

Houston, Stephen, David Stuart, and Karl Taube. 2006. *The Memory of Bones: Body, Being, and Experience among the Classic Maya*. Austin: University of Texas Press.

Houston, Stephen D., and Karl A. Taube. 2000. "An Archaeology of the Senses: Perceptions and Cultural Expression in Ancient Mesoamerica." *Cambridge Archaeological Journal* 10(2):261–294. https://doi.org/10.1017/S095977430000010X.

Hruby, Zachary. 2006. "The Organization of Chipped-Stone Economies at Piedras Negras, Guatemala." PhD dissertation, Department of Anthropology, University of California, Riverside.

Hruby, Zachary. 2007. "Ritualized Chipped-Stone Production at Piedras Negras, Guatemala." In *Rethinking Specialization in Complex Societies: Archaeological Analysis of the Social Meaning of Production*, ed. Zachary Hruby and Rowan K. Flad, 68–87. The Archeological Papers of the American Anthropological Association, No. 17. Arlington, VA: American Anthropological Association. https://doi.org/10.1525/ap3a.2007.17.1.68.

Hruby, Zachary, Helios J. Hernandez, and Brian Clark. 2007. "Análisis Preliminar de los artefactos líticos de Holmul, Cival, y La Sufricaya, Péten." In *XX Simposio de Investigaciones Arqueológicas en Guatemala, 2006*, ed. Juan Pedro Laporte,

Bárbara Arroyo, and Héctor Mejía, 1274–1283. Guatemala: Ministerio de Cultura y Deportes, Instituto de Antropología e Historia, Asociación Tikal, Fundación Arqueológica del Nuevo Mundo.

Hruby, Zachary, and Michelle Rich. 2014. "Flint for the Dead: Ritual Deposition of Production Debitage from El Perú-Waka', Burial 39." In *Archaeology at El Perú-Waka': Ancient Maya Performances of Ritual, Memory, and Power*, ed. Olivia C. Navarro-Farr and Michelle Rich, 167–183. Tucson: University of Arizona Press.

Hull, Kerry. 2005. *An Abbreviated Dictionary of Ch'orti' Maya*. Foundation for the Advancement of Mesoamerican Studies. Accessed May 21, 2016. www.famsi.org /reports/03031/03031.pdf.

Hyman, David S. 1970. *Precolumbian Cements: A Study in the Calcareous Cements in Prehispanic Mesoamerican Building Construction*. Baltimore, MD: John Hopkins University Press.

Inomata, Takeshi. 1997. "The Last Day of a Fortified Classic Maya center: Archaeological Investigations at Aguateca, Guatemala." *Ancient Mesoamerica* 8(02):337–351. https://doi.org/10.1017/S0956536100001772.

Inomata, Takeshi. 2001. "The Power and Ideology of Artistic Creation: Elite Craft Specialists in Classic Maya Society." *Current Anthropology* 42:321–349.

Inomata, Takeshi. 2003. "War, Destruction, and Abandonment: The Fall of the Classic Maya Center of Aguateca, Guatemala." In *The Archaeology of Settlement Abandonment in Middle America*, ed. Takeshi Inomata and Ronald W. Webb, 43–60. Salt Lake City: University of Utah Press.

Inomata, Takeshi. 2006. "Plaza, Performers, and Spectators: Political Theaters of the Classic Maya." *Current Anthropology* 47(5):805–842. https://doi.org/10.1086 /506279.

Inomata, Takeshi. 2014. "War, Violence, and Society in the Maya Lowlands." In *Embattled Places, Embattled Bodies: War In Pre-Columbian America*, ed. Andrew K. Scherer and John W. Verano, 25–56. Washington, DC: Dumbarton Oaks Research Library and Collection.

Inomata, Takeshi, and Stephen D. Houston. 2001. *Royal Courts of the Ancient Maya*. 2 vols. Boulder: Westview Press.

Inomata, Takeshi, Jessica MacLellan, and Melissa Burham. 2015. "The Construction of Public and Domestic Spheres in the Preclassic Maya Lowlands." *American Anthropologist* 117(3):519–534. https://doi.org/10.1111/aman.12285.

Inomata, Takeshi, Jessica MacLellan, Daniela Triadan, Jessica Munson, Melissa Burham, Kazuo Aoyama, Hiroo Nasu, Flory Pinzón, and Hitoshi Yonenobu. 2015. "The Development of Sedentary Communities in the Maya Lowlands: Co-Existing Mobile Groups and Public Ceremonies at Ceibal, Guatemala."

Proceedings of the National Academy of Sciences of the United States of America 112(14):4268–4273. https://doi.org/10.1073/pnas.1501212112.

Inomata, Takeshi, Erick Ponciano, Oswaldo Chinchilla, Otto Román, Véronique Breuil-Martínez, and Oscar Santos. 2004. "An Unfinished Temple at the Classic Maya Centre of Aguateca, Guatemala." *Antiquity* 78(302):798–811. https://doi.org /10.1017/S0003598X00113456.

Inomata, Takeshi, Daniela Triadan, Kazuo Aoyama, Victor Castillo, and Hitoshi Yonenobu. 2013. "Early Ceremonial Constructions at Ceibal, Guatemala, and the Origins of Lowland Maya Civilization." *Science* 340(6131):467–471. https://doi.org /10.1126/science.1234493.

Inomata, Takeshi, Daniela Triadan, and Otto Rodrigo Román. 2010. "Desarrollo de las comunidades preclásicas e interacciones entre las tierras bajas y el área olmeca." In *XXIII Simposio de Investigaciones Arqueológicas en Guatemala, 2009*, ed. B. Arroyo, A. Linares Palma, and L. Paiz Aragon, 47–61. Guatemala City: Museo Nacional de Arqueología y Etnología.

Ivic de Monterroso, Matilde. 2000. "Las figurillas de Piedras Negras: Un análisis preliminar." In *XIII Simposio de Investigaciones Arqueológicas en Guatemala, 1999*, ed. Juan Pedro Laporte, Héctor Escobedo, Bárbara Arroyo, and Ana Claudia de Suasnávar, 243–257. Guatemala: Museo Nacional de Arqueología y Etnología.

Ivic de Monterroso, Matilde. 2002. "Resultados de los análisis de las figurillas de Piedras Negras." In *XV Simposio de Investigaciones Arqueológicas en Guatemala, 2001*, ed. Juan Pedro Laporte, Héctor Escobedo, and Bárbara Arroyo, 480–494. Guatemala: Museo Nacional de Arqueología y Etnología.

Jackson, Sarah E. 2013. *Politics of the Maya Court: Hierarchy and Change in the Late Classic Period*. Austin: University of Texas Press.

Joffe, Alexander H. 1998. "Disembedded Capitals in Western Asian Perspective." *Comparative Studies in Society and History* 40(03):549–580. https://doi.org/10.1017 /S0010417598001406.

Johnson, Kevin D., Richard Terry, Mark Jackson, and Charles Golden. 2007. "Ancient Soil Resources of the Usumacinta River Region, Guatemala." *Journal of Archaeological Science* 34(7):1117–1129. https://doi.org/10.1016/j.jas.2006.10.004.

Jones, Christopher. 1996. *Excavations in the East Plaza of Tikal*. 2 vols. Tikal Report 16. Philadelphia: University Museum, University of Pennsylvania.

Jones, Grant D. 1998. *The Conquest of the Last Maya Kingdom*. Stanford, CA: Stanford University Press.

Jones, John G. 1994. "Pollen Evidence for Early Settlement and Agriculture in Northern Belize." *Palynology* 18(1):205–211. https://doi.org/10.1080/01916122.1994.9 989445.

Joyce, Rosemary A. 1993. "Women's Work: Images of Production and Reproduction in Pre-Hispanic Southern Central America." *Current Anthropology* 34(3):255–274. https://doi.org/10.1086/204167.

Joyce, Thomas A. 1933. "The Pottery Whistle-Figurines of Lubaantun." *Journal of the Royal Anthropological Institute of Great Britain and Ireland* 63:xv–xxv. https://doi.org/10.2307/2843907.

Just, Bryan, with contributions by Christina T. Halperin, Antonia E. Foias, and Sarah Nunberg. 2012. *Dancing into Dreams: Maya Vase Painting of the Ik' Kingdom.* Princeto, NJ: Princeton University Art Museum.

Kerr, Justin. 1989. "A Maya Vase from the Ik Site." *Record of the Art Museum, Princeton University* 48(2):32. https://doi.org/10.2307/3774732.

Killick, David. 2004. "Social Constructionist Approaches to the Study of Technology." *World Archaeology* 36(4):571–578. https://doi.org/10.1080/0043824042000303746.

King, Eleanor M. 2000. "The Organization of Late Classic Lithic Production at The Prehistoric Maya Site of Colha, Belize: A Study in Complexity and Hierarchy." PhD dissertation, Department of Anthropology, University of Pennsylvania, Philadelphia.

King, Stacie M., and Gonzalo Sánchez Santiago. 2011. "Soundscapes of the Everyday in Ancient Oaxaca, Mexico." *Archaeologies* 7(2):387–422. https://doi.org/10.1007/s11759-011-9171-y.

Kingsley, Melanie J. 2014. "In the Wake of 'Collapse': Life at El Zotz, Guatemala during the Early Postclassic Period." PhD dissertation, Department of Anthropology, Brandeis University, Waltham, MA.

Kingsley, Melanie J., and Rafael Cambranes. 2011. "Excavaciones en el Grupo Sur de El Zotz (Operación 6)." In *Proyecto Arqueológico "El Zotz" Informe No. 5: Temporada de Campo 2010,* ed. Jose Luis Garrido López, Stephen Houston, and Edwin Román, 163–198. Report submitted to the Guatemala Instituto de Antropología e Historia.

Kingsley, Melanie, Charles Golden, Andrew Scherer, and Luz Midilia Marroquin Franco. 2010. *Proyecto Regional Arqueológico Sierra Del Lacandón, 2010, Informe Preliminar No. 8.* Report submitted to the Guatemala Instituto de Antropología e Historia.

Kingsley, Melanie, Charles Golden, Andrew Scherer, and Luz Midilia Marroquin Franco. 2012. "Parallelism in Occupation: Tracking the Pre- and Post-Dynastic Evolution of Piedras Negras, Guatemala through its Secondary Site, El Porvenir." *Mexicon* 34(5):109–117.

Kingsley, Melanie, and André Rivas. 2012. "Excavaciones en el Grupo Sur." In *Proyecto Arqueológico "El Zotz" Informe No. 6, Temporada 2011,* ed. Jose Luis Garrido, Stephen Houston, Edwin Román, and Thomas Garrison, 107–138. Report submitted to the Guatemala Instituto de Antropología e Historia.

Knodell, Alex R., and Thomas G. Garrison. 2011. "Levantamiento topográfico de El Zotz." In *Proyecto Arqueológico "El Zotz" Informe No. 5: Temporada de Campo 2010*, ed. Jose Luis Garrido López, Stephen Houston, and Edwin Román, 387–394. Report submitted to the Guatemala Instituto de Antropología e Historia.

Koontz, Rex, Kathryn Reese-Taylor, and Annabeth Headrick, eds. 2001. *Landscape and Power in Ancient Mesoamerica*. Boulder: Westview Press.

Kováč, Milan, and Ernesto Arredondo, eds. 2011. *Nuevas excavaciones en Uaxactun III*. Bratislava, Slovakia: Slovak Archaeological and Historical Institute.

Krempel, Guido, and Albert Davletshin. 2014. "Tres fragmentos de la Estela 5 procedente del sitio Acté, Petén, Guatemala, y el pronombre ergativo de la segunda persona plural en la lengua jeroglífica maya." *Mexicon* 36(2):35–39.

Kruft, Hanno-Walter. 1994. *A History of Architectural Theory from Vitruvius to the Present*. Trans. Ronald Taylor, Elsie Callander, and Anthony Wood. London: Zwemmer; New York: Princeton Architectural Press.

Kwoka, Joshua J. 2014. "Ideological Presentism and the Study of Ancient Technology: Preclassic Maya Lithic Production at San Bartolo, Guatemala." PhD dissertation, Department of Anthropology, State University of New York, Buffalo.

Landels, John G. 2000. *Engineering in the Ancient World*. Revised Edition. Berkeley: University of California Press.

Laporte, Juan Pedro. 2006. "Trabajos no divulgados del Proyecto Nacional Tikal, Parte 4: Rescate en El Zotz, San José, Petén." In *XIX Simposio de Investigaciones Arqueológicas en Guatemala, 2005*, ed. Juan Pedro Laporte, Bárbara Arroyo, and Héctor Mejía, 877–894. Guatemala: Ministerio de Cultura y Deportes, IDAEH, Asociación Tikal, Fundación Arqueológica del Nuevo Mundo.

Laporte, Juan Pedro. 2007. *La Secuencia Cerámica del Sureste de Petén: Tipos, Cifras, Localidades, y la Historia del Asentamiento*. Monografías Atlas Arqueológico de Guatemala. Guatemala City: Instituto de Antropología e Historia.

Laporte, Juan Pedro. 2009. "El embrujo del tecolote y otras historietas: Algunas consideraciones sobre los silbatos del Clásico en Tikal." In *XXII Simposio de Investigaciones Arqueológicas en Guatemala, 2008*, ed. Juan Pedro Laporte, Bárbara Arroyo, and Héctor Mejía, 1021–1050. Guatemala: Museo Nacional de Arqueología y Etnología.

Laporte, Juan Pedro, and Vilma Fialko. 1985. *Reporte Arqueológico (1979–1984): Mundo Perdido y Zonas de Habitación, Tikal, Petén*. Guatemala City, Guatemala: Ministerios de Educación y Comunicaciones Transporte y Obras Públicas.

Laporte, Juan Pedro, and Vilma Fialko. 1995. "Un Reencuentro con Mundo Perdido, Tikal, Guatemala." *Ancient Mesoamerica* 6:41–94. https://doi.org/10.1017/S09565 36100002108.

Laporte, Juan Pedro, and Juan Antonio Valdés, eds. 1993. *Tikal y Uaxactun en el Preclásico*. DF, Mexico: Universidad Autonoma de Mexico.

Larsen, Clark Spencer. 2002. "Bioarchaeology: The Lives and Lifestyles of Past People." *Journal of Archaeological Research* 10(2):119–166. https://doi.org/10.102 3/A:1015267705803.

Larsen, Clark Spencer. 2006. "The Changing Face of Bioarchaeology: An Interdisciplinary Science." In *Bioarchaeology: The Contextual Analysis of Human Remains*, ed. Jane E. Buikstra and Lane A. Beck, 359–374. Burlington, MA: Academic Press.

Larsen, Clark S., Alfred W. Crosby, Mark C. Griffin, Dale L. Hutchinson, Christopher B. Ruff, Katherine F. Russell, Margaret J. Schoeninger, Leslie E. Sering, Scott W. Simpson, Jeffry L. Takács, et al. 2002. "A Biohistory of Health and Behavior in the Georgia Bight: The Agricultural Transition and the Impact of European Contact." In *Health and Nutrition in the Western Hemispher*, ed. Richard. H. Steckel and Jerome C. Rose, 406–439. Cambridge, UK: Cambridge University Press. https://doi.org/10.1017/CBO9780511549953.019.

LeCount, Lisa J. 1996. *Pottery and Power: Feasting, Gifting, and Displaying Wealth among the Late and Terminal Classic Lowland Maya.* Los Angeles: Department of Anthropology, University of California.

Lemonnier, Pierre. 1986. "The Study of Material Culture Today: Toward an Anthropology of Technical Systems." *Journal of Anthropological Archaeology* 5(2):147–186. https://doi.org/10.1016/0278-4165(86)90012-7.

Lemonnier, Pierre. 1992. "Leroi-Gourhan: Ethnologue des Techniques." *Les Nouvelles de l'Archéologie* 48(9):13–17.

Lemonnier, Pierre, ed. 1993. *Technological Choices: Transformation in Material Culture Since the Neolithic.* New York: Routledge.

Leroi-Gourhan, André. 1943. *Evolution et Techniques: l'Homme et la Matière.* Paris: Albin Michel.

Leroi-Gourhan, André. 1945. *Evolution et Techniques: Milieu et Techniques* Paris: Albin Michel.

Lesure, Richard G. 1997. "Early Formative Platforms at Paso de la Amada, Chiapas, Mexico." *Latin American Antiquity* 8(3):217–235. https://doi.org/10.2307/971653.

Lesure, Richard G. 1999. "Platform Architecture and Activity Patterns in an Early Mesoamerican Village in Chiapas, Mexico." *Journal of Field Archaeology* 26(4):391–406.

Lincoln, Bruce. 1994. *Authority: Construction and Corrosion.* Chicago, IL: University of Chicago Press.

Liu, Raymond, C. Edward Clapp, and H. H. Cheng. 1997. "Usefulness of the Carbon–13 Tracer Technique for Characterizing Terrestrial Carbon Pools." *Nutrient Cycling in Agroecosystems* 49(1/3):261–266. https://doi.org/10.1023/A:1009783825283.

Lohse, Jon C. 2010. "Archaic Origins of the Lowland Maya." *Latin American Antiquity* 21(3):312–352. https://doi.org/10.7183/1045-6635.21.3.312.

Looper, Matthew, and Yuri Polyukhovych. 2016. "Familial Relationship between Nobles of El Peru (Waka') and El Zotz (Pa'chan) as Recorded on a Polychrome Vessel." *Glyph Dweller Report* 47. Accessed Sept. 7, 2016. http://glyphdwellers.com/pdf/R47.pdf.

López Austin, Alfredo. 1988. *The Human Body and Ideology: Concepts of the Ancient Nahuas*. 2 vols. Trans. T. Ortiz de Montellano and B. Oritz de Montellano. Salt Lake City: University of Utah Press.

Lopez-Finn, Elliot M. 2014. "Defining the Red Background Style: The Production of Object and Identity in an Ancient Maya Court." Master's thesis, Department of Art and Art History, University of Texas at Austin.

López Varela, Sandra L. 1989. *Análisis y clasificación de la ceramic de un sitio maya del Clásico: Yaxchilan, México*. BAR International Series 535. Oxford, UK: Archaeopress.

Loten, Stanley H., and David M. Pendergast. 1984. *A Lexicon for Maya Architecture*. Royal Ontario Museum Archaeology Monograph No. 8. Toronto: Royal Ontario Museum.

Love, Bruce. 1987. *Glyph T93 and Maya Hand-Scattering Events*. Research Reports on Ancient Maya Writing 5. Washington, DC: Center for Maya Research.

Lucero, Lisa J. 1999. "Classic Lowland Maya Political Organization: A Review." *Journal of World Prehistory* 13(2):211–263. https://doi.org/10.1023/A:1022337629210.

Lucero, Lisa. 2001. *Social Integration in the Ancient Maya Hinterlands: Ceramic Variability in the Belize River Area*. Anthroplogical Resaerch Paper No. 53. Tempe: Arizona State University Press.

Lucero, Lisa J. 2003. "The Politics of Ritual: The Emergence of Classic Maya Rulers." *Current Anthropology* 44(4):523–558. https://doi.org/10.1086/375870.

Lundell, Charles L. 1937. *The Vegetation of Petén—with an appendix—Studies of Mexican and Central American Plants, I*. Publication 478. Washington, DC: Carnegie Institution of Washington.

Luzzadder-Beach, Sheryl, and Timothy Beach. 2008. "Water Chemistry Constraints and Possibilities for Ancient and Contemporary Maya Wetlands." *Journal of Ethnobiology* 28(2):211–230. https://doi.org/10.2993/0278-0771-28.2.211.

Luzzadder-Beach, Sheryl, and Timothy Beach. 2009. "Arising from the Wetlands: Mechanisms and Chronology of Landscape Aggradation in the Northern Coastal Plain of Belize." *Annals of the Association of American Geographers* 99(1):1–26. https://doi.org/10.1080/00045600802458830.

Luzzadder-Beach, Sheryl, Timothy Beach, and Nicholas P. Dunning. 2012. "Wetland Fields as Mirrors of Drought and the Maya Abandonment." *Proceedings of the National Academy of Sciences of the United States of America* 109(10):3646–3651. https://doi.org/10.1073/pnas.114919109.

Luzzadder-Beach, Sheryl, Timothy Beach, Scott Hutson, and Samantha Krause. 2016. "Sky-Earth, Lake-Sea: Climate and Water in Maya History and Landscape." *Antiquity* 90(350):426–442. https://doi.org/10.15184/aqy.2016.38.

Luzzadder-Beach, Sheryl, Timothy Beach, Thomas Garrison, Stephen Houston, James Doyle, Edwin Román, Steven Bozarth, Richard Terry, Samantha Krause, and Jonathan Flood. 2017. "Paleoecology and Geoarchaeology at El Palmar and the El Zotz Region, Guatemala." *Geoarchaeology: An International Journal* 32(1):90–106. https://doi.org/10.1002/gea.21587.

McAnany, Patricia A. 1990. "Water Storage in the Puuc Region of the Northern Maya Lowlands: A Key to Population Estimates and Architectural Variability." In *Precolumbian Population History in the Maya Lowlands*, ed. T. Patrick Culbert and Don S. Rice, 263–284. Albuquerque: University of New Mexico Press.

McAnany, Patricia A. 1998. "Ancestors and the Classic Maya Built Environment." In *Function and Meaning in Classic Maya Architecture*, ed. S. D. Houston, 271–298. Washington, DC: Dumbarton Oaks Research Library and Collection.

McAnany, Patricia A. 2013. *Living with the Ancestors: Kinship and Kingship in Ancient Maya Society*. Revised edition. Cambridge, UK: Cambridge University Press. https://doi.org/10.1017/CBO9781139017190.

McAnany, Patricia A., Rebecca Storey, and Angela K. Lockard. 1999. "Mortuary Ritual and Family Politics at Formative and Early Classic K'axob, Belize." *Ancient Mesoamerica* 10:129–146. https://doi.org/10.1017/S0956536199101081.

Mack, Alexandra. 2004. "One Landscape, Many Experiences: Differing Perspectives of the Temple Districts of Vijayanagara." *Journal of Archaeological Method and Theory* 11(1):59–81. https://doi.org/10.1023/B:JARM.0000014617.58744.1d.

MacLellan, Jessica, and Marta Alejandra Cordero. 2014. "Excavaciones en el Grupo Karinel (Plataforma 17-Base): Operación CB211." In *Proyecto Arqueológico Ceibal-Petexbatun: Informe de la Temporada de Campo 2014*, ed. Flory María Pizón and Takeshi Inomata, 76–103. Report submitted to the Guatemala Instituto de Arqueología e Historia.

Malacrino, Carmelo G. 2010. *Constructing the Ancient World: Architectural Techniques of the Greeks and Romans*. Trans. Jay Hyams. Los Angeles, CA: J. Paul Getty Museum.

Manahan, T. Kam, and Marcello A. Canuto. 2009. "Bracketing the Copan Dynasty: Late Preclassic and Early Postclassic Settlements at Copan, Honduras." *Latin American Antiquity* 20(04):553–580. https://doi.org/10.1017/S104566350000287X.

Marcus, Joyce. 1992. "Royal Families, Royal Texts: Examples from the Zapotec and Maya." In *Mesoamerican Elites: An Archaeological Assessment*, ed. D. Z. Chase and A. F. Chase, 221–241. Norman: University of Oklahoma Press.

Marcus, Joyce. 1998. "The Peaks and Valleys of Ancient States: An Extension of the Dynamic Model." In *Archaic States*, ed. Gary M. Feinman and Joyce Marcus, 59–94. Santa Fe, NM: School of American Research.

Margueron, Jean-Claude. 1994. "Fondations et refondations au Proche-Orient au Bronze Récent." In *Nuove Fondazioni nel Vicino Oriente Antico: Realtà e Ideologia*, ed. Stefania Mazzoni, 3–27. Pisa, Italy: Giardini.

Mark, Robert. 1990. *Light, Wind, and Structure: The Mystery of the Master Builders.* Cambridge, MA: MIT Press.

Mark, Robert, ed. 1993. *Architectural Technology up to the Scientific Revolution.* Cambridge, MA: MIT Press.

Marroquín, Elizabeth, Jose Luis Garrido, and Stephen D. Houston. 2011. "Excavaciones en la Acrópolis de El Zotz (Operación 2)." In *Proyecto Arqueológico "El Zotz" Informe No. 5: Temporada de Campo 2010*, ed. Jose Luis Garrido López, Stephen Houston, and Edwin Román, 11–66. Report submitted to the Guatemala Instituto de Antropología e Historia.

Martin, Simon. 2001. "Court and Realm: Architectural Signatures in the Classic Maya Southern Lowlands." In *Royal Courts of the Ancient Maya*, Volume 1: *Theory, Comparison, and Synthesis*, ed. Takeshi Inomata and Stephen Houston, 168–194. Boulder: Westview.

Martin, Simon. 2004. "A Broken Sky: The Ancient Name of Yaxchilan as *Pa' Chan*." *PARI Journal* 5(1):1–7.

Martin, Simon. 2005. "Of Snakes and Bats: Shifting Identities at Calakmul." *PARI Journal* 6(2):5–15.

Martin, Simon. 2016. "Reflections on the Archaeopolitical: Pursuing the Universal within a Unity of Opposites." In *Political Strategies in Pre-Columbian Mesoamerica*, ed. Sarah Kurnick and Joanne P. Baron, 241–277. Boulder: University Press of Colorado. https://doi.org/10.5876/9781607324164.c009.

Martin, Simon, and Dmitri Beliaev. 2016. "K'ahk' Ti' Ch'ich': A New Snake King from the Early Classic Period." Unpublished paper in possession of the authors.

Martin, Simon, and Nikolai Grube. 1994. "Evidence for Macro-Political Organization amongst Classic Maya Lowland States." Mesoweb. Accessed May 21, 2016. http://www.mesoweb.com/articles/martin/Macro-Politics.pdf.

Martin, Simon, and Nikolai Grube. 1995. "Superstates." *Archaeology* 48(6):41–46.

Martin, Simon, and Nikolai Grube. 2008. *Chronicle of the Maya Kings and Queens.* Rev. ed. New York: Thames and Hudson.

Martinelli, L. A., L.C.R. Pessenda, E. Espinoza, P. B. Camargo, E. C. Telles, C. C. Cerri, R. L. Victoria, R. Aravena, J. Richey, and S. Trumbore. 1996. "Carbon-13 Variation with Depth in Soils of Brazil and Climate Change during the Quaternary." *Oecologia* 106(3):376–381. https://doi.org/10.1007/BF00334565.

Masson, Marilyn A. 2001. "Changing Patterns of Ceramic Stylistic Diversity in the Pre-Hispanic Maya Lowlands." *Acta Archaeologica* 72(2):159–188. https://doi.org /10.1034/j.1600-0390.2001.720207.x.

Masson, Marilyn A. 2002. "Community Economy and the Mercantile Transformation in Postclassic Northeastern Belize." In *Ancient Maya Political Economies*, ed. Marilyn A. Masson and David A. Freidel, 335–364. Walnut Creek, CA: AltaMira Press.

Matos Moctezuma, Eduardo. 1992. "Aztec Main Pyramid: Ritual Architecture at Tenochtitlan." In *The Ancient Americas: Art from Sacred Landscapes*, ed. Richard F. Townsend, 186–195. Chicago, IL: Art Institute of Chicago.

Matute, Varinia, and James Doyle. 2008. "Sitio El Palmar (Operación 6)." In *Proyecto Arqueológico "El Zotz" Informe No. 1: Temporada de Campo 2008*, ed. Ernesto Arredondo Leiva and Stephen Houston, 135–152. Report submitted to the Guatemala Instituto de Antropología e Historia.

Mayer, Karl H. 1993. "Maya Inscriptions from El Zotz, Peten." *Mexicon* 15(1):4–5.

Mazzoni, Stefania. 1991. "Aramean and Luwian New Foundations." In *Nuove Fondazioni nel Vicino Oriente Antico: Realtà e Ideologia*, ed. Stefania Mazzoni, 319–340. Pisa, Italy: Giardin.

Meléndez, Juan Carlos, and Stephen Houston. 2008. "Acrópolis Central (Operación 2)." In *Proyecto Arqueológico "El Zotz" Informe No. 1: Temporada de Campo 2008*, ed. Ernesto Arredondo Leiva and Stephen Houston, 45–70. Report submitted to the Guatemala Instituto de Antropología e Historia.

Mesick, Cassandra L. 2012. "The Culture of Construction: Architectural Technology and Building Practice among the Classic Period Maya." PhD dissertation, Department of Anthropology, Brown University, Providence, RI.

Migdal, Joel. 1988. *Strong Societies and Weak States: State-Society Relations and State Capabilities in the Third World*. Princeton, NJ: Princeton University Press.

Milbrath, Susan, and Carlos Peraza Lope. 2003. "Revisiting Mayapan: Mexico's Last Maya Capital." *Ancient Mesoamerica* 14(01):1–46. https://doi.org/10.1017/S09565 36103132178.

Milbrath, Susan, and Carlos Peraza Lope. 2009. "Survival and Revival of Terminal Classic Traditions at Postclassic Mayapan." *Latin American Antiquity* 20(04):581–606. https://doi.org/10.1017/S1045663500002881.

Miles, Suzanna W. 1957. "The Sixteenth-Century Pokom-Maya: A Documentary Analysis of Social Structure and Archaeological Setting." *Transactions of the American Philosophical Society* 47(4):733–781. https://doi.org/10.2307/1005780.

Miller, Mary E. 1998. "A Design for Meaning in Maya Architecture." In *Function and Meaning in Classic Maya Architecture*, ed. Stephen D. Houston, 187–222. Washington, DC: Dumbarton Oaks Research Library and Collection.

Miller, Mary, and Karl Taube. 1993. *An Illustrated Dictionary of the Gods and Symbols of Ancient Mexico and the Maya*. New York: Thames and Hudson.

Miller, Thomas E. 1996. "Geologic and Hydrologic Controls on Karst and Cave Development in Belize." *Journal of Caves and Karst Studies* 58(2):100–120.

Miller, Virginia E. 1985. "The Dwarf Motif in Classic Maya Art." In *Fourth Palenque Round Table, 1980*, ed. Merle Greene Robertson and Elizabeth P. Benson, 141–153. San Francisco, CA: Pre-Columbian Art Research Institute.

Milner, George R., and Jesper L. Boldsen. 2012. "Transition Analysis: A Validation Study with Known-Age Modern American Skeletons." *American Journal of Physical Anthropology* 148(1):98–110. https://doi.org/10.1002/ajpa.22047.

Mock, Shirley B., and Debra S. Walker. 1998. *The Sowing and the Dawning: Termination, Dedication, and Transformation in the Archaeological and Ethnographic Record of Mesoamerica*. Albuquerque: University of New Mexico Press.

Moholy-Nagy, Hattula. 2002. *The Artifacts of Tikal: Utilitarian Artifacts and Unworked Material*. Tikal Report 27B. Philadelphia: University Museum, University of Pennsylvania.

Moholy-Nagy, Hattula. 2008. *The Artifacts of Tikal: Ornamental and Ceremonial Artifacts and Unworked Material*. Tikal Report 27A. Philadelphia: University Museum, University of Pennsylvania.

Moholy-Nagy, Hattula. 2012. *Historical Archaeology at Tikal, Guatemala*. Tikal Report 37. Philadelphia: University Museum, University of Pennsylvania. https://doi.org/10.9783/9781934536582.

Morgan, Morris H. 1960. *Vitruvius: De architectura (Ten Books on Architecture)*. New York: Dover Publications.

Morris, Earl H., Jean Charlot, and Ann Axtell Morris. 1931. *The Temple of the Warriors at Chichen Itzá, Yucatan*. 2 vols. Carnegie Institution of Washington Publication No. 406. Washington, DC: Carnegie Institution of Washington.

Morris, Walter F., Jr. 1985. "Fall Fashions: Lagartero Figurine Costume at the End of the Classic Period." In *Fifth Palenque Round Table, 1983*, ed. Virginia M. Fields, 245–254. San Francisco, CA: Pre-Columbian Art Research Institute.

Navarro-Farr, Olivia C. 2009. "Ritual, Process, and Continuity in the Late to Terminal Classic Transition: Investigations at Structure M13-1 in the Ancient Maya Site of El Perú-Waka', Petén, Guatemala." PhD dissertation, Department of Anthropology, Southern Methodist University, Dallas, TX.

Navarro-Farr, Olivia C., and Michelle Rich, eds. 2014. *Archaeology at El Perú-Waka': Ancient Maya Performances of Ritual, Memory, and Power*. Tucson: University of Arizona Press.

Nelson, Zachary, and James A. Doyle. 2008. "Programa de mapeo y reconocimiento." In *Proyecto Arqueológico "El Zotz" Informe No. 1: Temporada de Campo 2008*, ed.

Ernesto Arredondo Leiva and Stephen D. Houston, 153–160. Report submitted to the Instituto de Antropología e Historia, Guatemala.

Newman, Sarah E. 2011a. "Catálogo y Análisis Preliminar de la Cerámica de la Tumba Real, del grupo El Diablo." In *Proyecto Arqueológico "El Zotz" Informe No. 5: Temporada de Campo 2010*, ed. Jose Luis Garrido López, Stephen Houston, and Edwin Román, 479–522. Report submitted to the Guatemala Instituto de Antropología e Historia.

Newman, Sarah E. 2011b. "The Last Supper: The Role of Ceramic Serving Vessels in Ancient Maya Mortuary Practice." Master's thesis, Department of Anthropology, Brown University, Providence, RI.

Newman, Sarah E. 2015a. "Operación 26: Excavaciones en Estructura L8-17, Grupo Oeste de El Zotz." In *Proyecto Arqueológico El Zotz Informe Final 2014, Temporada de Campo #9*, ed. Jose Luis Garrido López, Edwin R. Román, Thomas G. Garrison, and Stephen D. Houston, 93–104. Report submitted to the Guatemala Instituto de Antropología e Historia.

Newman, Sarah E. 2015b. "Rethinking Refuse: A History of Maya Trash." PhD dissertation, Department of Anthropology, Brown University, Providence, RI.

Newman, Sarah, Stephen Houston, Jose Luis Garrido, Elizabeth Marroquín, Juan Carlos Meléndez, Elsa Damaris Menéndez, Griselda Pérez Robles, and Ewa Czapiewska. 2012. "Los procesos palaciegos: La Acrópolis de El Zotz." In *XXV Simposio de Investigaciones Arqueológicas en Guatemala, 2011*, ed. B. Arroyo, L. Paiz, and H. Mejía, 965–975. Guatemala City: Ministerio de Cultura y Deportes, Instituto de Antropologías e Historia, Asociación Tikal.

Newman, Sarah, Stephen Houston, Thomas Garrison, and Edwin Román. 2015. "Outfitting a Ruler." In *Temple of the Night Sun: A Royal Tomb at El Diablo, Guatemala*, by Stephen Houston, Sarah Newman, Edwin Román, and Thomas Garrison, 84–179. San Francisco, CA: Precolumbia Mesoweb Press.

Newman, Sarah, and Elsa Dámaris Menéndez. 2012. "Operaciones 2 y 12: Excavaciones en la Acrópolis y la Plazuela Noroeste." In *Proyecto Arqueológico El Zotz Informe No. 6: Temporada 2011*, ed. Jose Luis Garrido López, Stephen Houston, Edwin Román, and Thomas Garrison, 139–187. Report submitted to the Guatemala Instituto de Antropología e Historia.

Parker, Bradley J. 1997. "Garrisoning the Empire: Aspects of the Construction and Maintenance of Forts on the Assyrian Frontier." *Iraq* 59:77–87. https://doi.org/10.1017/S0021088900003363.

Parker, Geoffrey. 1998. *The Grand Strategy of Philip II*. New Haven, CT: Yale University Press.

Pendergast, David M. 1979. *Excavations at Altun Ha, Belize 1964–1970*. Toronto, Canada: Royal Ontario Museum.

Pendergast, David M. 1981. "Lamanai, Belize: Summary of Excavation Results, 1974–1980." *Journal of Field Archaeology* 8(1):29–53.

Pendergast, David M. 1982. *Excavations at Altun Ha, Belize 1964–1970. 2.* Toronto, Canada: Royal Ontario Museum.

Pendergast, David M. 1990. *Excavations at Altun Ha, Belize, 1964–1970. 3.* Toronto, Canada: Royal Ontario Museum.

Pennington, Terrence Dale, and José Sarukhán. 1968. *Arboles tropicales de México: Manual para la identificación de las principales especies.* Mexico, DF: Instituto Nacional de Investigaciones Forestales de México, Food and Agriculture Organization of the United Nations.

Pérez Calderón, Juan Carlos, ed. 2013. *Proyecto Regional Arqueológico El Perú-Waká, Informe No. 10, Temporada 2012.* Guatemala City: Informe presented to the Dirección General del Patrimonio Cultural y Natural de Guatemala.

Pérez Robles, Edwin Rolando. 2013. "La Restauración de dos Vasijas Cerámicas del Entierro 9 de Sitio Arqueológico 'El Zotz.'" Unpublished technical thesis, Portable Object Restoration, Universidad de San Carlos, Guatemala.

Pérez Robles, Griselda. 2011. "Diagnóstico de deterioro en el Templo M7-1 de El Zotz." In *Proyecto Arqueológico El Zotz: Informe No. 5, Temporada 2010,* ed. Jose Luis Garrido López, Stephen Houston, and Edwin Román, 523–568. Report submitted to the Guatemala Instituto de Antropología e Historia.

Pérez Robles, Griselda. 2014. "El Templo M7-1: Una propuesta de intervención para conservar y restaurar los edificios de El Zotz." Master's thesis, Restoration of Immovable Objects and Historical Centers, Universidad de San Carlos, Guatemala.

Pérez Robles, Griselda, Fabiola Quiroa, and Stephen Houston. 2009. "Operación 2: Excavaciones en la Acrópolis." In *Proyecto Arqueológico "El Zotz" Informe No. 4: Temporada 2009,* ed. Griselda Pérez Robles, Edwin Román, and Stephen Houston, 9–67. Report submitted to the Guatemala Instituto de Antropología e Historia.

Pérez Robles, Griselda, Edwin R. Román, and Stephen Houston, eds. 2009. *Proyecto Arqueológico "El Zotz" Informe No. 4: Temporada de Campo 2009.* Report presented to the Guatemala Instituto de Antropología e Historia.

Piedrasanta, Rony. 2012. "Excavaciones en Grupo El Tejón (Operación 17)." In *Proyecto Arqueológico El Zotz Informe No. 6: Temporada 2011,* ed. Jose Luis Garrido López, Stephen Houston, Edwin Román, and Thomas Garrison, 189–195. Report submitted to the Guatemala Instituto de Antropología e Historia.

Piedrasanta, Rony, Thomas Garrison, Edwin Román, and Stephen Houston. 2014. "Investigaciones recientes en el Grupo El Tejón, El Zotz, Petén, Guatemala." In *XXVII Simposio de Investigaciones Arqueologicas en Guatemala, 2013,* ed. Bárbara

Arroyo, Luis Méndez Salinas, and Andrea Rojas, 945–950. Guatemala: Ministerio de Cultura y Deportes, Instituto de Antropología e Historia, Asociación Tikal.

Piedrasanta, Rony, and Danilo Hernández. 2012. "Investigaciones en el Grupo El Tejón (Operación 20)." In *Proyecto Arqueológico El Zotz Informe No. 7: Temporada 2012*, ed. Jose Luis Garrido López, Thomas Garrison, Edwin Román, and Stephen Houston, 47–57. Report submitted to the Guatemala Instituto de Antropología e Historia.

Pope, Kevin O., Mary E. D. Pohl, John G. Jones, David L. Lentz, Christopher von Nagy, Francisco J. Vega, and Irvy R. Quitmyer. 2001. "Origin and Environmental Setting of Ancient Agriculture in the Lowlands of Mesoamerica." *Science* 292(5520):1370–1373. https://doi.org/10.1126/science.292.5520.1370.

Proskouriakoff, Tatiana. 1950. *A Study of Classic Maya Sculpture*. Carnegie Institution of Washington Publication No. 593. Washington, DC: Carnegie Institution of Washington.

Proskouriakoff, Tatiana. 1993. *Maya History*. Austin: University of Texas Press.

Prufer, Keith M., and James E. Brady. 2005. *Stone Houses and Earth Lords: Maya Religion in the Cave Context*. Boulder: University Press of Colorado.

Pugh, Timothy W., Prudence M. Rice, Evelyn Chan Nieto, and Don S. Rice. 2016. "A Chak'an Itza Center at Nixtun-Ch'ich', Petén, Guatemala." *Journal of Field Archaeology* 41(1):1–16. https://doi.org/10.1080/00934690.2015.1129253.

Quintana, Oscar, and Wolfgang Wurster. 2001. *Ciudades Mayas del Noreste de Peten, Guatemala: Un studio urbanístico comparative*. AVA—Materialien 59. Mainz am Rhein, Germany: Verlag Philipp von Zabern.

Quiroa, Fabiola, and Varinia Matute. 2008. "Programa de Pozos de Sondeo (Operación 1)." In *El Informe No. 1: Temporada de Campo 2008, Proyecto Arqueológico El Zotz*, ed. Ernesto Arrendondo and Stephen Houston, 13–44. Report submitted to the Guatemala Instituto de Antropología e Historia.

Rands, Robert. 1961. "Elaboration and Invention in Ceramic Traditions." *American Antiquity* 26(3-Part1):331–340. https://doi.org/10.2307/277400.

Rands, Robert L., and Barbara C. Rands. 1965. "Pottery Figurines of the Maya Lowlands." In *The Handbook of Middle American Indians*, ed. R. Wauchope, 535–560. New Orleans, LA: Middle American Research Institute.

Reents-Budet, Dorie, Stanley Guenter, Ronald L. Bishop, and M. James Blackman. 2012. "Identity and Interaction: Ceramic Styles and Social History of the Ik' Polity, Guatemala." In *Motul de San Jose: Politics, History, and Economy in a Classic Maya Polity*, ed. Antonia E. Foias and Kitty F. Emery, 67–93. Gainesville: University Press of Florida. https://doi.org/10.5744/florida/9780813041902.003.0003.

Reimer, Paula J., Edouard Bard, Alex Bayliss, J. Warren Beck, Paul G. Blackwell, Christopher Bronk Ramsey, Caitlin E. Buck, Hai Cheng, R. Lawrence Edwards,

Michael Friedrich, et al. 2013. "IntCal13 and Marine13 Radiocarbon Age Calibration Curves 0–50,000 Years Cal BP." *Radiocarbon* 55(4):1869–1887. https://doi.org/10.2458/azu_js_rc.55.16947.

Rice, Don S. 1986. "The Peten Postclassic: A Settlement Perspective." In *Late Lowland Maya Civilization: Classic to Postclassic*, ed. Jeremy A. Sabloff and E. Wyllys Andrews, 301–344. Albuquerque: University of New Mexico.

Rice, Don S. 1988. "Classic to Postclassic Household Transitions in the Central Peten, Guatemala." In *Household and Community in the Mesoamerican Past*, ed. Richard R. Wilk and Wendy Ashmore, 227–247. Albuquerque: University of New Mexico.

Rice, Don S., Prudence M. Rice, and Timothy Pugh. 1998. "Settlement Continuity and Change in the Central Petén Lakes Region: The Case of Zacpetén." In *Anatomía de una civilización: Aproximaciones interdisciplinarias a la cultura Maya*, ed. Andrés Ciudad Ruiz, Yolanda Fernández Marquínez, José Miguel García Campillo, Maria Josefa Iglesias Ponce de León, Alfonso Lacadena García-Gallo, and Luis T. Sanz Castro, 207–252. Madrid: Sociedad Española de Estudios Mayas.

Rice, Prudence M. 1980. "Peten Postclassic Poltery Production and Exchange: A View from Macanche." In *Models and Methods in Regional Exchange*, ed. by Robert Fry, 67–82. SAA Papers No. 1. Washington, DC: Society for American Archaeology.

Rice, Prudence M. 1987a. "Economic Change in the Lowland Maya Late Classic Period." In *Specialization, Exchange and Complex Societies*, ed. Elizabeth M. Brumfiel and Timothy K. Earle, 76–85. Cambridge, UK: Cambridge University Press.

Rice, Prudence M. 1987b. *Macanché Island, El Petén, Guatemala: Excavations, Pottery and Artifacts*. Gainesville: University of Florida Press.

Rice, Prudence M., William Y. Adams, Joseph W. Ball, Whitney M. Davis, Timothy Earle, Robert E. Fry, Ian Hodder, L. R. V. Joesink-Mandeville, Charles C. Kolb, Masae Nishimura, et al. 1981. "Evolution of Specialized Pottery Production: A Trial Model." *Current Anthropology* 22(3):219–240. https://doi.org/10.1086/202661.

Rice, Prudence M., Arthur A. Demarest, and Don S. Rice. 2004. "Terminal Classic and the 'Classic Maya Collapse' in Perspective." In *The Terminal Classic in the Maya Lowlands: Collapse, Transition, and Transformation*, ed. Arthur A. Demarest, Prudence M. Rice, and Don S. Rice, 1–11. Boulder: University Press of Colorado.

Rice, Prudence M., and Donald Forsyth. 2004. "Terminal Classic-Period Lowland Ceramics." In *The Terminal Classic in the Maya Lowlands: Collapse, Transition, and Transformation*, ed. Arthur A. Demarest, Prudence M. Rice, and Don S. Rice, 28–59. Boulder: University Press of Colorado.

Rice, Prudence M., and Don S. Rice. 1985. "Topoxte, Macanche, and the Central Peten Postclassic." In *The Lowland Maya Postclassic*, ed. Arlen F. Chase and Prudence M. Rice, 166–183. Austin: University of Texas Press.

Rice, Prudence M., and Don S. Rice. 2004. "Late Classic to Postclassic Transformations in the Peten Lakes Region." In *The Terminal Classic in the Maya
Lowlands: Collapse, Transition, and Transformation*, ed. Arthur A. Demarest, Prudence M. Rice, and Don S. Rice, 125–139. Boulder: University Press of
Colorado.

Rice, Prudence M., and Don S. Rice. 2009. *The Kowoj: Identity, Migration and Geopolitics in Late Postclassic Petén, Guatemala*. Boulder: University of Colorado Press.

Rich, Michelle E. 2011. "Ritual, Royalty, and Classic Period Politics: The Archaeology of the Mirador Group at El Perú-Waká, Petén, Guatemala." PhD dissertation,
Department of Anthropology, Southern Methodist University, Dallas, TX.

Ricketson, Jr. Oliver, and Edith Bayles Ricketson. 1937. *Uaxactun, Guatemala: Group
E, 1926–1931*. Washington, DC: Carnegie Institute of Washington.

Robertson, Merle Greene. 1985. "'57 Varieties': The Palenque Beauty Salon." In *Fourth
Palenque Round Table, 1980*, ed. Merle Greene Robertson and Elizabeth P. Benson,
29–44. San Francisco, CA: Pre-Columbian Art Research Institute.

Román-Ramírez, Edwin R. 2011. "Living the Sacred Landscape: The Process of
Abandonment of the Early Classic Maya Group of El Diablo at El Zotz, Petén,
Guatemala." Master's thesis, Teresa Lozano Long Institute for Latin American
Studies, University of Texas, Austin.

Román Ramírez, Edwin René. 2017. "The Early Classic Encounter: An Examination
of the Cultural and Historical Implications of an Ancient Maya Palace at El Diablo, El Zotz, Guatemala." PhD dissertation, Latin American Studies, University
of Texas at Austin. Austin, TX.

Román, Edwin, and Nicholas Carter. 2009. "Operación 4, Excavaciones en el Grupo
El Diablo." In *Proyecto Arqueológico "El Zotz" Informe No. 4: Temporada 2009*, ed.
Griselda Pérez Robles, Edwin Román, and Stephen Houston, 77–120. Report
submitted to the Guatemala Instituto de Antropología e Historia.

Román, Edwin, and Yeny Gutiérrez. 2016. "Excavaciones en el Grupo El Diablo
(Operación 19)." In *Proyecto Arqueológico El Zotz Informe Final, 10ma Tempo-
rada de Campo*, ed. Jose Luis Garrido López, Yeny Myshell Gutiérrez Castillo,
Edwin René Román Ramírez, Thomas Garrison, and Stephen Houston, 11–32.
Report submitted to the Guatemala Instituto de Antropología e Historia.

Román, Edwin, and Sarah Newman. 2011. "Excavaciones en el grupo El Diablo."
In *Proyecto Arqueológico "El Zotz" Informe No. 5: Temporada de Campo 2010*, ed.
Jose Luis Garrido López, Stephen Houston, and Edwin Román, 117–162. Report
submitted to the Guatemala Instituto de Antropología e Historia.

Román, Edwin, Sarah Newman, Stephen Houston, Thomas Garrison, Nicholas
Carter, Andrew Scherer, Zachary Hruby, and Catherine Magee. 2011. "El Diablo:
Grupo Cívico-Ceremonial del Clásico Temprano en El Zotz, El Petén." In *XXIV*

Simposio de Investigaciones Arqueologicas en Guatemala, 2010, ed. Bárbara Arroyo, Lorena Pais Aragón, Adriana Linares Palma, and Ana Lucía Arroyave, 471–476. Guatemala: Ministerio de Cultura y Deportes, Instituto de Antropología e Historia, Asociación Tikal.

Romero Molina, Javier. 1986. *Catálogo de la Colección de Dientes Mutilados Prehispánicos IV Parte*. México, DF: Instituto Nacional de Antropología e Historia.

Roys, Lawrence. 1934. "The Engineering Knowledge of the Maya." In *Contributions to American Archaeology* 2(6):27–105. Washington, DC: Carnegie Institution of Washington.

Rubertone, Patricia E. 1989. "Landscape as Artifact: Comments on 'The Archaeology of Landscape Treatment in Social, Economic, and Ideological Analysis'" *Historical Archaeology* 23(1):50–54. https://doi.org/10.1007/BF03374098.

Ruíz Aguilar, Maria Elena. 2004. "Materiales líticos asociados a una ofrenda del Clásico Temprano en El Zotz, Petén, Guatemala." *Los Investigadores de la Cultura Maya* 12(1):81–97.

Runggaldier, Astrid. 2009. "Memory and Materiality in Monumental Architecture: Construction and Reuse of a Late Preclassic Maya Palace at San Bartolo, Guatemala." PhD dissertation, Department of Archaeology, Boston University, Boston, MA.

Ruppert, Karl J. 1940. "A Special Assemblage of Maya Structures." In *The Maya and Their Neighbors: Essays on Middle American Anthropology and Archaeology*, ed. Ralph Linton, Samuel K. Lothrop, Harry Shapiro, and George C. Vaillant, 222–231. New York: Dover.

Ruscheinsky, Lynn M. 2003. "The Social Reproduction of Gender Identity through the Production and Reception of Lowland Maya Figurines." PhD dissertation, University of British Columbia.

Ruz Lhuillier, Alberto. 1973. *El Templo de las Inscripciones*. Mexico City: Instituto Nacional de Antropología e Historia.

Rzedowski, Jerzy, and Laura Huerta. 1978. *Vegetación de México*. Mexico, DF: Editorial Limusa.

Sabloff, Jeremy A. 1973. "Major Themes in the Past Hypotheses of the Maya Collapse." In *The Classic Maya Collapse*, ed. T. Patrick Culbert, 35–42. Albuquerque: University of New Mexico Press.

Sabloff, Jeremy A. 1975. *Excavations at Seibal, Department of Petén, Guatemala*, Number 2: *Ceramics*. Memoirs of the Peabody Museum of Archaeology and Ethnology Vol. 13. Cambridge, MA: Harvard University.

Sabloff, Jeremy A., ed. 2003. *Tikal: Dynasties, Foreigners, and Affairs of State: Advancing Maya Archaeology*. Santa Fe, NM: School of American Research Press.

Sabloff, Jeremy A., and Gordon R. Willey. 1967. "The Collapse of Maya Civilization in the Southern Lowlands: A Consideration of History and Process." *Southwestern Journal of Anthropology* 23(4):311–336. https://doi.org/10.1086/soutjanth.23.4.3629449.

Saturno, William A., David Stuart, and Boris Beltrán. 2006. "Early Maya Writing at San Bartolo, Guatemala." *Science* 311(5765):1281–1283. https://doi.org/10.1126 /science.1121745.

Saturno, William A., Karl A. Taube, and David Stuart. 2005. *The Murals of San Bartolo, El Petén, Guatemala*, Part 1: *The North Wall*. Ancient America No. 7. Barnardsville, NC: Center for Ancient American Studies.

Saul, Frank P. 1972. *The Human Skeletal Remains of Altar de Sacrificios: An Osteobiographic Analysis*. Papers of the Peabody Museum of Archaeology and Ethnology 63(2). Cambridge, MA: Harvard University.

Scarborough, Vernon L. 1998. "Ecology and Ritual: Water Management and the Maya." *Latin American Antiquity* 9(2):135–159. https://doi.org/10.2307/971991.

Scarborough, Vernon L., Nicholas P. Dunning, Kenneth B. Tankersley, Christopher Carr, Eric Weaver, Liwy Grazioso, Brian Lane, John G. Jones, Palma Buttles, Fred Valdez, et al. 2012. "Water and Sustainable Land Use at the Ancient Tropical City of Tikal, Guatemala." *Proceedings of the National Academy of Sciences of the United States of America* 109(31):12408–12413. https://doi.org/10.1073/pnas.1202881109.

Schele, Linda. 1995. "The Olmec Mountain and the Tree of Creation in Mesoamerican Cosmology." In *The Olmec World: Ritual and Rulership*, ed. Gillette G. Griffin, 105–117. Princeton, NJ: Princeton Art Museum; New York: Harry N. Abrams.

Scherer, Andrew. 2007. "Population Structure of the Classic Period Maya." *American Journal of Physical Anthropology* 132(3):367–380. https://doi.org/10.1002/ajpa.20535.

Scherer, Andrew. 2009. "Osteología de El Zotz, Bejucal, y El Palmar de las Temporadas de Campo 2008–2009." In *Proyecto Arqueológico "El Zotz" Informe No. 4: Temporada 2009*, ed. Griselda Pérez Robles, Edwin Román, and Stephen Houston, 321–334. Report submitted to the Guatemala Instituto de Antropología e Historia.

Scherer, Andrew K. 2012. "Osteología de El Zotz: Temporadas de Campo 2010–2011." In *Proyecto Arqueológico "El Zotz" Informe No. 6: Temporada de Campo 2011*, ed. Jose L. Garrido López, Stephen Houston and Edwin R. Román, 269–285. Report submitted to the Guatemala Instituto de Antropología e Historia.

Scherer, Andrew. 2014. "Osteología de El Zotz: Entierro 15 y huesos humanos de contextos no funerarios (2009–2012)." In *Proyecto Arqueológico El Zotz Informe Final 2013: Temporada de Campo #8*, ed. Jose Luis Garrido López, Thomas G. Garrison, Edwin R. Román, and Stephen Houston, 159–164. Report submitted to the Guatemala Instituto de Antropología e Historia.

Scherer, Andrew. 2015a. *Mortuary Landscapes of the Classic Maya: Rituals of Body and Soul*. Austin: University of Texas Press.

Scherer, Andrew. 2015b. "Osteology of Burial 9 and Associated Caches." In *Temple of the Night Sun: A Royal Tomb at El Diablo, Guatemala*, by Stephen Houston, Sarah Newman, Edwin Román, and Thomas Garrison, 180–207. San Francisco, CA: Precolumbia Mesoweb Press.

Scherer, Andrew. 2017. "Bioarchaeology and the Skeletons of the Pre-Columbian Maya." *Journal of Archaeological Research* 25(2):133–184. https://doi.org/10.1007/s10814-016-9098-3.

Scherer, Andrew K., and Alyce de Carteret. 2016. "Osteología de El Zotz: Temporadas de Campo 2014–2015." In *Proyecto Arqueológico El Zotz Informe Final: 10ma Temporada de Campo*, ed. Jose Luis Garrido López, Yeny Myshell Gutiérrez Castillo, Edwin René Román Ramirez, Thomas Garrison, and Stephen Houston, 157–171. Report submitted to the Guatemala Instituto de Antropología e Historia.

Scherer, Andrew K., and Chelsea Garrett. 2011a. "Osteología de El Zotz: Temporada de Campo 2010." In *Proyecto Arqueológico "El Zotz": Informe No. 5, Temporada 2010*, edited by Jose L. Garrido López, Stephen Houston and Edwin Román, 413–415. Report submitted to the Guatemala Instituto de Antropologia e Historia.

Scherer, Andrew K., and Chelsea Garrett. 2011b. "Osteología del Complejo El Diablo: Escondites y Entierro 9, El Zotz." In *Proyecto Arqueológico "El Zotz" Informe No. 5: Temporada de Campo 2010*, ed. Jose Luis Garrido López, Stephen Houston, and Edwin Román, 425–458. Report submitted to the Guatemala Instituto de Antropología e Historia.

Scherer, Andrew K., and Charles Golden. 2012. *Revisiting Maler's Usumacinta: Recent Archaeological Investigation in Chiapas, Mexico*. San Francisco, CA: The Pre-Columbian Art Research Institute.

Scherer, Andrew K., Charles Golden, Ana Lucía Arroyave Prera, and Griselda Pérez Robles. 2014. "Danse Macabre: Death, Community, and Kingdom at El Kinel, Guatemala." In *The Bioarchaeology of Space and Place: Ideology, Power and Meaning in Maya Mortuary Contexts*, ed. Gabriel D. Wrobel, 193–224. New York: Springer. https://doi.org/10.1007/978-1-4939-0479-2_8.

Scherer, Andrew, and Lori E. Wright. 2013. "Movilidad e Historia de Población en Tikal, Guatemala: Perspectivas desde la Biodistancia y el Análisis de los Isótopos de Estroncio." In *Afinidades Biológicas y Dinámicas Poblacionales entre los Antiguos Mayas: Una Visión Multidisciplinaria*, ed. Andrea Cucina, 57–72. Mérida, Mexico: Universidad Autónoma de Yucatán.

Scherer, Andrew K., Lori E. Wright, and Cassady J. Yoder. 2007. "Bioarchaeological Evidence for Social and Temporal Differences in Diet at Piedras Negras, Guatemala." *Latin American Antiquity* 18(1):85–104. https://doi.org/10.2307/25063087.

Schmidt, Peter, Mercedes de la Garza, and Enrique Nalda, eds. 1998. *Maya*. New York: Rizzoli.

Schortman, Edward M., and Patricia A. Urban. 1994. "Living on the Edge: Core/Periphery Relations in Ancient Southeastern Mesoamerica." *Current Anthropology* 35(4):401–430. https://doi.org/10.1086/204293.

Schuldenrein, Joseph, Rita P. Wright, M. Rafique Mughal, and M. Afzal Khan. 2004. "Landscapes, Soils, and Mound Histories of the Upper Indus Valley, Pakistan: New Insights on the Holocene Environments Near Ancient Harappa." *Journal of Archaeological Science* 31(6):777–797. https://doi.org/10.1016/j.jas.2003.10.015.

Schulze, Mark D., and David F. Whitacre. 1999. "A Classification and Ordination of the Tree Community of Tikal National Park, Petén, Guatemala." *Bulletin of the Florida Museum of Natural History* 41(3):169–297.

Schwartz, Glenn M., and John J. Nichols, eds. 2006. *After Collapse: The Regeneration of Complex Societies.* Tucson: University of Arizona Press.

Schwarz, Kevin R. 2009. "Eckixil: Understanding the Classic to Postclassic Survival and Transformation of a Peten Maya Village." *Latin American Antiquity* 20(03):413–441. https://doi.org/10.1017/S1045663500002789.

Scott, James. 1998. *Seeing Like a State: How Certain Schemes to Improve the Human Condition Have Failed.* New Haven, CT: Yale University Press.

Service, Elman R. 1962. *Primitive Social Organization: An Evolutionary Perspective.* New York: Random House.

Shackley, Stephen. 2011. "An Introduction to X-Ray Fluorescence (XRF) Analysis in Archaeology." In *X-Ray Fluorescence Spectrometry (XRF) in Geoarchaeology,* ed. M. Stephen Shackley, 7–44. New York: Springer. https://doi.org/10.1007/978-1-4419-6886-9_2.

Shackley, Stephen. 2012. "Source Provenience of Obsidian Artifacts from El Zotz, Guatemala." Unpublished report from The Geoarchaeological XRF Lab, Albuquerque, NM.

Sharer, Robert J., and Charles W. Golden. 2004. "Kingship and Polity: Conceptualizing the Maya Body Politic." In *Continuities and Changes in Maya Archaeology: Perspectives at the Millennium,* ed. Charles Golden and Greg Borstede, 23–50. New York: Routledge.

Sharer, Robert J., David W. Sedat, Loa P. Traxler, Julia C. Miller, and Ellen E. Bell. 2005. "Early Classic Royal Power in Copan: The Origins and Development of the Acropolis (ca. A.D. 250–600)." In *Copan: The History of an Ancient Maya Kingdom,* ed. E. Wyllys Andrews and William L. Fash, 139–199. Santa Fe, NM: School of American Research Press.

Smith, Adam T. 2003. *The Political Landscape: Constellations of Authority in Early Complex Polities.* Berkeley: University of California Press.

Smith, A. Ledyard. 1950. *Uaxactun, Guatemala: Excavations of 1931–1937.* Publication 588. Washington, DC: Carnegie Institute of Washington.

Smith, A. Ledyard. 1972. *Excavations at Altar de Sacrificios: Architecture, Settlement, Burials, and Caches.* Papers of the Peabody Museum 62. Cambridge, MA: Harvard University.

Smith, A. Ledyard, and Sylvanus G. Morley. 1932. *Two Recent Ceramic Finds at Uaxactun.* Contributions to American Archaeology no. 5. Publication 436. Washington, DC: Carnegie Institution of Washington.

Smith, Robert E. 1955. *Ceramic Sequence at Uaxactun, Guatemala.* 2 vols. Publication 20. New Orleans, LA: Middle American Research Institute, Tulane University.

Smith, Robert E., and James C. Gifford. 1966. *Maya Ceramic Varieties, Types, and Wares at Uaxactun: Supplement to* Ceramic Sequence at Uaxactun, Guatemala. Middle American Research Institute Publication No. 28. New Orleans, LA: Tulane University.

Smith, Robert E., Gordon R. Willey, and James C. Gifford. 1960. "The Type-Variety Concept as a Basis for the Analysis of Maya Pottery." *American Antiquity* 25(03):330–340. https://doi.org/10.2307/277516.

Soil Survey Staff. 1993. *Soil Survey Manual.* US Department of Agriculture Handbook 18. Washington, DC: US Department of Agriculture.

Soil Survey Staff. 2003. *Keys to Soil Taxonomy.* 9th ed. Blacksburg, VA: Pocahontas Press.

Solari, Amara. 2013. *Maya Ideologies of the Sacred: The Transfiguration of Space in Colonial Yucatan.* Austin: University of Texas Press.

Šprajc, Ivan, Carlos Morales Aguilar, and Richard D. Hansen. 2009. "Early Maya Astronomy and Urban Planning at El Mirador, Peten, Guatemala." *Anthropological Notebooks* 15(3):79–101.

Staller, John E., ed. 2008. *Pre-Columbian Landscapes of Creation and Origin.* New York: Springer. https://doi.org/10.1007/978-0-387-76910-3.

Stanton, Travis W., and Tomás Gallareta Negrón. 2001. "Warfare, Ceramic Economy, and the Itza: A Reconsideration of the Itza polity in ancient Yucatan." *Ancient Mesoamerica* 12(02):229–245. https://doi.org/10.1017/S0956536101122091.

Stephens, John Lloyd. 1841. *Incidents of Travel in Central America, Chiapas, and Yucatan.* 2 vols. New York: Harper & Brothers. https://doi.org/10.5962/bhl.title.84376.

Stephens, John Lloyd. 1843. *Incidents of Travel in Yucatán.* 2 vols. New York: Harper.

Stone, Andrea, and Marc Zender. 2011. *Reading Maya Art: A Hieroglyphic Guide to Ancient Maya Painting and Sculpture.* New York: Thames and Hudson.

Stone, Doris. 1977. *Pre-Columbian Man in Costa Rica.* Cambridge, MA: Peabody Museum Press, Peabody Museum of Archaeology and Ethnology, Harvard University.

Straight, Kirk D. 2007. "A House of Cards: Construction, Proportion, and Form at Temple XIX, Palenque, Chiapas, Mexico." In *Palenque: Recent Investigations at the Classic Maya Center*, ed. Damien B. Marken, 175–204. Lanham, MD: AltaMira Press.

Stross, Brian. 1997. "Mesoamerican Copal Resins." *U Mut Maya* 6:177–186.

Stuart, David. 1984. "Royal Auto-Sacrifice among the Maya: A Study of Image and Meaning." *Res: Anthropology and Aesthetics* 7/8:6–20. https://doi.org/10.1086/RESv n1ms20166705.

Stuart, David. 1998. "'The Fire Enters His House': Architecture and Ritual in Classic Maya Text." In *Function and Meaning in Classic Maya Architecture*, ed. Stephen D. Houston, 373–426. Washington, DC: Dumbarton Oaks Research Library and Collection.

Stuart, David. 2000. "'The Arrival of Strangers': Teotihuacan and Tollan in Classic Maya History." In *Mesoamerica's Classic Heritage from Teotihuacan to the Aztecs*, ed. Davíd Carrasco, Lindsay Jones, and Scott Sessions, 465–513. Boulder: University Press of Colorado.

Stuart, David. 2004. "The Beginning of the Copan Dynasty: A Review of the Hieroglyphic and Historical Evidence." In *Understanding Early Classic Copan*, ed. Ellen E. Bell, Marcello A. Canuto, and Robert J. Sharer, 215–247. Philadelphia: University of Pennsylvania Museum of Archaeology and Anthropology.

Stuart, David. 2005. "Ideology and Classic Maya Kingship." In *A Catalyst for Ideas: Anthropological Archaeology and the Legacy of Douglas W. Schwartz*, ed. Vernon L. Scarborough, 257–285. Santa Fe, NM: School of American Research.

Stuart, David. 2012a. "The Hieroglyphic Stairway at El Reinado, Guatemala." Accessed May 21, 2016. http://www.mesoweb.com/stuart/Reinado.pdf.

Stuart, David. 2012b. "The Name of Paper: The Mythology of Crowning and Royal Nomenclature on Palenque's Palace Tablet." In *Maya Archaeology 2*, ed. Charles Golden, Stephen Houston, and Joel Skidmore, 116–142. San Francisco, CA: Precolumbia Mesoweb Press.

Stuart, David. 2012c. "Notes on a New Text from La Corona." *Maya Decipherment: A Weblog on the Ancient Maya Script*. Accessed May 21, 2016. https://decipherment .wordpress.com/2012/06/30/notes-on-a-new-text-from-la-corona.

Stuart, David, and Stephen Houston. 1994. *Classic Maya Place Names*. Washington, DC: Dumbarton Oaks Research Library and Collection.

Suyuc-Ley, Edgar. 2011. "The Extraction of Obsidian at El Chayal, Guatemala." In *The Technology of Maya Civilization: Political Economy and Beyond in Lithic Studies*, ed. Zachary Hruby, Geoffrey Braswell, and Oswaldo Chinchilla, 130–142. Sheffield, UK: Equinox Publishing.

Sweetwood, Ryan V., Richard E. Terry, Timothy Beach, Bruce H. Dahlin, and David Hixson. 2009. "The Maya Footprint: Soil Resources of Chunchucmil, Yucatán,

Mexico." *Soil Science Society of America Journal* 73(4):1209–1220. https://doi.org/10
.2136/sssaj2008.0262.

Taube, Karl. 1985. "The Classic Maya Maize God: A Reappraisal." In *Fifth Palenque Round Table, 1983*, ed. Virginia M. Fields, 171–181. San Francisco, CA: Pre-Columbian Art Research Institute.

Taube, Karl. 1988. "A Study of Classic Maya Scaffold Sacrifice." In *Maya Iconography*, ed. Elizabeth P. Benson and Gillett G. Griffin, 330–351. Princeton, NJ: Princeton University Press.

Taube, Karl. 1992. *The Major Gods of Ancient Yucatan*. Washington, DC: Dumbarton Oaks Research Library and Collection.

Taube, Karl. 1998. "The Jade Hearth: Centrality, Rulership, and the Classic Maya Temple." In *Function and Meaning in Classic Maya Architecture*, ed. Stephen D. Houston. 427–478. Washington, DC: Dumbarton Oaks Research Library and Collection.

Taube, Karl. 2000. "Lightning Celts and Corn Fetishes: The Formative Olmec and the Development of Maize Symbolism in Mesoamerica and the American Southwest." In *Olmec Art and Archaeology in Mesoamerica*, ed. John E. Clark and Mary E. Pye, 297–337. New Haven, CT: Yale University Press.

Taube, Karl. 2003. "Ancient and Contemporary Maya Conceptions about Field and Forest." In *The Lowland Maya Area: Three Millennia at the Human-Wildland Interface*, ed. Arturo Gómez-Pompa, 461–492. Binghamton, NY: Food Products Press.

Taube, Karl. 2004a. "Flower Mountain: Concepts of Life, Beauty, and Paradise among the Classic Maya." *Res: Anthropology and Aesthetics* 45:69–98. https://doi.org/10.1086/RESv45n1ms20167622.

Taube, Karl. 2004b. "Structure 10L-16 and Its Early Classic Antecedents: Fire and the Evocation and Resurrection of K'inich Yax K'uk' Mo.'" In *Understanding Early Classic Copan*, ed. Ellen E. Bell, Marcello A. Canuto, and Robert J. Sharer, 265–296. Philadelphia: University of Pennsylvania Museum of Archaeology and Anthropology.

Taube, Karl, and Stephen Houston. 2015. "The Temple Stuccos." In *Temple of the Night Sun: A Royal Tomb at El Diablo, Guatemala*, by Stephen Houston, Sarah Newman, Edwin Román, and Thomas Garrison, 208–229. San Francisco, CA: Precolumbia Mesoweb Press.

Taube, Karl A., William A. Saturno, David Stuart, and Heather Hurst. 2010. *The Murals of San Bartolo, El Petén, Guatemala*, Part 2: *The West Wall. Ancient America 10*. Barnardsville, NC: Boundary End Archaeology Research Center.

Thompson, J. Eric S. 1966. *The Rise and Fall of Maya Civilization*. 2nd ed. Norman: University of Oklahoma Press.

Thompson, J. Eric S. 1970. *Maya History and Religion*. Norman: University of Oklahoma Press.

Tiesler, Vera. 2007. "Funerary or Nonfunerary? New References in Identifying Ancient Maya Sacrificial and Postsacrificial Behaviors from Human Assemblages." In *New Perspectives on Human Sacrifice and Ritual Body Treatments in Ancient Maya Society*, ed. Vera Tiesler and Aandrea Cucina, 14–44. New York: Springer. https://doi.org/10.1007/978-0-387-48871-4_2.

Tiesler, Vera. 2012. *Tranformarse en Maya: El Modelado Cefálico entro los Mayas Prehispánicos y Coloniales*. Mexico City: Universidad Nacional Autónoma de México.

Tiesler, Vera, and Andrea Cucina. 2006. "Procedures in Human Heart Extraction and Ritual Meaning: A Taphonomic Assessment of Anthropogenic Marks in Classic Maya Skeletons." *Latin American Antiquity* 17(4):493–510. https://doi.org/10.2307/25063069.

Tiesler, Vera, Andrea Cucina, T. Kam Manahan, T. Douglas Price, Traci Arden, and James H. Burton. 2010. "A Taphonomic Approach to Late Classic Maya Mortuary Practices at Xuenkal, Yucatán, Mexico." *Journal of Anthropological Archaeology* 35(4):365–379.

Tiesler, Vera, Andrea Cucina, and Arturo Romano Pacheco. 2004. "Who Was the Red Queen? Identity of the Female Maya Dignitary from the Sarcophagus Tomb of Temple XIII, Palenque, Mexico." *Homo* 55(1-2):65–76. https://doi.org/10.1016/j.jchb.2004.01.003.

Tilley, Christopher. 1994. *A Phenomenology of Landscape: Places, Paths and Monuments*. Providence, RI: Berg Publishing.

Tokovinine, Alexandre. 2008. "The Power of Place: Political Landscape and Identity in Classic Maya Inscriptions, Imagery, and Architecture." PhD dissertation, Department of Anthropology, Harvard University, Cambridge, MA.

Tokovinine, Alexandre, and Marc Zender. 2012. "Lords of Windy Water: The Royal Court of Motul de San José in Classic Maya Inscriptions." In *Motul de San José: Politics, History, and Economy in a Classic Maya Polity*, ed. Antonia E. Foias and Kitty F. Emery, 30–66. Gainesville: University Press of Florida. https://doi.org/10.5744/florida/9780813041902.003.0002.

Townsend, Richard F. 1982. "Pyramid and Sacred Mountain." In *Ethnoastronomy and Archaeoastronomy in the American Tropics*, ed. Anthony F. Aveni and Gary Urton, 37–62. New York Academy of Sciences Publication No. 385. New York: New York Academy of Sciences.

Tozzer, Alfred M. 1941. *Landa's relación de las cosas de Yucatán*. Papers of the Peabody Museum of Archaeology and Ethnology, Vol. 18. Cambridge, MA: Peabody Museum of Archaeology and Ethnology, Harvard University.

Triadan, Daniela. 2007. "Warriors, Nobles, Commoners and Beasts: Figurines from Elite Buildings at Aguateca, Guatemala." *Latin American Antiquity* 18(03):269–293. https://doi.org/10.2307/25478181.

Triadan, Daniela. 2014. "Figurines." In *Life and Politics at the Royal Court of Aguateca: Artifacts, Analytical Data, and Synthesis*, ed. Takeshi Inomata and Daniela Triadan, 9–38. Salt Lake City: University of Utah Press.

Urquizú, Mónica, and William A. Saturno. 2004. "Proyecto Arqueológico Regional San Bartolo: resultados de la segunda temporada de campo 2003." In *XVII Simposio de Investigaciones Arqueológicas en Guatemala, 2003*, ed. Juan Pedro Laporte, Bárbara Arroyo, Héctor L. Escobedo, and Héctor E. Mejía, 607–613. Guatemala: Ministerio de Cultura y Deportes, Instituto de Antropología e Historia, Asociación Tikal.

Valdés, Juan Antonio. 2005. "El Grupo A: Nacimiento y Ocaso de la Plaza Este." In *El periodo Clásico Temprano en Uaxactún, Guatemala*, ed. Juan Antonio Valdés, 27–68. Guatemala: Instituto de Investigaciones Antropológicas y Arqueológicas, Universidad de San Carlos.

Valdés, Juan Antonio, and Federico Fahsen. 1995. "The Reigning Dynasty of Uaxactun during the Early Classic: The Rulers and the Ruled." *Ancient Mesoamerica* 6:197–220. https://doi.org/10.1017/S0956536100002182.

Valdés, Juan Antonio, Mónica Urquizú, Horacio Martínez Paiz, and Carolina Díaz-Samayoa. 2001. "Lo que expresan las figurillas de Aguateca acerca del hombre y los animales." In *XIV Simposio de Investigaciones Arqueológicas en Guatemala, 2000*, ed. Juan Pedro Laporte, Ana Claudia de Suasnávar, and Bárbara Arroyo, 654–676. Guatemala: Ministerio de Cultura y Deportes, Instituto de Antropología e Historia, Asociación Tikal.

Villamil, Laura P. 2007. "Creating, Transforming, Rejecting and Reinterpreting Ancient Maya Urban Landscapes." In *Negotiating the Past in the Past: Identity, Memory, and Landscape in Archaeological Research*, ed. Norman Yoffee, 183–214. Tucson: University of Arizona Press.

Villela, Khristaan. 2011. *Ancient Civilizations of the Americas: Man, Nature, and Spirit in Pre-Columbian Art*. Shigaraki, Japan: Miho Museum.

Vogt, Evon Z. 1969. *Zinacantan: A Maya Community in the Highlands of Chiapas*. Cambridge, MA: Belnap Press of Harvard University. https://doi.org/10.4159/harvard.9780674436886.

Vogt, Evon Z. 1976. *Tortillas for the Gods: A Symbolic Analysis of Zinacantan Ritual*. Cambridge, MA: Harvard University Press.

Wagner, Philip L. 1964. "Natural Vegetation of Middle America." In *Natural Environment and Early Culture,*. Handbook of Middle American Indians, Vol. 1, ed. Robert C. West, 216–264. Austin: University of Texas Press.

Waldeck, Jean-Frédéric. 1838. *Voyage pittoresque et archéologique dans de Province d'Yucatan pendant les années 1834 et 1836*. Paris: Bellizard Dufour et Co.

Walker, Caitlin. 2008. "Análisis preliminar de los materiales cerámicos de la temporada de campo, 2008." In *Proyecto Arqueológico "El Zotz" Informe No. 1: Temporada de Campo 2008*, ed. Ernesto Arredondo Leiva and Stephen Houston, 71–94. Report submitted to the Guatemala Instituto de Antropología e Historia.

Walker, Caitlin. 2009. "Análisis de la cerámica de las temporadas 2008–2009." In *Proyecto Arqueológico "El Zotz" Informe No. 4: Temporada de Campo 2009*, ed. Griselda Pérez Robles, Edwin Román, and Stephen D. Houston, 295–306. Report submitted to the Guatemala Instituto de Antropología e Historia.

Walker, Caitlin. 2010. "A Ceramic Chronology of the El Zotz Region, Petén, Guatemala." Master's thesis, Department of Anthropology, Brown University, Providence, RI.

Webb, Elizabeth A., Henry P. Schwarcz, and Paul F. Healy. 2004. "Detection of Ancient Maize in Lowland Maya Soils Using Stable Carbon Isotopes: Evidence from Caracol, Belize." *Journal of Archaeological Science* 31(8):1039–1052. https://doi.org/10.1016/j.jas.2004.01.001.

Webb, Elizabeth A., Henry P. Schwarcz, Christopher T. Jensen, Richard E. Terry, Matthew D. Moriarty, and Kitty F. Emery. 2007. "Stable Carbon Isotopes Signature of Ancient Maize Agriculture in the Soils of Motul De San José, Guatemala." *Geoarchaeology: An International Journal* 22(3):291–312. https://doi.org/10.1002/gea.20154.

Weber, Max. 1978. *Economy and Society: An Outline of Interpretive Sociology*. Berkeley: University of California Press.

Webster, David. 1997. "City-States of the Maya." In *The Archaeology of City-States: Cross-Cultural Perspectives*, ed. Deborah Nichols and Thomas H. Charlton, 135–154. Washington, DC: Smithsonian Institution Press.

Webster, David. 2002. *The Fall of the Ancient Maya: Solving the Mystery of the Maya Collapse*. London: Thames and Hudson.

Webster, David, Timothy Murtha, Kirk D. Straight, Jay Silverstein, Horacio Martinez, Richard E. Terry, and Richard Burnett. 2007. "The Great Tikal Earthwork Revisited." *Journal of Field Archaeology* 32(1):41–64. https://doi.org/10.1179/009346907791071700.

Webster, David, Jay Silverstein, Timothy Murtha, Horacio Martinez, and Kirk Straight. 2004. *The Tikal Earthworks Revisited*. Occasional Papers in Anthropology No. 28. State College: Department of Anthropology, Pennsylvania State University.

Weeks, John M., Jane A. Hill, and Charles W. Golden, eds. 2005. *Piedras Negras Archaeology: 1931–1939*. Philadelphia: University of Pennsylvania Museum Press.

Weiss-Krejci, Estella. 2011. "The Role of Dead Bodies in Late Classic Maya Politics: Cross-Cultural Reflections on the Meaning of Tikal Altar 5." In *Living with the Dead: Mortuary Ritual in Mesoamerica*, ed. James L. Fitzsimmons and Izumi Shimada, 17–52. Tucson: University of Arizona Press.

Welsh, W. Bruce M. 1988. *An Analysis of Classic Lowland Maya Burials*. BAR International Series 409. Oxford, UK: British Archaeological Reports.

White, Christine D. 1988. "The Ancient Maya from Lamanai, Belize: Diet and Health Over 2000 Years." *Canadian Review of Physical Anthropology* 6(2):1–21.

White, Christine D., Paul F. Healy, and Henry P. Schwarcz. 1993. "Intensive Agriculture, Social Status, and Maya Diet at Pacbitun, Belize." *Journal of Anthropological Research* 49(4):347–375. https://doi.org/10.1086/jar.49.4.3630154.

White, Christine D., David M. Pendergast, Fred J. Longstaffe, and Kimberly R. Law. 2001. "Social Complexity and Food Systems at Altun Ha, Belize: The Isotopic Evidence." *Latin American Antiquity* 12(4):371–393. https://doi.org/10.2307/972085.

White, Tim D., Michael T. Black, and Pieter A. Folkens. 2011. *Human Osteology.* 3rd ed. Burlington, MA: Elsevier Academic Press.

Whittington, Stephen L. 1989. "Characteristics of Demography and Disease in Low Status Maya from Classic Period Copan, Honduras." PhD dissertation, Department of Anthropology, Pennsylvania State University, University Park.

Wilk, Richard. 1989. "Decision Making and Resource Flows within the Household: Beyond the Black Box." In *The Household Economy: Reconsidering the Domestic Mode of Production*, ed. Richard Wilk, 23–52. Boulder: Westview Press.

Wilkinson, T. J., Eleanor B. Wilkinson, Jason Ur, and Mark Altaweel. 2005. "Landscape and Settlement in the Neo-Assyrian Empire." *Bulletin of the American Schools of Oriental Research. American Schools of Oriental Research* 340:23–56.

Willey, Gordon R. 1972. *The Artifacts of Altar de Sacrificios.* Papers of the Peabody Museum of Archaeology and Ethnology 64. Cambridge, MA: Harvard University.

Willey, Gordon R. 1973. *The Altar de Sacrificios Excavations: General Summary and Conclusions.* Papers of the Peabody Museum of Archaeology and Ethnology, Harvard University 64(3). Cambridge, MA: Peabody Museum.

Willey, Gordon R. 1974. "Classic Maya Hiatus: A Rehearsal for the Collapse?" In *Mesoamerican Archaeology: New Approaches*, ed. Norman Hammond, 417–490. Austin: University of Texas Press.

Willey, Gordon R. 1978. *Excavations at Seibal, Department of Petén, Guatemala: Artifacts.* Memoirs of the Peabody Museum of Archaeology and Ethnology 14(1). Cambridge, MA: Harvard University.

Willey, Gordon R., T. Patrick Culbert, and Richard Adams. 1967. "Maya Lowland Ceramics: A Report from the 1965 Guatemala City Conference." *American Antiquity* 32(03):289–315. https://doi.org/10.2307/2694659.

Wolf, Eric. 1982. *Europe and the People without History.* Berkeley: University of California Press.

Wright, David R., Richard E. Terry, and Markus Eberl. 2009. "Soil Properties and Stable Carbon Isotope Analysis of Landscape Features in the Petexbatún Region of Guatemala." *Geoarchaeology: An International Journal* 24(4):466–491. https://doi.org/10.1002/gea.20275.

Wright, George R. H. 1985. *Ancient Building in South Syria and Palestine.* 2 vols. Leiden, Netherlands: Brill.

Wright, George R. H. 1992. *Ancient Building in Cyprus.* Leiden, Netherlands: Brill.

Wright, George R. H. 2000a. Ancient Building Technology, Vol. 1: *Historical Background.* Leiden, Netherlands: Brill.

Wright, George R. H. 2000b. Ancient Building Technology, Vol. 2: *Materials.* Leiden, Netherlands: Brill.

Wright, Lori E. 2004. "Osteological Investigations of Ancient Maya Lives." In *Continuities and Changes in Maya Archaeology,* ed. Charles W. Golden and Gregory Borgstede, 201–216. New York: Routledge.

Wright, Lori E. 2005. "Identifying Immigrants to Tikal, Guatemala: Defining Local Variability in Strontium Isotope Ratios of Human Tooth Enamel." *Journal of Archaeological Science* 32(4):555–566. https://doi.org/10.1016/j.jas.2004.11.011.

Wright, Lori E. 2006. *Diet, Health, and Status among the Pasión Maya: A Reappraisal of the Collapse.* Nashville, TN: Vanderbilt University Press.

Wright, Lori E. 2012. "Immigration to Tikal, Guatemala: Evidence from Stable Strontium and Oxygen Isotopes." *Journal of Anthropological Archaeology* 31(3):334–352. https://doi.org/10.1016/j.jaa.2012.02.001.

Wright, Lori E., and Christine D. White. 1996. "Human Biology in the Classic Maya Collapse: Evidence from Paleopathology and Paleodiet." *Journal of World Prehistory* 10(2):147–198. https://doi.org/10.1007/BF02221075.

Wrobel, Gabriel D., Marie E. Danforth, and Carl Armstrong. 2002. "Estimating Sex of Maya Skeletons by Discriminant Function Analysis of Long-Bone Measurements from the Protohistoric Maya Site of Tipu, Belize." *Ancient Mesoamerica* 13(02):255–263. https://doi.org/10.1017/S0956536102132044.

Yaeger, Jason. 2010. "Shifting Political Dynamics as Seen from the Xunantunich Palace." In *Classic Maya Provincial Politics: Xunantunich and its Hinterlands,* ed. Lisa J. LeCount and Jason Yaeger, 145–160. Tucson: University of Arizona Press.

Yaeger, Jason, and David Hodell. 2008. "The Collapse of Maya Civilization: Assessing the Interaction of Culture, Climate, and Environment." In *El Niño, Catastrophism, and Culture Change in Ancient America,* ed. David H. Sandweiss and Jeffrey Quilter, 187–242. Washington, DC: Dumbarton Oaks Research Library and Collection.

Yoffee, Norman. 2005. *Myths of the Archaic State: Evolution of the Earliest Cities, States, and Civilizations.* Cambridge, UK: Cambridge University Press. https://doi.org/10.1017/CBO9780511489662.

Zaro, Gregory, and Brett A. Houk. 2012. "The Growth and Decline of the Ancient Maya City of La Milpa, Belize: New Data and New Perspectives from the Southern Plazas." *Ancient Mesoamerica* 23(01):143–159. https://doi.org/10.1017/S0956536112000107.

Źrałka, Jaroslaw, and Bernard Hermes. 2012. "Great Development in Troubled Times: The Terminal Classic at the Maya Site of Nakum, Peten, Guatemala." *Ancient Mesoamerica* 23(01):161–187. https://doi.org/10.1017/S0956536112000120.

Źrałka, Jaroslaw, and Wieslaw Koszkul. 2010. "New Discoveries about the Ancient Maya: Excavations at Nakum, Guatemala." *Expedition* 52(2):21–32.

Timothy Beach holds a Centennial Chair in geography at the University of Texas, Austin, since 2014, after 21 years at Georgetown University, where he held the Cinco Hermanos Chair in environment and international affairs. He studies soils, geomorphology, geoarchaeology, paleoecology, and wetlands, focusing on the Maya and Mediterranean worlds. This research led to more than 100 peer-reviewed publications and hundreds of scientific presentations. He is an AAAS Fellow, a Guggenheim and Dumbarton Oaks Fellow, G. K. Gilbert co-Awardee in Geomorphology, Carl O. Sauer Distinguished Scholarship Awardee (2016), and has received Georgetown University's Distinguished Research Award (2010) and Georgetown University's School of Foreign Service's Faculty of the Year Award (2014).

Nicholas P. Carter is assistant professor of anthropology at Texas State University. He received his BA in philosophy from Our Lady of the Lake University in 2003, an MA in Latin American studies from the University of Texas, Austin, in 2008, an AM in anthropology from Brown University in 2010, and a PhD in anthropology from Brown in 2014.

Ewa Czapiewska-Halliday served as the ceramicist for phase I of the Proyecto Arqueológico El Zotz. She received a PhD from Institute of Archaeology, University College London, in 2018. Her dissertation, "The Study of Value: Social, Economic and Political Dimensions of Palace Complexes at El Zotz," focuses on the political economy of Maya pottery at El Zotz and the wider topic of Maya market distribution. She specializes in ancient Maya ceramics, theories of value, and data analytics to tackle the databases of ancient Maya sites. She heads and trains a team of data analysts in London.

Alyce de Carteret is a Postdoctoral Fellow in the Art of the Ancient Americas at the Los Angeles County Museum of Art (LACMA). She received her PhD in Anthropology from Brown University in 2017. Her research interests include Meso-american household archaeology and vernacular architecture, two topics explored in-depth by her doctoral dissertation, entitled "Building Communities: The Craft of Housebuilding among the Classic Maya." Since 2012 she has been a member of the Proyecto Arqueológico El Zotz and has conducted extensive excavations in the non-monumental residential sectors of the site. She graduated *magna cum laude* from Harvard University in 2010, and was awarded a MSt in Archaeology with Distinction from the University of Oxford in 2011.

William Delgado received his master's from the Department of Geography and the Environment at the University of Texas at Austin in 2017, and is currently a PhD student in the same program. He studies water resources and water infrastructure, specifically the application of renewable energy to power at reverse osmosis desalination plants in arid climates. His study area is the Kay Bailey Hutchison Desalination Plant in El Paso, Texas. He plans to broaden his studies at the doctoral level by assessing the feasibility of recycling brine from the desalination process into useful products such as mortar and analyzing the broader transboundary water issues between El Paso and its sister city across the US-Mexico border, Ciudad Juárez. His studies at El Zotz provide ideas as to how large water infrastructure supplies a given population.

Colin Doyle is a PhD student in the Department of Geography and the Environment at the University of Texas at Austin. His research focuses on the relationship between environmental hydrology and soil geomorphology with human systems. He received a BS in environmental biology from Georgetown University in 2013. He then worked for NASA's DEVELOP National Program and for Goddard Earth Science Technology and Research in the Hydrological Sciences Laboratory at NASA's Goddard Space Flight Center in Greenbelt, Maryland. At GSFC, Colin developed near real-time flood monitoring and socioeconomic impact assessment systems for Southeast Asia using satellite remote sensing and GIS technologies. He moved to UT-Austin to receive a MA from the Department of Geography and the Environment in 2017. His current research aims to understand the long-term effects of ancient Maya agriculture and water management on the modern environment. In addition, this research studies the development of ancient Maya agricultural and water management technologies in response to droughts, sea-level rise, and growing populations, and their influence on the early Anthropocene.

JAMES A. DOYLE is assistant curator for the Art of the Ancient Americas at The Metropolitan Museum of Art, having received his PhD in anthropology from Brown University. His expertise includes the art and archaeology of Mesoamerica, Central America, and Colombia, with a specialization in the ancient Maya. He is the author of many articles and the book *Architecture and the Origins of Preclassic Maya Politics* (2017). He also promotes the ancient Americas through blogs and social media.

LAURA GÁMEZ is a Guatemalan archaeologist, with a degree from the Universidad de San Carlos de Guatemala, as well as a certificate in advanced Latin American studies and a PhD from Pittsburgh University. Currently, she works at the Casa Herrera, a Guatemala-based extension of the Mesoamerican Center of the Department of Art and Art History at the University of Texas at Austin, and teaches at the universities of Rafael Landívar and Francisco Marroquín. Her field experience extends across several sites in the southern Maya Lowlands and Guatemalan Central Highlands.

JOSE LUIS GARRIDO received his *licenciatura* degree in archaeology from the Universidad de San Carlos de Guatemala. He has been an archaeologist or director on various projects, including Ixquisis, Salinas de los Nueve Cerros, Pompeya, Kaminaljuyu, San Bartolo, Cancuen, Motul de San José, Xilil, Ucanal, and El Zotz. He served as an archaeological technician for the Fundación de Antropología Forense de Guatemala. He has also supervised field training in Guatemala, as well as serving as a thesis reader for archaeology degree candidates at San Carlos. Since 2009, he has been a member of the Proyecto Arqueológico El Zotz as both an archaeologist and editor of the dig's annual reports, as well as vice president of the project's NGO. He collaborates with various energy and environment-related projects in Guatemala, and is a master's candidate in the Energy and Environment Program within the Faculty of Engineering at the Universidad de San Carlos. He has participated in meetings related to Guatemala's energy matrix, environment, and climate change.

THOMAS G. GARRISON is assistant professor in the Department of Geography and the Environment at the University of Texas at Austin. He previously taught at Ithaca College, the University of Southern California, and held postdoctoral fellowships at Brown University and Umeå Universitet, Sweden. In addition to his research in Guatemala, he has conducted field and laboratory work in Mexico, Belize, Honduras, and the United States. He received his PhD from Harvard University in 2007, writing his dissertation on the application of remote-sensing technologies to the settlement investigations at San Bartolo. He has collaborated with the Marshall Space and Flight Center, Jet Propulsion Laboratory, and the National Center for Airborne Laser Mapping to develop applications of remote-sensing technologies in archaeology. His research has been funded by the Fundación Patrimonio Cultural y Natural Maya (PACUNAM), National Science Foundation, Waitt Institute for Discovery, National Geographic, and the GEOS Foundation. Since 2012, he has served as the director of the Proyecto Arqueológico El Zotz, following three years of regional investigations around the site. He is a coauthor of *Temple of the Night Sun: A Royal Tomb at El Diablo, Guatemala* (2015).

YENY M. GUTIÉRREZ CASTILLO received her *licenciatura* in archaeology from the Universidad de San Carlos de Guatemala in 2015. During her studies, she worked with various archaeological projects in both the Maya Lowlands (El Zotz and San Bartolo) and the Highlands (Pompeya, Ixquisis), as well as participating in the investigation of colonial ruins. She presents her work regularly at the annual Simposio de Investigaciones Arqueológicas en Guatemala. Since 2010, her research has focused on paleomalacology, and she wrote her *licenciatura* thesis on the shells of El Zotz. Since 2016, she has been the codirector of the Proyecto Arqueológico El Zotz with Thomas Garrison.

STEPHEN HOUSTON serves as the Dupee Family Professor of Social Sciences at Brown University, where he also holds an appointment in anthropology. A specialist in Classic Maya civilization, writing systems, and indigenous representation, Houston is the author of many books and articles, including, most recently, *Temple of the Night Sun* (with several coauthors), *The Maya* (with Michael Coe, now in its ninth edition), and *The Life Within: Classic Maya and the Matter of Permanence*, winner of a PROSE Award in 2014. He was co-curator of a major show, *Fiery Pool: The Maya and the Mythic Sea*, exhibited at the Peabody-Essex Museum, the Kimbell, and the St. Louis Museum of Fine Arts. Houston has been honored with a MacArthur Fellowship, along with support from the Guggenheim Foundation, the National Science Foundation, Dumbarton Oaks, the National Gallery of Art, the Clark Art Institute, and the National Endowment for the Humanities. His current projects concern the central role of young men in Classic Maya civilization, the lives and roles of Maya sculptors, and the results of large-scale excavations at the dynastic center of Piedras Negras, Guatemala. In 2011, the President of Guatemala awarded Houston the Grand Cross of the Order of the Quetzal, that country's highest honor. He has also received the Tatiana Proskouriakoff Award from the Peabody Museum, Harvard University. Houston is a *summa cum laude* graduate of the University of Pennsylvania; his PhD, awarded in 1987, is from Yale.

ZACHARY HRUBY studies the archaeology of both Mesoamerica and North America, with specializations in the Maya area (southern Mexico, Guatemala, and Honduras) and the American West (California, Nevada, and the Pacific Northwest). His particular interest is Mesoamerican and Maya religion viewed through the lens of the archaeological record: ancient Maya texts, art, and ritual deposits (caches and burials). As a lithic analyst, he has worked with obsidian and flint materials from many Maya sites over the past 20 years, including Piedras Negras, El Perú-Waka', El Zotz, Holmul, Kaminaljuyu, and Motul de San José in Guatemala; Palenque, Pomona, Chunchucmil, and Vista Alegre in Mexico; and Copan and Río Amarillo in Honduras. These studies reveal broad economic patterns across the ancient Maya world and through time, as well as how lithic goods (jade, flint, and obsidian) were used in ritual contexts. Most recently, he has studied the largest-known obsidian cache from the Maya Lowlands, which consists of a deposit of over 500 obsidian macroblades, from the Grand Plaza at Copan, Honduras. Hruby, a 2006 Ph.D. from the University of California, Riverside, teaches anthropology at Northern Kentucky University.

MELANIE J. KINGSLEY holds a doctorate in anthropology from Brandeis University. Her research in Guatemala in the Usumacinta River region and at the site of El Zotz has focused on social and economic changes in Postclassic life among the Maya of Lowland Guatemala. She currently works and lives in Washington, DC.

SHERYL LUZZADDER-BEACH is professor of Geography and the Environment at the University of Texas at Austin, where she served as chair for 5 years. She is now President of the American Association of Geographers. She is also the Fellow of the C. B. Smith Sr. Centennial Chair in US-Mexico Relations at UT-Austin. Formerly, she taught for over 20 years at George Mason University, where she was professor of geography and also the associate provost for general education. She has taught at the University of Georgia, Humboldt State University, and the University of Minnesota, where she received her PhD. Her research and teaching specialties are in hydrology and water quality, geoarchaeology, earth systems science, spatial statistics, global change, and gender and science. Luzzadder-Beach has conducted field research in Mexico, Belize, Guatemala, California, Iceland, Italy, Turkey, and Syria. Her research has been supported by grants from the National Aeronautics and Space Administration, the National Geographic Society, the National Science Foundation, and by the University of Texas and George Mason University. Luzzadder-Beach and her coauthor Timothy Beach were awarded the 2010 G. K. Gilbert Award for Excellence in Research by the Association of American Geographers Geomorphology Specialty Group, and she was honored with the 2012 GMU College of Science Publication Excellence Award.

CASSANDRA MESICK BRAUN earned her MA and PhD in anthropology from Brown University, where she focused on precolumbian archaeology and architecture. After gaining museum experience at the Haffenreffer Museum of Anthropology and the Metropolitan Museum of Art, she became the curator of Global Indigenous Art at the University of Kansas's Spencer Museum of Art. She oversees a diverse collection of more than 10,000 works of art and material culture from the Americas, Africa, and Oceania, which she integrates into the exhibition, research, outreach, and teaching mission of the Museum. At the Spencer, Mesick Braun has organized six exhibitions and hosted five visiting artists, and she is currently working on an NEH-funded project about the educational experiences of African American and Native American families in Kansas from the mid-1800s to the present. Mesick Braun serves on the core faculty of the Center for Latin American and Caribbean Studies at the University of Kansas and teaches for the Honors and Museum Studies programs. She has coauthored *Veiled Brightness: A History of Ancient Maya Color* and has contributed to several volumes, including *Re-Presenting the Past: Archaeology through Text and Image* and *Fiery Pool: The Maya and the Mythic Sea.*

SARAH NEWMAN received her BA at Yale University (2007), her PhD from Brown University (2015), and is currently assistant professor of anthropology at the University of Chicago. She has conducted archaeological and zooarchaeological research in Mesoamerica since 2006, with a current field project at the site of Topoxte, Guatemala, and is a coauthor of *Temple of the Night Sun: A Royal Tomb at El Diablo, Guatemala* (2015). Her work has been supported by several grants and fellowships, including the US Department of State Fulbright Program, the National Science Foundation, the Dolores Zohrab Liebmann Foundation, the John Carter Brown Library, and, most recently, a 2017-2018 Richard Carley Hunt Fellowship from the Wenner-Gren Foundation to support the writing of her manuscript, Talking Trash: A History of Waste in Mesoamerica.

RONY E. PIEDRASANTA is studying for his *licenciatura* degree at the Universidad de San Carlos de Guatemala. He served for 10 years as a technician in forensic anthropology investigating human-rights violations that occurred during the Guatemalan civil war, especially in the Ixil genocide case, and has lent his expertise in this area to the Guatemalan National Police Historical Archive Project. His archaeological work includes fieldwork in the Middle Motagua, the Sierra Lacandon, Piedras Negras, Pompeya, Quirigua, and El Zotz, in addition to numerous colonial-period projects. He has acted as a consultant for socioeconomic planning for master planning of the Biotopo San Miguel la Palotada–El Zotz and the Biotopo Cerro Cahui. He has also assisted with the training of guides for community tourism programs and worked with assisting victims and communities affected by the Guatemalan civil war. He has published and presented his work throughout Guatemala.

EDWIN ROMÁN obtained his *licenciatura* degree in archaeology at the Universidad de San Carlos de Guatemala in 2006, and master's and doctoral degrees in Latin American studies at the University of Texas at Austin in 2011 and 2017, respectively. Román has participated on several archaeological projects in the Motagua Valley and in the Maya Lowlands, including San Bartolo, Sierra del Lacandon, and Cival. He served as the codirector of the Proyecto Arqueológico El Zotz with Stephen Houston (2009–2011) and Thomas Garrison (2012–2015). He recently completed his doctoral studies at the University of Texas at Austin, where his 2017 dissertation focused on how the Early Classic Maya were affected by the conquest of Tikal in AD 378 by Sihyaj K'ahk'.

ANDREW K. SCHERER is associate professor of Anthropology and Archaeology at Brown University. He has completed 16 seasons of archaeological fieldwork in the middle Usumacinta River basin of Guatemala and Mexico as the codirector of the Sierra del Lacandon Regional Archaeological Project and the Proyecto Arqueológico Busilja-Chocolja. He is author of *Mortuary Landscapes of the Classic Maya: Rituals of Body and Soul*, coauthor of *Revisiting Maler's Usumacinta: Recent Archaeological Investigations in Chiapas, Mexico* (with Charles Golden), and coeditor of *Embattled Bodies, Embattled Places: War in Pre-Columbian Mesoamerica and the Andes* (with John Verano). He has published a variety of articles pertaining to the archaeology of the western Maya Lowlands and is especially interested in the regional, diachronic, comparative study of ancient Maya polities. As a bioarchaeologist, he has researched diet and health at Piedras Negras, the population history of the Classic Maya Lowlands, violence at Colha, Belize, and royal mortuary rites at El Zotz, Guatemala. Scherer is a former fellow at Dumbarton Oaks Research Library and Collection. His research has been sponsored by the National Science Foundation, the Wenner-Gren Foundation, the National Geographic Society/Waitt Grants Program, and the Foundation for the Advancement of Mesoamerican Studies, Inc.

Sahcaba Molded-carved, 136 (fig.); shell, 270; skeletal, 338; stucco, 60 (fig.), 124, 291 (fig.); Terminal Classic, 268; vessel, 136 (fig.); zoomorphic, 270
Friedman, Jonathan: on self-definition, 158
Fundación Patrimonio Cultural y Natural Maya (PACUNAM), 10, 16, 24, 379

Gámez, Laura, 144, 291
Gann, Thomas, 116
Garrido López, Jose Luis, 73, 357, 370; work of, 325, 334, 335, 344
Garrison, Thomas G., 17, 22, 73, 90, 110, 236, 357; work of, 333, 336, 344, 347, 349, 350, 352
Geertz, Clifford, 18
Genovés, Santiago, 306
geochemistry, 165, 186
Geographic Information Systems (GIS), 21
George Mason University Water Quality Lab, 166
GF Instruments Magnetic Susceptibility Meter SM-20, 168
Gifford, James, 189, 190
Gillot Vassaux, Alejandro, 315, 321
glyphs, 21, 22, 26, 106, 135, 217, 225; bowls with, 206 (fig.); inscriptions, 207, 224; *mam*, 258; multicolored, 99
God L, 260, 266
Gómez, Oswaldo, 359
Graham, Ian, 16, 80, 90
Great Plaza, 358
Guatemalan Congress, 15
Guatemalan National Police, 357
Guderjan, Thomas H., 166
Guenter, Stanley P., 374
Gutiérrez Castillo, Yeny, 39, 340

HACH Conductivity Meter, 166
hairstyles, dress and, 259–60
Halperin, Christina, 153, 154, 261
hammerstones, 54
Harris Matrices, 280, 281 (fig.), 300
Hatfield, Ron, 28
Haviland, William, 358
headdresses, 106, 257, 262, 263 (fig.)
heads, 257 (table); anthropomorphic, 257; figurine, 258 (fig.); mold-made, 273
Healan, Daniel M., 156–57
hearth, jade, 371

heat, impact of, 290, 329
Hellmuth files, 23 (fig.)
hematite, 59, 85, 321; red, 315, 330, 343; specular, 315, 346
Hernández, Danilo, 343
heterarchy, 18–19
hierarchy, 19, 145–46
Hieroglyphic Stairway 1: 124
hieroglyphs, 20, 98, 210
history, 3, 4, 7, 137, 193, 229, 230; Classic, 21, 125; occupation, 28; scrim of, 21–27; sociopolitical, 359
Holmul, 249
Holmul Archaeological Project, 360n1
Hood, Darden, 28
household compounds, 109, 141, 147
Houston, Stephen, 16, 80, 87, 112, 122, 155, 265, 291, 322; work of, 12, 325, 349
Hruby, Zachary, 156, 363
huipils, 259, 261
humerus, 322, 325, 335, 338, 340, 343, 347, 348, 350, 351, 353
hydrogeology, 168

I10 Group, 12, 44, 376
iconography, 82–83, 84, 86, 194, 207, 225, 275, 276; style and, 255–68
IDAEH. See Instituto de Antropología e Historia de Guatemala
identity, 259, 273; ideological, 208; political, 208, 252; social, 252
ideology, 208, 283; involutionary, 249; religious, 230, 249
Ik' Emblem Glyph Style, 130
Ik' phase, 189, 349
Imix phase, 118, 189, 223
INAA. *See* Instrumental Neutron Activation Analysis
incensarios, 153–55; frog, 153 (fig.)
Infierno Black, 126, 202, 212, 217 (fig.)
Initial Series, 112
Inomata, Takeshi, 249
Instituto de Antropología e Historia de Guatemala (IDAEH), 5, 15, 16, 47, 205
Instrumental Neutron Activation Analysis (INAA), 47, 50 (fig.), 96, 111
INTCAL 12 Radiocarbon Age Calibration, 168
INTCAL 13 Calibration Curve, 28

Intertropical Convergence Zone (ITCZ), 164
iron/chromium ratios, comparison of, 50 (fig.)
Islas Gouged-incised, 220
isotopic ratios, 169, 183, 354
Itza Maya, 140, 141
Ixlu, 5, 137, 151
Ixtepeque, 131, 156, 254; artifact counts for, 251
    (fig.); obsidian from, 250
Izapa, 83

jade, 85, 154, 231, 270, 315, 334, 341, 342, 352–53,
    363, 364, 370
Jaguar God of the Underworld (JGU), 24–25,
    83, 84, 205
jaguars, anthropomorphic, 111
jars, 206; Aguila Orange, 197, 201 (fig.);
    Cambio, 205; Early Classic, 41, 183;
    Encanto, 205; monochrome, 131; Tinaja
    Red, 209 (fig.), 212; water, 210
Jasaw Chan K'awiil I, 112, 114, 375
Jasaw Chan K'awiil II, 137
Jester God, 135
JGU. *See* Jaguar God of the Underworld
Jimbal, 137
Joventud Group, 54
ju'n winikha'b ajaw, 97

Kaminaljuyu, 250
Kantunilkin, 275
k'atun, 111, 112, 137, 371
K'awiil, 135
ke-le-ma ch'o[ko], 23
keleem, 97
Kerr, Justin, 26, 99
K'ichee' Maya creation myth, 363
King James, 24
King, Stacie M., 275
kings: divine, 117; dynastic, 72, 91, 93, 364, 376;
    early seventh-century, 95–100
Kingsley, Melanie J., 142, 144, 145–46, 243
K'inich Bahlam I, 369
K'inich Janaab Pakal, tomb of, 356
K'inich Yax K'uk' Mo', 86
knappers, 228, 240, 243
knives, 85, 233
Kohunlich, 83
Kowoj Maya, 141
k'uhul, 22, 27
k'uhul ajaw, 20, 100, 374

K'uhul Ajaw Kan, 112
k'uhul-Pa'ka'n ajaw, 94, 97 (fig.), 115, 122, 374
K'uk' Chan, 112

La Avispa, 28, 46, 59, 61, 62, 63, 93, 236, 364, 380;
    activity at, 375; ceramics in, 362; dates of, 45;
    map of, 13 (fig.); occupation at, 110; PAEZ
    and, 230; population of, 47; pyramids, 68
La Avispa Str. P8-3: 365
La Avispa Str. P8-4: 61
La Avispa Str. P8-5: 61
La Avispa Str. P8-6: 61
La Brisanta, 6, 7, 376, 379
La Corona, 113, 374; Las Coronitas Group, 374
La Cuernavilla, 7, 168
La Cuernavilla Cival, 186, 380
La Florida, stelae/lintels at, 265
La Honradez, 367
La Joyanca, 111, 208
La Milpa, 125, 367
La Sufricaya, 86
La Tortuga, 111, 189, 224; ceramics at, 210–11,
    212; excavations at, 273; vessels at, 211
labor, 136, 156, 303; controlling, 134
Lacandon, 28, 43, 142, 377
Lagartero, figurines from, 261
Laguna El Palmar, 7, 28, 37, 52, 56, 61, 66, 68,
    167, 169, 362, 366; environmental evidence
    from, 51
lajas, 232, 322, 340, 343, 345, 349
Lake Peten Itza, 5, 158, 378
Lake Salpeten, 186
Lamanai, 112, 304
landscape, 110, 188, 283, 284, 300, 359, 379, 380;
    approach, 21; changing, 72, 361; Classic,
    280; natural resources of, 302; political, 71,
    286
Laporte, Juan Pedro, 16, 240, 262
Las Palmitas Group, 7, 11, 44, 56, 61, 68, 106,
    109, 114, 120, 131, 134, 135, 142, 189, 216, 217,
    218–20, 224, 225, 226, 230, 262, 280, 288, 297,
    298, 301, 358, 375, 376, 377, 380; buildings at,
    107, 285; burials at, 126; Caal-phase ceram-
    ics at, 202, 203–4 (table), 219; ceramics
    at, 210–11, 212, 222–23 (table); chert at, 231;
    construction at, 210; crypt at, 289 (fig.);
    Cucul-phase ceramics at, 213–15 (table),
    218, 219; dates of, 44; eastern plaza of, 107;
    El Zotz and, 285; floors at, 108; layout of,

metacarpals, 327, 345, 346, 349, 351
metatarsals, 321, 331, 335, 336, 345, 348
middens, 44, 45, 133, 272; Cucul-phase, 219; Late Classic, 220; South Group, 150 (fig.), 155, 226; Terminal Classic, 219, 220
Middle Postclassic, 150–51
Middle Preclassic, 28, 37, 41, 44, 46, 47, 49, 55, 55 (fig.), 56, 61, 68, 71, 144, 169, 172, 189, 244–45, 282–83; analysis of, 230; construction phase of, 54; dates for, 51; described, 362–63; population of, 51, 52; settlement during, 362; urbanization during, 171
Mirador Basin, 5, 27, 96, 110, 208
Miseria Appliquéd, 126
Mo' phase, 95, 98, 111, 114, 115, 189, 205, 206, 209, 221, 223, 224; first appearance of, 202
monkeys, 96, 266, 267, 271
monochromes, 125, 131, 148, 151, 152, 212, 323; black-slipped, 216; Caal, 206; decorated, 211; Late Classic, 211; red-slipped, 216, 217; Tinaja-group, 207
Monticulo Unslipped, 190
monumentalization, 56–57, 59, 61–62, 68, 71
monuments, 147, 362, 364; Classic, 124, 147; construction of, 94, 100–108, 125, 145, 283, 287, 293 (fig.); funerary, 80–81, 120, 368; inscribed, 116
morphology, 228, 233, 323, 326, 349
mortuary objects, 305, 307, 359
mortuary space, polarity of, 358
mortuary traditions, royal, 355
mosaics, 79, 85, 117, 164; jade, 66, 352, 370
Motul de San José, 106, 153, 209, 256, 261, 266
Muna Slate, 220
MUNAE. See Museo Nacional de Arqueología y Etnología
Mundo Perdido, 7, 47, 57, 59, 358
murals, 59, 86, 260, 261, 360n1; Early Classic, 262; Late Preclassic, 262
Museo Nacional de Arqueología y Etnología (MUNAE), 16, 79, 111, 135
Museo Popol Vuh, 22
Museu Barbier-Mueller, 14, 374

Nakbe, 52, 53, 54, 68, 71, 366
Nakum, 137, 138
Nakum Stela D, 137
Naranjo, 113, 138
Naranjo Stela 10:B4: 24

National Center for Airborne Laser Mapping (NCALM), 379
National Endowment for the Humanities, 16
National Gallery of Art (Australia), 13
National Science Foundation, 16
Nelson, Zachary, 17
neutron activation analysis, 206, 218
"New Archaeology," 304
Newman, Sarah, 62, 89, 332, 375; work of, 330, 331, 336, 339
Nixtun-Ch'ich, 5
North Acropolis, 358
North Atlantic Oscillation, 165
North Group, 106
Northwest Courtyard, 100, 103, 120, 122, 126, 130, 132, 134, 138, 142, 189, 218, 220, 224, 225, 230, 259, 274, 375, 376, 377; ceramics at, 212, 215–17; construction at, 205–10; Cucul assemblages at, 217; excavations in, 262; map of, 121 (fig.); obsidian in, 131; Saquij at, 198; sherds from, 216; stairway at, 125
nuclear assembly, 28, 288, 290, 291, 390

obsidian, 38, 84, 124, 131, 133, 228, 229, 231, 244, 254, 270, 341; analysis of, 155; Classic period, 239–40, 242–43, 251; distribution of, 250; Early Postclassic, 248; El Chayal, 156, 250; El Zotz, 250, 254; green, 64 (fig.), 334, 370; Guatemalan, 251 (fig.); Ixtepeque, 155, 156, 254; Mexican, 240, 250; nodules, 247; Otumba, 240, 251; overview, 248–51; Pachuca green, 251; Postclassic, 156, 240; Preclassic, 240, 250; production of, 159, 250; resource zone, 248; sources of, 157 (fig.), 241–42 (table), 249, 250–51; Terminal Postclassic, 248; Ucareo, 251; Zaragosa, 251
occupation, 71–73, 73–79, 91, 142–43, 158, 172, 221–22, 291, 362, 365, 378; Caal-phase, 110; Early Classic, 184, 193; Early Postclassic, 141, 149, 226; histories, 301–2; Late Classic, 110; Maya, 5, 28, 158; Middle Preclassic, 282–83; Postclassic, 158, 221, 272; Preclassic, 51; Saquij, 197, 198; Terminal Classic, 133.
ojo de reptil, 92, 368
ollas, 125, 195, 206, 210
organic matter, 168, 169, 185, 290, 291
osteoarthritis, 327, 331, 344
Otumba, 240, 250, 251
owls, 266, 267, 267 (fig.)